PRECISION FARMING

Techniques for Protected Cultivation

R. SURESH

Professor and Head
Department of Soil and Water Conservation Engineering
Dr. Rajendra Prasad Central Agricultural University, Pusa (Bihar)

S.K. NIRALA

Assistant Professor
Department of Soil and Water Conservation Engineering
Dr. Rajendra Prasad Central Agricultural University, Pusa (Bihar)

PHI Learning Private Limited

Delhi-110092
2025

In fond memory of ***Shri Asoke K. Ghosh*** *(October 1942–February 2024), Founder Chairman and Managing Director of PHI Learning, whose vision endlessly inspires.*

The Legacy Continues... .

Published by Pushpita Ghosh, PHI Learning Private Limited, Rimjhim House, 111, Patparganj Industrial Estate, Delhi-110092 and Printed by Syndicate Binders, A-20, Hosiery Complex, Noida, Phase-II Extension, Noida-201305 (N.C.R. Delhi).

₹850.00

PRECISION FARMING—TECHNIQUES FOR PROTECTED CULTIVATION
R. Suresh and S.K. Nirala

ISBN-978-81-19364-42-8 (Print Book)
ISBN-978-81-19364-24-4 (e-Book)

CONTENTS

Preface

The book entitled ***"Precision Farming Techniques for Protected Cultivation"*** is written for one of the courses of Under Graduate Agricultural Engineering degree programme recommended by Fifth Dean's Committee, ICAR, New Delhi. Book comprises total 13 chapters, namely: Protected Cultivation—Theory, Importance and Applications; Greenhouse—Concept, Classification and Uses; Greenhouse—Design and Construction; Greenhouse Heating System; Greenhouse Microclimate; Growing Media for Greenhouse Crops; Other Precision Farming Techniques—Poly tunnels, Shade Nets, Plastic Nets and Plastic Mulching; Greenhouse Irrigation Methods; Design of Drip and Micro-Sprinkler Systems; Fertigation to Greenhouse Crops; Water Quality for Greenhouse Crops; Greenhouse—Insects/Pests and Disease Management, besides Glossary and Subject index. Each chapter contains proper bibliography, figures, tables and the solved examples at appropriate places in the text, for better clarity of the subject, besides a good number of descriptive type and multiple-choice type questions. Book covers the entire syllabus of the said course.

The book will be highly useful for B. Tech. (Agricultural Engineering), B.Sc. (Agriculture) and B.Sc. (Horticulture) students of Agricultural Universities in India and Afro-Asian countries, as well. In addition, the candidates appearing in GATE, ARS, NET, JRF and SRF examinations, this book will also be very useful for their preparations.

In course of preparing manuscript of the book authors received so many suggestions from different individuals, they all are acknowledged hereby. Authors acknowledge to Dr. P. S. Pandey, Vice-Chancellor Dr. Rajendra Prasad Central Agricultural University, Pusa (Samastipur) Bihar, Dr. Ambrish Kumar, Dean, College of Agricultural Engineering and Technology, Dr. Maan Singh, Former Project Director, Water Technology Centre, IARI New Delhi, Dr. T.B.S. Rajput, Eminent Scientist (former), IARI, Dr. Neelam Patel, Principal Scientist, IARI New Delhi, NCPAH New Delhi, Dr. Md. Abbas Ahmad, Associate Professor, Department of Entomology, RPCAU, Pusa (Samastipur) for providing help in preparing the manuscript, and so many others for their moral supports.

Authors also feel proud to acknowledge all those professionals, scientists/researchers, progressive farmers, manufacturers and others who are contributing their efforts in development and dissemination of precision farming technologies to elevate agricultural production by using these technologies.

Last but not least, the authors also acknowledge the publisher PHI Learning Private Limited, New Delhi for taking keen interest to publish the book in a short course of time.

R. Suresh
S.K. Nirala

CHAPTER 1

Precision Farming—Concept and Applications

It is well known that the human population is continuously increasing at accelerated rate, worldwide. As per study conducted in United States of America about 83 million populations, each year is expected to add to the global population. Accordingly, the projected population by the year 2025 is likely to reach to the tune of 9.8 billion, which in turn to create the real-time challenge regarding economic, agricultural, and communal infrastructures, as well. Particularly, in developing countries the farming community will face the problems to enhance the crop productivity to meet the increasing demands. Apart from population growth, the drastic change in climate or global warming will also develop a brutal effect on crop yield, because of aberrant weather. Especially, the marginal and low-land holding farmers are expected to get badly suffer to enhance their crop productivity. Looking all these facts in view, it is to be very essential and important to enforce the technologies in agriculture sector for achieving the target of required food demand. In this scenario the scope of precision farming is vital, can be the game changer in agriculture sector. The precision farming technique encompasses all those interventions in agriculture which make possible the application of inputs to a precise level without any harm in crop production, besides maintaining the soil health, in order.

In normal agricultural practices for enhancing the crop productivity, the use of inputs such as fertilizers/chemicals, water, etc., is done in uncontrolled way, i.e., at very high rate by the growers. This leads to reduce the produce quality; deteriorate the soil health; pollute the groundwater and air; develop ecological imbalance and thus degrade the environment, ultimately. Development of these kinds of effect because of climate change or global warming is now becoming clearly visible, worldwide. Presently, everyone become very cautious about climate change or global warming. In this crucial situation to mitigate in-conducive effect of climate change the role of precision technologies can be very promising towards achieving a sustained crop yield and leaving the environment pollution free.

1.1 PRECISION FARMING—CONCEPT AND DEFINITION

The concept of precision agriculture was firstly emerged in the United States in the early 1980s; and applied to derive the input recommendation maps for correcting the doses of fertilizers and pH values towards a sustained and healthy agriculture. Later on, the yield sensors were also linked to the GPS; and precision farming technology took its final shape, usable for crop farming. The Precision Farming or Precision Agriculture is also called Satellite Farming, which signifies the farming management based on observing, measuring and responding to inter-and intra-field variability in the crop domain. It encompasses the decision support system for whole farm management system focusing the goal of return optimization against applied various inputs, besides preserving the input resources, as well. The management practice is counted as the Site-Specific Management (SSM).

Precision farming technology follows the Global Positioning System (GPS), which defines the characters temporally and spatially. In Precision Agriculture (PA) or farming the application of inputs like water, fertilizers, pesticides, etc. is done in very precise and correct amount to the crop and also at correct time, which effect on enhancement in crop productivity is very promising.

In nutshell, Precision Agriculture implies the management of field variations such as the soil, climate and water as accurately as possible to achieve high crop productivity in sustainable way; and simultaneously reducing the level of production cost and other in-conducive impacts on soil fauna. (https://www.scenario.co.za) Precision farming technique follows the adoption of technologies for a high level control measure to achieve better crop production per unit land mass on a site-specific, besides following others:

(i) More efficient application of inputs, i.e., the seed, fertilizer, etc.
(ii) More effective utilization of tillage equipments.
(iii) Improved crop and field measurements.
(iv) Better farm management decisions.

As for as definition of Precision farming is concerned there have been devised so many definitions by several individuals/institutions; few important definitions amongst them are presented below:

- The definition adopted by International Society of Precision Agriculture (https://www.ispag.org/) is "Precision Agriculture is a management strategy that gathers, processes and analyzes temporal, spatial and individual data and combines them with other information to support management decisions according to estimated variability for improved resource use efficiency, productivity, quality, profitability and sustainability of agricultural production."
- As per US Congress, "the Precision Agriculture is an evolving management strategy. Its main feature is decision making with regard to resource-use and not necessarily the adoption of information technology. The decisions could depend on changes on one field at a certain time in the season or changes over a season or seasons. Better solutions could provide many benefits (economic, environmental and social) that may or may not be known at present."
- As per Gebbers and Adamchuk (2010), "Precision Farming is an environment-friendly system solution that optimizes product quality and quantity while minimizing cost, human intervention and the variation caused by unpredictable nature."
- As per *Lowenberg-DeBoer* (2003), "Precision Farming is defined as an information technology applied to agriculture."

1.2 DIFFERENCE BETWEEN CONVENTIONAL FARMING AND PRECISION FARMING

In order to describe the differences between conventional and precision farming/agriculture, the following parameters are counted to deal:

1. Site selection
2. Soil preparation
3. Field preparation (ploughing/planking)
4. Seeding/planting
5. Irrigation
6. Fertilizer/pesticide application
7. Weed control
8. Crop harvesting

Considering aforesaid parameters, the differences between traditional and precision farming are presented in Table 1.1.

Table 1.1 Difference between conventional farming and precision farming techniques

S. No.	Particular	Conventional Farming	Precision Farming
1.	Site selection	♦ It is done, manually.	♦ It is done by means of drones and GPS.
2.	Soil preparation	♦ Soil preparation is carried out by mixing chemicals in the soil on the basis of previous experience.	♦ It is performed with the help of sensors, such as, (i) Temperature sensor, (ii) Humidity Sensor, (iii) Volatile matter sensor, etc.
3.	Field preparation–Ploughing and planking	♦ It is done with the help of tractor and bullock powers.	♦ Agricultural robots are used for automatic ploughing.
4.	Seeding and planting	♦ It is carried out, manually with the help of hand tools.	♦ The precision drills, broadcast seeders, seed drills, air seeders are used for seeding or planting work.
5.	Irrigation	♦ Traditional methods (flooding)	♦ Irrigation is performed by precision irrigation techniques such as drip and micro-sprinkler systems commanded by internet system.
6.	Application of fertilizer and pesticides	♦ It is carried out, manually by hand or spraying machine.	♦ It is done by using (i) UAVs and UGVs (ii) Sprayers (iii) GPS (iv) Smartphone and (v) Remote sensing

(*Contd.*)

S. No.	Particular	Conventional Farming	Precision Farming
7.	Weed control	♦ It is done by means of hand tools.	♦ The Blue River Technology and Nano Technologies Weeding Robot Oz are used for weed removal.
8.	Harvesting	♦ Crop harvesting is done, manually or by using mowers.	♦ It is done by using (i) Robotic pick and place arm (ii) Mechanical harvesting, (iii) Limb shaker (iv) Canopy shaker (v) Abscission Chemical

1.3 SALIENT FEATURES OF PRECISION FARMING TECHNOLOGY

Few important and focusing features of precision farming technology are narrated as under:

- It is an integrated crop management system, in which the kind and amount of inputs are matched with the actual requirement of the crop for a small segment of land within the farm.
- Precision agriculture is often referred to as GPS (Global Positioning System) agriculture or variable-rate farming.
- Precision farming/agriculture is described as the information and technology based farm management system for identification, analysis and management of spatial and temporal variability within field to achieve an optimum crop production, sustainability and protection of land resources by minimizing the level of production cost.
- Precision agriculture/farming is one of the approaches to manage the crop farm through interventions of information technology (IT) for insurance of an optimum dose of inputs to the crop and soil, which are actually required for a high crop yield and soil health, both (Bongiovanni, Lowenberg-DeBoer 2004).
- The main objective or goal of Precision agriculture is to ensure profitability, sustainability and protection of the environment.
- Approaches of precision agriculture include the assessment of real-time data about condition of standing crops, soil and air; severity of aberrant weather conditions and availability of labours and machineries along with their cost, as well.
- Optimization of long-term and site-specific farm productivity or increasing the production efficiency and produce quality, and simultaneously minimization of impacts on the environment.
- Precision farming technology is treated as one of the innovative approaches effective to reduce the production cost, risk, enhance productivity and profitability, and maintain sustainability, as well.
- Reducing pressure on agriculture by increasing work efficiency of machineries used and irrigation water cum nutrient use efficiencies. The use of precision based devices reduces the fuel consumption. Similarly, the variable rate application also reduces the use of inputs. This leads to cause a better saving of input costs; and accordingly the outcome gets increase, multifold.

1.4 PRECISION FARMING—MANDATES

The important mandates/objectives of precision farming technology are listed as under:

1. Optimization of field-level management activities mainly in following sectors:
   (i) In crop science sector, it requires to match the farming practices relevant or close to the crop requirements such as the water and nutrients/fertilizers.
   (ii) In case of environmental protection it requires to reduce the environmental risks by limiting or reducing the doses of chemicals/fertilizer application.
   (iii) In economics sector, boosting the competitiveness through introduction of efficient practices such as management of fertilizer application and other inputs.
2. Creation of information or data base related to the crop farming for the farmers/growers, i.e:
   - Creating farm records.
   - Improvement in decision-making
   - Fostering greater traceability
   - Enhancing marketing facility
   - Improving lease arrangements and relationship amongst landowners.
   - Enhancing inherent quality of farm produce, etc.

1.5 ADVANTAGES OF PRECISION FARMING

The main advantages offered by precision farming technique are divided into different perspectives, given as under:

(i) Agronomical perspective,
(ii) Technical perspective,
(iii) Environmental perspective, and
(iv) Economic perspective.

Besides, some of the other advantages of precision farming technology are narrated as under:

1. Solves the problem of farm labour scarcity.
2. Enables to preserve the variety of delicate crops.
3. Enhances crop yields.
4. Creates business opportunities.

Solving farm labour scarcity: The availability of efficient and productive labours to accomplish the farm operations properly and timely is one of the dominating issues in present scenario, across the world. In precision farming technology the introduction of robotics is one of the best substitutes of efficient and productive workforce, through which the agricultural activities can be carried out more precisely without fatigue and accurately as well. Although, the initial expenditure cost is very high in procurement of robots, but it is very reliable substitute of labours. In developing countries such as USA, Japan, China, etc. the intervention of robotics in agriculture sector has become old; however, in Indian context it has a lot of scopes.

Preserving the variety of delicate crops: In precision farming the preservation of delicate crops and their cultivation is possible by introduction of robotics. The researchers and manufacturing companies are also making their untiring efforts in robotics to develop such types of robot which can perform the operations in the manner just like human. The development of Fendt's Xaver Robot (in progress) is an example of it. This robot is designed for corn crop, is expected to launch in the upcoming years. In addition, in this line several other robots are also in pipeline for harvestings the fruit crops such as apple, strawberry, citric fruit, etc.

Enhancement in crop yield: Precision farming is technology based crop cultivation practice, in which the operations starting from land preparation to the crop harvesting are performed through precision tools comprising GPS, GIS VTR, sensors, etc. In addition, the activities of watering, weeding, fertilizing, crop protection, harvesting, etc. are also carried out at right time and in right way. This leads to create a very good effect on the crop, overall. The intervention of robotics technology is the key element in precision farming to cause multifold increase in crop yield or crop productivity.

Creation of business opportunity: In general, the precision farming technology encompasses precise and timely application of inputs such as water, fertilizers/nutrients, labours, etc.; and results a high crop yield with better quality produce. All these features push the farmers to go towards business oriented dealings in respect of crop produce to supply in the market. In addition, the farmers can also prefer the high valued vegetables, flowers, etc. to grow under protected environment using precision farming technique, for supplying the produce in market and realize better sale price.

1.6 DRAWBACK OF PRECISION FARMING

Few promising drawback of precision farming technique are given as under:

- High cost of establishment.
- Lack of technical expertise and awareness about technology.
- In case of small size field, its application is difficult.
- Imperfection regarding heterogeneity of cropping systems.

1.7 LIMITATIONS OF PRECISION FARMING

Being a tool of smart agriculture the precision farming technology involves few limitations, which are mentioned below:

- The tools/equipments such as GPS, GIS, Robots, etc. are costly items; or in other words they require huge amount of money to invest for purchasing them, which is not possible for the farmers of small land holding.
- Arrangement of training programmes on Precision Farming Technology to the users.
- Precision farming tools also require very sincere care and maintenance for their proper and smooth functioning, which is also money investing task as their care and maintenance is done by skilled person.
- The availability of Precision farming tools in nearby market is not so common.
- Farmers are expected to lose their engagement in farm activities, because of placing of Agribots like devices for perfuming the work.
- Requirement of wide publicity about its application at farmer's level.

1.8 PRECISION FARMING—IMPORTANCE IN INDIAN SCENARIO

In Indian context it is pertinent to say that to meet a huge demand of food grain of 480 MT by 2050 for feeding more than 170 corers population in the situation of increased biotic challenges and abiotic stresses experienced by the crops, the intervention/introduction or adoption of cutting edge technologies in crop farming system is to be very essential. The technology must be effective to enhance the production level, improve the produce quality, cause less use of chemicals/ fertilizers, etc.; and finally should result a high returns from the farming system adopted by the farmers. The horticultural crops such as fruits, flowers and vegetables are the prime crops, in which the application of modern technologies is very essential. The sugarcane is also one of the important crops, has a good potential for interventions of such technologies, as it is one of the most remunerative crops requiring high amount of irrigation and fertilizers during its crop period.

Precision farming is the technology in which the requisite inputs are applied in precise amount to the crop to realize an increased yield over traditional farming practices or technologies. In precision farming context the main constraint is small size land holding with the farmers in majority of the states. The land statistics of Indian states reveals that in majority of the states more than 58% land holdings have the size less than 1ha. The states comprising Punjab, Rajasthan, Haryana and Gujarat have more than 20% land (Agricultural lands) holding size more than 4 ha.

The application of Precision Farming (PA) as per crop concern, the commercial and horticultural crops have wide scope for use. In Indian context the sustainable precision farming technology is to be a most valuable innovation in farm management aspects. Furthermore, in present scenario the farmer's group is eager to follow the Precision farming technology to enhance their crop yield and produce quality, as well; and accordingly to realize a high benefit-to-cost (b/c) ratio. In nutshell, the PA technology meets the following requirements concern to agriculture:

- Increasing crop productivity level.
- Preventing the soil against erosion or degradation.
- Reducing fertilizer's/chemical's doses for application.
- Utilizing available water resources, efficiently.
- Disseminating modern farm technologies to improve crop yield and produce quality, as well.
- Reducing production cost.
- Developing favourable attitudes among farming community.
- Uplifting socio-economic condition of the farmers.

1.9 PRECISION FAMING—ADOPTION AT WORLD'S SCALE

At world scale, the precision farming technology has covered a good area in agriculture sector. However, the precursor countries are the United States, Canada and Australia among all. In European countries the United Kingdom was appeared first to introduce the PA system in agriculture, and the France was the second during 1997-1998. In Latin America the Argentina appeared a leading country to adopt Precision Farming technique in the mid 1990s. Similarly, the Brazil established a state-owned enterprise called Embrapa for conducting research on precision farming technique to develop a sustainable agriculture system for the country. Because of introduction of GPS and variable-rate spreading techniques, the precision farming technique got a new dimension for its broader applications. In France about 10% farmers are using variable-rate systems in their farming system. As demerit, the PA system requires huge investments on various devices such as GPS, advance computer system, etc. However, in developing countries the farmers are getting benefits by taking the help of mobile technology. The China is behind the Europe and United States regarding use of PA system, because of the reason that the Chinese agricultural system involves small-scale family-run farms, which causes restrictions in adoption of precision agriculture.

As for as, research on PA is concerned, it was started in the USA, Canada, Australia, and Western Europe, during mid-to late 1980s. Since, then it has been done enormous research across the world; and based on their recommendations or findings, its applications have also been done by the farmers to a significant level. However, very small number of farmers are still there, who have adopted the precision farming technologies for crop cultivation.

The implementation of precision farming technique is through use of machineries such as mounting type controllers and GPS to apply the inputs at variable rate. In this regard Naiqian et al. (2002) pointed that to the date the majority of application of precision farming is site-specific, which is mainly in the form of fertilizer application. Similarly, Heege, H. (ed.), (2013) also mentioned that the diverse type PA technologies, i.e., Variable rate technology (VRT) applications of fertilizers and herbicides are majorly in use across the world.

1.10 TECHNOLOGICAL INTERVENTIONS

The important technological interventions in precision faming are narrated as under,

Precision soil preparation: In agricultural farming for achieving a good crop yield the preparation of soil/field involves a high level importance. In regard to Precision Agriculture the preparation of soil is done in very precise way, keeping in view that the water stagnation at any spot in the field or in other words an improper water distribution in crop field should not be there. The water stagnation or non-uniform distribution of irrigation water takes place in undulated field, which causes so many d/s effects such as occurrence of soil erosion and non-uniformity in availability of nutrients and water to the crop, mainly. In context to precision farming the preparation of soil is carried out based on following information:

- Soil survey map comprising the soil type and topography, mainly.
- Soil physical property maps showing soil texture and available water capacity.
- Yield map of previous crop.

These information are helpful in prediction of yield potential and field management, besides to correct the agricultural practices and identify suitable implements to achieve most healthy soil preparation. In traditionally followed technologies for field preparation, the consumption of energy (labour and fuel) is very high depending on soil type and land topography. In result the benefit-cost ratio of crop production system gets declined, multifold.

Precision seeding: The seed rate, planting/sowing depth, row spacing, etc. are very sensitive factors affecting the crop yield, in addition to crop variety and nutrient application. In precision agriculture the rate of seeding is comparatively lesser than the traditional practices. Also, the depth of seed dropping and spacing is kept at an optimum range, by virtue of which the crop yield gets affected in positive sense. In precision agriculture, the precision seeding is ensured with the aid of geo-mapping, as follows:

(i) High seed rate in the soils with low yield potential,
(ii) Less seeds rate in soils having high yield potential, and
(iii) Application of fertilizers/chemicals with variable rate, technology (VRT) application.

In addition, the level of seed germination also ensures the crop productivity, which depends on the seed quality, soil and climate characteristics, and tillage practices followed to prepare the soil for sowing the seeds. In context to achieve proper result the seed sowing implements should be equipped with the technology or system to ensure effective and accurate sowing of seeds to satisfy the objective of precision agriculture.

Precision crop management: In order to achieve a good level of agricultural yield the crop management is very essential, which is carried out by means of following practices:

(i) Application of nutrients at right rate and right time using top-dressing method, and
(ii) Proper management of weeds, pests and diseases.

Accomplishment of above two requisites can be by following means:

(i) Using crop sensors,
(ii) Through optimized boundary spreading, and
(iii) Application of satellite steering systems, i.e., the Global Positioning System (GPS).

Precision harvesting: In crop production system the harvesting is one of the most critical activities. If it is not done at proper time the net crop yield is likely to get significantly affected. Sometimes, in absence of labour or harvesting machines the crop gets damage because of occurrence of rainfall or hail storm. Or sometimes, the crop is also harvested at improper stage. In result the net crop yield gets drastically reduced. In general, the harvesting speed/ rate, harvesting accuracy, timing, etc. are the overriding factors in crop harvesting process. In precision farming the crop harvesting is carried out by means of sensor equipped machines which harvesting capacity and other features are totally precision based.

1.11 EMERGING TECHNOLOGIES UNDER PRECISION FARMING

The emerging technologies associated to precision farming are narrated as under:

(i) Robot
(ii) Drones and satellite imaginary
(iii) Internet of things (IoT)
(iv) Smartphone
(v) Machine learning

Robots: Precision farming is basically automation based crop farming technique. Automation causes saving of time, water, fertilizer, energy and other inputs required in crop cultivation, besides increasing the crop productivity. In automation the robot plays significant role. Robot navigates the field and interprets the assigned task. In addition, robot also helps the farmers to control the weed problem from the crop; application of water, fertilizers and chemicals such as weedicides, fungicides, etc. In nutshell, the applications of robot in agriculture are as follows:

(i) Autonomous precision seeding
(ii) Application of fertilizers, nutrients/chemicals
(iii) Precision irrigation
(iv) Automation
(v) Harvesting and picking
(vi) Weed control
(vii) Crop monitoring
(viii) Nursery raising
(ix) Thinning and pruning
(x) Milking
(xi) Data collection
(xii) Mowing, pruning, seeding, spraying and thinning
(xiii) Phenotype
(xiv) Sorting and packing
(xv) Utility platforms

Drones and Satellite Imagery: Drones are Unmanned Aircraft Systems (UAS). It is a powerful tool that can be used for various purposes oriented to agriculture. In precision agriculture, its application is very wide. It provides real-time information. In agriculture sector its uses may be in following aspects:

- It can help the farmers to optimize various inputs such as seed, fertilizers, water, etc. for the crops.
- Provides very quick application of insecticides/pesticides to the infested crop.
- It saves time against crop scouting.
- Provides real-time observations on field crops.
- Accomplishes soil and field analysis.
- Performs crop monitoring, very accurately.
- It can also play role in livestock management.

Satellite imagery is the digital image of the earth's surface compiled from spectral data, collected by sensors. Spectral images are also taken for the crops grown or land use systems existing on the earth system. In precision farming these images constitute the information about status of the crop, attack of disease, etc. By imagery one can easily get the idea about health status of the crop. Its various uses are as follows:

- Satellite imagery can help in managing the natural environment.
- The yield map can allow for better targeting of fertilizer applications.
- It also allows to assess the crop yield, accurately.
- Satellite Imagery provides up-to-date information on moisture stress, disease incidence, structural anomalies, and nutrient's levels.
- The modern precision agriculture satellite imagery provides to get most accurate data.

Internet of things (IoT): It is a system comprising the features like computing devices, mechanical and digital machines, objects, animals or people provided with their unique identifiers, besides transferring the data over a network without requiring human-to-human or human-to-computer interactions. In the word "Internet of things" the "things" denotes to the followings:

(a) A person with heart monitor implant.
(b) A farm animal with a biochip transponder.
(c) An automobile along with built-in sensors to alert the driver when tyre pressure is low,
(d) The other natural or man-made object that can be assigned an Internet Protocol (IP) address and is able to transfer data over a network.

In agriculture IoT uses robots, drones, remote sensors, and computer imaging combined with continuously progressing machine learning and analytical tools. The functions of IoT are as under:

(i) Monitoring of crops
(ii) Surveying of field crops
(iii) Mapping of crop fields
(iv) Supplying farm management based data

Smartphone: It is also used as one of the important tools/technologies for discharging various purposes of precision farming system. Smartphone facilitates to operate the apps associated to agriculture. For meeting the farmer's requirement, the smartphones have been developed with different features suitable to agricultural activities. Mainly, the smartphones are categorized as per following features:

(i) Agriculture management information,
(ii) Agriculture information resource,
(iii) Agriculture calculator,
(iv) Agriculture news,
(v) Weather, and
(vi) m-government.

In addition to above categories of smartphones, they are also available for following works:

(i) Learning and reference,
(ii) Diseases and pests,
(iii) Market data,
(iv) Conference,
(v) Business, and
(vi) Field mapping.

***Applications of smartphones*:** The applications of smartphone for agricultural operations are categorized mainly in following three categories:

(i) Crop operations,
(ii) Farm management, and
(iii) Information system.

These applications are further elaborated as presented in Table 1.2.

Table 1.2 Applications of smartphone

S. No.	Applications
1.	Crop operations based applications (i) Decision making support at crop system level, (ii) Crop nutrition and fertilization, (iii) Crop irrigation, (iv) Crop growth and canopy management, and (v) Crop harvest.
2.	Farm management based applications (i) Efficient and effective farm resources, (ii) Machinery management, and (iii) Control of farm activities.
3.	Information system based applications (i) Providing essential information about agricultural system, (ii) Market information, (iii) Relevant news, (iv) Chat with experts, and (v) Climate information.

Machine learning: It is a branch of artificial intelligence (AI), in which with the aid of software the prediction of outcome is carried out more accurately without involvement of explicit programme. Using this tool a new output value is predicted based on the historic data as input. Machine learning is commonly used in conjunction with the drones, robots, and IoT, as well. In this technique the AI allows for the data input from each of the sources. The computer processes the information and communicates the action, back to the respective devices. Robots are allowed to deliver a perfect (precise) amount of fertilizers/chemicals; or to the IoT devices to provide a perfect quantity of water directly to the soil. Besides above, the machine learning can also predict the available nitrogen in soil media which is advantageous to prepare fertilization plan for the crop specific.

1.12 TOOLS AND MACHINERIES/DEVICES FOR PRECISION FARMING TECHNOLOGY

Precision Farming is totally technology based system, which comprises a set of tools and equipments for its implementation at field level. The essential tools and equipments required are listed as under:

1. Global Positioning System (GPS)
2. Geographic Information System (GIS)
3. Grid Sampling
4. Variable Rate Technology (VRT)
5. Yield Maps
6. Remote Sensors
7. Proximate Sensors
8. Computer Hardware and Software
9. Precision Irrigation Systems

Global Positioning System (GPS): This is one of the most important tools in precision farming technology, which is used in different agricultural processes to perform. GPS assembles a set of 24 satellites in the earth orbit at about 20,000 km altitude from earth surface, which transmit and receive the real-time data. The real-time data collected through GPS is being very accurate about position of the object, which in turn to result an efficient analysis and manipulation of geospatial data. The prediction accuracy of GPS varies within 10 to 15 m with reference to actual position of the object. GPS also facilitates precise mapping of farm activities. In addition, with the aid or help of software it also determines the status of standing crop in the field. In addition, GPS also enables to predict the requirement of inputs such as water, fertilizers, chemicals, pesticides, etc. for an individual part of the farm area. Accordingly, on the basis of obtained information the farmer can ensure himself to apply the inputs to the crop, very accurately at proper time schedule, which leads to return a good crop yield or production.

Geographic information system (GIS): This is a kind of software used in PA technology towards crop farming. In macro and micro level mapping of natural resources, it is used as one of the most important tools. In precision farming system it is also used for implementing and monitoring the farm activities at field scale. In nutshell, the activities such as field mapping, monitoring of crop at different stages, disease management, yield estimation, soil mapping, weed's mapping and hotspots for disease incidence can be suitably accomplished. Besides, it can also be used to facilitate the functions of import, export and processing of spatially and temporally distributed data.

Grid sampling: This is an important activity in PA technology to perform the operation smoothly and more precisely. Especially, it is important for soil sampling to analyze the soil properties. In gird sampling the entire field is fragmented into various grids. The size of grid may vary from 0.5 to 5 ha. Soil sampling is done within the grid area. The number of soil samples from the grid may be many. The collected soil samples are analyzed to determine the rate of fertilizer or nutrient requirement for the crop concern.

Variable rate technology (VRT): It is the technology which enables the application of materials at varying rates. In precision farming this is an important tool. In nutshell, VRT is a tool which allows a farmer to apply the inputs such as the water, fertilizers, chemicals and seeds at different rates as per requirement of the crop. Two types of VRT are commonly used in precision farming; they are namely, (i) Map based VRT; and (ii) Sensor based VRT, in which map based VRT performs the application on the basis of pre-generated map of the cropped field. On the other hand, the sensor-based VRT doesn't use the map, but performs the application by using sensors which determine the real-time soil properties or crop characteristics; and accordingly the control system predicts the inputs, required to apply.

Yield maps: The yield mapping or preparation of yield map is the key action for assessing the crop performance. This component is included to refine the PA system. The yield map signifies the potential of soil and other applied inputs to the crop to result the yield. In addition, it can also be used to demarcate the variations in soil, soil moisture content, etc. across the farm by correlating the crop yield obtained (Stafford, et,al. 1991). In context to precision farming technology the important components that constitute a part of yield map system, are narrated below:

- ***Grain flow sensors*:** These sensors are used to determine the overall amount of grain being harvested.

- ***Grain moisture sensors*:** These are equipped to determine the status of moisture content of the grain, and to compensate for variability of moisture levels.
- ***GPS antenna*:** It is placed to receive the satellite signals.
- ***Clean grain elevator speed sensors*:** These are used to enhance the accuracy of grain flow measurements.
- ***Yield monitor display*:** This is equipped with a GPS receiver. It records the data related to geo-referencing.
- ***Travel speed sensors*:** These sensors are used to determine the travel distance during specific logging intervals.
- ***Header position sensors*:** In system, these are used to distinguish the measurements, recorded during turns.

For a better result these sensors are required to calibrate very accurately, before placing them for use.

Remote sensors: In precision farming technique the remote sensing systems are used to generate a large volume of spectral data concern to the crop. The most widely used remote sensing systems are classified as under:

1. Platform based sensors, and
2. Other sensors.

The platform based sensors are mounted on satellites, aerial and ground based. Sometimes, the ground-based sensing systems are also known as proximal remote sensing systems, because they are located in close proximity to the target, i.e., the land surface or the plant. The ground-based platform sensors used for PA are further classified into following three categories:

(i) Hand hold,
(ii) Free standing, and
(iii) Mounted type.

The free standing type sensors are located in standing position in the crop field. Mounted type sensors are attached to the tractor or farm machinery. In recent, the aerial platforms including aircraft and unmanned aerial vehicles (UAVs) are also used in precision farming system. The aerial platforms like UAVs provide higher spatial resolutions, i.e., less than 5 m to that of the satellites.

Many of the satellites provide high spatial resolution, i.e., less than 5 m and temporal, i.e., for 1 day or say daily resolution images, in which most of them are rather coarse for many PA applications. The extent of appropriate spatiotemporal resolution required for PA system depends on host of the factors, such as management objectives, field size and the ability or capability of farm equipments to change the application rate of inputs such as irrigation, fertilizer, pesticide, etc. In case of estimation of crop biomass and yield, relatively high spatial resolution (1 to 3 m) is required as compared to the required resolution for application of fertilizers and irrigations (5 to 10 m) at varying rates. Similarly, in case of weed mapping and application of herbicide at varying rates the spatial resolution may vary from 5 to 50 cm.

Apart from above sensors the thermal infrared and microwave sensors are also used in PA system. Thermal infrared sensors are used to measure the energy emitted from the target (crops) to determine the temperature, which could further be used for determining the crop water stress, evapotranspiration (ET), and the irrigation requirement, as well.

The working principle of microwave type sensors is the same to the thermal infrared sensors, to measure the emitted energy from the land surface or the crop canopy surface. In PA system the microwave sensors are used to determine the level of soil moisture and the crop water use over a large area.

Proximate sensors: These sensors are used for measuring the soil parameters such as status of N in the soil and accordingly, the required amount of nitrogen for application to the crop; and the soil pH, besides the crop properties. Proximate sensors are attached to the tractor and pass over the field for measurement of respective soil or crop parameters.

Computer hardware and software: These are the tools used for analyzing the data and making them in presentable format such as maps, graphs, charts or reports, etc.; and also deriving conclusions from them.

Precision irrigation systems: Precision Irrigation is an innovative irrigation technique, through which water is precisely applied to the crops in terms of irrigation. This irrigation is beneficial to result a better crop yield through minimum water application. The drip and micro-sprinkler systems fall in the category of "Precision Irrigation" or "Variable Rate Irrigation" (VRI). The VRI system can be integrated to the micro-sprinklers, drip and overhead sprinklers by means of controllers and software.

1.13 FUTURE PROSPECT OF PRECISION FARMING

In agriculture sector, the future prospect of precision farming is very wide because of intervention of robotics and sensor based technologies. Few are mentioned as under:

1. Sensor based cropping,
2. Vertical farming,
3. Robotic swarms, and
4. Big data in farming.

Sensor based cropping: In traditional farming system the farmers adopt the practices as per guidelines provided by the scientists or the advisory framed by the state government agencies. For example the depth or number of irrigations, dose of fertilizers, plant protection measures, harvesting time, etc. for the crop concern are notified in terms of guidelines, which are as per scientific studies conducted at research institutions. On the other hand, in precision farming system most of the work activities are performed, sensor based (Ravi and Jagadeesha 2002). Sensors provide real time information. For example the information on existing moisture content, nutrients availability in the soil media and other characteristics of the soil are determined in the terms of real-time, which is most essential for their application at precise scale in accordance with the sensed values. This causes the input's saving to a large extent; and thus, making the crop farming more remunerative.

Scope of vertical farming: Vertical farming is one of the practices of growing crops in precision farming technique, in which crops are grown in vertically stacked layers. It is often practiced in a controlled-environment with the objective to optimize the plant growth. The soilless farming technique such as hydroponics, aquaponics and aeroponics are closely linked to the vertical farming system. The objective of vertical farming is to increase the crop yield per unit area. In this farming the problem of nutrients drainage form the soil is totally negated. The application of inputs such as fertilizers/nutrients, irrigation and others is carried out through drip system in precise amount as per sensed value by the sensor placed. This leads to reduce the rate of input application or in other words enhancing the level of net return from the crop. Nowadays, this form of crop farming is becoming very popular in the countries like China, USA and others, too.

Robotic swarms: It is the field of multi-robotics, in which large numbers of robots are coordinated in a distributed and decentralized manner. Swarm robotics act as a solution to the crops inspection for precision agriculture. The Swarm farming is the name emerged from the concept of swarm robotics. Swarm robotics generates the concept of multi-robots automated system. As the number of robots is increased (keeping the size of robot less) the capability of swarm entity gets increase. This leads to cast the solution, that would be about to impossible from a single robot. Using robotics swarm a large number of real-time data on different parameters can be collected from the field, which are shared to the cloud, analyzed and the results are generated in terms of excess moisture, nutrients deficiency, etc., on the basis of which, a suitable decision is taken in respect of their application as input to the crop. In this regard an international firm "FENDT" is working under a project called (MARS Mobile Agricultural Robot Swarms) funded by European Union.

Big data in farming: In precision farming there is collection and storage of large number of real-time data, because of use of sensors and robotic swarm in context to derive real-time decisions, quickly, with greater accuracy and to a precision level. A large number of data makes easy to provide more accurate feedback about the crop, which is beneficial to apply the measures against them in better way and in time, to mitigate the issues.

1.14 MAJOR CHALLENGES OF PRECISION FARMING

Precision farming is the crop farming technique, in which major inputs are applied to the crop in precise amount and ways, accurately. The technologies such as machine learning/ artificial intelligence, robotics, internet of things (IoT), sensors, etc. are the key tools in context to all agricultural operations including soil preparation, seed sowing/planting, watering, fertilizing, harvesting, as well. In application of precision farming technology for successful crop production, there are numerous constraints/challenges, which may discourage the users. Overall, in Indian contexts the followings are the main challenges associated to the application of precision farming techniques:

1. Educational Challenge
2. Economic Challenge

In India about 70% population lives in the rural areas, i.e., villages, where main occupation of the people is farming. The farmers are small, medium or large depending on their size of land holding. However, majority is of small farmers amongst total. Literacy level is also very poor. These factors in combination make the farmer's attitude unfavorable about crop farming under technological intervention. In present scenario, there have been developed enormous farmer's friendly technologies, which are very conducive to enhance the crop productivity along with saving of sufficient water, fertilizer and labour, as well. However, its adoption at country level is not satisfactory might be due to unawareness or lack of exposure about technologies. Regarding adoption of the technologies the farmers need to have innovative thoughts about crop farming system; otherwise, there is no conducive impact is expected to get happen on farming. The education plays significant role on this aspect. The lack of expertise on the subject concern, unavailability of qualified extension, electrical and electronic personnel, etc. are mainly because of poor education level in the area or region specific. These facts constitute a kind of educational challenge for adoption of precision farming technologies by farming community.

The economic challenge is also applied very seriously to the Indian farming communities regarding adoption of precision farming technique. The robots, sensors, GPS, GIS, drones, computer, etc. are the main devices used for application of the inputs in precise mode (Stafford, Ambler and Smith, 1991). These tools are costly items, which procurement at farmer's level is not possible. This fact also develops a kind of economic challenge for the farmers to introduce precision farming technique in their crop farming system.

1.15 SUGGESTIVE MEASURES FOR PROMOTION OF PRECISION FARMING TECHNIQUE

The Precision farming technique is one of the cutting edge technologies, causes enhancement in crop yield with better quality produce, high b/c ratio, water saving, nutrient saving, labour (energy) saving, etc. but still there is a large gap in its adoption level among the famers. There are few important points in terms of suggestions to promote the precision farming technology amongst farming community, narrated as under:

- Demarcate the niche areas, which could be promoted by precision farming for the crop specific.
- Formation of team of multidisciplinary professionals, such as agricultural scientists, engineers, manufacturers and economists; and conducting study to explore the possibilities of expansion of precision agriculture/farming scopes.
- Development of detail technical knowhow and making them available to the farmers, which could be beneficial for creating pilots projects or models at large scale.
- Arrangement of pilot studies on farmers' fields, in the mode of field level demonstration of promising results derived from the precision agriculture.
- Creation of awareness about importance of precision farming technique among farmers, regarding enhancement in crop yield, water saving, fertilizer saving, labour saving, etc.

1.16 PRECISION FARMING—STEPS

Precision farming accomplishes all those farm activities which are required to sow/plant the seeds, irrigation, weed management, fertilizing, insect/pest management, harvesting, threshing, etc. as done in traditional farming system in course of crop cultivation. However, in precision farming all these activities are performed in automated manner by means of sensors and other tools. The sequential steps involved in precision farming are given as under:

1. Locating land position
2. Soil sensing

3. Ploughing the soil and its leveling/planking
4. Seeding/planting
5. Applying irrigation
6. Application of fertilizers/nutrients and pesticides
7. Weed management
8. Crop harvesting

Locating land position: Precision farming is quite different over traditional farming in sense of application of requisite inputs in very precise way based on real-time time input data on existing status of moisture, nutrients, etc. in the soil media. On this ground the location of land position where PF technology is to be adopted becomes essential. Location somehow ascertains the availability of water, labour, transport and market connectivity, which are essential for establishment of PA system at field. The information about field location can be grasped by using the GPS. In this line the past experiences are also being most beneficial.

Soil sensing: This is one of the tasks in PA system. Soil sensing is carried out for determining the status of soil in respect of availability of moisture content, nutrients and others parameters in real-time. Soil sensing is done during course of cultivation by means of drones or robots loaded with sensors, by moving across the field. The sensors are linked to the micro-controller for processing the data, collected. Micro-controller is operated through a remote device, which is over a network of frequency. The soil sensing performs accurately when a large number of data is collected for making comparison or deriving the result (Pobkrut and Kerdcharoen, 2014).

The electronic nose (E-Nose) is another type of sensor used in precision farming technique, for determining the metallic fumes existing in the soil media. This information identifies the presence of mineral deposits if there in the soil. These sensors are placed in a chamber equipped with a fan, sense the odor with a change in airflow; on the basis of this the location of odour source is identified.

Ploughing and planking/leveling: This is the next step after locating the land position in PF system. Ploughing is the process of mechanical manipulation of soil favorable to a good germination of sown seeds. The ploughing operation consists of the processes such as breaking and loosening of the soil, and turning the same for removing/uprooting the weeds and simultaneously aerating the soil, as well. The loosened soil mass becomes well aerated, which is conducive to plant growth. Planking is done to level the ploughed surface, which is uneven. The big size soil clods appeared during ploughing operation, are also crushed during leveling operation. In addition the soil also becomes in compact form, effective to conserve the soil moisture content against evaporation loss. In precision farming the ploughing and leveling operations are performed by means of some special types of machines, are narrated as under:

***Agricultural robots*:** In precision farming these robots are used for various operations such as (i) ploughing; (ii) seed disbursing; (iii) fruit picking; and (iv) spraying of chemicals like pesticides, etc. In agricultural robots there is also the provision for manual control of the system, which is used as per requirement. In its operation, at beginning the robot tills the entire field and proceeds to plough, next. Simultaneously, during ploughing operation, the dispensing of seeds side by side is also accomplished. In its system an ultrasonic sensor is also equipped for continuously transferring the data to micro-controller (Raja and Karunakaran, 2017).

Seeding/Planting: In course of crop cultivation the seeds are directly sown in the well prepared field. While in case of planting the seedlings are prepared in the nursery, from where well developed seedlings are removed and transplanted to another field, such as in case of paddy crop. On the other hand, in precision farming technique the sowing of seeds or transplanting of seedlings is carried out by some special type of machines/implements. The commonly used machineries are described as under:

(i) *Air-assisted strip seeders*: The air-assisted strip seeders are used for direct seeding purpose. This machine is labour-saving and cost effective. Seeds are injected into the ports placed at the bottom, via blower. Its salient features are mentioned below:

(a) Base width: It is about 10 m, i.e., one side base width is 5 m.
(b) Seed dropping distance: It is about 30 cm.
(c) Field efficiency: It is about 70%.

(ii) *Broadcast seeders*: Broadcasting is also one of the traditional methods of seed sowing, done manually. However, this method has demerits about non-uniformity in sowing of seeds; and accordingly, there is also non-uniformity in germinated seedlings. In addition, the plant to plant and row to row spacing is also not maintained there. This causes no use of farm implements for inter-culturing operations in standing crop. Nowadays, various types of seeders have been developed for sowing the seeds. The broadcast seeders are one of them, which are used for sowing the seeds in broadcasting manner. These are designated as broadcast spreader or broadcaster, or even sometimes as the centrifugal fertilizer spreader, too. Apart from broadcasting the seeds these are also used for spreading the lime, fertilizer, sand, etc. Sometimes, these seeders are also used as the substitute of drop spreaders/seeders. The main demerit of this seeder is non-uniformity in distribution of seeds.

(iii) *Seed drill*: This is very common type of machine used for sowing the seeds. In precision farming the sowing operation is performed by seed drills of suitable field capacity, depending upon field size. The seed rate and seed to seed and row to row spacing are maintained by seed drills. In addition, the seed geometry (seed to seed and row to row spacing) can be easily adjusted as per requirement, which is done by replacing the seed metering device. The depth of seed dropping or placing in the soil is also maintained under seed drill sowing. Since, seeds are sown at a fixed geometry; therefore, germinated plants have a clear cut spacing in respect of their row to row and plants to plant. This feature makes the use of farm machineries for tillage operations, smoothly, in seed drill sown crop fields. The seed drills are also available in various types depending on use of power source for their operation, such as:

(i) Bullock drawn seed drill,
(ii) Power tiller operated, and
(iii) Tractor power operated seed drills.

Also, the zero till seed cum fertilizer drills are there, can be used for sowing purposes.

Irrigation: Application of water to the crop in terms of irrigation is very important work step in precision farming mode of crop cultivation. Conventionally, it is carried out by several methods following flooding approach. In context to precision farming the conventional methods are completely unsuitable, as there is no control on rate of water application, precisely. This leads to cause of improper application of irrigation to the crop; normally, greater in amount than the requirement, which is not acceptable in precision farming. The micro irrigation, i.e., the drip method is treated as one of the most suitable methods for precision irrigation. Drip system encompasses the provision for changing the rate of water application, besides so many other conducive features essential to precision farming. The drip system in context to precision farming, is narrated as under:

***Drip irrigation system*:** Although, the drip system involves the provision for varying the rate of water application by replacing the emitters of desired discharge rate, but by linking the system with internet module it can be made more versatile to precision farming, regarding control on water application at precision scale (Gaikwad et al., 2018). The view of drip system linked with internet module is presented in Figure 1.1. The module assembles following components:

(i) Power source (AC supply/solar power)
(ii) Power unit
(iii) Raspberry pi
(iv) Web server
(v) On/off switch
(vi) Sensor unit; and
(vii) Pumping unit

Power source: The AC power supply or solar power can be used for operating the system to perform irrigation, precisely. In drip module the power source is directly connected to the power unit.

Power unit: It is connected to the ON/OFF switch and Raspberry pi. Power unit receives the power or energy from the power source and supplies to the water pumping unit via ON/OFF switch.

Raspberry pi: This is linked to the Web server. Its function is to send the information to the sensor for sensing the concern character by using internet module. The sensed value by the sensor is directed to the Raspberry pi unit.

Web server: It receives the sensed value from Raspberry pi unit. Web server also compares the thought value of sensor and current value; and redirects the comparable values to the Raspberry pi unit. And finally, the Raspberry pi unit performs the function, accordingly.

Operation: The operation of drip module is presented as under:

(i) Form power source the power is supplied to the pumping unit via power unit and ON/OFF switch.
(ii) In On (switch) condition, the power unit gets link with the water pump. In OFF condition the power unit gets link with the Raspberry pi unit.
(iii) In OFF (switch) condition the Raspberry pi unit starts functioning, i.e., sends the information to the sensing unit comprising transpiration sensor, humidity sensor, moisture sensor, raindrop sensor, etc. for sensing respective parameters.
(iv) The sensed values by respective sensors are directed to the Raspberry pi unit.
(v) Now, Raspberry pi unit redirects these values to the web server.
(vi) The web server compares the thought values provided by the sensors and the current value. And sends the comparable values to the Raspberry pi unit.
(vii) Now, Raspberry pi unit takes the action to supply water for irrigation to the crop.

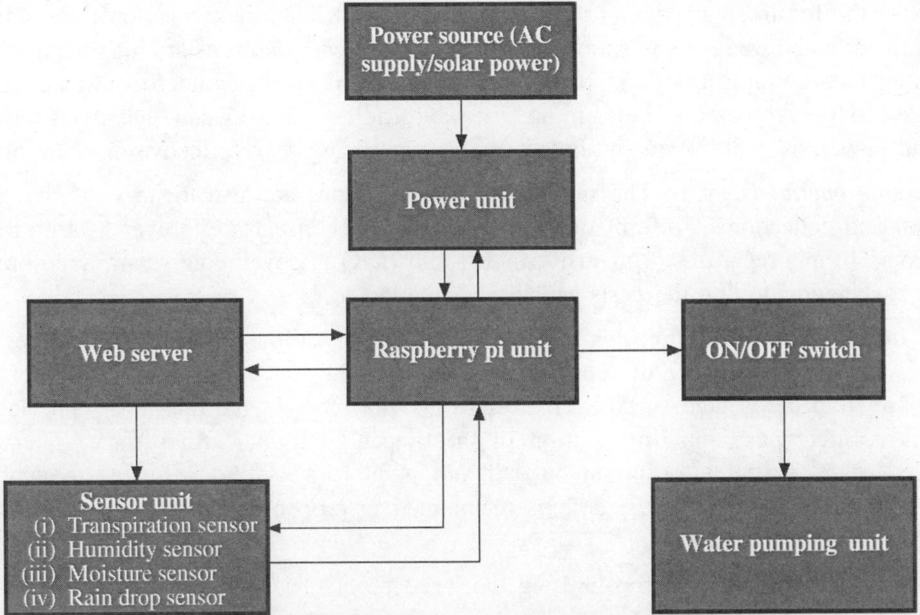

Figure 1.1 Block diagramme of drip system for precision irrigation

Application of Fertilizer/Nutrients/Chemicals: The application of fertilizers/nutrients or chemicals as insecticides or pesticides in proper dose and time to the crop for better yield is very essential. Manual application of these substances does not ensure to a precise amount. The drip system which is most suitable for irrigation and fertigation can be used for this purpose. In drip system there is a unit called "fertigation system" is used to apply fertilizers (soluble) or chemicals to the crop in controlled or precise way. In precision farming technique to manage a large area in respect of insect/pest management the commonly used tools are UAVs, UGVs, Patch sprayer, Canopy sprayer, GNSS and Mechanical/Thermal tools, are narrated as under:

Unmanned aerial vehicles (UAV) and unmanned ground vehicles (UGV): These are the remote controlled devices, are operated by well-trained pilot. These devices are used for collecting the information on various aspects related to crop grown. The unmanned aerial vehicles collect the information about incidence of insects/pests in the form of high-resolution images. The multi-spectral and hyper spectral imagery are normally preferred to predict the crop response in visible and near infra-red regime of electromagnetic spectrum. On the basis of images the status of crop due to any kind of incidence is analyzed; and according to that the requisite measures are applied on infested crop to control the problem from there. Since, information are in terms of images; therefore, the view about the content becomes very clear. Even from images the types of insects/pests in attack are also detected, accurately; based on which a correct selection of pesticide or fungicide is made easily. Above-mentioned vehicles, i.e., the UAVs and UGVs also carry the spraying devices for application of chemicals.

Sprayers: Sprayers are used for application of fertilizers and chemicals on standing crops. In precision agriculture/farming on the basis of data collected with the aid of prescribed tools or devices the fertilizers or chemicals are sprayed at controlled or precise rate over affected area of the crop. Nowadays, the sprayers equipped with several nozzles are integrated with the GPS navigation system through software, perform better result in context to fast application, coverage of large crop area and also in precise way, leading to save water, chemicals/fertilizers and man power, as well. Normally, boom sprayers are being more effective than the others.

***Smartphone operated apps*:** The smartphone operated apps are also found very effective in detection and collection of information about incidence of insects/pests over a large tract of field crops. In this regard the University of Lincoln (UK) is developing smartphone operated app for tacking/identifying the pests causing destruction of crops.

***GPS*:** In precision agriculture, this is used for predicting various crop based activities. This device is linked to a network of about 30 satellites, orbiting the earth at an altitude of about 20,000 km from the ground surface. GPS transmits and receives the real-time data, and also provides accurate positional information of the object lying on earth surface. The timely collection of geospatial information on soil and plant using GPS, facilitates to apply the measures, promptly. In result the crop is maintained in proper mode, to cause a good crop yield (Shanwad et al., 2002).

Weed removal/control: In crop farming the weed problem is one of the serious causes to decline the crop yield or productivity. Conventionally, there are so many practices or methods followed for eradication of weeds from the crop but they are not found fit for precision farming system. In precision farming the weed mapping showing the information on position, weed density/biomass and the species of weed, is done with the help of advance robotic technology. Besides, facilitating the weed control, the robotic technology is also being well suitable and an alternative to apply herbicides/pesticides. In addition, few more technologies are also there for weed control under precision farming. They are presented as under:

(a) ***Blue river technology*:** Blue river technology refers to the application of machine learning, robotics, and computer vision technologies to derive better decision on crop cultivation in precision mode. The tools such as See & Spray, computer vision, machine learning, and advanced robotic technology are used to distinguish the crops and weeds in cropped field; and accordingly the spraying of herbicides or other chemicals is done only on the surface area of weed growth in the field.

(b) ***Nano technology weeding robot Oz*:** It is another tool used for removing the weeds from cropped land. Its application in precision farming is highly justified. Various features of this device are enumerated as under:

- (i) It follows the crop row for its operation.
- (ii) During operation it is guided itself.
- (iii) It is capable to eradicate the weeds from crop rows without help of person.
- (iv) Oz works, autonomously.
- (v) It is easy-to-use tool.
- (vi) It reduces the risk of production loss, and helps to secure the income from the crop.
- (vii) The Oz robotic weeder is also capable to detect the obstacles, blocked tools, errors in row length, etc.
- (viii) It sends text messages to get alert by the operator.

Harvesting: The crop harvesting is one of the most labour-consuming agricultural activities. Nowadays, the harvesters are available, crop wise, e.g., the paddy harvester, reaper, mower, reaper cum binder, and combine harvesters, as well. These are suitable for conventional farming system, only. In precision farming the harvesting is carried out through robotic machines, is narrated as under:

***Robot with 4 degree of freedom manipulator*:** This harvesting tool was developed in Japan for harvesting Strawberry crop. It consists of square led-array and three sets of stereo vision cameras. In which 2 cameras are placed for identification and locating the position of the fruits, while third camera is equipped for locating the plant stems and their orientation. The data recorded by different cameras are analyzed and processed by the processor. And as per orientation of the stem, the effector is changed by tilting mechanism. In harvesting course as the stem comes under grab of the effector, that (stem) gets cut by the cutters. The cutters are equipped on grasping system. Finally, the harvested berries are collected into the tray (Hayashi et al., 2010).

In addition to above harvester, several other harvesting tools have also been developed, normally called as mechanical harvesters. These harvesters work on the principle of shaking the canopy of fruit tree. On shaking the fruits get pluck from the tree and dropped down. The dropped fruits are collected in a container in such a way that the damage of fruit may not be more. In addition, the canopy shakers have also been developed to harvest the fruits. In canopy shaker type harvesting machine the secondary limbs of fruit trees are shaken to precede for harvesting. This is manly used for orange harvesting.

PRACTICE QUESTIONS

Descriptive Type Questions

1. Define precision farming; and how it is different over conventional farming.
2. Narrate feasibility of precision farming in Indian farming context.
3. Spread light on future prospects of precision farming in Indian scenario.
4. Describe objectives and advantages of precision farming.
5. Describe tools and technologies of precision farming.
6. Describe precision farming steps in detail.
7. Explain emerging technologies with precision farming.

Multiple Choice Type Questions

1. Which of the following is the emerging technology associated to precision farming?
   (a) Smartphones (b) Robotics
   (c) Conservation technology (d) both (a) and (b)
2. Precision farming implies
   (a) Use of inputs in precise amount (b) Placing of seeds at right depth
   (c) Irrigation through drip system (d) All above
3. In precision farming technique the GPS is used for predicting
   (a) Various agricultural activities (b) Flood occurrence, mainly
   (c) Crop loss, mainly (d) Health hazards in rural areas, only

4. The ultimate objective of precision farming is to
   (a) Minimize crop loss, mainly (b) Enrich produce quality
   (c) Enhance crop productivity (d) both (b) and (c)
5. Precision farming techniques have broader scopes in
   (a) Farm mechanization (b) Horticultural crops
   (c) Drought monitoring (d) Flood management
6. Which of the following is the working structure/tool in precision farming?
   (a) Greenhouse (b) LASER leveler
   (c) Shade nets (d) All above
7. Which of the following is associated to the precision farming technique?
   (a) Robot (b) Smartphone
   (c) IoT (d) All above

Answers

1. d **2.** d **3.** a **4.** d **5.** a **6.** d **7.** d

BIBLIOGRAPHY

Bongiovanni, R., Lowenberg-DeBoer, J. (2004). Precision agriculture and sustainability. *Precision Agriculture*, 5, pp. 359–87.

Gaikwad Tararani1, Gandule Shital, Korabu Sofiya, Pawar Gouri, Prof. Vasekar S.R. (2018) Smart Drip Irrigation System using IoT. *International Research Journal of Engineering and Technology* (IRJET).

Gebbers, R. and Adamchuk, V. (2010). Precision Agriculture and Food Security. *Science*, Vol. 327, No. 5967, pp. 828–831, DOI: 10.1126/science.1183899.

Goldammer T. (2019). Greenhouse Management: A Guide to Operations and Technology. Apex Publishers, USA.

Hayashi, S., Shigematsu, K., Yamamoto, S., Kobayashi, K., Kohno, Y., Kamata, J., & Kurita, M. (2010). Evaluation of strawberry-harvesting robot in a field test. *Biosystems Engineering*, 105(2), 160–171.

Heege, H. (ed.) (2013). Precision in crop farming. Dordrecht: Springer. Hristov, K. (2011). Institutional problems small farms face when applying for assistance under the rural development program 2007–2013. *Trakia Journal of Sciences*, Vol. 9, Suppl. 3, pp. 83–87, ISSN 1313-7069, ISSN 1313-3551.

J. Raja, & W. Stanley Karunakaran (2017). Automatic Ploughing and Seeding Robot. *International Conference on Electrical, Information and Communication Technologies* (ICEICT 2017).

Lowenberg-DeBoer, J. (2003). Precision farming or convenience agriculture. In: Australian Agronomy Conference, 11, 2003, Geelong, Victoria. Solutions for better environment: proceedings. Geelong, Victoria: Australian Society of Agronomy.

Ravi, N. and Jagadeesha, C.J., (2002). Precision Agriculture, Training course on Remote Sensing and GIS Applications in Agriculture, May 27th–7th June, 2002. *RRSSC*- Bangalore, pp. 225–228.

Searcy, S., Schueller, J., Bae, Y., Borgelt, S., and Stout, B. (1989). Mapping of spatially variable yield during grain combining. *Transactions of the American Society of Agricultural Engineers*, 32(3), pp. 826–829.

Stafford, J., Ambler, B., and Smith, M. (1991). Sensing and mapping grain yield variation. *Proceedings of Symposium & Automated Agriculture for the 21st Century*, pp. 356–365. St Joseph, MI, USA: American Society of Agricultural Engineers.

T. Pobkrut and T. Kerdcharoen (2014). "Soil sensing survey robots based on electronic nose." 14th *International Conference on Control, Automation and Systems* (ICCAS 2014), Seoul, 2014, pp. 1604–1609.

U.K. Shanwad, V.C. Patil, G. S. Dasog, C.P. Mansur, and K. C. Shashidhar (2002). Global Positioning System (GPS) in Precision Agriculture. *The Asian GPS Conference* 2002, (October 24–25, 2002, New Delhi, India).

Precision pest control: smartphone app is the farmer's newest weapon in crop protection

http://www.lincoln.ac.uk//news/2019/01/1507.asp -via @lincolnlates

https://www.ispag.org/

https://www.scenario.co.za/en-ZA/News/Article/View/basic-concepts-of-precision-farming

http://www.senwes.co.za/en-za/products-services/agricultural-services)

Protected Cultivation– Theory, Importance and Applications

CHAPTER 2

The period through which we are passing ahead is under influence of ever increasing human population, drastic climate change, overall declining land holding per capita, pressure on natural resources, and very high demand of quality and fresh produce. In fulfilment of these requirements, traditional cultivation practices are about to incapable. The alternative is only to intervene the modern technologies of crop production in current farming system. The protected cultivation technique is one of them, which enables to meet the requirements with respect to better yield and produce quality, as well. In India about 9.2Mha land is engaged under vegetable cultivation; a part of this can be kept under protected cultivation for enhancing the national productivity and quality produce to meet the nation's demand.

At present in India around 40,000 ha land are kept under protected cultivation to grow the vegetable crops. Apart from enhancing crop productivity, protected cultivation is also beneficial to create self-employment among educated youths. Especially, for production of off-season vegetables, cut flowers, etc. the protected cultivation is reported to be the best practice. The research evidences show that this technique is capable to increase the water and nutrient use efficiencies and crop productivity by 3 to 5 times than the open field condition under varying climatic situations. Also, it can make available the product in market well in advance than the normal time. This leads to provide a better market price of the produce. For example the seedlings of vegetables and fruits such as papaya, brinjal, tomato, etc. can be successfully grown inside polyhouse and make available about two weeks earlier than the traditional practices. Accordingly the price of seedlings obtained from the purchaser will also be more than the normal selling time. The grown seedlings inside greenhouse are also free from disease, which creates an attraction for the purchaser. As for as suitable location for its adoption is concerned the urban and peri-urban areas adjoining to the major cities where market facilities are very prompt, this technology can be successfully adopted for cultivation. In contrast to various merits of protected cultivation there are certain demerits also such as it requires very careful planning, maintenance and management regarding cultivation timing and comparatively investment of greater capital cost for installation.

2.1 PROTECTED CULTIVATION

Few important points about protected cultivation are mentioned as under:

- This is a capital-intensive farming technique, in which the formed microclimate is fully atomized or controlled to clinch a high level of net return over traditional cultivation practices.
- The greenhouses, net houses, tunnels etc. are the innovative structures for protected cultivation, in which a controlled environment suitable to the crops is easily formulated, besides to protect the grown crop against adverse climatic conditions, insects/pests, as well,
- This cultivation technique ensures a high level of returns to the growers, because of higher yield and better quality produce.
- This cultivation also ensures efficient utilization of applied inputs such as water, fertilizers/nutrients and insecticides/pesticides as compared to the open field conditions.
- Also provides a kind of opportunity to gain high sale price of farm produce.

2.2 OBJECTIVES OF PROTECTED CULTIVATION

At present the protected cultivation has become a common name in crop farming domain, in which a farmer can easily control the required environment for better crop production and manage the operation, comfortably. In other words, it has now become as friendly use crop farming technique in developed countries. In this farming approach all the essential factors like temperature, humidity, light, etc. are regulated as per need of the crop stand. As compared to traditional practices it is healthier and results better yield or production in diverse conditions. In nutshell, it is an innovative crop farming technique, which is well capable to yield the quality produce of rare planting materials, enhance the crop production and provide so many favourable things from agriculture to different groups of stakeholders. The salient objectives of protected cultivation are enumerated as under:

(i) To protect the crops/plants from abiotic stress in terms of physical or non-living organisms such as temperature, excess/deficit water contents, hot and cold waves, etc.
(ii) To protect the crop/plants from biotic factors such as pest's attack, disease, etc.
(iii) To save the irrigation water and improve efficient water use.
(iv) To control the weed problems.
(v) To enhance the crop production potential.
(vi) To control or minimize the application of pesticides in crop production.
(vii) To produce export quality farm produce.
(viii) To promote high value and quality produce of horticultural crops.
(ix) To propagate healthy, uniform and disease-free planting materials.
(x) To improve germination percentage and provide better hardening.
(xi) To prepare disease-free yield and better planting materials.

2.3 IMPORTANCE OF PROTECTED CULTIVATION

In general, the protected cultivation is one of the cropping techniques, in which crops are grown in a controlled environment called micro-climate. The micro-climate is formed as per requirement of crop specific. The availability of humidity, temperature and soil moisture content is ascertained as per requirement of the crop. This feature leads to influence the growth and development of plant to an optimum range. The most commonly ways or means to accomplish the protected cultivation are the greenhouse/plastic house, net house, shade house and plastic mulching. The polyhouse or greenhouse is a framed structure covered with UV sheet of suitable thickness normally 200 to 250 micron. The solar heat intercepted within greenhouse is not escaped from there, in result the net temperature or heat content inside polyhouse or greenhouse becomes more than the outside. In addition, from the process of photosynthesis of plants or crops grown inside greenhouse the released carbon contents remain inside polyhouse, which is utilized during photosynthesis action, causes greater formation of synthates in the plants. This leads to cause the plant growth at higher rate than the outside the greenhouse or in open field condition.

The greenhouse use for protected cultivation was started during late 1950s and early 1960s mainly for vegetable production and propagation of cut-flowers and ornamental plants in the United Kingdom (UK) and the Netherlands. The Netherlands used (by 1960) glass-house on the area ranging from 5000 to 6000 ha for vegetable production of which about 75% area was under tomato cultivation. Also, the hydroponic cultivation (as one of the forms of protected cultivation) was started in the Netherlands in 1960s and from there the same got spread to many of the countries. By 1960 the United Kingdom had used about 2000ha greenhouses (Wittwer, 1981) for protected cultivation to grow vegetables and other commercial crops. Also, in USA the hydroponic cultivation started at wide scale in the late 1960s and early 1970s; more than 400ha area was engaged under hydroponic technology for cultivating vegetables such as tomato, cucumber and lettuce production. As per report of Wittwer and Castilla (1995) in USA about 2000ha area was engaged under greenhouse production of which about 95% for flowers, potted plants, ornamentals and bedding plants production. However, in current situation the area engaged under protected cultivation has been increased several folds to that of the above data. Wittwer (1981) reported that, globally by 1980s about 150,000ha area had been placed under greenhouses (glass, fibre glass, plastic) for production of high-valued commercial crops. The greenhouse area had been increased to the tune of about 280,000ha by 1995 across the world (Wittwer & Castilla, 1995). The other protected cultivation tools or structures such as plastic low tunnels, covers and plastic mulches, etc. were also used for protected cultivation later on to a large scale across the world. Overall, the adoption of protected cultivation tools/structures at global scale is presented in Table 2.1

Table 2.1 Extent of area covered under protected cultivation at global scale (Adopted from: Wittwer and Castilla, 1995)

Protected cultivation structure	Geographical Area covered (×1000ha)/Continents				
	Asia	Mediterranean*	North/South America	North Europe	Total
Direct cover (Floating type)	5.5	10.3	1.5[1]	27.0	44.3
Low tunnels (row covers)	143.4	90.5	20.0[2]	3.3	257.2
High tunnels	–	27.6[3]	–	–	27.6
Plastic houses	138.2	67.7	15.6	16.7	238.2
Glasshouses	3.0	7.9	4.0	25.8	40.7

1-Including France; 2-Crude value; 3-High tunnels are often taken together with plastic houses in the countries other than Mediterranean.

However, in current situation at world scale the greenhouse area has been spread on about 307,000ha out of which about 41,000ha is under glasshouses and about 266,000ha under polyhouses (plastic). Adopting protected cultivation technique different countries produce different crops at commercial level, which is summarized in Table 2.2.

Table 2.2 Crops grown adopting protected cultivation technique in the different countries across the world. (Adopted from: Wittwer and Castilla, 1995)

S. No.	Country	Crop
1.	Argentina, Belgium, Canada, Chile, China, Egypt, Finland, Germany, Greece, Israel, Italy, Japan, Morocco, Poland, Portugal, Saudi Arabia, Spain, The Netherlands, Tunisia, Ukraine, Former USSR, USA	Cucurbits
2.	Argentina, Belgium, Canada, Chile, China, Finland, Germany, Italy, Japan, Jordan, Morocco, Portugal, Spain, Tunisia	Strawberry
3.	Algeria, Argentina, Belgium, Bulgaria, Canada, Chile, China, Egypt, Finland, France, Germany, Great Britain, Greece, Italy, Japan, Jordan, Korea, Morocco, Poland, Portugal, Scandinavia, Spain, Taiwan,Tunisia, Ukraine, The Netherlands, Former USSR, USA	Solanaceous and Green beans
4.	Italy, Japan, Morocco, Portugal, Spain	Grapes and tree fruits
5.	Belgium, China, Egypt, Finland, France, Germany, Great Britain, Hungry Korea, Poland, Spain, The Netherlands and Former USSR, USA	Lettuce, cabbage, celery, radish, and asparagus
6.	Argentina, Belgium, Canada, Denmark, Egypt, Finland, Germany, Great Britain, Hungary Israel, Italy, Japan, Scandinavia, Spain, The Netherlands, USA	Flowers and ornamentals
7.	Argentina, Belgium, Canada, Denmark, France, Germany, Hungary Israel, Italy, Japan, Scandinavia, Spain, The Netherlands.	Bedding and potted plants

Overall, the salient points indicating the importance of protected cultivation in agriculture sector are presented below:

(i) The inconducive impact of climate change on crop can be nullified by means of protected cultivation practices.
(ii) The grown crop is under protection against cold, wind, storm, rain and frost.
(iii) The percentage germination of seeds is higher as compared to the traditional practices or in open field condition.
(iv) The crop growth is faster than the outside, and therefore, the crop reaches to its maturity, earlier.
(v) Improvement in produce quality.
(vi) Enhancement in crop yield.
(vii) Optimum use of water in irrigation.
(viii) Large amount of water saving, i.e., ranging from 40 to 50%.
(ix) Water and nutrient use efficiency is increased.

(x) Incidence of insects/pests is declined or eliminated from the crop.
(xi) Crop remains flourish throughout the year.
(xii) Best technology for high worth crops such as flowers, medicinal plants, etc.
(xiii) Appreciable saving of farm labours.
(xiv) Crop can be cultivated in aberrant weather conditions.
(xv) Few crops can be cultivated round the year to satisfy market demands.
(xvi) High valued and best quality produce, even organic crops can be fully grown for export markets under protected cultivation technique.
(xvii) Drastic improvement in farm income.
(xviii) Creates avenues for self-employment opportunities to the youth.
(xix) This technique is effective to environment control and allows the plants to grow any time during year.
(xx) It provides enhanced yield per unit area and per unit input cost.
(xxi) The yield quality is very high, i.e., free from pathogens, chemical residues, and also insect incidence.

2.4 ADVANTAGES OF PROTECTED CULTIVATION

In the technique of protected cultivation, the crop farming is done in protected environment, which may be in context to proper accomplishment of insect/pest management, nutrients/fertilizer and water application, as well. The supply of different inputs like water, fertilizers/chemicals/nutrients, etc. to the crop is also done in precise way to nullify the possibility of application of excess dose. This leads to proper utilization by the grown crop. Besides above, there are several other advantages due to protected cultivation, are presented below,

1. Early crop harvesting
2. Reduction in nutrients/fertilizer loss
3. Water saving
4. Weed control
5. Improvement in growth attributes of the crop
6. Enhancement in crop yield
7. Improvement in produce quality
8. Conducive effect on soil media

Early crop harvesting: This is one of the unique advantages offered by the protected cultivation technique. The reason behind this happening is the existing of better soil-plant-atmospheric environment for plant growth. Normally, either it is soil temperature or ambient temperature, is more in protected environment (greenhouse) than the open field, which leads to grow the crop more quickly. In result the respective growth stages fall early, causing the fruit setting and their maturity also take place at early date. As per research trials, the vegetables grown inside plastic tunnels, rain shelters or with plastic mulching the crop harvesting time falls 7 to 21 days earlier than the traditional practices or in open field condition. Also, the seedlings inside polyhouse or polytunnels get ready for transplanting 10 to 15 days before as compared to the open field condition. Either it is early crop harvesting or seedling raising, the protected cultivation (greenhouse) enables to provide better market price to the grower, because of their early supply in the market as compared to the normal time.

Reduction in nutrient's/fertilizer's loss: In traditional practices, it is very common that a large percentage of applied fertilizers or nutrients to the crop gets leach below the root zone due to flood irrigation or occurrence of heavy rainfall; and thus gets completely lost. On the other hand, in case of protected cultivation the applied fertilizers or chemicals do not leach because of heavy rainfall or application of greater irrigation water than the required amount. Because in protected farming the application of fertilizer and irrigation is carried out in very precise amount to the root zone, which are promptly and efficiently extracted by the crop root system or utilized by the crop. The soil is also protected against the rainfall, so there is complete check on nutrient's leaching due to rainfall. This feature accounts for saving of nutrients and water, both.

Water saving: In protected cultivation the saving of irrigation water is because of application of water as irrigation is through micro-irrigation system, i.e., drip and micro-sprinkler. In micro-irrigation the application of water to the crop is performed either daily or at alternate day. Since, irrigation interval is very short; therefore, the quantity of water to be applied is being very less, but that is sufficient to meet the daily water requirement of the crop/plant. Or it can be said that it is in precise amount. Besides, the irrigation water is dropped on the soil surface near to the stem, which immediately moves in the root zone, from where water gets efficiently extracted by the crop root system. Also, in widely spaced plantations such as orchards the water application is done exactly as per requirement of individual tree/plant; not on area basis. Say for example if in a field of 1 hectare size, there are total 2500 banana plants have been planted; and each plant requires 8 liters water on alternate day. Accordingly, to irrigate the entire 1-hectare banana orchard about 2500 × 8 = 200,00 liters of water will be required. On the other hand, for irrigating 1 hectare banana plantation using flooding method, several times more water will be required to flood the entre banana field. Especially, in drip method the water saving varies from 25 to 40% over flooding method (Suresh, 2010).

Weed control: Enormous weed control is achieved from the grown crop under protected cultivation. There are several reasons for this, such as (i) Limited or precise application of irrigation water to the crop root zone. (ii) Application of mulch, etc. In drip method the water in terms of irrigation is applied near to the plant stem which gets immediately enter the root zone. And rest part of field soil remains in dry condition, as result if any weed grows there, gets destroy due to non-availability of moisture content in the soil. In drip irrigated field the weeds are normally concentered near to the plant, as there is available some moisture content in the soil due to application of irrigation, frequently. Similarly, if drip system is installed along with black colour plastic mulch the weeds are suppressed below the mulch layer; and accordingly the weed problem is eliminated to large extent from the grown crop under protected cultivation. The research data reveals that due to drip irrigation along with plastic mulching about 45 to 50% weed control can be achieved.

Improvement in growth attributes: In protected cultivation, especially under polyhouse or greenhouse condition the increase in level of growth attributes of the crop or the plants such as plant height, number of branches, numbers of leaves, etc. are quite large in extent as compared to the outside condition. This is because of the reason that inside greenhouse the level of carbon contents is higher, as the released CO_2 during photosynthesis action from the crops or plants does not escape outside the greenhouse. The retained carbon is utilized in photosynthesis action, as result the formation synthates in plant body gets enhanced. This causes increase in growth attributes of the crop or the plant itself.

Enhancement in crop yield: The crop farming under protected condition through greenhouse, shade net, plastic mulching, etc. there is significant enhancement in crop yield. This is because of the reason that the grown crops are under protected mode against insects/pests and diseases. The application of requisite inputs either they are the irrigation water, fertilizer, nutrients or any others, required, is carried out properly at right time and also in right quantity. The crop growth is far better. Also, the weed infestation is very less. All the growth stages take place as per their time schedule. These favorable happenings with the crop leads to proper flowering, fruit/grain setting, poor fruit drop, etc.; and accordingly the extent of crop productivity gets multifold increased under protected cultivation condition.

Improvement in produce quality: In protected cultivation technique (greenhouse) the crop production zone is in protected mode, i.e., the crop is disease free; and also less subject to rot problem during rainy season. Because of these reasons the fruit or produce quality is found better to those of the produce obtained from open condition. In addition, the produce quality is also found better due to supply of requisite inputs to the crop at proper time, in proper quantity, and also by proper way. The vegetable's produce harvested under this condition is being more clean and free from diseases and rot's, as well.

Conducive effects on soil media: This focuses to the reduction in soil compaction, mainly. The structures used for protected cultivation such as the greenhouse, shade nets, tunnels, plastic mulching, etc. create cover on the top of open soil surface. In this condition the soil compaction due to direct hitting of raindrops is totally eliminated. Also, the soil remains in loose, friable, and well aerated condition. In result the root system gets access an adequate amount of oxygen and other inputs, promptly. Not only this, but also there is enhanced microbial activities in the soil media under protected cultivation.

2.5 DISADVANTAGES OF PROTECTED CULTIVATION

Apart from various advantages offered by the techniques of protected cultivation comprising enhancement in crop yield, improvement in produce quality, water and nutrient saving, weed control, etc., as described above, there are few disadvantages, too. These are narrated as under:

(i) High initial investment
(ii) High level management
(iii) Constraints of small land holding
(iv) Lack of system awareness

High initial investment: Broadly, the protected cultivation is performed through use of structures such as greenhouse, shade net house, polytunnels, etc., as well. In design and construction of these structures, there is involvement of money to invest. For example the construction of greenhouse or polyhouse requires its proper design, which cannot be done by the farmers; and accordingly, the construction work is assigned to carry out by some experienced companies. In this way the construction cost gets jump several times. Similarly, same thing is also applied to the construction of shade net house. Although, the construction of polytunnels can be done by the farmers itself, but the covering material needs to be purchased from the outside. In purchasing, there is investment of money, which may not be easy to the farmers. The application of mulching materials for crop growing such as plastic sheet of different thicknesses/ colours is also required to purchase from the market. Sometimes, the plastic mulch of desired thickness and colour is not found available in the local market, in result the application of mulch to control the weed problem, water conservation, etc. becomes impossible, is also considered as one of the important demerits of protected cultivation, to adopt.

High level management: Sometimes, the protected cultivation is also noted as Plasticulture technology. It offers several advantages in crop production over traditional farming. The use of greenhouse, shade net house, polytunnels, plastic mulching, etc. requires sincere care and management, timely. However, if it is ignored because of any reasons there is possibility of development of several inconducive effects in the structure, leading to failure in achieving the benefits to be offered by the system. For example, in case of greenhouse/shade net house/ polytunnel, if the cladding material is removed or torn at any place, is not properly removed, immediately, the whole greenhouse structure is likely to get damage due to incidence of occurring storm. Similarly, if mulching is not done in proper way or mulch is not properly retained by placing the soil materials, the mulch sheet is likely to get displaced from the place, which is totally undesirable. On this ground, the management of crop farming under protected cultivation system requires its maintenance from beginning to keep the system in condition, and thus, to achieve proper result in context to crop output.

2.6 LIMITATIONS OF PROTECTED CULTIVATION

Although, the technology of protected cultivation offers various advantages to the users, but there are few limitations also, are mentioned as under:

(i) High cost of infrastructure (capital cost).
(ii) Non-availability of skilled man power and their replacement locally.
(iii) Lack of technical knowledge on growing crops.
(iv) Operations are very intensive and require constant effort.
(v) Requires close supervision and monitoring.
(vi) Few pests and soil-borne pathogens are difficult to manage.
(vii) Repair and maintenance are major hurdles.
(viii) Requires assured marketing facility in nearby area.

2.7 PROTECTED CULTIVATION CRITERION

The technology of protected cultivation is quite different over traditional cultivation. Its application becomes conducive, only when, it is adopted under some well-defined guidelines. The guidelines are nothing but they are the criterion, narrated as under:

(i) Site condition
(ii) Soil characteristics
(iii) Pollination requisites
(iv) Crop priority
(v) Availability of sufficient financial resources

(vi) Good market facility
(vii) Proper linkage to roads/transport system
(viii) Institutional supports
(ix) Electricity availability

Site condition: The most appropriate site for using protected cultivation technique to grow the crops is judged by the following points:

(i) The field site should be free from gravels.
(ii) The crop field should be well drained, i.e., there should not be stagnation of rainwater, etc.
(iii) Site must be close to the market.
(iv) Site should be connected to the road or transportation system to transport the crop produce for sale purpose.
(v) Field should be north-to-south orientation for uniform plant stand and ripening as well.

Soil characteristics: Soil characteristics in favourable range, is one of the most important requirements of the crop production system. In protected cultivation practice the soil must be healthy in all the aspects. However, the soil health can be maintained by addition of organic matters, compost or FYM regularly. This makes the soil biologically active, with good structure and enables to hold the nutrients and water, sufficiently. As per research trials, it is recommended that the crop rotation should be followed in 1 or 2 years prior to planting. This practice is found to be effective for reducing the extent of soil pests, besides maintaining a good level of organic matter in the soil media.

Pollination requisites: In protected cultivation practice; especially under greenhouses/ polytunnels the problem of poor pollination is one of the major issues. Because of this effect the crop yield gets drastically reduced in most of the crops. In order to avoid this problem it is always suggested to cultivate those crops in greenhouse or polytunnel which are self-pollinated. Normally, the self-pollinated vegetables and leafy vegetables are found suitable and are also preferred to grow.

Crop priority: The following points are taken into consideration regarding setting priority on the crops to be grown under protected cultivation system:

1. High value crop
2. People's preference or high demand
3. HYV varieties
4. Low water requiring
5. Lesser crop period
6. Least susceptibility of insects and pests incidence.

Sufficient financial resource availability: As compared to traditional practices of crop farming, the requirement of financial input is more in protected cultivation, because of establishment of various structures such as greenhouse/shade net house, polytunnels, etc., to accomplish the crop cultivation. In this context the availability of banking facility, etc. can play an important role; they should be very prompt so that the farmers could get money from there on loan basis.

Market facility: The market facility plays very important role in agriculture sector to make prompt availability of various farming inputs such as fertilizers, nutrients, insecticides, pesticides, farm implements, fuels, etc. The market facility in nearby area provides a most suitable place for supply of crop produce (especially the off-season produce) and thus to receive a better sale price. Also, the spare parts of irrigation system (micro-irrigation) and other establishments is assured to get from the market in short time, which enables to remove the faults of the system in context to smooth functioning of same.

Proper linkage to roads/transport system: The connectivity of cropped area or farm to the roads and transport system is also one of the most important requisites of protected cultivation to realize a better income from the crop produce. In protected cultivation preference is always given to those crops to grow which are highly remunerative and off-season, as well. Therefore, it is very essential to transport such crop produce in that market from where they can be easily purchased by the persons at suitable sale price. Otherwise, the realization of good sale price or benefits from the produce becomes very difficult. The supply of crop produce from the field to the market depends very much on the available transport facility. Therefore, the transport vehicles such as mini trucks or other sources must be there at the field site.

Institutional support: It indicates to take supports of the existing research institutions in a short reach to provide solution or advice regarding crop cultivation, crop management, care and maintenance of different establishments such as greenhouse/polytunnel, micro-irrigation system, etc., in smooth way. This also makes the cultivation system better operative. These institutions also arrange the trainings on the subject concern, field demonstrations, and research trials, which build up a sound confidence level and also beneficial to convince the view of technology to the growers.

Electricity availability: Electricity at farm assures the availability of energy/power to operate the protected cultivation structures such as greenhouse and micro-irrigation system, as well. In the areas where electricity power facility is not available the fuel energy (petrol and diesel) based power sources are used for operating the system. Electrical power also assures so many other activities to get perform at the farm such as lighting facility inside greenhouse to develop a good effect on plant growth, flowering and others, too.

2.8 AREA COVERED UNDER PROTECTED CULTIVATION IN INDIA AND DIFFERENT COUNTRIES

In India during last decade under so many projects launched by the union ministries and state governments such as National Horticulture Mission (NHM), Precision Farming Development Centres, All India Coordinated Research Project on Water Management/Irrigation Water Management, AICRP on Horticulture, etc., there has been added one of the components related to the protected cultivation technique for research trials/demonstrations to disseminate the technology among farming community. In result there is intervening of this technology at farmer's field to an increased rate. As per report, by the end of 20th-century the area in India under protected cultivation was to the tune of about 110 ha and at the world scale it was more than 275,000 hectares. In Indian context the area under protected farming during 2007 to 2012 the Maharashtra and Gujarat had wide area coverage, i.e., 5,730.23ha in Maharashtra and 4,720.72ha in Gujarat (India). The extent of area engaged under protected cultivation by NHM in Maharashtra is shown in Table 2.3. Similarly, the world wide areas covered under protected cultivation are summarized in Table 2.4.

Table 2.3 Area achieved under protected cultivation by NHM in Maharashtra.

S. No.	Particular	Total area (ha)
1.	Greenhouse structure (fan & pad system)	41
2.	Naturally ventilated polyhouse	1639
3.	Shade net house	2747
4.	Plastic tunnel	51
5.	Anti-bird/anti-hail nets	219
6.	Planting material of high-value vegetables grown in polyhouse	341
7.	Planting material for flowers for polyhouse/shade net	623
8.	Plastic mulching	10364
	Total	16025

(Adopted from: National horticultural mission, 2005-06 to 2017-18)

Table 2.4 World wide area covered under protected cultivation

Country	Protected Cultivation Area (ha)
China	2,760,000
Korea	57,444
Spain	52,170
Japan	49,049
Turkey	33,515
Italy	26,500
Mexico	11,759
The Netherlands	10,370
France	9,620
United States	8,425

(Adopted from: https://www.tractorjunction.com/)

2.9 SITE SELECTION FOR PROTECTED CULTIVATION

Protected cultivation is accomplished by the tools of greenhouse, shade net house, polytunnels, plastic mulching, drip irrigation, raised bed farming, etc. In order to have better results in terms of enhanced crop yield, better produce quality and other beneficial effects, the site selection for establishment of greenhouse/shade net house is very essential. It is always suggested that before starting their construction the site must be property studied in respect of soil characteristics, exposure to sunlight, water quality, soil surface condition, availability of electricity, etc. If they are met at the site, then construction should be initiated; otherwise, there is possibility of getting failure of the constructed structure. In general, the followings are few important points in respect of site selection for construction of greenhouse or shade net house, to follow:

1. The construction site must have ample exposure to sunlight. This can be ascertained by the features such as not existence of tall trees, buildings or the leeward side of hills.
2. The lowlying area should be avoided as there is possibility of waterlogging problem, which is totally unacceptable to greenhouse.
3. The surface of site soil must be in level form. Normally, the slope 0 to 2% is found under acceptable range. However, if majority of the soil characteristics are in favorable range and surface slope is more, then by leveling the surface up to desired level, can be used for greenhouse or shed net house construction.
4. The pH and electrical conductivity (EC) of site soil should be from 6.0 to 6.5 and less than 0.5 dS/m, respectively.
5. At construction site the availability of good quality water in sufficient quantity must be there. As per research findings, for greenhouse operation the rate of water requirement varies from 1 to 21/m^2/day, which can also be adjusted depending on season and cultivation stage. In addition the pH and electrical conductivity (EC) of water should also be from 6.5 to 7.0 and less than 0.7 dS/m, respectively.
6. The availability of electricity at construction is essential for operation of greenhouse. The dependence on diesel or other fuels makes the cultivation costlier, which may not be justified.
7. The construction site must be linked to the proper transportation means such as heavy capacity truck, etc. Otherwise, there would be difficult in transportation of greenhouse produce to the market for sale.
8. At proposed site, there should be sufficient lands so that in future as per requirement the greenhouse construction may be easily expanded for greater areal extent. Also, the design criteria advocates that between two greenhouses there must be at least 10 to 15m gap, which also needs to follow during construction or expansion work in future.
9. The labour availability in nearby area is also one of the very important requisites for site selection in regards to greenhouse construction, as good number of labours is required in greenhouse based cultivation practices. The research findings suggest that for flower cultivation the required labour varies to the tune of 4 labourers/acre greenhouse area.
10. A good communication facility is also prerequisite for greenhouse construction.
11. The greenhouses/shade net houses are the costly establishment in protected cultivation technique. These structures are likely to get damage due to wind storms or high blowing winds. In order to avoid the effect of strong winds on these structures the plantation of wind break across the wind direction is very essential. These breaks dissipate the wind force; and check the structure against strong blowing winds. The plants to be used for establishment of wind break, should be tall and have strong root system to hold the soil, firmly. The species such as poplar, silver oak, casuarina, etc. can be suitably used for plantation. In this context, it is also suggested that the distance between greenhouse and the wind break should be about 20m at west side, provided the west winds are strongest.

2.10 PROTECTED CULTIVATION STRUCTURES/TOOLS

Protected cultivation (PC) is quite different over traditional practices. The crop growth, yield and its attributes water and nutrient use efficiency are dependent on the climate formed inside the structures used for. The formed climate is called micro-climate, which is governed by the structural features, soil and irrigation water applied. However, the required micro-climate varies with the crops, grown inside. For example the requirement of temperature, humidity, etc. is different for tomato to that of the capsicum. The degree of micro-climate also varies with the type of protected cultivation structures used. The PC structures comprises following main features/components in their design and construction:

(a) Assembles mainly three components, namely (i) Frame; (ii) Cladding material; and (iii) Ventilation/climate control systems. In which frame constitutes the super structure and protects the crop against various damaging factors such as wind, rain, snow, soil, climatic condition, and physical & chemical deteriorations, as well. Cladding or covering material is used to cover the super structure (frame). It is also to provide the required Photosynthetically Active Radiation (PAR) and trap sufficient amount of heat contents inside during cold weather condition and simultaneously to protect the grown crop from outside harsh weather conditions. The provision of ventilation is provided to control the micro-climate inside the structure; and thus to create a favourable environment for the crop or plant growth.

(b) The dimensions of various components, ventilation system, etc. are designed and constructed in such a way that they can modify or create the inside environment as per crop requirement, properly. Also, they can furnish sufficient structural stability/strength to the structure so that it can firmly stand in adverse situation of blowing wind, snow fall, intense or heavy rainfall, hailstorms, etc. Stability analysis of framed structure is carried out based on various loads acting on. Acting loads are mainly the dead load, live load, snow load and wind loads. The dead load fixes the service equipments such as heating, ventilation, air circulation, electrical, lighting, watering, etc. while live load accounts for repairs crews and hanging plants, etc.

The most common structures used for practicing the protected cultivation to grow the crops are narrated as under:

Polytunnels: These are common and low cost protected cultivation structure. Length of these structures is several times greater than their width. This features forms just like tunnel. Since polytunnel are covered by means of polythene sheets of suitable thickness; therefore these are designated as polytunnel. Height is kept in such a range that a person can easily perform the cultural operations, inside. Since, these are covered by plastic sheet, therefore inside temperature is little higher than the outside. This feature of polytunnel provides additional advantage in respect of enhanced temperature, inside.

Greenhouses: These are one of the main protected cultivation structures used for growing varieties of high valued crops. Greenhouses are the framed structure equipped with irrigation system, environment control or cooling/heating system, etc. Since, the involvement of construction cost to a high range; therefore, its use for growing crops is quite different than the traditional practices. Its constructional feature is just like a house, and is covered with UV stabilized polyethylene sheet of suitable thickness. Normally, 200 to 250 micro thickness UV sheets are used for its construction. There is also the provision of suitable size gate for going into or coming out from the polyhouse. The area enclosed within greenhouse is used for growing crops. Greenhouses can be of different types such as low cost, medium cost and high cost greenhouses. The variation in construction cost depends on the additional provision to be provided in them. High cost greenhouses consist of automated system comprising, cooling, irrigation or environment control, etc., while low cost or medium cost greenhouses do not have such systems.

Greenhouse offers several advantages associated to crop farming in protected mode, are narrated as under:

- It makes possible to cultivate off-season crops round the year.
- In harsh environmental conditions the crops can be successfully grown inside greenhouse.
- With the aid of greenhouse the export-quality produce can be successfully harvested.
- Best quality seedlings and planting materials can be raised using greenhouse.
- The crop production per unit area is higher in greenhouse.
- The grafts and propagation of quality planting materials can be easily prepared.
- The management of insect, pest and weed is easy.
- The b/c ratio of crop is much higher than the conventionally grown crops.
- Greenhouse technique creates employment opportunity for rural youth.

The description of greenhouse has been presented in Chapter-3.

Shade house: This is also known by several names such as shade net house or net house, green net house, etc. Shade net house is frame based structure covered with the nets or any other woven materials. The nets have perforations to facilitate penetration of solar radiation or sunlight, inside. Shade nets are manufactured by using UV treated 100% PE threads. They have different shade percentages or shade factors, i.e., 15%, 35%, 40%, 50% 75% and 90%. The 35% shade factor denotes the cut of light intensity by 35% and 65% to pass inside through net. The percentage perforations or shading percentage varies depending on the required shade in the net house. These nets lower the inside temperature by creating shading effect. The level of shading effect varies with the percentage perforations or shading factor of the net used. Like greenhouse a shade net house also creates micro-climate, inside but in poor range.

Mist chamber: This is also used as one of the structures under protected cultivation technique. Its main purpose is to develop a high level of humidity and without water droplet environment for proper propagation of delicate soft wood cuttings, vegetable crops, root plants and shrubs, mainly. In order to have a proper effect on propagating action the misting is accomplished in intermittent way with the help of high pressure pump using mist nozzles placed on pipeline. The misting frequency or interval is decided on the basis of ambient temperature and type of planting materials to be propagated. The application of water or drenching is avoided in mist chambers. Normally, for nursery works a mist chamber of 15 to 25 m^2 size is found sufficient. Mist chamber offers various advantages, listed as under:

- It enables to produce year-round planting materials.
- The success rate of plant propagation is very high.
- It reduced moisture loss from the plants, leading to cause better survival of root-cuttings.
- The hardening of tissue cultured plants can be successfully done using mist chamber.
- The desiccation or drying out of the plant materials is not there in mist chamber.
- The attack of pathogen, insect and pests is negated inside mist chamber.

Mulching: Mulching is an art of placing the mulch materials around the plant stem on soil surface to insulate and protect the plant root system against harsh weather condition. It works as a barrier to resists the solar radiation or sunlight/heat content in the soil and thus decline the evaporation from the soil media, leading to conserve the soil moisture contents. In addition, it also improves the soil's nutrient status by affecting the decomposition process of crop residues. Broadly, the mulch materials are in two main types, namely (i) Organic mulch; and (ii) Inorganic mulch. In which, the organic mulch is the biodegradable materials base product, such as grass clippings, wood chips, dried leaves, and straw, mainly. Inorganic mulches comprise the river rock, stones, crushed gravels, etc. With these types of mulching materials there is constraint about their availability in sufficient amount, for application. This results into not feasible to apply in large acreage of crops. However, this type of limitation is now removed by introduction of plastic much. Nowadays, plastic mulching has become very promising in agriculture because of so many reasons, are narrated as under.

Plastic mulching: The covering of cropped soil surface using polyethylene sheet or plastics is called plastic mulching. This technology is also called Plasticulture, is increasingly used for production of fresh vegetables. As per published data every year about 1 million ton of plastic film as mulch is used across the world (Yu et al., 2018) under Plasticulture. In Spain during 2012 more than 60,000 ha greenhouses have been constructed. Globally, the China is the highest user of plastic mulching, i.e. about 0.7 million ton that is around 40% of the world's level use (Daryanto et al., 2017). In recent years, the China, Japan, and South Korea used highest level of plastic film which is around 80% of world level plastic use (Ihuoma and Madramootoo 2017). Report advocates that on use of plastic mulching the Wheat and Maize production rate got enhanced to the tune of 33.2% and 33.7%, respectively (Chen et al., 2014) in China.

The beneficial effects of plastic mulching are mentioned as under:

- In dry land areas this is one of the promising techniques for water-saving, soil moisture conservation, temperature regulation and soil evaporation control.
- In rainfed areas this also plays significant role in water conservation
- As compared to organic mulches this is more effective in moisture conservation.
- It also causes soil erosion control.
- It declines the irrigation demands by conserving the moisture content in soil media.
- It keeps the soil-water-plant environment in optimum range for better plant growth.
- It insulates the soil media, leading to cause buffering action from the hot and cold temperatures.
- Impact of raindrop hitting causing soil/nutrients washing from the soil media also gets significantly reduced.
- It is found beneficial for improving the soil structure and nutrient cycling, especially by encouraging the earthworm activities in soil media.
- Mulching is also being beneficial to lower the pH level of soil media; in result the nutrient's availability for the plant gets increase. This effect is observed in case of organic mulches.
- Plastic mulches are being best fit for soil solarisation to kill the pathogens present in the soil.
- This also reduces fertilizer leaching.

Apart from various advantages offered by plastic mulching, there arc few disadvantages too, are cited below:

- Requirement of specialized equipments for mulching in field.
- Involvement of laying or installation cost.
- Removal of plastic mulch from the cropped field.
- Disposal of plastic mulch at safe place.
- Effective towards environmental pollution.

2.11 SCOPE OF PROTECTED CULTIVATION IN INDIA

At world scale the India is the second largest producer of vegetables; and China is the 1st largest grower. In present scenario the production of horticultural produce is continuously gaining importance, not in India but in majority of the countries across the world. As per statistics the India has achieved a record production in horticultural crops during 2017–18 to the tune of about 311.7 MT, which is about 3.7% higher than the previous year 2016–17 and about 10% higher than the past 5 years' average production. Amongst horticultural production the share of vegetables is highest, which is in the range of 59 to 61% over last five years period. As for as area engaged under vegetable cultivation is concerned, it was around 10.3 Mha during 2017–18 with an average production of 180.0 MT.

In recent few decades the vegetable production under organic mode is getting more and more popularity among users. Also the market for organic vegetables is increasing day- by- day at accelerated rate. In this way, the vegetable production is gaining better source of income (cash income) generation for the growers. On this ground the vegetable cultivation in organic mode is also adopted to a wide scale by the farming community at country level. On this aspect the data reveals that the India is at 9th rank about World's Organic Agricultural land and 1st for the total number of producers adopting the organic farming practices in vegetable production. The data advocates that during 2017–18 India produced about 1.70MT certified organic products; and around 4.58 lakh MT with the worth of ₹ 3453.48 crore was exported (http://apeda.gov.in).

The Indian statistics on organic farming states that the total area under organic certification is around 5.71 Mha. The Sikkim is the highest organic farming follower in the country (India), where total certified organic cultivable land is reported around 78,000ha with average land holding as 1.17 ha(www.apeda.gov.in).

Aforesaid description concludes that the adoption of protected cultivation technique in Indian scenario is more in vegetable production under organic mode. In developing countries including Indian sub-continent the vegetables are majorly cultivated by the small landholders under vulnerable climatic condition. This causes uncertainty in crop yield. The best solution to mitigate bad impact of the climate change or aberrant weather is the adoption of protected cultivation technique, in which crop is kept under protection mode by means of several structures such as, greenhouses, shade net houses, polytunnels and plastic mulching, mainly. In these structures the crop remains protected against insects/pests and inconducive environmental factors, as well. In nutshell, the crop becomes unaffected from the external happenings, and thus making the crop yield better. In line of protected cultivation, the World Greenhouse

Vegetable Statistics 2019 states that the world greenhouse vegetable area is spreading to the tune of around 4,96,800 ha (www.cuestaroble.com). Besides above, the followings narrations or points also add some more views on scope of protected cultivation in Indian agriculture:

(i) Problematic agroclimate
(ii) Demand of off-season and high value farm produce
(iii) Farm produce export
(iv) Demand of plant propagation
(v) Demand for biotechnology
(vi) Supply of rare and healthy planting materials

Problematic agroclimate: In Indian sub-continent the majority of suitable lands as per their land use capability (LUC) have been engaged for cultivation, either using traditional practices or by protected cultivation techniques. The left lands are those which are unsuitable for cultivation in normal way. The soils like barren, uncultivated fallow lands, desserts, etc. are available as the problem soils. Although, these lands are not directly suitable for cultivation point of view, but by application of protection cultivation techniques such as establishment of greenhouses/ shade net houses/polytunnels on such land segments, they can be made remunerative by growing high valued crops in protected environment. On this ground there is ample scope for protected cultivation technique to adopt by the farming community and realize better income from unexplored land mass. The major greenhouse areas covered under vegetable production at world scale are presented in Table 2.5.

Demand of off-season/high value farm produce: This is also one of the focusing points in respect of adoption of protected cultivation technique. Now days the demand of off-season farm produce such as vegetables and others is getting more and more from the young Indian population. The users groups such as hotels, restaurants, etc. are also putting their demand for off-season and high value farm produce to meet their requirement. This is the reason that the establishment of greenhouses around the metros or big cities has been started to a fast rate to cultivate such produce. The greenhouse is one of the most suitable structures to produce the off-season and high valued crops and supply them to the market for users. This provides strength for intervention of protected cultivation technique in Indian agriculture. The recommended flowers, vegetables, fruits and others are shown in Table 2.6

Farm produce export: The provision for export of farm produce is also one of the important steps to make the agriculture more remunerative. However, for export, the farm produce must have to qualify in respect to their quality. The export quality farm produce can be easily produced through greenhouse or application of protected cultivation practices. The cultivation of export quality off-season and high valued crops and preparation of cut-flowers can be suitably carried out under greenhouse environment.

Demand of plant propagation: Now days, the demand of quality seedlings or cuttings of high valued horticultural crops is at high scale throughout the world. For production of quality planting materials, there is requirement of high level management/control of environment, which is not possible in open conditions. The greenhouse is only the structure in which a desired micro-environment could be created and properly maintained to propagate the quality materials. This narrates to a good scope for protected cultivation in Indian agriculture.

Demand for biotechnology: The conductance of biotechnological studies in well-furnished laboratories is one of the requisites, but there is investment of huge amount of money in their establishment. However, a part of the works related to biotechnological studies such as hardening of tissue cultured plants prepared in TC labs can be accomplished in greenhouse structures, as hardening process requires a controlled environment which could be easily met in greenhouse.

Supply of rare and healthy planting materials: This is also one of the common demands in agriculture sector, which is not possible to generate in open condition. The best option is through protected cultivation via greenhouse interventions. In Indian geography there is ample scope for cultivation of healthful herbs and the rare plants like orchids to a wide range. The greenhouse technology which is associated to the protected cultivation can enable to provide the requisite environmental inputs or conditions required for intensive propagation of such plants.

Table 2.5 Major greenhouse vegetable production areas of the world (Adopted from: Sabir and Singh (2013).

Country	Area ('000 ha)	Country	Area ('000 ha)
China	81	Argentina	2.2
Spain	70.4	Chile	2.1
South Korea	47.0	Jordan	2.0
Japan	36.0	Belgium	1.6
Turkey	33.5	Russia	1.4
Italy	25.0	Germany	1.4
Morocco	16.5	Australia	1.3
France	10.0	Tunisia	1.3
Poland	5.2	Romania	1.3
Hungary	5.4	Egypt	1.2
Algeria	5.0	Canada	1.2
Greece	5.0	Bulgaria	1.1
Netherlands	4.6	Libya	1.0
Columbia	1.2	Serbia/Montenegro	1.0
Mexico	4.3	Lebanon	1.0
Israel	4.0	Brazil	1.0
Iran	4.0	United Arab Emirates	0.8
Palestine	3.3	India	0.7
Syria	3.1	New Zealand	0.7
Ukraine	2.7	United Kingdom	0.7
Ecuador	2.7	USA	0.7
Portugal	5	Moldova	0.5

Table 2.6 Recommended crops for protected cultivation

S. No.	Crop		
	Flower	**Vegetables**	**Fruits and others**
1.	Chrysanthemum	Tomato	Strawberry
2.	Carnation	Colored Capsicum (Yellow and Red)	Seedling raising-nursery and vegetables and flowers
3.	Gerbera	Bell Peppers	Hardening of Tissue cultured plants
4.	Rose	Cucumber,	Clonal for Forestry
5.	Lilium	Broccoli	Fruit Grafting such as Lemon, Citrus, Mango, Pomegranate, Guava, Litchi, etc.
6.	Orchid	Red Cabbage	
7.	Gladiolus, etc.	Leafy vegetables	
8.		Radish, etc.	

2.12 SOME IMPORTANT POINTS

- Indian agriculture sustains the livelihood of about 64% population and contributes approximately 26% to the gross domestic product.
- About 55% of total Indian population depends on farming.
- In India currently there is a substantial increase in food grain production, i.e., from about 51 MT (million tonnes) in the year 1950 to about 277 MT in 2017–18.
- In India about 80% land holdings fall in the category less than 2 ha, which are mostly rainfed and only 30% lands are under irrigated condition.
- India is the biggest producer of agricultural products.
- Asia and the Pacific regions account for more than 70% of the global agricultural population.
- Soil erosion due to water and wind is several times more than natural soil formation, i.e., 30 to 40 times.
- In India the agriculture sector creates the job opportunity to the tune of 90%.
- In India as per National Horticultural Database (NHD, 2014–15) the Tamil Nadu gained first rank for the area under flower cultivation followed by Karnataka and West Bengal. The floricultural products accounts for about 3.2% in export of total horticultural produce.
- Indian floriculture products account for about 0.6% in international market.
- As per APEDA (2016–17) the India's total export of floriculture was to the tune of ₹ 548.74 crore, in which dry flowers contribute about 70% revenue generation out of the total floricultural export. And India has the share of about 10% of the world's dry flower market.
- In India there is more than 300 floriculture export's oriented units. They are mostly located near to Mumbai, Pune, Bengaluru, Hyderabad and New Delhi.
- The export-quality flowers are mainly the bulbs, cut and loose flowers, dry flowers, ornamental plants and cut foliage produced under greenhouse cultivation.

- In Maharashtra, Tamil Nadu and Karnataka there is commercial production of floricultural crops, which meet the domestic and foreign market's demands.
- The Government of India has executed so many schemes to facilitate protected cultivation at central and state levels, such as National Horticulture Board (NHB), National Horticulture Mission (NHM), Mission for Integrated Development of Horticulture (MIDH) and Rashtriya Krishi Vikas Yojana (RKVY), mainly.

PRACTICE QUESTIONS

Descriptive Type Questions

1. Define protected cultivation and narrate its various objectives.
2. Write importance of protected cultivation in Indian scenario and extent of area covered in India and globally.
3. Describe scopes of protected cultivation in Indian agriculture.
4. Describe various advantages, disadvantages and limitations of protected cultivation practices.
5. Enlist the structures/tools used for protected cultivation.
6. Explain various criterions followed in protected cultivation.
7. Write short notes on following:
   (i) Greenhouse
   (ii) Shade nets
   (iii) Mist chamber
   (iv) Plastic mulching
   (v) Micro-irrigation

Multiple Choice Type Questions

1. Protected cultivation implies the crop protection against
   (a) Temperature (b) Weather condition
   (c) Insect and pest (d) All above
2. Which of the following is used as protected cultivation structure?
   (a) Plastic mulching (b) Storage structure
   (c) Greenhouse (d) Fertigation unit
3. The climate formed inside greenhouse is called
   (a) Weather (b) Greenhouse environment
   (c) Micro-climate (d) None of above
4. In protected cultivation the mist chamber is normally used for
   (a) Plant propagation (b) Hardening of plants
   (c) Climate modification (d) Flower cultivation
5. Plastic mulching saves the water against
   (a) Evaporation (b) ET
   (c) Percolation (d) All above

6. Which of the following crops can be successfully grown inside greenhouse?
   (a) Capsicum (b) Cucumber
   (c) Tomato (d) All above
7. Shade nets can be used for
   (a) Hardening of tissue cultured plants (b) Growing leafy vegetables
   (c) Plant propagation (d) All above
8. In protected cultivation the soil solarisation can done with the help of
   (a) Plastic mulch (b) Organic mulch
   (c) Heavy ploughing (d) All above
9. Mulching reduces
   (a) Weed growth (b) Nutrients loss
   (c) Water loss (d) All above
10. The best cultural practices to control the insect/pest incidence in greenhouse crops is
   (a) Cleaning of greenhouse surroundings (b) keeping greenhouse weed free
   (c) Proper irrigation (d) All above

Answers

1. d **2.** c **3.** c **4.** a **5.** a **6.** d **7.** d **8.** a **9.** d **10.** d

BIBLIOGRAPHY

Bakker, J.C. (1995). Greenhouse Climate Control: An Integrated Approach, Wageningen Press, Wageningen.

Chen LJ, Feng Q, and Li FR, Li CS (2014). A bidirectional model for simulating soil water flow and salt transport under mulched drip irrigation with saline water. Agric Water Manag. 146:24–33.

Daryanto S, Wang L, and Jacinthe P-A (2017). Can ridge-furrow plastic mulching replace irrigation in dryland wheat and maize cropping systems? Agric Water Manag [Internet]. 190:1–5.

Goldammer T. (2019). Greenhouse Management: A Guide to Operations and Technology. Apex Publishers, USA.

Ihuoma SO, and Madramootoo CA (2017). Recent advances in crop water stress detection. Comput Electron Agric [Internet]. 141:267–275. International Society of Arboriculture (ISA) (2005) Proper Mulching Techniques. P.

Sabir, N., & Singh, and B. (2013). Protected cultivation of vegetables in the global arena: A review. *Indian Journal of Agricultural Sciences*, 83(2), 123–135.

Suresh R. (2010). Micro Irrigation–Theory and Practice. Standard Publishers and Distributors, Delhi (India).

Wittwer SH, and Castilla N (1995). Protected cultivation of horticultural crops worldwide:
HortTechnology 5:6–23.

Wittwer, S.H. (1981). Advances in protected environments for plant growth, in Advances in Food Producing Systems for Arid and Semi-arid Lands. Academic Press, New York.

Wittwer SH, and Castilla N (1995). Protected cultivation of horticultural crops worldwide: HortTechnology 5:6–23.

Yu YY, Turner NC, Gong YH, Li FM, Fang C, Ge LJ, and Ye JS (2018). Benefits and limitations to straw-and plastic-film mulch on maize yield and water use efficiency: a meta-analysis across hydrothermal gradients. *Eur J Agron.* 99: 138–147.

www.apeda.gov.in

www.cuestaroble.com

https://www.tractorjunction.com/

CHAPTER 3

Greenhouse–Concept, Classification and Uses

The crop farming with good productivity is the function of interaction amongst soil-water-plant-atmosphere along with machineries' interventions. Achieving a good crop yield and quality produce is the demand of present era form agriculture. This is because of accelerating population growth. The soil which was long back with its original quality has now been completely changed, i.e., degraded. The soil productivity has been declined to such an extent that yield cannot be harvested without application of excess dose of inputs. Although, adopting these practices the crop yield has been increased but the produce quality does not fall in acceptable zone. However, produce is utilized by the people, compulsorily, because of no any option or alternative for survival. Although, in the direction of production of quality produce several attempts have been made by the researchers such as development package of practices concern to organic farming, adoption of protected cultivation, use of greenhouse technologies, etc. but their adoption rate at field level is not satisfactory, may be because of unawareness about them, financial matters, land based issues, etc.

Crop requires a well-defined climate around for its proper growth and development. In open field condition its formation or availability for growing a particular crop is not possible, naturally in changing climate scenario. In open field condition the successful crop farming is also at risk because of occurrence of aberrant weather. Besides, achieving a high production from agricultural crops is also one of the main objectives in present situation to feed ever-increasing population. These production based requisites can only met by interventions of cutting edge technologies in agriculture.

The greenhouse and protected cultivation techniques fall in this category, which have very strong potential to enhance crop productivity along with quality produce. Globally, these technologies have now been started utilizing for growing highly enumerative crops at large scale. As per research evidences the benefit-cost ratio is realized to the tune of more than 5.0 in most of the crops on using greenhouse and protected cultivation techniques. This chapter deals a complete view on greenhouse technology starting from greenhouse basics, history, advantages, classification to structural details, etc. in detail.

In nutshell a greenhouse encompasses following salient features advocating fruitfulness towards growing of high valued crops at commercial level:

- Greenhouse is a structure with walls and roof of transparent material, such as polyethylene (PE) and glass.
- It provides controlled and predictable conditions precisely for growing high valued crops.
- It provides favourable environmental conditions to plants for their proper growth and development.
- Enable to create a high temperature inside as compared to the outside, is one of the special characters.
- It has flexibility in its size and shape.
- On exposure to the sunlight, the greenhouse becomes significantly warmer than the external outside.
- It protects the crops from extreme weather—not only wind and temperature but also from the hail storm and insects/pests, too.
- A greenhouse creates an ideal micro-climate inside or around the plants.
- The inside micro-climate can be changed, manually and automatically, both.
- Greenhouse temperature and humidity can be regulated within.
- Greenhouse protects the plants from vagaries of weather or environment, i.e., wind, precipitation, excess solar radiation, temperature extremes and attack of pests and diseases.
- Greenhouse cladding materials are transparent in nature such as plastic, PVC sheet or glass. Because of this reason greenhouse cover transmits most of the sunlight inside, which is conducive to plant growth.
- The objects such as crop, floor and others lying inside greenhouse absorb the admitted sunlight and emit the long wave thermal radiations. The covering material has low transparency for long wave thermal radiation. In result there is trapping of solar energy inside. In result there is increase in greenhouse temperature. This effect is known as greenhouse effect.
- Greenhouse ensures year round crop production.
- Easy to control insect-pests and diseases infestation.
- Crop water requirement is less as compared to outside.
- Labour requirement is also less as compared to traditional farming system.
- Off-season vegetables cultivation is successfully done.
- The vegetables, flowers, seedling raising, graft preparation can be easily performed inside greenhouse.
- Develops Self-employment Avenue for rural youth.

3.1 GREENHOUSE HISTORY

Greenhouse is the framed or inflated structure covered with a transparent or translucent material; just in the form of house, utilized to grow the crops under at least partially controlled environmental conditions. In context to greenhouse history, the salient points are narrated below:

- In the 1st century the growing of off-season cucumbers under transparent stone for Emperor Tiberius is reported as the earliest protected agriculture.

- In 15th century the greenhouse with manually manipulated temperature was introduced.
- In 16th century, the practices of glass lanterns, bell jars and hot beds covered with glass were followed to protect the horticultural crops against cold, are the part and partial of protected cultivation technique.
- As per reported literature, in 17th century the low portable wooden frames covered with oiled translucent paper were used to warm the environment suitable to the crop grown is also an example related to greenhouse technology.
- A long ago during early 1960s in Japan the crops were saved against severe natural environment, using oil-paper and straw mats also casts an example towards greenhouse practicing.
- In the early 1960s in France and England the greenhouses were warm-up by using manure and covering with the glass panes.
- In 1900s firstly the greenhouses were constructed by using glass cover as cladding material for growing the crops such as melons, grapes, peaches and strawberries, and rarely for vegetable production.
- After the World War-II the protected agriculture was established with the use of polyethylene for greenhouse construction.
- In 1948 firstly the polyethylene (PE) film was used as greenhouse covering materials.
- Total area of glasshouses across the world (1987) was reported to the tune of 30,000 ha, majority of them were constructed in North-Western Europe. On the other hand, more than half of the world's area of plastic greenhouses was reported for Asian countries, in which the China was the largest covering country. The rate of development of greenhouse technology is faster in China than the other parts of the world.
- As per 1999 estimates, an area of 6,82,050 ha have been reported under plastic based greenhouses.
- In India as per 1994–95 estimates, about 100 ha area was under greenhouse cultivation.
- Since 1960, the greenhouse has become one of the most important technologies for protected cultivation.
- By the end of fifties of 20th century the greenhouse technology expanded to the north and central Europe, and also extended its influence and benefits to the Israel.

3.2 GREENHOUSE USES AT WORLD'S SCALE

Polyhouse or greenhouse is the house like structure covered with UV stabilized polyethylene sheet of suitable thickness or other cladding materials, constructed for growing high value crops. The cladding materials create greenhouse effect inside greenhouse, conducive to crop growth and development. Inside temperature of greenhouse is greater than the ambient temperature, is the boon for this structure. The greater inside temperature makes the greenhouse well suitable for cultivation of off-season crops successfully. In addition greenhouse also provides a protected environment for disease free crop cultivation, to a large extent. Because of so many conducive features, the greenhouse technology has now been spread throughout world at wide scale for growing variety of high valued commercial crops. However, the vegetables, tomatoes, cucumbers, capsicum, flower, etc. are the main crops grown in greenhouse. The country-wise use of greenhouse for growing different crops is shown in Table 3.1.

Table 3.1 Country-wise use of greenhouse for growing crops

S. No.	Country	Crops
1.	Canada	Flower cultivation and off-season vegetables tomatoes, cucumbers and capsicum, mainly
2.	Netherlands	Flowers and vegetables
3.	Gulf countries	Cut flowers and vegetables under extreme climatic conditions.
4.	Israel	Cut flowers, mainly
5.	Turkey	Cut flowers and vegetables
6.	Egypt	Cut flowers and vegetables in tunnel structure
7.	Japan	Fruit orchard, vegetables, cut flowers
8.	China	Fruit orchard, vegetables, cut flowers
9.	South Korea	Vegetables, cut flowers, etc.
10.	India	Vegetables, flowers, etc.
11.	USA	Vegetables, flowers, etc.

3.3 GREENHOUSE AREA COVERAGE—AT WORLD SCALE

Across the world more than 50 countries are growing crops on commercial scale using protected cultivation techniques. In Asia, the China and Japan are the largest users of greenhouse. The estimated areas under protected cultivation using greenhouse technology, worldwide, are presented in Table 3.2

Table 3.2 Estimated area under protected cultivation using greenhouses, worldwide

S. No.	Country	Area under protected cultivation ha (000)	Remark
1.	USA	0.70	Used under floriculture
2.	Spain	70.40	For growing watermelon, capsicum, strawberries, beans, cucumbers and tomatoes, etc.
3.	Italy	25.0	
4.	Canada	1.20	Mainly tomato, cucumbers and capsicum
5.	The Netherlands	4.60	Flowers and vegetables, mainly
6.	Israel	4.0	Cut flowers
7.	Turkey	33.50	Cut flowers and vegetables
8.	Egypt	1.20	Cut flowers and vegetables
9.	China	81.0	Grapes, cherry, Japanese persimmon, fig, loquat, lemon, mango
10.	Japan	36.0	Fruit, cut flowers and vegetables
11.	South Korea	47.0	Flowers and fruits

(*Source*: Hickman 2011)

3.4 GREENHOUSE, POLYHOUSE AND GLASSHOUSE—CONCEPT

Greenhouse is the house like framed structure covered with special type of covering material, which enables to create micro-climate inside. The structure may be erected with the help of metallic and non-metallic materials. The covering materials which are widely used in greenhouse construction are the UV Polyethylene film, glass, poly carbonate sheets, etc. The name greenhouse is due to formation of greenhouse effect inside.

Polyhouse is the house constructed with the help of Polyethylene (PE) film. This is one of the types of greenhouse. Polyhouse also involves greenhouse effect, conducive to crop farming.

Glasshouse is another structure also constitutes greenhouse effects inside. In glasshouse, the glass is used as covering material. As compared to glasshouse the polyhouse is more economical because of so many reasons such as easy in handling, involvement of less cost, more durable, etc.

3.5 BENEFITS OF GREENHOUSE

An appreciable benefit is realized in case of vegetable and flower cultivation inside greenhouse. In nutshell, the benefits borne by greenhouse use are narrated as under:

(i) High yield potential
(ii) Year round cultivation
(iii) Enhancement in produce quality
(iv) Off season cultivation
(v) Easy plant protection
(vi) Less water requirement
(vii) Weed free cultivation
(viii) Control on weather parameters, as well

High yield potential: For proper plant growth the presence of optimum environment comprising temperature, humidity, moisture content, sunlight, etc. is very essential, which is easily met inside greenhouse. This leads to better plant growth and timely appearance of all the stages of plant growth. In result, the crop yield becomes very promising. On the other hand, in open condition this is not met. Greenhouse technology is advantageous multifold; about 7 to 12 times higher yield can be possible through greenhouse use than the crops grown in open environment, depending on the type of greenhouse, type of crop and the equipped environmental control facilities, as well.

Year round cultivation: Greenhouse is one of the structures, in which there is the provision of self-monitored system to maintain the micro-climate as per requirement of the crop grown inside. In this way the required climate (temperature, humidity, sunlight) for growing the crop can be formed during any time span. On this ground, the year round cultivation becomes well possible inside greenhouse. This is the reason that the greenhouse has also been proved highly remunerative.

Enhanced produce quality: This is because of the reason that inside greenhouse the micro-climate suitable to a particular crop can be easily formed in automated greenhouses as and when required. In other words, there is no fluctuation in environmental factors. This leads to develop better plant/crop growth, appearance of crop growth stages well in time; proper fruit/grain setting and also the occurrence of crop maturity at right time. All these effects in combination result into better yield and high quality produce, both.

Off-season cultivation: Greenhouse is a special type structure, in which the retention of heat content is very large. In other words, the temperature inside greenhouse is more than the outside. This is because of the reason that the greenhouse covered with Polyethylene film (UV stabilized) when receives the sunlight from its top surface the heat contents infiltrate into greenhouse, where the objects like crop, floor surface and other substances absorb the heat; and simultaneously they also emit the heat from them, which does not escape from the greenhouse. This causes retention or storage of heat/temperature continuously in greenhouse structure. In result there is high temperature inside greenhouse as compared to the outside. Normally, the variation in inside and outside temperature is from 7 to 10°C. This temperature variation makes the greenhouse well suitable for growing off-season crops, i.e., the summer season crop can be grown in winter. Similarly, if greenhouse is well placed with the automatic system, the winter crops can be successfully grown in summer season; and so on.

Easy plant protection: The insect-pest attack and disease infestation are the main factors, against which the crops require their protection. Greenhouses are provided with insect screens to prevent entry of insects-pests in greenhouse. The disease infestation in greenhouse crops is due to unbalanced micro-climate in context to grown crop. In this regard, greenhouses are provided with automation system to control or modify the micro-climate as per requirement, instantly. This results into keeping the crop or plant always in protected mode. In general, the problem of insects/pests and diseases is very less in greenhouse, as compared to the crops grown in open field condition. In addition, greenhouse crops are also being safe against heavy rainfall, hail storms, etc.

Less crop water requirement: The water requirement of the crop grown inside greenhouse is less as compared to the outside. This is because of less evaporation loss from greenhouse production zone and also from the plant surface inside greenhouse. There is quite difference in Evapotranspiration (ET) requirement of the crop grown inside and outside in open field.

Weed free cultivation: In greenhouse the management of weeds is quite easy because of cultivation of crops in proper geometry. And the soil or growing media is also well treated.

Control on weather parameters: The weather parameters comprising temperature, humidity, sunlight, etc. can be suitably maintained as per requirement of the crop. For this purpose there are several means to place in greenhouse such as shade nets and automation system, as well. The shade nets develop cooling effect by creating shades in greenhouse. The automation system controls the micro-climate, automatically, as per requirement of the grown crop.

3.6 WORKING PRINCIPLE OF GREENHOUSE

Greenhouse is the framed structure covered with UV stabilized polyethylene sheet from the top, is erected in open atmosphere. The sunlight or solar radiation directly strike on the top surface, a part of which gets enter the greenhouse and rest part is reflected back to the atmosphere. The entered solar radiation/heat is absorbed by the crop and other objects lying there. The light entered the greenhouse is utilized in reference to (i) Intensity (brightness); (ii) Colour, and (iii) Amount by the crop. In plant growth and productivity, the light transmission in greenhouse is very important. The light intensity or solar radiation is mainly required to accomplish photosynthesis action, which in turn to affect the flowering and fruit setting as well.

In absence of adequate light intensity or solar radiation the plant growth becomes sluggish and unable to result good produce and quality, both. The transmission of adequate light in greenhouse depends on several factors, mainly related to the structural base and environmental factors. Especially, by using reflecting surfaces on north sides of greenhouses (in Northern Hemisphere) the amount of solar radiation or level of light availability to the greenhouse can be enhanced. Similarly, by putting the reflecting materials over the soil surface to reflect that light which is not intercepted by the crop, the availability of light can also be increased for the crop in greenhouse production area.

In greenhouse the conducive effect on crop is the function of formed micro-climate inside. The formation of micro-climate is due to incipient solar light. On striking solar light (radiation) a part of it is transmitted inside the greenhouse in terms of heat content through transparent covering material, i.e., the polyethylene film, which is absorbed there by the surfaces of crop canopies, floor of the production zone and other objects there, if any. In addition, these objects also emit the heat content from them, which is not escaped from the greenhouse area because of greenhouse cover. In result the inside temperature of greenhouse becomes more than the outside. This whole process is called "greenhouse effect", is always in operational mode in greenhouse. In nutshell, the formation of greenhouse effect is result of following two major reasons:

- ***Effect due to confinement*:** This is resulted because of reduction in air exchange with the outside environment; and
- ***Effect due to cover*:** The covering material used in greenhouse construction involves low transparency to far infrared radiation emitted by the objects inside greenhouse, while a high transparency to the sunlight. This feature of covering material is highly causative to create greenhouse effect in such structures.

3.7 GREENHOUSE EFFECT—GENERAL

In atmosphere the CO_2 shares about 0.035% (345 ppm) of the total gas contents. However, its percentage varies with the emission of pollutants and exhaust gases in the atmosphere. The CO_2 forms a kind of blanket at the outer periphery of atmosphere. In result there is retention of reflected solar radiation from the earth surface. This causes increase in atmospheric temperature. This whole process causing increase in ambient temperature because of formation of carbon dioxide blanket at the outer periphery of atmosphere is known as greenhouse effect. The CO_2 layer is transparent to the short wave radiation, while it is opaque to long wave radiations. The solar radiation falls in the category of short wavelength, while reflected solar radiation from the earth surface is in the form of long wavelength. Nowadays, this happening is designated as the global warming. The increase in atmospheric temperature with accelerating rate may lead to create the problem of melting of ice caps; and thereby rise in ocean level and submergence of coastal lines, as well.

In greenhouse structure, the reflected radiation/heat from soil surface and other objects lying there have long wave length, are not crossed outside from the covering materials. In result there is retention of heat contents within greenhouse; and accordingly there is increase in temperature. This is the process for development of greenhouse effect in greenhouse structure. For greenhouse crops this effect is treated as beneficial because there is positive effect on crop growth and development due to greenhouse effect.

3.8 GREENHOUSE GASSES

The gasses falling in the domain of greenhouse gas are mentioned below:

(i) Carbon dioxide (CO_2)
(ii) Methane (CH_4)
(iii) Nitrous oxide (N_2O)
(iv) Fluorinated gases.

- **Carbon dioxide (CO_2):** Its availability in the atmosphere is from the following sources,

  (i) Burning of fossil fuels such as coal, natural gas, and oil, solid waste, trees and other biological materials, and
  (ii) Certain chemical reactions such as in manufacturing of cement.

  Its consumption/sequestration from the atmosphere is through plants as the part of biological carbon cycle.

- **Methane (CH_4):** Its entry in the atmosphere is from the coal, natural gas and oil. In addition, it is also produced from the livestock and other agricultural activities, land use system and decay of organic wastes.
- **Nitrous oxide (N_2O):** This is emitted from the sources such as agricultural land uses, industrial activities, combustion of fossil fuels and solid wastes. In addition, it is also added from the treatment of wastewater.
- **Fluorinated gases:** The gases, namely (i) Hydro-fluorocarbons, (ii) Perfluoro-carbons, (iii) Sulphur Hexafluoride, and (iv) Nitrogen Trifluoride are the prominent greenhouse gases. These are emitted from industrial processes, mainly. Although, these gasses are emitted in very small amount but they are potent greenhouse gases. Because of this reason, sometimes, these gases are also designated as High Global Warming Potential (High GWP) gases. Effect of these gases depends on their concentration, which denotes the amount of a particular gas available in the air. Concentration of gas is measured in terms of part per million (ppm), parts per billion (ppb) and also parts per trillion (ppt). In which one ppm (part per million) is equal to one drop of water diluted in about 13 gallons of liquid.

As per overview of US in the year 2019 the distribution of greenhouse gasses in the atmosphere is shown in Table 3.3

Table 3.3 Distribution of greenhouse gasses

S. No.	Greenhouse gas	Distribution (%)
1.	Carbon Dioxide (CO_2)	80
2.	Methane (CH_4)	10
3.	Nitrous Oxide (N_2O)	7
4.	Fluorinated gases	3

3.9 TRANSMISSIVITY OF GREENHOUSE RADIATION

The amount of solar radiation entering to or transmitting into the greenhouse is called greenhouse transmissivity. The term "Greenhouse global transmissivity" is also associated to the radiation transmissivity, which is defined as the fraction of global solar radiation transmitted inside the greenhouse. The availability of maximum solar radiation inside greenhouse is desirable for better crop growth and development, especially during autumn and winter seasons. Solar radiation varies with the latitude of the place. For example, at the latitudes higher than 30° from the equator the solar radiation gets decrease for crop growth inside greenhouse. In general, the followings are the factors affecting transmissivity of solar radiation to greenhouse:

1. Climate conditions,
2. Position of the sun,
3. Geometry of greenhouse,
4. Greenhouse orientation,
5. Covering material (radiometric characteristics, cleanliness, water condensation on its inner surface), and
6. Structural elements and equipment inside.

Climatic condition: The climatic condition affecting transmissivity of solar radiation to greenhouse is mainly concern to the cloudiness and clear weather conditions. The magnitude of direct and diffused radiation coming to the greenhouse is more in clear days than the cloudy days. Accordingly, the transmitting of solar heat or radiation into the greenhouse production zone is comparatively more in clear days than the cloudy days. In completely cloudy days the solar radiation is being available in diffused form. In this condition, the available diffused solar radiation gets homogeneously distributed inside greenhouse. Overall, the average instantaneous transmissivity of solar radiation varies throughout the day depending on position of the Sun. Normally, on sunny days, the level of solar radiation gets slightly increase from dawn until noon, while it becomes low in later period until dusk.

Greenhouse geometry: Normally, greenhouses are constructed either in single span or more than one span. This difference in construction makes significant variation in amount of solar radiation availability to greenhouse production zone. In case of single-span greenhouse the radiation transmissivity is more to that of the multi-span greenhouse. This is because of creation of shadow effects between spans. Because of this reason the solar radiation transmissivity data of single-span greenhouse is not extrapolated or applied to the multi-span greenhouse.

Position of sun: It depends on date, time of day and latitude. All these factors significantly affect the level of incoming solar radiation from sun to the greenhouse body; and accordingly, to the amount of transmission of the same into the greenhouse.

Greenhouse orientation: Greenhouses are mainly constructed in the direction of east to west and north to south refers to the greenhouse orientation. The effect of orientation is mainly on transmissivity of solar radiation to the greenhouse. Its effect is very influencing during autumn and winter seasons under clear sky condition, especially when greenhouse is constructed in North-South direction. Normally, in this orientation greenhouse receives most photosynthetically active radiation (PAR) throughout the year. The North-South facing greenhouse has two surfaces for receiving sunlight or solar radiation, in which one is the East side roof surface which receives the radiation in morning session and second, is the west side roof surface, receives the radiation in afternoon session. During April to October when sun is located at the top in the sky, majority of the radiation enters the greenhouse from these two roof surfaces. However, with this orientation there is problem about reduction in level of solar radiation during April to October at 40°N latitude, when greenhouse temperature is very high. In general, the October to March period is very important regarding PAR transmission in greenhouse, as there is less availability of light because of small sun angle at latitude 40°N. Especially, in this situation a free-standing greenhouse at east-west orientation is more effective to receive good amount of solar radiation during October to March months. Although, in east–west oriented greenhouse the uniformity of radiation is less (on clear days) than the north–south oriented greenhouse but transmissivity rate is quite high in autumn season.

The uniformity of solar radiation in multi-span greenhouses constructed at east–west and north–south orientation can be attenuated by using following measures:

- Increasing greenhouse height, i.e., from 3.5 to 4.0 m at gutter,
- Keeping less span width, and
- Using plastic film with radiation diffusion characteristics.

Besides above the direction of prevailing wind is also counted in deciding the greenhouse orientation, because there is notable effect of wind velocity on transmission of solar radiation in the greenhouse. The orientation as per wind direction makes the greenhouse structure safe against mechanical damage. However, there is indirect effect on formation of greenhouse micro-climate and energy balance, as well. At this array of greenhouse orientation, the ventilation level should be reduced to keep the heat loss in suitable range.

Structural design: In structural design the inclination of rooftop is one of the main parameters affecting the interception and transmission of solar radiation to the greenhouse. At the condition of glazing surface (roof) perpendicular to the sun there is highest transmission of light/radiation energy in the greenhouse. Although, it takes place for a short time period during day hour, but it certainly does. In context to appropriate level of interception and transmission of solar light the design and construction of greenhouse should be done in such a way that, especially, during the months from October to March when greater amount of solar radiation is needed for crop growth and development, must be met out.

In addition, the closely placed supporting materials in frame structure of greenhouse also affect the light transmission. The selection of supporting materials should be as per covering sheet. However, the weight of structure should be under safe limit, i.e., is not much. The interior components such as supplemental light system, traditional overheating devices, thermal screens and others used in greenhouse also develop causative effects on radiation transmission. Basically these materials obstruct the PAR lighting.

Condensation effect: In greenhouse, condensation takes place at the inner surface of rooftop. This is useful in night hours to reduce the energy loss for direct radiation to the atmosphere from PE cover. On the other hand, in day hours an excess condensation declines the PAR transmission. Condensation effect also develops localized disease problem, especially when condensed water droplets fall on the canopy surface of plants inside greenhouse. This type of problem can be eliminated by using Infrared (IR) film as the cladding material in greenhouse construction.

3.10 GREENHOUSE ENVIRONMENTAL PARAMETERS

In greenhouse techniques for protected cultivation the following environmental factors play significant role to affect the yield and quality of the produce:

(i) Temperature,
(ii) Relative humidity,
(iii) Light,
(iv) Carbon dioxide (CO_2),
(v) Soil moisture content, and
(vi) Ventilation for gaseous exchange.

Temperature: In general, temperature is the indicator of level of heat present in the environment. In plant life the air temperature and soil temperature are very important. Each and every crop has its loving temperature range, in which they grow and flourish well. A little temperature variation can develop misconduct in plant growth processes. For example, the plant processes are stopped due to formation of ice with the tissues, leading to puncturing of cells due ice crystals. In addition, the enzymes which are biological reaction catalysts are also being very heat sensitive. Accordingly, they also become inactive in absence of proper temperature. As per research studies, the biochemical reactions in plant body are controlled by the enzymes. At each 10°C rise in temperature, the rate of reaction control by the enzyme may often be double or triple, till reaching of temperature to an optimum level. Further due to increase in temperature the reactions get suppress and stop, finally. In context to greenhouse corps, they grew in presence of day temperature, which is normally 3 to 6°C greater than the night temperature on cloudy days and about 8°C more on clear days. In general, the night temperature of greenhouse crops varies from 7 to 21°C. The temperature requirement for few greenhouse crops is mentioned Table 3.4.

Table 3.4 Temperature requirement of few greenhouse crops

S. No.	Greenhouse crop	Temperature (°C)
1.	Primula, matthiola incana and calceolaria	7
2.	Carnation and cineraria	10
3.	Rose	16
4.	Chrysanthemum and poinsettia	17 to 18
5.	African violet	21 to 22

In other words, the temperature is one of the most important environmental or weather parameters to affect the plant growth and development, both. In seed germination and plant's growth it is vital. The average temperature of greenhouse production zone should be in the range of 17 to 27°C, with about 10°C and 35°C as the lower and upper limits, respectively. The details about air and soil temperature are presented below:

***Air temperature*:** In soil-water-plant-atmosphere system the air temperature is the part of atmospheric temperature. In photosynthesis process, the temperature is very significant environmental factor. As per research evidence, an optimum photosynthesis takes place between 21 and 22°C. For proper flowering and fruit setting the optimum night temperature lies between

16 and 18°C. The level of optimum temperature is determined by the processes involved in utilization of assimilate products of photosynthesis. They are namely the distribution of dry matter to the shoots, leaves, roots and fruits.

The average temperature denotes 24-hour mean temperature. In most of the greenhouse crop production system there is close relationship between plant growth, yield and mean temperature. In vegetable corps the optimum 24-hour mean temperature varies between 21 and 23°C depending on the light intensity.

***Plant temperature*:** It affects the plant performance and yield, too. The actual leaf temperature is measured by using a device called "Infrared thermometer". The plant temperature is usually lying within a degree of air temperature. However, during intense light period the plant tissues are exposed to an intense heat. In this condition the plant temperature can reach from 10 to 12°C higher than the air temperature, which is inappropriate for plant. In this situation the lowering of greenhouse temperature can be done by using shade nets and evaporative cooling system.

***Soil temperature*:** Soil temperature maintains the soil media active, biologically. It is very essential for operating the soil based activities. A device called "soil thermometer" is used for measuring the soil temperature. Soil thermometer consists of a probe and screen. Soil temperature is measured by keeping the probe inside the soil. The sensor detects the temperature, which is displayed on the screen in degree Celsius (°C) unit.

Light: Light is the source of radiant energy. The light available to plants includes different wavelengths, in which one which is in visible nature and other is not in visible nature. The microwaves and infrared light are in non-visible nature. Plant uses the light for producing food through photosynthesis process. In addition, the spectral composition of light affects the morphological development of the plant, comprising the size or proportion of root and shoots growth. Plant intercepts and captures the radiant energy through special pigments. For example, in photosynthesis process the photosynthetic wavelengths (400–700 nm) activate the chlorophyll pigments, which transform the light energy into chemical energy. This leads to production of carbon molecules, i.e., the sugar. The formed sugar is then used to construct the other compounds; and finally the cells, tissues and organs such as the root, leaf, stem, flower and fruit are created in the plant.

Light is very essential for photosynthesis action in plants. The light energy, carbon dioxide (CO_2) and water are the basic elements of photosynthesis process, through which the formation of carbohydrates takes place. The formed carbohydrates from CO_2 and water in presence of chlorophyll along with light energy, causes plant growth and reproduction. Photosynthesis rate is governed by the available plant nutrients, water, carbon dioxide, light and temperature. The photosynthesis reaction is shown as under,

$$CO_2 + \text{Water}(H_2O) + \text{Light energy} \xrightarrow[\text{Plant nutrients}]{\text{Chlorophyll}} \text{Carbohydrates} + \text{Oxygen}$$

Above reaction advocates that if light intensity is diminished, the photosynthesis process gets decline. This causes reduction in plant growth. Similarly, if light intensity is very high than the optimal limit, the photosynthesis process also becomes slow, and thereby the plant growth declines in accordance with the same. At high light intensity condition the chloroplasts are injured, which poses its effect on photosynthesis action. Light intensity is expressed in the unit of "Lux", is an international unit. For greenhouse crops the suitable range of light intensity varies from 129.6klux on clear summer days to 3.2 klux on cloudy winter days. However, the requirement of light intensity for photosynthesis action varies considerably from crop to crop. For example the rose and carnation grow very well under summer light intensities, while others are not so.

***Light classification*:** Lights are classified as per their wavelength. All kinds of light are not being useful in photosynthesis process. Different types of lights and their specific features towards crop or plant growth are mentioned below:

(i) ***UV light*:** This light has short wavelength, i.e. less than 400nm. Its availability in large quantity is harmful to the plants.

(ii) ***Visible and white light*:** Its wavelength varies from 400 to 700nm. These lights are important for photosynthesis action.

(iii) ***Far red light*:** Its wavelength varies from 700 to 750nm. Its availability affects the plants, besides causing photosynthesis.

(iv) ***Infrared rays*:** These lights have longer wavelengths. These are not required in plant processes.

(v) ***Blue light*:** Its wavelength is short. In presence of blue light the rate of photosynthesis gets increase. However, blue light alone in photosynthesis process declines the plant growth. In result the plant becomes hard and dark in colour.

(vi) ***Red light*:** This has long wavelength. In presence of red light the plant growth becomes soft and internode distance is also lengthened. This results into tall height of the plants. In addition, red light is also beneficial to regulate the greenhouse temperature.

In general, the following three types of lights are more concern to the greenhouse:

(i) Visible light,

(ii) Blue light, and

(iii) Orange-red light.

***Visible light*:** This is most important light for greenhouse crops. In plants its main role is towards photosynthesis action. Its wavelength varies from 400 to 700 nm (nanometers). Sometimes, this light is also called Photosynthetically Active Radiation (PAR). Visible light acts as the source of energy for plants.

***Blue light*:** Its wavelength varies from 400 to 490 nm. The requirement of blue light is mainly during vegetative and foliage growth phases.

***Orange-red light*:** Its wavelength varies between 590 to700 nm. During flowering and fruiting phase its requirement is the main.

Although, the green light (490–580nm) is also there, but its effect on plant growth is very little, as the plants themselves are in green colour. The cell chloroplast absorbs the blue and red lights, and skips the green colour because they reflect that colour.

Relative humidity: Relative humidity denotes the presence of water contents in the air or to the atmosphere. In greenhouse domain the level of humidity is always higher to that of the ambient air. This is because of the reason that the greenhouse is in closed form, and continuously moisture (water content) is added to the greenhouse environment by crop ET process which does not escape from there. Although, some of the moisture is removed from ventilation and other points but a large percent of that is retained inside. In greenhouse the humidity level is also required to maintain, artificially, as per suitability or requirement of the grown crop. This is carried out by means of humidification or dehumidification process. The acceptable range of relative humidity for majority of the greenhouse crops varies from 50 to 80%. On the other hand, for plant's propagation points of view, it is up to 90% may be desirable.

Carbon dioxide (CO_2): Carbon is one of the main and essential elements for plant growth. In plants its availability is greater than the other elements. Out of the total dry matter in the plant about 40% is composed of carbon content. In atmosphere, under normal condition it is available in the form of gas, and in the concentration of 345 ppm. In photosynthesis process the plants consume the carbon contents and thereby the CO_2 level gets reduce to the level less than 200 ppm in the atmosphere. At lesser level of CO_2 than the ambient, the plant growth gets retard. In greenhouse, the CO_2 level can be increased by the provision of ventilation system. The outside air is allowed through ventilation to enter the greenhouse to maintain CO_2 level. However, in cold regions the maintenance of ambient CO_2 level by ventilation system is not found satisfactory, or normally being uneconomical, because of necessity of heating of incoming air to bring the temperature up. In such regions the CO_2 is added to the greenhouse from outside sources. The concentration of CO_2 in greenhouse also varies with the light intensity, temperature, nutrient levels, cultivar and degree of crop maturity. This is the reason that the exact amount of CO_2 level required for a crop does not remain same but varies throughout. As per research findings, majority of the crops respond better at the CO_2 level ranging from 1000 to 1200 ppm. The desired levels of climatic parameters inside greenhouse are presented in Table 3.5.

Table 3.5 Range of climatic parameters desired for greenhouse crops

S. No.	Climatic parameter	Desired range	Remark
1.	Wind velocity	Inflow: outflow as 1:1	Wind velocity affects the greenhouse temperature, relative humidity and concentration of CO_2 inside greenhouse.
2.	Carbon dioxide (CO_2)	350 to 1000 ppm	It is required for better photosynthesis in context to proper plant growth.
3.	Solar radiation/sunlight	50000 lux	It is required for photosynthesis, photomorphogenesis, photoperiodism, etc. processes.
4.	Temperature	18 to 25°C	This is important for cell division, elongation, respiration, photosynthesis, water uptake, transpiration, etc.
5.	Relative humidity (RH)	60 to 80%	This is desired for plant stability.

3.11 GREENHOUSE COMPONENTS

Greenhouse structure is just like a house used for growing the crops, inside. It assembles the frame structure; roof covered with covering material; a door for going in and coming out; storage space, soil for growing crops, ventilation system, cooling and heating devices, etc., mainly. The greenhouses are constructed in various sizes as per availability of land and requirement of the growers. The important components of greenhouse are given below:

1. Frame structure
2. Cover
3. Greenhouse floor
4. Ventilation system
5. Heating/cooling system
6. Watering system

Figure 3.1 depicts the components of greenhouse.

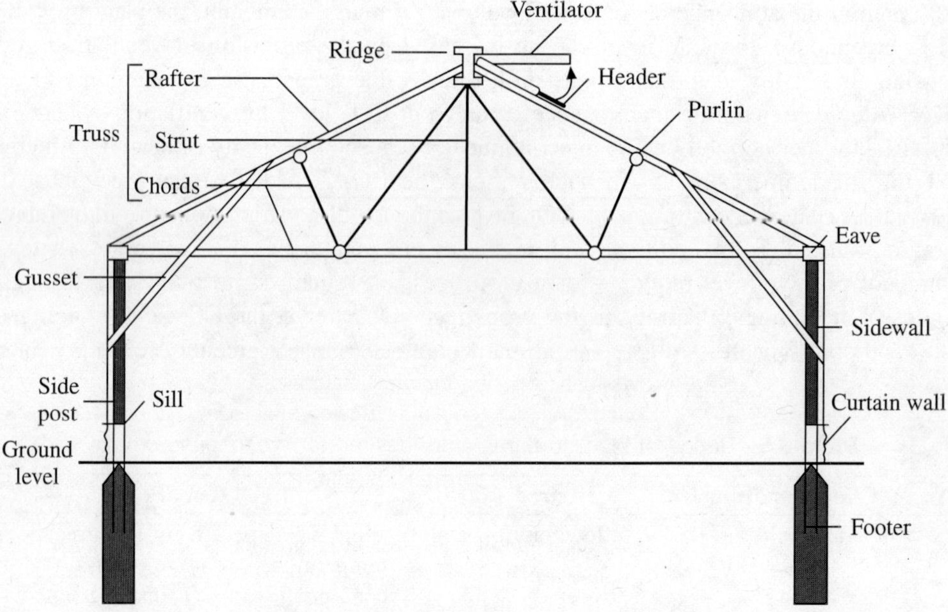

Figure 3.1 Structural details of greenhouse (*Source:* www.kirkwood.edu)

3.11.1 Frame Structure

This is one of the most important components of the greenhouse. The greenhouse stability and strength is mainly because of frame structure and materials, used. Structure is erected by using different kinds of materials such as the wooden, metallic, rigid PVC, aluminum; and sometimes, the masonry materials, also. The other components such as the cooling system, heating system, etc. are connected to the frame structure. Structure is erected on proper foundation to provide proper structural strength. The details are presented below:

(i) **Foundation:** Providing foundation to the greenhouse structure is for the purpose of sufficient structural strength and stability. The greenhouses are normally like to get failure against overturning. Foundation is prepared by using the concrete materials. The dimension of foundation may be to the tune of 60 cm (length) × 60 cm (breadth)

× 60 cm (depth) or 30 cm diameter and 1 m as the depth. In addition, the vertical poles are also placed to the height of 60 cm by PCC with 5 cm thickness to avoid the possibility of rusting problem in the erected poles.

(ii) **Structural components:** Structural components of greenhouse are shown in Figure 3.1. The rafters which are the primary vertical supports are generally placed on 2, 3 or 4 foot centers depending on strength requirement to hold the frame structure. Rafters may be in the form of truss, curved or arch, suitable to greenhouse span. The horizontal supports are casted by providing purlins that run from the rafter to rafter. The spacing between all structural components is kept to the tune of 4 to 8 feet based on the magnitude of greenhouse. Normally, purlins are suggested to add in the frame, especially, at the site where wind load is very heavy, for providing additional supports. Purlins are connected in the form of cross tie. The side posts and columns are used to provide vertical support to the structure. The sidewalls are provided to accomplish cooling effect through ventilation from sides. The details about other components are narrated in Table 3.6.

Table 3.6 Sub-components of frame structure of greenhouse

S. No.	Components	Remark
1.	Side wall	♦ It supports the truss and bears the weight of the greenhouse. ♦ It is set in concrete footings. ♦ Spaced 10 feet apart.
2.	Curtain wall	♦ The first several feet of sidewall above the soil line. ♦ It is made of solid building materials such as poured concrete, concrete blocks, bricks, or treated lumber.
3.	Sill	♦ It is top of curtain wall.
4.	Eave	♦ This is the point where sides join the roof of greenhouse, or top of the sides of greenhouse.
5.	Truss	♦ It is for supporting the weight of greenhouse roof. ♦ It consists of rafters, struts and chords.
6.	Purlin	♦ It runs along the length of greenhouse. ♦ It keeps the roof trusses, properly aligned.
7.	Ridge	♦ This is the point where the roofs come together at the top of greenhouse.
8.	Side posts and columns	♦ These are vertical supports, dictate the height of production area. ♦ Height may be from 1 to 10 feet. ♦ They directly influence the efficiency.
9.	Sash bar	♦ It runs perpendicular to purlins. ♦ Attached to the purlins. ♦ Holds the glazing in place.

3.11.2 Greenhouse Cover

Cladding materials play key role in creation of micro-climate inside greenhouse. In greenhouse construction, the cover is placed over the frame structure with the help of panel, to create roof.

The covering materials such as UV stabilized polyethylene (PE) film, glass, polycarbonate sheet, etc. are used for the purpose. However, amongst them the UV stabilized polyethylene film is very common. This is because of the reasons, such as (i) Easy in handling, and (ii) Availability at low price, etc. Sometimes, the greenhouse covering is also known as glazing. The UV stabilized PE film has a good property of transmitting the solar radiation (short wave length) to the greenhouse but highly resistant to the outgoing radiations (long wavelength).This effect causes temperature retention inside greenhouse. By virtue of this effect the greenhouse temperature becomes greater than the outside. This effect is known as "greenhouse effect", is conducive to greenhouse crops. Normally, the variation in inside and outside temperature is from 7 to 10°C in well designed and properly constructed greenhouse.

3.11.3 Greenhouse Floor

Greenhouse production zone comprises the soil surface and non-soil surfaces, both. The soil surface contains the soil area for crop growing, while non-soil surface assembles the concrete surfaces, stones slabs, bricks, sands, etc. inside greenhouse.

3.11.4 Greenhouse Ventilation

In greenhouse the ventilation system is mainly required for following purposes:

(i) Reducing greenhouse temperature by creating air exchange,
(ii) Replenishing CO_2 supply, and
(iii) Moderating relative humidity.

In greenhouse production zone the air temperature more than 35°C is not found suitable for majority of the crops. In high temperature condition the greenhouse crops get badly affected. Therefore, greenhouse cooling or temperature reduction becomes prime important. It is carried out by adding the provision of ventilation system in greenhouse structure. In greenhouse cooling the inside air temperature is brought below the upper limit of required temperature during spring and autumn seasons. The ventilation in greenhouse can be the natural and forced feed type. In which, the natural ventilation is being suitable for small greenhouses with less than 6m span width. Natural ventilations are found quite effective in spring and autumn seasons for crop framing points of view. The forced feed type ventilations such as the fan pad cooling system are suitable to use, when a precise control on air temperature, humidity and CO_2 level is required in greenhouse. These will be discussed in detail in forthcoming chapter. In nutshell, the importance and objectives of ventilation system in greenhouse are mentioned below:

- Regulating temperature to an optimal level as per crop requirement.
- Ensuring proper air circulation.
- Creating check against development of plant pathogens (such as *Botrytis cinerea*) preferring still air conditions.
- Supplying fresh air in greenhouse production zone.
- Enabling important pollinators to access greenhouse crops.

Ventilation system is the sub-part of greenhouse cooling system, is described in detail in forthcoming section 3.11.5.

3.11.5 Greenhouse Cooling/Heating System

In greenhouse performance towards better crop farming, the cooling system is one of the important components. Reason behind this may be described as, the cladding or glazing provided at the greenhouse roof top creates greater inside temperature than the outside, because of greenhouse effect. The variation in inside temperature is to the tune of 7 to 10°C. This heavy extent of temperature increment in production zone of greenhouse in summer season makes the crop damage in absence of cooling arrangement. In this condition, the provision of cooling system to save the crop damage or loss becomes very essential. This can be accomplished by various means such as use of shade nets, proper ventilation, placing of exhaust fan, use of cooling system, fogging or misting system and automated cooling system, as well. In temperate regions the provision of cooling system is most suitable, when temperature rises more than 40°C during summer season. On the other hand, in cold climates/regions the heating arrangement is essential in greenhouse to raise the inside temperature for successful crop production.

Types of cooling systems: These are given below:

(a) Fan-and Pad cooling system
(b) Fog cooling system
(c) Convection tube cooling
(d) Horizontal air flow cooling
(e) Greenhouse ventilation—Natural ventilation
(f) Roll up side passive ventilation system
(g) Forced ventilation system

Fan and pad cooling system: This kind of active summer cooling system, is in practice since 1954. This cooling is considered as one of the most suitable cooling systems for greenhouse. It works on the principle of evaporative cooling process, i.e., the required heat for evaporating the moisture is taken from the surrounding environment causing depression in temperature of surroundings. In evaporative cooling lesser the dryness of air, greater is the cooling. In this cooling process the maximum cooling can be achieved only up to the wet bulb temperature of incoming air. This is treated as one of the limitations of this method.

System comprises the pads, which are vertically mounted on the wall of greenhouse; and an exhaust fan placed on the wall just opposite to the wall mounted with pad. Pad is made of cross-fluted cellulose materials. The appearance of pad is just like corrugated card board. In operation the water is allowed to pass through the pad. The exhaust fan sucks the warm air from outside into the greenhouse through pad. The passing water through pad absorbs the heat content of striking warm air and also from the surroundings for its evaporation. This result into declination of surrounding's temperature. In this system, at the place of cooling pad the Khus-khus grass made mats can also be used. Fan pad cooling system is enabling to lower the temperature of greenhouse to the tune of about 80% of the difference between dry and wet bulb temperatures. This is because of the reason that complete evaporation of the water does not take place in this system.

Fog cooling system: This method follows the principle of evaporative cooling. It is commonly used in greenhouse crop farming. System consists of a high pressure pumping unit connected to the plastic tubing along with water emitting nozzles. On system operation, the water gets discharge from the nozzles in the form of very fine water droplets, which takes the form of "fog" in greenhouse. The mean diameter of water droplets forming the fogs is less than 10 micron. The generated fogs are dispersed in suspension form throughout greenhouse production zone; and accordingly, the entire environment inside greenhouse becomes cool down.

In fog cooling system, since, the plant foliage does not get wet with fogs; therefore, the incidence of disease and pest's attack is not on the grown crop inside greenhouse. This system can lower the temperature of incoming air by about 100% of the difference between dry bulb and wet bulb temperatures. This high range of cooling is because of complete evaporation of fine water droplets. This cooling system performs well for cooling the production zone to be used for seed germination and plant propagation, as well.

Convection tube cooling: In winter season the ambient temperature is lesser than the inside temperature of greenhouse, because of entrapment of solar heat. The entry of cold air from outside in greenhouse zone may be harmful for some of the crops. In this particular condition, the hot and cold spots in greenhouse may lead to cause uneven crop timing and quality, both. In order to avoid this possibility, the excessive cold air of outside is tempered to bring its temperature equal to inside air temperature. In nutshell, this whole process signifies the cooling process by mixing a low temperature air into warm air. This principle is applied in convection tube cooling method for greenhouse temperature control, in winter season. The convection tube cooling system comprises following components:

(i) Louvered air inlet
(ii) Polyethylene convection tube with air distribution holes
(iii) Pressurizing fan
(iv) Exhaust fan

At the condition, when temperature level inside greenhouse becomes more than the set value, the exhaust fan gets start; and thus there develops low pressure regime inside greenhouse. This leads to open the inlet and allowing to enter the cold air. The entered cold air is received by means of polyethylene convection tube operated by pressurizing fan. When cooling is not required the inlet louver gets close, but the pressurizing fan remains continue to circulate the air in greenhouse. In this cooling system, the cold air is mixed to the warm air of greenhouse, above plant canopy. Since, the density of cool mixed air mass is more; therefore, it gently flows down to the floor level. This causes a complete cooling of planted area. This method has merits that, as per requirement the temperature gradient can be minimized.

Horizontal air flow cooling: This is an alternative to convection tube cooling method. In this method many small horizontal fans are placed for circulating the air mass. The fans are arranged in such a way that air current gets directed along the greenhouse length and also parallel to the ground surface. The spacing between fans varies from 0.6 to 0.9 m. In greenhouse the fans are placed above the plant height and at about 15 m intervals. In greater width greenhouses more numbers of fan are required. HAF cooling system also employs the exhaust fans, inlet louvers and the controls like convection tube system. The louvers are located at higher level in greenhouse gables. On system operation the cold air is drawn due to air circulation developed by HAF fans. The louvered inlet, HAF fans and exhaust fan in combination distribute the cold air throughout greenhouse area, uniformly.

Ventilation System

Ventilation system allows the fresh air to enter the greenhouse by removing the air of undesirable properties exiting inside. In greenhouse the requirement of ventilation is felt essential to accomplish following purposes:

(i) Lowering the greenhouse temperature,
(ii) Replenishing CO_2 level, and
(iii) Controlling relative humidity as per crop requirement.

The above requirements vary greatly as per crops grown and season of the production, mainly. Ventilation systems are of following two types:

(i) Passive system, and
(ii) Active system.

The passive ventilation system refers to the natural ventilation, while active ventilation to the forced ventilation system. In greenhouse the natural type ventilations are very common.

Natural ventilation: This is provided in the side wall of greenhouse structure, which can be opened for ventilation purpose, depending on requirement. Ventilator facilitates to remove the warm air from the greenhouse. In fact as the air comes across the greenhouse that enters inside and gets mix with the warm air present there. The mixed air mass so, is removed either from the side ventilation or from the roof ventilation. The warm air is light in weight because of lesser density. In result it rises up in greenhouse and escaped from the roof ventilator.
The area of ventilation should be about 10% of total roof area. In winter season, for cooling points of view the south roof ventilator is opened, as per need. In case of summer cooling the south ventilator is opened first and then the north ventilator. However, for high level cooling (if required) the north and south ventilators, both are opened.

Roll up side passive ventilation: In this ventilation the air is allowed to flow across the plants. Ventilation level, i.e., on one side or both the sides or partial way can be adjusted as per temperature and prevailing wind and rain. In summer or during excessive heat, it can be rolled up to the top level. In order to check the entry of insects/pests from the open part of ventilation, that is properly netted or screened, using proper mesh size net. However, the aperture size of screen/net should be sufficient to permit the air flow, smoothly. This ventilation system is found effective in free standing greenhouses. In other words, the gutter connected greenhouses are not being fit for it.

Forced ventilation: This is the active type greenhouse ventilation. It consists of fans to expel the warm air from the greenhouse. This ventilation system produces uniform cooling of greenhouse environment. The summer fan-and-pad and fog cooling systems; and the winter convection tube and horizontal air flow cooling are the examples of forced cooling system.

3.11.6 Watering System

Greenhouse watering denotes the application of irrigation to the planted crops and also modifying the inside environment as per requirement of the crop. For this purpose the drip/sprinkler/foggers are commonly used. Manual application or flooding is totally avoided as there is more possibility of non-uniform application of irrigation. However, automated system is more suitable, in which sensors are provided to read the level of moisture deficit in growing media; and accordingly, to permit the system for supplying required depth of irrigation to the crop. In automated system the depth of water application is set to supply the requisite depth of irrigation. This removes the possibility of water loss and also the non-uniformity in application of water.

Micro-processors: These are used to receive the information on temperature, light intensity, rain and wind speed. They also permit to integrate the diverse range of devices, which is not possible with the thermostat. Micro-processors can also operate the ventilator's based information from the sensor for wind direction and speed. Similarly, a rain sensor can activate the ventilator to prevent the moisture sensitive crop against getting wet. A micro-processor can also be set to activate the CO_2 generator, especially, when light intensity exceeds a given set point, i.e., minimum level for photosynthesis.

Computers: Nowadays, the application of computer based control systems is frequently used across the world. Using computer system, the integrated control on temperature, humidity, irrigation and fertilization, CO_2, light and shade levels can be successfully accomplished for better crop yield. In other words, the precision level can be further enhanced. As per research data the growers can realize 15 to 50% savings in energy, water, chemical and pesticides in crop farming practices. In nutshell, the advantages of computerized control system equipped in greenhouse are narrated as under:

- It enables to provide all the information casting optimum environment.
- It facilitates to record, process, analyze and display the result.
- Using networking facility it can control remotely located greenhouses.
- Using software, it can predict anticipatory weather change beneficial to take measures against crop damage, etc.
- In context to adverse situation likely to occur, the computer can alarm the grower using software.

However, apart from various advantages there are few disadvantages too, are listed as under:

- Investment of high initial cost.
- Requirement of qualified operators to operate the system.
- High level of care and maintenance is required.
- Its suitability is confined to large-scale crop farming under precision technology.
- Not economical for seasonal production.

3.12 GREENHOUSE CLASSIFICATION

Nowadays, greenhouse becomes one of the most important precision farming tools for growing high valued crops, off-season cultivation, better productivity and quality produce. Initially, this was used to construct in a very simple way by covering the structure with the help of glass. Later on, based on research investigations a lot of improvements have been made in respect to its design and construction to improve its working performance, more applicability and for greater outcome. This was possible because of invention of UV polyethylene (PE) materials and automation system. All these interventions in greenhouse technology, grouped the greenhouse of various types or classes. Broadly, the greenhouses are classified based on different aspects, mentioned below:

1. Based on shape
   - (i) Lean-to type
   - (ii) Even span type
   - (iii) Uneven span type
   - (iv) Ridge and furrow type
   - (v) Saw tooth type
   - (vi) Quonset type
2. Based on utility
   - (i) With active heating
   - (ii) With active cooling
3. Based on construction materials, used
   - (i) Wooden frame structures
   - (ii) Pipe frame structures
   - (iii) Truss frame structures
4. Based on covering materials
   - (i) Glass greenhouses
   - (ii) Plastic film greenhouses
   - (iii) Rigid panel greenhouses

3.12.1 Greenhouse Classification Based on Shape

The cross sectional view of greenhouse depicts its overall shape. Cross section encompasses the width and height of the structure. Because of variations in width and height there is likely to change in overall appearance of the greenhouse. Accordingly, the cross section becomes as a basis for classification of greenhouse. Since, longitudinal section remains same almost in all the greenhouses; therefore, it is not counted for classification. In addition, the cross also provides the information about overall shape of the structural members, such as truss or hoop, etc. The common types of greenhouse based on shape are described as under:

Lean-to type greenhouse: This type of greenhouse is constructed against the side of already constructed building. In other words, it is constructed with the support of one or more sides of standing building. The other salient features of Lean-to type greenhouse are narrated as under:

- This greenhouse is usually attached to a house and may also to the other buildings.
- Building roof is extended using greenhouse cladding material to enclose the area properly.
- It faces south.
- It is limited to single or double-row plant benches.
- Its total width varies from 7 to 12 feet.
- Its length can be equal to length of the building.

The advantages of this greenhouse are as follows:

- Its facing is best to receive an adequate sunlight.
- Availability of electricity, water, and heat are ascertained to some extent.
- Construction cost is less.

It has following disadvantages:

- This type of greenhouses normally face the problem of limited space, limited light, limited ventilation and temperature control, as well.
- Its height is governed by the height of supporting wall of the building.
- In such greenhouses, the temperature control is tedious, because supporting wall of building can absorb the solar heat, while translucent cover of greenhouse may lose the heat rapidly.
- Also, it is a half greenhouse split along the peak of the building roof.

Even span type greenhouse: This is standard type greenhouse. It assembles full-size structure with two roof slopes of equal pitch and width. The other details of this greenhouse are presented below:

- Preferred to construct on level ground.
- Attached to the house at one gable end.
- 2 or 3 rows of plant benches can be easily accommodated in this greenhouse.
- Its construction cost is more than the lean-to type greenhouse. However, it involves greater flexibility in design.
- It accommodates more number of plants.
- Its design shape is better than the lean-to type greenhouse for air circulation and also to maintain a uniform temperature in winter.
- In single span greenhouse the length of span varies from 5 to 9 m, total length about 24 m and height varies from 2.5 to 4.3 m.

Uneven span type greenhouse: The important details of this type of greenhouse are mentioned below:

- These are not so common for use.
- These are constructed in hilly areas.
- Roof widths are not the same.
- This greenhouse does not provide scope for automation.

Ridge and furrow type greenhouse: Its top appearance is just like ridge and furrow combination. This is constructed by joining two or more number of A-frame greenhouses, lengthwise. On joining, there forms a furrow or valley between two ridges, called gutter. The gutter serves the purpose of rainwater disposal from greenhouse roof top. In this greenhouse the side walls are eliminated. This makes a large size interior of greenhouse. This greenhouse is well suitable to the Indian condition for use.

Saw tooth type greenhouse: To a large extent these are similar to the ridge and furrow type greenhouses. Its appearance is just like saw tooth, therefore, it is named as the saw tooth type greenhouse. These greenhouses have the provision of natural ventilation for lowering the inside temperature, suitable to greenhouse crops.

Quonset greenhouse: This is quite different over above types of greenhouses. In this greenhouse the frame structure consists of pipe arches or truss supported by the pipe purling running along the greenhouse length. Structure is covered with the help of polyethylene (PE) film. These may be constructed by connecting either the standing style or ridge and interlocking furrow based greenhouses. In comparison to gutter involving greenhouses its construction cost is less. Quonset type greenhouses are being useful for cultivating in a small isolated area.

3.12.2 Greenhouse Classification Based on Utility

In greenhouse the utility refers to the use of cooling or heating system for cooling or heating the greenhouse production zone as per requirement of the crop grown inside. Accordingly, under this head of classification, the greenhouses are described below,

Greenhouses with active heating system: These greenhouses are placed with heating arrangement for increasing the inside temperature depending on the requirement of the crop. At some places during night hours the greenhouse temperature gets sufficiently declined causing bad effect on crop growth due to freezing. In this condition, to avoid such possibility, the production area inside greenhouse requires heating. The heating requirement mainly depends on the rate of heat loss from the greenhouse. The heating arrangement may be accomplished by the provision of following systems:

(a) Double layer polyethylene
(b) Thermo pane glasses
(c) Heaters
(d) Central heating system
(e) Radiant heating system
(f) Solar heating system, etc.

Greenhouse with active cooling system: In general, the temperature inside greenhouse is greater than the outside because of greenhouse effect. In winter season the increased temperature is utilized for growing off-season crops, i.e., there is no harmful effect of increased temperature on the crop. On the other hand, in summer season the increased temperature becomes inconducive for crop growing. Therefore, in summer season, it becomes essential to reduce the greenhouse temperature for the level lesser than the outside temperature. The temperature reduction of greenhouse is carried out by use cooling systems. The commonly used cooling systems in greenhouse are given as under:

(i) Ventilation system
(ii) Shade nets
(iii) Fan and pad cooling system
(iv) Automated or air conditioning system

Besides, above it can also be accomplished by designing the greenhouse in such a way that the roof opening may be up to 40%; however, in some cases it is also up to 100%.

3.12.3 Greenhouse Classification Based on Structural Materials, Used

In greenhouse construction basically two types of materials are required. They are namely,

(i) Structural materials, and
(ii) Covering materials.

These two materials decide the type of greenhouse. In structural materials the woods, metallic pipe, etc. are commonly used for construction of frame structure. The span followed in greenhouse construction mainly governs the type structural materials for use. In case of greater span the material's selection is very important for structural strength point of view. There is a thumb rule, which states that greater the span, stronger to be the constructional materials. Normally, for greater span the sturdy truss type frame/structure is followed in construction of greenhouse. In contrast, for smaller span a simple design is followed, i.e., hoops. On the basis of structural materials used the greenhouses are classified as under:

(i) Wooden frame greenhouse,
(ii) Pipe frame greenhouse, and
(iii) Truss frame greenhouse.

Wooden frame greenhouse: This type of greenhouse comprises its span less than 6 m. Its frame is constructed with the help of wooden materials. Mainly, the side posts and columns are constructed with the help of wooden materials without truss. For this purpose the Pine wood is found most suitable and is commonly used. This is because of the reason that Pine wood is less expensive and also possesses the required structural strength. Overall, the following characteristics are taken into consideration, while selecting the wooden materials for constructing greenhouse:

(i) Local availability,
(ii) Good strength,
(iii) Durability, and
(iv) Machinability.

Pipe framed greenhouse: Frame structure of this greenhouse is erected by using the GI pipe of sufficient gauge. The span of greenhouse should be around 12 m. In frame the components such as the side posts, columns, cross ties and purlins are constructed with the help of pipes. Trusses are not required in this greenhouse.

Truss framed greenhouse: Span of this greenhouse is more than or equal to 15 m. Because of greater span these greenhouses require sufficient structural strength. It is met by providing truss in frame structure. Truss is formed by using the materials such as flat steel, tubular steel or angular steel. They are welded together encompassing the rafters, chords and struts. In which, the component called struts is provided as the support member for bearing compression. And chords are also placed as the support member for bearing tension. The angle iron purlins placed throughout greenhouse length are connected to each truss. In truss structured greenhouse, when truss frame is very wide, i.e., 21.3 m or more then columns are essentially provided. The glasshouses are mostly the truss framed as they are easy in fabrication to place the glass.

3.12.4 Greenhouse Classification Based on Covering Materials

The covering materials are quite different over structural materials (frame) in greenhouse construction. Cladding materials play significant role on greenhouse performance to result better yield and quality produce. To a large extent the formation of micro-climate in production zone of greenhouse, suitable to the crop concern depends very much on the characteristics of covering materials, used. Since, behaviour of greenhouse depends to a lot on the covering materials, used; therefore, this also forms a basis to classify the greenhouse. These greenhouses are described below:

Glass covered greenhouses: Theses greenhouses are covered from the top by glass made covers. Sometimes, they are also known as the glasshouse. Since, the formation of greenhouse effect is also in glasshouse; therefore, these are also kept in the category of greenhouse. The glass greenhouses are constructed in the forms of lean-to type, even span, ridge and furrow. Overall, the glass materials involve following merits:

- High interior light intensity.
- High air infiltration rate, leading to decline the inside relative humidity.
- Causes better control on disease incidence.

Plastic film greenhouses: Such types of greenhouses are constructed by using the flexible plastic films such as polyethylene, polyester and polyvinyl chloride (PVC). Nowadays, these greenhouses are highly popular in agriculture sector, as the plastics are cheaper, easily available and their handling is also very easy. The UV polyethylene films develop a good level of greenhouse effect, which produces better impact on crop yield and produce quality, as well. In this way, the role of plastic films is very significant in protected cultivation.

Rigid panel greenhouses: These greenhouses are constructed by using rigid panels made of polyvinyl chloride, fiber glass-reinforced plastics, acrylic and polycarbonate sheets as the covering materials. The Quonset type and ridge and furrow type greenhouses can be easily constructed by using rigid panels. These materials offer the advantages of greater resistant against breakage and uniform distribution of light intensity throughout greenhouse area as compared to the glasses or plastics as the covering material. The service life of a high grade panel is normally up to 20-year. The main demerit of rigid panels is attraction of dusts and also harboring the algae. This effect results into darkening the panels; and accordingly, there is reduction in radiation transmission.

3.13 GREENHOUSE CONSTRUCTION MATERIALS

Greenhouse is constructed on a frame structure, which is covered with the covering materials from the top and sides both. The frame structure is erected with the help of different kinds of materials such as wooden and non-wooden materials. The materials must be capable to develop a good level of mechanical strength in greenhouse; and accordingly making the structure safe against various causative forces, acting. The covering materials are mainly the plastic's based such as polyethylene films, etc. In nutshell, the materials to be used for construction of greenhouse are divided into two groups, namely:

(i) Framing materials, and
(ii) Covering materials.

Framing materials: The aluminum, steel, woods, etc. are commonly used for construction of greenhouse structures, in which, aluminum is the most durable and economical. In addition, aluminum is also available in different shapes and thicknesses, too. It can be suitably used for constructing different components such as rafters, side posts, etc. However, as compared to aluminum, the wood is not so common because it is likely to get deteriorate, quickly. For better result, the wood should be treated, very well. In general, the list of commonly used materials for greenhouse framework is presented in Table 3.7.

Table 3.7 List of frame materials for construction of greenhouse

S. No.	Materials	Remark
1.	Wood	The selection of materials should be as per strength requirement for the structure, expected life, materials' properties and cost mainly.
2.	Bamboo	
3.	Steel	
4.	Galvanized iron	
5.	Aluminum	
6.	Reinforced cement concrete (RCC)	

Wood and bamboo: These materials are used for construction of low cost greenhouse. The structure is erected with the help of side posts and columns, over which the polyethylene sheet is placed and fixed as the covering material. The wooden parts/components are properly treated with the chemicals before placing them in structure. This treatment makes the structure safe against mites and others. For this purpose the chromated copper arsenate and ammonical copper arsenate can be used. In addition, before placing the cover, the side posts and columns are also properly painted with white colour, because white colour improves the light intensity inside greenhouse. In woods, the pine and casuarina are most fit, as these are strong and less costly. The bamboos are used in tropical areas for constructing gable roof of greenhouse structure.

GI pipes, tubular steel and angle iron: In greenhouse construction these materials are generally used in the form of side posts, columns and purlins. The GI pipes are comparatively maintenance free.

Aluminum: It is used for truss making. Aluminum and steel made items are protected by painting with bitumen tar.

Reinforced cement concrete (RCC): Use of RCC is limited in construction of greenhouse. Mainly the foundation work is done with the help of RCC. In addition, the floors and benches are also constructed using RCC materials, especially in big size greenhouse.

Greenhouse Covering Materials

Covering materials play significant role in overall response or behaviour of greenhouse on crop yield. This is because of the reason that the covering materials enable to develop greenhouse effect and micro-climate conducive to the crop grown in greenhouse production zone. Covering materials are laid on the top and sides of the structure, receives the sunlight or solar radiation directly from the sun. A part of that solar radiation is transmitted into the greenhouse, which gets absorbed by the objects lying there. Further, these objects also emit the radiation, which does not escape from the greenhouse, i.e., retained there inside. The retained solar energy/heat develops heat content or temperature increment, called greenhouse effect. The enhancement in temperature varies to the tune of 7 to 10°C depending on the design and construction of greenhouse. Development of this effect is causative to create different kinds of climate which relative humidity is quite high, is called micro-climate. In nutshell, the covering or glazing affects the amount and type of solar radiation available in the greenhouse conducive to plant growth.

There are several covering materials available for use in construction of greenhouse. However, their selection is very important for getting better response on crop grown. Although, no covering material is ideal but priority should be given to that one, which could develop an optimal controlled environment; especially, in context to better transmissivity of solar radiation and formation of micro-climate, inside. In addition, some of the important points advocating favourable properties of covering materials are narrated as under:

- The covering material should be sufficiently capable to transmit the visible light to the greenhouse production zone for proper photosynthesis.
- It should absorb a small amount of UV rays from the solar radiation and also convert a portion of it to visible light useful for the plant's grown inside greenhouse.
- Cladding materials should have the property of reflection or absorption of IR radiation, because IR is not used by the crop, but produces heat content in greenhouse environment.
- The cost of material should also be less.
- The materials should have sufficient service life may be from 10 to 20 years.

Glass: Glass also involves the characteristics to develop micro-climate or greenhouse effect. Initially, the greenhouses were constructed by using the glasses as covering materials, called glasshouse. In present scenario, its use has become about to negligible, because of introduction of PE films. Nowadays, the materials, such as polyethylene, polycarbonate sheet, etc. are commonly used for greenhouse construction. Overall, in greenhouse construction the widely used glasses are given as under:

(i) Single drawn or float glass, and
(ii) Hammered and tempered glass.

***Single drawn glass*:** This is also known as float glass. Its thickness varies from 3 to 4 mm. This type of glass is made in traditional way; just by pulling the molten glass either by hand or by mechanical means. A coating of metal oxide having low emissivity is also provided on this glass, for the purpose of energy saving and adequate light transmittance.

***Hammered glass*:** This is also known as tempered glass. It is basically a casted glass with one face (exterior) as smooth and the other face (interior) is in rough texture. Its thickness varies to the tune of 4 mm, in translucent nature. Its light diffusivity is high as compared to the single dawn glass. This type of glass involves a high impact resistance. In the greenhouses expecting high wind load, snow fall/hail loading, the use of hammered glass is found most suitable.

Polyethylene film: This was developed in England during late 1930s. The commonly used plastics for greenhouse coverings are the thermoplastics. These plastics have the property of softness on heating and hardness on cooling. Its response on crop is also being best in all the respects. In addition, these are also being available in different thicknesses for various usages as per requirement. The followings are the reasons, by virtue of which the PE films are widely used in greenhouse construction:

- Construction cost of polyethylene covered greenhouse is comparatively less than the glass greenhouses.
- Heating cost is also being less (about 40%) as compared to the single-layer glass or fiberglass-reinforced plastic greenhouses.
- In PE films there is presence of UV inhibitor. Because of this property these plastic covers have a good range of service life, i.e., from 4 to 5 years. On the other hand, a simple plastic film may serve only one heating season.

The ultraviolet (UV) stabilized polyethylene sheets are available in widths up to 15.2 m and length to the tune of 30.5, 33.5, 45.7, 61 and 67m. However, few companies also manufacture in the length maximum up to 91.5m. UV-stabilized polyethylene films can transmit about 87% Photosynthetically Active Radiation (PAR) into the greenhouse. In PE films the occurrence of condensation is one of the big demerits. Because of this effect the incidence of disease, creation of waterlogging situation and deficiency of oxygen in the soil media may like to take place in greenhouse. In addition, due to condensation effect there is also declination in availability of proper light intensity inside growth hormone (GH) for better crop growth and development. However, at present a lot of advancements have been made in manufacturing PE films, making its perfection to a high level. These are pointed as under:

***PE with anti-fog surfactant*:** These PE films discourage the condensation effects. The anti-fog surfactant is built in the film or panel.

***PE with infrared (IR) blocking chemicals*:** These PE films used for covering the greenhouse, are very effective to check the radiant heat loss from the greenhouse. The range of heat loss control by these PE films is mentioned as under:

- About 50% radiant heats.
- As much as 25% of the total heat during cold and clear nights.
- About 15% heat on cloudy nights.

***IR absorbing polyethylene*:** It reduces the radiant heat loss and transmits about 82% PAR in the greenhouse.

Polyvinyl chloride film (PVC films): These are the UV light resistant films are found in the thickness of 0.2 to 0.3 mm. Service life of these films varies to the tune of 4 to 5 years. The cost of 0.3 mm PVC film is about three times greater than 0.15 mm thick polyethylene films. PVC films bear the electrical charge. This property makes this film to attract and hold the dust particles. This effect causes into reduction in light transmittance in dust loaded condition. Therefore, for proper light transmittance the washing of dust particles from these films is very essential.

Anti-dust films: The deposited dusts on covering materials (PE) directly reduce the light transmission to the greenhouse. As per research finding about 6% light transmission gets reduce after one year of exposure of plastic film in coastal Spain (Montero et al., 2001). In general, a plastic film attracts the dust particles because of poor electrical conductivity, which in turn to accumulate the static electricity on rubbing of two surfaces against each other or development of friction due to blowing wind. This is one of the important demerits of plastic films to be used for greenhouse construction. In order to remove this effect, i.e., poor electrical conductivity, some of the additives which increase the electrical conductivity, are placed to the interior or on the film surface.

Anti-drip films: The condensation of water vapours on the inner surface of plastic film placed as the greenhouse cover is very common. It develops negative effect on light transmissivity to the greenhouse production zone. Furthermore, due to falling of condensed water droplets onto the crop foliage there is incidence of fungal disease. As per study about 20% loss of PAR at incident radiation angle more than 15° is there because of condensation of water vapours. However, the radiation loss also varies with the drop size of condensed water. Castilla (2005) reported that the large size water drops cause less reduction in radiation loss as compared to the small size water drops, because of difference in contact angles of drops with the plastic film. In order to negate this effect the anti-drip additives, which modify the surface tension of water, are added to PE film to discourage the condensation of water vapors. However, these additives are likely to migrate towards the surface; and are washed out due to rainfall or condensed water.

Near infrared range (NIR) blocking plastic film: This is another plastic film used as covering material for greenhouse construction. NIR is that fraction of solar radiation which is not useful for photosynthesis action. Actually, out of total radiation energy falling on structure about 50% enters the greenhouse, which becomes useful for photosynthesis action is known as Photosynthetically Active Radiation (PAR) and remaining radiation energy is in the range of near infrared range (NIR). The NIR warms the greenhouse and crops both; and also contributes to evaporation.

Nowadays, some of the plastic films have been manufactured with NIR reflecting pigments in varying concentrations. These plastic films are advantageous to enhance the percentage of PAR by reducing the NIR; and accordingly to improve the crop behaviour in term of growth and other attributes.

Tefzel T2 film: These are the Ethylene Tetrafluoroethylene films, also used as the covering material in greenhouse construction. This is the latest development in context to greenhouse covering materials. At beginning this was used for covering the solar collector. It is available in the width of about 1.27m rolls. Because of this reason at every 1.27m clamping is required, which is not good for greenhouse construction points of view. The other characteristics of this film are narrated as under:

- Its service life may vary up to 20-years or so.
- Transmissivity of sunlight or solar energy may be about 95%, which is more than the other covering materials.
- It is more transparent to IR radiation as compared to the other plastics films.
- Heat trapping inside greenhouse during hot weather is comparatively less than the others.
- It requires less energy for cooling inside area of greenhouse.

Fiberglass-reinforced plastic (FRP) rigid panel: This is also used as one of the covering materials in greenhouse construction. The FRP rigid panels are available in flat and corrugated forms and also in variety of colours. The width and length of FRP is to the tune of 1.3 m and 7.3 m, respectively. In greenhouse construction, normally clear FRP panels are used. Light transmissivity of clear FRP panel varies from 88 to 90%, which is widely suitable to the greenhouse crops. On the other hand, light transmissivity is less in coloured FRP panels; normally, suitable to those greenhouse crops which require low light intensity. In many of the cases it is found more advantageous over plastic films regarding greenhouses construction. The advantages offered are listed as under:

- It is more resistant to the breakage likely to cause by hails or vandals.
- Distribution of light intensity is uniform throughout the greenhouse as compared to glass covering.
- Service life of better quality FRP can be up to 20 years. However, some inferior grade's FRP have their life from 5 to 10 years.
- These are flexible in nature. This feature causes easiness in casting of the shapes as per requirement. In addition, it also makes this as one of the most versatile covering materials.
- It can be suitably used for construction of inexpensive greenhouses.
- The cost (per unit area) of FRP greenhouse lies between plastic film greenhouse and glass greenhouse.
- It offers many advantages over glass greenhouse.

However, the incidence of etching and pitting due to dust abrasion and chemical pollution is considered as one of the main disadvantages offered by this material.

Acrylic and polycarbonate rigid-panel: In addition to the FRP panels, the Acrylic and Polycarbonate based Rigid-Panels are also used as the covering materials for greenhouses construction. Features of these two panels are as follows:

***Acrylic panels*:** These have following features,

- Available in two thicknesses, i.e. 16 mm and 18mm.
- These have about 83% PAR transmissivity.
- They have high light transmissivity.
- Service life is also more.
- Acrylic panels are also available with the coatings to prevent vapor condensation at inner surface.
- As demerit, these are highly inflammable.

***Polycarbonate panels*:** Specific features are as given as under:

- These are non-flammable.
- Mostly preferred for construction of commercial greenhouses due to low price
- They have greater resistance to hail damage.
- These panels are available in the thickness of 4, 6, 8, 10 and 16 mm.
- They also have the coatings to prevent vapour condensation.

The comparison of different covering materials used for greenhouse construction is presented in Table 3.8

Table 3.8 Comparison of covering materials used in greenhouse construction

S. No.	Covering material	Service life/durability (year)	Transmissivity (%)		Maintenance requirement
			Heat	Light	
1.	Polyethylene (PE)	1	70	90	Very high
2.	UV polyethylene	2	70	90	High
3.	Fiberglass	7	5	90	Low
4.	Tedlar coated fiberglass	15	5	90	Low
5.	Double strength glass	50	5	90	Low
6.	Polycarbonate	50	5	90	Very low

Insect Proof Screens

In greenhouse the placing of insect proof screens or nets is also required to prevent the invasion of pests. Screens are available in different size meshes. However, the mesh size of screen should be such that the entry of pests could be prevented, effectively. Overall, very fine mesh screens are desirable as the pests such as the whiteflies thrips, etc. are very small in size and they can be prevented, effectively, by using such screens. Although, these screens prevent the harmful effect borne by the insects/pests, but sometimes, they also create the problem regarding reduction in light transmission to the greenhouse. However, the main objective of insect proof screens is to prevent the entry of insects/pests in greenhouse. There are several parameters deciding the suitability of screen, mentioned as under:

(i) Porosity,
(ii) Mesh size,
(iii) Thread dimension (diameter or thickness),
(iv) Texture (woven, knitted, woven/knitted),
(v) Colour,
(vi) Light transmission/reflection, and
(vii) Resistance to airflow.

Porosity of screen defines the ratio of open area to the total area of screen. It expresses the relation of porosity with the mesh of screen. At greater mesh the porosity of screen is less and vice-versa. In general, most of the insect-proof screens either have square or rectangular openings, weaved with monofilament threads. Screens are generally characterized by the term called "mesh", which denotes the number of open spaces per inch length in each direction delineated by the threads. For example a 50-mesh screen denotes that there are 50 spaces per inch length of screen in warp and weft direction both. In greater mesh screen the size of opening is less as compared to the small mesh screen.

The insect-proof screens impose the effect on greenhouse ventilation because of increase in pressure drop on screen openings, which is governed by the screen porosity. The study on effect of screen porosity on ventilation rate and inside/outside temperature advocated that as the porosity gets increase the ventilation rate also gets increase while the inside/outside temperature difference becomes less. The porosity of woven screen, made of mono-filament thread comprising simple texture, can be determined by using the following relationship:

$$\varepsilon = \frac{(l - d)(m - d)}{m.l} \qquad \text{...(3.1)}$$

where,

l = distance between centre of the two adjacent weft threads
m = distance between centre of the two adjacent warp threads
d = thread diameter.

The screen used for preventing the thrips called anti-thrips screen, can reduce the ventilation to the tune of 60 to 70%. On the other hand, the antiphid screen can cause 40% reduction in ventilation rate (PérezParra et al., 2004).

PROBLEM 3.1 Determine the porosity of the insect proof net to be used in greenhouse as protectant. The distance between center of the two adjacent weft threads and wrap threads is 0.5 and 0.75 mm, respectively. Take the diameter of thread as 0.085 mm.

***Solution*:**

Given that,

(i) Distance between center of the two adjacent weft threads is 0.5 mm
(ii) Distance between center of the two adjacent wrap threads is 0.75 mm
(iii) Thread diameter is 0.085 mm

Using the following formula for determining the porosity of insect net,

$$\varepsilon = \frac{(l - d)(m - d)}{m.l}$$

in which l is given as 0.5 mm; m is as 0.75 mm and d as 0.085 mm. Substituting these value in above formula and after solving, we have,

$$\varepsilon = \frac{(0.5 - 0.085)(0.75 - 0.085)}{0.5 \times 0.75}$$

$$= \frac{0.415 \times 0.665}{0.375}$$

$$= 0.74 \text{ or } 75\% \quad \textbf{Ans.}$$

3.14 SELECTION OF COVERING MATERIALS

A greenhouse is considered to be most stable, when its structure is sufficiently strong, covered with a good quality covering material and is properly oriented as per guideline. Besides structural stability, the performance of structure should also be proper, is the basic requirement for construction of greenhouse. The greenhouse performance in respect to crop productivity depends very much on the covering materials used and orientation followed in construction. The covering materials affect the transmission of solar radiation to the greenhouse, on which the crop growth and development depends, mainly. In addition, the covering materials are also causative to develop proper micro-climate suitable to greenhouse crops. On this ground, the selection of covering or cladding material is carried out in such a way that it can meet the requirements in context to creation of micro-climate and transmission of solar radiation or sunlight for proper photosynthesis action in greenhouse. The major parameters counted for selection of greenhouse covering materials are described below:

Solar radiation transmission: The greenhouse offers its impact on crop by solar radiation transmitting behaviour, mainly. Conducting a good level of photosynthesis and thereby better crop growth and yield, is the prime objective of greenhouse. In this regard the covering material plays major role. The covering materials to be used must be capable to transmit a suitable wavelength light, which is usable to the plants grown inside greenhouse. The visible light which wavelength varies from 400 to 700 nanometers is very suitable to photosynthesis action called Photosynthetically Active Radiation (PAR), affects the plant growth. The other non-visible sunlight/radiation such as ultraviolet (UV), infrared (IR) and Far-Red (FR) wavebands are not desirable to the plants for growth point of views. The availability of solar radiation for proper plant growth also depends on latitude of the place concern. Especially, at the latitude greater than 25° from the equator the solar radiation can be the most limiting. Similarly, in the month of December, the availability of solar radiation gets reduce up to 30% than the amount available in the month of June at latitude 40° North, which is mainly because of poor sun angle and small day length. The media existing in the atmosphere acts as filtering source and availability of net amount of solar radiation at the earth system. A part of solar radiation emitted by the sun is filtered, and accordingly the proportion of PAR solar radiation gets change to that of the other radiation bands by filtering the UV radiations, etc. As per solar radiation statistics, above atmosphere about 38.2% solar radiation is being within the range of PAR waveband, which gets increase to the tune of 42.9% on reaching the ground surface, which may likely to get further change depending on the cloud presence, moisture content and pollution level, etc. Table 3.9 illustrates the statistics of solar radiation distribution above the atmosphere and at the earth system.

Table 3.9 Energy distribution of solar radiation above the atmosphere and at the earth's surface

Wave length (band)	Above atmosphere (Duffie and Beckman, 1980)	Earth surface (Thimijan and Heins, 1983)
	Energy distribution (%)	
UV (390–400 nm)	8.6	6.4
PAR (400–700 nm)	38.2	42.9
FR (700–850 nm)	16.5	15.2
IR (850–2800 rim)	33.9	34.2
Thermal (>2800 nm)	2.7	1.3

As for as distribution of solar radiation context to greenhouse is concerned, it depends on the covering materials placed on the greenhouse. The solar energy coming on the greenhouse cover is transmitted to the greenhouse, which is absorbed by the plants for their growth. The available solar radiation which plant utilizes is very limited, i.e. 1 to 5% only. Remaining is emitted as the thermal radiation (heat) effective to cause "greenhouse effect", favourable to greenhouse utilities. The development of greenhouse effect and its extent is very significant for crop cultivation point of view, which is dependent on heat transfer capability of the covering material. This advocates that the selection of covering materials, which could develop a favourable micro-climate for greenhouse crops, is most essential.

Transmittance of covering materials: On striking of direct or beam radiation (generated from the sun) to the greenhouse, there is transmission of direct and diffused solar radiations both at a time in the greenhouse. In which, the diffuse solar radiation is the scattered solar radiation. In many of the plastic films the amount of diffused radiation is more than the direct solar radiation. Transmission rate of solar radiation varies with the properties of covering material, is presented by the term called transmittance. The transmittance (τ) is the physical property of covering material, is defined as the ratio of the measured radiation intensity below and above the covering material in the same wavelength. It expressed by the following expression:

$$\tau = \frac{I}{I_0} \qquad \ldots(3.2)$$

In which, I is the measured radiation intensity below the covering material and to the measured radiation above the covering material. Transmittance is determined in terms of total radiation, i.e., the sum of direct and diffused radiation components, because in greenhouse the cover and structure directly affect the absolute amount. A high value of transmittance of covering material is more desirable. However, it should always be less than 100%. Radiation transmittance is also used as indicator of material's quality. At new and clean condition of covering material the transmittance level is quite high say up to 100%, but it gets decrease with laps of time because of deposition of unwanted materials like dust, carbon, etc. on covering material.

Using radiation transmittance the total energy for hourly, daily, seasonal or yearly basis can be determined. The hourly energy is determined by multiplying the hourly transmittance to the measured radiation above the covering material (I_0). It is given as under:

$$Total\ hourly\ energy = \tau_{hourly} \times I_0 \qquad \ldots(3.3)$$

The daily (for a particular day) energy available in greenhouse can be determined by adding hourly energy values for that particular day. Since, the plant photosynthesis efficiency also affects the total hourly energy available to the plant; therefore, it is also incorporated in the computation. Accordingly, the modified expression for total hourly energy is given as under:

$$Total\ hourly\ energy = \tau_{hourly} \times I_o \times n \qquad \ldots(3.4)$$

In which, n is the photosynthesis efficiency. There are several factors affecting the hourly radiation transmission; few important amongst them are given as under:

- Day of the year and hour of the day.
- Latitude of the place.
- Local weather condition of the place.
- Direct/diffuse solar radiation dominance.
- Radiation wavelength.
- Properties of covering materials at the date of installation and at the date of measurement. The material's properties of cover get deteriorate because of weathering, air pollutants, moisture condensation, and dust and dirt accumulation, etc.

In addition, the following points are also likely to affect the transmission of solar radiation in the greenhouse environment:

- Angle of greenhouse roof,
- Roof shape of greenhouse,
- Number and width of spans. The span width is the distance from gutter to gutter,
- Height of end wall of greenhouse,
- Length to width ratio of greenhouse structure, and
- Greenhouse orientation (compass).

3.15 ENERGY CONSERVATION IN GREENHOUSE

The conservation of energy inside greenhouse is important for crop point of view, especially in aberrant weather or variable weather conditions such as high wind, occurrence of hailstorm, snow fall and excessive heat or cold, as well. In greenhouse energy conservation the covering material plays major role. Because, it allows the energy contents to enter and retain in the greenhouse. Principally, the energy status of greenhouse is based on the amount of input and output energy. If amount of input energy is more than the outgoing energy (loss) the level of energy retained in the greenhouse will be more; and vice-versa. The level of available input energy to the greenhouse depends on the amount of solar radiation transmitted into, while output depends on the consumption made by the crop inside and energy lost from the other sources associated to greenhouse structure. The level of energy conservation in greenhouse can be assessed based on the energy balance approach, is described below.

Energy Balance

The energy balance or energy budget equation is presented by the following relationship:

$$\text{Input-output} = \text{Storage} \qquad ...(3.5)$$

In greenhouse the input energy components are the (i) Incoming solar radiation or energy; and (ii) Supplemental heat, if any; and the output energy is the energy consumed by the crops in their growth processes and loss due to structural faults; and storage energy is the surplus energy over the energy loss. The energy loss from greenhouse body is basically due to convection, radiation and infiltration, mainly through covering materials placed over the greenhouse structure. Applying equation (3.5) the energy balance for greenhouse can be written as under:

$$\text{Solar Energy} + \text{Supplemental Heat} = \text{Energy Losses} \qquad ...(3.6)$$

In which, the energy losses are due to following main agents:

(i) Convection,
(ii) Radiation, and
(iii) Infiltration mechanism.

In addition to the above sources of heat loss from the greenhouse, the condensation of vapour particles on the lower surface of covering material also causes heat loss indirectly from the greenhouse structure. This form of heat loss is termed as condensation heat loss.

Convective loss: It depends on the insulating effect of covering material. The level of insulation effect gets increase when a secondary layer is added to the primary (single) layer of covering material.

Radiation loss: It depends on the physical properties of covering material, which mainly signify the emissivity and transmissivity (infrared and thermal wavebands) of the same. Emissivity is the ability to emit the radiation. At greater emissivity the rate of radiation heat loss is more. Transmissivity is another property of covering material, which denotes the ability to transmit the radiation energy. In case of greenhouse heat loss, the transmissivity for infrared and thermal radiation is more concern to the heat loss. At greater transmissivity for infrared or thermal radiations, the rate of radiation heat loss from greenhouse gets enhance.

Infiltration loss: It is associated to the openings existing in the greenhouse structure including the covering material, besides the outside wind speed and its direction. The doors, heater intake/ exhaust openings, and fan/ventilator, cracks and joints, etc. are the key points to act as the openings for making infiltration heat loss from greenhouse structure.

Condensation loss: This is treated as the indirect heat loss from greenhouse. It is because of condensation of water vapors on the inner surface of covering material. The condensed water absorbs some energy, which becomes unutilized for heating greenhouse environment. In addition, a part of greenhouse energy or heat is also consumed to vaporize the moisture contents existing in the greenhouse, is treated as the part of energy loss. Basically, the change of water vapor to the liquid state results in release of energy is called latent heat. In nutshell, the energy loss in condensation refers to the loss of latent heat of water. However, condensation reduces the radiation heat loss by declining the transmission of infrared radiation.

3.16 INTERACTION AND INTEGRATION OF GLAZING/SUPER STRUCTURE

This is also very important regarding selection of covering materials to suit the super structure of greenhouse. This is mainly in respect to the GH weight to support the structure, spacing between glazing support bars and associated attachments, size and strength of supports, spacing between gutter and ridge, etc. The mismatch between interaction and integration of covering material and the erected super structure can cause the failure of greenhouse. Overall, the following factors are taken into consideration while selecting the covering material for greenhouse construction to grow the crop, successfully.

(i) Light intensity
(ii) Transmissivity of covering material
(iii) Weight of covering material and superstructure
(iv) Purpose of greenhouse construction
(v) Service life
(vi) Resistant to impact
(vii) Durability to outdoor weathering and thermal stability over wide range of temperature variations.
(viii) Transmissivity of visible light out of solar radiation for plant's utilization in photosynthesis action.

(ix) Little absorptivity of UV and converting a part of the same to fluoresce into visible light for plant use.

(x) Covering material should be able to reflect or absorb the infrared (IR) radiation, which is not useful for plants, but heats the greenhouse environment.

(xi) Low cost of materials.

(xii) Appreciable service life. At least in the range of 10 to 20 years.

(xiii) In the areas requiring high temperature such as in temperate regions the covering material should have the capability of greater light transmission and absorption of far IR.

(xiv) In addition, the heat loss due to conduction should also be minimum.

3.17 GREENHOUSE CROPS

Greenhouse is the structure, which involves its own climate, inside, is called micro-climate. The micro-climate may and may not be directly suitable to the grown crops. Greenhouse temperature is always greater than the outside, which is normally in the range of 7 to 10°C, depending on design and construction of greenhouse. This makes the greenhouse as different kinds of structure for crop growing, such as its suitability for off-season crop growing, mainly the summer crops in winter season, etc. In addition, an early seedling raising is also one of the merits of greenhouse. In nutshell, because of its unique features, there are certain crops which response are better to result a good yield and quality produce, are suggested to cultivate in greenhouse. The suitable crops which can be successfully grown in greenhouse are shown in Table 3.10,

Table 3.10 List of suitable greenhouse crops

S. No.	Crop	Name
1.	Fruits	(i) Papaya, (ii) Strawberry,
2.	Vegetables	(i) Tomato, (ii) Cauliflower, (iii) Cabbage, (iv) Capsicum, (v) Bitter gourd, (vi) Chili, (vii) Okra, (viii) Coriander, (ix) Spinach, etc.
3.	Flowers	(i) Carnation, (ii) Chrysanthemum, (iii) Gerbera, (iv) Gladiolus, (v) Marigold, (vi) Orchid, (vii) Rose, etc.

Greenhouse crops—As per temperature variation

As per temperature variation the greenhouse crops are divided in three main groups, narrated as under:

(i) Cold tolerant crops,
(ii) Cold temperate crops, and
(iii) Cold sensitive crops.

Cold-tolerant crops: In this category those crops are included which base temperature is around 4°C or less. These crops are grown at an average daily temperature ranging from 16 to 18°C. Development of these crops is less affected due to reduction in temperature. In addition, quality of these crops also becomes good when they are grown at the temperature ranging from 16 to 18°C, especially when daily light integral (DLI) is low (<10 mol/m^2/d).

Cold-temperate crops: The crops having their base temperature between 4 to 7°C are kept under this category of greenhouse crops. These crops are gown at average daily temperature ranging from 18 to 21°C.

Cold-sensitive crops: Base temperature of this category crops is around 8°C. These crops are grown at average daily temperature ranging from 21 to 24°C.

PRACTICE QUESTIONS

Descriptive Type Questions

1. Write evolution of greenhouse in agriculture.
2. Write importance and objectives of greenhouse.
3. Describe benefits and limitations of greenhouse
4. Describe greenhouse classifications, in detail.
5. Explain greenhouse effects and its working principle.
6. Narrate greenhouse micro-climate and its requirement.
7. Narrate greenhouse orientation and its effects on crops, grown.
8. Enlist the components of greenhouse and describe covering materials.
9. Describe classifications of greenhouse for protected cultivation.
10. Narrate different types of covering materials used in greenhouse construction.
11. Write suitable crops for greenhouse cultivation.
12. Write selection criterion followed for deciding the type of covering material for greenhouse construction.
13. Determine the porosity of the insect proof net to be used in greenhouse as protectant. The distance between center of the two adjacent weft threads and wrap threads is 0.45 and 0.60 mm, respectively. Take the diameter of thread as 0.075mm.

Multiple Choice Type Questions

1. Greenhouse may be the
   (a) Polyhouse (b) Glasshouse
   (c) Net house (d) both (a) and (b)

2. A polyhouse is known as greenhouse because of
   (a) Creation of greenhouse effect
   (b) Micro-climate formation
   (c) Greenish vegetation inside
   (d) Higher ET
3. Greenhouse is
   (a) Fabricated structure at the site
   (b) Framed structure
   (c) Constructed using metallic materials, only
   (d) Naturally ventilated, only
4. Greenhouse is used for growing
   (a) Highly remunerative crops
   (b) Cash crops, only
   (c) Tomato
   (d) Sugarcane
5. Inside temperature of greenhouse is greater than the outside, because of
   (a) Crop growing
   (b) Greenhouse effect
   (c) Growing media
   (d) Cladding material
6. Greenhouse effect causes increase in
   (a) Soil aeration
   (b) Solar radiation
   (c) Temperature
   (d) Relative humidity, only
7. In greenhouse the desired level of CO_2 concentration is
   (a) 100 ppm
   (b) 350 to 1000 ppm
   (c) 200 ppm
   (d) 150 ppm
8. The desired range of solar radiation in greenhouse is
   (a) 100 lux
   (b) 350 lux
   (c) 2000 lux
   (d) 50000 lux
9. The desired range of temperature inside greenhouse is
   (a) 18 to 25°C
   (b) 10°C
   (c) 35°C
   (d) 15°C
10. The desired level of relative humidity inside greenhouse is
    (a) 60 to 80%
    (b) 40 to 60%
    (c) 25 to 35%
    (d) 30 to 50%
11. The range of photosynthetic wavelength to activate the chlorophyll pigments, is
    (a) 400 to 700 nm
    (b) 250 nm
    (c) 200 nm
    (d) 750 nm
12. The wavelength of UV light is
    (a) 140 nm
    (b) Less than 400 nm
    (c) 200 nm
    (d) 750 nm
13. Photosynthetically Active Radiation is also called
    (a) Visible light
    (b) Orange light
    (c) Blue light
    (d) Green light
14. The percentage heat transmissivity of polyethylene (PE) is
    (a) 70
    (b) 65
    (c) 90
    (d) 75

15. Heat transmissivity of fiberglass as covering material is about

(a) 5% (b) 90%

(c) 25% (d) 75%

16. Heat transmissivity of Polycarbonate sheet used as covering material is about

(a) 5% (b) 90%

(c) 25% (d) 75%

17. The light transmissivity of fiberglass as covering material is about

(a) 5% (b) 90%

(c) 25% (d) 75%

18. The light transmissivity of polycarbonate sheet used as covering material is about

(a) 5% (b) 90%

(c) 25% (d) 75%

19. The percentage solar radiation consumed (of the total) by the plant is about

(a) 1 to 5% (b) 90%

(c) 25% (d) 75%

20. The range of temperature variation of greenhouse is

(a) 1 to 5°C (b) 10 to 15°C

(c) 7 to 10°C (d) 15 to 20°C

Answers

1. d	**2.** a	**3.** b	**4.** a	**5.** b	**6.** c	**7.** b	**8.** d	**9.** a	**10.** a
11. a	**12.** b	**13.** a	**14.** a	**15.** a	**16.** a	**17.** b	**18.** b	**19.** a	**20.** c

BIBLIOGRAPHY

Ametek, Inc.(1984). Solar Energy Handbook—Theory and Applications. Chilton Book Company, and coverings. *Foliage Digest* 15(l):1–3, in Florida Foliage 18(l):33–40.

Anonymous (2020). Food and Agriculture data, FAOSTAT, Rome.

Clark, M.M (1965). A two-season polyethylene film for greenhouse glazing. Proceedings of the Commercial Greenhouses. NRAES-3. The Northeast Regional Agricultural Engineering Service, Congress, Montreal, Quebec, Canada, pp. 129 to 134.

Dennis Decoteau (1998). "Plant Physiology: Manipulating Plant Growth with Solar Radiation." Greenhouse Glazing & Solar radiation Transmission Workshop, Centre for Controlled Environment Agriculture, Rutger University, Cook College. pp. 1 to 8.

Gray, H.E. (1992). Greenhouse glazing uncovered. Greenhouse Grower 10(8):5457.

Hickman (2011). A review of current data on international production of vegetable in greenhouse. www.cuestaroblecom. pp. 73.

J.A. and W.A. Beckman (1980). Solar Engineering of Thermal Processes. John Wiley & Sons, N.Y. Maitra, S., Shankar, T., Sairam, M., and Pine, S. (2020). Evaluation of gerbera

(*Gerbera jamesonii L.*) cultivars for growth, yield and flower quality under protected cultivation. *Indian Journal of Natural Sciences*, 10(60): 20271–20276.

Nicolas Castilla (2013). "Greenhouse Technology and Management." Ediciones Mundi-Prensa, Madrid (Spain) and Mexico. pp .77.

Prasad, S. and Kumar, U. (2007). Greenhouse Management for Horticultural Crops. 476 pages, Agrobios, India.

Proceedings of XI International Congress on the use of plastics in agriculture. Oxford & IBH Publishing Co. Pvt. Ltd. New Delhi, India. pp. G.31–G.59.

Radnor, P A. Ready, J. Personal Data. (2011); pages 20; https://gardeningtips.in/polyhouse-plant-nursery-setup-and-management, Accessed on October, 11, 2019.

Takakura, T., (1988). Protected cultivation in Japan. ACTA Horticulturae 230:29-37.

Thimijan, R.W. and R.D. Heins, (1983). Photometric, radiometric and quantum light units of through greenhouse glazings. Energy in Agriculture 6:121–132.

Ting, K.C. and G.A. Giacomelli, (1987a). Availability of solar photosynthetically active radiation. Transactions of the ASAE 30(5):14531457.

Zanon, M., (1990). Synergy between plastics research and protected agriculture. Proceedings of XI transmission in a greenhouse. Transactions of the ASAE 31(5):15401543.

Online sources

1. http://agritech.tnau.ac.in
2. http://home.howstuffworks.com
3. http://www.hgtv.com
4. http://en.wikipedia.org/wiki/Greenhouse

CHAPTER 4

Greenhouse— Design and Construction

Greenhouse is a structure in the form of house covered with cladding material, which is used for crop growing in protected environment. It constitutes a micro-climate inside, which is quite different from outside climate/environment. The formation of micro-climate is the function of inside temperature and relative humidity, which is always in changing mode depending on variations in moisture level and temperature, as well. The temperature variation depends on falling solar radiation on greenhouse roof and type of cladding material used for construction. On the other hand, the humidity varies with the level of moisture content present in the growing media, crop grown, and design and construction of greenhouse, mainly. The micro-climate plays key role on crop development and its productivity, as well. Besides, creating impact on micro-climate, the design and construction of greenhouse also causes its effects on longevity of the structure, too. Therefore, in greenhouse technology for its application to protected cultivation, the design and construction of structure considering all possible factors affecting is counted as very important. An improper design makes the structure faulty, which may be causative to result inconducive effect on crop farming. In nutshell, a properly designed and constructed greenhouse ensures following points, essential for better performance towards crop productivity:

- Withstand the load coming on the structure because of cladding materials, structural components, wind load, rainfall and hanging loads, as well.
- Interception of sufficient solar light by the structure, required for the grown crop inside.
- Minimum energy loss from the structure.
- Structural stability against various causative forces, acting.
- Sufficient service life of the structure to repay the invested cost.

4.1 GREENHOUSE DESIGN OBJECTIVES

The basic purpose of greenhouse construction is to cultivate most remunerative crops using precision farming technologies in protected environment, to realize better return from the grown crops. This is totally dependent on high yield and better quality produce, which is in real sense ascertained by the greenhouse application, provided it is properly designed and constructed at proper location or at the site. In nutshell, the main objectives of greenhouse design are pointed as under:

(i) To maximize transmittance of sunlight in greenhouse production zone along with adequate support.
(ii) To minimize the heat loss (in some cases) from the structure.
(iii) To allow maximum air exchange inside greenhouse.

4.2 GREENHOUSE DESIGN CRITERIA

Greenhouse is a costly structure for crop production. It involves sufficient money to invest for its construction. Therefore, its design and construction is carried in such a way that it can enable to perform better in sense of crop production or high level of monetary returns to the growers. In addition, the service life should also be long enough with least requirement of care and maintenance, as well. In order to accomplish all these requirements with the greenhouse, there have been devised some of the criterion regarding its design and construction (Castilla, (2013). These are narrated as under:

(i) Availability of maximum sunlight.
(ii) Avoiding shadow effects by reducing the number of elements in greenhouse construction.
(iii) Ensuring a good level of insulation to reduce heat loss from the greenhouse.
(iv) Affordable construction cost to bear by the growers.

In addition to above criterion, the following points are also advised to follow as the design criteria for greenhouse construction:

1. Greenhouse construction should be done in such a way that the cladding material remains unaffected by any cause; or in other words it must remain at its position. It could be achieved through properly fastening, and keeping airtight and wrinkle free. At this condition the wind effect on greenhouse structure is nullified.
2. Greenhouse must withstand against snow load, crop load and hanging type of loads, associated.
3. Those structural elements which are in contact to the covering materials (PE film) should be properly insulated.
4. Greenhouse should be airtight to check the night cooling. It is essential in the regions of low night temperature. In addition, the airtightness of structure also prevents escaping or leakage of CO_2 from greenhouse production zone.
5. Ventilation system should also be equipped with airtight vents.
6. Entry of rainwater should not be there.
7. Internal volume of greenhouse should be large enough to achieve high level thermal inertia and supports for the crop. The internal volume of greenhouse can be enhanced by increasing its height. However, greenhouse height must be in proper range; otherwise, there would be stability problem.
8. Greenhouse must be provided with the provision of rainwater harvesting using gutter system. The harvested rainwater can be used as supplement of irrigation water. As thumb rule, the size of gutter should be about 4 cm more to that of the size of drainpipe. The

size (cross-sectional area) of drain pipe should be about 7 cm^2 for each 10 m^2 area of the roof top. At this specification of drain pipe and gutter, the greenhouse can easily command the rainfall events having their intensity up to 7.5 cm/hour.

9. In order to make the provision of automation system in greenhouse the gutter height should be at least 3.7 m above the floor.
10. The greenhouse roof top should be inclined at an angle more than 26°. This is required to prevent dripping of condensed water on inner surface of roof top cover, over the crop canopies. However, it can also be removed by using anti-dripping PE films as the covering material.

Greenhouse design varies with the climatic conditions of the site specific. Considering this fact in view the design criterion have also been framed for different climatic conditions, are presented below:

4.2.1 Design Criterion—Mediterranean Climates

In general, the Mediterranean climates have following characteristics:

(i) Low temperature at night during winter months.
(ii) High temperature during day hours.
(iii) High humidity level at night, while low during day hours.
(iv) Reduced CO_2 level during day times

These characteristics have direct concern to the design of greenhouse. The design criterion of greenhouse suitable to this type of climatic condition are given as under:

(i) Provision of efficient ventilation is must to alleviate excess heat contents and extreme humidity level and also to prevent CO_2 deficiency in greenhouse production zone.
(ii) Ventilation area should be up to 30% of the floor area of greenhouse.
(iii) There should be the provision of rainwater collection from the rooftop of greenhouse.
(iv) Roof top should have proper inclination to prevent dripping of condensed water over crop canopy.
(v) The covering film must be fixed airtight to reduce thermal loss from the greenhouse.
(vi) There should be the provision of heating system to raise the inside temperature as per crop requirement, during winter months.

4.2.2 Design Criterion—Humid Climates

Humid climate is specified by the following characteristics, which affect the design of greenhouse structure.

(i) High rainfall
(ii) High relative humidity
(iii) High temperature during day and night both, round the year
(iv) Presence of high level of solar radiation; sometimes, it also becomes excessive.

The design criterion for greenhouse construction suitable to above characteristics or in humid climates is presented below:

(i) There should be provision of rainwater collection from greenhouse roof top.
(ii) Proper ventilation is essential, to provide.
(iii) Open area of ventilation should be placed with screen of suitable mesh to check the entry of insect pests.
(iv) Greenhouse height should be in optimum range to withstand against various forces acting over.

4.2.3 Design Criterion—Arid Climates (Desert)

Desert areas have following peculiar characteristics:

(i) Very high temperature as compared to other climatic regions.
(ii) Quite low relative humidity.
(iii) Very high wind velocity, loaded with sand contents.
(iv) Very low water potential.

Design criterions for arid climatic regions are as follows:

(i) Essential to provide high level of ventilation. In other words the ventilation capacity and efficiency both should be very high.
(ii) Provision of humidification system is essential, provided the ET is insufficient.
(iii) Provision of preventing heat loss at night hours. This can be accomplished by selecting proper covering materials and fixing the same, airtight.
(iv) Provision of water collection system to harvest the rainwater from rooftop.
(v) Sufficient structural strength to withstand strong blowing winds.

4.3 GREENHOUSE SITE SELECTION

The site condition for construction of greenhouse involves its prime importance, because after its construction, it has to be used for cultivation of remunerative crops. In general, the followings are some important points to follow, while selecting the site for greenhouse construction:

Solar radiation: At construction site the availability of sufficient sunlight is most essential, as the plants require sunlight for their photosynthesis action. In addition, some of the crops are very sensitive to the sunlight such as tomatoes, cucumbers, peppers, etc.; their yield gets reduce in the condition of poor sunlight availability. On this ground, the site location with high light intensity year-round is being most desirous for greenhouse establishment.

Soil: The pH and electrical conductivity (EC) are taken as the important parameters for defining soil suitability regarding greenhouse construction. The soil pH should be 5.5 to 6.5 and EC from 0.5 to 0.7 Mmhos. In addition, the ground slope should also be such that the land area may get easily drained.

Water: In greenhouse use the requirement of water is mainly for two works, namely (i) Irrigation of grown crop, and (ii) Cooling of production zone. In order to meet the requirement of water for these two need points there must be available sufficient water at the site. In addition, the water quality is also very important issue, because poor quality (chemically) water causes chocking of drippers, besides developing bad effects on crop growth and development. In general, the pH of irrigation water should be between 5.5–7.0 and EC between 0.1–0.3.

High wind areas: The strong wind passing through greenhouse is found inconducive in various aspects. A high wind is likely to "suck" the heat content away from the greenhouse. This is causative to increase the level of heat requirement to maintain the greenhouse temperature suitable to the grown crop. Furthermore, the high winds are damaging to the greenhouse structure, which is completely undesirable. On this ground, the areas having high wind loads should be avoided for selecting the site for greenhouse construction.

Large water bodies: The areas adjacent to the large water bodies are always under moderate temperature. For example the coastal areas tend to have smaller days along with greater night temperature difference as compared to the inland areas. In context to greenhouse construction; such sites are selected after careful studies on these aspects.

Electricity: At construction site the supply of electricity is must; otherwise, greenhouse operation will be hampered and crop productivity will also get reduce, significantly.

Transportation: The site should be connected to the roads for smooth transportation of greenhouse produce to the markets.

Communication: This is also one of the important requirements for selecting greenhouse site. In order to have better returns from greenhouse the communication must be very strong.

Man power: The availability of manpower at low cost at greenhouse site should be very prompt, so that the greenhouse cultivation related activities could be discharged smoothly at proper time schedule.

Obstruction: The site should also be free from the heavy obstructions such as building apartments, natural vegetations, etc. as these are causative to obstruct the sunlight to fall over greenhouse.

High pest incidence: This is also considered as one of the serious issues in context to construction of greenhouse. The insects/pests such as whiteflies, aphids, spider mites and thrips are more concern to infest the greenhouse crops. The agriculture production areas act as harboring point for insects/pests. Greenhouse construction site should be free from such locations.

Future expansion: Sometimes, the expansion of greenhouse is also required for cultivating high valued crops at large scale. In this condition there must be full scope for availability of sufficient land at the site of constructed greenhouse.

Presence of utilities: The utilities such as telephone service, electricity supply (3-phase), fuel supply, etc. are being very important and essential for successful operation of greenhouse. Therefore, before construction of greenhouse the availability of these utilities near to the site must be assured.

4.4 GREENHOUSE ORIENTATION

The availability of sunlight to greenhouse structure varies with its orientation. In greenhouse design and construction, the fixing of its orientation is considered to be very important, because on improper greenhouse orientation the availability of sunlight to meet the requirement of photosynthesis of grown crops gets reduce. In result the growth and development of crop/plant is declined, significantly. This leads to cause reduction in crop production. In order to make available the maximum amount of sunlight to greenhouse, the following modes of orientation are preferred:

1. East–west orientation—In this mode of orientation more sunlight gets available in winter season to free standing greenhouses constructed at the latitude of 40 degree angles. This reveals that the greenhouse should be constructed at east-west direction.
2. North–south orientation—In multi-span greenhouses along with gutter, this orientation is found most effective in context to receive maximum sunlight.
3. As per dominancy of strong blowing winds, the greenhouses should be constructed by keeping its longer axis perpendicular to the direction of blowing wind. This mode of orientation makes the greenhouse safe against heavy wind load.
4. Position of ventilation system also decides the greenhouse orientation. In naturally ventilated greenhouses the ventilation should be opened at leeward side of greenhouse. In other word, the east–west orientation is found fit for naturally ventilated type greenhouses.
5. As per climatic regions the greenhouse orientation varies. It is given as under,
   (a) In cold regions: east–west orientation.
   (b) In warm regions: north–south orientation.

4.5 GREENHOUSE COMPONENTS—STRUCTURAL

Greenhouse is a framed structure, which is erected with many components. The view of frame structure of greenhouse is shown in Figure 4.1. The details about different components are narrated in Table 4.1.

Table 4.1 Greenhouse components and their details

S. No.	Component	Details
1.	Side wall	♦ Its function is to support the trusses and also bear the G.H. (greenhouse) weight.
2.	Curtain wall	♦ It is constructed by using poured concrete, concrete blocks, and bricks or sometimes the lumber, also.
3.	Sill	♦ It is the top of curtain wall.
4.	Eave	♦ It is the top of G.H. sides, where it joins the roof.
5.	Truss	♦ It supports the weight of G.H. roof. ♦ The rafters, struts and chords are its sub-components.
6.	Purlin	♦ It is placed along greenhouse length. ♦ It keeps the roof trusses in proper alignment.
7.	Ridge	♦ This is the point at the top of G.H. where roofs meet together.
8.	Side posts and columns	♦ In G.H. frame structure these are the vertical supports, which constitute height of production area. ♦ Height ranges from 1 to 10 feet.

(Contd.)

S. No.	Component	Details
9.	Sash bar	♦ It is placed perpendicular to purlins. ♦ It holds glazing/covering materials in place. Sometimes, it is also used to catch the condensed water drops inside glass panel of G.H. For this purpose grooves called drip groove is made in sash bar. Location of sash bar is shown in Figure 4.2.

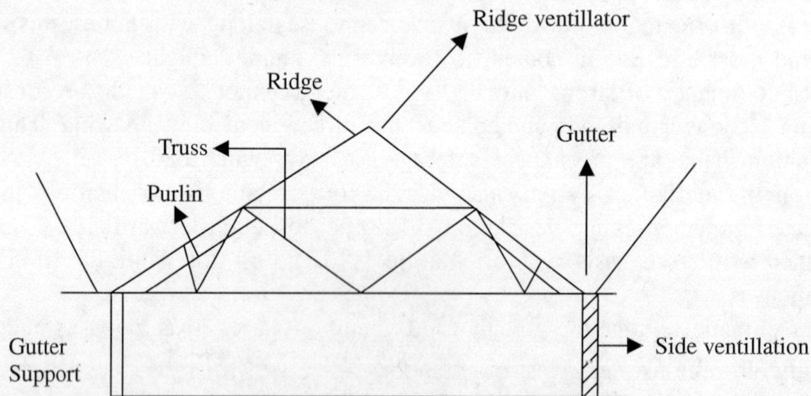

Figure 4.1 Structural components of greenhouse frame

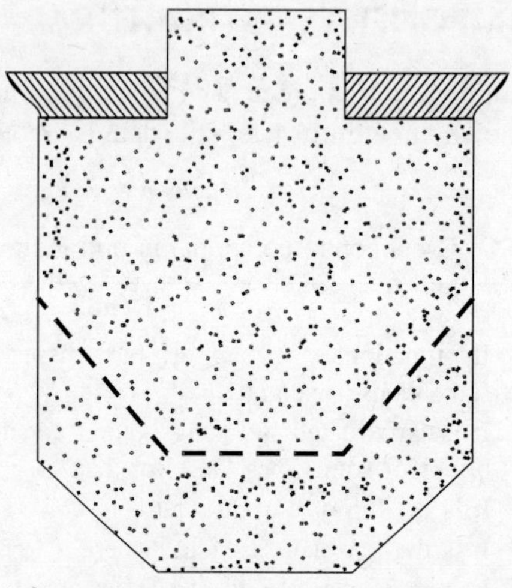

Sash bar used in greenhouse

Figure 4.2 View of sash bars.

4.6 TECHNICAL SPECIFICATIONS OF GREENHOUSE COMPONENTS

There are several design parameters, considered to define their specification in line of proper design and construction of greenhouse. Few important amongst them are mentioned in Table 4.2.

Table 4.2 List of greenhouse design parameters and their specification details

S. No.	Parameters	Technical specification
1.	Area	♦ The minimum greenhouse size (area) for growing commercial flowers for supplying to local or retail markets is 560 sqm (20 m × 28 m).
2.	Design	♦ Design is carried out for (i) Aerodynamic greenhouse structure, (ii) Galvanized tubular structure, and (iii) Naturally ventilated structures.
3.	Gutter height	♦ In greenhouse structures the function of gutter is to receive the rainwater from greenhouse top surface area and drain the same to a safe point. And also to prevent the rainwater dropping, inside. ♦ Minimum height is about 4.0 m from the ground surface. ♦ Its cross-section is in trapezoidal shape. ♦ Its width is about 60 cm, which is all along greenhouse length.
4.	Central height	♦ It is about 6.0 m from the ground surface with top ventilation system.
5.	Foundation	♦ Depth of foundation footing is about 60 cm. ♦ Footing diameter is kept to the tune of 40 cm.
6.	Ventilation system	♦ Three types of ventilations are provided in greenhouse structure; namely: (a) Ridge ventilation, (b) Open top ventilation, and (c) Side ventilations. ♦ Area of ventilation openings should be more than 19% of the area of greenhouse floor. ♦ The air exchange rate should be 50 to 60 times volume of greenhouse per hour.
7.	Frame structure	♦ Structure is designed to withstand the wind load or wind velocity 100 to 110 kmph. ♦ Greenhouse frame is erected by using Galvanized Iron pipe of diameter ranging from 0.5 to 2.0 inch and thickness about 2.0 mm. The GI pipes must be ISI marked (B class). ♦ The trusses, columns, beams (purlin) are constructed by using GI pipe. ♦ Structure parts are assembled by using M10 and M6 size nut bolts and clamps. ♦ Clamps are made of cold galvanized materials.
8.	Covering materials	♦ Greenhouses are constructed by using 3 layer UV stabilized polyethylene films. ♦ Thickness of PE film is 200 micron (800 gauge).
9.	Poly locks	♦ These are the fastening components, used for fixing the PE films on greenhouse frame. ♦ Poly locks are made of aluminum or steel.
10.	Zig-zag springs	♦ These are made of plastic coated steel material. ♦ Size is about 2 mm.
11.	Shade nets	♦ The plastic oven nets with 50% shading factor are used for purpose. ♦ After placing the shade nets on greenhouse structure, they are supported with the help of 2 mm thick GI wire. ♦ Normally, these are placed in foldable form using pulley arrangement.

(*Contd.*)

S. No.	Parameters	Technical specification
12.	Insect nets	♦ These are Rambo nets. ♦ Its specification is 60 Mesh.
13.	Irrigation cum fertigation system	♦ The drip and foggers are used for irrigation purpose in greenhouse. ♦ Fertigation system (venturi) is used for application of fertilizers to the grown crops along with irrigation water, inside greenhouse.

4.7 GREENHOUSE INTERIOR'S LAYOUTS

The interior of greenhouse constitutes crop production zone. A part of inner area is also used for other purposes such as benches for placing pots, movement path, etc. are the main greenhouse interiors. The production zone may be the original soil or sometimes the artificial growing media, too, depending on requirement. The important interior layout is the benches. The provision of benches is mainly for pot based plantations inside greenhouse. On the other hand, the bed plants are grown on the floor of greenhouse. Bedding system (raised bed) is mainly preferred for production of cut flowers.

Benches may be constructed with the help of wooden, metallic or even plastic materials, depending on their availability at low cost in nearby area. The bottom portion of bench is normally kept in mesh form. Inside greenhouse the benches are placed at some convenient height. However, it should be 50 to 100 cm from ground level. Placing of benches is advantageous in many regards such as prompt air circulation, easiness in doing cultural activities, etc.

4.8 LOADS ACTING ON GREENHOUSE STRUCTURE

Greenhouse structure is constructed in open environment, which bears a continuous thrust of several atmospheric variables. In result, the greenhouse is always at risk of its failure or damage due to effects of atmospheric agents. Considering this fact into account the design of greenhouse is performed by considering all the forces or loads likely to act on the structure. Normally, the following forces or loads are found acting on greenhouse structure:

(i) Dead load,
(ii) Live load,
(iii) Snow loads, and
(iv) Wind load.

These are described as under:

Dead loads: This is the total weight of structure. All the provisions comprising ventilation system, heating system, air circulation, irrigation system, lighting arrangements, etc. and the supporting crops such as tomatoes, cucumber, berries, etc. placed in the greenhouse are the part of dead load. On stability point of view, this load plays significant role. In design of greenhouse this is considered as one of important force components acting on greenhouse structure. The distribution of dead load among different components is presented in Table 4.3.

Table 4.3 Distribution of dead load across different components

S. No.	Component	Minimum dead load acting (N/m^2)
1.	Pipe frame and Polyethylene cover	100
2.	Truss frame and Lapped glass	250
3.	Supported crop—Tomatoes, cucumber, berries, etc.	200

Live loads: These are the temporary loads acting on the structure. The weights superimposed by use of hanging baskets, working persons inside greenhouse,shelves, repair materials used etc. are the components, contributing their loads in form of live loads on greenhouse structure. The minimum design live load contributed due to workers and repair materials, considered in design of greenhouse is about 250N/m^2.

Snow loads: In the snow covered regions or the regions having snow fall to the majority of the periods, the design of greenhouse structure is carried out by considering the snow loads as one of the important and major acting loads/forces. In snow covered regions the greenhouses are constructed by maintaining minimum 3.0 m gap or distance between them to allow deposition of snow and also for preventing the side wall against crushing due to sliding of snow from greenhouse roof top. In greenhouse design or construction the minimum snow load is considered to the tune of 750 N/m^2.

Wind load: Blowing wind causes direct thrust on greenhouse structure. Wind involves velocity or the energy thereby, called kinetic energy. The wind KE is converted into force on striking the structure. This impacting force is taken as the wind load acting on the structure. Wind load acts in the direction perpendicular to striking object. It develops lifting effect on greenhouse. In design of greenhouse the contribution of wind load is taken as 500N/m^2. Amongst different forces acting on greenhouse structure, the wind load is severe most. Greenhouse is designed to withstand wind load.

4.9 GREENHOUSE FOUNDATION

Greenhouse foundation must be sufficient to resist the overturning and acting loads/pressures due to structure, etc. In greenhouse construction the pier foundation is required for erecting the frame structure comprising hoops spaced at 1.0 m or more distance. In construction, the area between piers can be closed by providing curtain wall. Normally, 15 cm wall is being sufficient for building span up to 7.5 m; however for wider building span, 20 cm wall is more suitable. Also, if the members of frame structure are to be placed at the spacing lesser than 1.2 m, then either a continuous masonry or concrete wall should be constructed. The footing depth should be at least 60 cm below the ground surface; and sometimes it is kept below the frost level, also. The size of each individual pier footing should be abling to fit the load and soil condition of construction site. In addition, the pier may be constructed by using RCC, galvanized steel materials, concrete masonry or well treated wooden materials, too, depending on the requirement or availability of materials at reachable distance. The view of concrete masonry wall on concrete footing is shown in Figure 4.1. The foundation may be in following types depending on greenhouse structure to be constructed:

(a) Temporary foundation,
(b) Tubing or pipe foundation, and
(c) Concrete piper foundation.

Depending on greenhouse span and pier spacing, the size (diameter) of pier footing for average soil condition (122050 N/m^2) is presented in Table 4.4, can be followed in construction of greenhouse foundation.

Table 4.4 Specification of pier footing for average soil condition

Greenhouse span (cm)	Pier spacing (cm)					
	120	180	240	300	370	460
	Diameter of pier (cm)					
610	15	23	30	30	30	38
730	23	30	30	30	38	38
850	23	30	30	38	38	46
950	23	30	30	38	38	46
1100	23	30	38	38	46	SD
1220	30	30	38	38	46	SD
1400	30	38	38	46	46	SD
1830	30	46	46	46	SD	SD

(*Source*: (https://www.slideshare.net/pramodrai30/planning-and-design-of-greenhouse)

4.10 GREENHOUSE FLOOR

Greenhouse floor is divided into two main parts, namely (i) Production area floor; and (ii) Movement or pathway floor. The floor of production area may be the gravel, pea stone, rock materials, etc. Floor thickness may vary from 15 to 20 cm. Sometimes, a hard and smooth surface is also required. In this condition, with the help of porous concrete materials of uniform grading, 5 to 7.5 cm thick surface is constructed as the greenhouse floor. As precautionary measure, the floor surface must be provided with adequate slope to facilitate surface drainage. In addition, the surface should also be kept uniformly even to prevent puddling effect on greenhouse floor. The pathway or movement floor is constructed for discharging the greenhouse activities, i.e., the crop based activities and others. On an average, about 10% of the crop growing area is allowed as the service area in greenhouse system.

4.11 GREENHOUSE FRAME

Frame is the main component of greenhouse structure. Its mechanical strength ensures a good service life of structure. Mechanical strength of structure depends on the construction materials used, construction carefulness and fitting or fixing of different components, together. In general, the following materials are used for construction of greenhouse frame:

(i) Wood,
(ii) Aluminum,

(iii) Steel, and
(iv) Reinforced concrete.

Sometimes, frame is also constructed by using different materials, in combination.

Wood: It is used for construction of low cost greenhouse. In construction process, the wood based each components of structure are painted in proper thickness or preserved, first. This prevents the component against decay. As precautionary measure, the used chemical for preservation should be toxic free; otherwise, there may be injurious effect on the crop/plant and also to the working person inside greenhouse. However, some of the woods have the property of natural decay resistance, but they are costly enough. In greenhouse frame structure the components such as post beams, rafter system; post sand trusses or laminated arches, and rigid frames, are mainly constructed using wooden materials.

Aluminum and steel: These two materials are used for construction of medium and high cost greenhouses. Service life of constructed frame of these materials is comparatively longer than the wooden frames. The posts, beams, purlins, trusses and arches are constructed using Aluminum and steel materials. The constructed components should be protected against direct contact of soil, as there is possibility of formation of corrosion effect in the components. In addition, the constructed parts using either of the materials should also be painted with white colour paint to improve the level of light reflection in greenhouse. In metallic framed greenhouse the rate of heat loss is higher than the wooden structures. This advocates for using insulation in metallic structures. However, sometimes, the composite materials are also used for the purpose.

4.12 GREENHOUSE SHAPE

Deciding a proper shape of greenhouse is also one of the main design steps. The commonly used greenhouse shapes are mentioned in Table 4.5, below.

Table 4.5 Commonly used greenhouse shapes

S. No.	Greenhouse shape	Remark
1.	Solarium (Attached greenhouse) (i) Lean-to greenhouse	♦ These greenhouses are mainly attached to the existing structure.
2.	Free standing greenhouse (i) Quonset/Hoop shape (ii) Modified Quonset/Hoop shape (iii) Gable even span shape (iv) Gable uneven span shape	♦ These are separated from other buildings. ♦ The Quonset shape GHs are just like arch-shape, placed in row. ♦ The even span GHs are self-supporting with distance from ridge to eave is being equal.
3.	Connected greenhouses (i) Saw tooth shape (ii) Ridge and furrow (gutter connected) shape (iii) Barrel vault	♦ In this, several greenhouses are connected together. ♦ In saw tooth greenhouse the eave of lowest side wall allows natural ventilation. ♦ In ridge and furrow shape GH two or more even-span greenhouses are connected at the eaves.

4.13 GREENHOUSE SIZE

It mainly depends on the availability of land. In addition, the financial status and progressiveness of the grower are also overriding factors in deciding the size of greenhouse. However, as per expert's opinion, initially the greenhouse cultivation should be started by constructing low cost greenhouse, i.e., naturally ventilated type with minimum size of 100 sqm area. This is because of the reason that, it involves less capital investment in construction as compared to big size greenhouse; and also just for an experience about crop farming and net return likely to be realized with that. After full satisfaction, one should move for construction of bigger size greenhouse. The land availability can be ensured on lease basis for a particular period. The interest on use of greenhouse gets develops after realizing the benefits from the grown crops. The area of multi-span greenhouse is more than 200 sqm.

4.14 GREENHOUSE HEIGHT

In design of greenhouse, the height is considered as one of the key parameters. Greenhouse height is the central height, which is measured from ground surface to the top of roof at centre point. On greater height greenhouse the level of wind load is more, and vice-versa. Moreover, the height affects the greenhouse, in following aspects:

(i) Natural ventilation,
(ii) Stability of structure,
(iii) Stability of internal environment, and
(iv) Crop management.

Most commonly, the followed heights in greenhouse construction are given below:

(a) Naturally ventilated type small size greenhouses (area up to 250 sqm): It is 3.5 to 4.5 m.
(b) Big size greenhouses: It varies from 5.5 to 6.5 m.
(c) Greenhouse equipped with fan pad cooling system: The height should be slightly lesser than the naturally ventilated type G.H. However, in any case the height should not be more than 5.5 m.

Gutter height: In greenhouse the main purpose of gutter is to collect the rainwater from rooftop area and convey the same to collecting unit through conveyance pipeline. The discharge carrying capacity of gutter depends on runoff rate (rainwater) produced from greenhouse rooftop. The harvested rainwater can be suitably used for irrigating the crops grown inside greenhouse. As far as its height is concerned, it should be 2.5 to 3 m in small size greenhouse and 4.5 to 5 m in big size greenhouse.

4.15 COVERING MATERIALS

Covering material plays significant role in behaviour of greenhouse regarding formation of micro-climate in production zone of greenhouse. In nutshell, the level of greenhouse effect, and thereby the micro-climate is also governed by the type of cladding material used in construction of greenhouse. Broadly, the following types of cladding materials are commonly used in greenhouse construction:

(i) UV stabilized PE films,
(ii) Glasses, and
(iii) Rigid panels.

UV stabilized PE films: These films are in flexible nature, and are made of Low Density Polyethylene (LDPE), Linear Low Density Polyethylene (LLDPE), Ethylene-Vinyl Acetate (EVA) materials, etc. In natural way, these plastic films are very rapidly deteriorated due to exposure to sunlight. The sunlight contains Ultraviolet rays which are heat generating contents; and when they strike to the PE film, the PE molecules get highly energized. In result, they become susceptible to oxidation. This effect causes deterioration of PE film, which is not desirable to greenhouse structure. In order to avoid this inconducive effect, nowadays, PE films are manufactured in UV stabilized form, tough, clear and high PAR transmission, and they are also being very effective to develop a good level of greenhouse effect inside greenhouse. Normally, 200-micron thick UV stabilized PE films are used for G.H. construction.

In general, the selection of covering materials is carried out on the basis of following features:

(i) Light transmissivity
(ii) Weight per unit size
(iii) Resistant to blowing wind
(iv) Durability against weathering
(v) Thermal stability against temperature fluctuation

Besides above, the following ideal points should also be taken into consideration, while selecting the cladding materials for greenhouse construction:

(a) Purpose of greenhouse.
(b) Service life.
(c) Minimum heat loss through conduction.
(d) The cladding materials must be sufficiently able to transmit visible light of solar radiation to the plants for facilitating proper photosynthesis.
(e) Cladding material should be able to absorb few percentage of UV from sunlight and also to convert a portion of it into visible light for plant's use.
(f) Also, the plastic film must be capable to absorb IR radiation from sunlight. This is because of the reason that the IR radiations are not being useful for plant growth. On the other hand, they cause overheating effect on plants.
(g) The cost of material should also be low.
(h) Service life should be 10 to 20 years.

The service life of different cladding materials is mentioned in Table 4.6.

Table 4.6 Service life of different covering materials used for greenhouse construction

S. No.	Cladding materials	Service life
1.	Glass	20 years
2.	Acrylic sheet	20 years
3.	Polyethylene film	2 to 6 months

(Contd.)

S. No.	Cladding materials	Service life
4.	UV stabilized PE film	2 to 3 years
5.	Polycarbonate sheet	5 to 12 years
6.	Fiberglass	5 to 12 years

(*Source*: https://courseware.cutm.ac.in/wp-content/uploads/2020/06/LEC-6-PCPHT.pdf)

Greenhouse Roof Slope

The slope of GH roof top has its significance regarding transmittance of sunlight inside greenhouse and also yield of rainwater for harvesting point of view. The transmittance of solar radiation depends on the angle at which the solar rays strike the greenhouse surface. At the condition of glazing surface perpendicular to the solar rays the maximum amount of sunlight or solar radiation is transmitted into greenhouse production area. Figure 4.3 illustrates the view of solar radiation transmittance to greenhouse.

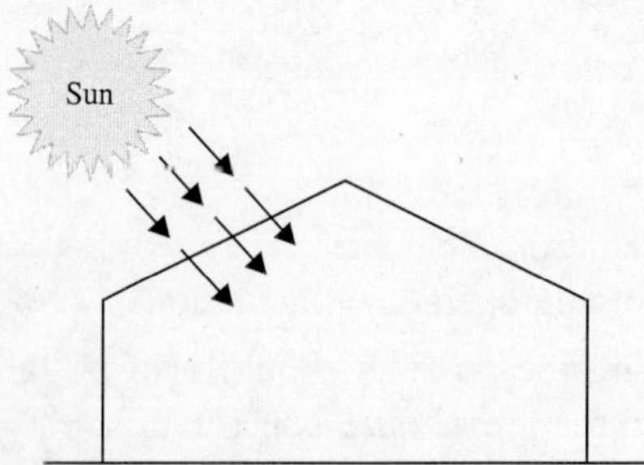

Figure 4.3 View of transmittance of solar radiation to greenhouse

4.16 ELECTRICITY POWER SUPPLY

The availability of assured power supply is one of the main requisites for greenhouse operation towards successful crop cultivation. This is specially required for following purposes:

(i) Operating drip system
(ii) Operating fogging system
(iii) Operating cooling system
(iv) Operating heating system
(v) Lighting arrangement

In order to meet the power requirements for above-mentioned greenhouse based operations, there should be adequate electrical power supply and its distribution system should also be near to the greenhouse site. In this context, the number and capacity (wattage) of electrical appliances such as motor, cooling/heating system, irrigation system, spaying system to be equipped in greenhouse must be known to determine the actual power requirement for greenhouse operation. Moreover, the power requirement varies with the size of greenhouse. As per size of greenhouse, the requirement of electrical power is presented in Table 4.7.

Table 4.7 Electrical power requirement as per size of greenhouse (Chandra, 1992)

Size of greenhouse (m^2)	Amp/Volt	Electrical power requirement
500	60/240	15
500 to 2000	100/240	24
2000 to 3000	150/240	36
3000 to 4000	200/240	48
4000 to 8000	400/240	96
8000 to 12000	600/240	145

4.17 GREENHOUSE IRRIGATION/WATERING SYSTEM

In greenhouse, the watering is required for irrigation of grown crop and climate control, mainly. The total amount of water availability at greenhouse is assessed based on the water requirement under different heads. Drip system is used for irrigating the crop, which should be capable to feed the required amount of water to the crop concerned. In addition, the quality of available water should also be well and must be determined carefully to avoid the possibility of inconducive effects on crop performance and drip system, as well. The silt free water is normally used for irrigating the crops through drip system. The water requirement of few greenhouse crops is given in Table 4.8.

Table 4.8 Maximum daily crop water requirement under greenhouse condition

Crop	Water requirement (lit/m^2)
Bench crops	16.0
Pot plants	20.0
Bedding plants	20.0
Chrysanthemums	41.0
Roses	29.0
Tomatoes	29.0

4.18 GREENHOUSE SAFETY CONSIDERATIONS

Greenhouse structure comprises its frame structure constructed by using metallic and non-metallic materials, as well. The covering material may be the PE films, glass, etc., is other than frame structure. The GH structure as a whole is always susceptible to get damaged because of so many agents, in which the strong blowing winds and hail storms are the main. However, the GH safety point is concerned; it is very important for greenhouse based crop farming system. In general, its safety is required in following broad aspects:

1. Safety against fire
2. Mechanical safety
3. Safety against electricity
4. Safety against chemical's application.

Safety against fire: The materials used for construction of greenhouses are the metallic and non-metallic. In which, metallic materials are mainly employed for construction of frame structure, and non-metallic materials for covering the frame structure, called cladding materials, i.e. the PE films, polycarbonate sheets, glasses, etc. The covering materials are very much prone to get lost due to fire incidence. Therefore, it is essentially required to keep them safe against fire incidence. In this context, it is always suggested, for not using any kind of fire based activities in and around the greenhouse structure. In addition, sometimes, due to electrical short-circuiting, there is also occurrence of fire incidence. In this regard the electrical circuits should always be kept in order.

Mechanical safety: This kind of greenhouse safety requires precaution against the sharp projected parts or edges of the frame structure, which may lead to cut or laceration in the PE cover, resulting in leakage effect in greenhouse. The formation of cut or laceration in structure creates inconducive effect on greenhouse performance to return a good crop yield. Basically, in this condition the maintenance of micro-climate to a favourable range, suitable to the crop concern becomes difficult, as there is gaseous exchange due to leakage. In addition, the G.H. also becomes structurally, unstable.

Safety against electricity: Greenhouse comprises machines/devices for operating the irrigation system, cooling system, heating systems, as well. These systems are operated mostly with the help of electrical power. In addition, the greenhouse environment is always at high level of moisture content. In this condition a loose electrical circuit may cause injurious effect. Or in other words, there is possibility of electricity based fire incidence in greenhouse. Not only this, the greenhouse operation also gets badly hamper. Normally, this problem is very common in highly fluctuating voltage conditions.

Safety against chemicals: Greenhouse constitutes a kind of well managed crop production system along with sustainable micro-climate. In which, the crops are cultivated by applying all the inputs, in precise way at predetermined time and schedule. The application of fertilizers, insecticides/pesticides, weedicides and others is done without any interruption. Especially, the insecticides/pesticides and weedicides pose injurious effect, if they come in contact to the human body. It may cause serious damage. In this context, it is therefore, suggested to apply the chemicals with great care.

4.19 GREENHOUSE SAFETY RULES

There are few important rules for smooth and safe use of greenhouse, which need to follow very carefully by the person, concern:

- Removal of any part from greenhouse should be avoided.
- Application of chemicals should be done with great care, as they are in concentrated form, which may injure.
- After leaving the greenhouse the hand should be washed, properly.
- Inside greenhouse the movement should be done with great care; otherwise, there is possibility of slippage because of wet soil surface, there.
- The setting of any parameter about greenhouse system (automated system) without specific authorization should be avoided.
- Lean on tables should also be avoided as there may be existence of dirt, wet surface, etc.

- During performing any work inside greenhouse the wearing of leather sole shoe should be avoided. In other words, the slippage resistant shoes should be preferred to wear.
- Since, in greenhouse there is electric power supply for operating different systems such as irrigation system, cooling system, heating systems, etc.; therefore, it needs to follow very sincere care about it. Otherwise, there is possibility of electrical shocks to the person concern.

PRACTICE QUESTIONS

Descriptive Type Questions

1. Describe different objectives of greenhouse design.
2. Describe selection of most suitable site for greenhouse construction.
3. Explain greenhouse orientation and its effect on crop performance.
4. Describe various criterion followed in design of greenhouse.
5. Describe design components of greenhouse construction.
6. Explain greenhouse frame structure.
7. Describe various loads acting on greenhouse structure.
8. Narrate cladding materials used for greenhouse construction, regarding its type and characteristics.
9. Describe shapes of greenhouses in common use.
10. Describe safety rules and measures used in greenhouse operation.

Multiple Choice Type Questions

1. The soil pH of greenhouse site should be
   (a) 5.5 to 6.5 (b) 7.0
   (c) 6.0 to 7.5 (d) 8.0
2. The EC of greenhouse soil should be
   (a) 0.5 to 0.7 Mmhos (b) 2.5 to 2.7 Mmhos
   (c) 1.5 to 2.7 Mmhos (d) 3.5 to 4.7 Mmhos
3. Which of the following parameters gets affected for the grown crop in greenhouse media?
   (a) Sunshine hour (b) Light duration
   (c) Solar radiation (d) Both (b) and (c)
4. In mediterrian climate the ventilation percentage of greenhouse should be about
   (a) 10% of the floor area (b) 30% of the floor area
   (c) 25% of the floor area (d) 15% of the floor area
5. Which of the following is interior of greenhouse layout?
   (a) Benches for placing pots (b) Pathway
   (c) Crop zone (d) Both (a) and (b)
6. In greenhouse structure the minimum dead load actin on truss frame and lapped glass is about
   (a) 200 N/m^2 (b) 350 N/m^2
   (c) 250 N/m^2 (d) 150 N/m^2

7. In design of greenhouse the minimum live load is taken as
(a) 200 N/m^2 (b) 250 N/m^2
(c) 350 N/m^2 (d) 150 N/m^2

8. In design of greenhouse the minimum snow load is taken as
(a) 750 N/m^2 (b) 250 N/m^2
(c) 350 N/m^2 (d) 150 N/m^2

9. In design of greenhouse the contribution of wind load is taken as
(a) 750 N/m^2 (b) 250 N/m^2
(c) 350 N/m^2 (d) 500 N/m^2

10. The floor thickness of greenhouse may be from
(a) 15 to 20 cm (b) 20 to 25 cm
(c) 5 to 10 cm (d) 25 to 30 cm

11. The area of multi-span greenhouse should be more than 200 sqm
(a) 200 sqm (b) 500 sqm
(c) 250 sqm (d) 300 sqm

12. The central height of naturally ventilated type small greenhouses (area up to 250 sqm) is
(a) 1.5 to 2.5 m (b) 3.5 to 4.5 m
(c) 2.5 to 5.5 m (d) 4.5 to 5.5 m

13. The central height of big size greenhouses is
(a) 5.5 to 6.5 m (b) 3.5 to 4.5 m
(c) 2.5 to 5.5 m (d) 4.5 to 5.5 m

14. The gutter height in small greenhouse varies from
(a) 5.5 to 6.5 m (b) 2.5 to 3.0 m
(c) 2.5 to 5.5 m (d) 4.5 to 5.5 m

15. The gutter height in large size greenhouse varies from
(a) 5.5 to 6.5 m (b) 2.5 to 3.0 m
(c) 2.5 to 5.5 m (d) 4.5 to 5.0 m

16. Thickness of UV stabilized PE film used for greenhouse covering is
(a) 200 micron (b) 150 micron
(c) 250 micron (d) 250 to 300 micron

17. The service life of UV stabilized PE film is
(a) 2 to 3 years (b) 1 to 1.5 years
(c) 6 to 12 months (d) 3 to 6 years

18. In greenhouse frame structure the sash bar is placed perpendicular to
(a) Gutter (b) Purlins
(c) Exhaust fan (d) Ridge

19. In greenhouse the function of side ventilation is to create
(a) Cooling effect (b) Gaseous exchange
(c) Heating effect (d) Both (a) and (b)

20. The service life fiberglass as covering material is

(a) 2 to 3 years (b) 1 to 1.5 years
(c) 5 to 12 years (d) 3 to 6 years

Answers

1. a	**2.** a	**3.** d	**4.** b	**5.** d	**6.** c	**7.** b	**8.** a	**9.** d	**10.** a
11. a	**12.** b	**13.** a	**14.** b	**15.** d	**16.** a	**17.** a	**18.** b	**19.** d	**20.** c

BIBLIOGRAPHY

Aldrich, R.A. and Bartok, J.W. (1992). Greenhouse engineering. Northeast Regional Agricultural Engineering Service, Cooperative Extension, Ithaca, NY, USA.

Al-Ibrahim, A., Al-Abbadi, N., and Al-Helal, I. (2006). PV greenhouse system—system description, performance and lesson learned. *Acta Hort.* 719:251–264.

Baeza, E.J., Pérez-Parra, J.J., Lopez, J.C., and Montero, J.I. (2006). CFD study of the natural ventilation performance of a Parral type greenhouse with different numbers of spans and roof vent configurations. *Acta Hort.* 719:333–340.

Bailey, B.J. (2000). Constraints, limitations and achievements in greenhouse natural ventilation. *Acta Hort.* 534:21–30.

Bakker, J.C., de Zwart, H.F., and Campen, J.B. (2006). Greenhouse cooling and heat recovery using fine wire heat exchangers in a closed pot plant greenhouse: design of an energy producing greenhouse. *Acta Hort.* 761:263–270.

Castilla, N. and Hernández, J. (2007). Greenhouse technological packages for high-quality crop production. *Acta Hort.* 761:285–297.

Kacira, M., Sase S., and Okushima, L. (2004). Effects of side vents and span numbers on wind-induced natural ventilation of a gothic multi-span greenhouse. *JARQ-Japan Agric. Res. Quart.* 38:227–233.

Nielsen, O.F. (2002). Natural ventilation of a greenhouse with top screen. *Biosyst. Eng.* 81: 443-452.

Suresh R. (2014). Micro Irrigation—Theory and Practice. Standard Publishers and distributors, Delhi.

Tanny, J., Teitel, M., Barak, M., Esquira, Y., and Amir R. (2008). The effect of height on screenhouse microclimate. *Acta Hort.* 801:107–114.

Zabeltitz, C. (2011). Integrated Greenhouse Systems for Mild Climates. Springer-Verlag, Heidelberg, Germany.

Teitel, M. (2001). The effect of insect-proof screens in roof openings on greenhouse microclimate. *Agric. For. Meteorol.* 110:13–25.

CHAPTER 5

Greenhouse Heating System

Greenhouse is a house like structure made of metallic and non-metallic materials, covered with a special type of covering material such as PE films, glasses, polycarbonate sheets, etc. A greenhouse creates the most favourable environment for better growth and development of crop. Greenhouse effect causes to raise the inside temperature which is advantageous to crop growth and development of crop. However, sometimes due to sudden drop in environmental temperature the greenhouse temperature becomes so low that the crop development gets hamper badly; and thus there is negative effect on crop yield. This type of problem mainly arises in cold regions or when length of cloudy weather prolongs for longer period of time, the planted greenhouse crops are badly hampered to result a good yield. In this condition of aberrant weather or season there is requirement of heating arrangement in greenhouse to raise the inside temperature, suitable to crop growth and development. This chapter presents the details about greenhouse heat loss, heating requirement, heating system/methods and selection on most suitable heating system amongst them.

5.1 GREENHOUSE HEATING

Greenhouse heating or temperature raising is an essential requirement for successful crop production in cold regions, where temperature remains below the desired range for majority of the months during year. In other words, in such regions for modification of micro-climate suitable to attain proper crop growth, the provision of heating system in greenhouse is very important. Greenhouse heating can be done by several means as per convenience or availability in the local market. However, that system is considered to be the most suitable, which is enable to provide a uniform temperature control without releasing any harmful gas or materials to the crop grown, there. In general, the most suitable heating sources to utilize for the purpose are the natural gas, LP gas, fuel oil, wood and electricity, mainly. Nowadays, a variety of heating systems have been devised for use, but their selection is more important. That system is rated as the most suitable which is highly efficient and capable to distribute the heat, uniformly throughout greenhouse production zone. Capacity of heating system depends on the heating requirement, which is based on heat loss from the structure. The heat loss from greenhouse structure, normally takes place by following three main processes:

(i) Conduction,
(ii) Convection, and
(iii) Radiation.

Conduction: In conduction process the transfer of heat is carried out through direct physical contact of the object or between the objects. The area of contact, length of travel, temperature difference and physical properties such as density, etc. affect the heat conduction rate. The rate of heat conduction from the object can be significantly reduced by using a poor heat conducting material. It can also be done by putting insulator in the heat flow path. The wood is very poor heat conductor.

Convection: In convection process the loss of heat takes place by moving the heat contents from warm zone to cold zone. In greenhouse, it mainly takes place through ventilation and infiltration action. The points of fans and air leakage are the prominent places for this mode of heat loss from greenhouse structure. It occurs along with air and vapour movement from greenhouse. The evaporation of water content consumes energy, i.e., there is energy loss while condensation releases the energy in greenhouse.

Radiation: In radiation process the heat transfer or loss takes place without contact of the objects, but through the air as the transferring media. The transfer of light energy in terms of solar radiation is an example. Radiation takes place in straight line mode. The radiant energy/heat gets reflected, transmitted and absorbed by the object on which it strikes. The absorbed radiant energy is converted into heat content in the object, which also releases energy in all the directions called radiant energy. The transfer of radiant heat/energy depends on the surface area of the object, temperature and characteristics as well. Transfer of radiant energy can be checked by putting a highly reflective opaque body in flow path. The opaque body causes high level of reflection of radiant energy back to the source.

5.2 GREENHOUSE HEAT LOSS AND ITS COMPUTATION

The loss of heat from greenhouse structure takes place through the processes of conduction, convection and radiation in presence of crop in production zone. In addition, there is also the occurrence of continuous heat exchange, causes heat loss from the greenhouse. Broadly, the heat loss from greenhouse takes place from following different ways:

(i) Heat loss due to conduction,
(ii) Heat loss from perimeter, and
(iii) Infiltration heat loss.

5.2.1 Heat Loss Due to Conduction

The solar radiation emitted by sunlight when strike the roof top, a part of it gets enter the greenhouse, which is absorbed by the vegetation (crop), soil media, fixtures, etc. existing there. The absorbed radiation generates heat content in them and warm-ups, accordingly. The warmed objects radiate some energy which gets escape outside the greenhouse. In this way, there happens energy or heat loss from greenhouse called radiant heat loss. The loss of radiant heat varies with the type of covering materials used, ambient temperature and amount of cloud cover present in the sky. Among different types of greenhouse covering materials the rigid plastic and glass have less than 4% thermal radiation to pass outside. In other words, these two covering materials generate high range of greenhouse effect in greenhouse structure. The view of greenhouse heat loss is presented in Figure 5.1.

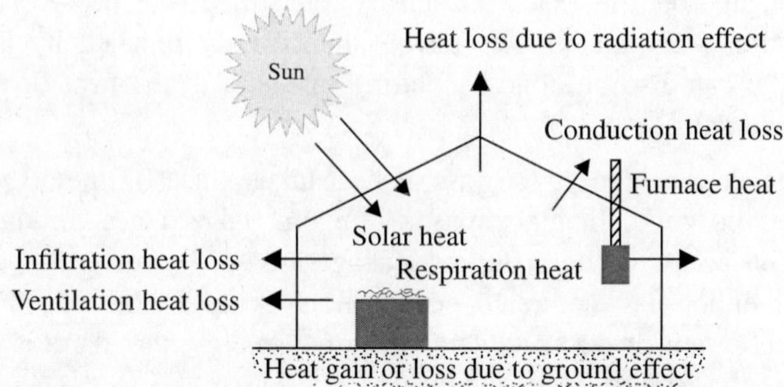

Figure 5.1 Figure showing heat loss from greenhouse structure

The extent of heat loss due to conduction can be computed by using the following relationship:

$$Q = A\left(\frac{T_i - T_o}{R}\right) \quad ...(5.1)$$

In which, Q is the heat loss (BTU per hour); A is the surface area of greenhouse (sq feet); R is the resistance to heat flow depends on the characteristics of material used and $(T_i - T_o)$ is the difference of air temperature between inside and outside greenhouse (°F). The value of R for different materials which are commonly used in construction of greenhouses are presented in Table 5.1, can be used for computing the value of heat loss from greenhouse.

Table 5.1 Values of R (resistance to heat flow) for different materials used in construction of greenhouse

S. No.	Greenhouse materials	Value of R*
1.	Glassfiber board, 1″	4.0
2.	Expanded polystyrene, 1″, cut surfaces	4.0
3.	Expanded polystyrene, 1″, smooth skin surface	5.0
4.	Expanded polystyrene, molded beads, 1″	3.6
5.	Expanded polyurethane, 1″	6.2
6.	Vermiculite, 1″	2.2
7.	Glassfiber blanket, 3–3.5″	11.0
8.	Glassfiber blanket, 5.0–6.5″	19.0
9.	Wall material	
	Concrete block, 8″	2.0
	Concrete block, 8″	14.3

(Contd.)

S. No.	Greenhouse materials	Value of R*
	Concrete, poured, 6″	1.25
	Concrete block or plywood, plus 1″ foamed urethane	7.69
	or plus 1″ polystyrene	5.0
	Greenhouse with thin thermal curtains	1.42–3.33
10.	Roof and wall material	
	Glass, single layer	0.91
	Glass, double layer, ¼″ space	2.00
	Polyethylene or other film, single layer	0.83
	Polyethylene or other film, double layer separated	1.43
	Polyethylene film, double layer, separated, over glass	2.00
	Fiberglass reinforced pane	0.83
	Double acrylic or polycarbonate	2.00
11.	Un-insulated	0.80
	Insulated	0.40

(*Source*: http://ecoursesonline.iasri.res.in/mod/page/view.php?id = 1637)
(* Includes effects of surface coefficients)

A high value of R indicates less heat flow from greenhouse. Similarly, the building materials when they are in wet condition also conduct the heat content.

PROBLEM 5.1 Determine the heat loss due to conduction from the greenhouse of 1500 sq feet surface area. Greenhouse is covered with polyethylene film (single layer). The inside and outside temperature of greenhouse is 98°F and 85°F, respectively. Take the value of R (resistance to heat flow) for Polyethylene film (single layer) as 0.83.

***Solution*:**

Given that,

(i) Surface area of greenhouse is 1500 sq feet
(ii) Inside temperature of greenhouse is 98°F
(iii) Outside temperature of greenhouse is 85°F
(iv) Resistance to heat flow for polyethylene film (single layer) is 0.83.

Using the following formula for determining the heat loss from the greenhouse due to conduction:

$$Q = A\left(\frac{T_i - T_o}{R}\right)$$

In which, A is the surface area of greenhouse is given as 1500 sq feet; T_i is the inside temperature of greenhouse is given as 98°F; T_o is the outside temperature is given as 85°F and R is the resistance to heat flow for polyethylene film (single layer) as 0.83. Substituting these values in above formula and after solving we have:

$$Q = 1500\left(\frac{98-85}{0.83}\right)\text{BTU per hour}$$

$$= 23493.97\ BTU \quad \textbf{Ans.}$$

PROBLEM 5.2 A greenhouse of 2000 sq feet size is constructed by using double layered (separated) polyethylene film. The inside and outside temperature of greenhouse is 37°C and 28°C, respectively. Determine the heat loss due to conduction effect from the greenhouse.

Solution:

Given that,

(i) Surface area of greenhouse is 2000 sq feet
(ii) Inside temperature of greenhouse is 37°C or 90°F
(iii) Outside temperature of greenhouse is 28°C or 78°F

Using the following formula for determining the heat loss from the greenhouse due to conduction,

$$Q = A\left(\frac{T_i - T_o}{R}\right)$$

In this equation, A is the surface area of greenhouse given as 2000 sq feet; T_i is the inside temperature of greenhouse given as 90°F; T_o is the outside temperature given as 78°F. Since, in polyhouse construction the used cladding material is double layered (separated) polyethylene film; therefore, the value of resistance to heat flow through polyethylene film is taken as 1.43 from the Table 5.1. Substituting these values in the formula; and after solving, the value of heat loss due to conductance is determined as under,

$$Q = 2000\left(\frac{90-78}{1.43}\right)\text{BTU per hour}$$

$$= 16783.22\ \text{BTU per hour} \quad \textbf{Ans.}$$

5.2.2 Perimeter Heat Loss

In greenhouse structure the possibility of heat loss is also from the ground, underneath. The following relationship can be used for computing the heat loss called as perimeter heat loss:

$$Q = P.L(T_i - T_o) \qquad \text{...(5.2)}$$

In which, Q is the perimeter heat loss (BTU per hour); P is the perimeter heat loss coefficient (BTU/ft °F hr); L is the distance around perimeter (feet) and ($T_i - T_o$) is the difference of air temperature between inside and outside greenhouse (°F).

PROBLEM 5.3 A greenhouse with 1500 sq feet surface is constructed, which perimeter is 450 feet. Determine its perimeter heat loss, if

(i) Inside temperature of greenhouse is 95°F
(ii) Outside temperature is 81°F
(iii) Greenhouse is constructed by using single layer polyethylene film

Take the value of perimeter heat loss coefficient 0.65BTU/ft °F hr.

***Solution*:**

Given that,

(i) Inside temperature of greenhouse is 95°F

(ii) Outside temperature is 81°F

(iii) Distance around greenhouse perimeter is 450 feet

(iv) Greenhouse is constructed by using single layer polyethylene film

(v) Value of perimeter heat loss coefficient 0.65 BTU/ft °F hr

Using following formula for determining the value perimeter heat loss from the greenhouse:

$$Q = P.L\left(T_i - T_o\right)\text{BTU per hour}$$

In which, Q is the perimeter heat loss (BTU per hour) is to be determined; P is the perimeter heat loss coefficient is given as 0.65 BTU/ft °F hr; L is the distance around greenhouse perimeter is given as 450 feet and $(T_i - T_o)$ is the difference of air temperature between inside and outside greenhouse is given as 14°F.

Substituting the values of respective parameters in formula and after solving, the value of perimeter heat loss is obtained as under:

$$Q = 0.65 \times 450 \times 14 \text{ BTU per hour}$$

$$= 4095 \text{ BTU per hour} \quad \textbf{Ans.}$$

5.2.3 Infiltration Heat Loss

The infiltration of air into greenhouse from outside environment is also one of important factors to cause heat loss. It mainly depends on the greenhouse age, greenhouse condition and type of greenhouse. These factors reveal to have the passage in greenhouse structure for entering the air from outside. For example an old greenhouse or that greenhouse which physical condition is not good, i.e., the cover has been cut from many places or the holes have been formed around the doors, a large amount of cold air from outside gets enter the greenhouse through these points, is main cause of heat loss form greenhouse. The entered cold air from outside gets mixed to the warm air contents of greenhouse, is the reason of heat loss, here. The view of greenhouse heat loss due to infiltration action is presented in Figure 5.2

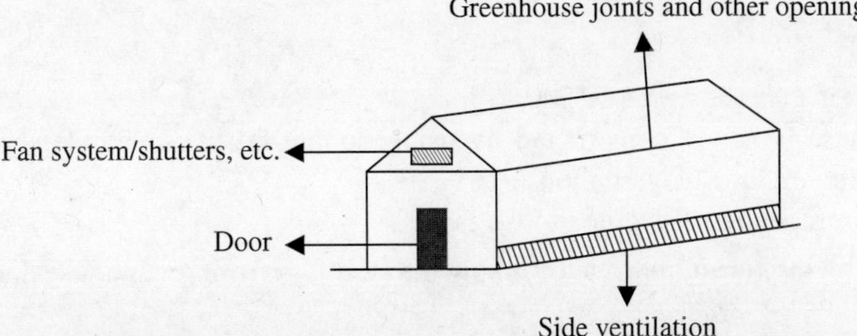

Figure 5.2 Greenhouse heat loss due to infiltration action

In addition, the provisions of ventilation system, inlet/outlet fan shutters, etc. are also very important causative factors to create heat loss because of infiltration action, as these provisions create passage to infiltrate the outside cold air into greenhouse.

Apart from the above the constructional features of greenhouse, construction materials used, ambient temperature and cloud cover in the atmosphere also affect the extent of heat loss from the greenhouse. These factors directly affect the greenhouse effect by varying the level of heat absorption and reflection of the heat back. The rigid plastic film and glass as covering materials exhibit high level of greenhouse effect, because these covering materials allow less than 4% thermal radiation to go outside in open atmosphere. The heat transfer or loss due to air infiltration is given by the following relationship:

$$Q = 0.02V \cdot C(T_i - T_o) \qquad \text{...(5.3)}$$

In which, V is the volume of inside area of greenhouse (cu ft); C is the number of air exchanges per hour and $(T_i - T_o)$ is the difference of air temperature between inside and outside greenhouse (°F). The number of air exchange per hour varies with the type and condition of greenhouse and the amount of wind passing through. The list of air exchange for greenhouse structure is presented in Table 5.2.

Table 5.2 List of natural air exchange for greenhouse

S. No.	Greenhouse construction	Number of air exchange per hour*
1.	New construction using glass/fiberglass	0.75 to 1
2.	New construction using double layer plastic film	0.5 to 1.0
3.	Old construction using glass and is under good maintenance	1 to 2
4.	Old construction using glass under poor condition	2 to 4

(*Source*: http://ecoursesonline.iasri.res.in/mod/page/view.php?id=1637)

* It is for the condition of low wind or greenhouse is protected from the wind

PROBLEM 5.4 Compute the extent of heat transfer or loss from the greenhouse due to infiltration action. Greenhouse is newly constructed by using double layer polyethylene film is under fully protected condition. The volume of greenhouse is about 31500 cft. Inside and outside temperature of greenhouse is 98°F and 80°F, respectively.

***Solution*:**

Given that,

(i) Volume of greenhouse is 31500 cft

(ii) Greenhouse is newly constructed by using double layer polyethylene film

(iii) Inside temperature of greenhouse is 98°F

(iv) Outside temperature of greenhouse is 80°F

Using the following formula for determining the heat loss from greenhouse due to infiltration action,

$$Q = 0.02V \cdot C(T_i - T_o)$$

In which, V is the volume of inside area of greenhouse is given as 31500 cu.ft; C is the number of air exchanges per hour is taken from the Table 5.2 as 0.65 and $(T_i - T_o)$ is the difference of air temperature between inside and outside greenhouse is given as 18°F.

Substituting these values in above formula; and after solving the amount of heat loss due to infiltration action is obtained as:

$$Q = 0.02 \times 31500 \times 0.65 \times 18 \text{ BTU per hour}$$
$$= 7371 \text{ BTU/hour} \quad \textbf{Ans.}$$

5.3 COMPUTATION OF GREENHOUSE HEAT REQUIREMENT

Inside greenhouse there is development of greenhouse effect, i.e., temperature increment, which is greater than the outside open environment. This effect is conducive for growth and development of greenhouse crops. However, there is negative variation in level of greenhouse temperature because of so many causes such as structural defects, vegetation inside, cloud covers, etc. mainly. This signifies the greenhouse heat loss. The declination in greenhouse temperature below the minimum required level affects the crop, significantly. In this situation there is requirement of heating arrangement in greenhouse for raising the inside temperature to the required level, suitable to grown crop. It is general concept that the heat requirement must be equal to the amount of heat loss from the greenhouse. On this ground, the heat requirement is determined as the amount of heat loss from greenhouse structure. The computation of greenhouse heat requirement is done under following steps:

Step (i): Compute the exposed surface area of greenhouse. This covers the entire surface area including side walls, and rooftop.

Step (ii): Compute the exposed surface area of other materials like concrete blocks, poured cement brick surfaces, etc.

Step (iii): Find the values of heat transfer coefficient of different materials used in greenhouse construction. It is shown in Table 5.1.

Step (iv): Determine the difference between highest temperature to be maintained inside greenhouse and the minimum outside night temperature. It is given as under:

T = (*Maximum temperature to be maintained inside greenhouse*
—Minimum outside night temperature)

Step (v): Compute the heat loss due to conduction effect for each of the greenhouse materials used. This is given by the equation (5.1), i.e.

$$Q = A\left(\frac{T_i - T_o}{R}\right)$$

In which, Q is the heat loss due to conduction effect (BT/h); T_i and T_o is the inside and outside temperature of greenhouse, respectively and R is the resistance to heat flow through covering materials.

Step (vi): Determine the volume of greenhouse.

Step (vii): Compute Infiltration heat loss using the equation (5.3), i.e.

$$Q_i = Q = 0.02V \cdot C(T_i - T_o)$$

The value of air exchange for greenhouse is given in Table 5.2.

Step (viii): Compute total greenhouse heat loss. It is the sum of heat loss due to conduction and infiltration action.

The solve example 5.5 illustrates the computation procedure of heat loss from the greenhouse.

PROBLEM 5.5 Compute total heat loss from the greenhouse. The details of greenhouse are given below

(i) Total surface area of greenhouse is 250 sq ft
(ii) Total volume of greenhouse is 45000 cft
(iii) Greenhouse is newly constructed by using double layer polyethylene film
(iv) Inside and outside temperature difference is about 20°F
(v) Take perimeter heat loss coefficient as 0.60
(vi) Total perimeter of greenhouse is 700 feet

***Solution*:**

Total heat loss is the sum of heat loss due to convection, perimeter and infiltration phenomena. The computation of different heat losses is shown as under:

1. Computation of convection heat loss—It is done by using the following formula,

$$Q = A\left(\frac{T_i - T_o}{R}\right)$$

In which, A is the surface area of greenhouse is given as 250 sq feet; $T_i - T_o$ is the inside and outside temperature difference of greenhouse is given as 20°F; and R is the resistance to heat flow for polyethylene film (double layer) as 1.43. Substituting these values in above formula and after solving we have:

$$Q = 250\left(\frac{20}{1.43}\right) \text{BTU per hour}$$

$$= 3496.5 \text{ BTU/hour}$$

2. Computation of perimeter heat loss—It is computed by using the following formula:

$$Q = P \cdot L(T_i - T_o) \text{ BTU per hour}$$

In which, P is the perimeter heat loss coefficient is given as 0.60 BTU/ft °F hr; L is the distance around greenhouse perimeter is given as 700 feet and $(T_i - T_o)$ is the difference of air temperature between inside and outside greenhouse is given as 20°F.

Substituting the values of respective parameters in formula and after solving, the perimeter heat loss is obtained as,

$$Q = 0.60 \times 700 \times 20 \text{ BTU per hour}$$

$$= 8400 \text{ BTU per hour}$$

3. Computation of infiltration heat loss—It is done by using the following formula:

$$Q = 0.02V.C(T_i - T_o)$$

In which, V is the volume of inside area of greenhouse is given as 45000 cu.ft; C is the number of air exchanges per hour is taken from the Table 5.2 as 0.60 and $(T_i - T_o)$ is the difference of air temperature between inside and outside greenhouse is given as 20°F.

Substituting these values in above formula; and after solving the amount of heat loss due to infiltration action is obtained as:

$$Q = 0.02 \times 45000 \times 0.60 \times 20 \text{ BTU per hour}$$
$$= 10800 \text{ BTU/hour}$$

Total heat loss from the greenhouse = (3496.5 + 8400 + 10800)
= 22696.5 BTU/hour **Ans.**

5.4 GREENHOUSE HEATING SYSTEM

The greenhouse heating system is treated as one of the accessories placed in greenhouse to modify its inside micro-climate suitable to crop growth and development. In cold regions where temperature falls far below the crop suitability range, the heating system is one of the most important components for successful crop production. A heating system which enables to create a uniform control on temperature without any harmful effect on the plants is considered to be the most desirable and acceptable system for greenhouse. In heating system the usable energy sources to raise the temperature are in varieties; however, the natural gas, LP gas, fuel oil, wood and electricity are the main and commonly used for the purpose.

In use of these energy sources there are many constraints for the users such as the labour cost, availability in nearby markets, convenience, investment and operating costs, mainly. In which, the labour cost can be controlled and justified to a large extent by the provision of automatic control system. As far as the use of heating system is concerned, depends on the level of heating requirement and the amount of heat loss from GH, mainly. There are varieties of heating systems available in the market, but the selection of most suitable amongst them is one of the most important tasks. The heating systems, those are commonly used for temperature raising of greenhouse production zone are given in Table 5.3.

Table. 5.3 Type of greenhouse heating systems

S. No.	Heating system
1.	Unit space heating system:
	(a) Vented type
	(i) Gravity vented unit heating system
	(ii) Power vented unit heating system
	(iii) Separated combustion unit heating system
	(iv) High efficiency condensing heating system
	(v) Portable unit heating system
	(b) Unvented type

(*Contd.*)

S. No.	Heating system
2.	Hot water system
3.	Steam heating system
4.	Unit radiant heating system
5.	Solar heating system

Unit space heating system: This type of heating system can be equipped at greenhouse floor or installed on the support. The other features of this heating system are narrated as under:

(i) This system can be operated with the help of natural or bottled gas or fuel.
(ii) It assembles fan system to spread the heat content uniformly throughout greenhouse area.
(iii) Its cost is less over other heating systems.
(iv) Its installation is very easy.
(v) It has sufficient scope for future expansion.

Unit space heating systems are of two types, namely (i) Vented type heating system; and (ii) Unvented type heating system. Vented type heating system transfers the heat in the form of combustion gas from outside into greenhouse area with the help of flue pipe. On the other hand, in unvented heating system the burning of gas and thereby exhausting of combustion gas is directly carried out in greenhouse, itself. In this way, total generated heat mass is utilized for heating the air contents inside greenhouse.

Vented type unit space heating devices are further classified in five different types, given as under:

(i) Gravity vented type heating system,
(ii) Power vented type heating system,
(iii) Separated combustion type heating system, and
(iv) High efficiency condensing heaters.

***Gravity vented unit heating system*:** It works on thermal buoyancy principles. In this system the greenhouse air is utilized for combustion of gas. It accounts only 2% (approx.) as efficiency loss. However, some of this type of heating system also uses continuous pilot lights for the purpose. Thermal efficiency of gravity vented type unit space heating system is about 80%. View of this heating system is presented in Figure 5.3.

Figure 5.3 View of gravity vented unit space heating system

***Power vented unit heaters*:** These heaters are equipped with a blower and small exhaust pipe passing through greenhouse wall, acts as vent damper, which is effective to minimize the level of thermal buoyancy loss. The function of blower is to blow the air content in correct amount for combustion and exhausting the flue gasses. The blower is operated at the time of heater firing. These heaters are often placed with an intermittent or electronic pilot to reduce the level of flameouts and pilot gas use. Thermal efficiency of this heating device is about 80%. View of power vented unit heater is illustrated in Figure 5.4.

Figure 5.4 View of power vented unit heating system

***Separated combustion unit heating system*:** This heating system is found suitable for greenhouse, where humidity level is high and environment is dusty or corrosive in nature. Thermal efficiency varies up to 80%. This heating system comprises a power vented exhaust. In addition, there is also separate air intake duct to facilitate air combustion. A tightly constructed greenhouse has low air infiltration, besides very high temperature. This leads to development of oxygen deficiency inside greenhouse, causing poor air combustion. However, this defect can be omitted by supplying the flue gases into greenhouse with the help of flue pipe. Sometimes, because of these activities there is formation of back draft of flue gas in greenhouse, which creates problem, especially in windy areas.

***High efficiency condensing heater*:** This heating system is quite old and is mostly used in residential furnaces for enhancing the level of heat contents. Working principle of this system is based on the concept of making condensation of some moisture contents out of the flue gas to decline the energy level, sufficiently. System consists of power vented exhaust and a separate air intake. In this heating device the hot air of greenhouse is not used for combustion purposes. A drain pipe is provided to dispose the acidic condensate. The yield of hot air per unit fuel consumption is very high. Its thermal efficiency is quite large as compared to the others, which is around 93%. However, system cost is very high.

***Portable unit heating system*:** Portable type unit heating devices are not used for heating to a large area, but often used for temporary and emergency heating purposes. These are operated with the help of kerosene oil or LPG gas. The unvented systems do not have air intake venting. Because of this reason they are not found suitable for closed structures. In emergency or temporary heating purpose these are operated by using only LPG gas fire unit along with the provision of open vent or open door for replacing the oxygen contents burned by heating system. Figure 5.5 illustrates the view of portable type unit heating system.

Hot water system: This heating system comprises pipeline placed around or periphery of the structure or under the benches. In which boiled or hot water is circulated. The heat content from hot water is emitted into the greenhouse area, causing rising of inside temperature. For yielding hot water a suitable capacity boiler is also equipped in the system. Although, heating rate of this system is slow, but uniformity of heat distribution throughout area is more as compared to the others. Also, its installation is simple, and care and maintenance is less. For small areas, it is well suitable to use for increasing environmental temperature.

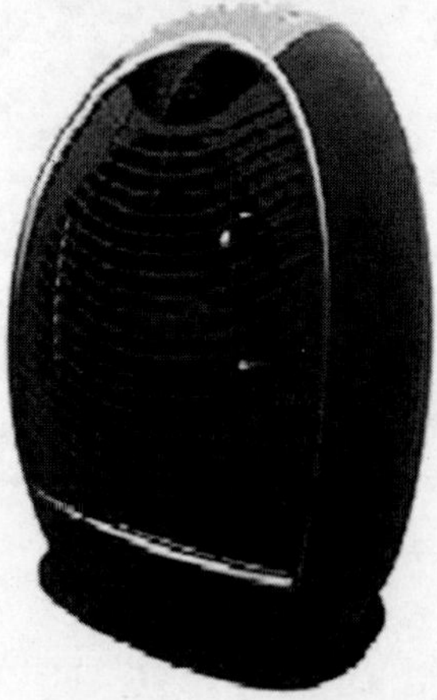

Figure 5.5 View of portable unit heater

Steam heating system: In this system steam is circulated through pipeline (steam line) in the greenhouse area. Heat gets emitted from the steam into the greenhouse; and accordingly, the inside temperature becomes high. For steam formation a boiler of suitable capacity is equipped in greenhouse. The boiler's capacity is decided on the basis of greenhouse size. This system is advantageous over hot water system in regards to fast heating of area and fast cooling of steam lines, as well. The steam lines may be the smooth or finned. In this heating system there is about 30% heat is at overhead and 70% is along the side walls. The steam line may be placed under the benches or overhead with fan forced unit heating elements. Its installation cost is high but service life is quite large. The distribution of steam or hot water can be done in various ways, such as:

(i) Pipe rail heating distribution
(ii) Hoist heating distribution
(iii) Under bench heat distribution
(iv) In floor heat distribution
(v) Overhead heat distribution
(vi) Perimeter heat distribution

Unit radiant heating system: Radiant heaters deliver the heat to the floor level; not to ceiling. This heating system is considered as one of the most efficient and effective systems. It is used to deliver the heat in very diverse conditions such as in warehouses, garages, storerooms, etc.

The hot gases are passed through radiant tubes under vacuum (negative) or power pressure (positive) effects. Radiant energy is dispersed with the help of reflectors, which are placed above radiant tubes. The radiant tubes act as the heat/energy source "sun". Facing of reflectors is towards floor area of greenhouse. The emitted radiant energy is absorbed by the objects of greenhouse, which gets converted into heat contents. The generated heat contents so, are further emitted by the objects in surrounding space. This leads to increase the temperature of surrounding air mass. In heating of air mass of greenhouse, there develops air stratification, i.e., there is temperature difference between floor area and ceiling of greenhouse. This effect results into significant reduction of heat loss, or in other words saving of heats, there. View of radiant energy heating system is shown in Figure 5.6.

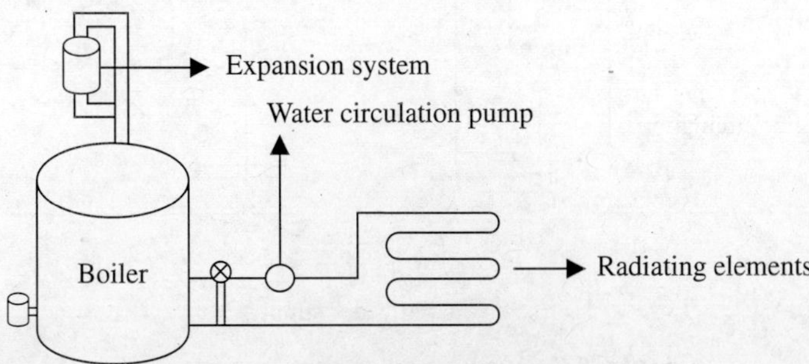

Figure 5.6 View of radiant heating system

Solar heating system: This heating system is used as one of the alternative arrangements for greenhouse heating. However, in use this not so common. Solar heating system comprises following components,

(i) Solar heat collector,
(ii) Heat storage facility,
(iii) Exchanger, etc.

In solar heating system the flat type solar collector is commonly used to collect the solar heat. It consists of a flat black plate, which may be made of rigid plastic film, plastic sheet, metal, or board, also. The flat plate solar collector is found most effective, when it is placed in the position perpendicular to the sun at solar noon. Its function is to absorb the solar energy. If it is located at proper orientation and place 20 to 50% heat requirement can be easily met. On sun side, it is covered with two or more number of transparent glasses or plastic layers, while on backside it is insulated. At back side of collector the copper tubes are mounted, through which water or air is passed. The purpose of cover is to trap the collected heat within the collector. The trapped heat within collector is absorbed by the copper tube placed on back side of plate, which is carried over to the heat storage facility by means of water or air as transporting media. In greenhouse case, it itself acts as solar collector. The collected solar heat inside greenhouse is stored in the soil media, plants, frame structure, floor, etc. Rest amount of solar heat is vented to the outside, which is directed to storage point. The exchanger transfers the solar heat to the greenhouse backup heater, and to supply the same to the greenhouse when solar heating does not suffice. View of solar heating system is shown in Figure 5.7.

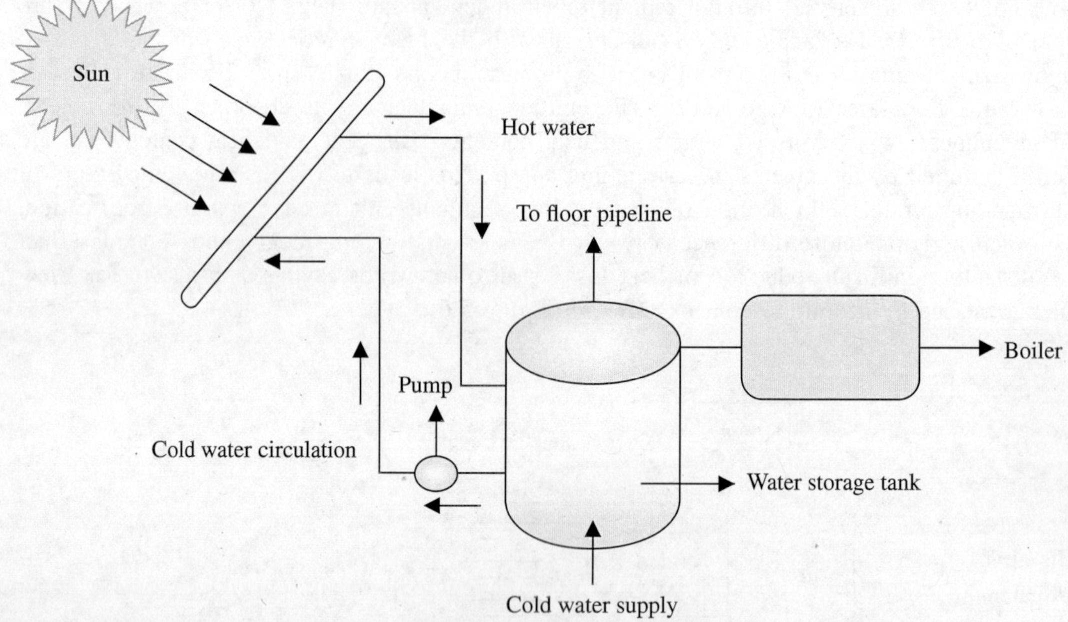

Figure 5.7 View of solar heating system

5.5 SELECTION OF GREENHOUSE HEATING SYSTEM

In context to selection of heating system for placing in the greenhouse, it is very essential to know the amount of heat loss. The heat loss from greenhouse denotes the requirement of heat for successful crop production. The computation of heat requirement should be done by considering the most adverse condition expected to occur in greenhouse production zone. In addition, it is also required to maintain a minimum temperature inside greenhouse by raising the greenhouse heat content. Say for example, if a grower just wants to save the crop from injury due to high temperature or the normal growth of the crop to continue, then he should have the information about minimum temperature on which the crop sustain. This information provides a guideline to the grower for maintaining at least that much temperature inside greenhouse to sustain the crop. Accordingly, additional heat is added to the greenhouse by means of heating system, placed.

The amount of heat required can be determined by multiplying the greenhouse area to the maximum temperature difference required to maintain inside. The determined heat amount is further multiplied by a factor called "Heat Transmission Factor" to assess the heat loss. The heat transfer factor depends on the covering materials, construction quality of the greenhouse and wind velocity, mainly. At high wind velocity the heat loss is more and vice- versa. Tables-5.4 and 5.5 present its values for different conditions.

Table 5.4 Value of heat transmission factor

S. No.	Particular	Heat transfer factor
1.	Covered with a single layer of PE film or rigid plastic	1.0 to 1.2
2.	Covered with a single layer of rigid plastic	1.0 to 1.2
3.	Construction quality is good, no leakage of air contents	1.0
4.	Construction quality is little less, more leakage of air contents	1.2

(*Source*: www.tnau.ac.in)

Table 5.5 Heat transmission factor depending on wind velocity

S. No.	Particular	Heat transfer factor
1.	GH is covered with double layer PE film with air space at least 3/4² but not more than 4²	0.75 to 0
2.	GH is glass glazed	1.1 to 1.4

Note that if GH is located at windy location and involves several leaks in body to infiltrate the air from outside about 10% more is added to the table value of heat transfer factor. On the other hand, if GH is highly protected by means of wind break or some other kinds of barriers, then a lower heat transmission factor of about 1.0 is used for computation. Similarly, if the heating system as central boiler is to be used then at least 25% is added to allow for heat loss for computing the size of boiler.

The selection of suitable heating system is carried on the basis of following important factors:

(i) Efficiency of heating system
(ii) Easiness in installation, operation and control
(iii) Uniformity in heat distribution
(iv) Scopes of further expansion
(v) Scopes for automated control

Heating efficiency is an important parameter for selecting the heating system for greenhouse. Heating efficiency should be matched with the greenhouse requirement. Although, manufacturer mentions the heating efficiency of the machine but it needs verification to make conformity on the same for the users.

The easiness in installation, operation and control is also most important requisites for heating machine, which must be fulfilled. A proper installation makes the machine efficient to discharge the rated efficiency. The operation should also be friendly. There should not be any sophistication in operation. Easy control on system should be friendly for operator.

A heating system is considered to be most desirable which heat distribution uniformity is high. For greenhouse this feature is very important regarding crop growth and development point of view. A heating machine with this feature should be given priority for selection.

In addition, the selection of that heating system should also be kept on priority, which has sufficient scope for future expansion, as per requirement of the site. For this purpose the study on temperature variation at least for 15 to 25 years of the site/area must be done.

This extracts very conducive information about temperature trend of the greenhouse location; and also to derive the decision about selection of suitable heating system for use in greenhouse.

The automation on system control is also one of the important requirements in selection of heating system. The provision of automation is mainly carried out by placing thermostat, which controls the operation of heating system. Normally, thermostats are placed at plant level and kept under protection against direct striking of sunrays. In context to greenhouse use the accuracy of thermostat should be within minimum 2 to 3°F.

5.6 GREENHOUSE HEATING METHODS

Broadly, the heating methods followed for greenhouse temperature control are given as under,

(i) Central heating,
(ii) Hot air heating, and
(iii) Electrical heating.

These are described as under:

5.6.1 Central Heating

In this method the warm water is circulated with the help of pipeline to the locations, where heating is required. It is accomplished by different ways, listed as under:

(i) Floor heating
(ii) Bed heating
(iii) Crop heating
(iv) Air heating
(v) Table heating

Floor heating: In this method, heating of greenhouse is carried out via its floor surface. The pipeline is placed below the greenhouse floor surface, through which warm water is allowed to flow. The PVC make pipeline is preferred for this purpose. The maximum temperature of water is maintained to the tune of 40°C.

Bed heating: In bed heating, the pipes are placed on greenhouse floor, and hot water is allowed to flow through that. In heating process the hot water heats the pipe. This results into emission of heats from hot pipes. The emitted heat gets spread in greenhouse area; and accordingly, there is increase in inside temperature of greenhouse production zone. In pipeline the maximum water temperature is maintained about 40°C.

Crop heating: In this heating method the pipes are laid in hanging position above the crop inside greenhouse. Sometimes, this form of arrangement of heating pipeline is also called lower net arrangement. The steel and aluminum pipes are found better as compared to the PVC pipes. The steel and aluminum pipes can be heated maximum up to 50°C, while in case of water it is maximum up to 40°C. Heated steel pipes emit the heat contents inside greenhouse, which becomes conducive to increase greenhouse temperature.

Air heating: This is also one of the methods, followed for greenhouse heating. In this method, the steel pipes are laid in hanging position over crops with the help of tension rod. The diameter of steel pipe is about 51 mm. Steel pipes are heated to the tune of 90°C, which emit the heat contents, by virtue which the air mass existing within greenhouse gets heated up.

Table heating: In this heating method the tables are fitted with aluminum supports, which are heated up to 70°C temperature with the help of PE tubes. Heated aluminum supports emit the heat contents. This leads to cause heating of the table, from where growing media gets heat for plant growth and development. This method is generally followed in that greenhouse in which growing media rests on the table.

5.6.2 Hot Air Heating

This heating method follows the use of hot air at the place of hot water. In greenhouse the ventilators are utilized for this purpose. Through ventilators the hot air is allowed to enter the greenhouse. Hot air is generated by using hot air heaters or blowers of suitable heating capacity. In this way, the inside environment of greenhouse gets heated or attains desired level of temperature. Normally, this method is selected for the purpose, when installation of central heating system is not being feasible or costly for the site. In addition, this method also involves some of the inconducive issues such as difficulty in adjustment of heat supply rate.

5.6.3 Electric Heating

In this heating method, electrical heating mats are used for the purpose. Electrical mats are fitted with heating elements, which gets heat up on supply of electrical current. This method is advantageous to heat a specific part of greenhouse production area rather entire area. The part, which requires heating, is placed with electrical mat, and by supplying electrical current in mat, the heating is accomplished. This method is also beneficial to better root and shoot growth of the plant.

PRACTICE QUESTIONS

Descriptive Type Questions

1. Heating requirement in greenhouse–why explain it.
2. Describe heat loss from the greenhouse.
3. Narrate computation of heat loss from greenhouse.
4. Explain the computation of heat loss due to conduction process.
5. Describe the method to determine the heating requirement of greenhouse.
6. Enlist greenhouse heating systems; and explain any one of them in detail.
7. Describe unit space heating system used in greenhouse.
8. Explain central heating system of greenhouse.

Multiple Choice Type Questions

1. In greenhouse the heat loss due to convection, mainly takes place through

   (a) Fans (b) Ventilation

   (c) Crops grown (d) Both (a) and (b)

2. The perimeter heat loss from greenhouse depends on
   (a) Inside and outside temperature difference
   (b) Inside relative humidity, only
   (c) Growing media temperature
   (d) Both (a) and (b)
3. Infiltration type heat loss from greenhouse is because of
   (a) Inside and outside temperature difference
   (b) Inside relative humidity, only
   (c) Entry of outside air into the greenhouse
   (d) Solar radiation.
4. In floor heating method the maximum temperature of water is maintained
   (a) 40°C (b) 20°C
   (c) 10°C (d) 15°C
5. In air heating method the steel pipes are heated to the temperature
   (a) 40°C (b) 90°C
   (c) 10°C (d) 15°C
6. In table heating method the aluminum pipes are heated to the temperature
   (a) 40°C (b) 90°C
   (c) 70°C (d) 15°C
7. Thermal efficiency of gravity vented type unit space heating system used in greenhouse, is about
   (a) 80% (b) 55%
   (c) 35% (d) 95%
8. Thermal efficiency of power vented unit heater type heating system used in greenhouse, is about
   (a) 80% (b) 55%
   (c) 65% (d) 95%
9. In bed heating method the maximum water temperature is maintained about
   (a) 10°C (b) 15°C
   (c) 20°C (d) 40°C
10. Thermal efficiency of high efficiency condensing heater used for greenhouse heating, is about
   (a) 80% (b) 55%
   (c) 93% (d) 95%

Answers

1. d **2.** a **3.** c **4.** a **5.** b **6.** c **7.** a **8.** a **9.** d **10.** c

BIBLIOGRAPHY

Buffington, D.E et al. (2013). Heating Greenhouses.

Scott Sanford (2011). Greenhouse Unit Heaters, Types, Placements & Efficiency

John Worley et al. (2011). "Greenhouse Heating, Cooling and ventilation", *Bulletin* 796, The University of Georgia and Ft. Valley State University, the U.S. Department of Agriculture and counties of the state cooperating.

Online source:

www.edis.ifis.ufl.edu/ae015

www.tnau.ac.in : Greenhouses and Post-Harvest Technology

www.radiantheater.net

http://blog.maripositas.org

http://ecoursesonline.iasri.res.in/mod/page/view.php?id=1637

CHAPTER 6

Greenhouse Micro-climate

A greenhouse forms its own climate/environment within, depending on inside weather condition on account of the grown crop, covering material and sunlight/solar radiation falling over the structure. The greenhouse environment is complex and dynamic in nature, affects the crop, significantly. The greenhouse climate is adjusted as per requirement of the crop to achieve proper growth and best yield, good quality produce and high return from the crops, grown. In nutshell, the climate or weather condition inside greenhouse affects the crop productivity and quality both, significantly. The weather parameters such as air temperature, humidity, light intensity, and Carbon dioxide (CO_2) concentration are the main. Besides climatic condition, the crop management practices followed also affects the crop behaviour to a wide range. In order to provide an efficient or improved management to the greenhouse crops, the sensor based monitoring systems have been developed, and are also used for management of greenhouse crops, nowadays.

6.1 FORMATION OF MICRO-CLIMATE

Greenhouse is restricted to a certain range of area, and is covered with a specific type of covering material such as Polyethylene/plastic film. The light or radiation emitted from the sun is transmitted to the greenhouse through covering material, by some percentage. The radiation penetrated into the greenhouse is absorbed by the growing media, crop and the other objects existing within. Simultaneously, there is also emission of radiation/heat from them, but that is not transmitted outside because of wavelength difference. In result, there is enhancement in inside heat/temperature (greenhouse effect). On enhancement in greenhouse temperature there is effect on the parameters such as humidity, moisture content, carbon dioxide, and solar radiation. These parameters in combination constitute a specific climate inside greenhouse. Since, extent of this constituted climate is restricted to a very limited areal extent, which is equal to the interior size of greenhouse; therefore, this is called micro-climate. Durability of micro-climate depends on the ambient temperature, crop grown, greenhouse construction, covering materials used, mainly. The extent and durability of micro-climate play significant role on crop physiology because of effects on photosynthetic action.

6.2 MICRO-CLIMATE PARAMETERS

The following parameters constitute the climate inside greenhouse at micro level, called micro-climate:

1. Solar radiation
2. Temperature
3. Relative humidity .
4. Sunlight
5. Carbon dioxide.

These are described as under:

6.2.1 Solar Radiation

It is one on the most important parameters constituting micro-climate inside greenhouse. The solar radiation is causative to produce dry matters in the plant body. The production of dry matters gets decrease linearly with decrease in solar radiation amount. As per experimental findings, the crop growth gets stop at compensation point, which attains at the light power ranging from 14 to 30 W/m^2. Especially, during winter season at high latitudes the production of dry matter in plants gets hamper in absence of artificial lights. In this regard Nisen et al. (1984) reported that for sufficient plant growth and flowering the minimum amount of daily global radiation should be from 2.0 to 2.3 kWh/m^2 day.

6.2.2 Temperature

The physiological growth such as germination, development and flowering, etc. are directly affected by the temperature. In addition, the transpiration rate and water requirement of crop/plant are also governed by the atmospheric temperature, because of variations in operation of stomatal activities during photosynthesis process. In greenhouse the extent of temperature requirement depends on the types of crops grown, as each and every crop responses differently to their development processes, depending on ambient temperature. Even, though there is effect on plant growth because of difference in day and night temperature and also on the average 24-hour temperature, as well. At low atmospheric temperature the growth rate and production of fruits and seeds are significantly affected.

The greenhouse temperature is the temperature existing inside the greenhouse, also causative to affect the crop yield. A high greenhouse temperature as compared to the outside which is not desirable to the crop needs immediate lowering to avoid mishappening to the grown crops. In general, majority of the greenhouse crops/plants are warm season species. These are adapted to an average temperature ranging from 20 to 30°C with lower and upper temperature limits between 10°C and 35°C, respectively. In the condition of higher temperature above defined limit, there requires cooling system in greenhouse to lower the temperature for the level, suitable to grown crop. On the other hand, when inside temperature is very less which is not suitable for the crops then heating system is required to increase the greenhouse temperature. Normally, when average minimum outside temperature becomes lesser than 10°C then heating system is essentially needed to raise the inside temperature especially during night hours. Further, the temperature range also decides the type of cooling system to be used for lowering the greenhouse temperature. Normally, in the condition of less than 27°C outside temperature the side ventilation (natural cooling) is found suitable to prevent the excessive inside temperature during day hours. Similarly, if average maximum outside temperature exceeds from 27 to 28°C then artificial cooling system is desirous. As per research findings, the maximum temperature greater than 35°C for a long period of time, is found harmful for many of the crops.

Temperature Effects

In greenhouse the temperature poses its effects in different ways on the grown crop. Some of the main amongst them are narrated as under:

- Plant growth and development are significantly affected.
- Seed germination, vegetative and ripening phases are severely affected.
- The seed germination and seedling growth at faster rate is more in warm environment condition.
- Warm temperature favors the photosynthesis.
- Warm temperature favours net growth in younger plants.
- Temperature influences the plant quality.
- The cool temperature produces high quality plants, especially in cold-tolerant crops.
- Warm temperature causes early maturity.
- High temperature reduces energy consumption.
- In addition warm temperature also reduces base period of the crop.

Plant Temperature

In crop production the importance of plant temperature is the same to the air temperature. The plant temperature depends on the air temperature, short wave radiation and transpiration. The atmospheric heat gets transfer from the air to the plant through convection process. The short wave radiation is not absorbed by the plant (leaves) for utilization in photosynthetic action, but that is reflected back to the atmosphere and also transmitted in plant body through leaf. This phenomenon increases the plant temperature. In accordance with the increase in level of solar radiation the plant temperature also gets increase, provided there is no dissipation of heat content through transpiration and convection processes. In presence of high intensity lighting the plant temperature also gets raise above atmospheric temperature.

Day-Night Temperature Differential (DIF): The day-night temperature difference (DIF) plays significant role on growth habit and flowering time of many ornamental plants and greenhouse crops. The day-night temperature difference is defined as the difference between day time and night time temperatures. DIF reduces the requirement of growth retardants. The height of plant can be reduced by reducing the level of daytime temperature or increasing the night-time temperature; or by making both the temperatures close to zero or negative day-night temperature difference. In contrast, the plant height can be increased by enhancing the day time temperature or decreasing the night-time temperature or by making both the temperatures close to zero or positive day-night temperature difference. DIF response varies with the crop species. Its major effects are observed in following attributes of the plants:

(i) Chlorophyll content
(ii) Length of internode
(iii) Lateral branching pattern
(iv) Height of the plant
(v) Orientation of leaf and shoots
(vi) Elongation pattern of petiole and flower stalk

Unfavourable Effects of DIF

The day-night temperature difference (DIF) may be the positive or negative, both, depending on variation in both the temperatures, individually. In case of negative or positive DIF, there is development of inconducive effects in the crop, are counted as unfavorable impact or sometimes, demerits, also. The negative DIF develops side effects in the crop in regards to following contexts:

(a) Reduction in leaf area
(b) Change in leaf orientation, i.e., possibility of horizontal leaf growth
(c) Downward curling of leaves
(d) Shoot orientation
(e) Reduction in chlorophyll content
(f) Reduction in composition of leaf nutrient
(g) Reduction in lateral branching
(h) Carbon partitioning.

Temperature drop (DIP): This is the lowering of temperature in the range of 2.8 to 8.3°C before sunrise for 2 to 3 hours duration in greenhouse environment. Its basic objective is to control the elongation of plant. The temperature drop can be accomplished by operating the exhaust fan equipped in the greenhouse. The operation of exhaust fan is continued for the duration till sufficient lowering of greenhouse temperature. A greater drop in temperature causes significant effect on plant height. However, the best and consistent result is realized when temperature drop is performed before the plant perceives the day start.

Average daily temperature: In greenhouse cultivation system the day temperature (DT) and night temperature (NT) are considered as one of the important parameters to effect on plant growth and development. The day temperature refers to the sunlight temperature, while night temperature denotes the temperature of darkness during night. In determining the effect of temperature on greenhouse crops the average daily temperature (ADT) is mainly taken into consideration. ADT is defined as the mean of the air temperature over 24-hour period as the plants integrates DT and NT over 24-hour period.

Relative humidity: Relative humidity is also taken as one of the important climatic parameters in context to productive crop farming under greenhouse techniques. Its effect is described by counting the parameter called Vapour Pressure Deficit (VPD), which is the difference of air moisture content and the moisture content that the air can hold at saturation stage. At high temperature and low humidity the VPD is high, affects the plant growth by creating high stomatal resistance and water stress, both. In this particular situation the rate of water loss through transpiration gets increase as compared to the rate of water absorption. In contrast, at low VPD the transpiration rate is less and there are physical disorders in plants. This advocates that by maintaining the VPD above some minimum value, the plants can be saved against water stress by ensuring the transpiration rate to an adequate level. As per reported research findings, for proper plant growth the relative humidity ranging from 60 to 90% is found suitable in greenhouse environment. In arid climate or when young plants bear small size leaves the relative humidity below 60% leads to cause water stress in the plant. Similarly, the relative humidity more than 90% especially during night when continued for long period of time causes development of fungal disease. A high relative humidity of greenhouse can be reduced by using heating arrangement.

6.2.3 Sunlight

The sunlight is essential to accomplish following plant growth processes, namely:

(i) Photosynthesis process,
(ii) Photomorphogenesis, and
(iii) Photoperiodism.

The variation in sunlight in any aspect develops direct effect on above-mentioned processes. In presence of sunlight the photosynthesis process converts the carbon dioxide (CO_2) into organic material and also releases the oxygen to the atmosphere. The sunlight acts as the primary energy source for actuating the photosynthesis process.

The photo morphogenesis reveals the process of development of plants under influence of different types of light. On the other hand, the photo periodism is the process that shows how the plant responds to the variations in day lengths and also whether it is seed or flower.

In context to the importance of light for horticultural aspects, mainly three properties of light are taken into considerations; they are namely:

1. Irradiance,
2. Spectral quality, and
3. Light duration.

These properties of light determine the presence of instantaneous and cumulative energy in greenhouse for photosynthesis process.

Light Quality

It denotes the wavelength (colors) of light. Its major importance is for photosynthesis and plant growth processes, as well. The light wavelength (color) is expressed as nanometer (nm). As per wavelength the light is divided in different qualities, given as under:

Visible light: It roughly corresponds to the Photosynthetically Active Radiation (PAR). The PAR is measured by using the quantum sensors along with filters by blocking the light outside the PAR wavebands. The wavelength of visible light varies from about 400 to 700 nm. PAR directly affects the photosynthesis or it drives the photosynthesis. About 50% of the energy coming from the sun falls within photosynthetic wavebands, while remaining 50% energy belongs to the short wavelengths (UV light) or the long wavelengths (infra-red radiation).

Blue light: The blue light is also known as the cool light. The most important wavelength of blue light varies from 430 to 450 nm. This light is very effective to cause vegetative growth, leaf growth, root growth and intense photosynthesis action. In nutshell, the blue lights have significant effects on plant growth.

Red light: In general, the longer wavelength lights are in red colour. The red and blue lights have largest impact on plant growth. The red light in combination of blue light encourages the appearance of flowering in the plants. The wavelength of red light varies from 600 to 700nm. The beneficial effects of red lights are as follows:

(i) Stem growth (diameter)
(ii) Formation of tuber and bulbs
(iii) Flowering
(iv) Fruit production
(v) Chlorophyll production
(vi) Promoting branches.

Far-red light: Its wavelength varies from 700 to 800 nm. This quality light is not photosynthetically active. It influences plant growth.

Green and yellow light: Wavelength of green light varies from 500 to 570 nm, while 570 to 600 nm of yellow light. The green colour light is reflected and results the plant to be in green colour; and it is least effective to plant growth.

Light Intensity

Light intensity is also expressed in the terms of light quantity, denotes the total amount of light received by the plants/objects on the earth system. It is useful in actuating photosynthesis process of the plant or in turn to produce the carbohydrates or increase the growth rate of plant. The light intensity can be different with respect to the time, i.e., the day, season, geographic location, distance from the equator, and weather, a well. During day hours, the intensity of sunlight gradually increases from sunrise to the mid of the day; and thereafter, it decreases slowly leading towards sunset. In addition, on a specific time or day during the year at which the sun-to-earth distance varies, there is also a slight variation in the intensity of sunlight. Generally, the sun to earth distance is very less in the month of January, while it is farthest in the early July.

Light Intensity and Plant Growth

At the light intensity below minimum level, the compensation or metabolic point of plant gets fall down. The compensation or metabolic point is the point at which the photosynthesis and respiration rates become equal to each other. At this particular point the leaves do not gain or lose the dry matter. The light compensation point varies with the type of plant, species and genera, as well. In the plants growing in shades the level of light compensation point is low, while it is high in the plants growing in full light conditions. Especially, in low light intensity condition the stem portion becomes elongated.

Light Requirements

It varies with the age of the plants because of variations in vegetative growth or in the canopy area. For example the light requirement of young plant is less as compared to the old plants only because of canopy variation. In context to the light requirement of plants few important points are narrated as under:

- The germination of seedling takes place at low level light intensity and also in the presence of artificial light.
- Once, the first true leaf gets appear the plant starts responding the sunlight and its intensity, both.
- Further, as the plant grows and the numbers of leaves get increase the plant requires more light.

Light duration: It signifies to the photoperiod, which is the time span during 24-hours, the plant is exposed to the sunlight. For example, an 8-hour photoperiod denotes 8 hours of sunlight received and 16 hours as darkness. The interval between sunrise and sunset is the daylight. The light duration is important in context to the plant growth. Light duration affects or controls the flowering. Besides, it also affects several other growth processes in many of the plants, such as:

(i) Internode length,
(ii) Tuber-rhizome and bulb formation,
(iii) Sex expression,
(iv) Formation of pigments like anthocyanin,
(v) Number of root nodules,
(vi) Size of root nodules,
(vii) Fruit setting,
(viii) Leaf fall, and
(ix) Dormancy.

Photoperiod Effects

Its effect on plant is very significant. On the basis of day length the plants are categorized in different classes such as:

(i) Long day plants,
(ii) Short day plants, and
(iii) Day-neutral plants.

In which, the long-day and short-day plants are associated to those crops which are very sensitive to the length of photoperiod. On the other hand, the day-neutral plants are insensitive to the photoperiod or they do not show Photoperiodism. In case of long-day plants the flowering takes place, only, when day length is longer than the critical number of hours allocated for them. As per research findings, in many of the long-day (LD) crops the long day takes place when length of photoperiod is atleast 14 to 16 hours; or in other words when length of dark period is less than 8 to 10 hours.

Formation of Artificial Short Days (Photoperiod)

This is required when length of natural day becomes long enough for greenhouse crops. In addition, when delay or prevention of flowering in long-day plants is desired, the creation of short-day artificially, is sought. In greenhouse production zone the creation of artificial short-day or photoperiod is accomplished by means of opaque materials, which block the light to penetrate in the greenhouse. Such opaque materials are known as black cloth or blackout cloth. The polyethylene films, knitted polyester and composite fabrics are commonly used for this purpose. In composite fabrics the strips are either aluminized or sometimes in opaque nature. The black cloths are placed over the plants in afternoon at the specific time. This causes reduction in length of natural days. Sometimes, individual benches or whole of the greenhouse is covered with black cloths for the purpose. This kind of arrangement is also found beneficial to cause heat delay during warm weather condition, i.e., when a high temperature (in excess of 29°C) for a long time period tends to cause delay or completely inhibit the initiation of flowering or few crops, too.

Formation of Artificial Long Day

This is required when because of short day there is a bad effect on plant growth or flowering behavior of the plant. The creation of artificial long day is done in different aspects, namely,

(i) Day-extension (DE),
(ii) Night interruption (NI), and
(iii) Cyclic lighting.

Day-extension (DE): In this case the lighting is done at the end of the day. DE is carried out to extend the length of natural day, which depends on the darkness period, a plant requires.

Night-interruption (NI): It is carried out by lighting during middle of the night, which is accomplished by providing a low intensity light. The night interruption is required when natural photoperiod is short. In short photoperiods the flowering gets hamper. In order to promote flowering, the night interruption becomes essential.

Cyclic lighting: It denotes the cyclic or intermittent photoperiodic lighting. This is basically an alternative to the long day lighting. In this form of lighting a series of short alternating light and dark cycle are arranged as the substitute of one continuous break. Cyclic lighting is used in the midnight, especially, where light is "on mode" for 10-minutes duration and 20-minutes in "off mode" in the span of 4-hours. This is based on the principle that the plants in general require at least 2 $\mu mol \cdot m^{-2} \cdot s^{-1}$ PPFD for minimum 5-minute at every 30-minute time span.

Lighting Options

In greenhouse cultivation the lighting options or the type of lighting to follow for controlling the photoperiods are narrated as under:

(i) Incandescent light bulbs
(ii) Compact fluorescent lights
(iii) High-intensity discharge lamps
(iv) Light-emitting diodes

Incandescent light bulbs: These bulbs are energy inefficient and have a broad range of wavelengths. However, these bulbs are low in context to blue light and emit large amount of heat contents. In greenhouse, its uses in terms of lighting options to control photoperiods are as follows:

(i) Providing Day Extension (DE)
(ii) For Night-Interruption (NI)
(iii) For cyclic lighting

Compact fluorescent lights: These are also known as CFL bulb. In greenhouse cultivation CFL bulbs are used for extending day length in some of the photoperiodic sensitive crops. It is often used alone; and sometimes, also in combination with the incandescent or halogen incandescent bulbs in case of specific crops.

High-intensity discharge lamps: The metal halide and high-pressure sodium (HPS) lamps fall in this category of lights, are effectively used in greenhouse. These lamps are mainly used for day length extension (DE) and also for night interruption (NI) lighting purposes.

Light-emitting diode: This is the LED bulb. In greenhouse this lighting system is considered as one of the important sources of light. This light involves following unique features, make it more viable for use:

(i) Long life span
(ii) Good energy efficient
(iii) Able to target specific wavelength of light in context to management of photoperiod for crop concern.

Light-emitting diodes (LEDs) have very wide range of applications including regulation of crop flowering, as well.

Daily Light Integral

The daily light integral (DLI) is defined as the amount of usable light received by the plant inside greenhouse depending on light intensity (instantaneous light) during day (24-hour) period. The usable light denotes the photosynthetically active radiation (PAR). DLI is expressed in the unit of moles of light per square meter per day. In nutshell, DLI is the function of light intensity and duration of light period. This parameter is important for monitoring the photosynthetic light in greenhouse production zone. The recommended range of DLI for different activities is shown in Table 6.1.

Table 6.1 Recommended range of DLI for different activities (Goldammer, 2019).

S. No.	Activities	Recommended DLI (mol/m^2/day)
1.	Seedlings propagation	6 to 8
2.	Young cuttings	6 to 8
3.	Older transplants, flowering annuals and small herbs	10 to 12

In many of the shade-loving indoor and ornamental plants the low value of DLI is also desirable. The day light integral (DLI) causes significant impacts on greenhouse crops such as:

(i) Root and shoot growth
(ii) Stem thickness
(iii) Plant height
(iv) Branching
(v) Flowering percentage or number of flowers
(vi) Flowering timings
(vii) Crop productivity
(viii) Produce quality

The presence of low light creates a number of in-conducive effects in plants. However, among all the slow growth and low production are the most influencing effects. In tomato a low DLI causes fruit quality degradation in context to sugar content, dry weight and flavor, as well.

The DLI can be determined or measured by using the sensors (quantum), Foot candle meter and DLI lamps. The quantum sensor measures the light used for photosynthesis (PAR) in the unit of micromoles (μmol) per square meter (m^{-2}) per second (s^{-1}), which is converted into $mol \cdot m^{-2} \cdot d^{-1}$ or moles/day.

Supplemental Lighting

In greenhouse cultivation the use of photoperiodic and supplemental lightings is mainly to enhance the plant growth cycle and season, as well. However, for extension of daylight hours or increase in DLI to improve or enhance the plant growth, the supplemental lighting is more effective than the photoperiodic lighting. Supplemental lighting is especially given priority when level of ambient daytime light becomes so low that the crop growth behaviour gets drastically change in negative sense. The expectance of low day time light is more common during winter season and in the early morning or late evening; and also during cloudy hours/days.

The application of supplemental lighting is only feasible when sunlight is limiting factor for crop productivity. However, if the status of other variables such as CO_2, water, nutrient, etc. is good, then role of supplemental lighting will not be so high in achieving desired crop productivity. However, before placing the supplemental lighting, the following points should be ascertained in prior:

(i) Average amount of available solar radiation at the place.

(ii) Type of greenhouse structure and covering materials to be used.

(iii) Greenhouse crops to be followed, as per requirement of light intensity, light duration or DLI of the crops.

(iv) Available space to place the light lamps in greenhouse. A poor space in small height greenhouse causes reduction in light availability for taller crops.

(v) Difference in amount of required light for grown crop and the available sunlight. In the condition of greater difference there is need of supplemental lighting.

As precautionary measure, when using supplemental lighting to enhance plant growth, the availability of sufficient CO_2 in greenhouse production zone is most essential, because in enough lighting condition the maintenance of CO_2 level in required range becomes limiting factor. The beneficial impacts of supplemental lighting are pointed as under:

- The length of light hour can be extended to the day light length.
- It compensates the light limiting effects of overcast weather.
- It enhances the level of available light energy.
- It can also increase the available light energy across the full visible spectrum or with specific spectrum range.

Greenhouses Lamp Lights

There are varieties of lamp lights for greenhouse use to enhance the crop productivity by enhancing the length of day light. The most suitable amongst them are listed as under:

(i) Incandescent bulbs
(ii) Halogen incandescent bulbs
(iii) Fluorescent lamps
(iv) T5 Full spectrum lamps
(v) Compact fluorescent lamps
(vi) High-intensity discharge lamps
  (a) Metal halide (MH)
  (b) High pressure sodium (HPS).
(vii) Light-emitting diodes

These are described below:

Incandescent bulbs: These are useful for phytochrome-dependent photoperiod control. For supplemental light these bulbs are not found suitable, because of following reasons:

(i) They produce excessive heat.
(ii) Light quality is very poor for crop growth and development.
(iii) They involve poor efficiency to covert the electricity into usable light, i.e., only 7% electrical power is converted into usable light, and rest is lost as heat to the atmosphere.
(iv) They produce large amount of red and infrared radiations.

Halogen incandescent bulbs: These bulbs are filled with halogen gas, which is mainly the Bromine or compounds of Bromine gas. Halogen incandescent bulbs are highly efficient than the incandescent bulbs. However, these bulbs produce large amount of far-red lights like incandescent bulbs.

Fluorescent bulbs: Light of this bulb gets spread to a large area. In other words, a single bulb is capable to illuminate a large space in uniform way. Also, it is being more efficient than the halogen bulbs. Fluorescent lamps are often used in growth chambers (rooms) and also in small capacity seed germination setups. They can be placed close to the plant foliage.

T5 Full spectrum lamps: These bulbs are in tubular shape. They provide full-spectrum lighting. In T5 the word "T" indicates the tubular shape and "5" refers to its diameter in eights of an inch, i.e., 5/8 inch. T5 full spectrum lamps can be suitably used for all kinds of plants; and are more efficient than the standard fluorescent tubes.

Compact fluorescent lamps: These are the improved version of fluorescent bulbs. In some of the applications these lamps are the replacement of incandescent bulbs. The other salient features of this type of bulbs are as follows:

(i) They provide full-spectrum lighting.
(ii) These are found best for greenhouse applications.
(iii) Light spreading is just like sunlight.
(iv) Its light is effective to the growth of young seedlings.

High-intensity discharge (HID) lamps: HID lamps are found suitable for supplemental lighting purposes in greenhouse farming. These bulbs emit high intensity lights. As compared to incandescent and fluorescent lamps the light intensity and efficiency is high of this type of lamp. In greenhouse these lamps are placed at about 2 feet or little more height above the top of the crop/plant, as they produce sufficient heat contents during lighting. At closer placing the plant canopies are likely to get injured/damage from lamp light heat. High-intensity discharge lamps are broadly in two types, given as under:

(i) Metal halide (MH) lamp, and
(ii) High-pressure sodium (HPS) lamp.

Metal halide (MH) lamp: These are high powered lamps, such as 1000W or more, provide enough red light output. MH lamps are used for following purposes:

(i) Commonly used during vegetative growth of the plants.
(ii) Found effective during flowering and fruiting stages.
(iii) Suitable for full-lifecycle lighting.

High pressure sodium (HPS) lamps: In commercial greenhouses these lamps are commonly used. HPS lamps mainly produce yellow and red end of the light spectrum, which is best fit for use during flowering and fruiting stages. HPS lamps may also be used as the supplement of fluorescent light, metal halide or other light sources having blue light. Using HPS lamps the good-quality plants can be successfully grown inside greenhouse.

Light-emitting diodes (LEDs) lamps: These lamps emit photon colors, which match to the important plant pigments, such as red and far-red absorbing phytochrome and the red and blue peaks of leaf photosynthetic action spectra, as well. LED lights do not produce the heat content in high range, is considered as one of the important features in context to its use in greenhouse cultivation. In addition, its standard operating temperature is also very less which is about 32°C, in comparison to HID lamps (315°C).

Greenhouse Lighting Control

The provision of artificial or supplemental lightings in greenhouse farming system is very conducive to raise the production potential of the grown crops, provided they are properly operated with great care. Therefore, it is always advised to operate the lighting system in precise manner as per requirement without any harmful effect. As for as greenhouse lighting control is concerned, the following points are very important to follow:

(i) The supplemental lighting should be done during day hours, when ambient daytime light level is so low that there is inverse effect on crop production. The possibility of low ambient daytime light level is normally observed in following situations:
   (a) During winter season,
   (b) In the early morning hours,
   (c) In the late evening hour, and
   (d) During cloudy days.

(ii) The best way of controlling lighting operation is either by using timer or by climate control system in greenhouse. However, it must be taken care about the point that there should also be some of the period of darkness. This is because of the reason that few crops do not tolerate continuous lighting. In greenhouse lighting operation through timer system, the following two options are strictly followed:
   (a) Lighting must be done from one hour before the sunset to the midnight or 2 am.
   (b) Lighting from 4 to 5 hours after sunset to 1-hour after sunrise.

Greenhouse Cardinal Temperature

Each and every greenhouse crop requires a cardinal temperature for its proper growth and development. In broad sense, the cardinal temperature for crop concern, is divided in three different ranges, given as under:

(i) Minimum cardinal temperature,
(ii) Optimum cardinal temperature, and
(iii) Maximum cardinal temperature.

Minimum cardinal temperature: It is also known as base temperature, refers to the lowest temperature at which the growing of plant gets stop. Its range varies crop species wise. As per research findings the minimum cardinal temperature for floricultural crops varies to the tune of −1°C to 12°C and for seed petunia it is 4°C. This indicates that at or below 4°C temperature the petunia stops growing.

Optimum cardinal temperature: It is the temperature at which the development of plant/crop is at highest rate. The optimum cardinal temperature of crop depends on season of the year, e.g., for cool season crops it is around 21°C. While for warm season crops, it is to the tune of 32°C. In this way, the optimum cardinal temperature of cool season crops is less as compared to the warm season crops. This is the reason that at lower temperature they tend to undergo heat stress symptoms.

Maximum cardinal temperature: It is the temperature at which the plant growth gets decrease due to reduction in photosynthesis rate. The maximum temperature stress gets develop in the crops, especially, when day and night temperatures exceed a well-defined crop specific temperature.

Measurement of Greenhouse Temperature

The measurement of greenhouse temperature is essential to have the information about existing micro-climate in greenhouse for the existing crop. And accordingly, to follow the measures for maintenance of that (micro-climate) suitable to the grown crop inside greenhouse; otherwise, there is possibility of inconducive effects on the crop. Amongst different climatic parameters the temperature is one of the main to affect the crop growth and maturation time or the cropping time. In greenhouse system the measurement of temperature is mainly done in respect of measuring the temperature of (i) Air; (ii) Growing media; and the (iii) Plants, as well. The methodologies or devices used for measuring the temperatures of above three items are described as under.

Air temperature: The air temperature causes its largest effect on shoot-tip temperature, light, humidity, media temperature and wind, as well. The sensors and thermocouples are two different devices, commonly used for measuring the air temperature. Sensors are properly shielded in an aspirated box or tube to keep the same free from sunlight. Only a constant stream of air is allowed to flow through the sensor. In addition, for an accurate measurement the chamber is also placed away from the heat pipes and walls; and also at some height above from the crop canopy. If temperature is measured at greater height from the crop canopy, the measurement will have few degrees more than the actual temperature to be at crop level. Therefore, the measuring height should neither be more nor less, but at an optimum height.

Thermocouples are also used as very common device for measuring the air temperature. It assembles two different kinds of metals combined together to produce voltage against their temperature difference. Nowadays, several types of thermocouples are available containing different types of metals, wire thicknesses, etc.; accordingly, they all have varying levels of measuring accuracies.

Media temperature: The information on media temperature is essential for determining growth patterns of plant concern. The temperature of growing media or the root zone is measured with the help of thermocouple and temperature probe as the most suitable and common devices. For taking measurements they are inserted into the media for the depth ranging from 1 to 2 inch, depending on container size. However, the measuring device should not touch the bottom of the container; otherwise, there is possibility of introduction of errors in measured temperature. The media temperature should be taken, frequently, to determine average daily temperature.

Plant temperature: The plant temperature acts as an indicator regarding development of the plant, concern. For example the temperature of growing point in plant body, determines the cell division. The plant temperature can be measured with the help of fine wired thermocouples, Infrared (IR) sensors and temperature sensors. For measuring the temperature of shoot tip the fine wired thermocouple is inserted in the stem below the shoot apex towards north side to shield the sunlight. Infrared (IR) sensors are used for measuring the plant canopy temperature. IR sensors are placed close to the plant canopy, i.e., within 3 feet at 45° depending on viewing angle of the sensor placed. As precautionary measure, the sensors should be periodically checked in context to their proper placement, so that the observations could be in accurate range.

Carbon dioxide (CO_2): Its necessity is in photosynthesis process. The concentration CO_2 is expressed in the unit of μmol mol^{-1}. In mild climatic regions during winter season the CO_2 level can drop to less than 200 μmol mol^{-1} At limiting concentration of CO_2 regarding photosynthesis point of view, the productivity of most of the vegetable crops gets significantly decrease. In greenhouse the availability of CO_2 concentration is found in varying range because of the grown crop. Especially, its level drops significantly below the outside level, when a dense crop is grown inside, even greenhouse is fully ventilated. As per De Pascale and Maggio, (2008) for proper growth and crop yield the optimal concentration of CO_2 should be in the range of 700 to 900 μmol mol^{-1}. And it is also suggested to keep the greenhouse CO_2 concentration at least equal to the outside level. In nutshell, to achieve a quality produce the concentration of CO_2 must be to a high level in greenhouse production zone/environment. As reported by Shanchez-Guerrero et al. (2005) about 20% fruit production (dry and fresh matter) can be enhanced by maintaining an increased CO_2 level either continuously or periodically.

6.3 MICRO-CLIMATE CONTROL

A plant requires carbon dioxide for its growth. In plant body the carbohydrate is formed by CO_2 and water. Plants consume CO_2 in photosynthesis process. In greenhouse environment the crop productivity can be significantly increased with proper management of CO_2, which can be done by feeding CO_2 from outside during daylight hours or in presence of artificial lights, if there is restriction to CO_2 entry from outside in the greenhouse. In greenhouse the concentration of CO_2 depends on the plant and day light conditions. At low light intensity the photosynthesis becomes slow; and accordingly the CO_2 uptake also gets drop in plant body. The provision of ventilation system plays a key role to control the CO_2 level in greenhouse production zone. In day light period when plants are exposed to high level of sunlight and photosynthesis is very active, the availability of CO_2 can be optimized with the help of direct control ventilation system.

Declining the extent of heat load or temperature is the major activity towards management of greenhouse climate, in hot climate condition. This can be carried out by reducing the level of incoming solar radiation to the greenhouse, removing excess heat through air exchange process and also by enhancing the percentage of energy sharing in the form of latent heat. The reduction in incoming solar radiation can be achieved by using the shade nets and also by painting the covering materials with lime or white paint. In general, the control of greenhouse micro-climate is carried out in following two ways:

(i) Decreasing the inside temperature, and
(ii) Increasing the inside temperature.

The increase or decrease of greenhouse temperature; or in other words the climate control, depends on the design and geographical location of the greenhouse. The climate control refers to control the associated climatic parameters of greenhouse productive zone, i.e., the soil and air temperature, relative humidity, CO_2 concentration, electrical conductivity (EC) and soil moisture, mainly. Each of these micro-climate parameters are maintained at their optimal level suitable to the grown crop, which varies with the type and stage of the crop.

6.3.1 Climate Control—In Terms of Cooling

In greenhouse by virtue of greenhouse effect the inside temperature or heat is always greater than the outside. On an average the difference of inside and outside temperature varies to the tune of 7 to 10°C depending on the design, construction and type of greenhouse. The increased temperature is beneficial in winter season to grow off-season crops, while in summer season the increased temperature becomes inconducive regarding crop growing points of view. Because in summer season the greenhouse temperature becomes so high, at which the heat tolerance of the crop becomes fail. At this particular situation the application of technologies for lowering the inside temperature of greenhouse is felt very essential for growing the crops, successfully. The methods or techniques used for reducing the greenhouse temperature are narrated as under:

Ventilation based cooling: In greenhouse the provision of side ventilation is mainly for the purpose of development of cooling effect in production zone. However, this is not being suitable for achieving the cooling effect to a greater extent in hot weather condition. Normally, mild cooling can be achieved by ventilation provision. This technique works on the principle of air exchange between inside and outside air content. The cooling effect inside greenhouse gets develop when outside air temperature is lesser than the inside air temperature; otherwise no. This cooling system is effective in reducing the heat load during high incidence of solar radiation to the greenhouse. It can be carried out by allowing the cool air from outside into the greenhouse in homogeneous way and simultaneously removing the hot air from the greenhouse through ventilation system. In greenhouse the following two forms of cooling systems are provided for lowering the inside temperature or controlling the micro-climate:

(i) Natural ventilation system, and
(ii) Forced ventilation system.

***Natural ventilation system*:** It directly affects the greenhouse micro-climate. In design and construction of greenhouses the provision of ventilation is considered as one of the most decisive factors, besides others. A well-designed ventilation system is fully capable to improve the status of micro-climate and also to optimize the energy consumption in crop farming. In natural ventilation system, a pressure difference is created because of wind and temperature gradients across inside and outside environment of greenhouse. The whole effect takes place through the openings existing in the greenhouse structure. Ventilation controls not only to the temperature but also to other parameters such as humidity and CO_2 concentration, which affect the growth and development of the crop both. The cooling efficiency of ventilation system is governed by so many factors like wind speed and its direction, temperature gradient between outside and inside greenhouse, design and presence or absence of crop inside, as well. The cooling efficiency of ventilation system can be accelerated by following ways:

Improving ventilation level: This can be done through roof vents, front doors and placing the fans in greenhouse structure. In greenhouse, the improvement in ventilation becomes essential when outside temperature is very high and also when a high level solar radiation is desired to achieve better plant growth.

Reducing pressure gradient: In greenhouse this is carried out by making the provision of ventilation openings near to the ground surface and also at the roof top. In this condition, the internal hot air is replaced by the outside cool air through ventilation opening provided at the roof, during hot sunny days with the aid of nominal wind. The flow of internal hot air to the upward direction and its removal from the greenhouse roof top opening is because of poor density of hot air. Simultaneously, the external cool air enters the greenhouse from the ventilation openings made at lower side near to the ground surface. In this way, there develops air circulation chain; and greenhouse environment becomes cool by exchanging the internal hot air with the outside cool air. Kittas et al. (2005) have suggested the following relationship to assess the greenhouse energy balance, which is beneficial for analyzing the greenhouse air temperature; and accordingly, to decide an appropriate measures for controlling temperature:

$$V_a = \frac{0.0003\tau R_{so-max}}{\Delta T} \quad \text{...(6.1)}$$

where,

V_a = Ratio of Q and Ag
Q = Ventilation air flow rate (m^3/s)
Ag = Surface (ground) area of greenhouse (m^2)
τ = Transmission coefficient to solar radiation of greenhouse
$R_{so\text{-max}}$ = Maximum outside solar radiation (W/m^2)
ΔT = Temperature difference between greenhouse and outside air content (°C).

In regards to achieve better cooling effect there has been made some guidelines associated to the design and construction of greenhouse placed with ventilation system. They are narrated as under:

- If possible the ventilators should be located at the ridge, on the side walls and the gable.

- Total ventilator area should be around 15 to 30% of greenhouse floor area, recommended by White and Aldrich (1975).
- Placing of insect proof nets in roof openings on greenhouse creates obstruction in flow of air causing reduction in velocity of air flow; and thus there is improper effect on temperature or micro-climate control.

This cooling system involves following important demerits:

(i) In case of improper or poor ventilation there is reduction in CO_2 level inside greenhouse.
(ii) Inadequate ventilation develops overheating effect inside greenhouse.
(iii) Poor ventilation causes excessive transpiration, which in turn to produce the problem of plant water stress and physiological disorders such as fruit cracking and abortion of flowers and fruits.

***Forced ventilation*:** This is also one of the ventilation means for lowering greenhouse temperature. In this system or method, air stream is created to flow inside greenhouse from the outside, with the help of exhaust fan. The fan is equipped at one side of the greenhouse; normally at wind side. This fan is called ventilation fan. In order to have better cooling effect in big size greenhouse, many such fans are equipped. The spacing of ventilation fan is kept to the tune of 8.0 to 10 m. Ventilation fans are operated with the help of electrical power. Opposite to fan side, the openings are provided to allow the air from outside in the greenhouse, called inlet openings. The area of inlet openings should be at least 1.25 times of fan area. Inlet openings are provided with the cover or lid, which automatically closes the inlet on stopping of exhaust fan.

On operation of exhaust fans the warm air is sucked from the greenhouse and removed outside. This develops a kind of pressure gradient between the air masses of inside and outside greenhouse. This pressure gradient develops force to suck the air from the outside and enter the same in greenhouse. Because of this effect the fresh air starts entering the greenhouse from the outside. The velocity of entering air stream in greenhouse should not be high, i.e., not more than 0.5 m/s. The air velocity may be adjusted by changing the inlet openings. As the cool air stream enters, the hot air mass existing in greenhouse gets replace with the cold air mass. This leads to develop cooling effect inside greenhouse. In this way, cooling system is operated till achieving the desired level of cooling effect inside greenhouse.

Shade covers: Lowering of greenhouse temperature by using shade covers is another means or method, besides ventilation approach. Shade covers develop cooling effect by creating shades inside greenhouse area and also by reflecting the solar radiation away from the structure. The shading covers may be placed inside or outside the greenhouse. Besides, the formation of shades also causes harmful effect to the grown crop, by creating effect on photosynthesis action, and accordingly reduction in plant growth, as well. This advocates that in selection of shading materials these points must be taken into consideration; otherwise, there would be inconducive effects on planted crops, which is not desirable for greenhouse system. For this purpose the shade nets which are commonly used in greenhouse, are narrated as under:

***Shade nets*:** These are found suitable and effective in the areas/places where temperature and solar radiation are adverse regarding crop farming under greenhouse technique, provided they are correctly selected and placed. As per research finding, the shade nets are not only effective to increase the crop productivity but also develop positive effect on produce quality to a wide range. Normally, its use is found more effective in the regions of hot and sunny climate. In cultivation of ornamental plants the use of nets in combination of other shading materials results very conducive impact on yield and produce quality, both. Nowadays, the shade nets are available in different colour combinations and extensive varieties of plastic nets along with varying optical characteristics for use under protected cultivation technique. Their proper selection is very important as the color and transparency level of covering materials affect the absorption, reflection and transmission of radiation to the structure, significantly. In addition, the coloured nets also simulate specific morphological and physiological reactions. This leads to qualitative improvement in crop produce (Shahak et al., 2002).

As for as, the placing of nets in greenhouse to modify the micro-climate or control the temperature, is concerned, they can be placed inside and outside of greenhouse, both. However, the shade nets placed inside greenhouse affect the wind speed; and thus reducing the CO_2 concentration near the leaf surface. Also, there is reduction in light intensity and its quality relevant to the greenhouse crops, because of covering or shading materials used. This may cause to decline the transpiration rate and enhancement in canopy temperature, thereby (Jakson et al., 1981).

Evaporative Cooling

Evaporative cooling applied to greenhouse is another method. It is superior over ventilation cooling method. This method follows the principle of conversion of sensible heat into latent heat via water evaporation. In greenhouse, it is carried out by means of directly supplying water using mist or fog, sprinkler or through evaporative pads.

In fogging system the water is sprayed in the form of very small droplets in the air above the plant canopy inside greenhouse. In this case the surface area of water contents gets increase and also become thoroughly in contact to the air. Because of this reason the evaporation efficiency gets enhance, several times. In addition to develop cooling effects, the fogging is also found beneficial to enhance the humidity level desirous to the plant growth. In fogging method there is uniformity in cooling throughout greenhouse area, inside.

The fan pad cooling system is also used in greenhouse for lowering the temperature or modifying the micro-climate. In this system, at one gable end the fan is mounted and just opposite side of the same, the pad system is placed. The fan and pad system is operated by using electrical power. Cooling pad is made of different types of materials, such as wood, wool, swelling clay minerals, etc. and specially impregnated cellulose paper. On system's operation, the water starts passing over the pad continuously; and at the same time the fan also sucks and removes the greenhouse hot air, outside. Because of this process there develops pressure gradient between greenhouse air and the outside air. The pressure inside greenhouse is lesser than the outside air. This leads to flow the air from outside into greenhouse passing through cooling pads. The air stream coming via cooling pad in the greenhouse production zone is the cooled air. In this way, on operation of the system for some time duration, the entire greenhouse area becomes cool or the inside micro-climate of greenhouse gets modify. Cooling efficiency depends on water flow rate, water distribution system, pump capacity, recirculation rate and output rate of the fan pad system, mainly. The fan pad cooling system can lower the greenhouse temperature up to 12°C even at very high ambient temperature. In addition this cooling system can also enhance the humidity up to the desired level.

6.3.2 Micro-climate Control—In Terms of Heating

In contrast to the cooling operations towards lowering the temperature or modification of greenhouse micro-climate, the heating of greenhouse also becomes essential in some of the special cases or locations, as well. Use of heating system is essential in the regions of cold climate, or when there is occurrence of prolong cloudy days. In such areas or situations, because of reduction or lowering of inside temperature the growth and development of the crop get drastically hampered. Although, its provision makes the production cost of greenhouse crops high, but its placement is essential to save the crop against failure. A detail description about greenhouse heating requirement, heating system, etc. has been presented in Chapter-5.

CO_2 Enrichment

In nutshell, the greenhouse environment or micro-climate should always be in favourable range for better photosynthesis or plant growth. In photosynthesis process the role of CO_2 is very important towards development of synthates causing plant growth. This advocates that the soundness of greenhouse micro-climate also depends on presence of CO_2 concentration in appropriate amount. In CO_2 deficient situation the growth process of plant gets affected. Therefore, to avoid this situation the CO_2 is added from outside to the greenhouse. For this purpose the pure liquid CO_2 is preferred. Its application in better way is done by using pipeline system, which is just similar to the fertigation system. The system assembles a gauge to report CO_2 concentration.

Lighting System

Light significantly affects the greenhouse micro-climate. Or in other words, the presence of light by its appropriate amount and intensity is very essential to accomplish sound photosynthesis action, and thus to cause better growth and crop yield as well. However, sometimes, the sunlight is not being available in appropriate amount and duration, in result the crop gets hamper. In this condition to avoid such possibility an artificial lighting arrangement is made in greenhouse structure. In this regard the LED bulbs, fluorescent lights, tube lamps, metal halide lamps or heat lamps can be suitably used. In general, the provision of lighting system in greenhouse becomes essential in following situations:

- In absence of natural light the artificial illumination is essential to apply.
- Greenhouse is overshaded.
- Commercial greenhouse crop production.
- In the areas receiving less than 4.5 hours average daily sunshine.
- In the greenhouse located at high latitudes and overcast weather.
- During winter and cloudy days.

Air Humidification

Air humidification is also the part of modification of greenhouse micro-climate. In greenhouse the fogging system is used for development of cooling effect and also for humidity control at a time, both. However, this system is not only for air humidification but also serves other purposes such as irrigation, temperature control, etc. Air humidification is accomplished by several means, such as:

(i) **Steam boilers:** These are often used in cold regions for air humidification. They supply the heat contents to the greenhouse environment and make the air mass, humid.

(ii) **Heaters:** These are used to produce the saturated vapour mass, which is diverted in the greenhouse for humidifying the air.

(iii) **High pressure humidifier:** This is used to change the water into very small droplets, which are propelled in the greenhouse to humidify the air mass.

(iv) **Pulsators:** In greenhouse these are also used for air humidification in context to modification of micro-climate.

Dehumidification

This is required to carry out, especially when, humidity level of greenhouse environment becomes so high that there is condensation of moisture content present and formation of water droplets at the inner surface of greenhouse cover. The condensation is the symptom of high humidity of environment. Condensation creates several problems regarding crop performance. In condensation process the water vapours are transformed into water droplets, which get settle on the surfaces/objects lying there. In greenhouse the surfaces such as inner surface of covering material, structural members, crop canopy and other objects are the main. In condensation process the warm and moist air comes in contact with the cold objects. When warm-moist air mass comes in contact to the cold object then it gets cooled down to the level of surface temperature of the object, concern. If temperature of the object is less than the dew point temperature the present vapour mass in the air gets condense on the object. In greenhouses the condensation rate is found heaviest from the period of sunset to several hours after sunrise. In greenhouse the requirement of dehumidification can be checked or prevented by using anti-drop/anti-dripping films as the covering material. The anti-dripping films contain special type of additives, which negate the formation of droplets.

6.3.3 Effect of Greenhouse Design Parameters on Micro-climate

The design parameters such as the shape, size, covering and shading materials used and fogging system equipped, etc. have their significant effect on formation of micro-clime, suitable to the crops grown inside greenhouse. Table 6.2 illustrates the effects on micro-climate due to different design parameters and change in climatic parameters, i.e., temperature, relative humidity and availability of solar radiation.

Table 6.2 Effect of greenhouse design and weather parameters on micro-climate

S. No.	Greenhouse design parameter	Temperature	Relative humidity	Solar radiation
1.	Shape–Quonset and saw tooth	♦ In saw tooth shape GH 3°C temperature lesser than the Quonset shape GH.	♦ In Quonset shape GH 13% RH is lesser than the saw tooth shape.	♦ In saw tooth shape GH 5 to 10% more solar radiation.

(Contd.)

S. No.	Greenhouse design parameter	Temperature	Relative humidity	Solar radiation
2.	Size	♦ In case of greater height GH less temperature at plant level, up to 2°C. ♦ In GH with the length more 20 m without adequate ventilation, there is increase in temperature.	♦ At lower height there is 10 to 12% high humidity.	♦ There is high level of solar radiation at upper 25% height as compared to lower heights.
3.	Cladding material-diffused and U.V. stabilized	♦ In case of UV stabilized clear film–slightly greater temperature is there as compared to the diffused film in summer and winter months, both. ♦ As compared to outside the maximum temperature reduction is observed in case of diffused film. while in UV stabilized films, it is less.	♦ A high humidity is noticed in UV film covered GH.	♦ In case of UV film covered GH about 80% solar energy reduction ♦ While, it is about 76% in case of diffused covers.
4.	Shading and fogging	♦ Using shading and fogging 3 to 4°C temperature can get reduce during peak of summer months.	♦ Using shading and fogging system the RH can get increase to the tune of 15 to 20%.	♦ No effect on solar radiation trapping is observed.

6.4 CLIMATE CONTROL SYSTEMS IN AUTOMATED GREENHOUSE

The successful crop cultivation in greenhouse requires maintenance of proper micro-climate as per crop's suitability. This is because of the reason that each and every crop follows its own climatic variable for its entire growth period. In greenhouse the production zone is a closed domain, which bears a well-defined environment with optimum climate (micro-climate) for plant growth. An optimum climate is formed by creating optimal control on indoor and outdoor environments. The indoor climate includes the parameters such as carbon dioxide (CO_2) concentration, relative humidity, solar radiation, vapor pressure deficit and temperature, while outdoor parameters are the wind speed and its direction, humidity, and rainfall, as well.

Greenhouse micro-climate is highly dynamic, which is in combination of physical processes, energy transfer and mass balance. Physical processes involve the energy transfer, i.e., the radiation, whereas the mass balance describes the water vapour fluxes and CO_2 concentration. In automated greenhouse the formation and monitoring of micro-climate is accomplished, automatically, with the help of the devices such as sensors, etc., are described below, in detail.

Sensors: These are the device, which produce electrical signals directly related to the parameters, to be measured. In greenhouse cultivation system these sensors are continuous type, which continuously measure the specific climatic parameter, i.e., the temperature, relative humidity, vapor pressure deficit (VPD), light intensity, electrical conductivity (EC), pH, carbon dioxide (CO_2) concentration, wind speed and its direction, and rainfall, as well. The types of sensors used are described below,

Types of Sensors

In general, the sensors are in two types, i.e.

(i) Continuous type, and
(ii) Discrete type sensors.

Continuous type sensors: These are the sensors, which produce continuous electrical signals in terms of voltage, current, conductivity, capacitance, or any other measurable electrical properties. Continuous sensors are used for collecting the details on information about the subject matter.

Discrete sensors: These are the mechanical or electronic switches used to indicate the thresholds, such as opening and closing of the devices like valves, alarms, etc. In addition, discrete seniors are also used to indicate the time instance when a threshold of an important state variable has been reached. For example to sense and switch-off the float, when water level in the tank is reached to the minimum desirable level, the used sensor is the discrete sensor. Similarly, for switching-off the tensiometer when soil moisture is above a desired threshold value, the used sensor is the discrete sensor. Besides above types of sensors, the other sensors are also categorized as per their measuring parameters, given in Table 6.3.

Table 6.3 Types of sensors

S. No.	Types of sensors
1.	Temperature sensors
	(i) Air temperature
	(ii) Plant temperature
	(iii) Substrate temperature
2.	Humidity sensors
3.	Light sensors
	(i) Pyrometers
	(ii) PAR sensors
4.	Carbon dioxide sensors
5.	Soil moisture sensors
5.	Tensiometer
6.	Electrical resistance blocks
7.	Dielectric sensors
8.	(i) Wind speed
	(ii) Direction sensors
9.	Precipitation sensors

Temperature sensors: Greenhouse is the structure in which a desirable temperature can be maintained or ascertained, suitable to the crop specific for proper growth and development. The formation of temperature inside greenhouse is largely governed by the frame structure, covering material, greenhouse effect, etc., mainly. The substrate temperature is conducive for propagation and seeds, mainly. This is because of the reason that for seed germination a specific substrate temperature is required. In nutshell, on the basis of temperature, the dryness/ coolness of the plant in comparison to air temperature can be assessed. The sensors used for temperature sensing are narrated as under:

***Air temperature sensors*:** The most commonly used temperature sensors are the thermostat. These are placed in suspended form close to the crop canopy. Since, in day's hour the sunlight strikes the sensor; therefore, there is possibility of introducing some error in measurement. On this ground, therefore, the thermostats/sensors are placed in aspirated box to nullify such effects on measurement. In aspirated box a fan is equipped to remove the air and results an actual ambient temperature measurement. The variation in temperature measurement with and without aspirant box is to the tune of 2 or 3°C and 4 or 5°C, respectively.

***Substrate temperature sensors*:** These sensors are used to measure the temperature of crop root zone area. In the aspects of plant health studies the information on root zone temperature is important. For this purpose the thermocouples as one of the substrate temperature sensors, are commonly used. Thermocouples are connected to the data logger with internal sensors.

***Plant temperature sensors*:** These sensors measure the plant temperature. The data on plant temperature is required for making analysis on various aspects such as formation of needful environment and management of disease effects, etc., mainly. The growth and development is largely affected by the plant temperature, as functioning of tissues gets directly affected by the plant temperature. Broadly, the significance of plant temperature is as follows:

(i) Leaf folding/unfolding,
(ii) Development of flower buds, and
(iii) Stem elongation.

Humidity sensors: Broadly, the sensing of greenhouse humidity is carried out by using following sensors:

(i) Capacitive sensors,
(ii) Resistive sensors, and
(iii) Wet/dry bulb sensors.

Out of above three sensors the capacitive and resistive type solid state sensors are fairly common, as they record reasonably accurate humidity value. In addition, their maintenance is also very less. Only cleaning once or twice in a year is sufficient.

Light sensors: In greenhouse environment the availability of optimum light is essential to enhance the plant growth and productivity, and simultaneously reduce the level of energy consumption. The measurement of light based information provides an idea about level of energy consumption and supplemental light required; and also frames guideline about positioning of light system in production zone of greenhouse. Broadly, the measurement of light is carried out in context to the plants, only, i.e.:

(i) Global radiation or the energy input, and
(ii) Photosynthetically Active Radiation (PAR).

The important light sensors are narrated as under:

(i) Pyranometer; and
(ii) PAR Sensors.

***Pyrometers*:** These are used to measure the global radiation, which is the most common light based information for greenhouse crop farming system. Pyrometers measure whole spectrum of energy producing light. The measured light energy is expressed in the unit of watts per square meter. However, the common unit is watts per square meter per second ($W/m^2/sec$).

***PAR Sensors*:** These are also known as the quantum sensors. They measure the Photosynthetically Active Radiation (PAR) which wave band varies from 400 to 700nm. The PAR is expressed in the unit of Micromoles per square meter per second ($\mu mol\ m^{-2}\ s^{-1}$) or sometimes micromoles per square meter per day ($mmol/m^2/day$). The PAR sensors were primarily meant for horticultural research applications to measure the PAR within canopies, greenhouses, growth and germination chambers, laboratory applications, light studies, etc. Besides, they are also used for comparing the PAR at various points across the plant canopy, under screens, etc; and also used to check the uniformity of PAR when new lighting system is introduced in greenhouse environment.

Carbon dioxide (CO_2) sensors: In greenhouse production zone the availability of desired level of CO_2 concentration is very essential for optimum plant growth and crop productivity. Therefore, to ascertain the exact availability of CO_2 the measurement with greater accuracy is most important. The Infrared Gas Analyzer (IRGA) is one of the most suitable sensors used for measurement of CO_2 concentration.

Tensiometer: This is one of the most commonly used sensors for determining the available moisture contents in soil media. It consists of plastic tube, one porous ceramic cup and vacuum gauge. The ceramic porous cup is placed at one end of the plastic tube and vacuum gauge is fitted to the other end of plastic tube. For taking measurement the tensiometer is inserted in the soil for the desired depth. As precautionary measure the tensiometer tube should be filled with water to remove the air contents, before placing in the soil. Tensiometer measures the soil moisture in terms of matric potential. On placing the TM in soil media (substrate) the water starts flowing into soil media from the tube. This leads to develop vacuum within the tube, which is measured by the vacuum gauge. The rate of water flow into the soil from tube depends on the moisture content available in the soil. A dry soil involves more water flow rate or greater pulling force applied by the soil; and accordingly the formation of vacuum pressure, too. The puling force applied is called matric potential. In this condition the level of vacuum pressure gets reduce.

Gypsum block sensor: This is the Electrical Resistance Block, is used for measuring and monitoring the soil moisture content. This device (sensor) comprises a plug or gypsum block equipped with two electrodes. It works on the principle that the resistance of an electrode-embedded porous block is proportional to the water content of porous block. This advocates that the drier the block, lower is the resistance across two embedded electrodes; and vice-versa. The level of electrical resistance between two electrodes is governed by the soil matric potential.

Dielectric sensors: These sensors measure the soil moisture contents in terms of dielectric constant. The dielectric constant is an electrical property, which is dependent on soil moisture content. On this ground, the dielectric constant of soil media is counted as the soil's ability to transmit electrical waves. At greater soil wetness the value of dielectric constant is more; and vice-versa. This sensor provides instantaneous observations on soil moisture. In this way, on the basis of instantaneous soil moisture content an immediate action can be taken to supply the irrigation.

Wind speed and direction sensors: Greenhouses are designed and constructed based on the consideration of wind load, besides several other factors. Therefore, the information on wind load and its direction for the construction site is very important. The measurements of wind speed and direction is performed by using the sensors. These sensors provide the information about unexpected occurrence of storms with swirling winds, which is essential to know in context to safety points of greenhouse. In many of the environment control computers there is a feature called "storm surge" dependent on weather station. The storm surge is a kind of protection feature, meant for taking safety action against high speed wind blow. At the condition of wind speed exceeding a preset threshold wind speed, the sensor allows to close the ridge vent of greenhouse for making the system safe.

Precipitation sensors: These sensors are placed outdoor at weather station for measuring the rainfall (precipitation). The simple rain "grids" as precipitation sensor is used for this purpose. These sensors are used to close or limit the roof vents or retractable roofs, when it is raining with high intensity.

6.5 GREENHOUSE INSTRUMENTS/EQUIPMENT

The main objective of monitoring of greenhouse micro-climate is to maximize the crop productivity. The temperature, relative humidity, soil moisture sunlight, CO_2 level, etc. are the main parameters, constitute the greenhouse micro-climate. In greenhouse production zone each and every parameter has its availability range depending on solar radiation, covering materials, frame structure, grown crops and others. A little variation in their level or concentration the micro-climate becomes inconducive. In this condition to have the information about their real time availability (quantity), the use of devices or equipments for measurement at the site, is essential. Normally, in greenhouse context, the following instruments/devices are commonly used for measurement of requisite parameters:

(i) Thermometer
(ii) Humidity meter
(iii) pH meter
(iv) Electrical conductivity (EC) meter
(v) Lux meter
(vi) CO_2 meter

These are described as under:

Thermometer: This is used for measuring the greenhouse temperature. In greenhouse cultivation system the availability of temperature in proper range is very important, as it poses significant effect on nutrient uptake, plant growth, pollination, fruit setting, fruit cracking, produce colour, flower size, stem length, etc. Therefore, the measurement of greenhouse temperature is essential. Different crops require different temperature, e.g., for flower's case the range of optimum temperature varies between 18 and 26°C.

In order to take measurement on temperature, the thermometer is placed at the centre of the greenhouse, at plant level. As precautionary measure, the thermometer should not be placed at sun facing. Otherwise, there would be erroneous measurement of temperature. Using thermometer the real-time temperature can be obtained.

Humidity meter: The measurement of humidity is done by using the device called "Hygrometer". It is very common device is used for measuring the relative humidity, both in open field and greenhouse. In greenhouse production zone the humidity is one of the important climatic parameters to affect the crop growth. Normally, best crop growth is attained at the humidity ranging between 60 and 80%. At high humidity level the transpiration rate gets reduce. This leads to decline the nutrient movement. In addition, at the humidity level less or above the desired level, there is incidence of pest and disease attack, also. Therefore, the measurement of humidity of greenhouse environment at regular interval is very essential to know the variations in humidity level; and accordingly, to take immediate measures for maintaining the required humidity level.

pH meter: This is the devise used for measuring the pH of growing media, water to be used for irrigation purposes and also of the nutrient solution. The pH indicates the acidity or basicity of the growing media and water used in greenhouse crops. For accurate measurement, the pH meter should be properly calibrated, before placing to use. The ideal pH level of soil to be used as growing media should be between 6.0–6.5. Similarly, in case of nutrient solution the pH should be in the range of 5.6 to 6.5 for better uptake or crop utilization. At low pH, there is increase in potential for leaching and nutrient loss such as calcium, magnesium, potassium and ammonium because of saturation of hydrogen ions. Similarly, at high media pH there is possibility of micro-nutrient's deficiency, even they are available in sufficient concentration in the growing media.

EC meter: It measures Electrical Conductivity (EC) or concentration of soluble salts in water, expressed in the unit of (mmhos/cm), (dS/m) and (mS/cm). The dS and mS denote the DeciSiemens and MilliSiemens, respectively. The EC value 1.0mS/cm of root zone indicates beginning of salt building in root zone, which can be removed by flushing the growing media, properly.

Lux meter: This device measures the visible light intensity in greenhouse production zone. It measures the light intensity in the unit of *lumen*. Lux meter assembles a silicon plate to sense the light. The term "Lux" denotes the number of Lumen per sqm surface area. In greenhouse the light intensity affects the photosynthesis action or in other words the plant growth, significantly. The availability of sunlight most conducive to a good level of photosynthesis action can be ascertained by measuring it in regular way, each and every day.

CO_2 meter (portable): This is the device used for measuring the availability of CO_2 concentration in greenhouse. The presence of CO_2 in an optimum range is essential to accomplish better photosynthesis action. Normally, in greenhouse during morning hours the level of CO_2 concentration is found to the tune of 1000 ppm (approx.), which gets decline as the day progresses ahead. The direct enrichment of CO_2 level can be done with the help of ventilation system of greenhouse.

6.6 GREENHOUSE FOGGING SYSTEM

This is one of the main systems for modifying the greenhouse micro-climate to a certain level. Fogging system performs artificial watering in the form fine droplets, beneficial to lower the temperature and modify the relative humidity of greenhouse, as well. In greenhouses the modification of micro-climate as per crop requirement, is mainly done with the help of fogging system. There are different types of fogging system; few main amongst them are narrated as under:

1. Nozzle system,
2. High speed fan, and
3. Compressed air system.

Nozzle system: In this fogging system, watering is done with the help of nozzle arrangement. Nozzles discharge the water in the form of very fine water droplets, which form fog like appearance inside greenhouse. The design of fogging system is performed based on the moisture requirement of production zone and level of cooling desired in greenhouse, mainly. The pipeline size, discharge capacity of nozzles, etc. are decided according to the maintenance of temperature and humidity level in context to modification of micro-clime inside greenhouse.

Fogging system mainly consists of following components:

(i) Pump,
(ii) Pipeline for water distribution, and
(iii) Nozzle.

***Pump*:** A high pressure pump, normally piston pump/reciprocating pump is used. Operating pressure of pump varies from 800 to 1200 psi. At this pressure the equipped nozzle discharges the water in the form of fine water droplets. The size of droplets varies to the tune of 10 to 20 micron diameter effective to form the fog very easily.

***Pipeline*:** The copper, stainless steel or re-enforced pipes in flexible nature are commonly used for water supply to the fogging system. The diameter of pipe varies to the tune of 1/4 in or 3/8 inch to supply the water at the rate of 1 to 2 gallons/hour/nozzle. In greenhouse production zone the pipes are placed at uniform interval above the crop grown.

***Nozzles*:** These are made of plastic, ceramic and stainless steel materials, as well. The emitted drop size varies from 4 to 6 micron. These are fixed at 0.6 to 0.8 m interval on the pipeline. In fogging system different types and sizes (aperture size) of nozzles are used. Normally, the nozzles used for cooling purposes, have the aperture (micro hole) size between 0.15–0.2 mm; while for moistening purposes the nozzle's aperture size is 0.3 mm. Similarly, in decorative fogging system the nozzles have 0.5 mm diameter aperture size.

Nozzles are equipped with anti-drip check valves. These valves check the water dripping after shutdown of the system operation. In addition, an integral strainer is also placed to the nozzle for preventing clogging problem. The clogging of nozzle is mainly because of deposition of chemical contents and particulate matters. The chemical deposits block the micro-holes and failure the fogging work. Such type of clogging is removed by chemical treatments and also by water flushing. The clogging because of particulate materials is removed by placing the filters in water supply unit (control unit).

High speed fan system: The fogs can also be formed by using high speed fan system. The water is channeled to the tips of fan blades. In result there is formation of fine water droplets, able to form the fog. This is because of the shearing action of very fast rotating fan's blades. The formed fog gets distributed in the entire greenhouse zone above crop canopy.

6.6.1 Benefits of Fogging

The advantages offered by fogging system in regards to greenhouse crops, are enumerated as under:

- The greenhouse temperature can be easily brought up to 5°C. In hot weather at low external humidity of about 20%, the temperature lowering up to 13°C can be easily done inside greenhouse.
- In greenhouse better moisture control can be carried out.
- The emitted droplets are in the size of 4 to 6 micron, which are very effective to form the fogs in greenhouse.
- The fogging system can be an autonomous to humidity sensors.
- Maintenance and operation cost is low.
- Greenhouse micro-climate can be modified as per requirement.
- Power consumption is less.
- Fogging system can be linked to the remote control unit for its smooth and easy operation.
- It enables to result high crop productivity.
- Develops proper growing environment for the crop concern, inside greenhouse.
- Reduces product spoilage.
- Improves crop yield and produce quality, both.
- Develops better environment for good plant growth and development.
- It regulates the temperature and humidity of greenhouse cropping zone.

6.6.2 Purpose of Fogging System

In greenhouse the purpose of using fogging system is to develop an optimum environment for crop growth and development by modifying the temperature and relative humidity; or in other words the micro-climate. In the shadow of these changes, there develops numerous effects related to the crop, are presented as under:

(a) Maintaining optimum growing condition,
(b) No water stress development,
(c) Humidity control,
(d) Temperature control, and
(e) Controlling moisture stress.

Maintaining optimum growing environment: Greenhouse as a whole is a crop production system comprises a well-defined micro-climate or environment within, suitable for crop cultivation. The variation in crop environment or micro-climate is because of grown crop, covering materials used and outside weather condition. Greenhouse production zone comprises soil or growing media, micro-climate and crop. Each and every greenhouse crop requires its own environmental condition, which is governed by the temperature and humidity to a large extent. The fogging is a kind of watering system, through which the water is sprayed in the form of very fine droplets with the aid of nozzles or some other means. The fine water droplets never come to the soil touch, but they remain in suspended form in the air, which appear in clustered way called fog. The formed fogs are causative to lower the temperature and raise the relative humidity of greenhouse environment. Because of variation in temperature and relative humidity inside greenhouse there is modification in micro-climate existing there. In this way by varying the temperature and relative humidity a requisite micro-climate for the grown crop can be formulated in greenhouse to achieve better crop yield.

No water stress development: The relative humidity inside greenhouse is more as compared to the outside. This is because of the reason that the growing media and crop, both are always in covered condition, and whatever water is applied to meet the irrigation requirement, is utilized by the crop, and a part of that is also returned back to the greenhouse, which does not escape outside but becomes beneficial to buildup humidity inside. At high humidity level the crop water requirement gets reduce. To a large extent the water balance of greenhouse remains unchanged during crop period. In nutshell, this advocates that the crop inside greenhouse is more or less being moisture stress free.

Humidity control: Humidity represents the presence of water contents in greenhouse air mass. This creates a great effect on micro-climate, existing there. In greenhouse the sources of addition of water content to the air mass are the water supplied for irrigation-cum-fertigation, soil moisture content and transpiration from the crop, mainly. The moisture content evaporated from the soil media, water vapours released through respiration and transpiration, water sprinkled from the sprinklers or foggers for temperature control, etc., get retain in the greenhouse air mass and constitutes humidity, there. The formed humidity is responsible to modify the greenhouse micro-climate. The fogging system is one of the most suitable means for humidity formation and thereby the micro-climate, both.

Temperature: Temperature reduction is another objective of fogging system in greenhouse. The fine water droplets emitted through foggers remain in suspension form in greenhouse air mass; and accordingly, there is lowering in temperature of greenhouse environment, besides raising the humidity level. In nutshell, the fogging system accomplishes the control on humidity and temperature, both, simultaneously. Apart from fogging system there are several other means, also available to cool or lower the greenhouse temperature such as misting system, ventilation system, fan pad cooling system, air conditioner, etc.

6.7 GREENHOUSE MISTING SYSTEM

This is also one of the means used for cooling or lowering the greenhouse temperature; and also for creating humidity to develop a suitable environment for growth and development of the crop grown. Misting system follows the principle of evaporative cooling. In misting system the water is sprayed with the help of pressure-increasing, minuscule nozzle. The super fine water droplets emitted by the nozzle are filled in the air mass and retained in suspension form, which gets appear in cluster mode is called mist. The formed mist gets quickly evaporated. In evaporation of mist mass there is requirement of heat content, which is met from the greenhouse air. In this way, the greenhouse temperature gets reduce or development of cooling effect in greenhouse environment.

6.7.1 Advantages of Misting System

Like fogging, the misting system is also being advantageous in various aspects, narrated as under,

- Development of humidity effect in greenhouse.
- Beneficial for raising seedlings and cuttings.
- Acts as tool for climate modification.
- Development of cooling effect in greenhouse.
- Beneficial for nurturing exotic or sensitive plants.

6.7.2 Difference between Fogging and Misting Systems

Although, the basic purpose of fogging and misting systems in greenhouse is the same, i.e. to develop a perfect environment for the crops grown to achieve a high crop productivity or b/c ratio, but there are some certain differences between them, are briefed as under,

S. No.	Feature	Fogger	Mister
1.	Ideal: For the plants susceptible to root disease.	Well suitable	Not so
2.	Suitability:		
	(i) Propagation of seeds and non-rooted cuttings	Well suitable	Not so
	(ii) Propagation of rooted cuttings	Not so	Well suitable
	(iii) Cooling and humidity Control	Well suitable	Well suitable
3.	Drop size:		
	(i) 50 to 100 micron diameter		✓
	(ii) 50 micron or less diameter	✓	

6.7.3 Misting System—Components

Misting system is the watering kit used in greenhouse for immediate lowering of temperature, creating humidity, etc., mainly. It comprises mainly the following components:

(i) Pipeline,
(ii) Nozzles,
(iii) Filter unit,
(iv) Pressure regulator,

(v) Solenoid valve, and
(vi) Timer or controller.

Pipeline: This is used for water supply to the system. The size of pipe is decided as per nozzle to be used for water misting.

Nozzles: There are several types of nozzles available to form mist in the greenhouse. However, the deflector or impingement types of nozzles are commonly used. These nozzles are operating at the pressure ranging from 30 to 60 psi. In system a leakage prevention device (LPD) is also used to check water dripping.

Filter: In misting system the purpose of filer is to remove the foreign materials such as soil particles, debris, etc. from the water, in context to avoid the possibility of nozzle clogging. For this purpose a 100 to 150 mesh strainer is placed in water pipeline at u/s end of the nozzle.

Installation should follow the manufacturer's recommendations. In greenhouse as per size of production area several such nozzles are placed at the grid of 3ft to 5ft at the height of 3 to 4 feet above the grown crop. And overlapping is kept to the tune of 100% or more for maintaining uniformity in water misting.

Solenoid valve: Its function is to turn the water flow "on or off". Normally, closing the valve with snapping action is more preferred. In addition, the voltage requirement of solenoid valve should also be the same as the time clock or the controller. In this context a 24 volt system is always found safer.

Timer or controller: The time clocks, timer, mechanical sensor, light-operated interval switch (LOIS), humidistat, etc. are the devices used as the controller in misting system. In which the *time clock* governs the time component for operation of misting system. The *timer* performs the function to turn on/off the misting. Mechanical sensor is placed in the plant canopy to collect the information on moisture content and accordingly to turn off/on the solenoid valve or the water supply thereby. In greenhouse the *LOIS sensor* is mounted below the glazing. The function of *humidistat* is to control the humidity level of greenhouse. Humidistat senses the humidity level and activates the solenoid valve to put it on or off position as per requirement. The controllers are equipped to command multiple zones of misting system as per requirement.

PRACTICE QUESTIONS

Descriptive Type Questions

1. Define greenhouse micro-climate and describe its parameters.
2. Describe significance of micro-climate on crop productivity.
3. Explain change dynamics of greenhouse micro-climate.
4. Explain importance of light in formation of greenhouse micro-climate.
5. Describe greenhouse climate modification as per crop requirement.
6. Enlist and make description about the instruments or devices required to control greenhouse micro-climate.
7. Narrate misting and fogging systems used for greenhouse temperature control.
8. Describe effect of greenhouse design on its micro-climate.

9. Describe climate control system in automated greenhouse.
10. Narrate greenhouse cardinal temperatures.

Multiple Choice Type Questions

1. Greenhouse climate is referred to as
   (a) Temporary climate (b) Micro-climate
   (c) Effective crop weather (d) None of above
2. Greenhouse climate composition includes the parameter
   (a) Rainfall (b) Wind velocity
   (c) Light concentration, only (d) Temperature
3. The solar radiation is causative to
   (a) Produce dry matters in plant (b) Initiate photosynthesis
   (c) water uptake (d) None of above
4. Temperature affects the
   (a) Germination (b) Plant growth
   (c) Flowering (d) All above
5. Plant temperature depends on
   (a) Air temperature (b) Short wave radiation
   (c) Transpiration (d) All above
6. Temperature drop is to lower the temperature in the range of
   (a) 2.8 to 8.3°C (b) 4 to 8°C
   (c) 2.0 to 5.0°C (d) 5 to 10°C
7. In greenhouse for proper plant growth the humidity level should be
   (a) 50 to 75% (b) 30 to 45%
   (c) 60 to 90% (d) 80 to 90%
8. Which of the following light corresponds the Photosynthetically Active Radiation (PAR)?
   (a) Visible light (b) Red light
   (c) Blue light (d) Far infrared light
9. Wavelength of visible light varies from
   (a) 250 to 300 nm (b) 500 to 650 nm
   (c) 400 to 700 nm (d) 150 to 300 nm
10. Wave length of blue light varies from
    (a) 250 to 300 nm (b) 500 to 650 nm
    (c) 430 to 450 nm (d) 150 to 300 nm
11. The effect of blue light is on
    (a) Plant growth (b) Flowering
    (c) Seed germination (d) Grain setting
12. The effect of red light is on
    (a) Plant growth (b) Flowering
    (c) Seed germination (d) Grain setting

13. The wavelength of red light is
(a) 600 to 700 nm (b) 500 to 650 nm
(c) 430 to 450 nm (d) 150 to 300 nm

14. In plant growth the light duration signifies the
(a) Photoperiod (b) Time between sunrise and sunset
(c) Duration of solar radiation (d) None of above

15. The minimum cardinal temperature for floricultural crops varies
(a) 3 to 5°C (b) 5 to 10°C
(c) –1°C to 12°C (d) 10 to 15°C

16. Role of CO_2 in photosynthesis process is
(a) Producing synthates (b) Vitamins
(c) Carbohydrates (d) Proteins

17. For proper growth and crop yield the optimum concentration of CO_2 should be
(a) 700–900 μmol mol^{-1} (b) 500–700 μmol mol^{-1}
(c) 200–300 μmol mol^{-1} (d) 150–200 μmol mol^{-1}

18. The required daily light integral (DLI) for seedling propagation is
(a) 10 to 15 mol/m^2/day (b) 6 to 8 mol/m^2/day
(c) 5 to 7 mol/m^2/day (d) 2.5 to 3.5 mol/m^2/day

19. The required daily light integral (DLI) for young cutting is
(a) 10 to 15 mol/m^2/day (b) 6 to 8 mol/m^2/day
(c) 5 to 7 mol/m^2/day (d) 2.5 to 3.5 mol/m^2/day

20. The wavelength of green light varies from
(a) 250 to 270 nm (b) 200 to 270 nm
(c) 400 to 500 nm (d) 500 to 570 nm

Answers

1. b	**2.** d	**3.** a	**4.** d	**5.** d	**6.** a	**7.** c	**8.** a	**9.** c	**10.** c
11. a	**12.** b	**13.** a	**14.** a	**15.** c	**16.** a	**17.** a	**18.** a	**19.** b	**20.** d

BIBLIOGRAPHY

Bansal, N.K., Minke, G. (1988). Climatic zone and rural housing in India. Scientific Series of International Bureau, Kern. Forschungszentrum, Anlage, Julich, Germany.

Contreras-Medina, L.M., Torres-Pacheco, I., Guevara-Gonzal-ez, R.G., RomeroTroncoso R.J., Terol-Villalobos, I.R., De Pascale, S.T., and Maggio, A. (2008). Plant stress management in semiarid greenhouses. *Acta Hortic.*, 797: 205–215.

Ellis, R.H., Hadley, P., Roberts, E.H., and Summerfield, R.J. (1980). Quantitative relations between temperature and crop development and growth. Climatic change and plant genetic Resources, Belhaven Press, Landon: 85–115.

Goldammer T. (2019). Greenhouse Management: A Guide to Operations and Technology. Apex Publishers, USA.

Jackson, R.D., Idso, S.B., Reginato, R.J., and Pinter, P.J. (1981). Canopy temperature as crop water stress indicator. *Water Res. Res.*, 17: 1133–1138.

Joliet, O. (1991). An improved static model for predicting the energy consumption of a greenhouse, *Agricultural and Forest Meteorol.*, 55: 265–294.

Katsoulas, N. Kittas, C. Tsirogiannis, H., and Kitta E, Savvas, D. (2007). Greenhouse microclimate and soilless pepper crop production and quality as affected fog evaporative cooling system. *Transaction of ASABE*, 50: 1831–1840.

Kittas, C., Boulard, T., Mermier, M., and Papadakis, G. (1996). Wind induced air exchange rates in a greenhouse tunnel with continuous side openings. *J. Agric. Eng. Res.*, 65: 37–49.

Kittas, C., Karamanis, M. & Katsoulas, N. (2005). Air temperature regime in a forced ventilated greenhouse with rose crop. Energy & Buildings, 37(8): 807–812.

Nisen, A., Sirjacobs, M., and von Zabeltitz, C. (1984). Protected cultivation in Mediterranean climate, greenhouses in Egypt. FAO, Rome.

Pearson, S., Hadley, P. and Wheldon, A.E. (1995). A model of the effect of day and night temperature on the height of chrysanthemum. *Acta Horticulturae*, 378: 71–80.

Rodríguez, F., Berenguel, M., and Arahal, M.R. (2001). Feedforward controllers for greenhouse climate control based on physical models.

Shahak, Y., Lahav, T., Spiegel, E., and PhilosophHadas, S. (2002). Growing aralia and monstera under colored shade nets. Olam Poreah, 13: 60–62.

Tap, F., van Willigenburg, L.G., and van Straten, G. (1996). Receding horizon optimal control of greenhouse climate based on the lazy man weather prediction, 13th IFAC World Congress; San Francisco; USA; pp. 387–392.

Tiwari, G.N. (2003). Greenhouse technology for controlled environment in India. Narosa Publishing House.

Zhang, S., Mahrer, and Y. Margolin, M. (1997). Predicting the microclimate inside a greenhouse: an application of a one dimensional numerical model in an unheated greenhouse, Agri. Forest Meteorol., 86: 291–297.

CHAPTER 7

Greenhouse – Growing Media

The soil is the natural growing media used for crop cultivation. Profitability of greenhouse cultivation depends to a lot on the growing media used for cultivation. The available soil within greenhouse structure acts as the common growing media for crop farming. In addition, several other media are also there for greenhouse farming. However, the natural soil with good quality is treated as suitable growing media for the purpose of greenhouse crop cultivation. Sometimes, the cultivation using greenhouse or protected cultivation techniques becomes constraint because of non-availability of suitable land site for construction, in context to better crop yield and produce quality as well. In this situation, the site soil which is unsuitable is not allowed for crop farming. The most suitable alternative is to use the other growing media for crop cultivation. The soilless growing media is one of the best substitutes, are widely used in greenhouse farming system. In addition, to go for multilayer crop farming inside greenhouse, the use of soilless growing media is more preferable than the soil media.

In greenhouse cultivation the growing media is counted as one of the main inputs, like others. The function of growing media is to provide a most favourable or an ideal environment for better root growth and development along with proper support to the plants, as well. In nutshell, it constitutes a kind of porous media within to retain water in terms of moisture content; to facilitate gaseous exchange and create most optimum water/nutrient-plant-environment for better plant growth. These contributions of growing media lead to accomplish the appearance of all growth stages well in time, resulting into the crop yield at potential level. Sometimes, the use of growing media becomes essential, because of vulnerability of site soil to the diseases and pests; and thus leading to cause unhealthy growths in the plants.

In agriculture sector, the growing media acting as one of the substitutes of soil has solved several problems related to the greenhouse cultivation. In result, the constraints of greenhouse technology towards crop cultivation in protected environment to achieve enhanced yield with better quality, are omitted.

Nowadays, various types of growing media have been developed for protected cultivation such as peat moss, vermiculite, perlite, shredded coconut husks/coco peat or composted materials along with starter nutrients and wetting agents, as well. These media have liberty for making their combinations as per requirement of the crop specific or the situation of crop cultivation. In comparison to natural soil, a growing media containing right proportion of different ingredients may have the following merits:

1. Enable to provide better aeration for root system.
2. Better drainage, causing no any misconduct.
3. Optimum water-holding capacity, conducive to create proper plant-water-atmosphere relationship.
4. Conducting better nutrient uptake.
5. Potential to develop resistance against diseases.
6. Resisting weed growths.

7.1 GROWING MEDIA—DEFINITION

In greenhouse production system a variety of inputs are required, in which growing media is one of the main. The field soils are generally not fit for container based crop farming because of improper aeration, drainage and water-holding capacity, mainly. In order to overcome these points, the soilless growing media have been developed, which are the best for greenhouse production system, provide increased yield with better quality produce.

The media or substrate, in which the plant can grow (root development) and extract the water and nutrients for survival and producing good yield, is called growing media. In greenhouse the use of growing media other than the soil has prime importance. The crop productivity in greenhouse environment depends very much on the type of growing media used for cultivation. The media flourishing a good root system is considered as the one of the most suitable means for cultivation of greenhouse crops. In this direction, therefore, the selection of suitable growing media is one of the important steps. Normally, for use in container based planting the growing media are available in following two forms:

1. Soil based growing media, and
2. Organic based growing media.

In soil based growing media the major component is the field soil. On the other hand, in organic based growing media the base material is the organic contents. The materials such as compost, peat, coconut coir, etc. fall in the category of organic materials. These are commonly used as the organic base for preparation of growing media. These organic materials are mixed to the inorganic ingredients to promote root growth and development in proper form. Besides organic materials, few industrial products such as peat moss, vermiculite and perlite are also used as the growing media. Overall, a growing media consisting two or more number of ingredients is considered to be the most favourable.

7.2 FUNCTIONS OF GROWING MEDIA

A growing media provides all the requisites required for crop growth, just like soil media. This advocates that its behaviour is more or less similar to the natural soil mass. In other worlds, a growing media encompasses water contents, gaseous exchange, facilitates nutrient's uptake by the plants and so many other activities which normally happens in natural soils. In nutshell, a growing media performs all those functions, which a soil does in respect to the plants or crop. Moreover, the major functions of growing media are given as under:

1. Physical support
2. Aeration
3. Proper water supply
4. Mineral/nutrient supply

Physical support: Although, growing media is highly porous in nature, but bears sufficient potential to support the plant, physically. In general, for better plant growth or to facilitate photosynthesis in optimum range, the young seedlings must be planted in upright position. This can be easily accomplished in growing media. The plant root system binds the media very tightly, creates a good support for the plant. Especially, in case of nurseries where a large number of seedlings or grafts are required to prepare, the use of growing media is most desirous. In such cases the growing media should be sufficiently strong/heavy to hold the plants upright, against wind blow. In this regard the bulk density is one of important characteristics of growing media, which should be in proper range to hold or support the plants in proper way.

Aeration: Growing media is a porous mass, involves good level of aeration or gaseous exchange capacity. For growing media a good level of aeration is most important. This is because of the reason that for plant growth a steady supply of oxygen contents through growing media is essential, which met, only when media is in porous nature. The O_2 is required to convert the photosynthates from leaves into energy for proper root development, besides water, nutrient and minerals uptake. In addition, the released CO_2 during photosynthesis action should also be dispersed into the atmosphere. An excess CO_2 concentration develops toxicity effect in soil media or in root zone, which is not desirous for proper plant growth. A prompt aeration of growing media always keeps this action in order. In growing media this whole process takes place in macro-pores or in air spaces.

Water supply: The supply of water content in proper way is very essential for plant growth in growing media. The root system takes the water from micro-pore spaces through fine roots. For soilless growing media this requirement is must. The growing media containing sufficient micro-pores to hold water is considered to be fit. In this condition there is prompt supply of water to the plant body from growing media. Some of the growing media contain high percentage of organic matters such as peat moss and composts, leading to hold the moisture content just like sponge. The planted crop may face little problem regarding extraction of water content in such growing media, if percentage micro-pores are less in extent. In nutshell, a proper or productive growing media should have adequate percentage of porosity to absorb and store large amount of water for plant use.

Mineral/nutrients supply: Like water supply, the supply of minerals and nutrients in proper way to the plants is also essential in context to their prompt growth and development. In crop farming, the majority of used minerals/nutrients are electrically charged ions. For example, Ammonium Nitrate (NH_4^+), Potassium (K^+), Calcium (Ca^{+2}), and Magnesium (Mg^{+2}) are the positively charged ions (cations), get attracted towards the negatively charged particles of growing media. In growing media the absorption capacity of cations is governed by the property called Cation Exchange Capacity (CEC), which varied from one growing media to another. Moreover, the growing media comprising peat moss, vermiculite and compost have high range of CEC and accordingly the absorption capacity of cation, too.

7.3 COMPOSITION OF GROWING MEDIA

In order to have a proper effect on plant growth the composition of growing media must be in proper range. However, many soilless cultures or substrates are used singly or in combination of other ingredients, depending on the requirement of the plant. In the case of ingredient's combination, the ratio between ingredients must be in proper range to meet the requirement of:

(i) Plant support
(ii) Aeration or gaseous exchange
(iii) Water-holding ability
(iv) Nutrients retention
(v) Weed control, etc.

As far as, the selection of components or ingredients is concerned, it depends on their availability and cost, as well. In standard composition of the materials comprising coco peat, vermiculite and perlite, their proportion is followed to the tune of 3:1:1 (volume or volume ratio). However, the followings few more points are also there to follow in deciding the composition of growing media ingredients:

- The seedling raising (nursery) can be carried out by using coco-peat alone as single ingredient/component. As precautionary measure the coco-peat must be treated with Calcium Nitrate at the rate of 50 g/kg to reduce electrical conductivity (EC) and pH level of the media.
- At the site, if plenty of timber trees are available the tree barks can also be used as the ingredient to prepare growing media, is being most economical as compared to the others. In preparation of growing media the sand is added to the bark materials. The sand gets settle down in the space and nests among the bark materials. This causes increment in surface area, and leads to provide better aeration and Water-holding per unit volume of substrate. Sometimes, the sphagnum peat moss is also mixed to the bark materials for enhancing water-holding capacity and nutrient retentivity in substrate.

7.4 TYPES OF GROWING MEDIA

In protected cultivation the following two types of growing media are commonly used:

(i) Soil, and
(ii) Soilless media.

7.4.1 Soil as Growing Media

It is very common form of growing media in open field condition and also for protected environment. Soil is the natural media encompasses all the components/ingredients required for plant growth. The water, nutrients and preventive treatments are additionally provided to the soil media as per requirement of the crops during farming. In general, the loamy and porous soils with rich in organic matter and pH around 7.0 are considered as most suitable. Also, the soil mixed with sand and FYM in the proportion of 2:1:1 is found better in context to:

(i) Better aeration,
(ii) Good water-holding capacity, and
(iii) Good supply of nutrients for plant uptake.

However, in use of soil as the growing media under protected environment, there are several problems in respect to following points:

- Difficult to maintain nutritive status.
- Not possible to maintain the desired level of pH and water-holding capacity.
- Problems due to soil-borne pathogens.
- Problems due to salinity or ill-drained soil condition posing the situation of poor soil aeration, porosity, nutrient uptake, etc.

Above-mentioned difficulties or problems borne by the natural soil as the growing are described under following heads:

1. Restricted volume
2. Imbalance of soil microorganisms
3. Problems with water and air
4. Problems with the maintenance of favourable characteristics
5. Variability and weeds
6. Sustainability concerns

Restricted volume: Protected cultivation is performed either through structures or under controlled environment. The requirement of soil media is in restricted volume. Normally, growing of plants (nursery) is carried out in small containers, in which a limited amount of soil is required to put. This results into availability of water, nutrients and other contents in very poor range, which get quickly reduced because of several reason like temperature, plant uptake, volatization, etc. This impact develops negative effects on crop growth and yield, as well, if required inputs are not applied at predetermined rate and schedule.

Imbalance of soil microorganisms: It is well known that a natural soil contains myriad of microorganisms, in which some are beneficial and some are not, may be pathogenic; yet they create a natural balance in the soil. But when a part the soils is placed in the pot or container of limited capacity for plant growing (nursery), the balance gets upset and poses several problems. Especially, at such situation the requirement of frequent irrigation and fertilization is essentially felt to provide to maintain the natural balance in terms of nutritive as well as moisture status of the soil media. In contrast, in the growing media, other than native soil, i.e., the soilless growing media, this type of happening is not there. As the requite inputs are applied afresh as per plant's requirement at the scheduled time; and accordingly, the possibility of occurrence of imbalance between the soil-water-plant-environment is not there.

Problems related to water and air: Native soils are in varying natures/types depending on distribution of sand, silt and clay percentage. All the soils are not fit for using as growing media for protected cultivation. Normally, the loamy soils are found to be most suitable. On the other hand, the clay and silty soils are not so, because they have very small particle size, lead to have aeration problem, drainage problems, etc. These soils also have the problems of shrinkage and swelling after drying and wetting, respectively, which are completely unfavorable for growing media. In addition, the circulation of air or gaseous exchange is also an important requisite for the growing media, is not met form heavy soils. The soil which could contain sufficient water and also release the same to the plant as per requirement, is very essential for a good growing media. The loamy soil is most suitable to use as growing media because it contains requisite features to a large extent.

Problems related to nutrients: The soil placed in pot or container as growing media does not provide the nutrients in proper quantity to the plant for its proper growth and development; and even some of the nutrients are immobile, too. As example, the clay soil absorbs the nutrients so strongly, but on demand of the plant that is not released. In result that becomes unavailable to the plant. On the other hand, in case of sandy soils the nutrients are poorly held, but existing nutrients are easily available to the plant for uptake. In addition, a large portion of available nutrients also gets leach below along with water in sandy soil. This advocates that there is likely of problems regarding unavailability of nutrients in proper quantity and time with such soils used as growing media.

Variability in soils: This is common phenomena that the soils are varying in types and characteristics, both. Accordingly, their response on crop production is always being different among them. In protected cultivation, the soils placed in containers as growing media behave different from container to container, crop to crop and even season to season. In this way, getting a consistent crop production using soil as GM is very difficult. In addition, the weed problem is also being high in range than the soilless growing media. A soil which involves high weed infestation, involves more cost of cultivation because of money investment in their control, excess nutrients application, and simultaneously reduction in crop yield, too. In contrast, this type of problem is very rare in soilless type growing media.

Sustainability concerns: In case of soil as growing media, the consideration of ecological sustainability is very important. The soils for using as GM, are taken from the top fertile layer. Accordingly, at most of places the sub-soil which is poor in fertility status, is left. In result there is depletion in nutrient's status of the lands, from where the soils are taken for using as growing media. As per report, in several countries millions of square meters of soil are mined each year for nurseries; and accordingly, leaving a huge acreage of land under nutrients depleted condition, which become unfit for plants (Wightman, 1999). In this condition to avoid the use of soil for growing media the ingredients comprising composts, bark, rice hulls, etc. are selected for preparing growing media to cultivate the crops under protected environment. However, if the use of media containing soil is compulsion then it should contain the soil at most in the range of 10 to 30%, which should also be amended with the help of organic ingredients for promoting aeration and drainage and also maintaining optimum water-holding capability.

7.4.2 Soilless Growing Media

The media other than the soil used for crop growing, is called soilless growing media, or sometimes, the soilless culture, also. It offers various advantages over soil media in context to protected cultivation, are mentioned below:

(i) It facilitates the nutritional requirement of plants in precise amount, frequently.
(ii) It creates an opportunity for pathogen-free cultivation.
(iii) Facilitate economical use of fertilizer/nutrients.
(iv) Labor saving against weeding and fertilizer application activities.
(v) Makes possible to save the basal doses of manures/fertilizers.
(vi) Facilitates or makes possible for crop cultivation in problematic soil conditions

7.5 PROPERTIES OF GROWING MEDIA

Properties of growing media are divided in following three categories:

1. Physical properties,
2. Chemical properties, and
3. Biological properties.

7.5.1 Physical Properties

In context to physical properties of growing media the followings are mainly taken into consideration:

1. Water-holding capacity,
2. Aeration,
3. Porosity, and
4. Bulk density.

Water-holding capacity (WHC): The water-holding capacity of porous media is defined as the percentage of total pore space filled with the water after drainage of gravitational water from the media, concern. In porous media the pore spaces are in varying sizes, i.e., few are bigger, few are medium and few are very small (micro) in size. The water available in big or medium size pore spaces are easily drained due to gravity effect, while the water available in micro-pore spaces are retained and hold up against gravity force. This forms moisture content in the media and is available for plant uptake. A good growing media should have high water-holding capacity. In artificial growing media this is artificially constituted by adding suitable ingredients. As example a peat moss particle holds more water as compared to the similar size pumice piece. In addition to the effects of ingredients, the compaction level also affects the WHC. However, due to excess compaction the particles of growing media are likely to get damage, which in turn to cause percentage reduction in macro pore spaces. This change in growing media affects aeration or gaseous exchange. Furthermore, because of compaction the water-holding capacity of media gets increase, but for root development it creates suffocation. Also, the height of container holding the growing media affects its WHC. A short container filled with the same GM is likely to have waterlogging problem, while in tall size container it is not so.

Aeration: The growing media must have the property of proper aeration to conduct gaseous exchange. In growing media aeration effect is developed because of macro-pore spaces, as these are bigger in size. On watering, the stored water in macro-pores gets drain due to gravity effect. In result, they become empty, i.e., without water. Accordingly, these empty macro-pore spaces get filled with the air contents comprising oxygen. This whole process is considered as aeration in growing media.

Aeration is very important for proper and healthy root development, besides dissipating the released CO_2 from respiration action. Especially, for preparation of root cuttings the growing media should have high percentage of macro-pores to create better aeration effect.

Porosity: The porosity and bulk density are related to each other. In general, the porosity of a porous media expresses the space occupied by the voids or filled with water or gaseous contents. It is the sum of the space under macro-pores and micro-pores. Practically, majority of the soilless media contain the pore spaces to the tune of 60 to 80% of total volume. A part of these pore spaces is filled with the air and rest by the water and root contents. The pore spaces facilitate to provide adequate quantity of oxygen for growth. In addition, the root system also gives off CO_2, which exchange is essential, is also accomplished in pore spaces. The total available pore spaces in growing media determines the rate of gaseous exchange and drainage behavior. However, an adequate distribution between large and small pore spaces is essential.

Porosity of media affects the water-holding capacity and aeration, significantly. For a growing media to perform better in respect of plant growth and yield, the porosity level should always be in optimum range. In growing media, the porosity can be developed by varying the ingredients to be used for preparing growing media. In this respect, the following points should be taken into consideration, while preparing the growing media:

1. Growing media containing large size particles involves more aeration and poor water-holding capacity.
2. Growing media with smaller size particles involves less aeration and more water-holding capacity.

The growing media with above two features are not being well for crop growing points of view, because of the following reasons:

(i) In both the features of GM, there would be restriction on plant growth.
(ii) In first case of GM, there would be quick drying or loss of water contents.
(iii) In second case of GM, there is likely to develop waterlogging situation, which is injurious to the plant health.

This advocates that the growing media (GM) should be formed by using single component with ideal particle size to constitute proper water-holding capacity. Normally, the water-holding capacity ranging from 0.8 to 6 mm is found okay in respect to develop better aeration in growing media fit to proper plant growth.

Bulk density(BD): BD is also one of the important physical properties of the growing media to cause better plant growth; and thus to result a conducive crop yield. It is defined as the weight per unit volume of porous media. An excessive bulk density of growing media denotes compaction, which is not fit for proper plant growth and development. Bulk density depends on the inherent bulk density of the ingredients and their arrangement in mass. In respect to provide a firm physical support to the plants the bulk density (weight) of growing media should always be in high range. However, it creates problem in handling and shipping of GM.

7.5.2 Chemical Properties

The important chemical properties of growing media fit to cause a proper plant growth and yield, are narrated as under:

1. Fertility status
2. pH
3. Cation Exchange Capacity (CEC)
4. Electrical Conductivity (EC)

Fertility status: It is well known that soon after emergence, the young growing plants/ seedlings extract the nutrients from the seeds. After that, they depend on the nutrients available in growing media. On fertility status of growing media, the following points are importantly considered to follow:

- Many people prefer to use the GM having inherently low fertility status such as peat-vermiculite. This is just to discourage the problem "damping-off" during establishment phase; and also to supply the fertilizers (soluble) as per requirement of the media during crop life cycle.
- In case of non-availability of requisite fertilizers or because of their high cost, the organic manures or compost can be suitably added to the growing media to maintain its required fertility status.
- Furthermore, few plants grow better in low fertilization case; accordingly, the fertility status of GM should be kept low.
- Also, the beneficial microorganisms such as mycorrhizal fungi require low fertility level to get establish. In this condition a low fertility status of GM may be OK.

pH: It is used as an index to measure the acidity or alkalinity level of growing media. The pH value varies minimum 0 to maximum 14. On the basis of pH, the growing media are characterized as under:

1. pH below 7: indicates acidic nature.
2. pH above 7: indicates alkaline nature.

The pH level of growing media plays role on plant's growth by creating effects or control on nutrient's availability to the plants for their uptake. As per research findings, majority of the native plants tend to grow at the pH between 5.5 and 6.5. On the other hand, some of the species are tolerant to high/low pH levels, also. Few other observations on pH are as follows,

(i) At high pH level the availability of Phosphorus gets declined because it gets bind with the Iron and Aluminum ions at low pH level and with the Calcium at high pH level.
(ii) The availability of Nitrogen is about to uniform at all pH levels.
(iii) pH affects the availability of micro-nutrients such as Iron. At high pH the iron gets converted into Iron Chloride, which is most common showing nutrient deficiency in nursery stocks.
(iv) The effect of pH on availability of Sulphur and Calcium is not so influencing.

Apart from above, the extremely high as well as extremely low pH levels affect majority of the pathogens and beneficial microorganisms present in the soil media. Especially, at low pH the young plants are likely to damping-off fungi.

Also, the most desirable extent of pH level for different targets are presented in Table 7.1.

Table 7.1 Level of pH requirement of growing media for different targets

S. No.	Target	pH
1.	General purpose	5.2 to 6.2*
2.	Seed germination	5.0 to 6.0**
3.	Root cuttings	5.0 to 6.0

*With a target of 5.8 when wetting out
**With a target wet-out at 5.6

Interpretation of pH

The pH value of any medium or solution, in spite to depict the salinity and alkalinity status of the same, it also predicts the availability of nutrients to the plant, present in growing media. The H^+ concentration primarily affects the exchange complex and also to the nutrient's solubility. At low pH the solubility of some nutrients such as Iron and few other micro-nutrients is found to a greater range. However, many elements are also found insoluble at the pH less than 4.2. This advocates that, it is very essential to optimize the pH value of growing media in proper range to ensure the availability of all essential nutrients/elements present in the growing media, to the plants for their uptake. The range of pH values for soilless growing media, required for proper plant growth and development is presented in Table 7.2.

Table 7.2 Range of pH values for soilless media

pH value of soilless media	Category (rating)
4.5 or less	Extremely low
4.6–4.7	Very low
4.8–4.9	Low
5.0–5.1	Slightly low
5.2–5.5	Optimum
5.6–5.8	Slightly high
5.9–6.3	High
6.4–6.8	Very high
6.9 and more	Extremely high

Modification of pH

Sometimes, the growing media to be used for crop growing does not contain proper pH, in result there is development of harmful effect on plant response by affecting the nutrient's availability. In this condition, it is urgently required to modify the pH level of growing media. This is carried out by mixing the chemical substances, as described below:

Limestone: This is the Calcium Carbonate ($CaCO_3$) is also known as ground limestone. Limestone is very common material, used for raising the pH of growing media. The effectiveness depends on its purity level, which is assessed by determining the value of Calcium Carbonate Equivalent (CCE). One Calcium Carbonate Equivalent is equal to 50.045 grams of $CaCO_3$.

Hydrated lime: This is the Calcium Hydroxide, is also used for modifying the pH of growing media. Hydrated lime is mainly used for fast reduction in pH value. In comparison to limestone, it shares more ions to the soluble salts available in growing media, because of this reason its amount is reduced by 33 to 50% as compared to the ground limestone, for application.

Dolomite: It is the Calcium/Magnesium Carbonate, is also used for raising the pH level of growing media. Its action is same to the limestone. This solves two purposes, i.e. (i) modifies (increase) the pH value, and (ii) adds magnesium, essential for plant growth. This is the reason that dolomite is particularly preferred in the condition when Magnesium content is not available in the soluble/granular fertilizers to be used for fertigation thorough drip system. Its quantity is determined on the basis of CEC and existing pH of the growing media.

Sometimes, the growing media involves high pH, which is not deemed fit for the plant. In this condition, the lowering of media pH is essentially required. For this purpose, the Agricultural Sulphur or Flowers of Sulphur is used. It does the action by converting the Agricultural Sulphur into Sulphur Dioxide, which depends very much on the availability of bacteria in growing media. Because of this reason the rate of lowering of pH is low, in this case.

Cation Exchange Capacity (CEC): In growing media, its function or importance is to hold the positively charged ions. It also reflects the nutrients storage capacity of growing media. In other words, it depicts fertigation requirement for the grown plants in growing media. In general, majority of the growing media are inherently infertile. In this condition, the role of CEC is very important to attract the contrasting (positive) charged ions. In crop farming under protected environment using artificial growing media the plant root system exchanges excess charged ions for forming charged nutrient ions, which are transported to the foliage for growth and development of the plant. In container or pot nurseries, the used growing media requires very high level of CEC, because on watering (irrigation) the leaching of nutrients from container is at very high rate.

Electrical Conductivity (EC): It represents the salinity status of growing media. EC also shows the ability of soil water to carry electrical current and the nutrients available for plant's uptake. The electrical conductivity of growing media should be in proper range to have better effect in terms of plant growth and the yield, also. The range of electrical conductivity categorizing the salinity status of growing media is presented in Table 7.3, could be followed for testing the growing media. Also, the desired level of EC for different targets is shown in Table 7.4.

Table 7.3 Range of EC for defining the salinity level of growing media

Electrical Conductivity EC, (μS/cm)	Salinity level
0 to 1200	Low
1200 to 2500	Normal
2500 to 3000	High
3000 to 4000	Excessive
More than 4000	Lethal

(*Source*: Timmer and Parton, 1982)

Table 7.4 Range of EC requirement of growing media for different targets

S. No.	Target	EC(mmhos/cm)
1.	General purpose	1.0–2.0
2.	Seed germination	0.5–1.1
3.	Propagation	0.5–1.1

7.5.3 Biological Properties

This is very common that, the growing media used for crop cultivation under protected mode are likely to contain the pathogenic bacteria or fungi with them. As such they are not fit to use. They must be treated through sterilization or pasteurization techniques before use. However, the growing media which are organic based, are mostly found free from pathogens or weed seeds, need not to sterilize or pasteurize. Similarly, the vermiculite and perlite are already sterilized during their manufacturing process, by exposing to the temperature as high as 1,000°C. Similarly, well prepared composts are also being pest free, as most of the pathogens are killed during composting process. In addition, several beneficial microorganisms are also added in composting process, which enrich compost's quality. Furthermore, the composts prepared with the help of barks of some tree species, contain sufficient amount of microbes, which are effective to suppress the fungal pathogens and nematodes, as well (Castillo 2004).

7.6 INGREDIENTS OF GROWING MEDIA

The ingredients used for preparation of growing media are divided in following two groups:

(i) Organic ingredients, and
(ii) Inorganic ingredients,

These are described as under.

7.6.1 Organic Ingredients

The most commonly used organic ingredients for preparing growing media to cultivate the crop under protected mode are the compost, coconut coir, peat moss, bark, rice hulls, sawdust and locally available materials. The ingredients must have the following properties:

(i) Light in weight,
(ii) High water-holding capacity and CEC, and
(iii) Minor amount of mineral nutrients, as well.

However, some of the organic ingredients require screening or composting of local raw materials to be used, which should be essentially done before their use. The common organic ingredients are narrated as under:

Peat: It is one of the main components for most of the soilless growing media. It is mainly derived from the remains of aquatic, marsh, bog, swamp vegetations, etc. preserved in water in partially decomposed state. Since, the sources of peat are different; therefore, their nutrient status also varies, widely. In addition, their decomposition level, minerals availability and acidity status also affect the nutrients status in peats.

Peat moss: It is the decomposed organic matter. The most common plant material in peat moss is the Sphagnum moss. In present practice, the Sphagnum peat moss is commonly used as organic ingredient for preparing growing media. Peat mosses have varying physical and chemical properties. The pH of Sphagnum peat moss varies from 3.0 to 4.0, i.e., acidic in nature. The pH level can be brought to the level, best for most of the crops by treating with the help of dolomite at the rate of 8 to 20 kg/m^3. In the areas having alkaline water, its application at low rate is found suitable. Due to low pH, the peat mosses are being free from pathogenic diseases. Various advantages of Peat Moss are mentioned below:

***Managing pH*:** This is an attractive point of Peat Moss. In the plants requiring acidic environment, this could be the best for use. In other sense, it can also be used to neutralize the alkalinity of soil media by declining the pH level.

***Excellent water-holding capacity*:** The excellent water retention capacity is an important feature of Peat Moss, but little bit poor regarding drainage point of view. However, its drainage potential can be enhanced by adding sand contents.

***Disease-resistant*:** Peat mosses are available in sterilized form. In result, there is no need of taking additional measures for sterilization or pasteurization to make it disease resistant. This property makes it an excellent growing media. Peat Moss is taken as one of the best ingredients for development of young plant roots. Because of this feature, sometimes, it is also used for seedling preparation.

***Suitable for hydroponic*:** Peat moss provides an excellent result in hydroponic or soilless media based crop farming system. The plant root system gets promptly develop, as result the nutrients uptake, plant growth and yields are found in better range.

***No compaction*:** Peat Moss is free from compaction effect. It can be placed very smoothly in spongy form on top soil surface. In clay soils it acts as soil conditioner.

Apart from above advantages the Peat Moss also involves some disadvantages, too; they are mainly (i) Not suitable to certain plants to grow such as lavender, ginger, daylilies, blackberries, and raspberries; and (ii) problem regarding soil cracking.

Compost: It is also used as ingredient for preparation of growing media. This is prepared by decomposing organic materials. The suitable raw materials which can be used for composting are given in Table 7.5.

Table 7.5 List of raw materials used for composting

S. No.	Raw materials
1.	Plant waste
	(i) Vegetable/fruit scraps
	(ii) Leaves
	(iii) Weeds
	(iv) Orchard pruning
	(v) Straw
	(vi) Tree bark

(Contd.)

S. No.	Raw materials
2.	Agricultural byproducts
	(i) Coffee pulp
	(ii) Sugarcane bagasse
	(iii) Rice hulls
	(iv) Wooden waste
	(v) Sawdust
3.	Animal waste
	(i) Manures
	(ii) Feathers
	(iii) Bedding
4.	Aquatic weeds
	(i) Fish part
	(ii) Sea weeds

In order to prepare compost the raw materials are chopped or cut into small pieces, normally 1 to 5 cm in length and piled to allow them for decomposing. As precautionary measure, the piles are mixed at some suitable time interval to maintain proper aeration. At the same time the moisture level of piled materials is also maintained to the tune of about 50%. During composting process, the temperature of piled materials gets change over time because of microbial decomposition. Initially, within few days, the temperature is likely to rise from 38 to 49°C due to decomposition of smaller and easily degradable materials. Thereafter, the temperature gets rise in the range of 54 to 65°C due to decay of greater amount of materials. Further, the maximum temperature equal to 71°C of pile is maintained for a long period of time to kill the weed seeds and the fungal pathogens, also. Finally, temperatures gets declined to about 40°C, which further reduced during "curing operation". The monitoring of temperature can be done with the help of thermometer. In this way, the compost (mature) can be produced in the period of 2 to 4 months in humid tropics. The ratio between amount of prepared compost and the raw materials used is 2:3 by volume. The prepared compost (mature) should not be used or incorporated in growing media, immediately. Before use, it should be assured that there is no any unpleasant odor or heat content in the prepared compost (mature). It can be checked by the colour of the compost. Good quality compost comprises dark colour and a strong earthy smell. Also, the texture of compost must be friable and crumby nature. In addition, the earthworms and soil insects are also being available in the compost, signify the completion of composting process; and accordingly, the prepared compost becomes ready to use. The prepared compost is being hot and leaves a short of smell like manure or ammonia.

The quality of compost can be assessed by determining the C/N ratio, which predicts the level of available nitrogen, i.e., in limiting amount or excessive. Regarding C/N ratio value the predictions are as below:

S. No.	C:N ratio	Prediction
1.	High	Risk of non-availability of nitrogen to the plants.
2.	Greater than 15 : 1	Immobilization of available nitrogen.
3.	Below 15 : 1	Nitrogen becomes available for plant uptake.
4.	As low as 10 : 1	Compost is considered equivalent to fertilizers.

The composts prepared using the raw material "wood wastes" like sawdust, etc. have very high C:N ratio to the tune of 400:1 to 1,300:1. The C:N ratio of compost prepared by using the tree bark, is considerably lesser than the sawdust, i.e., from 70 : 1 to 500 : 1, is broadly preferred for horticultural purposes.

The important characteristics of compost as one of the ingredients of growing media are mentioned as under:

(i) The bulk density and porosity are varying depending on the raw materials used for composting.
(ii) pH varies from 6 to 8.
(iii) Cation Exchange capacity (CEC) is high in range.

Shredded barks: The shredded barks used as ingredients of growing media play significant role in improving the status of aeration of growing media. It also changes the quality of growing media significantly, after its decomposition. The bark may be the fresh, aged or composted. The aged barks involve less humus and greater nitrogen depletion as compared to the composted barks.

Pine bark: This is also used as the component for preparing growing media. Normally, pine barks are preferred over hardwood bark, as it has tendency to resist more against decomposition and also contains less leachable organic acids. The Pine barks are stripped from the trees and are milled to a granular level. Thereafter, milled bark materials are screened into different sizes as per requirement. A good growing media contains 70 to 80% (by volume) of Pine bark's particles ranging from 0.6 to 9.5 mm size. At coarse size milled bark materials, the water retention is not being adequate for plant growth.

Hardwood bark: This is also used as one of the excellent organic substrate ingredients or components for preparation of growing media. The bark is mechanically processed for milling into small particles. The proportion of milled particle's size out of the total bark materials used, is as per below:

S. No.	Particle size (mm)	Percentage of total bark materials
1.	12.7	55%
2.	Larger than 3.2	10%
3.	0.8	35%

Coconut coir: This is another organic ingredient used for preparation of growing media. The coco based byproduct such as coco coir, coir dust, coco peat, or simply coir, etc. are considered as one of the excellent organic materials for preparing potted type growing media. The physical and chemical properties of coir are about close to the Peat Moss. Its pH generally varies from 6 to 7, which is higher than the Sphagnum Peat Moss. Because of this reason the requirement of Limestone to modify its pH level is very less. Its quality has been proved to be the best over others. Its various conducive/desirous qualities are narrated as under:

- High water-holding capacity.
- pH varies from 6 to 7.
- CEC is low in range.

- EC in acceptable range.
- Excellent drainage characteristics.
- Free from weeds and pathogens.
- Involvement of physical resiliency.
- Slow decomposition characteristics.
- Easy wettability.

Sawdust: A raw sawdust bears high C:N ratio value, which impact is negative in context to nutrients (mainly nitrogen) availability in growing media. However, its properties can be improved by composting it. In general, the quality of sawdusts and their suitability are being different depending on the types of wood materials, used. This is because of the reason that the origin source (wood) of respective sawdust involves different chemical properties. This advocates that the growing media constituted by using different sourced sawdust contains different qualitative status, which may or may not be suitable for plant growth and development. For example, the sawdust from the trees of coastal area can contain high level of salt contents; accordingly, the quality of prepared growing media using this sawdust may not be fit for use, because of consisting of high concentration of salt contents. It is therefore, suggested that before using the sawdust for preparation of growing media, its source must be determined, and quality of the same should also be properly assessed. If chemical properties are found Okay, then it should be allowed to use for the purpose; otherwise no. Moreover, its important properties are pointed as under:

- Bulk density is low in range.
- Porosity is high (air) while moderate for water contents.
- pH varies from 3 to 6.
- Cation Exchange Capacity (CEC) is also in low range.

Rice hulls: It is the sheaths of rice grains, treated as the waste product. Rice hulls are used for various purposes such as mulching, fuel and also as one of the ingredients of growing media. These are easily decomposed and add organic contents to the soil. As ingredient, these are mainly used with the locally available peat for preparing growing media. Research finding reveals that in nurseries these are also used for composting purpose. In growing media, the rice hulls are used for creating drainage and aeration properties. Especially, in peat based growing media the large size particles of parboiled fresh rice hulls can be more effective to increase the drainage as well as aeration effects, without nitrogen immobilization. Also, the rice hulls are used as one of the economical ingredients for perlite. Few important characteristics are listed below:

- Bulk density is low.
- Porosity is low (air) while moderate for water contents.
- pH varies from 5 to 6.
- Cation Exchange Capacity (CEC) is also low.

7.6.2 Inorganic Ingredients

The use of inorganic ingredients is mainly to modify or maintain the structural system of growing media, enable to create an optimum level of aeration and drainage, as well. In other words, these are used to maintain the structure of macro-pore spaces in proper order. Many of the inorganic ingredients involve very low range of Cation Exchange Capacity (CEC) and they provide inert base (chemically) to the growing media. Similarly, few have high range of bulk density, beneficial to develop structural strength. The inorganic ingredients, which are commonly used for preparing growing media are the gravel, sand, vermiculite, perlite, pumice, and polystyrene beads. These are described below:

Vermiculite: It is hydrated Aluminum-Iron-Magnesium Silicate material, is commonly used as inorganic ingredient for preparing growing media. Based on the particle size, these are produced or prepared in four different grades. Particle size affects the aeration and water-holding capacity of the growing media. In which grade-2 is preferred, when more aeration is required in growing media. Grade-3 vermiculite results a high water-holding capacity in growing media. In many of the nurseries located in temperate regions 1:1 mixture of Peat Moss and coarse Vermiculite is preferred. Vermiculite offers various advantages over others, are narrated as under:

***Merits*:**

- It has low bulk density.
- Water-holding capacity is high, which is about five times of its weight.
- pH is neutral (6 to 8)
- Cation Exchange Capacity (CEC) is also high; accordingly, holds good amount of nutrients as reserve stock for later release.
- Potassium and Magnesium are in small amount. The other nutrients are needed as supplement from the fertilizer's source.
- It can absorb the water ranging from 40 to 54 liters/m^3.

***Demerits*:** Few important demerits are pointed as under:

- It has poor physical stability after wetting.
- Once it is mixed, wetted and compressed, does not gain physical character.
- If moist vermiculite is compressed, then there is expansion of particles. This may lead to collapse and slipping apart.

Perlite: It is basically a volcanic origin siliceous material. In growing media its function is to increase the aeration level. It is mixed in the range of 10 to 30%. Perlites are available in different grades but they are not standardized. The size of particles is different in different grades perlites. Normally, for preparation of growing media 6 & 8 grade perlites, which are known as "propagation grade", are preferred to use. The important characteristics of perlite are mentioned as under:

- Adheres water to their surfaces.
- Perlite does not absorb water.
- Bulk density is very low.
- It makes the growing media highly drained and light weight.
- It is rigid and does not get compress, easily.
- It contains good porosity.
- It is completely sterilized.
- Its CEC is minimum.
- Its pH varies from 6 to 8.

- During its mixing there is possibility of lung irritation, as it contains very fine particles that get mixed in the air stream and entered the lung through breathing.

Pumice and Cinder: These two are also the inorganic ingredients used for preparation of growing media. Both are the volcanic rocks, in which Pumice majorly consists of Silicon Dioxide and Aluminum Oxide. In addition, the iron, calcium, magnesium and sodium are also there in Pumice, but in small quantity. Important properties of Pumice are briefed as under:

- Pumice particles are porous in nature.
- Improves aeration and porosity.
- Retains sufficient water.
- Resists compaction effect.
- Bulk density is low.
- Porosity (water) is also low, but for air contents it is high.
- pH varies from 6 to 8.
- CEC is also low.

Cinder is often known as Scoria, is also a volcanic rock. It is commonly used for preparing growing media in volcanic areas.

Sands: It is another inorganic ingredient, which is readily available and is being inexpensive as compared to the others. Sands are derived from calcareous sources, i.e., the coral or lime-stones, are rich in Calcium Carbonate ($CaCO_3$). Its suitability mainly depends on types, particle size, etc. During preparation of growing media this is used for enhancing porosity level. In contrast, the fine sands (0.05 to 0.25 mm size) enter the existing pore spaces, leading to reduce the aeration percentage and drainage behavior of growing media. The medium size sands are also being suitable to enhance the porosity level. In course of preparation of growing media using sands as one of the ingredients, it is always suggested to wash and sterilize/pasteurize the sands before mixing in the media. As demerit, sands add weight to the growing media, which is not desirable. The main characteristics of sands are mentioned, below:

(i) Bulk density is very high.
(ii) Porosity to retain water is moderate.
(iii) Porosity for air content is high.
(iv) pH is highly variable.
(v) CEC is low.

Polystyrene: It is also known by its trade name Styrofoam, also used as inorganic component for preparation of growing media. Its few important properties are listed as under,

- It increases aeration and drainage behavior of growing media.
- It reduces the bulk density.
- It is highly resistant to decomposition.
- It is not biodegradable.

7.7 TREATMENT OF INGREDIENTS

This is considered as one of the most important steps under formulation of growing media to be used for cultivation of high valued crops in protected environment, i.e. the greenhouse. Since, preparation of growing media involves expenditure of money; therefore, it is always expected that its use must be remunerative multifold over the expenditure incurred. This is only possible when formulated growing media performs well. The performance of growing media depends to a lot on the quality and quantity of the ingredients used. Quality of ingredients is mainly judged on the basis of their disease freeness, etc. On this ground, the treatment of ingredients to be used becomes very essential to ensure a good quality. Treatments must be done before their use. Broadly, the treatments are carried out in following aspects:

1. Flushing or removal of salts.
2. Pasteurization for killing or removing unwanted organisms.
3. Shifting or screening.

Flushing of salts: This treatment is carried out for removal of salt contents from the ingredients to be used for preparing growing media. It is essential to treat the ingredients, otherwise; the present salt content can develop negative effect on plant growth due to salinity/alkalinity effects. Normally, the ingredients such as coir, sand, sawdust, etc. taken from near to the ocean, and the composts having excessive soluble salts are essentially treated for removing the salts from them. The flushing is one of the methods followed for this purpose. In this method the salt contents are removed by flushing the ingredients using fresh water. This action is continued till concentration of salt becomes lesser than the critical limit. The flushing can be accomplished by leaching the salt content with the help of rainwater or fresh water.

Sterilization: It refers to the process by which all forms of microbial lives are removed from the objects. In other words, a micro-biologically sterilized item is free from any kind of living microorganisms. In sterilization process the microorganisms may be killed, inhibited or removed by exposing the materials to the lethal agents and also in the form of elimination of cells from the medium, physically. The lethal agents may be the physical, chemical/ionic and also in the form of liquid, as well. The process of soil sterilization is presented below:

***Soil sterilization*:** Most often the soil media used for plant's growing or cultivation, is congenial for growth of microorganisms such as the bacteria, fungi, actinomycetes, protozoa, viruses, insects, nematodes and weed seeds, as well. Among the microorganisms present in soil media, few may be in the form of beneficial and few non-beneficial (harmful). The non-beneficial microorganisms are mainly the pathogens, nematodes, insects, etc. cause disease problems in crops/plants. Removal of these non-beneficial microorganisms from growing media is very essential for attaining a proper growth in the plants. The sterilization/pasteurization is one of the most appropriate treatments for this, can be suitably used for the purpose.

***Methods*:** Several methods/techniques and treatment agents are available for disinfection or sterilization of soil media. Among them each and every method/agent has its own limit for application. However, selecting a most suitable method is one of the main tasks. However, the followings are few important points, taken into consideration, while selecting the method,

(i) Desired efficiency
(ii) Applicability
(iii) Toxicity level
(iv) Availability
(v) Cost involved
(vi) Effects on objects, etc.

Most commonly the sterilization of soil or substrate is carried by the methods of (i) soil solarisation; and (ii) chemical (fumigants) treatments, are described as under:

Soil solarisation: This is one of the most-friendly used techniques for soil sterilization. Although, it is not a foolproof technique for soil sterilization, but kills so many harmful bacteria and pathogens, present in the soil media, effectively. In this method, the lethal agent to be used is the high intensity solar radiation, which likely to available during summer months, i.e., from April to June. Using this method, the plant pathogenic organisms, insect pests, nematodes, and weeds are removed or controlled. This is carried out by means of fine transparent polyethylene films of about 25-micron thickness. In nutshell, this method is known as soil solarisation. The following steps can be followed for solarisation of soil media:

Step (i): Plough the field to a proper depth so that the harmful bacteria and pathogens existing in the soil can get exposed to the sunlight.

Step (ii): Provide a light irrigation to the ploughed field. This is for creating moisture content in the soil media, which causes increase in moist temperature in soil, effective to kill the unwanted microorganisms.

Step (iii): Cover the ploughed field with the help of 25-micron thick transparent UV stabilized polyethylene film for the period of 20 to 30 days. It should always be taken care that the edges of poly films must be properly covered with the soil, so that the air may not enter in the covered soil mass.

Soil Sterilization by Chemicals

The chemicals, namely Formaldehyde and Hydrogen Peroxide are commonly used for sterilization of soil media. This is presented as under.

(1) Formaldehyde: It is one of the best sterilizing agents, used for this purpose. It kills the harmful soil microbes, very effectively. In market, Formaldehyde is available as aqueous solution of Formalin which contains 37 to 40% formaldehyde. Sterilization procedure is shown under following steps:

Step (i): Prepare the solution by mixing 4 liters Formalin in about 19 liters water.

Step (ii): Take the soil or root substrate from the field.

Step (iii): Pour the soil or root substrate in the solution or spray on the soil @5 ml/m^2. Application rate is decided on the basis of soil moisture content, soil depth and soil types, as well.

Step (iv): Cover the treated soil or root substrate with a thin plastic film to retain the generated fumes below plastic cover.

Step (v): Remove the plastic film after 7-days period, i.e., removal of Formaldehyde fume. Normally, complete removal of Formaldehyde smell or fume from the soil takes place in 15 to 20 days period.

Once the sterilization process is over, the sowing or planting operation can be done, thereafter. This method involves following limitations:

- Its effect on nematode is not so impressive.
- In standing crop it is avoided to follow because Formalin is a biocide, which inhibits the plant growth.

- It reduces the activities of living organisms present in the soil media.
- It is also detrimental to the health and safety concern.

(2) Hydrogen Peroxide: In this sterilization, the soil is treated with the help of Hydrogen Peroxide containing Nano particle Silver. This can be accomplished very easily with the help of drip system assembled with fertigation unit. The Hydrogen Peroxide solution kept in tank, is connected to the fertigation system, which automatically delivers the solution to the soil. As precautionary measures the soil bed should be lightly watered before applying Hydrogen Peroxide treatment. The recommended dose of solution varies from 35 to 40 ml/sqm. After treatment is completed, the operations such as sowing/planting can be started from the next day.

Pasteurization: In pasteurization the pathogenic fungi and bacteria are removed from the ingredients. However, for growing plants the complete sterilization of media is not desirable, as there is existence of several beneficial microorganisms that can be antagonistic to pathogens. The inorganic ingredients such as Vermiculite and Perlite are inherently sterilized. In contrast, the organic ingredients are always under suspicion about presence of pathogens, etc. Similarly, in case of composts the pathogens and the other available pests get destroy during composting process due to release of intense heat. The field soils, used for preparing growing media are essentially required to pasteurize, as there is full possibility of existence of pathogens and so many other damaging bacteria, too.

The heat pasteurization is commonly used for treatment. The availability of heat can be assured from the sources such as moist heat from steam, aerated steam, boiling water heat, dry heat from flame, electric pasteurizers, microwave ovens and the solar heat, as well. At commercial level the pasteurization of growing media and ingredients is done by using expensive equipments. At small scale the manual method is more feasible. In which small batches of media are spread in the form of thin layer, normally not more than 15cm deep, below a black colour polyethylene/plastic tarp placed on inclined platform, in open ground to create maximum exposure of sunlight. In this process the temperature ranging from 60 to 80°C is retained for about 30-minute duration to kill the pathogens or bacteria present in the soil media. The range of temperature required for pasteurizing a particular target from the ingredients is shown in Table 7.6. After sterilization treatment is over, the sterilized materials are placed to the mixing place, and are allowed to cool, properly. And finally the pasteurized soil is used for preparing the growing media.

Table 7.6 Range of temperature required to pasteurize the materials (Baker (1957)

S. No.	Target	Temperature (°C)
1.	Fungal pathogens and Nematodes	47 to 59
2.	Insects	60 to 70
3.	All Bacteria	70 to 81
4.	Most weed seeds	70 to 81
5.	Viruses	70 to 81
6.	Resistant weed seeds and viruses	94 to 100

Note: The heating should be continued till achieving the mentioned temperature for at least 30-minutes duration.

Screening: This treatment is followed to the ingredients such as soil, sand, and cinder, mainly. Screening is carried out for obtaining a desired particle size of the given ingredient, suitable to growing media. The small or fine size particles are likely to choke the drainage path (holes) and also hinder the aeration, are not being fit for media preparation. Similarly, the large particles develop big size voids, affect the root development, are also not being fit for growing media formulation. The medium size particles are desirable. In order to achieve this size particle, the screening of ingredients is carried out in two steps. In first step, the screening is done by using small size mesh to remove unwanted small size materials. And in second step the large size mesh is used to remove the big size materials from the ingredients of first step screening. In this way, after second screening step the medium size materials are left, which are used for preparing growing media.

7.8 PREPARATION OF GROWING MEDIA

In general, the following three types of growing media are very common for container type of nurseries:

Seed propagating media: This type of growing media is prepared for seed propagation or seed germination or establishment of germinants called sprouting seeds. For better result, these growing media must be sterilized. In addition, they should also have a good level of fine texture for maintaining high moisture content in the surroundings of germinating seeds.

Root cutting media: This type of growing media is prepared for root cuttings. The growing media should be highly porous to prevent waterlogging, beside causing a good aeration for root development.

Transplant media: This type of growing media is developed for transplanting small seedlings or root cuttings in a big size container. The growing media should be coarser in nature.

Preparing Methods

The preparation of growing media by mixing the ingredients in proper quantity is the primary step. A little variation in ingredients to suit the requirement, makes the media inefficient to create proper effects on the plant growth or yield potential, as well. The mixing of ingredients for media preparation should be accomplished by an experienced person, who can ensure the quantity of ingredient and mixing them, properly. Mixing of ingredients should be done in such a way that there is uniformity in distribution. In addition, the occurrence of problems such as compaction, contamination, etc. may not be there in growing media. In general, the mixing of ingredients is carried out by using the following methods:

(i) Manual method, and
(ii) Mechanical method.

Manual method: This method follows the mixing works by hand. It is being suitable for preparation of small batches of growing media. The required ingredients/components and amendments (if require) are taken by volume or weight basis and are mixed together in a bucket, manually. In case of large batches, the components are kept on clean and hard surface, and are mixed together by using hand shovel. The ingredients are piled on one another; and lastly the amendments are broadcasted or spread uniformly over the piled materials. Thereafter, using large scoop shovel the piled materials along with amendment is turned and mixed thoroughly. Mixing should be started from the edge of piled ingredients. However, care must be taken that all piled ingredients should be properly mixed by repeating the process several times. As per observation, few of organic ingredients repel water content on their drying. In this case the piled materials should be frequently misted with the help of water at a certain interval. This process is repeated till the completion of ingredient's mixing in proper way.

Mechanical method: In case of large batches of nursery raising using growing media, huge amount of ingredients is required to mix for preparation of growing media. In this condition manual method is not found okay. The mixing machine is found well to use for this purpose. Normally, the cement mixer can be well for mixing of huge quantity of materials. However, excessive mixing should be avoided, as there is possibility of breakdown of ingredients to small size. This possibility is more common in case of Vermiculite and Peat Moss ingredients. Also, an overmixed material is likely to get compact very soon, after its filling in the container. The compaction of growing media always causes reduction in aeration level along with development of water stagnation in container, which is injurious to the plant health. The methods followed for preparation of different forms of growing media is presented in Table 7.7.

Table 7.7 Methods for preparing different types of growing media

Media type	Properties	Examples of media (by volume)	Reference
Seed propagation	♦ Maintains uniform moisture around germinating seeds, which is not too wet or too dry ♦ No fertilizer ♦ Free from pests and diseases.	♦ 3-parts Perlite and 1-part coarse Vermiculite (for beach plants). ♦ 4-parts Perlite and 1-part Peat. ♦ 3-parts small rinsed Cinders and 1 part Peat and 1-part Perlite.	Lilleeng-Rosenberger (2005)
		♦ Fine, washed quartz sand (0.5 to 1 mm)] (100% sand needs frequent watering).	Jaenicke (1999)
Rooting cuttings	♦ Porous to prevent water-logging and to allow a good level of aeration for proper root formation and also to provide support to the cuttings. ♦ Free from diseases and weed seeds.	♦ 3-parts Perlite and 1-part Vermiculite. ♦ 3-parts small rinsed Cinders and 1-part Peat and 1-part Perlite. ♦ 100% rinsed small cinder (but needs frequent misting).	Lilleeng-Rosenberger (2005)
		♦ 100% washed quartz sand (2 mm).	Jaenicke (1999)
		♦ 1-part grit or fine gravel and 1-part washed sand and 1-part aged sawdust. ♦ 1-part grit or fine gravel and 1-part aged sawdust.	Longman (1998)
Transplant	♦ Coarser and heavy enough to keep the plants upright. ♦ It may contain some nutrients.	♦ 1-part Peat and 1-part Vermiculite. ♦ 2-parts Cinder or perlite to 1-part well-decayed compost and 1-part Peat.	Lilleeng-Rosenberger (2005)

(Contd.)

Media type	Properties	Examples of media (by volume)	Reference
	♦ Free from diseases and weed seeds.	♦ 1-part coarse sand, 2-parts Coconut coir, 1-part topsoil/duff.	Miller and Jones (1995)
		♦ 2-parts bagasse to 1-part rice hulls and 1-part alluvial soil.	
		♦ 1-part well-composed grasses and 1-part rice hulls or Pumice.	
		♦ 3-parts composed bark and 1-part sand and 1-part shale.	
		♦ 2-parts well-decayed compost and 2-parts sand and 1-part clay soil.	Wightman (1999)
		♦ 3-parts coir and 1-part compost.	Lovelace (2011)
		♦ 30% composted rice hulls, 50% pine bark, and 20% sand.	

7.8.1 Use of Amendments

The ingredients of growing media also comprises few amendments to use, besides several organic and inorganic constituents (ingredients). This is to add some additional properties in growing media required for proper plant growth and development. Amendments are added as supplemental material to the tune of less than 10%. Overall, the percentage contribution of organic and inorganic components is quite large to that of the amendments. In amendment's application three points are always considered, namely (i) To what it will accomplish; (ii) Its necessity; and (iii) Its injury effects. The list of commonly used amendments for preparation of growing media is illustrated in Table 7.8.

Table 7.8 List of commonly used amendments for preparation of growing media

S. No.	Amendment
1.	Dolomitic limestone
2.	Starter fertilizers
3.	Controlled-release fertilizers
4.	Surfactants
5.	Hydrophilic gels
6.	Mycorrhizal Inoculum
7.	Rock Phosphate
8.	Other amendments

Dolomitic limestone: This is also called "lime". It is used for raising the pH level and adding Calcium content as one of requisite nutrients for plant growth and development. In general, it is recommended to use in the condition when the plant to be grown, requires neutral or alkaline pH medium.

Starter fertilizers: Addition of this amendment becomes essential, when fertigation to the grown plant is not possible due to some reasons. Although, few growing media are already provided with some quantity of fertilizers, but to ensure the availability of fertilizers/mineral nutrients to the young developing plants for their quick access, the use of starter fertilizer becomes essential in the growing media. Also, it is very important to note that the addition of fertilizers (soluble) in large quantity is injurious to the plant, as they develop salt toxicity effect in media.

Controlled-Release Fertilizer (CRF): These are granulated fertilizers, release the nutrients gradually in the soil. CRFs are also known as controlled-availability fertilizer, delayed-release fertilizer, metered-release fertilizer, and sometimes, also as the slow-acting fertilizer. These fertilizers are used to improve the nutrient use efficiency of the plants.

Surfactants: These are the chemical amendments, also known as wetting agents. Surfactants are used to increase the wettability of few hydrophobic organic materials, such as Peat Moss and Pine bark and also for breaking the surface tension of water. However, these are not recommended for general use like others, because in some cases they showed adverse effects on plant growth. This advocate that prior to use this material, it is very essential to get assure that really it is needed or not. It is also advised that before using, the experiences of growers must be collected on its use and impacts for taking proper decision about its application.

Hydrophilic gels: These are the "hydrogels". Chemically, they are cross-linked polymers. Hydrogels have the property to absorb the water many times of their own weight. They are used to enhance the water-holding capacity of growing media. And accordingly to make available the moisture contents to the plants for longer periods. In nutshell, the hydrogels are the plant saving materials against moisture stress.

Mycorrhizal inoculum: The mycorrhizal plays role in providing essential elements and water to the plants, in addition to contribute for soil formation. In growing media, these are used for inoculation of native plants with the mycorrhizal fungi. These are incorporated in the ingredients of growing media during their mixing operation. However, these are not suggested for their general use. Prior to use this material as one of the amendments, its necessity must be verified. If it is really required, then should be added; otherwise, no. As per research study, it has been noticed that the association of Arbuscular Mycorrhiza Fungi (AMF) is effective to increase the plant height, stem diameter, number of leaves per plant, shoot and root biomass, total root length, total root projected area, total root surface area and total root volume, significantly (Wu and Zou, 2010; Wu et al., 2011a).

Rock phosphate: This amendment is used for increasing the availability of phosphorus in the growing media. However, its concentration should not be more than the requirement of the plant specific; otherwise, it may create hindrance in development of mycorrhizae; and also interfere the absorption of mineral nutrients (Wilkerson 2011).

Other amendments: In addition to afore-mentioned amendments used in growing media, some of the other amendments are also there, required to supplement in growing media for enhancing yield potential, water/nutrient use efficiencies, as well. These are mainly the worm castings, bone meal, kelp, guano, humic acid, compost tea, etc. used for the purpose.

7.9 EFFECT OF GROWING MEDIA CHARACTERISTICS

A growing media offers its effect on plant growth and development by its components/ ingredients, mixed. The water, air, nutrients and support are the essential requisites for plant.

In which, the requirement of water, air and support are met from the components/ingredients constituting growing media. On the other hand, the nutrients are provided from the fertilizer thorough fertilization or fertigation process. The variations in supply rate of water, air and nutrients affect the plant development. Broadly, the effect of growing media on plant growth is because of the following factors:

(i) Media components and their ratio,
(ii) Media column height in containers,
(iii) Growing media handling, and
(iv) Irrigation practices followed.

Media components and their ratio: In general, the growing media are formulated in such a way that an optimum level of porosity and thereby the water retention and aeration could be ascertained. In protected cultivation, especially under greenhouse farming system, the container filled with growing media utilizes a variety of ingredients/media comprising the soilless and soil media as well. In which, the commonly used soilless components are the Peat Moss, Vermiculite, Perlite, Coconut coir, compost, tree barks and many others. In contrast, the field soils are not found fit as they do not fulfill the requirement of aeration, drainage and water-holding capacity after filling in the container. In addition, they also need to pasteurize or fumigate to kill the pathogens, weeds and other harmful organisms present in the soil.

In addition to the selection of suitable ingredients for preparation of growing media, a proper proportion or ratio between them is also being most essential to discharge better performance by the prepared media. Most commonly, to use the media in container for greenhouse cultivation, the share of peat moss varies to the tune of 30 to 60% as singly or in combination with the Pine bark in compost form. In respect to media component and their ratio affecting the plant growth, few important points are mentioned below to follow, strictly:

- The pH is maintained to the tune of 6.0 (approx.). However, for most of the greenhouse crops the initial pH should be between 5.8 and 6.2. This is because of the reason that most of the media components are acidic in nature. The pH adjustment can be done by using the limestone.
- The level of initial wetting of growing media such as the Peat Moss and Pine bark, can be enhanced by adding non-ionic wetting agents.

Media column height in containers: The height of media column in container affects the quantum of air/water contents available in the domain of plant root system. In case of tall column height, the ratio between water-filled pore space to the air-filled space is less. This results into more aeration of root zone. In this case there is small part of saturation of media near to the bottom of the container, after drainage. On the other hand, in short height column growing media the extent of saturation zone is to a large extent of total volume of media, results into poor aeration for plant growth.

Growing media handling: The method followed to handle the growing media mainly affects its compaction level. The compaction level changes the air exchange, water-holding capacity; and thereby several other parameters, associated to the growing media. Compaction declines the aeration percentage because of drastic reduction in quantity of big size pore spaces in growing media. The effect on compaction due to media handling can be checked by lightly filling the materials in container and brushing off the excess materials from the container's top. In addition, the following points are also needs to follow, carefully, in this regard:

- At any time, the growing media containers should not be stacked.
- In Peat-based mixes the addition of water before filling the plug trays (container) results into swelling of the media. This leads to develop more aeration effect.
- In large containers the moistening of media before filling, is not found beneficial.

Irrigation practices: It is one of the important requirements for greenhouse cultivation using artificial growing media. Providing irrigation by correct amount and at proper schedule keeps the plants moisture stress free. In general, out of total water applied to the media a part of that is available to the plant uptake. In this regard, as per research trial it has been pointed that, a container of about 15cm height (6 inch) filled with growing media, when watered to a saturation level, about 60% voids are filled with water after allowing drainage of excess water, of which about 70% is available and rest is unavailable water. Amongst different growing media the peat has relatively highest level of unavailable water content as compared to the rock, at a given matric tension. Overall, the variability in water availability is being different to different types of media components. This advocates that the irrigation schedule is different for each growing media component. The "wettability" is another important characteristic of growing media, regarding supply of water in terms of irrigation, which is defined as the ability of a dry media to absorb water, when moistened. The wettability of media can be increased by using surfactant, occasionally. Surfactant facilitates to rewet the media quickly.

7.10 TESTING OF GROWING MEDIA

Once, the growing media is prepared by mixing the required ingredients, adopting proper procedure, its testing in context to response on the plants, is essential. This is because of the reason that each individual growing media shows its different response depending on quality of the ingredients used for preparation. For example in case of homemade ingredients such as compost, the quality may vary significantly as per types of materials used for composting. Accordingly, the growing media prepared by using the compost material has different potential to develop the effects on plant growth and development, as compared to the growing media prepared using the ingredients other than compost. Similarly, in case of purchased growing media there is always possibility of uncertainty in their quality. On these grounds, the testing of prepared or purchased growing media is felt essential. Testing provides conformity on quality of the object, concern. In general, the testing of growing media is carried out in following respects:

(i) Plant bioassay test, and
(ii) Test for EC.

Plant bioassay test: This is the one of the easiest and effective tests, suggested by Grubinger (2007). In this method, the sample of growing media to be used for growing the plant is collected from the container. And the seed, which is abundantly available and is fast-growing, is sown in the collected growing media. After sowing, the performance of plant in various aspects is noticed as the observation. Mostly, the following observations are taken at week period:

- Whether seed germination is at par to the expected one or not.
- Is there damping off, as the seeds grow?
- Is there incidence of pests, etc. on the germinated seedlings?
- Is the growing media stable or compacted/uncompacted or waterlogged?

The collected information on aforesaid points, provides an idea about proper or ill-functioning of the growing media in context to plant growth and development.

EC Test: This test is carried out for determining the salinity status of growing media to be used, because salinity affects the development and health of the plants. An excessive salt contents in growing media can damage the crop or even destroy the young plants, too. It is advised to measure the salinity level in routine way before and during crop cycle, so that a correct dose of fertilizers/nutrients could be applied to the crop at scheduled time. In growing media, the arising of salt problem is from different sources, such as:

(i) Ingredient's side,
(ii) Water to be used for irrigation,
(iii) From the mixed fertilizers.

The measurement of EC is done by using the Electrical Conductivity meter. The measured EC data is maintained in the form of record for the entire crop cycle, as it is likely to change in accordance to the application of fertilizers/nutrients and water for irrigation. For example, if as per observation it is noticed that the growth of plant is declining during a given time period and during the same time the EC level of growing media is also dropping; then this advocates about insufficient availability of nutrients in growing media. And as per this observation the dose of fertilizers/nutrients is increased to fulfil nutrient's deficiency. In contrast, if plant growth is declining while EC level is more or in increasing trend, then it indicates the situation of development of salt's toxicity in growing media. At this condition, the availability of excess salts needs to be leached out from the container. In this way, the EC data provides a kind of guidelines for proper application of fertilizers/nutrients; and accordingly the management of salinity status of growing media, to have a proper effect on overall development of the crop and realizing a good yield, as well.

7.11 SAFETY CONSIDERATIONS

The handling or use of soilless type growing media, especially, requires safety measures in context to health aspects of the person, attached. The dusts associated to the ingredient's mixing during media preparation is more concerned, in this regard. Especially, the Perlite dust is very harmful, as it has the potential for development of silicosis effect in lungs. Actually, Perlite dust contains silica, which gets inhaled in the lungs. This leads to cause inflammation problem. In order to avoid such harmful effects, the follow-up of safety measures becomes essential. In this context, the important safety measures are suggested as under:

- The work place should be properly ventilated.
- Working person should wear protective dust mask and safety glasses.
- Growing media should be misted with water.
- Work place should also be lightly water sprinkled to reduce the dust blow.

- The worker with cuts or abrasions in the body parts, especially in the hands should be more causes about careful handling of Sphagnum peat moss, as there is possibility of attack of fungal pathogens on cut body parts. In addition, the fungal spores can also invade the cuts and be inhaled in the lungs, too.
- The storage of Peat moss and peat-based growing media should be done in dry condition.
- In order to remove the possibility of infection in the hands and other exposed body parts, they must be washed with the soap, after preparing and filling the growing media in container.
- If there any injury happens during working with the growing media, that must be treated, immediately, with suitable disinfectant such as iodine tincture, etc.
- The workplace should also be properly cleaned.

PRACTICE QUESTIONS

Descriptive Type Questions

1. What is growing media? Write its importance in greenhouse farming.
2. Write various functions of growing media.
3. Describe the properties of growing media, required to better crop response.
4. Narrate biological properties of growing media.
5. Describe different ingredients used for preparing growing media.
6. Explain the methodologies used for preparation of growing media.
7. Narrate different amendments used in preparation of growing media.
8. Describe various types of growing media used for greenhouse cultivation.
9. Explain soil sterilization, its importance, and methodologies used.
10. Describe different treatments of ingredients used for preparation of growing media.
11. Explain testing procedures of growing media.

Multiple Choice Type Questions

1. Use of growing media for crop growing is very common in
   (a) Shade nets (b) Greenhouses
   (c) Plastic mulching (d) Mist chamber
2. Important requirement of growing media is
   (a) Free from waterlogging (b) Good root development potential
   (c) Better aeration (d) All above
3. In majority of the soilless media the percentage pore space varies from
   (a) 60 to 80% (b) 30 to 35%
   (c) 45 to 60% (d) 80 to 85%
4. A growing media with pH below 7 is
   (a) Acidic in nature (b) Neutral
   (c) Alkaline in nature (d) Highly sodic in nature

5. A growing media with pH above 7 is
   (a) Acidic in nature (b) Neutral
   (c) Alkaline in nature (d) Highly sodic in nature
6. Majority of the native plants tend to grow at the pH between
   (a) 5.5 and 6.5 (b) 4 and 4.5
   (c) 6 and 7 (d) 7 and 10
7. In growing media, the pH level affects the availability of micro-nutrients, such as
   (a) Iron (b) Phosphorus
   (c) Manganese (d) Potash
8. In greenhouse farming system, for general purpose the media pH should be from
   (a) 5.0 to 6.0 (b) 5.2 to 6.2
   (c) 3.0 to 4.0 (d) 4.0 to 5.0
9. In greenhouse farming system, for proper seed germination the media pH should be from
   (a) 5.0 to 6.0 (b) 5.2 to 6.2
   (c) 3.0 to 4.0 (d) 4.0 to 5.0
10. In greenhouse farming system, for proper rooting the media pH should be from
   (a) 5.0 to 6.0 (b) 5.2 to 6.2
   (c) 3.0 to 4.0 (d) 4.0 to 5.0
11. The modification of growing media pH can be done by using
   (a) Dolomite (b) Hydrated lime
   (c) Limestone (d) All above
12. In growing media, the function of EC is to hold the
   (a) Positively charged ions (b) Micro-nutrients
   (c) Negatively charged ions (d) Water contents
13. For general use the EC (mmhos/cm) of growing media should be
   (a) 1.0 to 2.0 (b) 1.5 to 4.0
   (c) 0.5 to 1.1 (d) 3.0 to 4.5
14. For proper seed germination the EC (mmhos/cm) of growing media should be
   (a) 1.0 to 2.0 (b) 1.5 to 4.0
   (c) 0.5 to 1.1 (d) 3.0 to 4.5
15. For proper plant propagation the EC (mmhos/cm) of growing media should be
   (a) 1.0 to 2.0 (b) 1.5 to 4.0
   (c) 0.5 to 1.1 (d) 3.0 to 4.5
16. Which of the following is the organic ingredient used for preparation of growing media?
   (a) Peat (b) Peat moss
   (c) Non-composting materials (d) both (a) and (b)
17. The quality of compost is judged by the parameter
   (a) C/N ratio (b) Water-holding capacity
   (c) Porosity (d) All above

18. At the C/N ratio greater than 15:1, the nitrogen becomes
(a) Faster mobile (b) Leachable
(c) Immobile (d) All above

19. On which of the following C/N ratio the nitrogen becomes available for plant uptake?
(a) Below 15:1 (b) Above 15:1
(c) 15:1 (d) 1:15

20. Which of the following is used as inorganic ingredient for preparing growing media?
(a) Perlite (b) Vermiculite
(c) Sands (d) All above

21. The pH of Vermiculite varies from
(a) 6 to 8 (b) More than 7
(c) 3 to 5 (d) 10

22. Sterilization of growing media is done for removing
(a) Microorganism (b) Pathogens
(c) Non-beneficial microorganism (d) Both (a) and (b)

23. Which of the following soil is used for preparing growing media?
(a) Sandy soil, only (b) Loamy soil
(c) Silty soil (d) Clay soil

24. Which of the following is used for soil sterilization?
(a) Hydrogen Peroxide (b) Formaldehyde
(c) Methane (d) Both (a) and (b)

25. For soil sterilization against fungal pathogens, the required temperature is
(a) 47 to 59°C (b) 30 to 45°C
(c) 25 to 35°C (d) 40 to 50°C

26. For soil sterilization against insect pests, the required temperature is
(a) 47 to 59°C (b) 60 to 70°C
(c) 25 to 35°C (d) 40 to 50°C

27. For soil sterilization against bacteria, the required temperature is
(a) 47 to 59°C (b) 60 to 70°C
(c) 70 to 81°C (d) 40 to 50°C

28. For soil sterilization against most of the weeds, the required temperature is
(a) 70 to 81°C (b) 40 to 55°C
(c) 50 to 61°C (d) 35 to 55°C

29. For soil sterilization against viruses, the required temperature is
(a) 30 to 45°C (b) 70 to 81°C
(c) 50 to 61°C (d) 35 to 55°C

30. For soil sterilization against resistant weeds and viruses, the required temperature is
(a) 30 to 45°C (b) 70 to 81°C
(c) 94 to 100°C (d) 35 to 55°C

Answers

1. b	**2.** d	**3.** a	**4.** a	**5.** c	**6.** a	**7.** a	**8.** b	**9.** a	**10.** a
11. d	**12.** a	**13.** a	**14.** c	**15.** c	**16.** d	**17.** a	**18.** c	**19.** a	**20.** d
21. a	**22.** c	**23.** b	**24.** d	**25.** a	**26.** b	**27.** c	**28.** a	**29.** b	**30.** c

BIBLIOGRAPHY

Baker, K.F. (1957). The U.C. system for producing healthy container-grown plants through the use of clean soil, clean stock, and sanitation. University of California, Division of Agricultural Sciences, Manual 23. Berkeley, CA: University of California. 332 p.

Buamscha, G., and Altland, J. (2005). Pumice and the Oregon nursery industry. Digger. 49(6): 18–27.

Bunt, A.C. (1988). Media and mixes for container grown plants. London, United Kingdom: Unwin Hyman. 309 p.

Castillo, J.V. (2004). Inoculating composted pine bark with beneficial organisms to make a disease suppressive compost for container production in Mexican forest nurseries. *Native Plants Journal*. 5(2): 181–185.

Dumroese, R.K., Luna, T., and Landis, T.D. (2008). Nursery manual for native plants: volume 1, a guide for tribal nurseries. Agriculture Handbook 730. Washington, DC: U.S. Department of Agriculture, Forest Service. 302 p.

Evans, M.R., Konduru, S., and Stamps, R.H. (1996). Source variation in physical and chemical properties of coconut coir dust. *Hort-Science*. 31: 965–967.

Goldammer T. (2019). Greenhouse Management: A Guide to Operations and Technology. Apex Publishers, USA

Grubinger, V. (2007). Potting mixes for organic growers. Brattle-boro, VT: University of Vermont Extension. http://www.uvm. edu/vtvegandberry/factsheets/pottingmix.html. (August 2011).

Jaenicke, H. (1999). Good tree nursery practices: practical guidelines for research nurseries. International Centre for Research in Agro-forestry. Nairobi, Kenya: Majestic Printing Works. 93 p.

Johnson, P. (1968). Horticultural and agricultural uses of sawdust and soil amendments. National City, CA: Paul Johnson. 46 p.

Landis, T.D. (1995). Improving polybag culture for sustainable nurseries. Forest Nursery Notes. (July 1995): 6–7.

Lilleeng-Rosenberger, K. (2005). Growing Hawaii's native plants. Honolulu, HI; Mutual Publishing.

Lovelace, W. (2011). Personal communication (with Thomas Lovelace, W. Kuczmarski, D. (1994). The use of composted rice hulls in rooting and potting media. International Plant Propagators' Society, Combined Proceedings. 42: 449–450.

Martin, D.L., and Gershuny, G. (1992). The Rodale book of composting. Emmaus, PA: Rodale Press. 278 p.

Mastalerz, J.W. (1977). The greenhouse environment. New York: John Wiley & Sons. 629 p.

Miller, J.H.; and Jones, N. (1995). Organic and compost-based growing media for tree seedling nurseries. World Bank Tech. Pap. No. 264, Forestry Series. Washington, DC: The World Bank. 75 p.

Schundler Company (2002). Perlite health issues: studies and effects. Edison, New Jersey: The Schundler Company http://www. schundler.com/perlitehealth.htm. (February 2002).

Timmer, V.R.; and Parton, W.J. (1982). Monitoring nutrient status of containerized seedlings. In: Proceedings, Ontario Ministry of Natural Resources Nurseryman's Meeting, 1982 June, Thunder Bay, ON. Toronto, ON, Canada: Ontario Ministry of Natural Resources: 48–58.

Whitcomb, C.E. (2003). Plant production in containers II. Stillwater, OK: Lacebark Publications. 1,129 p.

Wightman, K.E. (1999). Good tree nursery practices: practical guidelines for community nurseries. International Centre for Research in Agroforestry. Nairobi, Kenya: Majestic Printing Works. 93 p.

Wilson, S.B., and Stoffella, P.J. (2006). Using compost for container production of ornamental wetland and flatwood species native to Florida. *Native Plants Journal.* 7: 293–300.

Wu, Q.S., and Zou, Y.N., (2010). Beneficial roles of arbuscular mycorrhizas in citrus seedlings at temperature stress. *Scientia Horticulturae* 125, 289–293.

Wu, Q.S., Zou, Y.N., He, X.H., and Luo, P., (2011a). Arbuscular mycorrhizal fungi can alter some root characters and physiological status in trifoliate orange (*Poncirus trifoliata* L. Raf.) seedlings. Plant Growth Regulation 65, 273–278.

CHAPTER 8

Polytunnels, Shade Nets, Plastic Nets and Plastic Mulching

The polytunnels and shade nets/net houses are the low cost structures used for crop farming under protected cultivation. The farmers can get easily constructed with the help of village persons. These two are considered as the farmer's friendly structures for protected cultivation. Polytunnels are covered with the help of Polyethylene films as the covering material. These are commonly used for garden, mainly to grow the vegetables and seedling raising, as well. Its construction involves a curved frame structure erected on soil surface, covered with a single piece plastic film of suitable thickness. The plastic film is properly stretched over the curved frame; and edges are anchored in the ground by placing the soil materials. The frame structure is mainly constructed with the help of galvanised steel tubes or bars or strips. The bigger polytunnels also consist of ventilation panels, sliding doors, ready-covered panels; and sometimes, also the rigid PVC covering. The function of polytunnels is for growing leafy vegetables and also for seedling raising. In addition, polytunnel also acts as rain shelter. Because of this feature, they can be suitably used for high quality seedling raising without damaging effect of heavy rains.

Shade nets are also the frame based structure, little super in action than the polytunnels. In shade net construction the plastic thread made nets are used as the covering material. The nets are in different colours. They cause their effects on the crop by creating cooling effect, because of formation of shades on the crop, inside. This chapter deals with the details of polytunnels and shade nets, plastic nets and plastic mulching as the technologies used for protected cultivation.

8.1 POLYTUNNEL

In appearance polytunnels are just like tunnel, i.e., length is very long in comparison to width. These are open and ventilated structures. The control of micro-climate is not completely, but to a part or partial. Polytunnels are constructed in varying sizes and for different purposes. The low and high tunnels are very common in use, for growing vegetables, horticultural fruit crops, raising of planting materials, etc. mainly. These are the low cost structures for protected cultivation; fully enable to meet the farmer's requirements in term of growing high quality or high valued crops in protected environment at low cost investment. Because of this reason it is treated as the novel structure.

A properly constructed polytunnel is effective to enhance the temperature inside; and thus leading to raise the soil temperature, also. However, the range of temperature increment in polytunnel is quite low as compared to the greenhouse. Besides, the polytunnels are being well to retain the moisture content in soil media and also provide protection to the crop against serious heat, strong winds, intense rainfall, concentrated sunlight, hail storms, cold waves, etc. as well. View of polytunnel is shown in Figure 8.1.

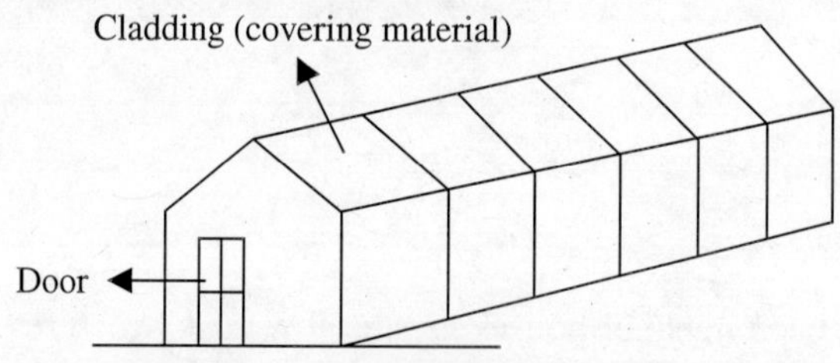

Figure 8.1 View of polytunnel

8.1.1 Benefits of Polytunnel

Like greenhouse, the polytunnels also play very significant role in crop production with enhanced production and quality produce. More or less the advantages offered by the protected cultivation in gross, are also applied to the crop cultivation under polytunnels. The focusing benefits, realized on use of polytunnels, are described as under:

1. Provides protection to the grown crops against strong wind, frost, heavy rain events as well, because grown crops are under protected environment.
2. Optimizes the crop growing season. Research evidence advocates that the polytunnels are well enabled to extend the growing duration of the crop. For example, the courgettes planted in the month of May could be ready to harvest by mid-June, i.e., 6 to 8 weeks earlier than the outdoor crops.
3. Polytunnel can provide fresh yield of leafy vegetables, green salads starting from November to the spring season, continuously.
4. The crops which are normally not being flourish out door they can be easily grown by use of polytunnels. The crops such as peppers, cucumbers, tomatoes, melons, aubergines, okra, flowers and herbs can be suitably grown using polytunnels.
5. The raising seedlings of desired vegetables and flowers can be easily possible through use of polytunnels.
6. The production of quality seedlings, i.e., the organic seedlings/plantlets can be raised at low cost with or without heating propagating facility.
7. The drying of farm produce can be accomplished under polytunnels during wet weather, summer or winter season, successfully.
8. The cost of cultivation per square meter is less than the greenhouse.
9. Since, the size of polytunnel varies from small to big; therefore, it provides scope for small farmers to cultivate the crops adopting protected cultivation technique.

10. Early seedlings can be easily raised by adopting this structure, because the range of inside temperature and soil warmness is being most favourable to create a better micro-climate.
11. The closely spaced crops can also be grown inside polytunnel placed with micro-irrigation system for watering.
12. The graft of fruits and flowers can be successfully prepared.
13. The supply of quality vegetables and flowers is possible, year round.
14. The effect of aberrant weather condition and environmental factors such as extreme temperature, extreme humidity, etc., climate type, i.e., the arid climate, humid climate and semi-arid is not there on grown crops.
15. Creates opportunity for the growers to take multiple crops during the year.
16. Using polytunnels the growers can realize better return during off-season.
17. Provides quite good profit per unit land area, better utilization of water and energy, as well.
18. Using polytunnel as the tool, the crop cultivation can be possible on the lands situated at high altitudes, and also in desert lands.
19. Through polytunnels the vertical farming of horticultural crops can be accomplished with the aid of aeroponics, hydroponics, etc.
20. Polytunnels can also facilitate to produce quality seeds (disease free) of costly vegetables.
21. The management/control of insect pests, disease, etc. in grown crops can be easily possible.

8.1.2 Limitations of Polytunnels

Apart from various advantages or benefits offered by polytunnel as one of the protected cultivation techniques/tools for cultivation of high valued crops, there are few important limitations regarding its use. They are narrated as under:

(i) For a small farmer this is capital expensive technique.
(ii) Requires close supervision of structure and grown crops, as well.
(iii) The soil-borne microbes may be troublesome for the grown crop.
(iv) There is more possibility of tearing of polyethylene film or cladding material during strong wind blow, if proper arrangement is not there against that.
(v) The cultural operations in low height polytunnels are not so easy to perform.
(vi) Requires very prompt repair and maintenance.

8.1.3 Drawback of Polytunnels

The important ones are as follows:

- There is large use of plastic films which poses bad effects on environment.
- Flooding method of irrigation is not well to use; the drip system is only good to use. This makes it very costly for the farmers to use for growing crops, frequently. In polytunnels the ventilation is very poor. In result, there generates a favourable environment for occurrence of fungal diseases.

- In polytunnels there must be the provision of doors, to ensure proper air circulation in production area.
- Due to deposition of dusts/soil particles and fungal effect on top of the plastic film, the effect of polytunnel on grown crop does not meet well, because in this condition of cover the transmission of sunlight in polytunnels gets decline, significantly. This situation alarms for washing or removal of all the depositions from the top of polytunnel cover.

8.1.4 Differences between Polytunnel and Greenhouse

It is general observation that many of the growers use the polytunnels like greenhouse, which is not proper. Between both the structures, there are fundamental differences, are narrated as under:

Structural difference: The polytunnel and greenhouse are the framed structure but their design is different. The major differences are pointed as under:

(i) The design and construction is quite different between twos.

(ii) Greenhouses have the provision of automated cooling system, while polytunnel is naturally cooled system.

(iii) The life span of greenhouse is quite large to that of the polytunnels.

(iv) The small size polytunnel can be easily shifted to other locations, while greenhouse no.

(v) The height and other specifications are greater in range in greenhouses, making them suitable for growing perennial crops such as grape vines or other climbers, while polytunnels are not fit for them to grow, commonly.

(vi) The cladding material in case of polytunnels is the polyethylene or plastic film. On the other hand in greenhouses there is choice on cladding materials such as the Ultraviolet (UV) stabilized polyethylene film, polycarbonate sheet, glasses, etc. Behaviour of all these covering materials in respect of catching or emitting the solar radiation is quite different.

(vii) The heating and cooling of air contents inside polytunnels is quicker than the greenhouses.

(viii) The range of temperature inside polytunnel is lesser than the greenhouse.

(ix) The electricity facility is not as essential as in case of greenhouse.

(x) The unit construction cost of polytunnel is much lesser than the greenhouses.

(xi) In construction of polytunnels the technical expertise is not so important. On the other hand, in case of greenhouse, it is very essential to have.

8.1.5 Polytunnel Covering Material

The material (film) used for covering the frame of polytunnel is referred to as the covering material. This is also called cladding material. In construction of polytunnels the plastic films of suitable thickness are commonly used. The salient features of cladding materials are presented below:

(i) Broadly, the polyethylene films (PE) with different extra additives are commonly employed in construction of polytunnels. The requirement of extra additives is only for increasing the life span of film and also for better performance in respect of intercepting the solar radiation and making its conducive effect on the crops grown, inside.

(ii) The addition of UVI (Ultra Violet Inhibitor) in PE films is causative to prolong the service life of the cover. This nullifies the impact of heat contents of sunlight on PE sheet; otherwise, there is development of sagging effect in PE film, which makes the structure not so effective. Also, there is another additive called Ethylene Vinyl Acetate (EVA) which is incorporated for improving strength and flexibility of covering material, besides reducing heat loss from the structure.

(iii) The covering material is also specified by its thickness, which is expressed in terms of either 'micron' or 'gauge'. Normally, in the market 150 to 180 micron or 600 to 720 gauge PE films are easily available. A covering film of greater micron comprises more thickness, better service life and more costs; and vice-versa. Broadly, in construction of polytunnels the PE films of 180 micron or 720 gauges are widely used. Its minimum expected life varies from 3 to 4 years.

(iv) It is general observation that the plastic film tends to get degrade quickly at the joint place on metallic frame of the structure due to heating or tearing effect. In result, the whole structure becomes at the verge of destruction. This type of shortcoming can be rectified or checked by using anti-hot-spot tapes. For this purpose, special foam tapes are available, which reduce the transmission of heat from metal to the plastic film. In addition, the adhesive foam tape can also be used as insulator between plastic film and the metal frame. Its surface casting is being slippery in nature, which is causative to reduce the abrasion effect. The above two effects are being significant to extend the life span of cover.

(v) As precautionary measure, the cladding material or plastic film should be placed on the frame structure during sunny time.

(vi) The laying of plastic film on frame structure should be as tight/stretch as maximum possible; otherwise, it is likely to blow away due to ballooning effect.

8.1.6 Construction Criterion of Polytunnels

Polytunnels are the structures or tools used for crop growing under protected environment. In order to make the structure most causative to result better performance regarding crop growth and development to enhance the crop yield, the design and construction must be done in most efficient way adopting technical expertise. In context to design and construction of polytunnels there have been formulated few important guidelines to follow, are mentioned as under:

- As an important criterion, the polytunnel should be constructed in north-west facing to protect it from the wind. And also the polytunnel should be kept open in east and south directions for receiving more sunlight and ventilation, too.
- The soil surface on which the tunnel is required to construct must be well prepared and bed should also be furnished for transplanting or sowing the seeds.

- The selection of polyethylene film (covering material) must be done well in advance.
- The shape of tunnels should also be decided prior to start its construction.

8.1.7 Polytunnel Types

Polytunnels are in following two types:

(i) Low polytunnel, and
(ii) High polytunnel.

Low Tunnels

Low tunnels are called 'miniature greenhouse'. Since, it covers the rows of plants; therefore, sometimes, it is also known as row covers. Its appearance is just like hoop. The low tunnels are mainly the row-cover type. The height of low tunnel is normally to the tune of 1 m or little less. Inside on plinth area a strip of soil surface is also left to provide passage for moving to perform cultural operations in the grown crops. Tunnels are covered with the plastic sheet of suitable thickness. Normally UV stabilized polythene sheets are preferred as the cladding material for construction of polytunnels. The temperature inside tunnels is more (nominal) than the outside, which is very conducive to grow off-season crops. Polytunnels are found beneficial for growing seedlings of vegetables such as brinjal, tomato, capsicum, etc. which are protected from the rainfall and hail storms. In addition to polythene sheets the other covering materials such as Ethylene Vinyl Acetate (EVA), Copolymer, Polyvinyl Chloride (PVC) and conventional PE are also used for construction of low tunnels for facilitating protected cultivation.

Construction: Its structure is made of steel wire, bamboo strip and also by cane in arc or hoop shape. The central height of arc or hoop is about 100 cm. From the top the clean plastic film or net is stretched over the hoop. The cover protects the plants against frost, wind, insect pests, etc. The thickness of plastic cover or sheet or cladding material is about 50-micron. The edges of plastic sheet are covered with the soil materials so that plastic cover may retain at its proper position. For this purpose, a trench of 20 to 40 cm deep is dug at the periphery of polytunnel structure. The plastic sheet is properly stretched in the trench and covered by placing the earth materials over that in trench. The plastic sheet is removed from the trench when plants start flowering, so that in pollination there may not be any hindrance to pollinating agents/insects. The polytunnel is provided with the holes on the side opposite to the movement of solar sun. These holes are called ventilation hole. The area of ventilation is kept about 4% of surface area of the tunnel (plinth). Nowadays, the use non-woven or spun-bonded fabric materials are also used for this purpose. These fabrics are porous is nature and very light in weight, found more suitable for ventilation purpose. The polytunnel with these provisions enables to create a micro-climate inside, beneficial to the grown crops. In order to facilitate irrigation to the crop inside polytunnel, the drip system is most suitable means of irrigation. Polytunnel crop field is linked to the drip tubing for watering.

Use: The tunnels are not being used for growing flowers. In general, the crops such as melons, cucumber, tomato, strawberry, pepper, beans, squash and sweet corn are most suitable to cultivate in polytunnels. The yield and produce quality both are very good as compared to the yield harvested under traditional practices.

Advantages: The advantages offered by low tunnels are narrated as under:

1. The low tunnels are found more responsive to result good yield, especially in winter season for growing early cucurbits.
2. These are being best in action to protect the crop against wind, rain, frost and snow.
3. These are found suitable for raising healthy nursery and early vegetable crops.
4. Low tunnels enable to maintain optimum temperature for healthy plant growth.
5. They help to better nutrient uptake by the plants.

High Tunnels

These tunnels are also called walk-in tunnels. Constructional features are the same to the low polytunnels. Difference is only in respect of height, which is more than the low tunnels. The optimum size of high tunnel is as follows:

(i) Size (area)–60 to 75 sqm
(ii) Width–2 to 2.5 m
(iii) Length–30 m
(iv) Central height–2 to 2.5 m. Normally, the height should be sufficient for walking a person comfortably inside tunnel, to perform cultural operations.

The moderate height crops are recommended to grow in these tunnels. The cladding/covering material is the same, i.e., the U.V stabilized polyethylene sheet. The height is sufficient to perform cultural practices, smoothly. The off-season cultivation of vegetables and preparation of flower seedlings can be suitably done in such type of polytunnel. Construction cost of this is more than the low tunnels.

Advantages: Various advantages offered by high polytunnels are given as under:

- A person can easily perform the cultural operations required for the grown crops.
- A high range of benefit can be realized by using this type of polytunnel by growing off-season vegetables and preparing flower's seedlings.
- These are the low-cost structure can be easily constructed by the village people, itself.
- Its design is very simple.

8.1.8 Irrigation and Fertilization Practices

Polytunnels are the structure constructed for cultivation of quite different types of the crops, i.e., the high valued or most remunerative crops. Overall, the main objective is to enhance the crop yield and produce quality, both. In order to achieve these objectives the irrigation and fertilization must be performed in efficient way and at proper time schedule. In addition, the application of fertilizer should neither be more nor less than the actual requirement. The irrigation by flooding is not found suitable, because there is always possibility of excess application of water, due to which there may be the problem of water ponding on soil surface, injurious to the grown crops. Similarly, the application of fertilizers, manually to the crop also likely to poses non-uniformity in application, makes effect on plant growth and yield, as well.

Considering all above facts in respect of irrigation and fertilization to the crops grown inside polytunnel, the best option is use of micro-irrigation (MI) technique. The MI system comprises two components for emitting water in terms of irrigation to the crop; in which one is the drip system; and other is the micro-sprinkler system. The drip system is used for irrigating the crops planted in rows such as vegetables, flowers, etc. On the other hand, the micro-sprinklers are used for closely grown crops, not planted in rows.

In micro-irrigation system the control unit is assembled with the fertigation unit (venturi attachment), which is connected to the fertilizer tank filled with the fertilizer solution of required concentration. On operation of the system the fertilizer solution kept in fertilizer tank, is sucked by the venturi attachment, and the same gets mix to the irrigation water. Finally, the fertilizer along with irrigation water is delivered to the plant. This process of fertilizer application is called fertigation. Micro-irrigation system performs the irrigation and fertigation in very precise way. The loss of water and fertilizer is about to negligible. The vegetable crops such as okra, tomato, brinjal, etc. can be irrigated by drip system, while leafy vegetables such as Palak, Methi, cumin, etc. by micro-sprinklers. In nutshell, the MI system is found well suitable to irrigate the crops grown in polytunnels.

8.1.9 Suitable Polytunnel Crops

The suitability of crop for successful cultivation in any environment or region depends on climatic condition of that particular region or the area, concerned. The polytunnel is a structure which is covered with the help of polyethylene film of suitable thickness. On striking of sunlight over the top surface of PE film, a part of solar energy gets transmit inside the tunnel, which causes to form a kind of micro-climate, there. This micro-climate comprises a particular temperature, humidity and light intensity. If the available temperature, humidity and light intensity inside tunnel is favourable for the grown crop, the crop successfully returns a good production; otherwise, no. On the basis of micro-climate available inside polytunnel, the list of suitable crops in context to vegetables, flowers and fruits is given in Table 8.1.

Table 8.1 List of recommended crops for cultivation in polytunnels

S. No.	Crop type	Suitable Crops
1.	Vegetables	Tomato, Cucumber, Capsicum (colored), Red cabbage, Radish, Spinach, leafy vegetables.
2.	Flowers	Gerbera, Gladiolus, rose, Chrysanthemum, Carnation
3.	Fruits	Sapota, Strawberry

8.1.10 Polytunnel's Micro-climate

Each and every crop either it is grown out side in open environment or in protected environment, requires a particular climate for its proper growth and development. On this basis, the crops are divided in two broad categorizes, namely (i) *Rabi*; and (ii) *Kharif* crops in Indian cropping system. In protected cultivation adopting polytunnels as one of the tools, the crops to be grown also require a specific climate comprising the parameters, temperature, humidity and light intensity, mainly. In absence or availability of inappropriate parameters by their magnitude inside polytunnel, there is a drastic effect on crop growth and yield, as well. As per extensive studies conducted on this aspect, there have been recommended the values of different climatic parameters suitable to different crops grown in polytunnels, is presented in Table 8.2.

Table 8.2 Recommended values of different climatic parameters for the common crops grown in polytunnels

S. No.	Crop	Humidity (%)	Temperature (°C)		Light intensity (lux)
			Day hour	Night hour	
1.	Tomato	50–65	22–27	15–19	50000–60000
2.	Cucumber	60–65	24–27	18–19	50000–60000
3.	Capsicum	50–65	21–24	18–20	50000–60000
4.	Nursery	50–65	22–27	16–19	50000–60000
5.	Carnation	60–65	16–20	10–12	40000–50000
6.	Chrysanthemum				
	6a. Cut flower	60–65	22–24	15–16	35000–40000
	6b. Pot	60–65	23–26	16–19	35000–40000

8.1.11 Crop Cultivation in Polytunnel

Polytunnels are small size framed structure behave just like greenhouse in terms of creating protected environment against insect/pests, rain, hail and also the micro-climate suitable to grow high value commercial crops with enhanced yield and better quality produce. Especially, in Northern India the crops such as tomato, cherry tomato, coloured capsicum, parthenocarpic cucumbers, French beans (pole type), winter watermelon, muskmelon and strawberries can be successfully grown in polytunnels. In addition, the grafted fruit plants can also be produced year round, successfully in polytunnels. The details about crop cycle, fertigation schedule, etc. for different suitable crops in polytunnel environment are described below:

Crop cycle: The crops such as tomato, cucumber, cauliflower, leafy vegetables, okra, muskmelon, water melon, flowers, etc. are suitably cultivated inside polytunnel. In addition, the propagation of planting materials of fruits can also be successfully done by use of polytunnels. The crop cycle which reveals year-round cultivation needs to develop for better monitory realization from the grown crops and efficient use of the structure, simultaneously. On the basis of recommended crops, a tentative crop cycle is mentioned below in Table 8.3, can be followed to achieve beneficial effects on yield potential and better quality produce, as well.

Table 8.3 Tentative crop cycle for some of the recommended crops

S. No.	Crop	Period/Crop cycle	
		Transplanting	Harvesting
1.	Tomato	August–September	April–May
		April–May	July–August
		February	May–June

(*Contd.*)

S. No.	Crop	Period/Crop cycle	
		Transplanting	Harvesting
2.	Cucumber, Cauliflower	November-December	March–April
	Leafy vegetables, Okra	April-May	October-November
3.	Propagation of planting materials of fruits	Round the year	
4	Muskmelon/Watermelon	February–March	June
5	Flowers	Round the year	

8.1.12 Polytunnel Fertigation Schedule

The application of fertilizers through fertigation technique is found better in all the aspects in case of protected cultivation using polytunnels. The basal doses should be furnished by soil incorporation and rest through fertigation technique. In fertigation the liquid or water soluble fertilizers are used. A proper concentration solution of given fertilizer is prepared and placed in fertilizer tank, is connected to the drip system. On operation of the system a requisite amount of fertilizer gets supplied to each individual plant. This application is done as per predecided fertigation schedule of the crop concerned. Table 8.4 illustrates the fertigation schedule as per crop stage, could be followed to obtain a beneficial impact on the grown crop.

Table 8.4 Fertigation schedule as per crop stage

S. No.	Crop stage	N:P:K	Recommended dose (g per 500 sq. m)
1.	Planting to first flowering	19 : 19 : 19	250
2.	First flowering to fruit set	19:19:19 46:0:0 0:0:50	100 175 275

8.1.13 Polytunnel Crops Varieties and Fertigation Schedule

In this regards few important crops are described as under:

Tomato: The hybrid varieties of tomato are recommended to grow inside polytunnels under protected environment. Few important hybrid varieties of tomato are mentioned in Table 8.5 to grow in greenhouse/polytunnels (height at least 3 m). The selected varieties should have the yield potential to the tune of 170 t/ha and crop duration may be at least six months.

Table 8.5 Hybrid varieties of tomato recommended for greenhouse/polytunnel cultivation

Tomato	Tomato cherry
(i) Naveen (Indo American)	(i) BR 124 (Holland)
(ii) Sartaj (Beejo Sheetal)	(ii) Pusa Cherry Type (IARI, Pusa)

(*Contd.*)

Tomato	Tomato cherry
(iii) Avinash II (Syngenta)	(iii) Olle
(iii) Himsona (Syngenta)	(iv) Seran
(iv) Himshikhar (Syngenta)	(v) Regy
(v) GS 600 (Golden Seed Company)	
(vi) Shreshtha (Syngenta)	
(vii) Tolstoi (CEU)	

Coloured Capsicum: Its botanical name is *Capsicum annum*, is commonly grown in winter or cool season. Coloured capsicum is also known as Sweet Pepper or sometime, the Bell Pepper, also. In greenhouse or polytunnel conditions the recommended varieties of capsicum for North Indian climatic conditions are listed in Table 8.6.

Table 8.6 Recommended varieties of coloured capsicum for cultivation in greenhouse/polytunnel

Capsicum variety		
Yellow fruited	**Red fruited**	**Green fruited**
(i) Orobelle	(i) Bombay, 3019	(i) California wonder
(ii) Super Gold	(ii) Tanvi	(ii) Bharat
(iii) NS (285 and 280), 3020	(iii) Torkel	(iii) Indra
(iv) Yellow Wonder		(iv) Pusa Deepti
		(v) Green Gold

***Fertigation*:** The water soluble or liquid fertilizers are applied through fertigation technique with the aid of drip system. It is done twice a week. The recommended dose of fertilizers as per defined schedule is mentioned in Table 8.7.

Table 8.7 Recommended dose of fertilizer (N:P:K) to be applied at different growth stages of the crop

S. No.	Crop stage	N:P:K	Recommended dose (gram per 500 sqm)
1.	Planting	19:19:19	500
	till fruit setting	0:0:50	250
2.	Fruit setting	19:19:19	500
	until	46:0:0	100
	first picking	0:0:50	250
3.	After first	19:19:19	450
	picking	46:0:0	500
	to the end of season	0:0:50	250

Parthenocarpic Cucumber: It involves the characteristics of high cross-pollinated habits. In order to avoid the use of pollinators due to this particular characteristic, it is especially cultivated in protected environment. In North Indian climatic condition, the Parthenocarpic cucumbers have been found to produce better yield under protected cultivation mode. The recommended varieties providing a good yield in greenhouse/polytunnel situation are listed in Table 8.8.

Table 8.8 Recommended varieties of Parthenocarpic Cucumber for greenhouse/polytunnel situation

S. No.	Varieties
1.	Hilton (C.E.V)
2.	Kiyan (Syngenta)
3.	Isatis (Syngenta)
4.	Multistar C.E.V)
5.	Deltastar (C.E.V)
6.	Sunstar (Rizwan)
7.	Kingstar (Rizwan)
8.	Hasan (Holland

***Fertigation*:** Application of fertigation is done twice a week using drip system. The fertilizers and their recommended dose as per predetermined schedule are mentioned in Table 8.9.

Table 8.9 Recommended dose of fertilizer for Parthenocarpic Cucumber crop

Days after transplanting	N:P:K	Dose (gram/500 sqm)
0 to 14 Days	19:19:19	500
14 to 35 Days	13:0:45	200
	46:0:0	100
35 to till the end of crop	13:00:45	500
	46:0:0	150

8.2 NET HOUSE

This is another structure used for protected cultivation. Its construction is same to the greenhouse, but in this structure the cladding material is the plastic thread made net at the place of UV stabilized polyethylene film. The nets are made of different colours combination threads; for example green and black; green and green; black and black. The shading percentage of nets varies. Shed net house are mainly used for growing leafy vegetables, preparation of grafts, hardening of T.C. plantlets, growing of cucumber, etc., mainly.

Its structure is made of GI pipe, angle iron, wood or bamboo materials. The whole structure is erected on the ground surface with some foundation. The frame structure is covered with the help of cladding material "plastic made net". The net comprises 100% Polyethylene thread with specialized UV treatment. The nets have different shading percentages. They create partially controlled micro-environment inside house by cutting the light intensity, which is effective to reduce the heat content for the crop during daytime; or in other words develop cooling effect. This feature makes possible to cultivate year-round seasonal/off-seasonal crops. View of shade net house is shown in Figure 8.2.

8.2.1 Types of Net House

Net houses are classified as per cladding (covering) material used in construction. They are given as under:

(i) Insect-proof net house, and
(ii) Shade net house.

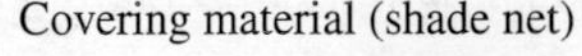

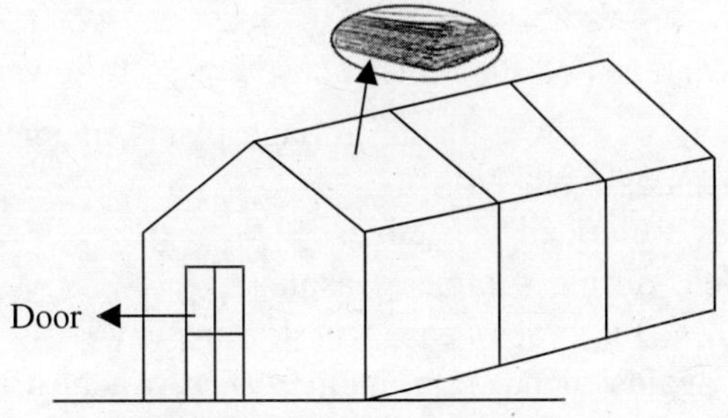

Figure 8.2 View of net house

Insect-proof net house: It can be a temporary or permanent structure, but with different designs. Also, it can be a walk-in tunnel form and shape with double door facility at one end. The structure is erected on the ground surface and is covered with the help of UV-stabilized insect-proof net. The net mesh varies from 40 to 50% effective to control the insect pests and diseases. The minimum size of this type of net house is 100 sqm as the plinth area. This type of net house as permanent structures are constructed in two different designs, namely; (i) Flat roof net house with central height ranging from 3.5 to 4 m; and (ii) Dome-shaped net house with central height from 4.5 to 5 m. Among these two, the dome-shaped insect-proof net houses are more popular.

Use: (i) These net houses are mainly used for producing quality produce and seedling growing.
(ii) Off-season cultivation.

Advantages: The main advantages of insect-proof net houses are as follows:

1. Off-season cultivation of crops.
2. Production of quality seedlings.
3. Control of insect pests and diseases.

Shade net house: Such type of net houses are constructed for protecting the plants from intensive solar heats or radiations. Its frame structure is made of wood, stone, bamboo or GI pipes. In constructing the net house using bamboo or wooden materials, the bamboo/wooden poles are firstly treated with the turpentine and tar to the side which is to be inserted in the soil. This treatment must be done before inserting the poles into the ground. For insertion a proper size hole is drilled in the soil. The erected frame structure is covered with the help of cladding material, which is the shade net. These nets are available in different colour combinations and shading percentages, such as 15%, 35%, 40%, 50% 75% and 90%. A shade net with 40% shade percentage denotes that it cuts 40% light intensity and allows 60% light intensity to the net house. The requirement of light intensity varies with the types of crop. Accordingly, the selection of shade net of a given shade factor or percentage suitable to the given crop, is most essential. Moreover the selection of shade net in accordance with the colour and shade factor is the location and season-specific. The shade nets are found in different types, such as (i) Green × Black; (ii) Black × Black; (iii) White × Black; (iv) Green × Green.

Uses: These structures are used for hardening of planting materials raised inside the greenhouse.

***Advantages*:** Various advantages of shade net house are as follows:

- Beneficial for raising of flower plants, foliage plants, medicinal and aromatic plants, vegetables and spices as well.
- Raising nurseries of fruits and vegetables.
- Enhancing crop yield during summer season.
- Provides protection to the crops against pest's incidence.
- Protects the crops against wind, rain, hail, frost, snow, bird and insects.
- Production of graft saplings.
- Reducing mortality of grafted saplings during hot weather conditions.
- Hardening of tissue cultured (TC) plants.
- Quality drying of agro-products.
- Creating favourable micro-climate/environment for Vermicomposting.

8.2.2 Types of Shade Nets

The shade nets are available in different colours and their combinations. The most commonly available nets are in the colours of white, black, red, blue, yellow and green; and also in their combinations. However, the commonly used shade nets for construction of net houses are given in Table 8.10, below:

Table 8.10 Types of shade nets; their characteristics and use

S. No.	Colour combination	Characteristics	Uses
1.	Green × Black	It cutoff unwanted ultraviolet rays and provides aesthetic look.	Used in Grapes for creation of shade to the crop and also for drying purposes.
2.	Black × Black	These nets absorb and radiate the heat contents inside the net house.	Used in nursery raising.
3.	White × Black	These nets diffuse the light inside the net house.	These are mainly used for flowers such as Gerbera, Anthurium, etc.
4.	Green × Green	These shade nets enhance the photosynthesis process.	Normally, used in ornamental plants.

Plastic Nets

The plastic nets/shade nets were developed about 30-years back for the purpose to provide a kind of protection to the crops/plants from a harsh climate. In agriculture the main use of these nets is for raising horticultural crops in protected mode. The plastic nets are extensively used to protect the plants from intense solar radiation, especially, in summer months. The transmissivity of solar radiation is the one of the most important parameters, characterizing the suitability of net for agricultural purposes.

In other words, the shade nets reduce the intensity of direct sunlight to the net house as per requirement of the grown crops. Shade nets are the plastic fiber-based product, are manufactured by knitting the plastic threads. Plastic nets have fixed percentages of porosity for allowing the sunlight, air and gaseous contents through. Porosity of net enables to develop shading effect on the ground surface or on the object below it. Sometimes, these nets are also called agricultural nets, as these are used for agricultural production by creating a kind of protected environment to the crops grown. The nets are mainly manufactured with the help of high density polyethylene (HDPE) and Polypropylene (PP) threads.

Applications: In agriculture, the main applications of plastic nets are as follows:

***Crop protection*:** Broadly, the grown crops are required their protection in two aspects; namely (i) Protection against hail, strong blowing winds, intense rainfall events, etc.; and (ii) Protection against insect pests and birds, as well.

***Environment control*:** Plastic nets are very effective to create shading effects below the net layer; and accordingly, reduce the temperature level. On this ground, these nets are also used to nullify the effect of extreme temperatures, especially, in case of fruit crops. In greenhouses, the shading nets are also used to modify the micro-climate, i.e., to lower the temperature.

***Crop cultivation*:** In mild-temperate regions the plastic nets are successfully used for growing leafy vegetables, etc.

***Hardening of seedlings*:** These nets are also found suitable to acclimatize the newborne seedlings, especially, the tissue cultured plants. Acclimatization is essential to reduce the level of mortality of the seedlings after their transplanting in open field. The tissue cultured plants are developed in a controlled environment, where temperature, humidity and other parameters are well-defined (controlled) as per requirement. If such plants are directly transplanted in the field, they are likely to get failure to survive because of sudden change of environment. Therefore, to avoid this situation the hardening of TC plants is essentially carried out.

Shade Net Characteristics

The plastic nets/agricultural nets are characterized by different features as shown in following table.

S. No.	Characteristics
1.	Kind of threads/fabrics used
2.	Shape and dimension of fibers
3.	Meshing
4.	Weight
5.	Colour
6.	Shading factor
7.	Durability
8.	Porosity/air permeability
9.	Stress and strength at break and elongation

The length and breadth of plastic net varies from one manufacturing company to another. There is no standard dimension. However, depending on the type of plastic net, the width varies from 1 to 6 m and also from 12 to 20 m. The length varies from 25 to 300 m. However, the width of net can be enlarged by joining more number of net units, together.

Fibers and mesh size: The net thickness is governed by the thickness of single thread. The thread thickness varies from 0.25 to 0.32 mm. Mesh size is the distance between two threads in wrap or weft direction. The mesh size of different types of nets is shown in Table 8.11.

Table 8.11 Net types and their mesh size

S. No.	Net type	Mesh size for wrap and weft (mm)
1.	Insect nets	0.2 to 3.1
2.	Shade nets	1.7 to 7.0
3.	Anti-hail nets	2.5 to 4.0
4.	Windbreak nets	1.8 to 7.0
5.	Anti-birds nets	30 to 40

Weight: The weight of plastic net depends on the thickness of plastic threads used, kind of fabric and the mesh size. The weight generally varies from 15 g/m^2 to 325 g/m^2.

Shading factor: It denotes the ability of net to absorb/reflect the part of solar radiation out of the total. Shading factor of a particular plastic net is time dependent, not the constant. In other words, it is not constant but changes with the daytime, incidence angle of solar beam, orientation and location, as well. In addition, it also varies with the requirement of the crop concerned. Shade percentage is counted as an index for characterizing the type of nets. In market various shade percentage (35%, 50%, 65%, 75%, etc.) plastic nets are available. As per research findings, for most of the fruits and vegetables the plastic nets having 20 to 40% shade percentage are found most suitable. A net having 35% shade percentage denotes 35% sunlight cutting and rest 65% allowing to enter the structure.

Air permeability: It is the ability of plastic net to pass the air through it. Air permeability of net depends on several factors, such as air viscosity and speed, size and shape of threads used for manufacturing, mesh size and the texture of the net as well. The net permeability influences the pressure likely to be exerted on the net and also on the level of micro-climate (air velocity, humidity, temperature, etc.) likely to be formulated inside. The air permeability of net used as thermal net varies from 10 to 11m^2 and in case of insect nets it is less than 10 to 8m^2.

Colour: The colored nets are used to modify the spectral transmittance of solar radiation to develop light-induced effects on the plants, in terms of increasing the size of fruit and also for controlling the crop production period (Shahak et al., 2002). Furthermore, these are also used for modifying the flowering period and quality production of cut flowers. In manufacturing of plastic nets using HDPE threads, the color of net is developed by mixing the chromatic additives to HDPE grains. Agricultural nets are found in following common colors:

(i) Black
(ii) Green
(iii) Transparent or clear
(iv) Red
(v) Yellow

(vi) Grey
(vii) Silver, etc.

The uses of different color nets are summarized in Table 8.12.

Table 8.12 Uses of different color plastic nets

S. No.	Plastic net with colour	Uses/effects
1.	Black	Used for shade creation to lower the temperature.
2.	Red	Plant growth simulation
3.	Yellow	Plant growth simulation
4.	Blue	Used for dwarfism in ornamental plants
5.	Grey	Used to stimulate branching and produce `bushy' plants with short branches and small leaves.
6.	Silver	Used as thermal screen inside greenhouse and outside as a shading membrane.
7.	Transparent	Used to heat up the soil and killing the harmful soil born lives.

Durability: This character of plastic net depends on the stability of mechanical properties of high density polyethylene (HDPE), i.e., on its resisting capability against UV radiation. The UV radiation is considered as one of the main agents causing degradation in HDPE. The UV degradation resistance is judged in terms of amount of kilolangley (kly) required to reduce the tensile strength of net to 50% of its original value. The kilolangley denotes the global incident solar irradiation. One kilolangley is equal to 1 kcal/cm^2 = 41.84 MJ/m^2. The commercial plastic nets have the value of solar radiation resistance to the tune of 400 to 800kly; and at this level of solar radiation resistance the durability of polymer is about 5 to 6 years in mild climate, i.e., in Mediterranean areas having yearly solar radiation resistance from 100 to 120kly/yr. And in tropical areas with solar radiation resistance from 140 to 160kly/year the durability may vary from 3 to 4 years. In addition to solar radiation resistance, the durability of net also depends on the contact nature (type) with the frame materials (metal or wood), atmospheric temperature, and use of pesticides (sulphur and/or chlorine mix), as well.

Porosity and solidity: The porosity and solidity both are associated to each other in reciprocal mode. In which, the porosity represents the percentage void space occupied out of total surface area of net. It is defined as the ratio of open area (voids) to the total area of net. The porosity of plastic net can be determined by the methods; namely (i) Radiation balance method; (ii) Interception of solar radiation method; and (iii) Analysis of image of the material, as well.

The solidity ratio is used as the parameter to evaluate the wind force acting on porous structures. It is defined as the ratio of fabric area to the total area of net sample. It is basically, complementary to the porosity of net sample.

Raw materials used: The most commonly used raw material for manufacturing agricultural nets (Plastic net) is the high density polyethylene (HDPE), which is a non-toxic and can be used in direct contact with the plants without any harmful effect. In addition, it is easily convertible, water proof and highly durable. It also bears good mechanical characteristics such as tensile stress (σ) as 20/37MPa; elongation at break (ε) is 200/600%, etc. The other details of PE are as below.

Polyethylene: It is the polyolefin characterized by light in weight and highly durable and can be used for multi-purposes such as manufacturing frozen food bags, bottles, cereal liners, yogurt containers, etc. The PE plastics are associated to different crystalline structures. The HDPE, LDPE, LLDPE, etc. are sub-forms of PE plastics. These are constructed by the process of polymerization of ethylene. Polyethylene plastics are found in different types. The most common amongst them are given as under:

1. Low-density polyethylene (LDPE)
2. Linear low-density polyethylene (LLDPE)
3. High-density polyethylene (HDPE)
4. Ultra-high-molecular-weight polyethylene (UHMWPE)

In addition, the PE plastics are also available in following more types:

(i) Medium-density polyethylene (MDPE)
(ii) Ultra low-density polyethylene (ULDPE)
(iii) High-molecular-weight polyethylene (HMWPE)
(iv) Metallocene polyethylene (mPE)
(v) Chlorinated polyethylene (CPE)

The differences between LDPE, LLDPE and HDPE films are presented in Table 8.13.

Table 8.13 Difference between LDPE, LLDPE and HDPE films

S. No.	Property	Low-Density Polyethylene (LDPE)	Linear Low-Density Polyethylene (LLDPE)	High-Density Polyethylene (HDPE)
1.	Structure	♦ It involves high degree of short chain branching and long chain branching.	♦ It involves only high degree of short chain branching.	♦ It comprises linear or low degree of short chain branching.
2.	Density	♦ Its density varies from 0.910 to 0.925 g/cm^3.	♦ Its varies to the tune of 0.91 to 0.94 g/cm^3	♦ It varies from 0.941 to 0.965 g/cm^3.
3.	Crystallinity	♦ It has low crystallinity and high amorphous, which varies from 50 to 60% crystalline.	♦ It has semi-crystalline, level, i.e., between 35 to 60%.	♦ It involves high crystalline and low amorphous, i.e., less than 90% crystalline.
4.	Characteristics	♦ It is flexible. ♦ It has good transparency level. ♦ It is a good moisture barrier. ♦ At low temperature its impact strength is high. ♦ For acids, bases and vegetable oils its resistance is very high.	As compared to LDPE, it involves: ♦ High tensile strength. ♦ High impact strength. ♦ High puncture resistance.	♦ It offers excellent chemical resistance. ♦ High tensile strength. ♦ Excellent moisture barrier properties. ♦ Hard to semi-flexible.

In addition, the biodegradable (starch based) materials are also used for manufacturing agricultural nets. The biodegradable nets are likely to mix in the soil media, till the end of their use. Or in other words, the nets made of biodegradable materials are decayed directly in the soil. In addition, they can also be used for preparing composts along with organic materials such as food and vegetable's residues and manure. The prepared compost so, is being carbon-rich. Moreover, in comparison to plastic nets the biodegradable films/nets are not so common in use, because of their high cost and also due to deterioration in physical and mechanical properties on continuous exposition to the solar radiation.

Types of Plastic Nets

Plastic nets are in different types depending on their uses, colours and broadly the agricultural concerns, as given in Table 8.14.

Table 8.14 Types of plastic nets

S. No.	Types of plastic nets
1.0	As per uses
	(i) Insect nets
	(ii) Shade nets
	(iii) Anti-hail nets
	(iv) Anti-rain nets
	(v) Anti-frost nets
	(vi) Windbreak nets
	(vii) Anti-birds nets
2.0	As per colour
	(i) Green nets
	(ii) Black nets
	(iii) Red nets
	(iv) Yellow nets
	(v) Blue nets
	(vi) Grey nets
	(vii) Silver nets
	(viii) Transparent nets
3.0	Agricultural nets
	(i) Flat woven nets
	(ii) English woven nets
	(iii) Raschel loom nets

Insect nets: These nets are also known as anti-insect nets are used to prevent the crop against incidence of insect. On use of this net, the application of insecticides is not require to a large extent. In this way, these nets not only prevent the crop from the insects for enhancing the crop productivity, but they are also enabling to improve the produce quality. In nutshell, the other benefits offered by insect nets are enumerated as under:

- These are the perfect means to keep the insect pests away from the crops.
- Avoid the use of harmful chemicals such as insecticides/pesticides to the soil via crop.
- Nets are perforated; because of this reason the crops have a good exposure to the natural environment/surroundings.

- Nets are UV stabilized, enhances the service life more than 3 to 5 years.
- Nets enable to maintain a good environment inside for optimum growth of the crop.
- These nets are cost effective (friendly), and are preferred to use.

Shade nets: These are special type of plastic nets used for protecting the plants from intense solar temperature, especially, during summer months. For this particular objective, these nets are preferably used to operate the greenhouse. Or in other words, these are used for lowering the greenhouse temperature, as for the grown crop inside greenhouse a particular range of temperature is required for their proper growth or development. These nets are placed inside and outside greenhouse, both as per range of temperature lowering. The development of cooling effect or temperature lowering is based on the fact of creating shades on the working surface/area of the greenhouse. On development of shades, there is direct reduction in temperature.

The importance of shade nets is multifold folds, i.e. (i) Protect the crop from harsh temperature; (ii) Enhance the crop production; and (iii) Improve the produce quality. The other beneficial effects of shade nets are pointed as under:

- Provides better ventilation and air circulation to the crop.
- Obstructs the wind blow; and thus saves the crop, too.
- Easy to handle and use for the purpose, because of its light weight.
- Provides UV protection to the crop.
- Chemically resistant against most of the horticultural chemicals.
- Effective to reduce the soil moisture loss, because of causing poor evaporation.

Anti-hail nets: Anti-hail nets are used to prevent the crop against the damages likely to be due to occurrence of hails. The horticultural crops mainly the fruits such the grapes, peaches, apricots, apples and cherries are protected against hail storm by covering their tree canopies using these nets. The percent perforations in these nets are different than the other nets. These nets are placed over the orchard of concern fruit with the help of proper supports that may of wooden materials, metallic and sometimes, the masonry, also. The greenhouse constructed with the help of glass panels, are also protected by means of anti-hail plastic nets. In greenhouses, the anti-hail nets also cause reduction of incoming solar radiation, especially, during summer months, when control of inside temperature is essential.

Anti-rain nets: These nets are used to avoid the crop damages because of occurrence of intense rainfalls. However, these nets are combined with the anti-hail nets. The horticultural crops such as cherries, etc. are mostly protected by mean of these nets.

Anti-frost nets: The anti-frost nets are basically the non-woven sheets. These nets are spread over the crop to avoid the possibility of damages likely to be due to occurrence of frost.

Windbreak nets: These nets are used to protect the crop against strong blowing winds, which are likely to damage or destroy the crops. Normally, in the condition of standing crop the plant's branches get break and flowers are removed from them due to strong winds, is called mechanical damage. Similarly, there is also happened biological consequence due to strong blowing winds; they are the high evapotranspirational loss, difficulties in pollination, etc. These wind generated problems can be easily removed by using these nets. In addition, these nets also offer following additional advantages in context to agriculture:

- These nets play key role to increase the produce quality by protecting the produce/fruits from dust, salt, sands, etc.

- They reduce the wind load on greenhouse structures.
- They decline the extent of heat loss from animals due to ventilation in open livestock farms.

Anti-bird nets: The bird harboring and thereby the damage to the crop, is very serious type of consequence in crop farming. The overall crop productivity gets directly hampered due to this incidence. In order to avoid such circumstances the crop field is covered with the plastic net (anti-bird net), which checks the birds to enter the crop field. The size of net perforation is kept in such a range that the birds may not pass through.

The percentage shading and UV resistance of different types of nets are mentioned in Table 8.15.

Table 8.15 Shading percentage and UV resistance of different plastic nets

S. No.	Plastic Nets	Shading percentage	UV resistance (kly)
1.	Shade nets	25 to 90	400 to 800
2.	Anti-hail nets	10 to 25	400 to 800
3.	Anti-insect nets	10 to 20	400 to 600
4.	Wind break nets	30 to 70	400 to 800
5.	Anti-bird nets	5 to 15	300 to 600

(*Source*: Castellano and Russo, 2005).

Green nets: These nets are extensively used in agriculture, especially, in floriculture. Green nets are mainly used to protect the green vegetables and fresh foods against dry and extreme moist conditions. These are also being effective to ensure enhancement in plant's growth/development, besides optimum use of water by the grown crop. In market these nets are available with 35%, 50%, 75%, and 90% shading factor in rolls. One roll comprises about 50 m length of green net.

Black nets: These nets are being in black colour, both the sides. Black nets are commonly used for creating shading effect. Because of black colour, these nets are also found very effective to reduce the interception of solar radiations, leading to cause lowering of temperature, inside. In plastic net the black colour is derived by means of an additive called 'carbon black', which also acts as UV-stabilizer. Durability of black colour nets is comparatively greater than the transparent nets, because of its UV behaviour caused by black carbon. The quantity of black carbon in plastic net varies to the tune of less than 1%. A high quantity of black carbon in plastic net makes it very poor against mechanical stability.

Red nets: These nets are named after their colour as red, are mainly used for stimulating the crop/plant growth. Besides, these are also used for packaging the crop produce such as potato, onion, turmeric, etc.

Yellow nets: Like red nets, the yellow nets are also used for stimulating the crop/plant growth.

Blue nets: These nets are blue in colour, mainly used for dwarfism in ornamental plants.

Grey nets: Grey nets are mainly used for stimulating the branches in crops/plants. Besides, they are also applied to produce 'bushy' plants with short branches and small leaves. In addition, for modification in flowering period and enhancing the quality of cut flowers, the grey colour plastic nets are found best, to use.

Silver nets: Silver nets are manufactured by extruding the HDPE tape fiber with the aluminum layer. These nets have the characteristics of high solar radiation reflectance. These are used both the inside and outside the greenhouse. Inside greenhouse they are used as the thermal screen, and outside as the shading membrane.

Transparent nets: These plastic nets are transparent without colour. Transparent nets are not causative to create shading effect on the ground surface. Such plastic nets are mainly used for temperature rising.

8.3 PLASTIC MULCHING

The polyethylene (PE) as the plastic film/sheet was developed in the year 1938. The introduction of plastic film as plastic mulch in vegetable cultivation was introduced in 1950s, through which a significant enhancement in commercial crop production was achieved (Lamont 2017). The production of plastic films at world scale to the tune of 360 million tonnes was done in the year 2018, which was distributed in Asia 51%, Europe 17%, North American Free Trade Agreement (NAFTA) 18%, Africa 7%, Commonwealth of Independent States (CIS) 3%, and Latin America 4% (PEMRG, 2019). In agriculture sector about 4% plastic-based fabricated products are used in various forms such as plastic mulching (PEMRG, 2019). Plastic mulch directly affects the micro-climate below mulch cover and around the plant by modifying the energy or radiation budget; and also declines the soil water loss by reducing the evaporation.

The plastic mulch is considered as the type of inorganic mulch material. In plastic mulching the plastic sheet of suitable thickness is used for mulching purpose, which is spread over the mulching surface. The objective and function of plastic mulching are the same to the general mulching practices. Nowadays, plastic mulches are found available in different colours and thicknesses, at low cost. It results its instant effect on water conservation. However, they also develop negative impacts on surrounding environment. Now days, the application of plastic mulching in standing crop has been spread worldwide at large scale for instant benefits in terms of yield enhancement, early maturing of the crop, quality improvement, increased water/nutrient use efficiency, etc. mainly.

In contrast, the plastic mulches also impose several inconducive d/s effects in long-term use; they are detailed as under:

(i) Adverse impact on soil health and environment, both, which may be because of plastic additives.
(ii) Enhancement in pesticidal runoff and fragmented plastic residues in soil media, which become a kind of challenge to overcome its effect on soil properties.
(iii) Plastic mulches have potential to alter the quality of soil by shifting the edaphic bio-coenosis, i.e., the mycotoxigenic fungi.
(iv) Depleting organic matters existing in soil media.
(v) Increasing soil water repellency.
(vi) Enhancing the release of greenhouse gases.
(vii) Declining soil quality.

View of plastic mulching is shown in Figure 8.3.

Figure 8.3 View of plastic mulching

8.3.1 Plastic Mulching—Benefits

Its various benefits are as follows:

(i) Soil structure improvement
(ii) Soil insulation
(iii) Weed control
(iv) Fast crop/plant growth
(v) Improvement in crop produce
(vi) Reduction in root damage
(vii) Irrigation water saving

Soil structure improvement: In this context, the impact of mulching is promising. Plastic mulching is causative to prevent the soil from crumping effects. Also, it makes the soil mass able to trap the moisture and heat contents, which are favourable to limit the loss of plant nutrients. In addition, plastic mulching also discourages the people and pets from moving through mulched area, and accordingly, keeps the soil structure, safe.

Soil insulation: Plastic mulches act as insulating materials to raise the temperature level of soil media. It is well known that most of the plants are temperature sensitive; they cannot tolerate winter colds. For these crops the plastic mulches can be successfully used to insulate the soil; and accordingly, raise the temperature of the same. The reason behind this effect is that, when solar radiation/heat strike the upper surface of plastic mulch, a part of that heat mass gets enter below the plastic cover, which is absorbed by the soil mass. A part of absorbed heat contents is retained there; and rest part of that is emitted from the soil. The emitted heat content is retained below the plastic layer. This leads to raise the soil temperature. Experimentally, it has been observed that due to plastic mulching there is enhancement in soil temperature to the tune of about 5°F. In this way, in the crops which are winter cold's sensitive the plastic mulching can be beneficial to save them. The soil insulation effect can also be beneficial in case of fruit bearing trees.

Irrigation water saving: The treatment of plastic mulching + drip irrigation has been found to be most effective for saving irrigation water in horticultural crops. On an average, it varies from 35 to 40% as compared to the flooding method of irrigation. The reason may be because of control on evaporation loss due to plastic mulching, mainly. In addition, the water loss due to deep percolation is completely eliminated in drip system along with plastic mulching. The saved irrigation water can be utilized for extension of irrigated area under drip system.

Weed control: The plastic mulching is very significant to control the weed problems. The plastic mulching in combination of drip system has been found to be most effective to control the weeds, which may be in the range of 40 to 55% over untreated (control) traditional practices. The reason behind this effect may be explained as; the plastic mulch (black colour) prevents the plant to get the sunlight, required for photosynthesis process. In result, the weeds are deprived of sunlight; and accordingly, they start dying. In due course of time the entire weed population gets destroy from the field because of mulching treatment.

Early crop maturity: Plastic mulching causes fast growth of plants. This results into early appearance of different growth stages; and accordingly, the maturity of the crop, too. This is because of the reason that plastic mulch heat ups the soil media, which activates the growth process very promptly by creating most favourable soil-water-plant-atmosphere environment. This effect is highly visible in vegetables. The research evidences on this aspect advocate that on use of plastic mulch the crop maturity could be attained 1 to 2 weeks, earlier than the traditional practices.

Improvement in produce quality: A noticeable effect of plastic mulching has been recorded in vegetables regarding improvement in produce quality. In strawberry cultivation the plastic mulching is found very effective. In mulched condition, the berries rest on the mulch surface, i.e., not in soil touch, as result the overall cleanliness and quality of berries is very attractive. In addition, on plastic mulching the possibility insect pests is also declined to an appreciable extent; as the incidence of insect pests deteriorates the fruit quality, significantly.

Reduction in root damage: In standing crop the main cause of root damage is the inter-culturing operations, because soil becomes in disturbed condition. On the other hand, in mulched condition the soil adjacent to the plant is covered with the plastic mulch; and accordingly, the soil remains undisturbed. The inter-culturing operations are performed in the space out from the mulched part. In undisturbed soil below the mulch layer, the plant roots are fully able to grow and spread to the deeper layers, effective to extract the moisture and nutrients for plant uptake and their proper growth, too.

8.3.2 Drawback of Plastic Mulch

The following features of plastic mulch and thereby mulching in standing crop denote its drawback/demerits/disadvantages:

(i) Not eco-friendly.
(ii) Difficult to dispose-off.
(iii) Excessive heat formation.
(iv) Requires trained person for mulching.
(v) Alters hydrological behaviour of land.

Not eco-friendly: Plastic mulches are petroleum based products. These are not biodegradable in nature. They remain in soil media for a long period of time, and create so many inconducive effects on soil health. Because of this reason, it is always suggested that after using as mulch, they must be removed from the field, to avoid forthcoming bad effects likely to be developed there in the field soil.

Difficult to disposed-off: The plastic mulch or plastic based products such as poly bags, etc. create their disposal problem. In drainage line the poly bags form balloon due to filling of water in them, which occupy the flow space of drainage system. This leads to reduce the flow carrying capacity, causing drainage problem, there. In worse situation, the drainage line gets completely choked due to this type of occurrence. Instant removal or disposal of this problem is very difficult. For this machines are required. Similarly, from cropped field the removal of plastic mulch after their use is also cumbersome task. Machines are also not there which could be used for removing that from the field. Alternative is only manual method, in which there is time and money loss.

Excessive heat formation: Plastic mulch allows a part of sunlight or solar heat to enter below the mulch layer, because of its transmissivity property. The heat contents from below the mulch are not escaped. In result the inside temperature gets exceed the outside (open field) temperature. As per research findings about 2 to 3°C temperature is more below the plastic mulch layer to that of the outside temperature. This range of temperature increment may be more in case of thin and white colour plastic mulch. The increased temperature warm ups the soil significantly, which develops inconducive effects on temperature sensitive crops. On this ground, the black plastic mulch is only suggested to use in heat-loving crops such as melons, tomatoes, peppers, and others. In contrast, the black plastic mulches are not recommended for use in cool-season crops such as lettuce, peas, and tubers, as they are likely to die due to excessive heat.

Requirement of skilled person for mulching: The application of plastic mulching in cropped field is mainly for the purposes, such as (i) Moisture conservation; and (ii) Weed control. Mulching effects on these contents gets happen properly and significantly, when mulching is done in proper way; otherwise no. Therefore, to accomplish the laying of mulch or mulching work the need of skilled person is essential. This poses the problem of extra financial burden, is considered as one of the demerits of plastic mulching.

8.4 COLORED PLASTIC MULCH

The mulch is a Germanic word, which represents the meaning as "soft" indicating spongy layer as found in the forest ecosystem. The definition of mulch encompasses as the material, which is applied to or grow upon the soil surface for achieving the effects in terms of preventing drought stress, protection against cold or freezing, improving chemical, physical and biological properties of the soil, disease control, and enhancing the crop productivities, as well. In this context, Li et al. (2004) and Franquera (2015) observed that the colored plastic mulch improves the micro-climate around the plants leading to increase the cell expansion, by virtue of which there is appreciable growth and development in the plants. As per source of production and nature, the plastics are reproduced in the form of polyethylene, polyamides, polypropylene, polycarbonate, expanded polystyrene, polyethylene terephthalate, etc. In addition, the plastic films are also started manufacturing in different colors such as black, white, red, yellow, orange, etc. And they are started using in agriculture as the plastic mulch for mulching works. In present scenario, the mostly used colored plastic film as mulch material are black, white, green, brown, red, silver, and blue, mainly. The colours of plastic mulch are effective in respect of light absorption and crop physiology, as well. The impacts of colored plastic mulch have been quantified by different individuals in variety of the crops. Overall, the black color plastic mulch is the most available and widely used as compared to the others. The black plastic mulch absorbs the UV, visible and infrared (IR) wavelengths of solar radiation, efficiently. The variation in colour of plastic mulch affects the spectral balance, quality, and quantity of light absorption which affect the pattern of plant growth/development including the yield, too. The features of different colors plastic mulch are narrated as under:

Black plastic mulch: The black color plastic mulch is very effective to increase the soil temperature or heat contents in soil media, as it absorbs large amount of solar radiation. In other words, the black plastic mulch is used to increase the absorption of light and temperature, both. Also, it is used for weed control. In black colour plastic mulching the photosynthesis rate gets reduced to a large extent, leads to affect the plant growth, significantly.

White plastic mulch: This color plastic mulch is just reverse in behaviour to the black color plastic mulch. It creates cooling effect in the soil. It is mostly used in those crops, which require less soil heating.

Red plastic mulch: Red color plastic mulch is found most efficient in absorbing the solar radiation as compared to the black, blue, green, and yellow color plastic mulches. The trend of solar radiation transmittance depending upon color of the mulch is expressed as black<blue<yellow<green<red<transparent plastic mulches. As for as energy balance is concerned, it is in the order of red>transparent>green>blue>yellow>black.

The colored plastic mulch affects the light absorptivity, light reflectivity, soil water loss, soil temperature, plant morphology, and weed control, significantly. This is because of the reason that there is wide variation in absorption and reflection of Far-red to red FR:R ratio, leading to cause photochromic regulation. A plant receiving high FR:R light will show increase in plant height and above-ground biomass.

8.4.1 Effect of Colored Plastic Mulch

The effects of coloured plastic mulch are narrated as under:

Soil temperature: The soil temperature is counted as one of the main properties of the growing media affecting the crop attributes including production, as well. As per various researches and their recommendations, the role of soil temperature is mainly in respect of nutrient uptake, water absorption, root growth, and life of soil microorganisms. The colored plastic mulch alters the soil temperature to a wide extent. In this context, it has been reported that the colored plastic mulch enable to result a high level of soil temperature than the bare soil. The blue color plastic mulch results more temperature to that of the red color plastic mulch. Furthermore, by another study it is reported that the highest range of temperature increment is observed in case of clear (transparent) plastic mulch, while there is no difference in temperature under black plastic mulch and the bare soil. In addition, it is also reported that a high level of soil temperature is recorded in case of black plastic mulch to those of the olive, silver, white, and blue color plastic mulches. In contrast, the brown and blue color plastic mulch resulted higher soil temperature as compared to others including black colour mulch. The variation in soil temperature by same color plastic mulch is because of change in soil type and climatic conditions of the area, specific. In tomato and radish crops, it is very prominent to reduce the temperature level of root zone soil due to development of full canopy causing shading effect, and also due to restriction in direct interception of solar radiation and heat transfer from open atmosphere to the soil media. In this case by use of colored plastic mulch this type of misconduct can be eliminated, as they can easily enhance the soil temperature.

Soil water: The water is an important requisite for all the living creatures on the earth system. No one can survive without water. In agriculture same view is also applied. It is reported that of the total available water on earth system maximum portion of that is consumed in agriculture for crop farming. In a plant's life the main role of water is for hydration, transpiration, and production of dry matters. In plant body by maintaining an optimum level of water content the plant growth/development and yield could be enhanced to a significant level. This could be achieved through proper management of water by minimizing the water loss from any source at field level. On this aspect enormous research works have been done across the world. From majority of the researches, it is pointed that the practice of plastic mulching is one of the most suitable means to enhance the availability of water for plants by removing or minimizing the water loss. In mulching practice the surrounding soil mass of the plant is covered with the plastic film, because of which the impact of wind and weed population, etc. on evaporation loss, is nullified to a large extent. In context to control on water loss the impact of colored plastic mulch is highly significant. They play leading role towards effective water use, check on water loss; and ultimately enhancing the water use efficiency in majority of the crops.

Water use efficiency: It is one of the indexes used for assessing the water productivity, i.e., yield per unit quantity of water used. This is particularly applied when crop production is performed under limited water supply conditions such as in arid and semi-arid areas where water availability is very limited. In order to sustain the crop yield the water saving is an important task in crop production system in these areas. And accordingly, the use of water saving technologies is quite significant. In these areas the crop yield is linearly related to the available water. The extent of water availability can be extended to some extent by reducing the water loss, which may be ascertained by using mulch (plastic). Plastic mulching causes poor exposure of land mass to the solar radiation and wind which are water loss making agents. From a field experiment Li et al. (2018) noticed that the water use efficiency gets increase (31%) in potato crop on use of black and white colour plastic mulches to that of the non-mulched condition, which is because of reduction in evaporation loss from the soil surface. They also reported that between black and white colours plastic mulch the rate of evapotranspiration is higher (202 to 442.6 mm) in black plastic mulch than the white colour plastic mulch (142.8 to 436.1 mm).

The colored plastic mulch affects the Photosynthetically Active Radiation (PAR). Accordingly, the variation in colours of plastic mulch will cause increase or decrease in transmittance, absorbance, and reflectance of short and long wave radiations. At high reflection in PAR the soil temperature is declined, while moisture content is increased in root zone of the plant. Among silver, white and black colored plastic mulches, the silver color plastic mulch is being higher in reflecting PAR than the black and white color plastic mulches. Therefore, the silver color plastic mulch can be used to reduce the temperature of root zone and water loss, both. Furthermore, the colored plastic mulching is being effective to decrease the bulk density, increase soil porosity, enhance the level of nutrient status, decrease evaporation, enhance infiltration, redistribute the soil moisture and relieve the water stress. All these in combination increase the water use efficiency. In this context, through an experiment Lamont (2003) pointed that in bell paper, the use of plastic mulch resulted 33 to 52% more efficient irrigation water use as compared to unmulched field.

Plant growth and development: The effects of environment and edaphic factors on growth and development of the crops are very significant. There are several methods to modify the impact of these factors. However, the plastic mulches have been reported to be very effective in enhancing the growth and development of vegetables, and other crops. As per research findings, the white colored plastic mulch causes earlier branching in the plants as compared to the black plastic mulch. Similarly, it is also reported that the colored plastic mulch increases the leaf area of watermelon and potato plants leading to increase the photosynthesis rate, yield, and produce quality, as well. Similarly, Jahan et al. (2018) also reported that in lettuce crop the number of leaves, length of leaf, and width of leave were noted quite higher in range in case of black colored plastic mulch as compared to the white, blue, silver, and olive colour plastic mulching, which was mainly due to development of an optimum growth environment encompassing adequate soil moisture content and temperature in root zone of the crop. In onion crop as reported by Sarkar (2019) the plant height, number of leaves, and fresh root biomass were observed to a greater extent in case of silver colored plastic mulching, while the highest root length of onion was noticed under black color plastic mulching than the silver colour, which was due to greater soil temperature in case black plastic mulching. Overall, as conclusion, in majority of the cases the colored plastic mulch enables to develop positive impacts on mean soil temperature and growth parameters, causative to enhance the yield potential. However, the black color plastic mulch is more responsive to enhance the growth attributes of plant.

Crop yield: The status of root zone temperature is very much responsive to affect the plant physiology in terms of root development, soil aeration, and water and nutrient/mineral uptake. This also leads to affect the crop yield in significant manner. In this regard Díaz-Pérez (2010) through an experiment pointed that in pepper there is significant effect of colored plastic mulch on its fruit yield. In hot (summer) weather the yield was higher in case of silver color plastic mulching than the black plastic mulching. On the other hand, in the cool (winter) condition, it was higher in case of black plastic mulching. Similarly, as per Ashrafuzzaman (2011) in chili crop a better response in terms of highest number of fruits and increase in yield was noticed in black color plastic mulch, besides highest level of chlorophyll a and b and total chlorophyll contents. The reason behind this fact was associated to the spectral distribution of reflected light from the surface of colour film. Increased chlorophyll content is causative to affect the process of photosynthesis; and thereby, the crop yield, too.

In another research trial conducted by Li et al. (2018), it is found that in potato crop at the mean air temperature more than 20°C the yield was quite higher in case of black color plastic mulch in contrast to white color plastic mulch, while it was higher in case of white color plastic mulching when air temperature was lesser than 20°C.

Produce quality: The colored plastic mulches also put their effects on quality of the crop produce. On this aspect several research trials have been done worldwide, showed their significant effects on produce quality. In a field study on watermelon Shaikh and Fouda (2008) found that there was increase in dry matter percentage, and vitamin-C in the treatment of black color plastic mulching. Also, in lettuce crop there was increase in vitamin-C and phenolic contents, when black color plastic film was applied for mulching. Sarkar et al. (2018) also mentioned that in onion crop the treatment of silver polyethylene mulch resulted increase in total soluble solids (TSS), reduced sugar content, vitamin-C and pyruvates, because of change in reflectance pattern of light which causes improvement in microbial activities towards enhancing S and K activity (photosynthesis).

Weed control: The effect of plastic mulching on weed control is promising. This has been proved across the world by conducting field trials and demonstrations. The reason behind this may be the effects on photosynthesis action, development of shading effect and poor germination of weed's seeds. In this line few important findings reported by the scientists are presented hereby. Rajablarijani et al. (2014) reported that the plastic mulching has positive impacts on weed suppression because of shading effects causing reduction in weed germination and their seedling growth, besides creating effects on photosynthesis action, also. Similarly, as per Mahajan (2007), in ginger crop the plastic mulch reduced the weed's dry matter by 63.8% as compared to unmulched field. Similarly, Lamont (2005) in a field experiment found that the impact of black and clear plastic mulches was positive to reduce the weed infestation, which was mainly because of their effectiveness towards warming the soil and enhancing the temperature of root zone soil mass. However, between black and clear mulch the impact of black color plastic mulch was better to reduce the weed control.

Diseases and insect pest control: The effect of plastic machining has also been noticed to a large extent on disease as well as insect pest's control. The aphid as the crop pest is severely affected on application of plastic mulching. Farias-Larios and Orozco-Santos (1997) found that amongst different colors plastic mulch the clear plastic mulch is most effective to repel this particular pest to that of the black color plastic mulch. On the other hand, Dickerson (2002) observed that, the yellow color plastic mulch causes negative impact on insect pest control. It attracts the green pea aphids, striped and spotted cucumber beetles. Brown et al (2019) reported that among colored plastic mulches, the white and clear plastic mulches are highly effective to reduce the incidence of viral diseases, whitefly population, and aphid population as well. Also, in some of the crops the repelling Aphids reduce the incidence of viral diseases. The infestation by thrips was reported low in red, green, and black color plastic mulches.

Extension of crop period: The effect or benefit of plastic mulching has also been observed regarding extension of crop period. On using black color plastic mulching the soil temperature gets increase due to more absorption or trapping of incoming solar radiations. The warm soil mass allows to fall earlier planting date/seed germination, which tends to speed up early plant growth. In case of white or silver color plastic mulching in summer season, there is reduction in soil temperature, because of reflection of solar radiation from the top of mulch surface. Use of this mulch could be better in winter season to raise the soil temperature. In an experiment conducted at Utah, the plastic mulching resulted 2 to 3 weeks earlier crop maturity, than the crops grown in unmulched condition.

Leaching reduction: Research evidences advocate that the plastic mulching causes reduction in leaching of fertilizers/nutrients applied to the crop. In mulching case if drip system has been used for irrigating/fertigating the crop, the possibility of fertilizer leaching is completely negated as the fertilizers/nutrients are applied in very precise amount through irrigation water (fertigation), which is retained in the root zone and does not move beyond that, i.e., there is no leaching of water + nutrients. In addition, the applied nutrients are instantly utilized by the grown crops. This also denotes the possibility of nutrient's availability for leaching, is not there.

Reduction in soil compaction: In mulched condition, the soil is in covered form, i.e., there is no direct impact of any foreign agents. In rainy season the plastic mulch also acts as rain protector for soil media. In this situation, the soil becomes free from rain drop impact. The soil compaction due to rainfall occurrence is very common, because rain drops falling from the height offer impacting force on the top of soil mass. In result, the coarser soil particles get break into fine particles, which settle down in the inter-connected void's path. In this way, the top soil surface becomes compact in nature. In mulched condition the soil is lying under protected condition against foot trafficking and rainfall. This leads to keep the soil mass in loose, friable, and well-aerated condition. In this featured soils the root development, plant growth, nutrient's uptake, etc. are in quite improved range.

8.4.2 Comparison between Organic and Plastic Mulches

The organic mulches are quite different than the plastic mulches in terms of their effects on crops, cost, service life, etc. Table 8.16. illustrates few important differences between organic and plastic mulches.

Table 8.16 Difference between organic and plastic mulch

S. No.	Parameter	Organic mulch	Plastic mulch
1.	Materials that can be used	Bio-based cellulose, chips, leaf, paper, etc.	Acetate, polyethylene, polymeric materials.
2.	Durability	Not fixed (Temporary) They get decay over time.	Long-lasting, 2 to 3 crop seasons depending upon thickness of film.
3.	Mulch thickness	Normally, 3 to 5 cm depends on application rate.	Depends on thickness of the plastic film. 5 to 100 micron thickness can be used for mulching.
4.	Color	Natural, i.e., depends on the color of the parent materials.	Several colors such as black, silver, white, red, blues, yellow, etc.
5.	Weed control	Weed control is there, but lesser than plastic mulching	High level of weed control, except in case of transparent or clear film plastic mulch.

(Contd.)

S. No.	Parameter	Organic mulch	Plastic mulch
6.	Soil solarisation	Not effective or not applied.	Most effective for soil solarisation. Transparent and thin plastic films are most suitable.
7.	Pest management	Effective to reduce thrips and fungal diseases.	Reduces thrips, spider mites and whiteflies.
8.	Fragments	Fully degradable.	Non-degradable to soil
9.	Availability	These are locally available materials.	These are purchase items, i.e., not available as local materials.
10.	Priority mulch materials	Normally, the rice husk, wheat straw, sugarcane leaves, etc. are commonly used.	Plastic film/mulch materials.
11.	Price and its laying cost	Cheaper than the others.	Expensive
12.	Labour requirement for laying	Not so high.	Large number of labour requirement for placing in field.
13.	Plant growth	Moderate in range.	Very good response on crop/plant growth.
14.	Moisture conservation	Moderate in range.	Significant moisture conservation.
15.	Environmental effect	Not so.	Develops environmental effect (pollution).

8.4.3 Selection of Plastic Mulch

The plastic mulches are available in different features such as (i) Smoothness ;(ii) Thickness; and (iii) Colors, as well, which make them different with respect to their behaviour or effect on crop, concerned. The selection of suitable plastic film for using as mulch material, based on above three parameters, is described below:

Types of plastic film: Normally, the plastic films are found in two main forms or types, i.e., (i) Smooth plastic films; and (ii) Embossed plastic films. In which, the smooth plastic films are very common and easily available in local market. These are plane with smooth surface, are commonly used for mulching purpose. Also, they are cheaper than the embossed plastic films. The surface of embossed plastic films is corrugated and comprises stretches. Because of this reason these plastic films are less prone to wind fatigue/cracking. Also, they do not expand or contract under fluctuating temperature condition. Considering these features and others of plastic films one can easily select the plastic films for mulching purposes.

Thickness of film: The thickness of plastic film to be used for mulching purposes varies from 25 to 100 microns. Thickness affects the strength and durability of the plastic film. However, cost of film varies with the thickness. A 25-micron thick plastic film involves less cost than the 50, 75 or 100-microns thick plastic films. Thickness of film also decides its application for mulching in different crops. In short duration crops say for 3-months or little more, such as in vegetables like okra, brinjal, tomato, potato, etc. 25-micron thick plastic films are better to use for mulching, but in the crops having their duration more say year or so, a greater thickness plastic film, i.e., 75–100-microns thick plastic films are suggested to use. In banana, normally, more than 100-micron thick poly films are used for mulching, because banana suckers easily tear the thin films. The clear thin plastic films (25-micron) are being suitable for soil solarisation.

Film's color: In context to mulching, the plastic films are available in different colors such as black, white, red, yellow, blue, gray, and orange. Each color plastic films have their individual effects on the crop, concerned. Amongst different colors plastic films, the black plastic films are widely used for mulching purposes. The clear and white plastic films are selected in certain conditions; normally, for soil solarisation but their thickness must be very less say 25-micron or so. Apart from above, the green and brown infrared transmitting (IRT) plastic films are also in option for use. The IRT plastic films allow soil warming to a significant level; and thus affect the weed growth. The black color plastic films are used for weed control, as they retard photosynthesis action of the weeds. In nutshell, the effect of different colors plastic films is shown in Table 8.17.

Table 8.17 Effect of different colors plastic films (Angima 2009, Penn State Extension 2015, and Sanders 2001)

S. No.	Mulch property	Color of plastic film			
		Black	**Clear**	**White/Silver**	**Infrared transmitting (IRT)**
1.	Soil temperature	#Increases in the range of 3 to 5°F	#Increases in the range of 6 to 14°F	Decreases in the range of −2 to 0.7°F	#Increases from 5 to 8°F
2.	Light reflectivity	Low	Low	High	Low
3.	Light absorptivity	High	Low	Low	High
4.	Light transmission	Low	Very High	Low	High
5.	Weed suppression	Excellent	Poor	Excellent	Excellent

2 to 4 inch soil depth

8.5 BIODEGRADABLE PLASTIC MULCH

The plastic mulch, which is commonly used in agriculture, especially, in horticultural crops for achieving the target of water saving, weed control, yield increment, better produce quality, soil temperature increment; or in nutshell, for creating most conducive soil-water-plant environment for proper growth and development of the crop, is the low cost polyethylene (PE) film. PE is the petrochemical based product. Although, because of its various positive features its use is versatile in agriculture sector, but because of its non-degradable characteristics there are so many bad effects get developed at d/s, which make it injurious for human being. The environmental pollution is one of the main amongst them. Experimental evidences advocate that on prolong use of plastic much, the soil-plant environment gets badly degraded; and accordingly, the soil becomes unsuitable for cultivation points of view. In a research conducted in China, it is found that the long-term use of plastic mulch resulted the accumulation of plastic residuals in the soil @ 50 to 260 kg/m^2 in top soil (0–20 cm) depth inhibiting the plant growth (Liu E.K. et al., 2014). In addition, the PE is also found chemically inert, affects the soil and may also enter the food chain (Barnes et al., 2009; Teuten et al., 2009). Besides, plastic mulches also add plasticizing agents in soil media and pollute it.

In contrast, the biodegradable plastic mulch (BDM) overcomes all the demerits posed by conventional polyethylene (PE) mulch. In normal course, the BDMs are tilled, which get mixed in soil media in due course of time. In this way, BDM also develops impact on soil ecosystem. Research findings pointed that the BDMs influence the soil microbial communities by developing surface barrier before their incorporation in the soil. This leads to affect the soil micro-climate like PE films. Furthermore, after incorporation in soil, there is direct addition of carbon, microorganisms, additives, and adherent chemicals, which is inconducive for soil health. The incorporation of BDM in soil can also result increment of microbial activities and fungal taxa.

8.5.1 Materials Used for BDM

The biodegradable mulches (BDMs) are formed by bio-based polymers derived from the microbes or plants, or fossil-sourced materials. The common bio-based polymers used for manufacturing BDMs are Polylactic acid (PLA), starch, cellulose, Poly-Hydroxyalkanoates (PHA), etc. mainly. In case of fossil-sourced polyesters used for manufacturing the BDMs the common contents are Polybutylene succinate (PBS), Poly (butylene succinate-co-adipate) (PBSA), and Poly (butylene-adipate-co-terephthalate) (PBAT) (Kasirajan and Ngouajio, 2012). The polymers used for making the BDM, contain ester bonds or Polysaccharides, are amenable to microbial hydrolysis.

8.5.2 Effects of Biodegradable Mulch

The function and objective of biodegradable mulch (BDM) and Polyethylene (PE) mulch are the same. Both the mulches affect the soil ecosystem and activate the microbial community by modifying the soil micro-climate. In process, these mulches form the barrier between soil surface and the atmosphere; and intercept the solar radiation. A part of intercepted solar radiation gets penetrate into the soil media and heat up the same. This results into increase in soil temperature. On increase or alteration in soil temperature the microbial activities of soil gets initiated at fast rate. Simultaneously, there is also happening of evaporation of soil moisture content due to temperature effect. The evaporated water mass retains below the BDM barrier. In other words, there is no evaporation loss. This advocates the water saving due to use of biodegradable mulching.

The color (black) of BDM mulch resists the solar light to enter below. In result there is effect on photosynthesis action. A reduced photosynthesis causes suppression of weeds. The extent of change or modification in above aspects depends on the physico-chemical properties of BDMs. Biodegradable mulches are permeable in nature, this causes less accumulation of Carbon dioxide (CO_2) below the mulch barrier. In result, the formation of synthates in plant body is less; and accordingly, there is negative effect on plant growth and development. Comparatively, the extent of development of above-mentioned effects is more pronounced in PE mulch than the biodegradable mulch. The beneficial feature of biodegradable mulch is their decomposition in soil media; and accordingly, no harmful effects on environment, thereby. However, the cost is quite high over PE mulch.

8.6 MULCHING CONSIDERATIONS

Prior to place the plastic mulch in the crop for achieving the set of objectives, the followings are the important points to consider before starting mulching operation:

1. Soil preparedness
2. Irrigation provision
3. Fertilizer application
4. Bed shaping
5. Placing, anchoring and earthing
6. Provision for wind break

Soil Preparedness: It indicates the view that before laying the plastic mulch in the field, the soil must be prepared in such a way that the planting or sowing of seed could be done, directly. In other words, it can be stated that:

(i) The organic matters or plant residues should be well decomposed in the soil media.
(ii) The soil must be friable.
(iii) The soil must be clod-free.
(iv) The grass or weed residues, stones/pebbles should not be on the soil surface as these objects make difficult in laying the plastic mulch.
(v) The soil should contain proper moisture content, so that if planting or sowing is required immediately, that could be easily performed. However, the soil condition "too wet" or "too dry" should be avoided.

Irrigation provision: The plastic mulching + drip system is an essential combination. In which, the function of drip system is to supply irrigation to the planted crop; while mulching acts as protectant against water and nutrients loss. In plastic mulched crop the application of irrigation by flooding technique is not recommended, because of non-uniformity in distribution of irrigation water. Therefore, in mulched crop the provision of drip system is essential. The plastic mulch causes barrier against water flow. Similarly, placing the drip tube (laterals) above plastic mulch is also not being proper. As in this condition, the water emitted from the emitter/dripper gets collected over the plastic mulch, which is not met to the crop root system. The laterals should be placed before laying the plastic film. Or in other words, the mulch should be placed above lateral lines, around the plants.

Fertilizer application: In field the laying of plastic mulch is carried out after thorough preparation of field and installation of tubing (drip system), properly. In course of field preparation the recommended basal dose of fertilizers should also be incorporated in the soil before placing the plastic mulch. The routine fertilizer application is accomplished with the help of fertigation unit attached to the drip system. In fertigation unit the venturi attachment is equipped, which sucks the solution from fertilizer tank and delvers the same to the water supply line; and finally, same is delivered to the plant through drippers.

Bed shaping: In order to have a better response of mulching on crop, the planting of seedlings or sowing of seeds is carried out on properly formed raised beds, as laying of plastic mulch is accomplished in better way on raised beds. The width of raised bed depends on the crop geometry (row to row spacing) and number of rows of the crop to be accommodated in the bed, mainly. In majority of the vegetable crops, including tomato, squash, melons, etc. for single row plantation the width of raised bed is followed to the tune of 2 to 3 feet. On the other hand, for plantation (double row) of peppers and eggplants the width of raised bed is kept 3 feet.

Placing, anchoring and earthing: The placing, anchoring and earthing of plastic film on raised bed, done in proper way, adds quality in mulching work, is being most favourable to result a better effect on the crop. The laying of plastic mulch should be done in such a way that the mulch must be properly stretched on bed surface and firmly secured from all the sides/edges and make a good level of contact with the soil of bed surface. A proper contact between the soil and plastic film/mulch assures a good level of heat transfer in soil media; and thereby, proper increment in soil temperature, too. Loosely placed plastic mulch is always under risk of damage due to ballooning effect. Especially, in case of weed control a proper contact between the soil and plastic film is very essential, because when weeds get germinate below the mulch they immediately come in contact to the plastic film. In result they get burn/damage due to heated surface of plastic mulch. In sunny days, the temperature of top surface of black color plastic film raised up 130°F, which is sufficient to burn the tender seedlings. In the condition, when soil contact is not proper with plastic mulch, then there left some clear cut space between soil surface and plastic film (mulch). This leftover space forms air pocket. In this way, the entire mulched area includes a large number of such air pockets. This creates unproductive effects on mulched crops. Actually, the available air contents in these pockets get heated up to a high temperature level. The heated air content starts moving below the mulch layer. This leads to cause desiccation of tender seedlings/plantlets, there.

Provision of windbreak: This kind of provision is felt essential for mulched crop fields, to keep the mulching work safe against strong blowing winds. The windbreak may be established by erecting a kind of vegetative barrier at the field boundary across the direction of prevailing wind. For this purpose the use of locally available trees or shrubs is found better, as their survival is very easy. The formed wind break directly obstructs the incoming strong wind currents, and saves the mulching work.

PRACTICE QUESTIONS

Descriptive Type Questions

1. Describe polytunnel—Its importance, uses, advantages and limitations.
2. Write the difference between polytunnel and greenhouse; and also describe various types of polytunnels used under protected farming.
3. Describe construction criterion of polytunnel.
4. What is the shade house; and also writes its importance and uses in agriculture.
5. Narrate the advantages and uses of net house.
6. Describe the characteristics of plastic nets.
7. Describe the type of plastic nets commonly used in construction of net house.
8. What is plastic mulching; and also write its importance in agriculture?

9. Write various advantages and disadvantages of plastic mulching.
10. Describe applications and effects of coloured plastic mulch.
11. What is biodegradable mulch; and write its similarity with plastic mulch?
12. Write various advantages and disadvantages of biodegradable mulch.

Multiple Choice Type Questions

1. Which of the following statements is correct for polytunnel?
   (a) Central height is very less
   (b) Cladding materials are different
   (c) Length is longer than the width
   (d) Only used for growing leafy vegetables
2. Which of the following crop is found best for growing in polytunnel?
   (a) Cucumber
   (b) Flowers
   (c) Melon
   (d) All above
3. The thickness of PE film used for construction of polytunnel is normally
   (a) 180 micron
   (b) 720 gauge
   (c) 450 micron
   (d) Both (a) and (b)
4. Which of the following polytunnel is called "miniature greenhouse"?
   (a) Low polytunnel
   (b) High polytunnel
   (c) Medium polytunnel
   (d) None of above
5. The height of low polytunnel is normally up to
   (a) 2 m
   (b) 1 m or little less
   (c) 2.5 m
   (d) 3.0 m
6. The commonly used covering material in construction of polytunnel is
   (a) Polythene sheets
   (b) Ethylenevinyl Acetate (EVA),
   (c) Conventional PE
   (d) All above
7. The size of high polytunnel varies to the tune of
   (a) 60 to 75 sqm
   (b) 150 to 250 sqm
   (c) 250 to 300 sqm
   (d) At least 500 sqm
8. The width of high polytunnel is in the range of
   (a) 1.5 to 2.5 m
   (b) 2.5 to 5.0 m
   (c) 5.0 to 10 m
   (d) 2 to 2.5 m
9. The length of high polytunnel is kept to the tune of
   (a) 150 m
   (b) 30 m
   (c) 200 m
   (d) 250 m
10. The central height of high polytunnel varies up to
    (a) 1.5 m
    (b) 3.0 m
    (c) 2 to 2.5 m
    (d) 1.0 m
11. Which of the following flower can be grown in polytunnels?
    (a) Gerbera and Chrysanthemum
    (b) Rose and Carnation
    (c) Gladiolus
    (d) All above

12. Which of the following fruit can be grown in polytunnels?
    (a) Strawberry (b) Sapota
    (c) Guava (d) Both (a) and (b)
13. Which of the following covering material is used for construction of net house?
    (a) Plastic net with 100% PE thread (b) Fiberglass
    (c) UV sheet (d) Glass
14. In insect proof net house the mesh of net varies from
    (a) 40 to 50% (b) 15 to 25%
    (c) 30 to 35% (d) 60 to 70%
15. A shade net with 40% shading percentage denotes
    (a) 40% light intensity is cut
    (b) 40% incoming temperature is intercepted
    (c) 60% light intensity is allowed to pass, inside
    (d) Both (a) and (c)
16. The "Green × Black" colour combination plastic nets can be used for
    (a) Nursery raising (b) Grape cultivation
    (c) Gerbera cultivation (d) All above
17. The "Black × Black" colour combination plastic nets can be used for
    (a) Nursery raising (b) Grape cultivation
    (c) Gerbera cultivation (d) All above
18. The "White × Black" colour combination plastic nets can be used for
    (a) Nursery raising (b) Grape cultivation
    (c) Gerbera cultivation (d) All above
19. The "Green × Green" colour combination plastic nets can be used for
    (a) Nursery raising (b) Grape cultivation
    (c) Ornamental plants growing (d) All above
20. The mesh size of shade net varies from
    (a) 1.7 to 7.0 mm (b) 2.5 to 4.0 mm
    (c) 0.2 to 3.1 mm (d) 1.8 to 7.0 mm
21. The mesh size of anti-hail nets varies from
    (a) 1.7 to 7.0 mm (b) 2.5 to 4.0 mm
    (c) 0.2 to 3.1 mm (d) 1.8 to 7.0 mm
22. The mesh size of anti-birds nets varies from
    (a) 30 to 40 mm (b) 2.5 to 4.0 mm
    (c) 1.7 to 7.0 mm (d) 1.8 to 7.0 mm
23. The shading percentage of anti-birds nets varies from
    (a) 25 to 90 (b) 10 to 20
    (c) 10 to 25 (d) 5 to 15
24. The shading percentage of anti-insects nets varies from
    (a) 25 to 90 (b) 10 to 20
    (c) 10 to 25 (d) 5 to 15

25. The shading percentage of anti-hail nets varies from
(a) 25 to 90 (b) 10 to 20
(c) 10 to 25 (d) 5 to 15

26. The percentage of black carbon in plastic nets varies from
(a) Less than 1% (b) 2 to 5%
(c) More than 1% (d) 3 to 4.5%

27. Plastic mulching is done for
(a) Fertilizer saving, mainly (b) Water saving, mainly
(c) Weed control, mainly (d) All above

28. Black colour plastic mulch is used for
(a) Fertilizer saving, mainly (b) Water saving, mainly
(c) Weed control, mainly (d) All above

29. Thickness of plastic mulch varies from
(a) 5 to 100 micron (b) 20 to 50 micron
(c) 10 to 20 micron (d) 50 to 75 micron

30. The bio-degradable mulches are constructed by using
(a) Agricultural residues (b) Bio-based polymers
(c) Petrochemicals (d) All above

Answers

1. c	**2.** d	**3.** d	**4.** a	**5.** b	**6.** d	**7.** a	**8.** d	**9.** b	**10.** c
11. d	**12.** d	**13.** a	**14.** a	**15.** d	**16.** b	**17.** a	**18.** c	**19.** c	**20.** a
21. b	**22.** a	**23.** d	**24.** b	**25.** c	**26.** a	**27.** d	**28.** c	**29.** a	**30.** b

BIBLIOGRAPHY

Arin, L., and Ankara, S. (2001). Effect of low tunnel, mulch and pruning on the yield and earliness to tomato in unheated greenhouse. *J. Appl. Hort.*, Lucknow, **3**: 23–27.

Bas, T. (1991). Possibilities of Using Different Organic and Inorganic Materials for Greenhouse cucumber production. Ph.D Thesis. Ege Univ., Izmir.

Bhattacharyya, P. (2012). Planting the seeds for prosperity. Livemint.com. *HT Media.* Retrieved November 23.

Del Amor, F.M., Ortuño, G., Gómez, M.D., Vicente, F., and García, A.J. (2007). Yield and fruit quality response of sweet pepper plants cultivated in environmentally friendly substrates. *Acta Hort.*, **761**: 527–531.

Enoch, H.Z., and Enoch, Y. (1999). The history and geography of greenhouse, In: G. Stanhill and H.Z. Enoch (eds). Greenhouse ecosystems. Elsevier, Amsterdam, The Netherlands. November, pp. 1–15.

Goldammer T. (2019). Greenhouse Management: A Guide to Operations and Technology. Apex Publishers, USA.

Gyan P. Mishra, Narendra Singh, Hitesh Kumar, and Shashi Bala Singh. (2007). Protected cultivation for Food and Nutritional Security at Ladakh. *Defence Science Journal*, **61**(2): 219–225.

Harel, D., Fadida, H., Alik, S., Gantzand, S., and Shilo, K. (2014). The effect of mean daily temperature and relative humidityon pollen, fruit set and yield of tomato Grown in commercial protected cultivation. *Agronomy*, **4**: 167–177.

Isaac, S.R. (2015). Performance Evaluation of Leafy Vegetables in Naturally Ventilated Polyhouses, *International Journal of Research Studies in Agricultural Sciences*, **1**(3): 1–4.

Ken-Bar. (2004). Low tunnel–hoop supported row covers. *Acta Horticultrae*, **491**: 87–91.

Libik, A. and Siwek, P. (1994). Changes in soil temperature affected by the application of plastic covers in field production of lettuce and water melon. *Acta Hort*., 371: 269–273.

Maitra, S., Shankar, T., Sairam, M., and Pine, S. (2020). Evaluation of Gerbera (*Gerbera jamesonii L.*) Cultivars for growth, yield and flower quality under protected cultivation. *Indian Journal of Natural Sciences*, **10**(60): 20271–20276.

Maughan, T.L. (2013). Optimizing systems for cold climate strawberry production. MS Thesis. Utah State University. Logan, Utah, pp. 2034.

Monteiro, J.E.B.A., Silva, I.J.O., and Piedade, S.M. (2002). Perforated plastic film for low tunnels cultivated with lettuce. Revista Brasileira-de-Engenharia *Agricola-Ambiental*, **6**: 535–538.

Saini, A.K. and Singh, K.G. (2001). In: Annual report of All India Coordinated Research, Project on application of plastics in agriculture, pp. 69–74.

Shahi, S. (2009). Protective cultivation–A key for sustainable production in North western Himalayas. *Himalayan Ecology*, **12**(2): 1–5.

Shiraiwa, N., Kashima, Y., Itai, A., and Tanabe, K. (2007). Effects of tunnel covering plastic films and fertilization methods on growth, bolting and yield in Welsh onion (*Allium fistulosum L.*) harvested in early summer. *Horticulture Research*, Japan, **6**: 17.

Singh, A.A., Syndor, B.C., Deka, R.K., Singh, R.K. and Patel, R.K., (2012). The effect of microclimate inside low tunnels on off season production of strawberry (*Frageria × ananassa Duch.*). *Scientia Horticulturae*, **144**: 36-41.

Singh, R.K. and Satpathy, K.K. (2005). Scope and adoption of plastic culture technology in north-east hill region. In: Agricultural mechanization in North East India, ICAR, Research Complex for NEH region, Barapani, pp. 114-21.

Streck, L., Schneider, F.M., Buriol, G.A., Luzza, J., and Sandri, M.A. (2007). A system grow lettuce inside low plastic tunnels. *Ciencia Rural*, **37**: 667–675.

Suresh R. (2010). Micro Irrigation—Theory and Practice. Standard Publishers Distributors, Nai Sarak, Delhi.

United States Department of Agriculture (USDA) (2009). USDA to launch high tunnel pilot study to increase availability of locally grown foods (Press release). Washington, DC. Archived from the original on January 31, 2010.

Wien, H.C. (2009). Micro environmental variations within the high tunnel. *Horticulture Science*, **44**: 235-238.

Wien, H.C., Reid, J.E., Rasmussen, C., and Orzolek, M.D. (2006). Use of low tunnels to improve plant growth in high tunnels, pp. 1–4.

https://www.indiamart.com/proddetail/plastic-mulching-paper-sheet-22797512830.html

https://blog.firsttunnels.co.uk/polytunnel-polythene-types/)

CHAPTER 9

Greenhouse Irrigation Methods

Greenhouse is frame-based structure appearing just like house, is used for crop growing in a controlled environment under protected condition. The crop grown inside greenhouse requires proper inputs in scheduled manner. Amongst various inputs required, the irrigation is one on the main. If irrigation in proper amount and at scheduled time is not provided, the crop yield gets drastically hampered. In addition, the irrigation and other inputs are also required to apply in precise manner, frequently. Especially, the irrigation needs to apply at high frequency or close interval so that there would not be the moisture stress in root zone of the crop. The irrigation scheduling at daily or alternate day is found better for greenhouse crops. At this irrigation schedule the water is applied on daily basis or alternate day for the amount equal to the daily water requirement of the crop, which is very small, say for few liters or so. This small quantity of water application is beneficial in management of micro-clime inside greenhouse. It mainly affects the humidity level of greenhouse. The application of irrigation by traditional methods such as flooding, border, check basin, furrow method, etc. is not found okay for greenhouse crops. The micro-irrigation comprising drip and micro-sprinkler system is only the technique, which is found most suitable for watering greenhouse crops. The micro-irrigation satisfies mostly all the requirements of precise application of irrigation water and fertilizers/nutrients to the greenhouse crops. On daily basis, with little irrigation amount, it can be successfully accomplished by using micro-irrigation. In addition, the micro-irrigation system also includes the provision for application of fertilizers/nutrients along with irrigation water called fertigation, is an additional benefit towards greenhouse crop farming. In a closed production zone such as in greenhouse the micro-irrigation system is well suitable for development of micro-climate as per requirement of the crop concern. In this chapter the irrigation methods comprising drip, micro-sprinkler and others have been narrated in detail.

9.1 IRRIGATION FUNDAMENTAL

There are few important terminologies to know for better understanding about irrigation, are narrated as below:

Irrigation frequency: It denotes the time interval between irrigations to be done. In greenhouse crop irrigation the physical characteristics of growing media used play significant role in deciding the irrigation frequency. In which the water-holding capacity and drainage ability of growing media are the overriding factors. Water-holding capacity determines the water retention in media after providing irrigation to them. Drainage ability of growing media is important particularly, when there is problem of availability of soluble salts in irrigation water. However, sometimes, the occurrence of nutritional problems such as the deficiency of magnesium and micro-nutrient's also arises, because of excess leaching from the media. In order to overcome such situations, the consideration of drainage ability of growing media is taken into consideration.

Irrigation amount: This is very important to know the amount of water to be applied as irrigation to the crop. Although, the timing and modes of irrigation are also important, but irrigation amount is dominating over these two parameters. For irrigation of greenhouse crop, normally 10 to 15% extra water than the holding capacity of the media/container is applied. This is just to cause leaching action for removing the possibility of salt accumulation in growing media or container.

Growing media condition: Irrigation of greenhouse crops in proper way also depends on the condition of media used for growing the crop. Especially, irrigation efficiency gets significantly affected because of media condition. For example, the peat moss, bark and other organic substances used in soilless growing media, involve water repelling features or in other words they have hydrophobic characteristics. These constituents on excessive drying have difficulty to wet, smoothly. This peculiar property advocates to follow the irrigation, very carefully in such growing media. However, this could be resolved by applying some wetting agents to cause appropriate level of water absorption in growing media.

Media porosity and water-holding capacity (WHC): Porosity represents the space available to store water, nutrients and air contents in porous media. The porosity and water-holding capacity are interrelated to each other. In other words, the porosity determines the water-holding capacity of growing media. In this way, the porosity and WHC in combine form affect the irrigation, significantly. At optimum level of porosity and WHC for a given growing media constitutes sufficient pores spaces to allow adequate salt leaching and gaseous transformation, besides forming a good level of water-holding capacity. This leads to reduce the irrigation frequency.

Water quality: Water quality signifies the availability of foreign materials, mainly the soluble salts in the water to be used for irrigation. It largely affects the irrigation. In the situation of using salty water for irrigation, about 10 to 15% extra water is applied to the growing media for removing or leaching the salt contents from the media container. In addition, the wetting and drying of growing media should also be reduced to avoid the possibility of increase in relative concentration of salt contents. In water quality context, it is always advised for testing its quality on regular basis, to remove the possibility of development of water quality-based problems in growing media.

9.2 GREENHOUSE IRRIGATION RULES

The crops grown in greenhouse environment have quite different climate/environment for their growth and development. However, within protected environment they require proper irrigation water management, nutrient management, insect-pest management, and weed management as well to result optimum crop production. As for as irrigation application is concerned, the grown crop never response well in case of under- and overirrigations. In other words, the grown crop requires an optimum dose of inputs at proper schedule; otherwise, there develops negative impacts on crop yield. In order to have better impact of irrigation on crop productivity, the following rules have been framed for watering of greenhouse crop:

Rule No (i): Use a well-drained and good structured root substrate

In greenhouse farming system to perform the irrigation efficiently the root substrate to be used, must have the property of prompt drainage along with good structure. A good structure for media denotes to have sufficient moisture retention capacity and aeration for gaseous exchange. This feature develops most efficient soil-water-plant environment for conducive plant growth and development. The combination of coarse textured and highly stable structure in optimum range constitutes such type of substrate.

Rule No (ii): Perform thorough watering at the schedule time

The partial watering is always avoided. However, as per rule 10 to 15% excess water should be applied. The following points should also be followed in context to irrigation of greenhouse crops:

- In watering process, the water should flow from the bottom of the pots.
- In case of bedding system of plantations, the root zone should be thoroughly wetted.
- Water requirement of soil-based substrates should be at the rate of 20 l/m^2 of bench area and 0.3 to 0.35 liter per 16.5 cm diameter container.

Rule No (iii): Do watering immediately before occurrence of moisture stress

This irrigation rule advocates that the watering must be done just before start of moisture stress in plant. The moisture stress can be observed in the form of foliar-based symptoms such as change in texture, colour and turbidity level. However, these symptoms vary from crop to crop. In some of the crops there is no any moisture stress symptom is seen in the form of change in texture, color or turbidity. The most accurate way to assess the situation of moisture stress in growing media is by taking the weight of substrate at some predetermined interval.

9.3 MICRO-IRRIGATION

In micro-irrigation the term "micro" refers to very small or very low application of water, which is performed in the form of continuous drips, tiny streams or miniature spray above or below the soil surface. The application of water in micro form satisfies the requirement of precision irrigation. Micro-irrigation method is very effective to save the irrigation water and also enhance water cum fertilizer use efficiency in greenhouse environment. In addition, it also reduces the weed control, soil erosion and overall cost of cultivation, as well. This irrigation is suitably used in greenhouse crop production system. The important features of micro-irrigation are narrated as under:

- Water distribution is carried out through pipeline system under suitable pressure range.
- System is operated with the help of suitable capacity pumping unit to build up sufficient pressure in pipeline for proper water discharge at delivery points.

- Irrigation is applied in the form of drop (drip method) or spray (micro-sprinklers) to the crop.
- Rate of water application is low.
- The air exchange and water balance within root zone is at optimum level.
- Water application is done at frequent interval depending on water requirement of the crop.
- Applied water is instantly extracted by the root system for crop growth.
- No water wastage in terms of runoff, deep percolation, etc.
- Root zone soil is always at field capacity. This is the reason that plant growth is very fast in MIS case.
- Nutrients or fertilizer's loss is negligible.
- The crop yield is very high.
- Produce quality is far better.

9.3.1 Classification of Micro-irrigation

Micro-irrigation comprises following two irrigation methods:

(i) Drip irrigation, and
(ii) Micro-sprinkler irrigation method.

These two methods are described as under:

Drip Irrigation

This is one of the types of micro-irrigation, is also called trickle irrigation. In this irrigation method water is directly applied to the crop root zone in the form of drops by means of emitter/dripper at frequent time intervals. Drippers may be placed over or below the soil surface. The drippers placed on the soil surface are called online drippers, while those placed below the soil surface are known as inline drippers. In drip irrigation the rate of water application is less than infiltration rate of water in growing media. The water emitted from drippers gets move in soil media largely in the form of unsaturated flow. Emitted water wets the root zone vertically by gravity flow and laterally due to capillary action. The movement of water in vertical and horizontal or lateral direction depends on the soil types and rate of water emission from emitters. As example the lateral movement of water is more in medium to heavy soils than the sandy soils. Similarly, at high discharge rate the water moves downward, more as compared to the lateral or horizontal movement.

Drip system consists of control unit, pipeline, emission device and accessories, mainly. The control unit assembles the filters—sand filter, disc filter and hydro-cyclone filters, fertigation unit, pressure gauge, etc. mainly. The function of filter is to remove foreign materials from the water to be used for irrigation. These filters are placed at the u/s end of the pipeline. Fertigation unit comprises injection system, i.e., venturi and fertilizer tank. Pipeline assembles the main line, sub-main line and the laterals. Laterals are laid along the rows of plantation. Drippers are placed on the lateral pipe near to the plants. The water source may be the tube well, pond water, canal water, spring water or harvested rainwater, depending on their availability at the field. The energy source may be the fuel (diesel and petrol) and electricity-based pumping units. On system operation, the water from source is extracted by the pumping unit and delivered to the filtering unit, where water is filtered and clean water is directed to pass in the main line. The water from main line is delivered to the sub-main line and from there to the laterals. Finally, lateral water is dropped near to the plant stem through drip. The water soluble fertilizers/liquid fertilizers and other chemicals (nutrients) are also applied with the help of fertigation unit. The water soluble fertilizers and liquid fertilizers are used for fertigation.

Advantages of Drip Method

Drip system is precision irrigation method, provides significant advantages in various aspects, which cannot be compared with flood irrigation methods. In brief some of the important advantages are narrated as under:

- Excellent control on water application.
- Irrigation is possible on daily basis.
- The water loss likely to be due to evaporation, seepage and deep percolation is completely eliminated.
- In field the soil moisture deficit at micro-level can be easily removed by scheduling the irrigation at daily basis.
- Drip system encompasses fertigation unit, through which the water soluble or liquid fertilizers can be easily applied to the crop in precise way.
- In drip method the fertilizers and nutrients are directly applied to the crop root zone, which becomes readily available to the plants.
- Application of saline water can also be possible without any harmful effect.
- This method causes ample water saving, fertilizer saving, energy saving and labor savings, as well.
- The line sown crops like sugarcane, papaya, banana, guava, flowers, etc. are easily irrigated by drip method.
- Land levelness is not so essential.
- The soil erosion problem is completely negated.
- Weed problem is very less.
- Water application efficiency and water use efficiency, both are very high.
- High crop yield.
- Better produce quality.
- Drip irrigation is only the method for irrigation of greenhouse crops.
- Low pressure requirement.
- Labour consumption is less.

***Disadvantage*:** The disadvantages of drip method are pointed as under:

- High initial cost; varies with the crop geometry.
- At low pressure it causes poor water distribution.
- Clean water, i.e., free from soil particle and physical impurities, is essential.
- The chocked emitters due to chemical deposits cannot be completely cleaned.
- Its use for irrigating high water requiring crops, such as paddy, etc. is not suitable.

***Suitability*:** Suitability of drip irrigation method is predicted on various aspects, such as:

(i) Crop
(ii) Soil

(iii) Slopes
(iv) Water

Suitable crops: Drip system is found most suitable for row crops. The fruit crops, vegetables and flowers are most suitable to irrigate by this method. However, in terms of preference the high valued crops are always preferred for irrigation using drip method.

Suitable slopes: At medium slope this can be placed for irrigating the crops. However, in undulating land topography where crops are planted along the contour, the lateral lines should be laid along them; otherwise, there is possibility of pressure variation on the emitters, causing non-uniformity in water emitting from the emitters.

Suitable soils: In most of the soils the drip method is found fit for irrigating the crops. However, in clay soils the low discharge emitters are used to keep the rate of water application low. At high discharge condition there is water ponding on the soil surface or formation of over land flow. This leads to cause water loss which is not desirable with drip method. On the other hand, in sandy soils high discharge emitters are placed to ensure adequate lateral wetting of soil in the root zone. Overall, the loamy soils are found best for drip irrigation method.

Suitable water: Drip method requires quality water, i.e., the water must be silt or sediment free and salt free, also. The soil particles available in water tend to choke the emitters. Similarly, the chemical contents present in the water are also likely to get deposit in the pipeline and emitters in the form of precipitates; and accordingly there is blockage of emitters. The aperture size of emitters varies from 0.2 to 2.0 mm are very prone to get chock due to entry of small soil particles.

Limitations of Drip Irrigation

Besides, several advantages offered by drip method in respect of water saving, nutrient saving, labour saving energy savings, etc. and potential increase in crop productivity, there are some prominent limitations regarding application of this technology. These are mentioned below:

Emitter's clogging: This is very serious limitation of drip system, which removal by the farmer becomes difficult unless support of subject expert.

Pipeline damage: The plastic pipeline used in drip system is more likely to get damage because of rodents. A small hole made in the pipeline creates very serious effect on water distribution and application to the crop, too. In this condition there is water loss and less pressure development in pipeline. This results into reduction in water dripping rate of drippers.

Elevation effect: The effect of surface elevation on performance of drip system is not so influencing. However, in highly undulating terrains such as in hilly tracts where slope is very steep and irregular, there is significant effect on water distribution and application both to the crop.

Salt accumulation: In drip irrigated field there is possibility of salt accumulation in crop root zone. This is because of the reason that in the condition of saline water use for irrigation, the water content is extracted by the crop, but salt contents remain in the soil (root zone), which does not leach below. This results into accumulation of salts in root zone of the crop.

High initial cost: Drip system consists of plastic tubing of different sizes and control unit comprising different filters and fertigation unit, involves high initial cost for establishment.

This makes the poor or medium farmers difficult to install the system for irrigating the crops. However, few states in country providing subsidy on drip system. Utilizing subsidy scheme majority of the interested growers are using this method for irrigating the crops.

Other causes: In the situation of failure of drip system the crop faces a high level of moisture stress, because of not supply of water to the crop. Since, drip irrigated crops have the habit of daily water feeding; therefore, a long gap in water application develops bad effect on crop response.

Drip System—Components

Broadly, a drip system comprises following main components:

1. Water source
2. Pumping unit
3. Pipeline system
   - (i) Main pipeline
   - (ii) Sub-main pipeline
   - (iii) Laterals
4. Emitters
5. Accessories: In accessories different types of valves, pressure regulator, filters, pressure gauge, fertilizer applicator, etc. are included.

Figure 9.1 shows the components of drip system.

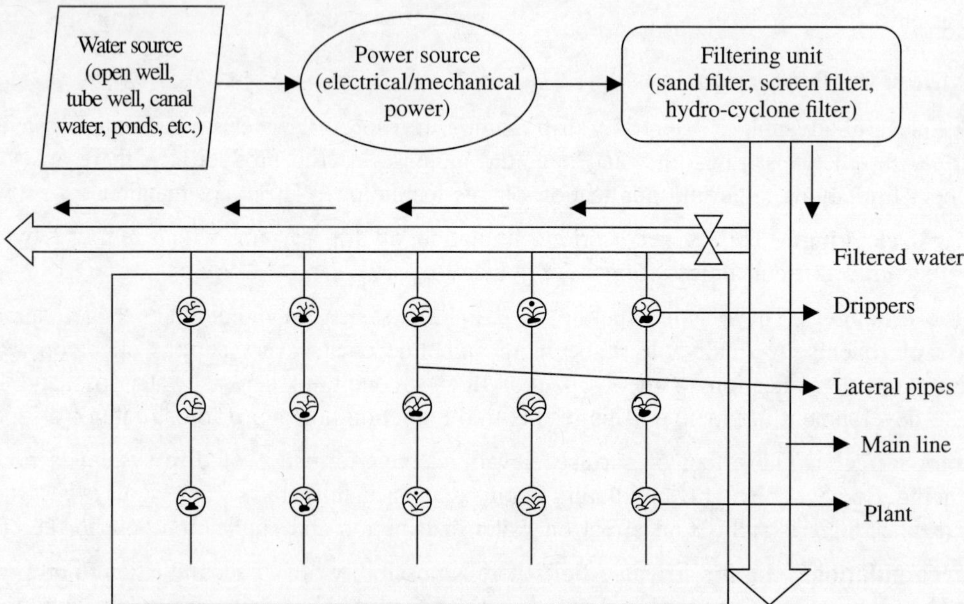

Figure 9.1 View of drip system installed in the field

Water source: Any water body with good quality water can be used as the water source for irrigating the crops. The groundwater and pond's water, dug wells, canal water, etc. are very common for using by this method. Also, the harvested rainwater in ponds, tanks, etc. can be used with drip system. In low rainfall regions, i.e., the arid and semi-arid areas where rainfall is less, the rainwater is harvested in depressed area or in ponds. These harvested water can also be used for irrigation using drip method. In canal command areas where irrigation is performed through canal water supply; this water can also be used for the purpose. However, the water must be of good quality, both physically and chemically. The groundwater with heavy silt load is not suitable, as silt particles are so fine in size that they are not absolutely filtered with the commonly used filters (sand and screen filters). In this case, a special type of filter called hydro-cyclone filter is used to remove the silt particles from the water and then it is allowed to use for irrigation through drip method.

Pump: The centrifugal pump is commonly used as the power source to lift the water from water source and deliver the same to the plant via pipeline system. The pump size/capacity depends on the depth of water-table and extent of crop area to be irrigated by the system. Sometimes, the overhead tank is also used as the water source. In this condition the water form overhead tank flows to the pipeline under gravity effect; accordingly, the need of pump is not essential. However, the height of water tank must be at least to that extent, at which the required pressure at emitter's level could be easily formed. For example, to create the pressure in the range of 1.5 to 2.0 kg/sqcm which is normally required in case of drip method, the height of water tank must be at least 15 m or more from the ground level; otherwise, the required pressure would not get develop at the emitter; and accordingly the rate of water emission from the emitter will get affected.

Pipeline System: Drip method is totally pipeline based system. The PVC made pipes are commonly used for the purpose. The drip pipeline system is divided in following three sub-sections, namely:

(i) Main pipeline,
(ii) Sub-main pipeline, and
(iii) Lateral line.

***Main pipeline*:** This part of pipeline unit is directly connected to the control head. It directly receives the filtered water from screen filter or source with the aid of pumping unit. The water from main pipeline is delivered to the sub-main pipeline. The size of main pipeline is greater than the sub-main pipe and laterals. In order to conduct the water with proper flow rate, the main pipeline is placed at little higher elevation than the sub-main and laterals. The main pipeline is installed at proper depth below the ground surface.

***Sub-main line*:** This is connected by one end from the main pipeline and other end is placed with end cap. Laterals are connected to sub-main line. Sub-main pipe directly receives the water from main pipe and delvers the same to the laterals. The size (diameter) of sub-main is lesser than the main pipe but greater than the laterals. However, the size of sub-main is decided on the basis of crop water requirement and size of lateral pipe. Overall, the size of sub-main varies from 25 to 50 mm diameter. This pipeline is also installed below the ground surface at some suitable depth, normally 35 to 40 cm, so that during tillage operation the pipeline may not get disturb.

***Lateral*:** Laterals are connected to the sub-main pipeline. However, in absence of sub-main line due to small size of field, the laterals are directly connected to the main pipe. Laterals may be placed above or below the ground surface along the rows of plantation. The laterals placed on ground surface are called online laterals, and that which is placed below the ground is called inline lateral. In inline laterals the emitters are inbuilt in pipe. Depending upon layout of the field and size of sub-main pipe the laterals are fitted on front and back sides of the sub-main line. Usually, the size of lateral pipe which is commonly used, varies to the tune of 9, 12 and 15 mm diameter. The view of main, sub-main pipe and laterals is shown in Figure 9.1.

Emitter: This is an important component of drip system, also called dripper, drip nozzle, trickler, etc. Emitters are placed on the laterals at regular interval as per plant spacing. In online laterals they are placed on the soil surface near to the plant/tree stem. Emitters receive the water from lateral and deliver the water to the plant at its base on the soil surface. Emitting of water is in the form of droplets and at very slow rate. Emitters are found in different emitting capacities ranging from 2 to more than 10 lph (common). These contain very fine holes to emit the water. Average diameter of openings in emitter varies from 0.0025 to 0.25 mm. Because of this reason emitters are very prone to get clog due to entry of fine soil particles; and also sometime due to deposition of chemical contents called precipitates. Figure 9.2 shows the view of different types of emitter.

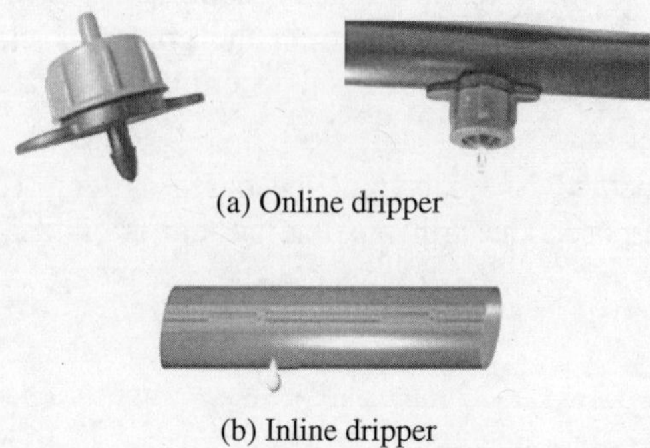

(a) Online dripper

(b) Inline dripper

Figure 9.2 View of (a) online dripper/emitter, and (b) inline dripper

Emitters' classification: Emitters are in different types or classes as shown in Table 9.1.

Table 9.1 Classification of emitters

S. No.	Emitters' classification	Remark
1.	As per discharge rate	
	(i) Low discharge emitter	4 lph
	(ii) Medium discharge emitter	4 to 10 lph
	(iii) High discharge emitter	More than 10 lph
2.	As per operating pressure	
	(i) Low pressure emitter	2 to 5 mm
	(ii) High pressure emitter	8 to 15 mm
3.	As per water emitting principle	
	(i) Orifice type	

(Contd.)

S. No.	Emitters' classification	Remark
	(ii) Perforated pipe type	
	(iii) Doubled wall type	
	(iv) Long path type, etc.	
4.	As per position	
	Online dripper/emitter	
	Inline dripper/emitter	

Control Unit

This component is treated as the heart of drip system. It is directly connected with the water source via pumping unit placed on a well-located firm foundation. The main function of control unit is to filter the water through different filters and allowing the clean water to the water distribution system, i.e., the main, sub-main, laterals and emitters. In addition, control unit also assembles the fertigation system for application of fertilizers/chemicals to the crop along with irrigation water. The associated components of control unit are described below:

(i) Filters
(ii) Fertigation system
(iii) Pressure gauge.

Filter: This is very important and essential component of drip system, is used for filtering or cleaning the water before allowing to pipeline system for irrigating the crops. In its absence there is always possibility of clogging of drippers; and thereby the failure of system as well. In drip system the filtering of water is carried out in different stages namely (i) Filtering of coarser materials like debris or sand particles, etc.; (ii) Filtering of fine particles; and (iii) Filtering of silt particle (suspended materials). These filtering operations are accomplished by using different types of filters, mentioned as under:

(i) Sand or gravel filter
(ii) Screen filter; and
(iii) Disc filter
(iv) Hydro-cyclone filter

Gravel or media filter: This filter is placed for primary filtration of water to be used for irrigation purpose. This filter consists of fine gravels or coarse quartz sands. The size of grain varies from 1.5 to 4 mm in diameter. The sand grains are free from $CaCO_3$. The shape of filter is in cylindrical form. Gravel filters are used for removing the materials such as algae and other organic contents, fine sands, etc. from the water. Normally, the canal water, open well water, etc. in which growth of algae is expected to take place, are filtered by using gravel or media filters. The water is allowed to passes through gravel mass placed in filter. In course of water passing the existing impurities are filtered out from the water and the clean water is discharged through the outlet, linked to the screen or hydro-cyclone filter. In order to measure the head loss across the filter, pressure gauge is also placed at the inlet and outlet ends of the filter. Head loss is because of deposition of filtered materials in sand media. In case of greater head loss, i.e., more than 30KPa, the filter requires back washing for cleaning point of view. Media filter is illustrated in Figure 9.3(a).

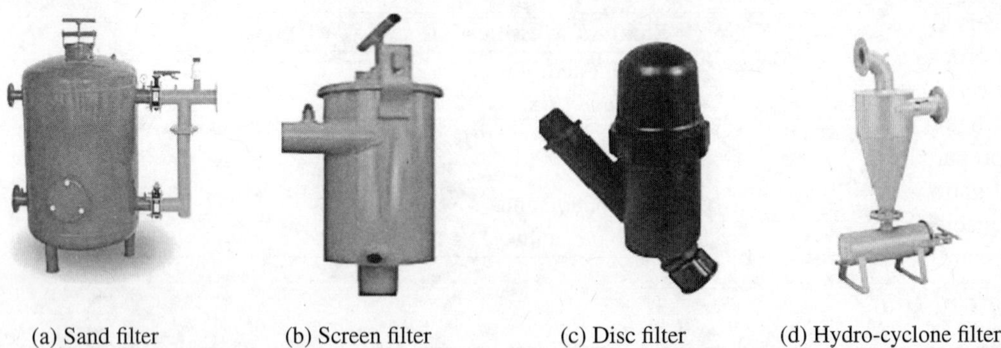

(a) Sand filter (b) Screen filter (c) Disc filter (d) Hydro-cyclone filter

Figure 9.3 Different types of filters used in drip irrigation system

***Screen filter*:** This filter is used for final filtration of water. In nutshell, this filter acts as the safeguard against clogging of drip pipeline system. Screen filter removes those impurities which are not filtered in media filter. The shape of screen filter is usually cylindrical, and is made of non-corrosive metal or plastic materials. Screen filters are found in different capacities and screen sizes. Normally, screen size varies from 20 to 200 mesh. View of screen filter is presented in Figure 9.3(b).

***Disc filter*:** This filter consists of stacks of grooved ring shaped discs, placed in a cylindrical container. Disc filters are very effective to remove or filter the debris, organic materials and algae from the water. During filtering operation, the discs are pressed together because of passing of water. This action leads to filter the foreign materials present in the water. The size of disc varies from 25 to 400 micron. In the alignment of two adjacent discs there forms an angle, which results a series of cavity in varying size. The cavity causes partial change in flow regime, i.e., the turbulent flow. Disc filters are cleaned by using back flushing method. For better result the back flushing should be done at high pressure ranging from 2 to 3 kg/sqcm. View of disc filter is illustrated in Figure 9.3(c).

***Hydro-cyclone filter*:** This is also known as centrifugal filter. This filter is effective to remove the fine sands, fine gravels and high density materials existing in the water. Working principle of this filter is just like cream separator. Irrigation water is allowed from the top (cone) of filter, tangentially, which gets thoroughly churned there, by centrifugal force created due to circular motion of water in the filter. This leads to separate the materials from the water. Finally, the separated materials get collected in a narrow vessel located at the filter bottom; from where they are removed through outlet. View of hydro-cyclone filter is shown in Figure 9.3(d).

In control unit the media filter is placed at d/s of water source for filtering the coarser materials like debris or any other existing in the water. The screen and hydro-cyclone filters are located at u/s of main pipeline to filter suspended particles left in filtered water from the media filter.

Fertigation Unit

Fertigation is the application of fertilizer to the crop along with irrigation water. It is carried out by the system called Fertigation unit, which is the part of control head of drip system. It is very important component of drip system to apply the fertilizers/nutrients in precise way to the crop along with irrigation water. In control head the fertigation unit is generally equipped between media filter and screen/hydro-cyclone filter. The water soluble fertilizers and liquid fertilizers are used for fertigation purpose. The fertilizer solution with appropriate concentration is prepared and placed in the fertilizer tank, which is connected to the venture arrangement. For fertigation the drip system is started first, and then fertilizer tank filled with fertilizer solution is connected to the venture. During operation the water flow gets start, which develops differential pressure across venture. In result the fertilizer solution is sucked and mixed in flowing water. In this way, the fertilizer along with irrigation water is delivered to the plant through drippers placed near to plant stem.

There are different types of fertigation devices, but Venturi System is the most common amongst them is described below.

Venturi injector: Venturi injector injects the fertilizer solution by creating vacuum or low pressure zone across. The venturi arrangement is installed on by-pass line along with gate valve or pressure-regulating device. During operation of drip system, the fertilizer solution is sucked and transferred to the irrigation water flow at constriction point of venturi. In this way, the fertilizer solution gets mixed in the irrigation water; and is delivered to the plant through emitters. Injection rate depends on operating pressure, venturi size, etc., mainly. The pressure variation should normally be in the range of 20 to 50% of the inlet pressure. Injection rate can be controlled by the following ways:

(i) Changing the injector flow rate.
(ii) Adjusting operating pressure.
(iii) Adjusting control valve located at discharge line.

View of venturi injector is shown in Figure 9.4

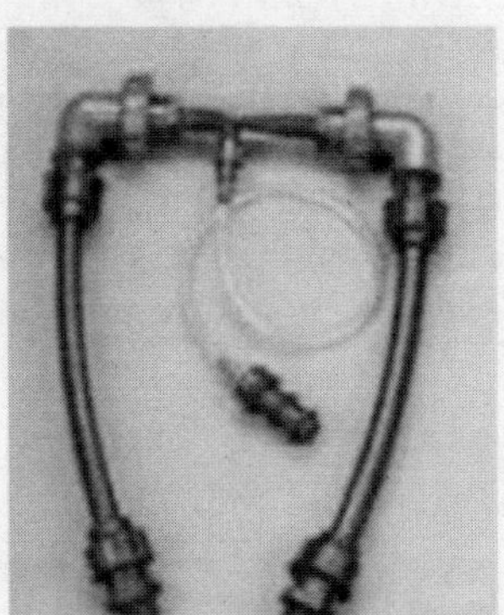

Figure 9.4 View venturi attachment as fertigation unit

Pressure gauge: This is equipped for measuring pressure under which water is flowing through drip pipeline. Pressure gauge consists of a dial on which pressure (kg/sq.cm) is indicated during system operation. Pressure affects the flow rate, especially at the emitter. Pressure gauge gives the information about flow pressure in control unit and also in pipeline system. On the basis of measured pressure the requirement of filter cleaning and discharge variation at emitting point, is determined. Pressure variation is regulated by adjusting the discharge rate at the control unit.

Accessories: The fittings and so many others parts such as the joints, i.e., the T-joints, nipples, female adopter, male insert adopter, main-sub main connections, sub-main-manifold, sub-main lateral connections, etc. are mainly used as the accessories in drip system. Details about accessories used in drip/micro-irrigation system are narrated in Table 9.2.

Table 9.2 List of drip/micro-irrigation accessories and their functions

S. No.	Accessory	Remark (function)
1.	Control valves/Ball valves	♦ Used to control the pipe flow. ♦ In MIS this is placed in filtration system, mainline, and also in sub-main pipeline. ♦ These are made of gun metal, PVC and cast iron, mainly. ♦ Its size varies from ½" to more than 5''.
2.	Flush valves	♦ These are placed at the end sub-main line. ♦ Its function is to flush the water and remove the foreign materials from pipeline.
3.	Air release cum vacuum breaker valves	♦ These are placed at the highest point in main pipeline. ♦ These are also placed in quite greater length sub-main pipeline.
4.	Non-return valves	♦ These are used in rising main pipeline. ♦ Its main function is to prevent pump damage because of water hammer.
5.	Gromate and take-off	♦ Gromate acts as seal for sub-main pipeline. ♦ These are used to connect the lateral pipe with sub-main line. ♦ For its placing in sub-main line a hole of required size is drilled with the help of hand drill machine. ♦ Gromate is fixed in the drilled hole. ♦ Take off valve is pressed in the gromate. ♦ Size of gromate varies with the size of lateral pipeline, i.e., 12, 16 and 20 mm.
6.	End caps or end sets	♦ These are used to close the ends of lateral pipes. ♦ These can also be used to flush the line.

Types of Drip System

Broadly, drip irrigation system is classified in following two types:

(i) Surface drip system, and
(ii) Sub-surface drip system.

Besides above, the drip system is also classified as under:

(i) Online drip system,
(ii) Inline drip system, and
(iii) Gravity fed drip system.

Surface drip system: In this drip system the laterals are placed on the soil surface passing along the crop rows. The drippers/emitters are placed near the plant stem on soil surface. This drip system is widely used in perennial and annual crops for supplying irrigation water.

Perennial crops are those which live for more than two years. On the other hand, the annual crops are those which gets germinate, flower, produce seeds and also die in one-year duration. The drippers or emitters used in this system are made of High Density Polyethylene (HDPE) plastic. In dripper the water enters at pressure about 1kg/sqcm and discharges the water at zero pressure in the form of droplets. The view of surface drip system is shown in Figure 9.1.

Sub-surface drip system: In sub-surface drip system the laterals along with inbuilt emitters, are buried in the soil and irrigation is applied directly to the root zone. This drip system avoids the possibility of water loss due to evaporation. In result the water application efficiency becomes very high as compared to surface drip method. The other features of this drip system are narrated as under:

(i) Emitters are embedded in the soil at regular location.
(ii) Its design is same to the surface drip method. However, drip tubes are placed at 97 to 213 cm spacing below the soil at 15 to 25 cm depth.
(iii) The loss of irrigation water due to evaporation gets minimized to a large extent.
(iv) Efficient water utilization by the crop as compared to the surface drip method.
(v) The effects such as surface crusting and accumulation of water on soil surface is not found in case of sub-surface drip irrigation.
(vi) Water application is very efficient and uniform.
(vii) About 25 to 50% water saving or conservation can be easily achieved by this irrigation method.

Online drip irrigation: In online drip irrigation method the drippers are placed externally on the lateral lines at design intervals as per crop geometry. The emitters are placed on the laterals by inserting the emitters' barb-shaped base in the drilled hole. The diameter of lateral pipe varies between 12 and 20 mm. The online drippers deliver the water either in the form of small water stream or water drops on the soil. The applied water moves through the soil media by capillary action and forms a wet zone around root zone in oval or circular shape. The size of wetted zone depends on the soil type, dripper flow rate and irrigation schedule, mainly. The other features are same to the surface drip system. The online drip system has advantage regarding easy cleaning of drippers in case of their clogging, as compared to the sub-surface drip system. In addition, the dripper's spacing can also be changed to accommodate the areal extent of crop root zone. More commonly, the orchards, vineyards, nurseries and also in artificial landscapes this system can be suitably used for watering. In addition, in horticultural plantations such as mango, guava, coconut, orange, lemon/citrus, papaya, banana, sapota, aonla, bamboo, grapes, etc. it can also be used for irrigating the plants.

In-line drip irrigation: In this type of drip system the drippers are inbuilt or fixed at designed interval in the lateral pipe. Dripper's spacing is fixed on the basis of crop water requirement and water-holding capacity of the soil concerned. Dripper spacing is permanently fixed. The emitter's flow rate depends on the inlet pressure. Inline drippers are available in the discharge capacity of 0.8 to 4.0 lph. The other components such as the control unit, fertigation unit, filtering unit, main, sub-main and accessories are the same. Normally, in the crops such as sugarcane, ground nut, vegetables, flowers, cotton, tomato, broccoli, celery, cauliflower, spinach, kohlrabi, leaf lettuce, etc. the inline drip system is commonly used for watering purpose.

Gravity fed drip irrigation: Sometimes, this drip method is also known as family drip system. This is low-cost drip system, is used for a very small size field or in the kitchen garden. In the area ranging from 500 to 1000 sqm, this type of drip irrigation can be successfully used for irrigation purpose. Also, to demonstrate the drip technology or its working principle it can be used as a module. The main components of this drip system are the (i) water tank placed at designed height as per pressure required at emitter point; (ii) filtering unit; (iii) shutoff valves; (iv) main pipeline; (v) laterals (vi) emitters; and (vii) accessories as well. The possibility of sub-main line is about to no because of very small size field. The water from tank is circulated automatically due to gravity effect to the pipeline and finally that gets delivered to the plant in terms of irrigation.

Sprinkler Irrigation System

This is the irrigation method, in which water is applied in the form of rainfall over the standing crop either in open field or inside greenhouse. This method is found suitable for most of the row crops, field crops and also to the tree crops. A mild undulating land topography does not create significant effect on uniformity in water application. However, a high wind velocity causes drastic effect on uniformity of water application. Normally, in high wind zone this method is not recommended to use for irrigation, because of non-uniformity in water application due to distortion in falling water droplets on soil surface. In addition, in high wind condition there is also ample water loss due to evaporation effect. In general, the size of water droplets formed through sprinkler nozzles varies to the tune of 0.5 to 4 mm, which get easily evaporate due to blowing winds. The size of water droplets can be controlled by varying the pressure and nozzle size.

Water application in terms of irrigation is measured as mm/hour, which denotes that a given mm depth of water is sprinkled on the soil surface in one-hour duration for watering the crop. For maintaining all-round application of water to the crop the sprinklers are arranged or spaced at such spacing that there is overlapping of water fall. Application rate can be modified by changing the nozzles size, operating pressure and sprinkler distance, as well. However, water application rate should not exceed the infiltration rate of water; otherwise, there is formation of overland flow on the soil surface, leading to generate soil erosion or soil loss and surface sealing problem, thereby. In contrast, i.e., when application rate is less than the infiltration rate then there is shortage of water application, which may cause moisture stress in crop root zone; and also damaging the crop, accordingly. At greater pressure the drop size gets reduce, while at lesser pressure the drop size becomes more. In this way, the drop size also affects the water distribution or application uniformity. Furthermore, at falling of big size water droplets there is occurrence of soil erosion, which is not acceptable. It is, therefore, suggested to go for designing the sprinkler system by considering the pressures as one of the main criterion.

Types of Sprinkler System

Broadly, the sprinkler irrigation system is found in following types:

(i) Centre pivot system
(ii) Towable pivot system
(iii) Rain gun system
(iv) Impact sprinkler system

(v) Pop-up sprinkler system
(vi) Linear move sprinkler system

These are narrated as under,

Centre pivot sprinkler system: It consists of main pipeline, sprinkler head, and supporting structure, mainly. The mainline distributes the water to the pipeline; sprinkler head sprinkles the water and supporting structure holds the weight acting between towers. In addition to the above components, the system also comprises drive unit assembling the beam, drive train, wheels and the towers, as well. In this sprinkler system a single lateral is there, which is placed on or supported by towers. The lateral line is fixed at one end, and by other end it is rotated around a fixed point called central point. The central point is also called pivot point. The rotation of lateral pipe around pivot is carried out with the help of drive towers, which are self-propelled. This sprinkler system is capable of high efficiency water application.

Towable pivot: This type of sprinkler system is similar to the centre pivot system. However, in towable pivot system the pivot is towed away by means of tractor. This sprinkler system comprises 3 to 4 number of wheels in centre of the pivot. The wheels facilitate the movement of pivot from one place to another, which is done by pulling it with tractor power. In this way, it makes the irrigation, economical.

Rain gun: This is quite different over sprinkler system. It applies the water in the form of mist or fog beam. Water discharge rate is less than 175 lph. Rain guns are used to irrigate the trees having big canopy and also to those crops which are widely spaced. In fruit trees such as citrus, mango, guava, avocado, etc. the rain guns are widely used for irrigation. However, the field crops such as groundnut, onion, potato, sugarcane, cotton and the plantation crops like coffee and tea are also being most suitable for irrigation using rain guns.

Rain guns have very small or fine size passage to sprinkle the water. Because of this reason the water to be used for irrigation that must be filtered by filtering units. Normally, 60 to 80 mesh or 250 to 177 micron filters are used for this purpose. The minimum operating pressure of rain gun varies from 1.5 to 2 kg/cm^2. Its head is mounted on plastic made piles at 20 to 30 cm height above the ground surface.

Impact sprinkler: This type of sprinkler system is driven or operated in circular motion with the help of outgoing water force. Its one arm is extended from the head, which is repeatedly pushed back in the water stream with the aid of spring force. On striking of extended arm with the water stream, the stream water gets scatter and reorient the water flow. This leads to cause uniform water spreading around sprinkler head on ground surface. The impact type sprinkler systems are recommended for applying irrigation to the closely spaced crops such as leafy vegetables, potato, cotton, oil seeds, pulses cereals, fodder crops, etc.

Pop-up sprinkler: These sprinklers are mostly suitable for watering the lawns, seasonal flowers and planting beds as well. It assembles the components such as inlet, body, cap, wiper seal, riser and nozzle. In addition, an adjustment screw is also provided in the system to adjust the radius of water spreading.

Linear move sprinkler: Its constructional feature is almost same to the centre pivot sprinkler system. However, in this case no any end of lateral pipe is fixed. This sprinkler system comprises a series of towers in suspended form, moving laterally in row direction. The sprinkler line moves down the soil surface just perpendicular to the lateral line. Hosepipe or open ditch pickup is placed to the lateral pipe for delivering the water. Its hosepipe is in flexible form. Because of this reason it can be easily wrapped at the end of watering task. The linear move sprinkler systems have high efficiency of water application. As demerit this sprinkler system involves high expenditure of money for its installation.

Micro-sprinklers: These are different than the general sprinkler system, commonly known as sprinkler or water spray heads. They apply water to the crop by spreading in air in predetermined pattern. As per pattern of water spray the micro-sprinklers are also known as the mini-spray, micro-spray, jet or spinner. The micro-sprinkler heads are connected to the lateral pipe with the help of micro-tube. The micro-tubes are small diameter PVC pipe. In order to apply irrigation the micro-sprinkler heads are mounted on a riser or support stake. The height of riser or support stake varies from 25 to 30 cm. Micro-sprinklers require low energy to sprinkle the water. Normally, the pressure requirement to operate the system varies from 1 to 3 kg/cm^2. Its discharge varies to the tune of 40 to 75 lph. The micro-sprinklers are found well suitable for watering the crops having shallow rooting system. The crops such as garlic, onion, leafy vegetables, etc. are most common.

There are several types of micro-sprinklers used for watering the greenhouse crops; however, the followings are very common in use.

Bubblers**:** This is also one of the forms of micro-sprinkler, used for watering the greenhouse crops. The area coverage of this device is large as compared to the micro-sprinklers. Water spreading pattern is just like umbrella. The flow regulation is done by varying the pressure, through diaphragm material inbuilt inside emitting tool. The deflection of water is accomplished with the aid of small orifice. The bubblers are placed with single or multiple port outlets for spraying water, smoothly. In bubbler irrigation the water is applied in the form of small water stream with the help of small diameter tube. The diameter of tube varies from 1 to 13 mm. Sometimes, the commercially available emitters are also used for this purpose. As precautionary measures, in this irrigation small size basins or furrows are also required for controlling the water distribution on soil surface, as water application rate is greater than the infiltration rate. In practice, the following types of bubblers are commonly used for irrigation:

(i) Low head or gravity type bubbler-it requires the pressure about 10 kPa
(ii) Pressurized or high head bubbler-It requires the pressure from 50 to 150 kPa
(iii) Adjustable flow type bubbler
(iv) Pressure compensating type bubbler

The design of pressurized bubbler system is same to the micro-irrigation system.

Spray irrigation**:** It is carried out by means of the devices such as jets, foggers or misters. In this irrigation the water is applied to a part or fraction of the soil surface, and is continued to complete the irrigation of the required area. The water spraying is performed with the help of micro-sprayer system containing a series of nozzles. These nozzles have quite large area coverage in comparison to drip system.

9.3.2 Advantages of Micro-Irrigation

In general, the micro-irrigation (MI) system offers a large number of advantageous in various aspects, narrated as under:

(i) Uniformity in water application
(ii) Water saving
(iii) Energy saving
(iv) Better nutrients use efficiency
(v) Reduction in weed and disease problems
(vi) Improvement in soil salinity tolerance
(vii) Regulation in water flow rate using automation system
(viii) No constraints about land topography and soil types
(ix) Reduction in labour cost
(x) Improvement in yield and produce quality.

Uniformity in water application: Water application uniformity denotes equal amount of water supply to each of the plants in the field. Micro-irrigation method ensures this to a large-extent. This feature designates this irrigation method as one of the most efficient irrigation methods involving no wastage of water, nutrients and energy, as well. Not only this, but the other benefits such as better and uniform crop yield is also realized because of uniform water application.

Water saving: The water application in terms of irrigation to the crop by this method is quite different than the other practices. In MI system the water distribution from water source to the crop level is done by using plastic tubing. This completely avoids the possibility of water distribution loss. In drip irrigation the amount of water requirement for crop irrigation is assessed on the basis of the number of plants in the field, but not on the basis of area of the crop field. This also reduces the level of water requirement for irrigating the crop. The possibility of water loss due to evaporation is also very less, because of wetting of limited soil area (in drip method). In addition, the other sources of water loss such as formation of runoff and water collection at tail end of the field is also not there in MI system, results the water saving to an appreciable limit. All these points reveal the benefits of MI system over other irrigation practices. As per research findings on this aspect about 25 to 40% water saving can be realized through micro-irrigation as compared to the overhead sprinkler method and about 45 to 60% water saving than the surface irrigation methods.

Energy saving: The operation of MI system is normally done either by using the electricity or the fuels such as diesel and petrol, mainly. The consumption of electrical power or fuel energy is very less in MI system over traditional methods for irrigating the same acreage of crop field. This is because of the reasons that there is no effect of surface undulation on water movement in the field. In addition, the water is applied to each individual plant; the soil flooding is not done. The occurrence of water loss due to percolation is also not there. In nutshell, the system operation is done for a limited time period, results into less consumption of energy. Furthermore, the drip or MI system requires less operating pressure, i.e., 2 to 4 bar, is also one of the causes to reduce the level of energy consumption.

Better nutrient's use: In micro-irrigation system (MIS) the application of fertilizers or nutrients is carried out through fertigation unit. The requisite dose of fertilizer is delivered to the plant root zone along with irrigation water. Its effect on plant growth and other parameters is far better than the broadcasting method. In MI system (drip) the required amount of fertilizer is determined based on the number of plants; not on the extent of area as in case of traditional practices. This directly saves the fertilizer to an appreciable level. As per research findings about 25 to 50% fertilizer's saving can be realized through MI system over traditional practices. Besides application of fertilizers, the other chemicals such as herbicides, insecticides, fungicides, etc. are also applied with MI system, which is causative to result a better response on the crop yield and produce quality, as well.

Reduction in weed and disease problem: In cropped field the weed growth is very serious type of problem. Its control at proper time and in proper way is very essential; otherwise, there is drastic effect on crop yield. In this aspect the MI system plays significant role. In MI case (drip) the application of irrigation water is done near to the plant stem in root zone area. This results into wetting of soil for a very limited extent, i.e., near to the plant, only; and other parts of field remains dry. In this situation, the weed growth gets decline to a large extent due to absence of moisture in soil. Normally, weed problem is dominating in the areas of high soil moisture content. Similarly, the problem of disease infestation is also more in high humidity condition. In MI irrigated crop field the humidity level is always less as compared to the flooding irrigated field. This leads to reduce the problem of disease incidence on crop. In addition, the attack of insects/pests is also controlled in absence of weeds as they do not get shelter for breeding and other activities.

Regulation of water flow rate: The provision of automation is well compatible to the MI system. This makes the micro-irrigation system, fully controlled. In other words, through automation the application of irrigation at any time during 24-hour can be easily accomplished. In automation system there is provision to set the time of irrigation (irrigation schedule) with the aid of timer, which opens/closes the valve to release/stop the water flow in pipeline. Similarly, a program can also be made to run the system at night hours to reduce the water loss due to evaporation. In MI system the provision of automation can be easily equipped with the help of electrical solenoid valves and a controller unit.

No constraints of topography and soil type: In application of micro-irrigation system, either it is drip system or micro-sprinkler; there is no significant effect of land topography and soil types. Both the methods work well in all topographical conditions, provided the system is properly designed, installed and managed. In clay soil the rate of water application should be maintained low because of poor water infiltration rate; otherwise, at high application rate there would be the formation of surface flow (excess water). On the other hand, in sandy or loamy soils the application rate should be little more as these soils involve high infiltration rate, to accommodate the excess water application. In nutshell, the water application should be as per infiltration rate; i.e., water application rate should never be more than the infiltration rate.

Reduction in labour cost: Normally, for performing irrigation the labours are required for watch and ward of the irrigation water supply. For example, in traditional methods the water is directed to the crop field through earthen channels, which are more likely to get cut from some points; and thus, flowing of water from there, becomes waste. In order to watch such locations and take appropriate measures against water cut, if any, the labours are required to engage, essentially. On the other hand, in micro-irrigation the irrigation water is directed to the crop field through plastic pipeline system, in which the occurrence of above problems is about to negligible, provided the attack of rodent is not there on plastic pipeline. In addition, by the provision of automation the irrigation through MI system becomes fully controlled by the machine itself; and accordingly, the requirement of labour engagement is not there. Furthermore, the weed problem, insects/pests or disease infestation is also less in micro-irrigated field. This factor also cuts the employment of labours.

Improvement in yield and its quality: Micro-irrigation supplies the water, fertilizers and other requisite inputs to the crop in precise amount at right time and at closer interval throughout the crop period. In this way, the development of moisture and nutrient stress in the crop root zone is completely negated. The weeds problem, insects/pests and disease attack is also reduced to a significant level. The application of water and fertilizer or nutrients is also performed at uniform rate. All these factors in combination become very conducive to enhance the crop productivity. Since, the crop field always remains disease free; therefore, the crop produce quality is also found better than the traditionally grown crops.

9.4 OTHER IRRIGATION METHODS

In greenhouse to irrigate the crops the following methods are also used other than drip methods:

(i) Hand watering,
(ii) Perimeter watering,
(iii) Overhead sprinklers, and
(iv) Boom watering.

These are described below:

Hand watering: This is also one of the irrigation methods, often used for irrigating greenhouse crops. It is most traditional method, is used in very small size crop field. Normally, the seed beds, potted plants, etc. are watered by hand watering method. On use of this practice, there is possibility of over- or under-irrigation of the crop, depending on the expertise of the person involve. The over- and under-irrigation, both are totally unfit for the crop. In over-irrigation there is drainage issue. In absence of proper drainage there is water-logging effects. On the other hand, in under-irrigation situation there is development of moisture stress in the crop root zone, leads to generate the effect on crop growth and development. In addition, the span of irrigation time is also very large, which is not justified.

Perimeter watering: This type of irrigation is used in the crops grown or planted on the benches or beds in the greenhouse. In order to irrigate the crop the plastic (PE) made pipe is placed at the perimeter of the bench. The nozzles are fitted in the pipeline. On system operation the water from nozzles is sprayed on the soil surface and below the crop foliage. The nozzles used to spray the water are at the trajectory of 180, 90 or 45 degree angles. Nozzles are arranged in staggered form across the bench soil. In this form of nozzle's arrangement there is uniformity in water spaying on the bench soil.

Overhead sprinklers: In greenhouse farming system few crops require their canopy in wet condition. For such crops the overhead water sprinkling is one of the best methods. The leafy vegetables, azalea liners, etc. are being most suitable for irrigation by using this technique. In this irrigation, the pipeline is placed along the centre of the bed. The overhead sprinklers/ nozzles are placed with the help of risers. The riser height should be greater than the normal height of the grown crop. In bedding plants about 60 cm height of riser is found sufficient.

The overhead nozzles throw the water at 360 degree angels. Discharge capacity of overhead sprinkler should also be sufficient to meet the requirement.

Boom watering: This irrigation system consists of pipeline, equipped with boom system, which is extended from one side of greenhouse bay to the other. Pipeline is placed with the nozzles of suitable capacity, which function is to spray the water or fertilizer/chemical solution over the seedlings/vegetations. For smooth operation the system is equipped on a rail system. It facilitates to cover the entire bay of greenhouse. The water or fertilizer application rate is adjusted by controlling the system speed on the rail. This method is followed for watering the seedlings grown in the plug tray. The size of plug tray is about 30 × 61 sqcm and height 1.3 to 3.8 cm. A plug tray of above specification contains 800 to 1003 cells for seedling growing, in which each individual cell acts as one unit for single seedling.

9.5 AUTOMATED IRRIGATION SYSTEM

This is one of the new developments in irrigation sector. The automation makes the irrigation system fully controlled, mechanically. It facilitates followings jobs, automatically:

- Application of water or irrigation to the crops as per pre-scheduled time.
- Also, ensures the application of fertilizers or nutrients at predetermined time in exact amount.
- Watering to the crop is exactly as per requirement without aid of human labor.
- In greenhouse, it enables to modify the micro-climate as per need of the grown crop.

Its application offers following main advantages:

- In greenhouse the provision of automation can be easily placed to control the water application through different irrigation systems comprising misting, booms, etc. Similarly, in sub-surface watering system including drip, NFT, cascade floors, etc. the automated system can be successfully equipped.
- Automation reduces labour engagement.
- Introduction of human-based errors in irrigation practices is also reduced to a large extent.
- The water and fertilizer savings can be achieved to a significant level.
- Automation enables to save the time likely to be incurred under irrigation and fertigation, both. It is done by clustering the crops of same nature in zone form; and accordingly applying the irrigation, zone wise.
- In automation system the amount of water and nutrients received by a plant specific can be easily determined or monitored with the help of sensors.
- In automation there is provision to monitor the remotely located crops.
- The management of crops in context to irrigation, fertigation, insect/pest, etc. is easily possible.
- Possibility of water loss is least in case of automated irrigation.
- The crop yield is enhanced multifold as compared to the normal greenhouse farming system.
- On application of automation system the crop return becomes very high.

PRACTICE QUESTIONS

Descriptive Type Questions

1. Describe greenhouse irrigation rules in detail.
2. Narrate micro-irrigation—its suitability, limitations and advantages.
3. Describe micro-irrigation components.
4. Narrate different types of filters used in micro-irrigation system.
5. Classify micro-irrigation and explain drip irrigation.
6. Explain micro-sprinkler irrigation.
7. Describe installation of micro-irrigation system.
8. Describe care and maintenance of micro-irrigation system.
9. Explain chemical treatment of MI system.
10. Explain automated micro-irrigation system.

Multiple Choice Type Questions

1. Which of the following irrigation method is used in greenhouse?
   (a) Pitcher irrigation (b) Drip irrigation
   (c) Flooding (d) Furrow irrigation
2. Which of the following irrigation method is the form of micro-irrigation?
   (a) Pitcher irrigation (b) Drip irrigation
   (c) Micro-sprinkler irrigation (d) Both (b) and (c)
3. Drip irrigation is also known as
   (a) Pitcher irrigation (b) Micro irrigation
   (c) Frequent irrigation (d) Both (b) and (c)
4. In MI technique which of the following component is considered as the heart of the system
   (a) Dripper (b) Filters
   (c) Fertigation system (d) Pumping unit
5. Drip irrigation is suitable for which of the following greenhouse crop?
   (a) Leafy vegetables (b) Flowers
   (c) Capsicum (d) Both (b) and (c)
6. In MI system the ball valve is placed at
   (a) Inlet end of sub-main (b) Before sand filter
   (c) Lateral line (d) Main line
7. In MI system the air release valve is placed in
   (a) Sub-main line (b) Control unit
   (c) Lateral line (d) Main line
8. In MI system the purpose of flush valve is to
   (a) Filter the foreign materials (b) Control root intrusion
   (c) Flush the deposited materials in sub-main pipeline (d) Maintain pressure in sub-main line

9. In chemical treatment for removing precipitates from pipeline, the used chemical is
(a) Sulphuric acid only (b) Hydrochloride (HCl)
(c) Chlorine (d) Nitric acid

10. The requirement of filter cleaning is assessed based on the
(a) Pressure difference across filter (b) Emitter's clogging
(c) Low discharge rate of emitter (d) No water flow from filter

Answers

1. b **2.** d **3.** d **4.** b **5.** d **6.** a **7.** a **8.** c **9.** b **10.** a

BIBLIOGRAPHY

Anonymous (2004). Report of the Task Force on Micro-irrigation, Ministry of Agriculture, Dept. of Agriculture & cooperation, Govt. of India, New Delhi, Jan, 2004.

Goldammer T. (2019). Greenhouse Management: A Guide to Operations and Technology. Apex Publishers, USA.

Hamish, F. (1977). Main line installation, in Drip/Trickle Irrigation No. 5, Vol. 2, No. 2, 1977, Pub. International Drip Irrigation Asso., P.O. Box 288, Bloomington, California-92316 (714) 877–4405: 12.

James, L. G. (1988). Principles of Farm Irrigation System Design, John Willey & Sons, Inc. New York.

Michael, A. M. (2010). Irrigation Theory and Practice, Vikas Publishing House Pvt. Ltd, Delhi, India: 643–645.

Suresh R. (2010). Micro Irrigation–Theory and Practice, Standard Publishers Distributors, Delhi.

Tiwari. K. N. (2009). Pressurized Irrigation, Precision Farming Development Center IIT Kharagpur Publication No. PFDC/IIT KGP/2/2009: 27–32.

United States Department of Agriculture, Soil Conservation Service (1984). Trickle Irrigation. US Dept. of Agriculture, Soil Conservation Service, National Engineering Handbook Chapter 15, Section 15. U.S.D.A., S.C.S., Washington, D.C: 129.

http://fvtchort.wikispaces.com/Soils+Group+1)

www.ag.ndsu.edu/pubs/ageng/**irrigate**/ae1243w.htm 16th Aug, 2012.

Design of Drip and Micro-Sprinkler Irrigation Systems

CHAPTER 10

Greenhouse is the framed structure, provides space for cultivation in protected environment. The size or areal extent of greenhouse is not as the open field but it is in limited form. The crops grown are quite different in terms of yield potential and produce quality than the general crops grown in open field condition. Normally, vegetables, flower and highly remunerative crops are preferred to cultivate. In greenhouse cultivation, it is always tried to provide all the required inputs in precise way at scheduled time without failing to achieve high returns from the grown crop. The greenhouse cultivation is considered to be successful, when benefit-cost ratio of the crop is realized up to 5 or more as compared to the crops grown in traditional way, outside.

The application of water and nutrients/fertilizers in greenhouse crop is carried out in precise way, is one of the important facts. As far as the water application or irrigation to the greenhouse crops is concerned, the use of micro-irrigation technique comprising drip and micro-sprinkler is mandatory. Flooding method is completely avoided to use in greenhouse, as this method never satisfy the requirement of precision application.

The drip irrigation is known as the most precise irrigation method used in protected cultivation to achieve better crop yield and water-cum-nutrient use efficiency, as well. It comprises plastic tubing and emitters for water distribution/application, set of filters for removing physical impurities from water and fertigation system for nutrients application, mainly. The water quality plays very important role in context to work efficiency of the drip system. In nutshell, drip system is an integral component of greenhouse, is described in terms of its various components, design, installation and care maintenance in this chapter.

10.1 DRIP IRRIGATION SYSTEM

This is the form of micro irrigation, is also known as frequent irrigation. Drip method is most suitable for application of irrigation and nutrients in precise manner to the crop. System comprises plastic tubing for water supply from water source to the drippers. Water is delivered to the plant through emitters/drippers placed close to the plant stem on the soil surface. The emitted water gets infiltrate into the root zone and becomes available to the plant for uptake.

Drip system also comprises fertigation unit, through which the fertilizers or nutrients are applied to the crop along with irrigation water, called fertigation.

In this method the water loss during irrigation is about to negligible. The conveyance loss is completely eliminated. The loss of water because of deep percolation or seepage is also not there in this irrigation method, as the quantity of water applied is very small in amount. Applied water gets remain in root zone domain. No excess water is available for movement as deep percolation, or others. Similarly, the movement of nutrient downward beyond the root zone domain is also not there in drip irrigation method.

10.2 DESIGN OF DRIP SYSTEM

10.2.1 Design Considerations—General

Design of drip system is done to achieve better performance of the system on crop yield and returns thereby. In this regard several points have been framed to follow for design of drip system; few important points amongst them are narrated as under:

- Efficiency of filtration.
- Permissible variations in pressure head.
- Maintenance of operating pressure.
- Proper control on flow or pressure.
- Relationship between discharge and pressure at the pump or hydrant supplying water to the system.
- Chemical treatment to prevent mineral deposits.
- Use of secondary safety screening.
- Flow monitoring.

10.2.2 Wetting Pattern

On drip system operation the water gets emitted near to the plant stem through emitter. Emitted water wets small portion of soil, horizontally; and expands to some depth below the soil; and forms just like inverted bulb shape wetted area, which is around root zone. The extent of wetted area out of the total cropped area depends on the emitter's discharge rate at emission point, emitter's spacing and soil types, mainly. Wetted area is defined as an average watered area below the soil. It is determined by considering the wetted area at the depth ranging from 15 to 30 cm below the emitter divided by total area under crop. A high value of wetted area advocates more volume of water storage and vice-versa. As per research findings, in widely spaced crops the percentage wetted area should be less than 67% so that the soil strips between crop rows may be in dry condition; and thus to eliminate the cultural practices from there. Also, in the condition of low wetted area the water loss due to evaporation becomes less. In closely grown crops and lateral's spacing less than 1.8 m the wetted area often approaches 100%. The extent of wetted area can be computed as under:

Case (i) Straight single lateral system: For this condition the wetted area can be computed by using the following formula:

$$P_w = \frac{N_p S_e \cdot w}{S_p S_r} \times 100 \qquad \ldots(10.1)$$

in which, P_w is the wetted area (%); N_p is the number of emitters per tree; S_p is the spacing of plant (m); S_r is the spacing of row (m); S_e is the emitter's spacing (m) and w is the wetted width(m).

Case (ii): Spray emitters: In case of spray emitters the wetted area can be determined by using the following formula:

$$P_w = \frac{N_p\left[A_p + \dfrac{(S_e \cdot PS)}{2}\right]}{S_p S_r} \times 100 \qquad \ldots(10.2)$$

in which, P_w is the wetted area of soil (%); N_p is the number of spraying emitters per tree; S_p is the spacing of plant (m); S_r is the spacing of row (m); S_e is the emitter's spacing (m); A_p is the surface area of soil wetted by the sprayers (m^2) and PS is the perimeter of wetted area by sprayer (m).

As per research findings, James (1998) determined the expected maximum diameter of wetted area due to single emission (emitter) in different soils with varying characteristics, i.e. homogenous, varying soil layers with low density and soil layers with medium density, is shown in Table 10.1.

Table 10.1 Expected maximum diameter of wetted area due to single emission (emitter) in different soils with varying characteristics at emitter discharge rate 4 lph (James, 1998)

S. No.	Sand/rooting depth/soil texture	Soil characteristics		
		Homogeneous	Varying layers, generally low density	Varying layers, generally medium density
		Soil depth 75 cm		
1.	Coarse	45	75	110
2.	Medium	90	120	150
3.	Fine	107	150	180
		Soil depth 150 cm		
4.	Coarse	75	140	180
5.	Medium	120	215	275
6.	Fine	150	200	245

PROBLEM 10.1 In a fruit orchard the trees are planted at 10 m × 10 m geometry. The age of trees is about 10 yeras. Each fruit tree is equipped with 2 numbers of emitters for watering. The emitters are placed at 10 m spacing on lateral lines. The average water wetting is recoded as 0.75 m. Determine percentage wetted area of dripper.

Solution:

Given that,

(i) Pant to plant spacing = 10 m
(ii) Row to row spacing = 10 m
(iii) Numbers of emitters per tree = 2
(iv) Average wetted width = 1.75 m

Using the following formula for determining the percentage wetted area:

$$P_w = \frac{N_p S_e \cdot w}{S_p S_r} \times 100$$

in which, P_w is the wetted area (%) to be determined; N_p is the number of emitters per tree is given as 2; S_p is the spacing of plant is given as 10 m; S_r is the spacing of row is given as 10 m; S_e is the emitter's spacing is given as 10 m and w is the wetted width is as 1.75 m. Substituting these values in above formula, and solving, we have,

$$P_w = \frac{2 \times 10 \times 1.75}{10 \times 10} \times 100$$

$$= 35\% \quad \textbf{Ans.}$$

PROBLEM 10.2 Determine percentage wetted area of micro-sprinkler system, installed in the orchard having plant to plant and row to row spacing as 2.5 m. The other details are mentioned below,

(i) Numbers of micro-sprinkler per tree is 1
(ii) Surface area wetted by micro-sprinkler is 2.25 sqm
(iii) Spacing of micro-sprinkler 1.5m
(iv) Wetted perimeter is 4.75m
(v) Row to row spacing 2.5m
(vi) Plant to plant spacing is 2.5m

Solution:

Using the following formula for determining percentage wetted area:

$$P_w = \frac{N_p \left[A_p + \frac{(S_e \cdot PS)}{2} \right]}{S_p S_r} \times 100$$

In which, P_w is the wetted area of soil (%) is to be determined; N_p is the number of micro-sprinkler per tree is given as 1; S_p is the spacing of plant is given as 2.5 m; S_r is the spacing of row is given as 2.5 m; S_e is the micro-sprinkler spacing 1.5 m; A_p is the surface area of soil wetted by the sprayers is given as 2.25 m^2 and PS is the perimeter of wetted area by micro-sprinkler is given as 4.75 m.

Substituting these values in above formula and solving, we have:

$$P_w = \frac{1 \left[2.25 + \frac{(1.5 \times 4.75)}{2} \right]}{2.5 \times 2.5} \times 100 = 93 \quad \textbf{Ans.}$$

10.2.3 Crop Water Requirement

It is the amount of water including rainfall, required to meet the ET demand of the crop concerned without significant reduction in yield. The crop water requirement varies with the irrigation method, followed. For example, in drip method it is less as compared to the surface (flooding) and sprinkler irrigation methods. This is because of the reason that the extent of wetted area is less in drip method, while in others two it is quite large causing more water loss due to evaporation and percolation.

Computation of Crop Water Requirement (CWR)

Broadly, CWR is the crop evapotranspiration (ET_{crop}) refers to the sum of water amount required for meeting evaporating demand from the soil surface and transpiration loss from the crops grown under optimum soil water, excellent management and environmental conditions to achieve full production under given climatic conditions. The weather parameters, crop characteristics, management and environmental aspects are the overriding factors affecting the *ET*. In weather parameters the solar radiation, air temperature, humidity and wind speed are the main. *ET* crop can be computed as the product of reference *ET* and the crop coefficient (K_c), expressed as under:

$$ET_c = ET_o{\cdot}K_c \qquad \text{...(10.3)}$$

in which, ET_o is the reference evapotranspiration which denotes the evaporating power of atmosphere at a specific location and time during the year and K_c is the crop coefficient. The reference ET is the ET from a standardized vegetated surface. In other words, ET_o refers to the evapotranspiration rate from a reference surface which does not face the moisture stress or water shortage. It is affected by the climatic parameters and does not depend on crop characteristics and soil factors as well.

Crop coefficient: It depends on crop characteristics affecting evaporation rate from open soil surface. This is because of change in vegetative growth; and accordingly variations in extent of soil surface cover. This advocates that the K_c value of a given crop gets change throughout its various growth stages. It is affected by a host of factors such as crop type, crop height, albedo (reflectance) of the crop-soil surface, aerodynamic factors, leaf area, stomatal properties and crop stages (Allen et al., 1998). In determining ET crop the trend of K_c curve should be derived, which can be done with the help of K_c values at initial stage, mid stage and the end stage of the crop concern. The trend of K_c curve for entire growth stage is shown in Figure 10.1.

Once the value of K_c and ET_o is determined the *ET* crop is computed by multiplying them together. However, the crop evapotranspiration (ET_c) can also be computed by using the FAO Penman–Monteith method (Allen et al., 1998) based on the climatic data. The computing formula is given below:

$$ET_c = K_c \frac{0.408\,\Delta(R_n - G) + \gamma\left(\dfrac{900}{T_{\text{Mean}}} + 273\right)u_2(e_s - e_a)}{\Delta + \gamma(1 + 0.34\,u_2)} \qquad \text{...(10.4)}$$

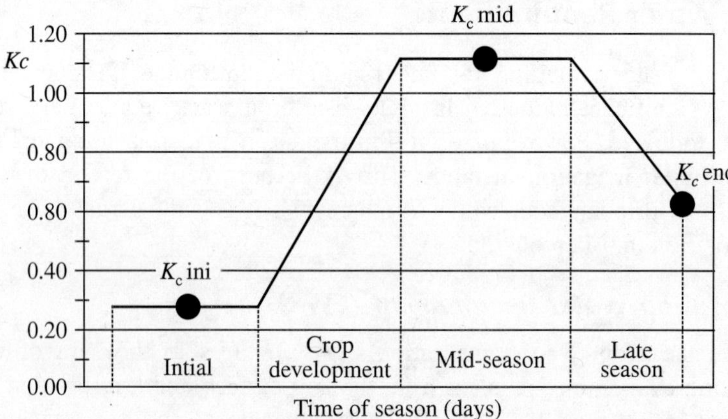

Figure 10.1 View of crop coefficient curve
(*Source*: https://www.fao.org/3/X0490E/x0490e0b.htm)

where,

ET_c = Crop evapotranspiration under standard condition (mm day^{-1})
R_n = Net radiation available at the crop surface (MJ m^{-2} day^{-1})
G = Soil heat flux density (MJ m^{-2} day^{-1}) which is relatively small and is ignored for day period
T_{mean} = Mean daily air temperature at 2 m height from the ground surface (°C)
u_2 = Wind speed at 2 m height (m s^{-1})
$(e_s - e_a)$ = Vapor pressure deficit (kPa)
Δ = Slope of vapor pressure curve (kPa °C^{-1})
γ = Psychometric constant (kPa °C^{-1})
K_c = Crop coefficient, varies between 0.45 and 1.05.

10.2.4 Net Depth Per Irrigation

Application of irrigation through drip is quite different than the flooding or other methods. In drip method water is applied to a point specific, i.e., near to the plant stem; accordingly, a very small part of soil area gets wet. On this ground, it is therefore essential to modify or adjust the relationship/formula used for determining the depth or volume of water per irrigation and irrigation interval, etc. by considering the point water application. The formula for maximum net depth of irrigation is given below. It can be used after adjusting the point water application.

$$d_{max} = \frac{MAD}{100} \cdot W_a \cdot Z \qquad \ldots(10.5)$$

in which, dmax is the maximum net depth of water application per irrigation (mm); MAD is the management allowable moisture deficit (%); W_a is the available water-holding capacity of the soil (mm/m) and Z is the rooting depth (m). Maximum net depth of water application refers to the amount of water required to replace the moisture deficit equal to management allowable deficit (MAD) developed in the root zone. The computed value of d_{max} by above formula stands for the entire cropped area; not for the wetted area only. Accordingly, by counting the percentage wetted area out of the total cropped area, the above relationship is modified and expressed as under:

$$d_{max} = \frac{MAD}{100} \cdot \frac{P_w}{100} \cdot W_a \cdot Z \qquad \text{...(10.6)}$$

This formula can be used for computing the maximum depth of water application per irrigation through drip system.

The net depth of water application per irrigation to meet the consumptive use requirement, is given by the following relationship:

$$d_{net} = d_{avg} \cdot f' \qquad \text{...(10.7)}$$

in which d_{net} is the net depth of water application per irrigation (mm); d_{avg} is the average depth of water application per irrigation (mm) and f' is the irrigation frequency or interval (days).

PROBLEM 10.3 Determine maximum net depth of water application per irrigation, if management allowable deficit is about 45%; the available water-holding capacity of soil is 70 mm/m and rooting depth is 0.75 m. Soil is sandy loam.

***Solution*:**

Given that,

(i) Management allowable deficit (MAD) = 45%

(ii) Available water-holding capacity of soil (Wa) = 70 mm/m

(iii) Rooting depth (Z) = 0.75 m

Using the following formula for determining maximum net depth of water application per irrigation:

$$d_{max} = \frac{MAD}{100} \cdot W_a \cdot Z$$

in which, d_{max} is the maximum net depth of water application per irrigation (mm) to be determined; *MAD* is the management allowable moisture deficit is given as 45%; W_a is the available water-holding capacity of the soil is given as 70 mm/m and *Z* is the rooting depth is given as 0.75 m.

Substituting these values in above formula, and after solving, we have,

$$d_{max} = \frac{45}{100} \times 70 \times 0.75$$

$$= 23.63 \text{ mm} \quad \textbf{Ans.}$$

PROBLEM 10.4 Compute maximum net depth of water application per irrigation through drip system. The requisite details are as follows:

(i) Soil is sandy loam

(ii) Percentage wetted area is 80%

(iii) Management allowable deficit is 40%

(iv) Rooting depth is 0.75 m

(v) Available water-holding capacity of soil is 70 mm/m.

***Solution*:**

The computation of maximum net depth of water application per irrigation is carried out by using the following formula:

$$d_{max} = \frac{MAD}{100} \cdot \frac{P_w}{100} \cdot W_a \cdot Z$$

in which the values of associated parameters are given as, MAD = 40%; P_w = 80%; W_a = 70 mm/m and Z as 0.75 m.

Substituting these values in the formula, and solving the same, the value of maximum net depth of water application per irrigation is obtained as:

$$d_{max} = \frac{40}{100} \times \frac{80}{100} \times 70 \times 0.75 \text{ mm}$$

$$= 16.8 \text{ mm} \quad \textbf{Ans.}$$

Average daily transpiration loss: The average daily transpiration loss (T_d) during peak use period is given by the following relationship,

$$T_d = \frac{d_{avg}}{f_x} \qquad \text{...(10.8)}$$

In which f_x irrigation frequency or interval. In design of pipeline sizing the value of T_d is taken for mature crop. In case of irrigation interval 1-day as normally followed in drip method the value of d_{net} is taken equal to T_d for simplifying design process, as suggested by Keller and Bliesner (1990).

10.2.5 Gross Irrigation Requirement

The gross irrigation requirement in terms of depth depends on the net irrigation depth and irrigation efficiency. The formula for computing the gross depth of irrigation requirement is given below:

$$d = \frac{d_{net} \cdot T_d}{\frac{E_{ff}}{100}} \qquad \text{...(10.9)}$$

In which, d is the gross depth of water application, is also given allowances for leaching requirement and unavoidable deep percolation losses. The relationship for gross depth of irrigation based on consideration of leaching requirement is presented as under:

In the condition when leaching requirement (LR) is more than 1 or $T_r < 0.9/(1.0 - LR_i)$ the relationship for gross depth of irrigation is expressed as under:

$$d = \frac{100 \cdot d_{net}}{E_u(1 - LR_i)} \qquad \text{...(10.10)}$$

And, the maximum gross daily irrigation requirement per irrigation (mm) is given by:

$$d' = \frac{T_d}{E_u(1 - LR_i)} \qquad \text{...(10.11)}$$

in which, d is the gross depth of water application per irrigation (mm); d_{net} is the net depth of water application per irrigation to satisfy consumptive use requirement (mm); d' is the maximum gross daily irrigation requirement (mm); T_d is the average daily transpiration loss during peak-use period (mm); E_u is the emission uniformity (%) and LR_i is the leaching requirement under drip irrigation.

PROBLEM 10.5 Find the value of gross depth of water application, if the net irrigation depth and irrigation efficiency is 15 mm and 85% (drip system), respectively. Irrigation is applied at daily basis.

Solution:

The expression of gross irrigation depth is given by the following equation:

$$d = \frac{d_{net} \cdot T_d}{\frac{E_{ff}}{100}}$$

The values of associated parameters are given as d_{net} = 15 mm and e_{ff} = 85%. The transpiration loss, i.e., T_d is taken same to the d_{net} as 15 mm. This is because of the reason that, in drip irrigation the depth of transpiration loss is taken equal to the net depth of water application, when irrigation interval is very less say for example daily or at 1-day interval. Accordingly, the gross depth of water application is obtained as,

$$d = \frac{15 \times 15}{0.85} = 265 \text{ mm} \quad \textbf{Ans.}$$

PROBLEM 10.6 Determine gross depth of irrigation for the condition when there is leaching requirement. The net depth of water application is 15 mm. The leaching fraction to be maintained is 0.30 in case of container type growing media. Take emission uniformity as 85%.

Solution:

The expression of gross depth of water application, counting leaching requirement of growing media is given as under:

$$d = \frac{100 \cdot d_{net}}{E_u (1 - LR_i)}$$

in which the values of associated parameters are as d_{net} = 15 mm; E_u = 85% and LR_i as 0.30. Substituting these values in the formula and solving, we have:

$$d = \frac{100 \times 15}{85(1 - 0.3)}$$

$$= 25.21 \text{ mm} \quad \textbf{Ans.}$$

PROBLEM 10.7 Compute gross depth of water application per irrigation by drip method, followed for watering container type growing media placed inside greenhouse. The irrigation interval is followed, as daily basis. The net depth of water application is 15 mm. Emission uniformity of drip system is 85%. Assume leaching requirement as 0.35.

Solution:

The expression of maximum gross daily irrigation requirement per irrigation (mm) counting leaching requirement is given as under:

$$d' = \frac{T_d}{E_u (1 - LR_i)}$$

in which, T_d is the average daily transpiration loss during peak-use period is taken equal to the net depth of water application is given as 15 mm; E_u is the emission uniformity is given as 85% and LR_i is the leaching fraction is given as 0.35. Substituting these values in above expression, and solving, we have:

$$d' = \frac{15}{0.85(1-0.35)}$$

$$= 27.15 \text{ mm} \quad \textbf{Ans.}$$

10.2.6 Gross Volume of Water

It is very useful parameter for selecting the emitters of a given discharge capacity. The gross volume of water required per plant per day is given by the following relationship:

$$V_{gross} = K.d'S_p \cdot S_r \qquad ...(10.12)$$

in which, V_{gross} is the gross volume of water required per plant per day; K is the constant taken as 1.0; d' is the maximum gross daily irrigation requirement (mm); S_p is the plant to plant spacing (m) and S_r is the row to row spacing (m).

10.2.7 Drip System Capacity

The capacity of drip irrigation system denotes the total discharge available at the control unit to meet the requirement of the plants in the field. This information is required to determine the pump capacity and design of pipeline system including selection of emitters, as well. System capacity is determined by multiplying the number of emitters operating at a time to the average discharge rate of the emitters. Keller and Bliesner (1990) suggested following relationship for determining the discharge capacity of drip system, considering uniform spacing between laterals:

$$Q_s = K\frac{A \cdot q_s}{N_s \cdot S_e \cdot S_l} \qquad ...(10.13)$$

in which, Q_s is the system capacity (lps); q_s is the average emitter discharge (lph); K is the constant taken as 2.778; S_e is the emitter spacing (m); A is the field area (ha) ; S_l is the lateral spacing (m) and N_s is the number of operating emitters. However, the discharge capacity of drip system is taken 10 to 20% extra than the computed rate from the equation (10.13). This is to adjust the variations in emitter's discharge rate because of clogging due to sedimentation and other reasons.

PROBLEM 10.8 At a given farm the greenhouses have been constructed on about 5 ha area. The drip system is planned to install for watering the greenhouse crops. Determine the capacity of drip system, if average emitter discharge to be required is 8 lph; emitter spacing as 0.45 m; lateral spacing to be 0.75 m and total number of emitters to be operated at a time for watering is 125.

***Solution*:**

Given that,

(i) Total area of field = 5 ha or 50000 sqm
(ii) Emitter's discharge rate = 8 lph
(iii) Number of emitters to be operated at a time = 125
(iv) Lateral spacing = 0.75 m
(v) Emitter spacing = 0.45 m

Using the following formula for determining capacity of drip system:

$$Q_s = K \frac{A \cdot q_s}{N_s \cdot S_e \cdot S_l}$$

in which, Q_s is the system capacity (lps) to be determined; q_s is the average emitter discharge is given as 8 lph; K is the constant taken as 2.778; S_e is the emitter spacing given as 0.45 m; A is the field area given as 5ha; S_l is the lateral spacing given as 0.75 m and N_s is the number of operating emitters at a time to be operated is given as 125.
Substituting these values in above formula and after solving, we have:

$$Q_s = 2.778 \times \frac{5 \times 8}{125 \times 0.45 \times 0.75} \text{lps}$$

$$= 2.65 \text{ lps} \quad \textbf{Ans.}$$

10.2.8 Emitter's Selection

The selection of suitable size emitter in drip system is very important for supplying irrigation to the crop at requisite rate, uniformly throughout the crop field. In addition, the efficiency of drip system is also governed to a large extent on emitter's sizing. Overall, the following characteristics are commonly taken into consideration while selecting the emitters:

(i) Manufacturing characteristics,
(ii) Hydraulic characteristics, and
(iii) Operational characteristics.

Manufacturing Characteristics

The uniformity in water emission of drip system depends to some extent on manufacturing characteristics of the emission component. The manufacturing variations cause change in discharge rate of emitter. This leads to vary the water application uniformity among emitters of the same type and same discharge capacity operated at same pressure. The variation in manufacturing characteristics in emitters and other components is mainly due to following probable reasons:

- Change in manufacturing temperature.
- Damage in molds used for construction.
- Non-uniformity in mixing of raw materials. However, in case of manufacturing pressure compensation type emitters this problem is eliminated by mixing the elastomeric materials in raw materials to be used for emitter's manufacturing.
- Difficulty in manufacturing with consistent dimensions of the components.
- Variations in aperture size, shape and final finish of the components.

- Inability to maintain a constant pressure and temperature during molding and welding processes.
- Inconsistency of the materials used for manufacturing.

In order to signify the quantum of manufacturing effect on system performance a statistical factor called manufacturing coefficient of variation (C_{vm}) is introduced, which is defined as the ratio of standard deviation to the mean discharge rate of the emitter. The emitters having low C_{vm} should be selected for system use.

Hydraulic Characteristics

Hydraulic characteristics signify the effect of frictional resistance on passing flow. In drip emitters, the flow is regulated by dissipating the flow energy through frictional resistance. In case of low flow emitters (laminar flow emitters) such as micro-tubes and spiral path emitters, the regulation of flow is carried out by dissipation of flow energy through frictional resistance developed by the walls of water flow passage. In laminar flow emitters the flow path is long and narrow, causing large amount of frictional resistance acting on the water flow.

In case of turbulent flow emitters such as the orifice, nozzle emitters, tortuous path emitters and jets or sprayers, the regulation of water flow is accomplished by dissipating the flow energy through frictional effect created by the walls of water flow path and also by the resistance between the particles itself during their turbulent motion.

Hydraulic characteristics are directly related to the mode of water flow inside the emitter. A term called Reynolds number (R_e) is used to define the hydraulic characteristics, is expressed by the following relationship:

$$R_e = \frac{v \cdot d}{\vartheta} \quad \text{...(10.14)}$$

in which R_e is the Reynolds number; v is the velocity of water flow through emitter (m/s), d is the diameter of emitter (m), ϑ is the kinematic viscosity of water (m^2/s). On the basis of R_e the flow regimes are classified as shown in Table 10.2.

Table 10.2 Classification of flow regimes based on Reynolds number

S. No.	Reynolds Number	Flow regime
1.	$R_e < 2000$	Laminar flow
2.	$2000 \leq R_e \leq 4000$	Unstable flow
3.	$4000 \leq R_e \leq 10{,}000$	Partially turbulent
4.	$10{,}000 \leq R_e$	Fully turbulent

Operational Characteristics

Operational characteristics advocate the resistivity and maintenance of physical features of emitters throughout their service life against extreme environmental conditions to sustain consistent flow. In this context, various indices are used to evaluate operational characteristics of emitters. However, the followings indices are the main amongst them:

- Coefficient of manufacturing variation (CV),
- Emission uniformity (EU), and
- Emitter flow variation (q_{var}).

10.2.9 Emitter's Spacing

Emitter spacing is decided on the basis of soil-water properties of the site, specific rooting system of the crop and climatic characteristics, affecting the extent to which the crop depends on irrigation. For application of irrigation for the same time span and water volume a narrow spacing between drippers on lateral line, renders a narrower and deeper water wetting pattern. In case of close dripper spacing the soil wetting by dripper gets increase due to overlapping of adjacent soil wetted area, which is not desirable. Because at overlapping condition a large amount of applied irrigation water starts flowing downward beyond root zone, i.e., water loss. In case of widely spaced drippers, there is shallow wetting pattern, which may also not fit for the crop. It is, therefore, suggested to keep the dripper spacing at optimum range so that above mentioned demerits may not develop. Overall, depending on emitter discharge capacity and soil type the typical spacing of emitters at different discharge rates and soil types is presented in Table 10.3.

Table 10.3 Emitter's spacing depending on discharge rate and soil types

Soil type	Emitter's spacing (m)	
	2.0 lph	**4.0 lph**
Sandy soil (Coarse textured)	0.30	0.60
Loam soil (Medium textured)	0.60	1.00
Clay soil (Fine textured)	1.00	1.30

(*Source*: www.irrigationtutorial.com/drip)

10.2.10 Emitter's Selection

Broadly, the selection of emitter is carried out based on following two aspects:

- As per soil type, and
- As per crop geometry.

As per soil types: The soil types play key role in selection of drippers of suitable discharge capacity. The clay soil involves the property of slow water absorption, and thereby the occurrence of overland flow or excess water flow on the soil surface. For such soils the drippers of 2 lph discharge capacity are found more appropriate. On the other hand, the sandy soils have greater ability to absorb the water, and accordingly the formation of excess water to flow over the soil surface in the form of overland flow is nil. In sandy soils the emitters of 4 to 8 lph discharge capacity response well; and are selected for placing in system.

The loam soils are considered as ideal between clay and sandy soils about water transmission behaviour. In this soil the water absorption rate is greater than the clay soil but lesser than the sandy soil. In addition, the movement of water is also in uniform pattern as compared to those twos. The water retention/holding and draining ability is in medium range. In this soil the emitters of 2 to 4 lph discharge capacity are found better to install for watering purpose. In nutshell, the selection of emitters as per soil types is summarized in Table 10.4.

Table 10.4 Emitter's selection as per soil types

S. No.	Soil type	Emitter's size (lph)
1.	Clay soil	2.0
2.	Sandy soil	4.0 to 8.0
3.	Loam soil	2.0 to 4.0

As per crop geometry: In widely spaced crops or plantations such as Mango, Citrus, Litchi, Sapota the drip system is equipped @1 or more number of emitters (per tree) of high discharge capacity ranging from 4 to 8 lph for watering to meet the water requirement. On the other hand, in close growing crops such as Spinach, Coriander, Methi, etc. the system is provided with micro-sprinklers for watering the crops.

10.2.11 Emitter's Discharge Capacity

The following relationship can be used for determining the emitter's discharge capacity:

$$Q = \frac{A \times d}{H \times E_a} \quad ...(10.15)$$

in which, Q is the discharge capacity of the emitter (lph); A is the extent of area to be irrigated (sqm); d is the depth of water application (m); H is the irrigation time (hour) and E_a is the application efficiency. The extent of area irrigated by the emitters is given by the following expression:

$$A = \frac{L \times S \times W_p}{100 \times N_e} \quad ...(10.16)$$

in which, A is the area irrigated (m^2); L is the row spacing (m); S is the emitter's spacing (m); W_p is the cropped area being irrigated (%); and N_e is the number of emitters. The percentage crop area being irrigated varies with the crop types and growth stage. In widely spaced crops the value of W_p varies between 40 to 60% while in closely spaced crop it is from 70 to 90%.

PROBLEM 10.9 Determine the emitters discharge capacity, if the area of field is 2500 sqm; depth of water application is 5 mm; irrigation duration is 1.5 h and water application efficiency is 85%. Total number of emitters placed in the area is 1000.

***Solution*:**

Given that,

(i) Area of the field = 2500 sqm
(ii) Depth of water to be applied = 5 mm
(iii) Duration of irrigation = 1.5 hour
(iv) Water application efficiency = 85%

Using the following formula for computing emitter's discharge capacity:

$$Q = \frac{A \times d}{H \times E_a}$$

in which, Q is the discharge capacity of the emitter (lph) to be determined; A is the extent of area to be irrigated is given as 2500 sqm; d is the depth of water application is given as 5 mm; H is the irrigation time is given as 1.5 hour and E_a is the application efficiency is 85%. Substituting these values in above formula, and after solving, we have:

$$Q = \frac{2500 \times 5}{1.5 \times 0.85}$$

= 9803.92 lph to be discharged through 1000 numbers of emitter, accordingly the discharge rate to be from single emitter is 9.8 say 10 lph. **Ans.**

10.2.12 Number of Emitters

It depends on the requirement of water wetting level in horizontal and vertical directions in root zone area of the crop concern. The following formula can be used for determining the number of equally spaced emitters on a single lateral line:

$$N_e = \frac{100 \cdot W_p \cdot S \cdot L}{D_w \cdot S_e}, \text{ when } S_e \leq 0.8 D_w \qquad \text{...(10.17)}$$

in which, D_w is the maximum diameter of wetted circle by the emitter at single emission point; S_e is the emitter's spacing (cm); W_P is the percent of S times L irrigated; L is the row spacing (m) and S is the emitter's spacing (m). In the case when system is equipped with double laterals or Zigzag, pigtail, or multi exit layouts, the formula for determining the number of water emitting device (micro-sprinkler) is given as under:

$$N_e = \frac{W_p \cdot S \cdot L}{100\left(A_s + \frac{D_w \cdot P_s}{2 \times 100}\right)} \qquad \text{...(10.18)}$$

and

$$S_e = D_T + \frac{D_W}{2 \times 100} \qquad \text{...(10.19)}$$

in which, A_S is the wetted area by a single micro-sprinkler (m^2); P_S is the perimeter of wetted area by the micro-sprinkler (m) and D_T is the distance of water throw or sprinkling (m).

10.2.13 Emission Uniformity

This term is used to denote the uniformity of emitter discharge in drip irrigation. EU of drip irrigation depends on several factors such as:

- Change in topographical elevation causing hydraulic variations.
- Frictional loss in pipeline.
- Variations in discharge at a given operating pressure, because of manufacturing defects, clogging, water temperature and aging as well.

The following relationship can be used for determining the emission uniformity of drip irrigation:

- EU relationship suggested by Keller and Karmeli (1975):

$$EU = 100\left\{1 - 1.27(C_{vm})N_e^{-0.5}\right\}\left(\frac{q_n}{\bar{q}}\right) \qquad ...(10.20)$$

where,

C_{vm} = Manufacturing coefficient of variation for point source or line source emitters
N_e = Number of emitters per emission point
q_n = Minimum emitter discharge rate (lph)
$\bar{q}$ = Mean emitter discharge rate (lph)

The equation 10.20 of EU is based on the ratio of the discharge rate for lowest 25% of emitters to the average discharge rate. Above equation reveals that on increasing the number of emitters at emission point, the level of EU gets increase.

- Nakayama et al. (1979) suggested the term "Coefficient of Design Uniformity" (C_{ud}) to denote emission uniformity of drip irrigation system. The relationship is mentioned as under:

$$C_{ud} = 100\left[1 - 0.789(C_{vm})N_e^{-0.5}\right] \qquad ...(10.21)$$

This equation is based on the deviation of discharge from the average rate.

PROBLEM 10.10 In greenhouse the drip system is installed for watering the crops Determine Emission uniformity of drip irrigation. The requisite details are as follows:

(i) Number of emitter per container is 1
(ii) Minimum discharge rate of emitter is 3.25 lph
(iii) Mean emitter discharge rate is 4 lph

Assume manufacturing coefficient of variation of emitters (line source) is about 0.55.

***Solution*:**

Using the following formula for determining emission uniformity of drip irrigation as suggested by Keller and Karmeli (1975):

$$EU = 100\left\{1 - 1.27(C_{vm})N_e^{-0.5}\right\}\left(\frac{q_n}{\bar{q}}\right)$$

in which, C_{vm} is the manufacturing coefficient of variation of line source emitters is given as 0.55; N_e is the number of emitters per emission point is given as 1; q_n is the minimum emitter discharge rate is given as 3.25 lph; $\bar{q}$ is the mean emitter discharge rate is given as 4 lph. Substituting these values in above relationship and after solving, we have:

$$EU = 100\left\{1 - 1.27(0.55)1^{-0.5}\right\}\left(\frac{3.25}{4}\right)$$

$$= 24.4\% \quad \textbf{Ans.}$$

PROBLEM 10.11 Determine emission uniformity of drip irrigation used in greenhouse for irrigating the crops. The number of emitters per container is used as 1. Take manufacturing coefficient of variation of line source emitters as 0.55.

***Solution*:**

Using the following formula for determining emission uniformity of drip irrigation as suggested by Nakayama et al. (1979):

$$C_{ud} = 100\left[1 - 0.789\left(C_{vm}\right)N_e^{-0.5}\right]$$

in which, C_{vm} is the manufacturing coefficient of variation of line source emitters is given as 0.55 and N_e is the number of emitters per emission point is given as 1. Substituting these values in above relationship and after solving, we have:

$$C_{ud} = 100\left[1 - 0.789(0.55)1^{-0.5}\right]$$

$$= 57\% \quad \textbf{Ans.}$$

10.2.14 Head-Discharge Relationship of Emitter

Emitter's discharge varies with the flow pressure. Discharge variation should not be in such a range that the emission uniformity (EU) becomes unacceptable. The relationship between head and discharge acts as tool for predicting instant discharge rate passing through drip system at the given pressure head. Therefore, the development of pressure head versus discharge relationship is essential to approximate discharge variation corresponding to existing pressure head during system operation. The general form of relationship between pressure head and emitter discharge is presented as under:

$$Q = C_d \cdot H^x \qquad \text{...(10.22)}$$

in which, Q is the emitter's discharge rate; H is the operating pressure head; C_d is the coefficient of discharge and x is the exponent. The values of exponent (x) for the given flow regimes and types of emitters are presented in Table 10.5.

Table 10.5 Values of exponents (x) for the given flow regime and emitter's type

S. No.	Value of exponent x	Flow regime	Emitter's type
1.	0.0,0.1,0.2, and 0.3	Variable flow path	Pressure Compensating
2.	0.4	Vortex flow	Vortex
3.	0.5	Fully turbulent flow	Orifice tortuous
4.	0.6,0.7 and 0.8	Mostly turbulent flow	Long or spiral path
5.	0.9	Mostly laminar flow	Micro-tube
6.	1.0	Fully laminar flow	Capillary

(*Source*: www. agridrip.com/page/437645582)

A lower EU than the recommended one, can be improved by using, as per below:

(i) Large diameter lateral pipe.
(ii) Shorter laterals.
(iii) Pressure compensating emitters.
(iv) Emitter with low C_{vm}.

10.2.15 Hydraulics of Drip Pipeline System

Drip system comprises a network of plastic/PVC pipeline consisting of main line, sub-main line and laterals. The design of drip pipeline system should be done in such a way that at each section of field there must be uniformity in emitter's discharge. Mostly, the variation in emitter's discharge is because of pressure difference between head and tail ends of the lateral pipeline. The maximum allowable pressure difference across the whole system is counted to the tune of 20%. On the other hand, the pressure difference between head end and tail end of lateral lines should not exceed 10%. The pressure head loss can be determined by using the relationship, available. In pipeline system the occurrence of head loss is because of frictional resistance offered by the wall roughness of pipeline on water flow. In addition, the obstacles countered across the flow path such as the turns, bends, expansions, contractions of pipes, etc. also increase the level of head loss against flow. The factors affecting head loss in pipeline system are presented in Table 10.6.

Table 10.6 List of factors affecting head loss in pipeline system

S. No.	Factors affecting head loss
1.	Pipe length
2.	Pipe diameter
3.	Wall roughness of the pipeline
4.	Rate of water/liquid flow through pipeline
5.	Water/liquid viscosity

10.2.16 Pressure Variation in Pipeline

In drip pipeline system the analysis of pressure variation is very important to know whether it is in allowable limit or not. Greater variation of pressure causes non-uniformity in emitter's discharge or water application. The main agents responsible to cause pressure variation in pipeline are the friction loss in pipes and fittings and topographical difference of the field. The friction head reduces the flow pressure in d/s direction, while change in topographical elevation decrease or increase the pressure, both, depending on the position of pipe running, i.e., uphill or downhill, respectively. The following relationship can be used for determining the pressure difference between two points along the pipeline:

$$P_d = P_u - 9.81(h_l \pm \Delta Z) \qquad \text{...(10.23)}$$

in which, P_d is the pressure at downstream position (kPa); P_u is the pressure at upstream position (kPa); h_1 is the energy loss in pipeline between up and downstream points (m) and ΔZ is the elevation difference (m) which is +ve for uphill running of pipeline and −ve for downhill pipeline running. The computation of energy loss in pipeline is described below:

Energy loss: The energy loss in pipeline is because of frictional head, treated as the major energy loss. It is presented by the following relationship:

$$h_l = FH_f + M_l \qquad \text{...(10.24)}$$

in which, F is the constant; H_f is the friction head loss between up and downstream points in pipeline (m); M_l is the minor head loss caused by fittings of pipeline. The computation of major and minor head losses is narrated as under:

Computation of major head loss: It is carried out by using the universal equation called Hazen-Williams equation is mentioned as under:

$$H_f(100) = K\left(\frac{Q}{C}\right)^{1.852} . D^{-4.871} . F \quad ...(10.25)$$

in which, $H_f(100)$ is the friction head loss per 100 m pipe length (m/100m); K is the constant taken as 1.22×10^{12} in metric unit; Q is the pipe flow rate (lps); C is the friction coefficient; D is the internal diameter of pipeline (mm) and F is the reduction factor. At high C the head loss is less and vice-versa. The reduction factor (F) signifies that as the pipe length gets increase the discharge becomes less due to emitting outlets. This leads to cause the drop in total energy lesser than the computed value from the equation (10.25). In order to avoid this effect a factor called reduction factor (F) is introduced in above equation. William-Hazen equation holds good for a limited range of temperature and flow pattern. The constant K of William-Hazen equation can be computed by using the following relationship:

$$K = (0.285C)^{-1.855} \quad ...(10.26)$$

in which, C is the friction coefficient, depends on the construction material and diameter of the pipe used.

Especially, for small diameter pipes such as laterals, the Darcy-Welsbach equation is considered to be as the most fit for computing head loss due to friction effect, is described by the following equation:

$$H_f = f\left(\frac{LV^2}{2gd}\right) \quad ...(10.27)$$

in which, H_f is the head loss in pipeline (m); f is the Darcy-Weisbach friction factor; L is the pipe length (m); V is the flow velocity (m/s); g is the acceleration due to gravity (9.81m/s^2); d is the internal diameter of pipeline (m). As per this equation the head loss gets increase with increase of friction factor (f). The value of friction factor (f) of Darcy-Weisbach equation can be computed by using the following relationship given by Colebrook-White:

$$\frac{1}{\sqrt{f}} = 1.14 - 2\log_{10}\left(\frac{e}{D} + \frac{9.35}{R_e\sqrt{f}}\right) \quad \text{for } R_e > 4000 \quad ...(10.28)$$

in which, e is the roughness coefficient equivalent to the size of sand grain. The value of e for different materials used for pipe construction is given in Table 10.7.

Table 10.7 Value of e for computing friction factor (f) of Darcy-Welsbach equation

S. No.	Material used for pipe construction	Value of e
1.	Plastic	0.003
2.	Commercial steel, wrought iron	0.03
3.	Galvanized iron	0.06
4.	Aluminum	0.10
5.	Concrete	0.30
6.	Corrugated metal steel	30.0

Computation of Minor Head Losses

In pipeline system the minor head losses are developed because of fittings/bends placed and transitions in the flow. It becomes effective when flow velocity gets high because of fittings or bends and flow transitions. In design of pipeline the minor head losses are counted in terms of equivalent length of pipe that adds a virtual length of straight pipe of accessory diameter to the pipe under design.

The Scobey equation can be used for computing the head loss due to friction, is given by the following expression:

$$H_f = \frac{(K)(c)(L)(Q^m)}{d^2 + n} \quad \text{...(10.29)}$$

In which, H_f is the friction head loss; K is the friction factor depends on the material used for pipe manufacturing; L is the pipe length (m); Q is the flow rate (lpm); d is the inner diameter of pipe (mm) and c, m, and n are the constants, given as 610042,1.90 and 1.10, respectively. The friction factor (K) of Scobey formula can be computed by using the following relationship,

$$K = \frac{K_s}{348} \quad \text{...(10.30)}$$

in which K_s is the friction factor depends on the diameter of pipe and construction materials, used.

In drip pipeline system comprising main, sub-main and laterals the quantum of friction loss gets reduce as compared to the pipeline having same diameter, length and construction materials, with no discharge variation. This is because of the reason that the total flow is divided into different branches, i.e., the sub-main, laterals and emitters, resulting into continuous declination in flow rate towards d/s side.

Christensen Formula

Christensen (1942) developed an empirical relationship for computing friction loss in pipeline equipped with several outlets at equal spacing and discharging constant flow. The relationship is given as under:

$$H_f = F \cdot K \frac{\frac{L}{100} - \left(\frac{Q^m}{C}\right)}{D^{2m+n}} \quad \text{...(10.31)}$$

in which, H_f is the friction loss in pipeline of length L placed with several outlets at equal interval and discharging the flow at uniform rate; F is the adjustment factor to correct the friction loss computed by the formula; K is the constant; L is the length of lateral pipeline; Q is the total flow in pipeline; C is the retardance coefficient; D is the pipe diameter; m is the velocity exponent and n is the exponent. In above equation the value of adjustment factor (F) is taken as 1 when there is no any outlet between u/s and d/s end of the pipeline. However, for the condition when the distance from pipeline to the first outlet is equal to the outlet spacing, the value of F can be computed by using the following formula (Christensen, 1942):

$$F = \frac{1}{m+1} + \frac{1}{2N} + \frac{\sqrt{m-1}}{6N^2} \quad \text{...(10.32)}$$

in which, m is the exponent and N is the total number of outlets, i.e., the emitters, sprinklers, etc.

Similarly, when the distance from the pipeline to the first outlet is half of outlet spacing the adjustment factor (F) can be computed by using the formula, given as under:

$$F = \frac{1}{(2N-1)} + \frac{2}{(2N-1)N^m} \sum_{i=1}^{N-1} (N-1)^m \qquad \text{...(10.33)}$$

PROBLEM 10.12 Determine the pressure developed at d/s part of 70 m lateral length. The energy loss in lateral pipeline between u/s and d/s end is about 0.15 m. The pipeline is running uphill with the elevation difference of 0.25 m. Take pressure at u/s end of pipe as 98 kpa.

Solution:

Given that,

(i) Lateral length is 70 m

(ii) Energy loss between u/s and d/s end of pipe is 0.15 m

(iii) Elevation difference between the points is 0.25 m

(iv) Pressure at u/s end of pipe is 98 Kpa.

Using the following relationship for determining the pressure difference between two points along the lateral pipeline:

$$P_d = P_u - 9.81(h_l \pm \Delta Z)$$

in which, P_d is the pressure at downstream position (kPa) to be determined; P_u is the pressure at upstream end is given as 98kPa; h_l is the energy loss in pipeline between u/s and downstream points is given as 0.15 and ΔZ is the elevation difference between the points is given as 0.25 m, which is taken as +ve for uphill running of pipeline. Substituting these values in above formula and after solving, we have:

$$P_d = 98 - 9.81(0.15 + 0.25) \text{ Kpa} = 94.1 \text{ Kpa} \quad \textbf{Ans.}$$

PROBLEM 10.13 Find out energy loss in lateral pipeline of 100 m length, if the friction head loss between u/s and downstream points in pipeline is 0.15 m and the minor head loss due to fittings, etc. is 0.17 m.

Solution:

Given that,

(i) Length of lateral pipeline = 100 m

(ii) Friction head loss between u/s and downstream points in pipeline = 0.15 m

(iii) Minor head loss due to fittings, etc. = 0.17 m

Using the following formula for determining the energy loss because of frictional head:

$$h_l = FH_f + M_l$$

in which, F is the constant is assumed as 0.35 ; H_f is the friction head loss between up and downstream points in pipeline is given as 0.15 m and M_l is the minor head loss caused by fittings of pipeline is given as 0.17 m. Substituting these values in above formula and after solving, we have:

$$h_l = 0.35 \times 0.15 + 0.17$$
$$= 0.22 \text{ m} \quad \textbf{Ans.}$$

PROBLEM 10.14 Calculate the friction loss in lateral pipe of 250 m length and 12 cm diameter. In lateral pipe total 15 micro-sprinklers are installed for watering. Sprinkler discharge rate is 40 lpm. Take the value of friction factor of pipe as 0.04.

***Solution*:**

Given that,

(i) Sprinkler discharge rate = 40 lpm
(ii) Length of lateral pipe = 250 m
(iii) Total number of sprinklers placed in lateral pipe = 15
(iv) Size (dia.) of lateral pipe = 0.12 m
(v) Friction factor of pipe = 0.04

Friction loss of lateral pipeline is computed by using the following formula:

$$H_f = \frac{fLQ^2}{\left(\frac{\pi}{4}\right)^2 2.g.d^5}$$

in which, the values of different parameters are given as friction factor (f) of pipe as 0.04; length of lateral pipe (L) as 250 m and discharge rate of lateral line (Q) as 0.01 m^3/s. Substituting these values in the formula and solving, we have

$$H_f = \frac{0.04 \times 250 \times 0.01^2}{\left(\frac{\pi}{4}\right)^2 \times 2 \times 9.81 \times 0.12^5}$$

$$= 3.32 \text{ m or } 332 \text{ cm} \quad \textbf{Ans.}$$

PROBLEM 10.15 In a sprinkler pipeline system total 15 number of micro-sprinklers are placed at lateral line. Determine adjusted value of frictional head loss in lateral pipeline. Assume frictional head loss in lateral line as 15 mm.

***Solution*:**

Given that,

(i) Number of sprinklers placed at lateral pipe = 15
(ii) Frictional head loss in lateral line = 15 mm or 0.015

Using the following formula for determining adjusted frictional head loss in lateral pipeline due to outlets:

$$H_{fad} = FH_f$$

In which, F is the factor and H_f is the friction head loss. The factor F is computed by using the following formula:

$$F = \frac{1}{m+1} + \frac{1}{2N} + \frac{\sqrt{m-1}}{6N^2}$$

in which, m is the exponent is taken as 2 and N is the number of outlets given as 15 (sprinkler set). Substituting these values in above equation and solving, we have:

$$F = \frac{1}{2+1} + \frac{1}{2 \times 15} + \frac{\sqrt{2-1}}{6 \times 15^2} = 0.36$$

Therefore, $H_{f.ad} = 0.36 \times 0.015$
$= 0.0054$ m **Ans.**

PROBLEM 10.16 Find out the magnitude of pressure drop due to friction loss in lateral pipeline. The length of lateral pipe is 40 m and its diameter is 16 mm. Total 25 drippers are placed at 1.5 m spacing. The rate of water passing through lateral is 65 lps.

***Solution*:**

Given that,

(i) Length of lateral pipe = 40 m
(ii) Diameter of lateral pipe = 16 mm
(iii) Number of emitters placed at lateral = 25
(iv) Emitter spacing = 1.5 m
(v) Emitter's discharge rate = 0.65 lps

Using the following formula for determining the extent of pressure drop due to friction loss:

$$\Delta H = 3.98 \times 10^5 \times \frac{Q^{1.852}.L}{D^{4.871}}$$

in which, the discharge rate (Q) flowing through lateral line is 0.65 lps; length of lateral pipe (L) is 40 m; the internal diameter of lateral pipe (D) is given as 16 mm. Substituting these values in the formula and solving, we have:

$$\Delta H = 3.98 \times 10^5 \times \frac{0.65^{1.852} \times 40}{16^{4.871}}$$

$= 9.76$ m **Ans.**

10.2.17 Design of Pipeline System

Drip system consists of following pipeline systems for design:

(i) Main pipeline,
(ii) Sub-main pipeline, and
(iii) Lateral pipeline.

Design is performed from tail end to head end of pipeline, presented below.

Design of Lateral Pipeline

In drip pipeline system the lateral line acts as the hydraulic link between the main or sub-main pipeline and the emitters. The emitters, either they are online or inline, are fitted/inbuilt to the laterals. The laterals are connected to the sub-main or directly to the main pipeline depending on the geometry of field with the help of "T", unions, etc. The diameter of lateral line varies from 12 to 16 mm. In general, the followings are the focusing points to consider for lateral design:

- Flow rate,
- Inlet pressure,

- Location of manifold,
- Length, and
- Pressure variation within.

The design should ensure a uniform emitting of water from the emitters placed on the lateral. The pressure variation is computed by determining the head loss in the lateral. In laterals the regime of water flow may likely to be in the modes of laminar or turbulent flow; and accordingly, the Darcy-Welsbach equation may be used for determining the head loss developed due to frictional effect in the pipe used as lateral. At the field slope less than 3% facing lateral direction, the laterals can be connected both the sides of the manifold. The spacing of manifold is decided as per field geometry and lateral hydraulics. The lateral length varies with the field size. However, lateral length should be such that there would be minimum head loss, and accordingly, the variations in pressure or discharge at emitting point is also minimum. The friction factor (Darcy-Weisbach) for small diameter pipeline is determined by counting the flow regimes. The flow regime is predicted based on the parameter called Reynolds number (*Re*), which is expressed by the following relationship:

$$R_e = \left(\frac{\rho \cdot D \cdot V}{K \cdot \mu}\right) \qquad \text{...(10.34)}$$

In which, R_e is the Reynold's number; ρ is the density of water (g/cm$^{3)}$; D is the diameter of pipe (cm); V is the average flow velocity (cm/s); K is the unit constant (10 with these units) and μ is the viscosity of the fluid (N.s/m^2). On the basis of determined R_e value the flow regime is decided. And for the same flow regime the friction factor (f) is computed by using the respective relationship, narrated as under:

***Friction factor for laminar flow regime*:** The R_e for laminar flow regime varies to the tune of less than 2000. The friction factor relationship for this flow regime is given as under:

$$f = \frac{64}{R_e} \qquad \text{...(10.35)}$$

***Friction factor for turbulent flow regime*:** The range of R_e for turbulent flow regime is between 2000 and 10,0000. For this flow regime the friction factor is computed by using the following formula:

$$f = 0.32\, R_e^{-0.25} \qquad \text{...(10.36)}$$

***Friction factor for fully turbulent flow regime*:** For this flow regime the value of R_e is greater than 100000. The friction factor computing formula for this flow regime is given as under:

$$f = 0.80 + 2\, log\left(\frac{R_e}{\sqrt{f}}\right) \qquad \text{...(10.36)}$$

Design of Sub-Main Line

Design of sub-main pipeline is same to the lateral line. As per Keller and Karmeli (1975) the energy loss in lateral and sub-main line varies to the tune of 55% and 45% of total allowable energy loss, respectively. Overall, the extent of energy loss in sub-main pipeline depends on its length, which should not exceed the allowable limit.

In the case when laterals are placed on the steep slopes, each individual lateral line requires pressure/flow regulation for uniform water application through emitters. In this particular case the length and diameter of sub-main line is determined in such a way that there would be a balance between the cost of energy and pipe, both. On undulating land surface, the position of sub-main inlet is decided on the basis of field slope. Laterals are laid along the contour and sub-main is positioned facing the field slope. In sloppy sub-main, the inlet is fixed in such a way that the uphill running length of sub-main line would be shorter than the downhill running length. In the case of sub-main to be laid on gentle sloping surface or on level land the inlet should be fixed at the center of sub-main line.

The size of sub-main pipeline is determined by using the Hazen-Williams equation and considering the roughness coefficient (C) between 140 and 150 for PVC made pipes. The energy loss is determined same to the laterals. The loss of energy in sub-main because of lateral connection depends on the type of connections used, i.e., tee, elbow, bends, etc. The total sub-main-energy loss includes the energy loss in filters, pressure valves, and other minor losses.

Design of Main Pipeline

The design of main pipeline is carried out on the basis of total discharge to be handled for meeting the irrigation requirement at tail end, i.e.

Discharge capacity of main line = Total discharge passing through sub-main lines.

As precautionary measures the energy loss in main pipeline should not be so to affect the water application uniformity at emitter's level. Besides, above the size of main pipeline should also be based on the comparison between power cost and capital cost, which must be minimum over the lifetime of pipeline. For detail knowhow the reader can refer the book "Micro-irrigation—Theory and Practice written by Suresh (2014).

10.2.18 Installation of Drip System

A proper installation of drip system plays significant role in smooth operation, working performance and extent of service life, as well. In micro-irrigation system the following components are installed with proper attention, as per below:

1. ***Control unit or head assembly*:** This component comprises the pumping set, water meter, non-return valve, different filters, fertigation assembly, flow control valve, air release valve and pressure release valves. These are installed on firm surface.
2. ***Pipeline*:** It comprises the main, sub-mains, laterals and emitters/micro-sprinklers. These are installed below the soil at suitable depth except lateral. Laterals are placed above or below the soil depending on type of laterals (inline or online) to be used.
3. ***Accessories*:** The accessories such as elbows, reducers, etc. are placed as per predicted locations.

The installation of different components of MI system in sequence, is narrated as under:

- Installation of filters
- Installation of fertigation unit

- Installation of main pipeline
- Installation of sub-main pipeline
- Installation or laying of laterals
- Fixing of emitters/drippers and accessories

Installation of Filters

In MI/drip system the sand filter, screen filter and hydro-cyclone filters are commonly used. These filters are placed on a firm surface of concrete or brick materials. This is required to make the control system safe against any kind of vibrations occurring because of their body weight during operation. The delivery pipe of pumping system is connected to the filters. Thereafter, the main-pipeline is directly connected to the screen filter. This arrangement confirms the flow of filtered water to the pipeline system.

Installation of Fertigation Unit

The purpose of fertigation unit is to apply fertilizers or nutrients to the plants in prescribed dose along with irrigation water. In MI system fertigation unit is placed between sand filter and screen filter. In order to conduct proper fertilizer distribution through this unit, the following two points are essentially followed:

- The fertilizer solution must pass through at least two 90-degree bends or turns so that the mixing of fertilizer solution in irrigation water may be in proper form in a short time span, and
- The undissolved materials should not be allowed to enter the main pipeline, directly.

In order to meet these points the fertigation unit is placed at u/s end of the screen filter. The exact location of fertigation unit is between the sand and screen filters.

Installation of Main Pipeline

In MI system the main pipeline receives the water from pumping unit via filters in the form of clean water, which is directed to the sub-main pipelines, ahead. The main pipeline is permanently installed below the soil at some proper depth, normally at minimum depth of 50 cm from the top soil surface, to keep the pipeline unaffected by farm machineries during farm operations, and also from harvesting tools used for harvesting the crop. The installation is carried out by making the trench of predetermined depth. The trench width should be such that the working person can easily move through it. After construction of trench the main pipe is laid in that, properly and earth materials are placed over the pipe in trench.

In context to the depth of pipe or earth cover on the pipe, the USSCS has framed guidelines for placing a minimum depth of earth cover depending on the pipe size (Fred Hamish, 1977), is presented in Table 10.8. However, if the main pipeline is made of the materials other than PVC, i.e., the HDPE or GI, the pipeline may not be essentially requiring to install below the ground. However, for safety points of view it is advised to place them underground at some suitable depth.

Table 10.8 Minimum depth of earth cover depending on size of the pipe

S. No.	Pipe diameter (mm)	Depth of earth cover on pipe (mm)
1.	12 to 60	450
2.	60 to 100	600
3.	more than 600	750

(*Source*: (Fred Hamish, 1977)

Installation of Sub-Main Pipeline

The sub-main pipelines are also installed permanently, underground. In field the position of sub-main pipeline is just across the rows of plantation. The installation of sub-main line is accomplished by adopting all the points suggested by USSCS regarding minimum depth of earth cover to be on the pipe. The sub-main line is connected by its one end from the main pipe-line. As precautionary measure, the pipe must be cleaned by removing the foreign materials existing inside the pipe such as mud or others, before connecting with the main pipeline. The accessories such as gate valve, ball valve, air release valve, flush valve, etc. are also fixed in the sub-main pipeline at their defined locations. The locations of different accessories are mentioned below:

- ***Ball valve*:** It is placed at the inlet end of sub-main pipe.
- ***Air release valve*:** It is placed after ball valve in sub-man pipeline.
- ***Flush valve*:** It is fixed at the end of each sub-main line.

The covering of sub-main pipeline with earth materials is done after fitting all the requisite accessories and laterals; otherwise, their fitting will be difficult.

Installation of Lateral Lines

Laterals are connected to the sub-main line. Their location is fixed as per rows of planation. At each row there is one lateral line. Fitting of lateral with the sub-main line is done by making holes on the sub-main pipe, just across the respective rows using hand drill machine. Thereafter, in drilled hole the gromate take off called GTO is fitted. The lateral pipe is inserted in sub-main pipe through GTO. Since, GTO is made of rubber; therefore, there is created water leak proof connection between lateral and sub-main pipe. The size of hole to be drilled in sub-main line is decided on the basis of size of GTO and lateral pipe to be used. For example, for 8 mm size (ID) GTO about 11.9mm size hole is being appropriate. After placing the laterals on respective rows of plantation the other end of laterals is fitted with end plug. The laterals can be flushed by removing the end plug. As precautionary measure, an extra length of lateral pipe is provided at the end of each row to accommodate shrinkage in pipe. This is called shrinkage allowance.

Fitting of Emitters/Drippers and Accessories

In MI system the emitters are used to drop or deliver the water near plant stem in root zone area. Emitters receive the water from the lateral pipe. These are fitted on lateral pipe near to the respective plants. Fitting of emitter/dripper is carried out by puncturing the lateral pipe, manually. The fitting should be started from sub-main side. During puncturing the flow of water through lateral should be continued, as it makes easy to puncture the pipe. The puncturing should be done sideways as per position of the plant. The drippers should be fixed in the punctured holes after completion of entire puncturing works in the lateral line. The emitter's fitting should be preceded towards sub-main side. In fitting work, firstly, the dripper point should be pushed inside the lateral through punctured hole and thereafter slightly pulled outward. This makes proper fitting of dripper along with water leak connection, too.

The micro-sprinklers are also fitted to laterals at desired point with the help of micro-tube. One end of micro-tube is placed to the lateral and other end is fitted with the micro-sprinkler. In case of wetting of tree canopy several micro-sprinklers are placed over the canopy with the help of stakes, tied to the tree branches.

10.3 DESIGN OF MICRO-SPRINKLER SYSTEM

The micro-sprinkler is one of the components of micro-irrigation system. It also applies irrigation water in precise amount at controlled rate as per requirement of the crop. In greenhouse irrigation system the drip and micro-sprinkler are commonly used as irrigation tools. The design of micro-sprinkler system is the same to the drip system. The components comprising control unit, filters and pipeline including main, sub-main and laterals are the same both in drip and micro sprinkler system. Difference is in respect of water emitting device, only. In micro-sprinkler system at the place emitter/dripper the micro-sprinklers are used with the help of micro tubes. Micro-tube is connected to the lateral pipe. In order to accomplish irrigation the micro-sprinkler head is placed at some height from the ground surface using riser or stake. This makes unobstructed water sprinkling over crop canopy. The height of riser is about 50 cm or so. The selection of micro-sprinkler is done on the basis of discharge rate or depth of water application required to the crop. The closely grown crops such as leafy vegetables are irrigated using micro-sprinklers. Spacing between two micro-sprinklers is fixed in such a way that there is complete wetting of cropped area. The number of required micro-sprinklers is determined based on total cropped area and the area covered by single micro-sprinkler. Total crop area divided by area covered from single micro-sprinkler gives the number of required micro-sprinklers.

The hydraulics of main, sub-main and lateral pipelines is the same to the drip pipe line system. The evaluation of irrigation uniformity is also carried out by adopting the same procedure as described in drip design case.

10.4 TESTING OF SYSTEM INSTALLATION

Testing of system (MI) installation is essential to ascertain proper functioning of different components. This is done as per below:

- Ensure that all the valves are in open mode.
- Allow the water flow through system.
- Flush the main, sub-main and laterals, completely.
- Close the flush valve and end caps.
- Check the pressure with the help of pressure gauge equipped in the system. And get it ensure that the pressure at selected point is well as per design norm.
- Also check the functioning of filters, different valves and fertigation unit placed in MI system.

The installed system is considered to be fit for operation, when it is ensured that all the components of MI system are properly functioning and existing pressure is also in required range.

10.5 SYSTEM OPERATION

Once, the MI system is installed at the site, and its testing whether each and every component are properly functioning or not is also done, then it is assumed that the system is ready for operation to irrigate the crop. In context to operation of MI system the followings are few important points to follow, for keeping the system long lasting and trouble free:

- Keep all the data record regarding design, evaluation and testing derived from the designer, installer and dealer's sides for future need if any misconduct is developed in the system.
- Maintain the time of operation of different sub-units considering climatic variables such as rainfall, etc.
- Keep the record of time schedule about operation of different valves.
- Determine the volume of water required to apply each and every setting and sub-unit. It is just to ensure the supply of desired quantity of water.
- Record the pressure reading from the pressure gauge. This is to have the information about proper functioning of the system.
- Check all the components for their proper functioning.
- Check the emitters for their discharge deliverance. This should be done by selecting the drippers, randomly in the field and measuring their discharge rates.
- Evaluate the uniformity of water emission/application of drippers and micro-sprinklers.
- Also evaluate the working of fertigation unit by determining its application rate.

10.6 CARE AND MAINTENANCE OF MI SYSTEM

MI system handles the water and chemicals (fertilizers) to deliver the plants in terms of irrigation and fertigation. The major defects in system gets introduce mainly because of following causative factors, which immediately require their remedy, anyhow; otherwise, there is development of serious problems; and accordingly making the system permanently failure to work:

- Clogging
- Pipe breakage
- Component removal
- Root intrusion, etc.

The component-wise care and maintenance of MI system is narrated as under:

Emitter: This is one of the important components of MI system. The water delivery to the plant at desired rate is accomplished by this component. A little mistake in its placement or misconduct in water emission may cause significant effect on uniformity in irrigation application. Normally, the followings are few important symptoms which indicate improper functioning of emitters, and they need to follow the measures to remove, immediately:

(i) *Improper water wetting*: This is because of not functioning of emitter well to emit the water. In this condition, emitter should be replaced, immediately. This defect may also be due to development of improper pressure, which could be solved by properly cleaning of emitter. The emitter's cleaning is carried out in various ways depending on the type of blockage. For example, if clogging is simply due to entry of soil particles then by flushing action it can be easily removed. On the other hand, if it is because of deposition of chemical contents (precipitate) then chemical method called acid treatment is performed for removing the blockage.

(ii) *Disturbance in emitter's placement*: This is also one of the serious issues to take care, promptly. The best solution for this problem is to install the emitter accurately at proper place or position.

(iii) *Leakage from emitter's connection point*: This is because of improper fitting of emitter to the lateral pipe. This problem can be rectified by pushing and pulling the emitter in the hole at lateral pipe.

Filter: This is one of the most important components, generally known as the heart of MI system. Its proper functioning ensures better performance of MIS. In the condition of improper filtering of water to be delivered to the plant through emitter, the emitter holes are likely to get block due to entry of soil particles. Ultimately, this leads to cause failure of MI system. The essentiality and timing of filter cleaning is decided based on the level of pressure difference across the filter.

In MIS there are three types of filters, namely (i) Sand filter; (2) Screen/Disc filter (3) Hydro-cyclone filters are used. Their care and maintenance is done as per below:

***Sand filter*:** This filter is used for removing the silts, dirt and organic materials from irrigation water. These filtered materials get deposit in sand filter during course of irrigation. Slowly and slowly the level of deposition becomes very much in filter. This leads into pressure drop across the filter, causes effect on discharge rate of pipeline system. In this condition the requirement of filter cleaning becomes essential to keep the performance on water application, proper. As per American Society of Agricultural Engineers (ASAE) the pressure drop should not exceed 70 kPa. The filter cleaning by back flushing/washing technique is found better.

The back washing should be done every day for 5-minutes period. In back washing process the water is allowed to pass through lid of the filter instead of flush or backwash valve. In addition, the sands existing at filter bed is also stirred up to the level of filter candle. During stirring action, care must be taken that the candle may not get damage. In this action the deposited sands at deeper depth inside sand filter gets free, and removed away through water via filter lid. Similarly, if irrigation water contains sufficient amount of organic contents, the sand filter should be cleaned by thorough washing, using clean water. Sometimes, the sand level in filter gets decrease; and thereby filtering performance becomes slow. In this condition, same grade sand should be filled in the filter up to required level.

***Screen/Disc filter*:** The flushing is most appropriate cleaning action for screen or disc filters. Its cleaning requirement is predicted by knowing the pressure drop. The flushing of screen filter becomes essential when pressure drop is more than 0.5 kg/cm^2. It is carried out by keeping the filter lid open, so that the deposited dirt and silt particles could get easily removed through that. Also, the filter elements such as screen and discs are taken out from the filter, and they are properly cleaned with the help of flowing clean water. Prior to start cleaning of screen or disc the rubber seal pack placed on both the ends of screen should be carefully removed. And after cleaning of screen/disc, they should again be fitted at the place, properly; otherwise, there is possibility of water leakage and damage of the same, too.

***Hydro-cyclone filter*:** This filter is placed after sand and screen filters. Its use becomes essential when irrigation water contains heavy load of fine sands. As compared to sand and screen or disc filters this requires less maintenance. However, after performing irrigation, the deposited dirt or sands inside flow chamber of HC filter should be properly washed. This can be done by keeping the flush valve open and allowing the water flow through the filter.

Fertigation unit: In micro-irrigation system, the venturi is commonly used for fertigation purpose. On performing fertigation, the suction port of venturi normally gets clogged. This clogging is removed by allowing clean water for 10 to 15-minute period before and after fertigation work. In addition, the following points are also taken into consideration regarding maintenance of fertigation unit:

- In course of fertigation the lid of fertilizer tank should be kept fully tight.
- The leakage in fertigation unit should be regularly watched; and if there, that must be removed, immediately.

Sub-main and lateral pipeline: Sometimes, the silt and other foreign materials are not properly filtered by the filters equipped in MI system; and they are escaped and delivered to the water in main pipeline. These escaped materials get deposit in sub-main and also in lateral pipes. In addition, there is also the formation of slimes or pastes because of algal and bacterial growth in pipeline. All these factors cause plugging problem. The cleaning of deposited materials inside sub-main and laterals is removed by flushing action using fresh water. Flushing of sub-main line is carried out by opening the flush valve to remove the flushed materials. The laterals are flushed by removing the end caps and allowing fresh water to pass through the same. Flushing should be continued till coming out of clean water from pipeline.

10.6.1 Chemical Treatments

In MI system, the clogging or plugging problem, especially in emitters, also takes place because of deposition of chemical precipitates. Normally, the carbonates and bicarbonates of Iron, Calcium and Manganese salts are very much susceptible to get precipitate. In addition, the clogging also takes place due to growth of microorganisms and Iron and Sulphur slimes. Such forms of clogging cannot be cleaned properly by flushing action. The best alternative is the chemical treatment, only. This is carried out with the help of chemicals such as "Chloride and Chlorine, mainly. In which Chloride treatment (acid treatment) is done for cleaning the chemical deposits or precipitates; while Chlorine treatment is performed for removing the organic and other kinds of deposits such as bacterial slimes. The treatment should be carried out at some interval, which may be based on clogging level and water quality. The acid and chlorine treatments are described below.

10.6.2 Acid Treatment

For this purpose, the Hydrochloride (HCl) acid is used. HCl of suitable concentration is injected in the pipeline at recommended rate. Thereafter system is stopped for about 24-hour duration.

After end of 24-hour the system is flushed off by keeping the flush valve of sub-main line and end caps of lateral lines in open condition. This treatment is continued till achieving the pH level as 4.0 of water at the end of pipe. In acid treatment there is a thumb rule that it should be carried out once in 10-day.

10.6.3 Chlorine Treatment

Chlorine treatment is done once in 15-day. In this chemical treatment the bleaching powder is used as the source of chlorine. A solution of bleaching powder is prepared by dissolving in the water. The prepared solution is injected in the pipeline system for about half hour (30-minute) duration. Injection rate depends on pH of water flowing through pipeline. At high pH more amount of chlorine is required for treatment. After injection of solution, system is stopped for about 24-hour duration to get dissolve the deposited materials in pipeline. After end of 24-hour system is flushed by opening the flush valve (sub-main line) and end caps of lateral lines. The recommended dose of chlorine solution for treatment is shown in Table 10.9.

Table 10.9 Recommended dose of chlorine solution for plugging treatment

S. No.	Forms of clogging	Recommended dose (Chlorine)	Remark
1.	Algal	0.5 to 1.0 ppm	Application of dose should be done, continuously.
		20 ppm	Application should be for 20 minutes at the end of each irrigation cycle.
2.	Slimes	1.0 ppm	Free residual chlorine is maintained at each lateral end.
3.	Iron precipitates	0.64 times the Fe^{++}	1.0 ppm free residual chlorine is maintained at the end of each lateral.

Injection rate of chlorine solution is governed by the system flow rate. It can be determined by using the following relationship:

$$q_c = 6 \times 10^{-3} \frac{u \cdot q_s}{c} \qquad \ldots(10.37)$$

in which q_c is the injection rate of chemical to be used; u is the desired concentration of chemical in irrigation water (ppm); q_s is the water flow rate (lpm) and c is the concentration of chemical in solution ready for injection (%).

10.7 PUMP SELECTION

The selection of pump is the last step of MI system design. Broadly, the MIS is operated with the help of external power source such as electrical motors or fuel-based engines. The purpose of pumping system is to suck the water from source and distribute that in pipeline, i.e., from the main line to the emitters via sub-main in such a way that there would be uniformity in application rate throughout cropped field. In market there is a wide range of pump's availability in respect to power and discharge capacity. However, their proper selection to meet the requirement is most important. In this context there have been framed some guidelines for selection of pumping unit; few important amongst them are narrated below:

- Sufficient pressure to achieve better discharge
- Available power source
- Power consumption
- Cost of pumping unit
- Frequency of operation
- Reliability

10.8 POWER REQUIREMENT OF PUMPING UNIT

The power required to discharge the water from the pump is called water horsepower or sometimes the water power, too. It is computed on the basis of discharge rate and pumping head. The following formula can be used for determining the required power of pumping system:

$$W_p = \frac{Q \cdot H}{360} \qquad \ldots(10.38)$$

in which, W_p is the required power of pumping unit (Kilowatt); Q is the pump discharge rate or pumping capacity (m^3/h) and H is the pumping head (m) also called dynamic head of the pump. The total dynamic head (TDC) is given by the following formula:

$$H_t = H_n + H_m + H_j + H_s \qquad \ldots(10.39)$$

in which H_t is the total dynamic head (design head) in m; H_n is the maximum head required at the main pipeline to operate the drip/micro-sprinklers at requisite pressure (m); H_m is the maximum head loss due to friction in main pipeline and suction line (m); H_j is the elevation difference between pump and the junction point of lateral and main pipeline (m) and H_s is the suction head(m). The relationship between TDC and pump capacity is illustrated graphically in Figure 10.2.

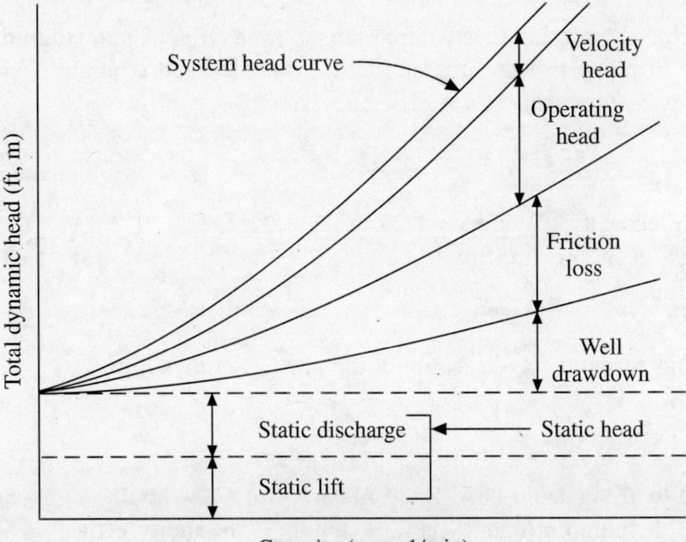

Figure 10.2 System curve showing the relationship between TDC and Pump capacity (*Source*: Haman et al., 1992)

PROBLEM 10.17 Compute the required power (kilowatt) of pumping system to be used for supplying water at the rate of 15.0 m^3/h. The pumping head is 7.5 m.

***Solution*:**

Given that,

(i) Pumping rate = 15^3/h
(ii) Pumping head = 7.5 m

Using the following formula for determining the power of pumping unit:

$$W_p = \frac{Q \cdot H}{360}$$

in which, W_p is the required power of pumping unit (Kilowatt) to be determined; Q is the pump discharge rate is given as 5 m^3/h and H is the pumping head is given as 7.5 m. Substituting these values in the formula and solving, we have:

$$W_p = \frac{15 \times 7.5}{360} = 0.314 \text{ Kilowatt} \quad \textbf{Ans.}$$

10.9 HORSEPOWER OF PUMPING UNIT

It is computed by using the following formula:

$$HP = \frac{Q \cdot H}{75 \cdot n_p n_m} \qquad \text{...(10.40)}$$

in which, H is the total head acting on the pump; Q is the discharge capacity of drip/sprinkler system (liter per sec); n_p is the pump efficiency (fraction) and n_m is the motor efficiency (fraction).

PROBLEM 10.18 Determine the required horsepower (HP) of pumping unit, if the desired discharge capacity of pump is 1.25 m^3/s and total available head at pump is about 55 m. Take the pump efficiency as 60% and motor efficiency as 65%.

***Solution*:**

Given that,

(i) Discharge capacity of pump = 1.25 m^3/s
(ii) Total head at pump = 55 m
(iii) Pump efficiency = 60%
(iv) Motor efficiency = 65%

Using following formula for determining the size (HP) of pump:

$$HP = \frac{Q \cdot H}{75 \cdot n_p \, n_m}$$

in which, H is the total available head is given as 55 m; Q is the discharge capacity of pump is 1.25 m^3/s); n_p is the pump efficiency is 60% and n_m is the motor efficiency is given as 65%. Substituting these values in above formula and solving, we have:

$$HP = \frac{55 \times 1.25}{75 \times 0.60 \times 0.65} = 2.35$$

$$= 2.35 \text{ HP} \quad \textbf{Ans.}$$

PRACTICE QUESTIONS

Descriptive Type Questions

1. Describe different considerations followed in design of drip irrigation system.
2. Describe water wetting pattern of drip irrigation and its consideration in design.
3. What do you mean by crop water requirement and net irrigation requirement?
4. Describe hydraulics of pipeline in drip irrigation/sprinkler system.
5. Explain design of main, sub-main and lateral pipelines of drip system.
6. Explain design capacity of drip system.
7. Describe the design of micro-sprinkler irrigation system.
8. Explain installation of drip and micro-sprinkler system.
9. Describe care and maintenance of drip/micro-sprinkler system.
10. Describe cleaning of filters used in drip/micro-sprinkler system.
11. Describe power requirement or size of pumping unit to be used for operating drip system.

Multiple Choice Type Questions

1. Wetting pattern of drip irrigation gets affected due to
   (a) Dripper flow rate (b) Soil types
   (c) Size of pumping unit (d) Both (a) and (b)
2. Capacity of drip irrigation system denotes
   (a) Total discharge available at the control unit
   (b) Total discharge available at emitting point
   (c) Total discharge available at lateral line
   (d) Total discharge available at sub-main line
3. Christensen (1942) formula computes
   (a) Friction loss in pipeline (b) Flow regime in pipeline
   (c) Discharge coefficient (d) Irrigation efficiency
4. The main pipeline is connected to the
   (a) Sand filter (b) Hydro-cyclone only
   (c) Screen filter (d) Both (a) and (b)
5. Scobey formula computes
   (a) Friction head loss (b) Friction coefficient
   (c) Friction factor (d) Pipe size
6. The diameter of lateral line varies from
   (a) 15 to 25 mm (b) 10 to 12 mm
   (c) 12 to 16 mm (d) 20 to 300 mm
7. Ball valve is placed at the inlet end of
   (a) Main pipe (b) Sub-main pipe
   (c) Lateral line (d) None of above

8. Air release valve is placed after ball valve in

(a) Sub-main pipe (b) Main pipe
(c) Lateral line (d) None of above

9. The flush valve is fixed at the end of each

(a) Lateral line (b) Main pipe
(c) Sub-main pipe (d) None of above

10. The gromate take off (GTO) is used for connecting

(a) Sub-main line (b) Emitters in laterals
(c) Laterals in sub-main line (d) Both (a) and (b)

11. Selection of pumping unit is done on the basis of

(a) Dripper flow rate (b) Soil types
(c) System capacity (d) Both (a) and (b)

12. Horsepower of pump depends on

(a) Total dynamic head (b) Soil types
(c) Discharge rate (d) Both (a) and (c)

13. The depth of earth fill on drip pipeline depends on

(a) Pipe diameter (b) Soil type
(c) Pipe length (d) Soil moisture content

14. Chlorine treatment is done for removing

(a) Chemical clogging (b) Physical plugins
(c) Bacteriological clogging (d) All above

15. Acid treatment (HCl) is done at the interval of

(a) 10-day (b) 30-day
(c) 15-day (d) 20-day

Answers

1. d **2.** d **3.** a **4.** c **5.** a **6.** c **7.** b **8.** a **9.** c **10.** c
11. c **12.** d **13.** a **14.** c **15.** a

BIBLIOGRAPHY

Allen, R.G., Pereira, L., Raes, D., and Smith, M., (1998). Crop evapotranspiration guidelines for computing crop water requirements. *FAO Irrigation and Drainage Paper* 56. UN-FAO, Rome, Italy.

Doorenbos, J. and Pruitt, W. O. (1977). Crop water requirements. *Irrigation and Drainage Paper No.* 24, (rev.) FAO, Rome, Italy. 144 p.

Goldammer T. (2019). Greenhouse Management: A Guide to Operations and Technology. Apex Publishers, USA.

Goldberg Dan, Gornat B, and Rimon D (1976). Drip irrigation Principles Design and Agricultural Practices. Drip Irrigation Scientific Publication, Kfar Shmaryahes, Israel 68–90.

Haman, D.Z., Zaxuta, F.S., and Izuno, F.T. (1992). Selection of Centrifugal Pumping Equipment. *Extension circular* 1048. IFAS. University of Florida, Gainesville, FL 32611.

Hamish, F. (1977). Main Line Installation, in Drip/Trickle Irrigation No.5(2), 2Pub. *International Drip Irrigation Asso.*, P.O. Box 288, Bloomington, California-92316 (714) 877–4405, p. 12.

Howell T.A, Stevenson D.S, Aljibury F.K., Giltin H.M, Wu I.P, Warrick A.W., and Raats P.A.C (1980). Design and Operation of Trickle (Drip) System (In Design and Operation of Farm Irrigation System, Chapter 16; edited by Jensen, M.E.) *ASAE Monograph* 3, ASAE Michigan USA.

James L.G. (1998). Principles of irrigation system Design, John Wiley, New York.

James, L.G. (1988). Principles of Farm Irrigation System Design, John Willey & sons, Inc. New York.

Keller, J. and Bliesner R.D. (1990). Sprinkler and trickle irrigation. AVI, Van Nostrand Reinhold, New York.

Keller, J. and Karmeli, D. (1975). Trickle Irrigation Design, Rain Bird Sprinkler Manufacturing Corporation, Glendora, California, USA.

Keller, J. and Karmeli, D. (1975). Trickle Irrigation Design. Rain Bird Sprinkler Manufacturing Corporation Glendora, California, U.S.A, 46–49.

Kenworthy, A. L. (1972). Trickle Irrigation—The Concept and Guidelines for Use. *Research report No.* 165, *Farm Science.*, Michigan State University. East Lansing, Michigan.

Michael, A. M. (2010). Irrigation Theory and Practice, Vikas Publishing House Pvt. Ltd, Delhi, India.

Nakayama, F.S., Bucks, D.A., and Clements, A.J., (1979). Assessing Trickle Emitter Application Uniformity. *Trans. ASAE* 22(4): 816-821.

Soil Conservation Service. (1984). Procedures for Collecting Soil Samples and Methods of Analysis for Soil Survey. USDA-SCS, *Soil Survey Investigations Report No.* 1. GPO, Washington, DC.

Soil Conservation Service. (1984). Procedures for Collecting Soil Samples and Methods of Analysis for Soil Survey. USDA-SCS, *Soil Survey Investigations Report No.* 1. GPO, Washington, DC.

Suresh R. (2010).Micro-Irrigation—Theory and Practice. Standard publishers Distributors, Nai Sarak, Delhi.

Tiwari, K. N. (2009). Pressurized Irrigation, Precision Farming Development Center Publication No. PFDC/IIT KGP/2/2009 Agricultural & Food Engineering Department, IIT Kharagpur.

Tiwari, K.N. (2007). Pressurized Irrigation, Scientific Publication No. PFDC/IITKGP/1/2007, Precision Farming Development (NCPAH), IIT Kharagpur, India.

United States Department of Agriculture, Soil Conservation Service (1984), Trickle Irrigation.

US Dept. of Agriculture, Soil Conservation Service, National Engineering Handbook Chapter 15, Section 15. U.S.D.A., S.C.S., Washington, D.C., pp.129.

http://www. Rainfornet.com/services/pump-training/#System Curve

http://www.agridrip.com/page/437645582

http://www.irrigationdirect.com

http://www.irrigationtutorial.com/drip

https://www.fao.org/3/X0490E/x0490e0b.htm)

CHAPTER 11

Fertigation of Greenhouse Crops

Greenhouse is covered with a special type of cladding or covering material, mainly the UV stabilized polyethylene film. It creates a protected environment with micro-climate suitable to variety of the commercial crops to grow, inside. Since, greenhouse is a costly structure to facilitate crop growing; therefore, the measures associated to enhance the crop productivity, are essentially followed to the greenhouse crops. The irrigation and fertilization are the two important inputs, applied in proper amount and time schedule, plays significant role in maximizing crop yield along with better quality produce.

Fertigation is the art of fertilizer application to the crop, in which prefixed dose of fertilizers are applied along with irrigation water to the crops grown, inside greenhouse. This is accomplished with the help of a special attachment to control unit of drip system is called fertigation unit. Through this system the fertilizers in the form of solution of requisite concentration are placed in the fertilizer tank, connected to the drip control unit. On system operation, the fertilizer solution gets automatically sucked from the fertilizer tank, and is delivered into irrigation pipeline. The mixed fertilizer solution in irrigation water is ultimately delivered near to the crop/plant on soil surface, which enters the root zone. Fertigation technique provides a best means to apply the fertilizers and other nutrients, uniformly to all the greenhouse crops/plants. Its benefits are multifold, such as fertilizer saving, labour saving, enhancement in crop productivity, etc. in significant range. This chapter emphasizes the presentation and discussion associated to fertigation including compatible fertilizers, methodologies used, merits and demerits, essential nutrients and their deficiency symptoms, growing media—its components and others related to the greenhouse cultivation.

11.1 ESSENTIAL ELEMENTS FOR PLANT GROWTH

In general, a plant requires total 16 elements for its normal growth and reproduction. In fertigation scheme, these are provided to the crop or plant through fertilizers in combination at a well-defined schedule. The application is done in prescribed dose; not in excess. The list of 16 elements is shown in Table 11.1.

Table 11.1 List of essential elements for plant growth and reproduction

S. No.	Name of element	S. No.	Name of element	Remark
1.	Carbon (C)	9.	Magnesium (Mg)	Out of 16 elements the Carbon (C), Hydrogen (H) and Oxygen (O_2) are largely met from the air (Carbon dioxide, CO_2) and water (H_2O). The remaining elements are called mineral nutrients, are met from different sources.
2.	Hydrogen (H)	10.	Iron (Fe)	
3.	Oxygen (O)	11.	Boron (B)	
4.	Phosphorus (P)	12.	Manganese (Mn)	
5.	Potassium (K)	13.	Copper (Cu)	
6.	Nitrogen (N)	14.	Zinc (Zn)	
7.	Sulphur (S)	15.	Molybdenum (Mo)	
8.	Calcium (Ca)	16.	Chlorine (Cl)	

(*Source*: Goldammer T., 2019)

Besides, the sources to supply the 16 elements for plant growth a small amount of them is also received from the growing media, used for crop growing. However, most of them (13 mineral elements) are fulfilled through fertilizers. Among mineral elements the Nitrogen (N), Phosphorus (P), Potash (K), Sulphur (S), Calcium (Ca), and Magnesium (Mg) are counted as the macro-nutrients. It is only because of the reason that as compared to other elements their required amount for the crop or plant is more. The other elements, i.e., the Iron (Fe), Boron (B), Manganese (Mn), Copper (Cu), Zinc (Zn), Molybdenum (Mo) and Chlorine (Cl) are counted as micro-nutrients, as their required amount for plant growth is very small; normally in ppm (parts per million). The inorganic sources of micro-nutrients are listed in Table 11.2.

Table 11.2 Inorganic sources of micro-nutrients

Material		Element (%)	Water solubility (g/100g H_2O)	Temp °C
	Sources of Boron			
Granular Borax	$NaB_4O_7 \cdot 10H_2O$	11.3	2.5	1
Sodium Tetra Borate Anhydrous	NaB_4O_7	21.5	1.3	0
Solubor	$NaB_4O_{15} \cdot 4H_2O$	20.5	22	30
Ammonium Pentaborate	$NH_4B_5O_8 \cdot 4H_2O$	19.9	7	18
	Sources of Copper			
Copper Sulphate	$CuSO_4 \cdot 5H_2O$	25.0	24	0
Cuprous Oxide	Cu_2O	88.8	1	
Cupric Oxide	CuO	79.8	1	
Cuprous Chloride	Cu_2Cl_2	64.2	1.5	25
Cupric Chloride	$CuCl_2$	47.2	71	0
	Sources of Iron			
Ferrous Sulphate	$FeSO_4 \cdot 7H_2O$	20.1	33	0
Ferric Sulphate	$Fe_2(SO_4)_3 \cdot 9H_2O$	19.9	440	20
Iron Oxalate	$Fe_2(C_2O_4)_3$	30.0	Very soluble	
Ferrous Ammonium Sulphate	$Fe(NH_4)_2(SO_4)_2 \cdot 6H_2O$	14.2	18	0
Ferric Chloride	$FeCl_2$	34.4	74	

(Contd.)

Material		Element (%)	Water solubility (g/100g H_2O)	Temp °C
	Sources of Zinc			
Zinc Sulphate	$ZnSO_4 \cdot H_2O$	36.4	89	100
Zinc Oxide	ZnO	80.3	1	
Zinc Carbonate	$ZnCO_3$	52.1	0.001	16
Zinc Chloride	$ZnCl_2$	48.0	432	25
Zinc Oxysulphate	$ZnO \cdot ZnSO_4$	53.8		
Zinc Ammonium Sulphate	$ZnSO_4 \cdot (NH_4)_2SO_4 \cdot 6H_2O_2$	16.3	9.6	0
Zinc Nitrate	$Zn(NO_3)_2 \cdot 6H_2O$	22.0	324	20

11.2 SIGNIFICANCE OF ELEMENTS

The element-wise significance or roles in context to plant growth are described as under:

Carbon (C): It is derived from CO_2 available in the atmosphere through photosynthesis action conducted by living plants. This produces one of the components of all organic compounds such as sugar, protein, and organic acids as well. In plants these compounds are served to use in the form of structural components for actuating enzymatic reactions, and also as genetic materials. As per research evidences, the plant growth gets accelerate when level of ambient CO_2 is available in the range of 800 to 1000 ppm. This range of CO_2 concentration could be easily generated inside greenhouse. The sources of carbon for greenhouse are pointed as under:

- ***Atmosphere*:** The normal CO_2 level in the atmosphere is about 350 ppm.
- ***Injecting CO_2*:** In greenhouse the level of CO_2 can be enhanced by injecting it, artificially, which is commonly practised for winter greenhouse vegetable cultivation. As precautionary measure, the CO_2 injection should be accomplished during day light, because injected CO_2 will likely to get utilize in photosynthesis process, which happens in presence of sunlight. Also, the injection of CO_2 should be done within canopy of the plant, from where the entry of CO_2 in the plant leaves becomes easy and to a greater rate.
- ***Burning of natural gas or Propane*:** The level of CO_2 inside greenhouse can also be increased by burning the natural gas or propane (liquid) using special type of CO_2 burner.

Hydrogen (H): This also constitutes as one of the components of organic compounds releasing carbon. In addition, hydrogen ions also cause electro-chemical reaction in maintaining charge balance across cell membrane.

Oxygen (O): In plant body its presence is essential to actuate many of the plant bio-chemical reactions. Oxygen is considered as the third element in typical organic molecules (sugar).

Phosphorus (P): Its important roles in context to plant growth are as follows:

- Used in many of the energies transfer compounds.
- Important in regards to nucleic acids formation.
- Beneficial in building blocks for genetic code material.

Potassium (K): In plant's body, its roles are narrated as under:

(i) Activates many of the enzymatic reactions.
(ii) Maintains turgor level in guard cells. The guard cells are being around the stomata. The turgor level of guard cells controls the stomatal opening. The flow of K in and out of the guard cells, affects the turgor level. This leads to affect the level of gaseous and water vapour exchange between plant body and the atmosphere.

Nitrogen (N): It is very common and an important element in context to plant growth. It is found in many of the compounds. In chlorophyll, i.e., the green pigments in plant, amino acids, proteins, nucleic acids and organic acids, N is available. In vegetative growth nitrogen plays significant role.

Sulphur (S): This is an important component of sulphur containing amino acids such as Methionine. In addition, it is also found available in certain enzymes of Sulfhydryl group.

Calcium (Ca): In plants its main roles are pointed as under:

(i) Development of cell wall.
(ii) Used as co-factor in certain enzymatic reactions.
(iii) Regulation of cell processes mediated by molecule called Calmodulin.

Magnesium (Mg): It is also counted as one of the important elements for plant growth. In plant cell, it is located in the centre of chlorophyll molecule. In certain enzymatic reactions magnesium is required to use as co-factor.

Iron (Fe): Its important uses in plant body, are as follows:

- Uses in bio-chemical reactions forming chlorophyll.
- Acts as the part of one of the enzymes, which is responsible to modify the nitrate-nitrogen to ammoniacal nitrogen.
- In addition to above, the catalase and peroxidase also require Mg.

Boron (B): This is one of the micro-nutrients, essential for plant growth. Although, its clearcut function in plant body is not well known, but it is important to apply for development of normal meristem in young parts of the plant such as the root tips.

Manganese (Mn): Its importance is in many of the enzymatic reactions involving energy compounds Adenosine Triphosphate (ATP). In addition, it also activates several enzymes. Manganese is also found involve in the processes of electron transport system in photosynthesis.

Copper (Cu): This is the component of several enzymes in plant body. In addition, it also constitutes a part of protein in electron transport system in photosynthesis.

Zinc (Zn): It is associated to activate several enzymes. In plant, it is required for synthesis of indole acetic acid, which is a growth regulator. In nutshell, it is beneficial for plant growth.

Molybdenum (Mo): It is one of the micro-nutrients used as constituent of enzyme associated to the nitrogen metabolism. In addition, molybdenum is also found important regarding nitrate reductase.

Chlorine (Cl): It plays an important role in photosynthesis process. In addition, it also acts as counter ion in K fluxes, involved in cell turgor.

11.3 PLANT NUTRIENTS

Broadly, the plant nutrients are grouped in following three groups:

1. Primary nutrients,
2. Secondary nutrients, and
3. Micro nutrients.

Table 11.3. Illustrates the nutrients falling under different categories.

Table 11.3 List of nutrients falling under different categories

S. No.	Nutrients category	Nutrients	Remark
1.	Primary nutrients	(i) Nitrogen (N) (ii) Phosphorus (P) (iii) Potassium (K)	♦ Nitrogen is an integral part of plant protein. And also one of structural components of chlorophyll molecules required for photosynthesis action. ♦ Potassium is important to cause stomatal opening and closing.
2.	Secondary nutrients	(i) Calcium (Ca) (ii) Magnesium (Mg) (iii) Sulphur (S)	♦ Magnesium is the structural component of chlorophyll molecules required for photosynthesis action.
3.	Micronutrients	(i) Boron (B) (ii) Copper (Cu) (iii) Iron (Fe) (iv) Chloride (Cl) (v) Manganese (Mn) (vi) Molybdenum (Mo) (vii) Zinc (Zn)	♦ Micro-nutrients are also called trace elements. ♦ These are needed in very small (micro) amount to the plant

11.4 PLANT NUTRITION

Maintenance of adequate nutrient level in crop root zone is an essential and important issue to achieve the crop productivity in optimum range. In greenhouse cultivation this has special attention for the growers; otherwise, the crop productivity or b/c ratio gets badly affected. In general, the plant nutrition in greenhouse is carried out based on two main aspects, narrated as under.

Aspect (1): Availability of overall nutrients to the plant: In crop cycle or period the requirement of nutrient varies. A high rate of nutrient application is needed as the plant growth and fruit load get increase. The plant growth can be controlled by reducing the application of mineral nutrients, while other nutrients may be in sufficient amount. This advocates that a single nutritional element may be the most effective factor to limit the plant growth, even on availability of other elements in sufficient amount in root zone.

Aspect (2): Availability of nutrients in optimum ratio or in balance form: In this aspect of plant nutrition the vegetative and reproductive growth is developed by making available the nutrients in an optimum range. This feature is the key factor to keep the crop productivity for a long term. In imbalance situation (excess or deficient) of nutrients there is development of severe nutrient's deficiency or toxicity to the plant. In order to avoid the nutrient's imbalance, the growers need to have very alert regarding monitoring of nutrients' status in growing media, throughout crop period. It can be monitored by determining the EC and pH of growing media. In which the electrical conductivity (EC) is a good indicator of overall nutrients status. On the other hand, pH denotes the availability of individual nutrient to the plant for uptake. In this way, due to variation in pH value the nutrients balance of growing media gets change.

11.5 PLANT NUTRITION BASICS

The basic inorganic fertilizers are the salts. The salts are chemical compounds comprising positively and negatively charged ions (one, each). The positively charged ion is called cation and negatively charged ion is anion. For example, in the fertilizer salt named Calcium Nitrate, contains one Calcium cation and one Nitrate anion. On placing of salts in growing media the two ions get separate from each other and dissolve in the water. The dissolved ions in water are taken up by the plant's root system, which are further distributed in the plant body. In taking most of the ions, the plant applies sufficient energy or force. After entering the ions in plant body, they form useful compounds for plant growth. As an example, in plant metabolism (photosynthesis) process the water (Hydrogen and Oxygen) gets combine with the Carbon dioxide (Carbon and Oxygen) and forms starch or sugar (Carbon, Hydrogen and Oxygen), leads to develop plant growth. Similarly, it can also be explained by taking another example on formation of chlorophyll molecule. A chlorophyll molecule contains 55-carbon atoms; 60-hydrogen atoms; 5-oxygen atoms; 4-nitrogen atoms and 1-magnesium atom. In order to form 1-chlorophyll molecule:

- The leaves must have to take the CO_2 to meet the requirement of carbon and oxygen.
- The leaves should also have to take the Nitrogen and Magnesium, which is met from the inorganic fertilizers.
- The roots must have to take up water for hydrogen and oxygen from soil media.

Out of various nutrients, some nutrients are utilized to generate new tissues useful for growth; while others are either deposited or fixed in the older plant tissues. This fact is used as the basis for detecting nutrient's deficiency in the plant. As example, in case of deficiency of immobile nutrients the deficiency symptoms is found to visible in new growths of the plant in terms of yellowing or chlorosis, because the older tissues of the plant hold the immobile nutrients. Similarly, the deficiency symptoms of mobile nutrients are visible in older leaves. It is because of the reason that in plant the movement of mobile nutrients takes place from older leaves to the new leaves.

In nutshell, the plants require variety of nutrients for their growth and development, however, the carbon, hydrogen and oxygen are required in greater amount than the others. A plant takes these three elements from the H_2O and CO_2. The other elements such as the nitrogen, phosphorus, potassium, calcium, magnesium and sulphur are required in little large amount called macro-nutrients; are provided from external sources. And the iron, manganese, copper, zinc, boron, chloride, molybdenum, etc. are required in small amount to the plant, called micro-nutrients.

11.6 MOVEMENT OF NUTRIENT WITHIN PLANT BODY

On application of nutrients from external sources or already available in growing media, the root system takes the nutrients from there. The entered nutrients in the plant get movement from root to the growing parts of the plant through xylem. In addition, some of the nutrients also move to the developing or growing leaves or flowers from the older leaves, especially, when there is deficiency of that particular nutrient. The older leaves act as nutrients' source while growing leaves or flowers as the sink. On the basis of assessment of nutrient's movement, the deficiency symptoms in plant can be easily diagnosed. The deficiency of fast moving nutrients causes to affect the lower leaves.

11.7 GROWING MEDIA pH AND NUTRIENT'S AVAILABILITY

It represents the concentration of Hydrogen (H^+) ion in growing media. pH decides the acidity/alkalinity status of growing media. At greater H^+ ion concentration the solution becomes more acidic in nature. In addition, pH also controls the nutrient's uptake. In the condition of undesirable pH, the individual nutrients cannot be taken up by the plant. This leads to develop nutrient deficiency in the plant. In other words, at high or low pH conditions there develops nutrient imbalance. Overall, the nutrient's uptake varies with a wide range of pH, mentioned below:

Nitrogen and Potassium: These are readily available at wide range of pH.

Phosphorus: It is readily available at low pH. In general, in greenhouse crops the phosphorus problems is not common.

Calcium and Magnesium: These are readily available at high pH range.

Minor nutrients: The iron, manganese, boron, zinc and copper are readily available at a low pH. In addition, the toxicities of minor nutrients are also found at low pH, i.e., less than 6.5.

11.8 NUTRIENT'S DEFICIENCY

Nutrient deficiency in the crop grown either inside greenhouse or outside in open field, develops a great effect on growth and yield of the crop, as well. In greenhouse cultivation, this possibility is always tried to overcome by anyhow, so that the production of the grown crop may not get hamper or decline. The growers should be very attentive in this respect, to look into. As for as, nutrient is concerned, total 26 numbers of nutrients are required for proper growth and development of the crop/plant. Out of them, if there is deficiency in any case of the nutrients, certainly, there borne effects on grown crop.

11.8.1 Determining Nutrient Deficiency

In order to maintain proper plant growth, the diagnosis of nutritional deficiency and supplying the deficient nutrients, accordingly is very essential. However, by keeping the proper record of day-to-day activities comprising application of nutrients as well as development of misconducts like nutrients deficiency, etc. in crop farming can be removed, smoothly. Sometimes, the symptom also gets develop because of combine effect of pesticide's toxicity and disease. Apart from above, the symptom of nutritional disorder is often species or cultivar dependent. In this condition, the growers need to have complete exposure about nutritional deficiencies on crop-to-crop scale. Also, the disorder of each individual nutrient leaves a well-defined pattern of symptom. In general, the mobile elements (nutrient) in plant body induce the deficiency in lower or older leaves, first. On the other hand, the immobile elements induce the deficiency in younger of upper leaves.

There has been devised several tools/methods to detect correct nutritional deficiency in the plant. Some of them are described below:

(i) Visual diagnosis
(ii) Media testing
(iii) Tissue analysis

Visual diagnosis: This is done just visualizing the plant physiology at the site. However, it is not so reliable. This method requires a considerable experience about the disease, crop, cultivar and the condition or environment in which the crop is grown. It is a thumb rule that in case of the nutrients with high mobility the symptom of shortage is first visible in older of lower leaves, while in case of poor mobility of nutrients through phloem the deficiency symptoms appear first in new growths, i.e., in upper parts of the plant.

Media testing: In this method, the deficiency of nutrients is determined by collecting the samples of plant body and analyzing them in laboratory. This is more accurate method to determine the nutrient deficiency, but costlier than the others. The samples are collected from randomly selected pots within the unit, and are mixed together. The sampling unit may be the part of an individual crop species planted at the same time and are kept under same treatment. The collected samples are analyzed in the laboratory to determine the status of available nutrients in the plant body.

Tissue analysis: In this method of determining nutrients' deficiency/concentration or potentially toxic elements existing in the plant, the leaves are taken as the representative part of the plant to analyze. Although, different parts have different levels of nutrients, but leaf tissue is preferred for determining the nutrients uptake from the media. Presence of mineral contents, i.e., the macro-nutrients such as nitrogen, phosphorus, potassium, etc. is expressed in terms of percentage on dry weight basis. On the other hand, the micro-nutrients (iron, manganese, copper, zinc, boron and molybdenum) are expressed in terms of mg/g; or sometimes, parts per million (ppm) of dry matter of the plant, also. For analyses the samples are taken from the most recently matured leaves, as they provide best indication of nutritional status of the plant. In addition, sometimes, the petiole of the leaf is also taken for analyses purposes.

11.8.2 Common Nutrient's Deficiency Symptoms

Deficiency symptom is closely related to the effects of nutrient in the plant body, which could be because of deficient or excess availability of nutrients. Broadly, the symptoms generated due to nutrient deficiencies in the plant, are noticed in following forms:

(i) Stunted growth,
(ii) Chlorosis,
(iii) Interveinal chlorosis,
(iv) Purplish-red colouring, and
(v) Necrosis.

Amongst above symptoms the appearing of stunting type growth is very common, because of deficiency of nutrient's involved in many of the plant's functions, such as (i) Stem elongation, (ii) Photosynthesis, and (iii) Protein production, as well. In this particular case, the plant growth becomes slow; and accordingly, the plant height and stature also get reduce. The nutrient's-wise deficiency symptoms are described as under:

Phosphorus: It is very fast moving element in the plant body, and is absorbed in the form of $H_2PO_4^{-1}$ or HPO_4^{-2} with the aid of active energy-requiring process. Availability of excess P in the root zone leads to cause reduction in plant growth due to restriction in Zn, Fe, and Cu uptake. The phosphorus uptake is reduced due to high level of pH of rooting media and also because of media coolness. In this regard, it is therefore, essential to maintain the pH of hydroponic solution between 5.6 to 6.0 for proper uptake of phosphorus. Also, in case of seedling development the media temperature should not be less than 60°F for a long period. Its deficiency in the plant is noticed by following symptoms:

- Phosphorus deficiency is observed in the older leaves of the plant, as it is translocated out of these leaves to meet the requirement of new growths.
- Appearance of stunting and reddish colour of the leaves, due to increase in the level of anthocyanin pigments.
- Development of purplish colour underside of the petiole or leaf stem, which may likely to get spread to the main veins of the leaf, later on.

In deficient leaves the percentage *P* is about 0.1% by dry weight. On the other hand, in most-recently matured leaves in majority of the vegetables, it varies from 0.25 to 0.6% *P* on dry weight basis.

Sometimes, the petioles and leaf midribs of young leaves of full-grown plant also show minor purpling, which occurs during late fall because of lowering of temperature. This symptom is not associated to the *P* deficiency as it takes place in young plants' leaves. This type of problem gets remove soon after rising in temperature.

Potassium: It is also in mobile nature; and promptly transported to the quite new generated tissues (young). Potassium is absorbed in large quantity through active uptake process. The *K* in a deficient plant leave is found less than 1.5%. Deficiency of *K* in the plant or crops can be visualized by the following symptoms:

- Initially, its deficiency is appeared on lower leaves in the form of marginal flecking or mottling. Also, the margin of older leaves become yellow.
- The chlorosis extends towards mid portion of the foliage with increase in severity of deficiency.
- A prolong deficiency is noticed by the symptom of necrosis along the leaf margins; and also the appearance of plants, slightly wilted.
- In extreme deficient situation, there is drop of older leaves.

- In tomato the *K* deficiency leads to blotchy ripening of fruits. And the colour of tomato fruits is not to the normal red colour. An excess level of K in the growing media (hydroponics and rockwool) is likely to decline the uptake of Mg or Ca, etc.

Nitrogen: Plants absorb the nitrogen mainly in the form of Nitrate (NO_3) or Ammonium (NH_4). In greenhouse where inside temperature is more than 7 to 10°C than the outside most of the greenhouse crops absorb the nitrogen in NO_3 form. On the other hand, in cool environment (less than 55°F) the plant absorbs the nitrogen in NH_4 form, which is easier to absorb than NO_3 form. At approaching neutral pH state, the uptake of NH_4 is found best; and it gets decline with the drop in pH level. In contrast, the uptake of NO_3 is better at greater acidic pH state. Moreover, the N uptake gets increase when it is available in both the forms, i.e., NH_4 and NO_3 simultaneously, in growing media. On absorption of NH_4 there is release of H ion which leads to maintain the electrical balance. In this condition the pH level of growing media gets reduce. In contrast, on NO_3 absorption the pH level of media gets increase due to availability of increased OH-ions. In case of tomato an excess N (especially under warm and sunny weather) causes "bullish" plants. In normal case, the magnitude of N in leaves varies between 2% and 5% on dry weight basis.

The deficiency of N in the plant is noticed, mainly by the following symptoms:

- Initially, its effect is stared from the lower leaves.
- Yellowing (chlorosis) of the leaves.
- Becoming of entire plant light green. However, this effect is most visible in older foliage.
- Appearance of small size flowers.
- In tomato there is red coloration to the petioles and leaf veins.
- In prolong N deficiency case there is dropping of leaves from the plant.

Sulphur: As compared to the *N* and *K*, it is not so mobile in the plant. It is mainly absorbed in sulphate (SO_4) form. The level of sulphur in plant leaves varies between 0.2% and 0.5% on dry weight basis, which is at par to the *P* level. In growing media, the plants can easily tolerate its high level. Because of this reason, there is wide use of sulphur containing materials to fulfil the requirement of nutrients such as Mg and micronutrients, as well. In this particular condition the possibility of sulphur deficiency is not so common in greenhouse crops, especially in the vegetables. Few important symptoms of sulphur deficiency in plants are mentioned below:

- General yellowing of the leaves.
- Its deficiency occurs on the upper leaves of the plants.

Calcium: Its uptake is broadly governed by the transpiration process. In other words, the movement of calcium is towards high transpiration zone, which is largely affected by the presence of expanding types leaves in the plant. In root system zone, its most of the uptake takes place from the region just behind the tip of the root. This character is beneficial to the greenhouse vegetables, because by keeping the healthy root system of the plant in growing media the crop productivity could be sufficiently enhanced by checking calcium deficiency, in this way. The calcium concentration in normal and most-recently matured leaves varies to the tune of 1.0% to 5.0%. Its uptake is affected by the ions such as NH_4, Mg and K. In many of the cases the deficiency of calcium is associated to the low pH of growing media.

The important deficiency symptoms of calcium are mentioned as under:

- Its deficiency symptom gets start first on the new growths.
- Development of necrosis of new leaves or lead to curled.
- Reduction in plant growth.
- Development of short clubby roots.
- In Lettuce and Cole crops the tips get burn.
- In tomato there is occurrence of Blossom-end-rot problem.

Magnesium: As compared to the calcium, it is relatively less (amount) absorbed by the plant. Its absorption is also highly affected by the presence of K, Ca and NH_4 ions. The movement of Mg in plant body is more to that of the Ca. In normal leaves the quantity of Mg varies from 0.2% to 0.8% by dry weight. Generally, its deficiency takes place, either when fertigation programme does not include the application of fertilizers containing Mg element or supply of excess K, Ca, or NH_4 in fertigation. The common symptoms of Mg deficiency in plants are narrated as under:

- Its deficiency appears first on the lower leaves of the plant.
- There is interveinal chlorosism; and thus leading to bleaching and necrosis of the affected areas.
- In tomato crops the leaves are appeared to a mild purpling at the affected area.

Manganese: Its absorption is in the form of Mn^{2+} ions. The cations such as Ca and Mg affect its uptake, significantly. Relatively, it is being immobile in the plant body. In most of the plant's leaves its normal concentration varies to the tune of 30 to 125 ppm. Its high concentration, i.e., 800 to 1000 ppm becomes injurious or toxic to many of the plants. In addition, its excess in nutrient's solution leads to reduce the intake of Fe. In soil media the solubility of Mn gets increase at low pH. The Mn deficiency is mainly due to inadequate availability of its concentration in solution; and also, sometimes, due to competition effects of ions. The symptoms of Mn deficiency are mentioned as under:

- Its effects get seen on the upper leaves.
- Deficiency of Mn is found in terms of interveinal chlorosis.
- Toxicity is noticed as the marginal leaf necrosis in many plants.

Zinc: Its uptake is affected by the concentration of P in growing media. It is also not being highly mobile in the plant body. In a normal leave its concentration varies from 25 to 50 ppm. However, its availability in high concentration becomes injurious or toxic to many of the plants. Normally, at high concentration situation the root development gets hamper and leaves also appear in small size with chlorotic. Zinc deficiency may be due to several reason such as (i) decrease in temperature or increased cold; (ii) wet growing media; (iii) due to very high pH media; and (iv) due to growing media having excessive P. The deficiency of Zn results following symptoms:

- Leaves appear with interveinal chlorosis.
- Appearance of plants with shortened internodes.

Copper: It is taken in very small quantity by the plants. Its uptake is strongly affected by Zn and pH of the growing media. Copper (Cu) is also not being highly mobile in the plant body. In contrast, some of the Cu are likely to get translocate from older leaves to new ones. In plants, its availability varies to the tune of 5 to 20 ppm. Its deficiency leads to cause chlorosis and elongation effects in the leaves. However, in acidic media its excess availability can be injurious to the plant, or in nutshell, becomes toxic.

Molybdenum: It is absorbed in the form of Molybdate MoO_4^{2-}. In presence of sulphate its uptake rate can be suppressed. In plants its concentration or availability is normally less than 1 ppm. The effect of Mo deficiency first appears in the middle and older leaves. Normally, in Mo deficiency condition the leaves become chlorotic and margins are rolled. The Mo deficiency is more pronounced in acidic environment.

Boron: It is not mobile in the plant. Its uptake and transport features are common to Ca. In normal leaves the concentration of Boron varies from 20 to 40 ppm. However, its high concentration leads to cause toxicity. Deficiency of Boron is visualized by the following symptoms,

- Its deficiency affects more to the young growing parts such as the buds, leaf tips and margins, as well.
- Leaf tips become chlorotic and eventually die.
- In tomato the leaves and stem become brittle.
- The rose flowers are normally malformed.
- Stem tips get die; and there is growth in shoots, immediately below.
- New foliage becomes thick and quickly chlorotic.

Chlorine: Its requirement for a plant is very less as compared to the other nutrients. Accordingly, its deficiency is seen very rare in the crops/plants. In addition, it is commonly available in the fertilizers, water, air, and the media as well. The list of mobile and immobile elements in soil media is presented in Table 11.4.

Table 11.4 List of mobile and immobile fertilizers/micro-nutrients in soil media

S. No.	Mobile fertilizer	S. No.	Immobile fertilizer
1.	Nitrogen	1.	Calcium
2.	Phosphorus	2.	Iron
3.	Potassium	3.	Manganese
4.	Magnesium	4.	Zinc
5.	Sulphur	5.	Copper
		6.	Boron
		7.	Molybdenum

11.9 EFFECT OF EXCESS APPLICATION OF FERTILIZERS

This is common thinking of the growers that by increasing the fertilizer dose they can harvest better crop yield. However, this practice always results untold damage or loss of the crop. In real sense an excess application of fertilizer to the crop than its actual requirement, develops injurious effect on overall development and growth of the crop. Sometimes, in few crops there is burning effect gets form in absence of irrigation. The effect of excess dose of fertilizers is narrated in Table 11.5.

Table 11.5 Effect of excess dose of fertilizers on crop

S. No.	Fertilizer	Effect
1.	Nitrogen	♦ Plants attain vigorous growth with dark-green leaves that are often crisp and break easily. ♦ Excess N may inhibit the root action. In result there may be typical symptoms of iron chlorosis. And the plants may like to wilt excessively which recovery is not possible. ♦ An excess N may also lead to cause the problem of yellowing of top foliage, which is very common in *Chrysanthemums* and *Snapdragons*.
2.	Phosphorus	♦ Its excess dose causes to precipitate the Iron from the soil solution. And thus make it insoluble and unavailable to the plant. Accordingly, there is development of iron chlorosis.
3.	Potassium	♦ Its dose greater than the requirement inhibits the root action. ♦ Also, causes chlorosis and wilting of the plant.
4.	Calcium	♦ There is increase in pH of soil media. ♦ Development of Iron chlorosis in many of the plants, called overliming injury.
5.	Iron	♦ In excess availability of Iron there is little danger of plants when pH of soil solution is in normal range because the phosphorus/calcium gets precipitate from the soil solution. ♦ At the pH level 5.0 or less the iron becomes soluble. This leads to cause the appearance of *Hydrangeas* brown dots on the leaves.
6.	Sulphate	♦ A high concentration of sulphate may lead to decline the pH of growing media. ♦ At more than 600 ppm concentration, it becomes toxic to most of the plants.
7.	Boron	♦ At excess ppm, it becomes toxic to most of the plants. ♦ In roses the margin of lower leaves turn black and remaining leaves turn into yellow colour; and they drop down, also.
8.	Aluminium	♦ It is not troublesome except on *Hydrangeas*. ♦ Roots are burnt and plants also get wilt.

11.10 REMEDIAL MEASURES AGAINST EXCESS APPLICATION OF FERTILIZER

In greenhouse cultivation the maintenance of fertility level in optimum range is very essential; otherwise, there is development of inconducive effects on crop yield. There are some remedial measures against unexpected application of excessive fertilizers in course of crop cultivation under greenhouse environment, are shown in Table 11.6.

Table 11.6 Remedial measures against excessive applied fertilizers

S. No.	Excessive applied fertilizer	Remedial measures
1.	Nitrogen	♦ Leaching with heavy watering. ♦ Using straw mulch.
2.	Phosphorus	♦ Treatment with lime or iron sulphate.

(*Contd.*)

S. No.	Excessive applied fertilizer	Remedial measures
3.	Potassium	♦ Leaching treatment to decline the effect. However, in clay soil it is not being effective.
4.	Calcium	♦ Acidification of soil media.
5.	Iron	♦ Increasing the pH. ♦ Addition of phosphorus.
6.	Sulphates	♦ Leaching with heavy watering. ♦ Avoiding the use of sulphate forms of fertilizers.
7.	Boron	♦ Use of water glass, or sodium silicate in soil media.
8.	Aluminium	♦ Increasing pH of soil media. ♦ Addition of phosphorus.
9.	Soluble salts	♦ Leaching with heavy watering.

11.11 MEASURES TO REDUCE NUTRIENT'S LOSS

Although, the nutrients are applied to the crop or plant as per their recommended dose, with the view that they all will be utilized by the crop, but still a certain part of the applied nutrients gets lost because of several reasons. This leads to cause deficiency of nutrients in the plant. In this situation, it is very essential to check the loss of nutrients. There are various measures to follow towards control of nutrient's loss, given as under:

(i) Reducing leaching rate
(ii) Use of low phosphorus
(iii) Use of drip system
(iv) Pot spacing
(v) Saucers and trays
(vi) Capillary mats
(vii) Matching fertilizer application with plant nutrient needs
(viii) Nutrient balance sheets

Reducing leaching: In course of watering and fertigation to the plant or crop, a fraction of applied nutrients is lost due to leaching action from the growing media. In general, in greenhouse cultivation using growing media the leaching varies from 10 to 15% which is in terms of leaching fraction (LF) as 0.1 to 0.15, is recommended for the purpose to drain the excess salt contents from the pots. On the other hand, in actual sense the majority of the growers follow the leaching fraction to the tune of 0.4 to 0.6 which is much high, causing a significant loss of nutrients from the media. In context to control the nutrients loss the leaching fraction must be zero, provided the applied nutrients are fully utilized by the grown crop. The best means to check or control the leaching fraction is the use of drip irrigation for watering and fertigating the crop. The watering done by drip system is at precise rate and the amount is as per requirement of the crop/plant. This leads to avoid the possibility of excess application of water as irrigation. Furthermore, there is also no leaching of water and thereby the applied fertilizer, too. The reduction in leaching is beneficial to decrease the fertigation and frequency of irrigation, both. However, in this condition, there develops harmful effect regarding increase in level of salt content in growing media. In order to avoid this possibility, the fertigation rate is decreased at least 25%. However, at zero leaching fraction the frequent monitoring of salt status in growing media is essential; otherwise, in ignorance situation the level of salt may rise to a high level, which may endanger the crop.

Use of low phosphorus: It is general observation that in greenhouse cropping system the use of phosphorus is carried out by greater amount than the actual requirement of the crop. This can be avoided by applying in low doses that can be totally utilized by the crop without leaving any excess amount. There are several low phosphorus containing fertilizers such as 15-0-15, 20-1-20, 20-2-20, etc. may be included in fertigation programme. On use of these phosphorus fertilizers, there is reduction in level of P availability in the effluent water of growing media.

Use of drip system: The drip system is a tool which is used for irrigation and fertigation to the crop in very precise way, but at lesser time gap. In use of this system the application of water and fertilizer is done exactly to the required depth/amount as per crop concern. The possibility of excess water or fertilizer in the root zone is about to completely negated. In other words, the development of water or nutrient leaching effect is declined or reduced to a significant level. Also, in drip system the spilling of water and fertilizer from the pot is not there. This also leads to check the nutrients loss. In greenhouse cultivation the watering and fertigation done through drip system, is treated as one of the best ways.

Pot spacing: This is also one of the methods followed for controlling the nutrient loss. In this method, some empty pots are taken and placed at some suitable spacing. The square pots are found better than the other shape pots. The pots are arranged in staggered form to collect the leachate content. The spacing must be such that there may not be any problem in watering the crop. At closer spacing the loss of water and fertilizer is less.

Use of saucers or trays: In this method the saucers or collection trays are used for collecting the spills from the pots. The collected water is conveyed to the base of the pot. If the captured material is very much in amount, then that can be recycled for application. However, if it is less in amount, is absorbed by the pot itself which gets utilized by the grown plant. In this way, there is about to no loss of water and fertilizer, both.

Use of capillary mats: These are used for watering and fertilizing the plants in the form of sub- irrigation. In addition, these are also used for watering the plants grown in the pots. The water is applied from the top, which gets met to the plant by capillary action. The applied water from the top is soaked and held up by the mat. In this method the possibility of water spilling is completely negated. The soaking capacity of capillary mats is very high. After soaking capacity is saturated the water starts dripping below, which is utilized by the grown crop.

Fertilizer matching with plant nutrient's need: Application of fertilizer by matching the plant's nutrient need, is also one of the effective steps in reducing the nutrients loss. In this approach, that fertilizer is selected for application, which actually contains the desired nutrient; otherwise, the applied fertilizer or nutrient becomes useless in context to the plant or crop concerned. In addition, the fertilizer amount and time of application should also be decided before fertigating. In nutshell, a complete fertigation programme or schedule should be prepared for the crop to be grown.

11.12 FERTIGATION—CONCEPT

It is the application of fertilizers to the crop/plant along with irrigation water through drip irrigation system. In drip system a separate sub-system called fertigation unit (venturi) is assembled to fertigate the crop. Fertigation provides an economical means to apply fertilizer with sufficient saving in crop farming, both in open field and greenhouse environment. The nutrient loss due to overleaching and evaporations effect is completely omitted in drip method.

Fertigation is also called chemigation, in which the fertilizers/nutrients (chemicals) are simultaneously applied along with irrigation water to the crop. This is done with the help of drip irrigation system. In fertigation process the requisite amount of nutrient is delivered to the plant. In fertigation process the amount of nutrient dose can be easily adjusted as per crop growth stage. The nutrient's use efficiency gets enhance several-folds through fertigation technique. The fertilizers or nutrients to be fertigated must be fully soluble in the water. However, liquid fertilizers are also available, they can be directly used for fertigation. The selected fertilizers should be compatible to the irrigation water. Through fertigation the macro-nutrients such as nitrogen, potassium, phosphorus and magnesium can also be successfully applied. On the other hand, the micro-nutrients, i.e., the boron, zinc, iron, calcium manganese and copper can be applied through micro-sprinkler system in the form of foliar application. The other chemicals such as chlorine, acid, herbicides, nematicides, fungicides, etc. can also be applied through fertigation technique.

Advantages/Disadvantages

The advantages offered by fertigation are narrated as under:

- Saves fertilizer amount and time both.
- Greater uniformity in application as compared to the other techniques such aircraft or sprayers, etc.
- Makes prompt availability of nutrients to the plants for their uptake.
- It is compatible to the reduced or zero tillage practices.
- No effect of field undulations.
- Zero mechanical damage to the crop during fertigation, which is normally found in case of spraying, etc.
- No any kind of chemical reaction or injury to the person engaged for fertigation work.
- No possibility of environmental hazard.
- It provides a means for reducing the crop photo-toxicity.
- It saves the fertilization cost up to 40%, or sometimes more, also.
- It saves the energy consumption up to 90%.
- Effects on crop yield and quality are very significant.

In contrast to various advantages, fertigation practice also involves few disadvantages, too, are mentioned below:

- Needs skilled staff for operating the system.
- Preparation of fertilizer solution as per required concentration is very difficult.
- Besides control unit of drip system, this is an additional unit, requires money investment for its procurement.

- There is possibility of chemical reactions with the components of drip system.
- Insoluble fertilizers cannot be used.

11.12.1 Fertigation Considerations

The main objective of fertigation is to apply the requisite fertilizers in correct amount and at scheduled time, very efficiently in uniform way to the grown crop. In this context the important points to follow are mentioned as under:

- Protection assurance to the person engaged for fertigation operation.
- Awareness about danger during application of fertilizers/chemicals.
- Essentiality of equipment's calibration.
- Fertigation should be exactly as per schedule and in proper amount.
- Proper concentration of fertilizer solution.
- System should be properly designed and maintained.

11.12.2 Fertigation Depth

Fertigation depth denotes the depth to which the applied nutrients may lie in the growing media. However, the availability of nutrients in the effective root zone of the plant is most desirable. The loss of nutrients due to leaching effect must not be there. In this context there are few important points, which are required to follow for achieving better fertigation effect on the plant.

- System discharge rate
- Irrigation duration
- Soil texture or type
- Moisture status of soil media.

11.12.3 Fertigation Equipment

Fertigation is performed by means of a device called "Injectors", which are available in variety. Different injectors have their own merits and demerits. Therefore, selecting a most suitable injector in all the respects is most important, because it affects the fertigation quality, i.e., uniformity and depth, both. In general, the followings are few salient points, followed in selection of fertigation equipment:

- Crop types
- Available irrigation system for use
- System flow or discharge rate
- System operating pressure
- Chemicals/fertilizers to be used
- Power source at the site
- Operating duration
- Safety measures, etc.

The list of injectors used for fertigation is shown in Table 11.7.

Table 11.7 List of injectors used for fertigation

S. No.	Injectors	Remark
1.0	Based on the feeder system	
1.1	Constant rate feeder	♦ Injection rate is constant even on varying flow rate of irrigation system.
1.2	Constant ratio feeder	♦ The proportion of chemical injection and flow rate of irrigation system is constant.
2.0	Based on use of energy source	
2.1	Active injectors	♦ These are the pumps or compressors, acting as external power source. ♦ These develop the pressure greater than the existing pressure in the irrigation line.
2.1.1	Injection pumps, diaphragm pumps and piston pumps	♦ These pumps have the provision for adjusting the injection rate as per requirement.
2.1.2	Water powered injector	♦ These injectors do not expel water but utilize the pressure of irrigation line.
2.1.3	Compressor injector	♦ These injectors utilize the compressor to develop pressure in the chemical tank. ♦ Because of greater pressure than the irrigation pipeline the flow of chemical from tank to the irrigation pipeline gets start.
2.2	Passive injector	♦ This injector utilizes the pressure of irrigation pipeline to suck the solution from the tank.
2.2.1	Pitot tube injector	♦ Working principle is same to the passive injector. ♦ These are not being suitable for travelling gun type sprinkler system.
2.2.2	Pressure differential injectors	
2.2.2.1	Venturi injector	♦ Injection of fertilizer is carried out by creating vacuum in the venturi. ♦ The solution is automatically sucked from the tank, which gets mixed in the irrigation water, and finally delivered to the plant.

The venturi injector type fertigation system, is more common to use for fertigation purpose, is described below:

Venturi injector: This is the pressure differential type injector, is commonly used for fertigation purpose. It works on the principle that due to fast flowing water (irrigation water) through pipeline, a poor pressure zone is created in the side of flow line. The venturing arrangement linked with fertilizer tank, is fixed to the water flow line. On system operation there develops a pressure gradient, i.e., the pressure adjacent to the water flow line is very less while it is more at fertilizer tank. This pressure gradient leads to suck the fertiliser solution from the fertilizer tank. The sucked fertilizer solution gets delivered to the irrigation water flow line, where fertilizer solution is mixed in the irrigation water. In this way, the water along with fertilizer content is delivered near to the plant through drippers. For better working performance, the pressure drop in venture arrangement should normally be in the range of 20 to 50% of the pressure at inlet. This fertigation system consists of provisions to regulate the fertilizer injection rate. They are given as under:

(i) Regulating the injector flow rate.
(ii) Adjustment in operating pressure of system.
(iii) Adjustment in control valve at discharge line.
(iv) Placing a metering valve on suction line.

Specification of different modules of venture injectors is presented in Table 11.8.

Table 11.8 Details of different modules of Venturi injector

Model	Size in/out (inch)	Pressure differential (%)	Flow through injector @ 50 Psi (gpm)	Injection rate(l/h)
283	½″	26	0.5	23
384	½″	25	2.1	38
484	½″-3/4″	18	3.4	64
584	¾″	18	6.4	95
878	1″	16	12	227
1078	1″	16	17	284
1583	1 ½″	18	34	680
2081	2″	18	101	1890
384-x	½″	50	2.1	132
885-x	1″	32	12	530
1585-x	1 ½″	35	69	1325
2083-B	2″	67	29	4275

Calibration of Injector

In order to have a better result on fertigation using this technique, the calibration of injector is very essential. The calibration should be done before using the device for fertigation work. It involves following steps:

Step (1): Determine the area or number of plants to be fertigated.
Step (2): Determine the amount of fertilizer to be applied per unit area (ha or acre) or per plant.
Step (3): Calculate the total amount of fertilizer's required.
Step (4): Determine injection time duration for fertigating total fertilizer (h).
Step (5): Decide the chemical composition and concentration of solution.
Step (6): Determine and fix the injection rate, which can be obtained by using the following formula:

$$I_r = \frac{A \cdot Q_c}{C \cdot T} \qquad \text{...(11.1)}$$

in which, I_r is the injection rate (lpm); Q_c is the amount of fertilizer to be fertigated (Kg/ha); A is the cropped area; C is the concentration of fertilizer solution (kg/l) and T is the injection duration (h).

PROBLEM 11.1 Banana crop planted at 1.5 m × 1.5 m spacing is to be fertigated. The row length is fixed about 60 m and total number of rows is 25. The system flow rate is expected to be 6 lpm. The normal operating time period is to be followed is 1.0 hour. Determine the injection rate, if operating pressure to be maintained is 12 Psi. The fertilizers to be used are (i) 300g N; 300g (P_2O_5) and 500g (K_2O) in total 20 equal doses.

***Solution*:**

Requisite computations are shown as under:

1. *Total number of plants required to fertigate*: It is determined by multiplying the number of plants per row and total number of rows, i.e.

   = Number of plants per row × Number of rows

   = (60/ 1.5) × 25

   = 1000

2. *Fertilizer's amount to be applied*: The fertilizer amount per application is given by the following formula,

   = (Amount per plant × Number of plants)/(Number of applications × Solution density)

   (i) *Nitrogen(N) dose*: It is computed as under

   = (300 × 1000)/(20 × 1370)

   = 10.94 liters solution

   (Assume density of solution as 1370g/liter)

   (ii) *Phosphorus (P) dose*: It is given as

   = (300 × 1000)/(20 × 1370)

   = 10.94 liters solution

   (Assume density of solution as 1370g/liter)

   (iii) *Potash (K) dose*: It is computed as

   = (500 × 1000)/(20 × 1370)

   = 18.25 liters solution

   (Assume density of solution as 1370g/liter)

3. *Irrigation rate*: It should be such that total solution could be finished in 30 minutes cycle., i.e.

   = 18.25 × 60/30

   = 36.5 litres per hour

11.13 ACIDITY AND BASICITY OF FERTILIZERS

On application of fertilizers to the crop or in the soil, there may be increase or decrease in the level of pH of growing media depending on fertilizer's acidity or basicity. It is the reason that the fertilizers are rated by their potential acidity/basicity. Largely, the acidity or basicity of fertilizer is determined by the amount and the sources of nitrogen. In general, a fertilizer that contains more amount of Urea and Ammoniacal nitrogen is found in acidic nature. On the other hand, the fertilizer which contains primarily the nitrate (nitrogen) is being in basicity nature. The potential acidity and basicity of fertilizer is denoted by a number, which refers to the amount of limestone ($CaCO_3$) available in one ton of fertilizer. The limestone neutralizes the potential acidity. For example the potential acidity of fertilizer 15-16-17 is 215 pounds (lbs) $CaCO_3$, denotes that 215 pounds $CaCO_3$ is present in one ton of the fertilizer. This also advocates that 215 pounds limestone will be required to neutralize the acidic effect of the fertilizer 15-16-17 on 1-ton of its application in growing media. Similarly, the other fertilizer 15-0-15, which basicity is 420 pounds of $CaCO_3$ per ton of fertilizer, increases the pH value of growing media. In this condition, to neutralize the pH level the limestone is required to the tune of 420 pounds. In this way, more is the potential acidity number, greater will be the effect of fertilizer on pH value.

11.13 COMMON FERTILIZERS

Commercially, there are varieties of Nitrogenous, Phosphoric and Potassic fertilizers are available in the market, in granular and liquid forms. Amongst granular fertilizers, all are not being suitable for fertigation. Only those are being suitable which are soluble in water. The insoluble fertilizers are not suitable for fertigation. On the other hand, the liquid fertilizers are solely fit for fertigation. Some of the important fertilizers are narrated as under:

Peat-lite special: These are found in two categories of constituent's proportions, namely (i) 15-16-17; and (ii) 20-10-20. For routine fertilization purpose these are very common and popular fertilizers among all for spring crops. In both the fertilizers, the nitrate percentage is more than 50%. Demerit of these fertilizers is to raise the concentration of Fe and Mn to toxic level at low pH, as they have high range of these trace elements. Both fertilizers, i.e., 15-16-17 and 20-10-20 are in acid forming nature. However, the 20-10-20 fertilizer is more acidic than the 15-16-17 fertilizer.

15-15-15 Geranium special: This is also referred to "Triple 15", is considered as one of the good alternatives to the Peat-Lite Special fertilizer. This fertilizer is suitable for the sensitive crops to the toxicities of trace elements, as the level of trace elements added by this fertilizer is very less as compared to the Peat-Lite Specials fertilizer. Although, this fertilizer is also in the nature of acid forming, but its potential acidity is slightly higher than the 15-16-17 fertilizer.

20-20-20 General purpose: This fertilizer poses the risk of ammonium toxicity in soilless media because it contains 75% ammonium and urea. However, in the growing media containing soil, there is no formation of such type of problem. Regarding use of this fertilizer, it is always suggested to go for testing the growing medium about availability of ammonium in that, particularly during low temperature or cool conditions. Furthermore, it also suggested to add the trace elements in growing media. Potential acidity of this fertilizer is being high as compared to the other fertilizers.

Low Phosphorus fertilizers: In this category, the fertilizers namely 20-0-20, 20-1-20 and 15-0-15 are most common. Besides, using these as the fertilizers for fertigation to the crops, they can also be used as an alternative to the chemical growth regulators, especially, in bedding plants. This role on growth regulation by using phosphorus fertilizer is called "phosphorus starvation". On continuous use of these fertilizers in growing media with low P, there is more possibility of development of risk about P deficiency in the planted crops. Few specific properties of above-mentioned phosphoric fertilizers are pointed, below:

S. No.	Fertilizer	Properties
1.	15-0-15	♦ It is basic fertilizer, contains about 95% nitrate. ♦ It supplies calcium, also.
2.	20-0-20	♦ It is a neutral fertilizer, contains about 50% nitrate. ♦ It supplies calcium, also.
3.	20-1-20	♦ It is an acidic fertilizer. ♦ It does not supply Ca. ♦ It contains about 70% nitrate.

Calcium nitrate and potassium nitrate: Use of these fertilizers in combination reduces the possibility of development of toxicity effects due to trace elements in growing media. The Calcium Nitrate can also be used as an alternative to the Peat-Lite Specials to add Ca content in growing media, which counters the acidic effect of Peat-Lite. For use of these two fertilizers, it is suggested that the superphosphates and trace element fertilizers must be added in the growing media, when both are required to use in combination as the sole fertilizer.

Controlled release fertilizers: These fertilizers are quite different over the others. They have outer coating or shell like an M&M candy, which is released due to effects of temperature and soil moisture content. The purpose of coating is to protect the nutrients in the "prill" against releasing at a time, immediately. On application, as the fertilizer grain comes in contact to the soil, the moisture content enters the prill and develops pressure, inside. In result the ingredients in the prill materials start escaping through the pores existing in the coating. The release of nutrients depends on the coating. The basic principle of controlled release fertilizer is protecting the soluble nutrient against its release at once by providing a kind of protective cover, is called controlled release.

Organic fertilizers: In greenhouse cultivation practices, apart from use of chemical fertilizers to nourish the crop, the organic fertilizers are also used, especially, in vegetable production. The organic fertilizers are mixed in the growing media components before planting the seedlings. The bulk fertilizers such as the dried blood, bone meal and rock phosphate, etc. can be used for this purpose. In addition, the organic fertilizers such as fish emulsion can also be used after planting to supply nutrients to the plants. The quantity of organic fertilizers to be applied depends on the requirement of the plant, which can be ascertained by analysing the nutrient's status of the growing media. In general, the deficiency of nitrogen is very common, which can be easily and immediately met by using inorganic fertilizers. The availability or release of N from most of the organic fertilizers is very slow.

Liquid fertilizers: These are in the form of solution, which may contain multi or single nutrient's concentration. In real sense liquid fertilizers are the true solutions, which contain plant nutrients. The liquid fertilizers offer many advantages over granular fertilizers such as labor saving, efficient application, etc. by fertigation system. In addition, its other merits are narrated as under:

- Suitable to fertigate the crops through drip and sprinkler systems.
- These are excellent carrier of herbicides and micro-nutrients, both.
- Plants utilize efficiently.
- They become easily available to the root system, very soon.

The list of fertilizer solution or liquid fertilizers is shown in Table 11.9

Table 11.9 List of liquid fertilizer/fertilizer solution

S. No.	Fertilizer solution	% Nutrient	Density Kg/Litre
1.	Nitrogen		
1.1	Urea solution	23% N	1.14
1.2		20% N	1.12
1.3	Ammonium Nitrate	20% N	1.27
1.4	N Solution	33% N	1.27
1.5	Urea Ammonium Nitrate	28% N	1.28
1.6		32% N	1.33
1.7	Ammonium Nitrate Ammonia	37% N	1.19
1.8		41% N	1.14
1.9	Calcium Ammonium Nitrate	17% N	
1.10	Aqua Ammonia	20% N	0.91
		24% N	0.90
2.0	Phosphorus		
2.1	Phosphoric Acid	52% P_2O_5	
		68% P_2O_5	
		75% P_2O_5	
2.2	Ammonium Polyphosphate	8%N	1.26
		24% P_2O_5	
		9%N	1.36
		30% P_2O_5	
		10%N	1.37
		34% P_2O_5	
		11%N	1.41
		37% P_2O_5	
3.0	Potassium		
3.1	Potassium Ammonium Phosphate	15% N	
		15% P_2O_5	
		10% K_2O	
		10% N	
		10% P_2O_5	
		10% K_2O	
		15% N	
		8% P_2O_5	
		4% K_2O	

Suspension fertilizers: These fertilizers are also in liquid form, but a part of plant nutrients is available in suspended form, hold by suspending agents. In other words, suspension fertilizers contain undissolved nutrients. These fertilizers are dissolved in sufficient water to ensure that the fertilizer contents have been fully dissolved, before their application to the crop/plants through fertigation.

Granular fertilizers: These are in dry pellet (solid) or granule form (circular or any form) coated with some special type of conditioner to keep them free from moisture absorption from the atmosphere. The dry fertilizer with non-dissolving coating materials are allowed for 6 to 8 hours for settling purpose, prior to putting for application via drip system (fertigation unit); otherwise, there is possibility of choking of the system. In order to use these fertilizers for fertigation, they are first dissolved in the water for preparing solution. Solubility of fertilizer refers to the mass of fertilizer dissolved in a unit volume of water, depends very much on the water temperature. The solubility status of some of the fertilizers is shown in Table 11.10. In context to fertigation, the granular fertilizers should meet the following requirements:

- Enable to meet the crop requirement.
- Easy in handling.
- Easily soluble in water.

The list of granular fertilizers is shown in Table 11.10.

Table 11.10 List of granular fertilizers and their properties

S. No.	Fertilizer	Element (%)	Solubility (g/100 g) H_2O	Temp (°C)
1.	Ammonia, NH_3	80%N	90	0
2.	Ammonium Nitrate, NH_4NO_3	34%N	118	0
			187	20
			590	80
3.	Ammonium Sulphate, $(NH_4)_2SO_4$	21%N	71	0
		24%	95	80
4.	Calcium Carbonate (Limestone), $CaCO_3$	–	0.0006	0
5.	Calcium Metaphosphate $Ca(PO_3)_2$	–	0.0001	0
6.	Calcium Nitrate, $Ca(NO_3)_24H_2O$	15·5%N	134	0
			364	100
7.	Calcium Sulphate, $CaSO_4{\cdot}2H_2O$		0.24	0
8.	Copper Sulphate, $CuSO_4{\cdot}5H_2O$		32	0
9.	Di-Ammonium Phosphate, $(NH_4)_2HPO_4$	18%N	25	0
		20%P		
10.	Di-Calcium Phosphate, $CaHOP_4{\cdot}2H_2O$		0.02	0
11.	Magnesia, MgO		0.0006	0
12.	Magnesium Sulphate, $MgSO_4{\cdot}7H_2O$		85	0
13.	Manganese Sulphate, $MnSO_3{\cdot}45H_2O$		105	0
14.	Mono-Ammonium Phosphate, $NH_4H_2PO_4$	11%N	43	0
		22%P		
15.	Mono-Calcium Phosphate, $CaH_4(PO_4)_2H_2O$	20%P	Varies	
16.	Potassium Chloride, KCl	60%K_2O	28	0
			51	80
17.	Potassium Nitrate, KNO_3	13%N	13	0
		46%K_2O	169	80
18.	Potassium Sulphate, K_2SO_4	53%K_2O	8	0
19.	Sodium Nitrate, $NaNO_3$	16%N	73	0

(*Contd.*)

S. No.	Fertilizer	Element (%)	Solubility (g/100 g) H_2O	Temp (°C)
20	Urea, $Co(NH_2)_2$	46%N	67	0
			108	20
			167	40
21.	Zinc Sulphate, $ZnSO_4 \cdot 6H_2O$		70	0

11.14 FERTILIZER SELECTION CRITERIA

There are large numbers of nitrogenous, phosphoric and potashic fertilizers are available both in solid and liquid (solution) forms, suitable to apply through fertigation to the crops either they are in open condition or in greenhouse environment. Overall, the suitability of fertilizer for fertigation depends very much on the physio-chemical properties of the fertilizer, concerned. As compared to liquid fertilizers, the granular fertilizers are less expensive. Accordingly, their use is more justified, provided they are completely soluble in the water for preparing their solution to put for fertigation. In addition, some of the fertilizers are not being compatible, because of formation of compounds in insoluble nature and precipitates, too, during preparation of their solution by mixing two or more fertilizers, together at a time. The formed precipitates attract the nutrients and make them unavailable for plant uptake. Also, precipitates cause clogging problem in irrigation pipeline system. On this ground, it is very important to assess the solubility of fertilizers in respect of their fully dissolving nature in water, formation of insoluble compounds or precipitates in solution, etc. The solubility of fertilizer varies fertilizer to fertilizer. In nutshell, the selection of fertilizer is carried out based on the following criterion:

(i) Solubility.
(ii) Effect of chemicals on the crop as well as on the soil, too.
(iii) Type of irrigation system to be used.
(iv) Compatibility with the water to be used.
(v) State of fertilizer.
(vi) Storage requirement.
(vii) Easiness in handling.
(viii) Injection method to be followed.
(ix) Fertilizer cost.
(x) Effects on growing or soil media.

A fertilizer is considered to be the best for fertigation, which is readily soluble in the water; and remains for a long duration in solution. The fertilizer should be such that it can provide good effect on the crop; and at the same time no any bad effect on the soil, too. In addition, the fertilizer to be applied should be fully compatible with irrigation water; otherwise, there may be the possibility of chemical reactions between the chemical contents of fertilizer and the water, as well. The selection of fertilizer should also be based on the type of fertigation system to be used, because fertilizer application uniformity, application efficiency, etc. are found different in different fertigation systems. The fertilizer also determines its handling, fertigation method and application (injection) rate. Fertilizer should be such that all these requisites could be easily met in better way.

11.15 FERTILIZER COMPATIBILITY

The fertilizers which are soluble in water are being suitable for fertigation. However, few fertilizers react at higher concentration and form insoluble precipitates. The formed precipitates can tie up with the nutrients and clog the irrigation system. For example, on mixing of Ammonium sulphate $(NH_4)_2SO_4$ and Potassium chloride (KCl), there is formation of Potassium sulphate (K_2SO_4) compound, which is insoluble in nature, i.e., the precipitate. This precipitate may clog the system; and thus making the whole irrigation system un-operational.

Fertilizer solubility: The fertilizers in highly soluble nature are being suitable for fertigation; otherwise, there is creation of plugging problem in irrigation system. The dry or granular fertilizers differ in their solubility in water media. The solubility depends to a lot on physical properties of water, temperature of water to be used for irrigation and pH, as well. Temperature affects the solubility, i.e., at high temperature solubility is more; and vice-versa. However, some of the fertilizers develop cooling effect in solution after their dissolving in water such as the Urea, Ammonium nitrate, Calcium nitrate, and Potassium nitrate. In this situation, it may not be possible to dissolve the fertilizer in more quantity to achieve the desired concentration of fertilizer solution. The solubility of different fertilizers is shown in Table 11.10.

11.16 FERTILIZER EFFICIENCY ENHANCEMENT

It is very common that the growers apply the fertilizers in excess doses than their actual requirement of the crop, without considering the rate and frequency of fertigation. In this particular situation the loss of fertilizer takes place to a significant level, besides deteriorating the growing media. In order to control such type of fertilization based problems, the nutrient management plays a good role.

Nutrient management advocates to efficient use of fertilizer and reducing the nutrient loss by utilizing maximum part of applied fertilizers by the crop or retaining that in the container against leaching. In nutrient management the following points are very important to follow, which are beneficial to enhance the fertilizer use efficiency:

- Apply the fertilizer as per requirement of the crop.
- Control the nutrient's loss from growing media container.
- Control the nutrient and water loss from irrigation and leaching action.

11.17 GREENHOUSE FERTILIZATION PROGRAM

In order to have proper plant growth and thereby the yield potential, the maintenance of requisite nutrient status in greenhouse growing media is most essential. Also, to apply the fertilizers the framing of fertigation program, considering various associated points is most important. In general, the application of fertilizers or chemicals to the greenhouse crops is carried out as per below:

(i) Pre-plant fertilization, and
(ii) Post-plant fertilization.

In pre-plant fertilization the application of fertilizers is done before planting the crops/ seedlings in growing media. This fertilization schedule is beneficial to ensure the availability of minerals/nutrients at the beginning to grow the plant in healthy environment. In addition, some of the growing media such as the peat moss and pine bark contain acidic components, which acidity level is required to decline for attaining a proper plant growth. This can be done by adding Dolomitic Limestone (agricultural limestone). The Dolomite Limestone increases the media pH. The addition of amendments is done before plantation of the seedlings.

In post-fertilization the application of fertilizers is performed after transplanting the seedlings in growing media. It is very common practice in greenhouse farming system. Application of fertilizers/nutrients is continued throughout the crop period using proper dose, and as per predetermined fertigation schedule. This practice is beneficial to make available the essential nutrients to the plant throughout crop period.

11.18 FERTIGATION FREQUENCY

In greenhouse cultivation the fertigation frequency is followed in such a way that there may not develop nutrient deficiency in root zone to affect the plant growth. Normally, on this aspect two approaches are used to decide a proper fertigation frequency, given below:

(i) Constant fertigation, and
(ii) Scheduled fertigation.

In constant fertigation the application of nutrients is performed in the form of diluted solution of fertilizer at each irrigation by using drip system. In this case a close fertigation frequency is followed. The possibility of nutrient deficiency and damage to the crop due to concentration of chemical is about to nil, is considered as one of the merits of this fertigation approach.

In scheduled fertigation the fertilizers are applied in the form of more concentrated solution at predetermined periodic interval; normally on weekly interval, i.e., once in a week. However, in few cases, it is also done at peak periods of reproductive growth stages of the crop, concerned.

11.19 FERTIGATION RATE

It is decided after fixing the fertigation schedule. In greenhouse cultivation the rate of fertigation is often expressed in terms of ppm, equivalent to 1 mg/lit, which expresses the concentration of fertilizer, concerned. Fertigation rate depends on so many factors, such as the crop types, pre-plant fertilization, weather condition, growth stage, desired growth rate, and also leaching percentage of fertilizer. In absence of pre-fertigation, the concentration of fertilizers in post-fertigation schedule is increased; and even sometimes, the fertigation is started, earlier.

The fertilizer leaching denotes the amount or proportion of applied fertilizer solution lost from the media container by leaching below. It is strongly affected by the volume of water applied to the media container. Reduction in leaching denotes to the retaining of nutrient applied to the plant; or in other words reducing the fertilizer loss/cost. In this way, by keeping the fertilizer leaching fraction, small, the application of fertilizer solution with low concentration can be very effective, as compared to the application of high concentration fertilizer.

Moreover, the nutrient's requirement of greenhouse crops is being more during fast growth stages of the crop/plant; and vice-versa. Accordingly, the fertigation rate should be adjusted, carefully. By the way, if a high fertigation rate is followed during slow growth period, there is deposition of excess soluble salts in the growing media, may lead to cause inconducive effects on plant growth. Similarly, if a low fertigation rate is followed during fast growth period, then there is development nutrient's deficiency in the plant.

11.20 FERTIGATION OF NITROGENOUS FERTILIZERS

In general, majority of the granular nitrogenous fertilizers are readily dissolve in the water. This feature makes these fertilizers to use for fertigation to the crops, smoothly. However, amongst different nitrogenous fertilizers, the urea ($NH_2.CO.NH_2$) which contains about 46%N is very common, because of its high level of solubility in the water. Its important characteristics in context to fertigation are enumerated as under:

- Acts as neutral molecule in the solution.
- It does not ionize.
- Easily fertigated with best performance.
- It can be mixed with other nitrogenous fertilizers for preparing solution, such as with the ammonium nitrate.
- Its molecules are retained in the soil solution, causing their movement in the direction of irrigation water flow in soil media.

Few important points in respect of fertigation of other nitrogenous fertilizers are mentioned below:

Urea: Its fertigation in accurate way depends on emitter discharge rate, irrigation frequency, soil's physical properties and EC, as well.

Anhydrous ammonia: It is found in gaseous form at normal air pressure, is treated as hazardous fertilizer. Actually, when Anhydrous Ammonia is dissolved in water, forms Aqua-ammonia. And on fertigation, it gets volatize and accordingly declines the level of fertilizer use efficiency. Because of this reason, this fertilizer is not recommended for fertigation purpose.

Ammonia fertilizers: On fertigation these are likely to get concentrate in the soil as they are being immobile in nature. In addition, at high temperature and alkaline nature of soil media, this fertilizer is also volatilizing at fast rate. This results into loss of fertilizer. However, applying through fertigation using drip system this loss can be controlled by using plastic mulch.

11.21 FERTIGATION OF PHOSPHORIC FERTILIZERS

Phosphoric fertilizers are available in varieties. And most of them are soluble in the water. However, few of them are not found suitable for fertigation because of some important reasons. As per research evidences, it has been reported that the concentrated phosphorus solution fertigated though drip system can move up to 20 cm in horizontal direction, and about 30 cm in vertical direction from the emitting point in soil media. In case of fertigation of phosphoric fertilizers the following points need to follow, to have better effect:

- The pH of irrigation water rich in calcium and magnesium contents, should be very low.
- The fertilizer must be compatible to irrigation water quality.
- Prior to fertigation the Precipitation test of fertilizer should be essentially done, to know the possibility of formation of precipitation; and accordingly, to take measure against that, if there.

In context to fertigation, few important views on phosphoric fertilizers (granular) are mentioned, below.

S. No.	Fertilizer	Remarks
1.	Ammonium phosphate	♦ Highly soluble in water.
2.	Ammonium sulphate	♦ Commonly used for fertigation.
3.	Mono-ammonium phosphate	
4.	Di-ammonium phosphate	
5.	Phosphoric acid	♦ Good for fertigation. ♦ Declines pH of injected solution.
6.	Treble Superphosphate	♦ Not suitable for fertigation.

11.22 FERTIGATION OF POTASSIC FERTILIZERS

Amongst various Potassic fertilizers the Potassium chloride, Potassium Sulphate and Potassium Nitrate are most commercially available. These fertilizers are also highly soluble in the water at any pH level. In soil media the potassium contents are adsorbed by the cation exchange process as the ammonium contents. Its fertigation through drip system is found better as compared to other methods. Potassium ion (K^+) has lesser affinity with the soil colloids than the ammonium ions (NH_4^+). In regards to fertigation of potassium fertilizers few important points are mentioned below:

S. No.	Fertilizer	Remark
1.	Potassium sulphate	Suitable for fertigation in fruit crops and strawberry.
2.	Potassium nitrate	Suitable for fertigation.
3.	Potassium chloride	Not recommended for fertigation in fruit crops and strawberry.

11.23 CHEMIGATION OF MICRO-NUTRIENTS

The dose of micro-nutrients varies in very little amount for the crops/plants. In general, its application through chemigation technique is not found well, because chemigated nutrient contents do not move easily in the soil media. This leads to improper distribution of micro-nutrients in the root zone. The foliar application is found best in respect to better and prompt response to the crops. However, some of the micro-nutrients such as iron, zinc copper, manganese, etc. are recommended to apply though chemigation process using drip system.

11.23.1 Problems Related to Nutrients Application (Chemigation)

The associated problems with nutrients chemigation are cited in Table 11.11.

Table 11.11 Associated problem with the chemigation

S. No.	Nutrients/Chemicals	Problems
1.	Nitrogen	♦ It gets deposit or accumulate at the wetted periphery of soil volume. In result the roots existing at the periphery of wetted zone access more amount of nitrogen. ♦ Its loss takes place due to leaching and de-nitrification.
2.	Phosphorus	♦ It likely to accumulate near the dripper (in case of drip system). ♦ In low pH zone near to the dripper, there is high fixation of P.
3.	Potassium	♦ It moves laterally and also in downward direction, as result its accumulation near to emitter, is not there. ♦ As compared to N and P its distribution is more uniform.
4.	Micro-nutrients	♦ If these are fertigated or applied thorough drip system, they are likely to get deposit near to drippers. However, this is except Boron. ♦ The Boron as micro-nutrient gets lost mainly due to leaching action in coarse textured soils such as sandy soils with very poor organic contents. ♦ The chelated micro-nutrients Fe and Zn can move from the dripper point, but not far away from the root zone area.

11.24 INSECTIGATION

It is the application of insecticides through irrigation system such as (i) Sprinkler system; and (ii) Drip system. Insectigation is carried out to control the insect's problem from greenhouse environment in very effective manner. This method enables to save the cultivation cost more than the traditional methods. Insecticides are injected in undiluted or diluted form. Dilution is done with the help of water or oil. Studies on this aspect suggest that the insecticides which are soluble in water but insoluble in oil, are being best for insectigation. The insectigation can be smoothly accomplished by using the centre pivot type sprinkler system.

11.25 FUNGIGATION

It is the application of fungicides to the infected crops or plants through irrigation system (sprinkler). The centre pivot, side roll and hand move sprinkler systems are the best tools for this purpose. In fungigation the coverage of treated area is more concerned, which must be large enough. It is governed by so many factors, such as:

- Fungicide formulation,
- Water quantity, and
- Irrigation uniformity.

Fungicide formulation is assumed to be more appropriate or the best, in which the applied materials using foliar application are not easily washed, and also less requirement of water. Similarly, for soil application the formulation should ensure that the applied materials must be washed to a large extent, and they should also be deposited on the soil surface.

Fertilizer concentration: The concentration of fertilizer in irrigation water should not be so high, because at high concentration the root system is likely to get damage from the chemicals, applied. The concentration should not exceed 5%. In most of the crops, the fertilizer concentration 1 to 2% in irrigation water is found to be in acceptable range. At high concentration the plant roots are likely to burn. However, burring level varies with the types of crop, fertilizers used and irrigation practices, followed, as well.

11.26 INJURY OF GREENHOUSE PLANTS BY TOXIC GASES

The newly grown plants are delicious; and are very sensitive to the environment. A clean or unpolluted environment is very effective to result healthy growth and better crop yield. The gasses which are injurious or toxic to most of the plants, are narrated as under:

Natural gas: It causes injury to the greenhouse plants. Natural gas normally contains about 95% Methane and 4 to 5% Ethane, which act as toxic elements for most of the greenhouse plants. As per research evidences, a very small concentration of gas (1 part of natural gas in 10,000 to 100,000 part air) is being sufficient to damage the greenhouse plants. The gaseous injuries are at dominating scale, especially, during winter season when greenhouse ventilators are kept close to raise the inside temperature. The toxic effect of natural gas in different crops are pointed below,

***Tomato*:** Leaves get turn down because of epinastic response. This causes increase in growth of leave's petiole on upper side.

***Carnation*:** In this crop a low concentration can develop long stigmas. However, this symptom also borne in bright weather and unshaded greenhouses. In prolong exposed condition the newly borne buds are likely to fail even at the concentration of 1 part to 100,000 part air.

***Rose*:** The effects of natural gas in rose may be as below:

- The foliage of upper shoots exhibits epinasty.
- The petiole bends downward.
- There is large number of leaf drops.
- The colour of flower often fades.
- The bulbous plants develop twisted foliage.
- In addition, the flowers do not open properly.

Ethylene gas: This gas is released by the plants through metabolic process, in very small amount. Its effects are observed in the form of dropping of flowers after pollination. In carnation species of flower there is appearance of "sleepy", i.e., the end of petal's curl, inward.

Sulphur dioxide: It poses toxic effect on the plants at very low concentration. This gas enters the plant body through the space of stomatal openings; and destroys the cells located in nearby area. This leads to develop the patches of dead tissues on the leaf surface in scattered way.

The effect of Sulphur dioxide is more in middle aged leaves to that of the young leaves. In the localities, where burning of coal is very common, the development of this effect is highly pronounced.

Mercury damage: This gas damages the plants in vapour form. The effect of mercury damage can be controlled by removing all mercury traces from the area. Sometimes, it is also carried out by covering the soil surface, which is under mercury spilled. In addition, the paint containing mercury contents, used as fungicide, should also be stopped to apply in rose houses. Because of mercury traces the newly appeared rose buds turn into yellow colour; and later on they also become blackish. Also, in some cases the flower colour turns into dark and leaves are scorched.

2,4-D: It creates its damaging effect on the plants in the form of bending, curling, and malformations of leaves, stems, flowers or bracts, as well. In greenhouse environment the entry of 2, 4, D-fume or drift is more common when this chemical is sprayed in nearby areas of greenhouse.

Phenol compounds: The materials which contain phenol or its derivatives, should be avoided to apply in greenhouse crops, as they are toxic to the plants. The tar, carbolic acid, pentachlorophenol, etc. are the phenol containing materials, should never be used. Similarly, the wood preservatives which contain the phenol compounds, should also not be allowed to use.

The PGRs which are chemical based, used for regulating the plant growth, are also being effective to manage the crop in greenhouse environment. In addition, there are various cultural activities also found beneficial in reducing cost of cultivation, besides improvement in health of growing media. Important activities in this sense are mentioned below:

(i) Size of container
(ii) Plant density
(iii) Irrigation practices
(iv) Fertigation/nutrient management
(v) Mechanical conditioning—Pinching, brushing, etc.
(vi) Temperature management
(vii) Light quality and quantity

These are described as under:

Container size: It is well known that the root growth plays significant role in development of plant. Accordingly, by restricting the root growth in greenhouse media the plant growth could be easily controlled, which can be accomplished by using a small size pot for growing purpose. This can also be done by increasing the number of plants in the pot or per pot. However, this practice is found suitable, when there is no restriction on application of nutrients and availability of sufficient lights, there.

Plant density: The plant density signifies the interval between plants. It is also one of the important ways to control plant growth. Plant density affects the level of availability of light, water, nutrients, etc. to an individual plant. At greater density or lesser plant spacing the plant becomes tall in height and lesser in girth (diameter); and vice-versa.

Irrigation practices: Irrigation is the practice of supplying water to the crop, also causes significant effect on plant's growth. In this practice by controlling the irrigation, a situation of moisture stress is developed in the root zone. However, the level of moisture stress should not be so high to cause plant's wilting. Normally, mid-to-moderate moisture stress is desirable for this purpose, which can be developed by continuously keeping the root zone dry and immediately applying the irrigation just before the plant starts wilting or as per appearance of wilting symptom in the plant.

Fertilization: The application of fertilizers to the crop or plant also imposes significant effect on plant growth. In general, among different fertilizers the nitrogen is very effective to plant growth. The growth can be easily checked by restricting the nitrogen level. A prolong deficiency of nitrogen in growing media results the plant height very small. The creation of phosphorus deficiency is comparatively difficult than the nitrogen. However, if it is succeeded to create mild to moderate phosphorus deficiency in root zone, a desirable reduction in plant growth could be easily accomplished, without any foliar symptoms.

Mechanical conditioning: This practice refers to change the structure of plant, i.e., the shape and size of the plant canopy, stem length, etc. plays significant role in regulating the plant growth. The pinching and brushing are the two main methods used for this purpose, are described below:

***Pinching*:** This is a common practice in many of the greenhouse crops. It is carried out to reduce the plant height, besides promoting the appearance of branches and also creating the plant shape in proper form and size, both. In pinching operation, the tips of the plants are removed, manually, which is effective to increase the number of branch formations. Pinching is also done for removing the apical dominance of the shoot to prevent branching. The apical dominance is associated to the production of natural plant hormone called "auxin" and young leaves. In this way, by removing the tips/terminal growing points and young leaves through pinching action, the source of "auxin" is terminated; and accordingly allowing the dormant buds to grow, below the pinch. Pinching time is very important related to branching and flowering time.

***Brushing*:** This is done for reducing the plant height, leaf area and dry weight of the plant, beside increasing the strength of stem and petiole, as well. In nutshell, the main objective of brushing is to bend the plant without breaking the leaves/stems or causing any types of damage to the plant.

Light quantity, quality and photo period: In addition to various activities described so far in regards to control the plant growth in greenhouse environment, it can also be achieved by regulating the light quality, quantity and photosynthesis period of the plant, as these are very effective to cause significant effect on plant growth and overall development of the plant. Effects of these parameters are narrated as under:

***Light quantity*:** It denotes the intensity or concentration of sunlight coming on the greenhouse structure and ultimately transmitting into cropped zone, inside. Light intensity varies with the season of the year. The stem elongation can be reduced by increasing the amount of light to receive the plant.

***Light quality*:** It refers to the wavelength/color of the light reaching the plant surface. The proportion of red to far red light affects the elongation or stretch of the plant, even branching is also affected in many of the plants.

***Photoperiod*:** It reveals the light duration, which is the time period up to which a plant is exposed to the sunlight. The photo period (long days or short days) can be manipulated as per requirement of the crop, by means of black plastic sheet or the cloth, itself.

Temperature: The temperature inside greenhouse is always greater than the outside, because of cladding material's characteristics (UV polyethylene). Greenhouse temperature is one of the important factors affecting the plant growth, can be modified by using various tools or techniques, such as shade nets, fan pad cooling system, etc.

11.27 PLANT GROWTH REGULATORS

PGRs are the chemicals, used to regulate or control the plant growth, in few specialized aspects such as stem length, rooting, flowering, leaf abscission, fruiting, cold hardiness, etc. However, in greenhouse cultivation the main objective of PGR is to retard the plant growth; or in other words they are used as "Growth Retardants." The plant growth regulator reduces or regulates the plant height by inhibiting the gibberellins production, which is hormone responsive regarding cell elongation. In general, the primary effect of PGR is on stem, petiole and peduncle elongation. On application of growth regulators, the leaf geometry also gets affected in following aspects:

- Leaf expansion gets reduce, leading to shorten the leaf length.
- Leaf thickness gets increase.
- Color of leaf becomes dark-green.
- Declination of water requirement due to reduction in transpiration rate.

11.27.1 Purpose and Uses of PGRs

In greenhouse cultivation system the main use/purpose of PGRs is to retard the plant growth by controlling the stem elongation. The other purposes of PGRs are as follows:

- Promoting root development.
- Elongating stem length.
- Aborting flower buds.
- Promoting branch appearance.
- Inhibiting plant growth.
- Improvement in plant appearance, i.e., the size and shape.

As for as uses are concerned, the followings are the well-recognized uses of PGRs in context to control the plant growth:

1. Shoot growth regulation.
2. Increasing lateral branching.
3. Enhancing flowering.
4. Removal of flowers.
5. Other uses.

Shoot growth regulation: In majority of the greenhouse crops the plant growth regulators (PGRs) are used for regulating the shoot growth (stretch) of container plants. Such PGRs are called growth retardants. They control the plant height by inhibiting the gibberellin production, which is the primary plant hormone causing cell elongation.

Increasing lateral branching: This is required in floricultural crops to enhance the number of flowers appearance in the plant. For this purpose, the important PGRs are named below:

(i) Ethephon (Florel),
(ii) Benzyladenine (BA; Configure),
(iii) Dikegulac sodium (Atrimmec or Augeo), and
(iv) Methyl esters (Off-Shoot-O).

Since, these PGRs inhibit the growth of terminal shoots or increase the growth of lateral buds; therefore, sometimes, these are also known as chemical pinchers.

Plant flowering: The number of flowers in a plant can also be enhanced by using PGRs. For this purpose, the important PGRs are given as under:

(i) Florgib 4L
(ii) ProGibb T&O
(iii) GA3 4%: it contains the growth promoter as Gibberellic Acid (GA3).

Removal of flowers: The removal of flowers is preferably required for stock plants in respect to cuttings of vegetatively propagated ornamental plants such as *Verbena* or *Lantana*, mainly. This can also be done by using the PGR, named Ethephon (Florel) which is a primary compound. On its application, the absorbed Ethephon by the plant gets converted into ethylene (gaseous form) which acts as the natural hormone, is effective to activate many of the processes associated to the plant, besides growth regulation.

Other uses: Bedsides aforesaid uses of PGRs, some of the PGRs are also applied for reducing the yellowing of lower leaves of the plant.

11.27.2 Factors Affecting to PGR Response

In general, all those factors which affect the plant growth and development in respect to rate and quality, are also found to affect the plant's response to plant growth regulators, applied. The growers should consider all of them related to their greenhouse crops. In nutshell, the factors affecting to PGRs response are shown in Table 11.12.

Table 11.12 Factors affecting PGR's response on crop growth

S. No.	Factor	Sub-factor
1.	Plant factors	(i) Plant species (ii) Plant growth stage (iii) Plant vigor (iv) Plant size
2.	Environmental factors	(i) Temperature (ii) Light (iii) Growing media (iv) Water quality and quantity
3.	Physical and chemical factors	(i) Residual chemical effect (ii) Application rate (iii) Time of application (iv) Doses (v) Chemical uptake and translocation (vi) Coverage (vii) Spray droplet size

Plant Factors

The plant species, growth stage, vigor, size, etc. affect the PGR's response on plant growth, are described as under:

Plant species: Majority of the plant species have their different growth habits. In addition, they also have varying sensitiveness in context to chemical and environmental variabilities. Because of this reason the effect of a particular PGR may be to a good range on given plant species, while the same may not be so on another species. Similarly, a given rate of application of PGR may be effective on one cultivar, but that may not be for another cultivar of the same species.

Plant growth stage: In general, a plant passes through a series of growth stages. In sequence they are as follows:

(i) Stem extension,
(ii) Elongation of internode,
(iii) Leaf expansion,
(iv) Bud formation,
(v) Bud opening/flowering, and
(vi) Physiological maturity.

In warm environment along with high light intensity the rate of physiological development/ growth becomes rapid to that of the cool and low light condition over a given time period.

Plant vigor: The plant vigor also impacts the PGR's response on growth aspect. Comparatively, a plant with vigorous growth habit requires high rate of PGR application than those having poor growth habit. Accordingly, in low vigor crops or plants a low rate of PGR is recommended for application; and vice-versa.

Plant size: The rate of PGR application is also decided on the basis of plant size. A small size plant requires low rate of PGR application than the large size plants. For example, to achieve a given level of growth control in the plant grown in 15 cm size growing pot requires more drench or spray of PGR as compared to the plant with same cultivar grown in 10 cm size pot for achieving same level of control on the plant growth.

Environmental Factors

The environmental factors encompassing temperature, light, growing media, water quality and quantity, etc. also affect the requirement of PGR for its proper response on plant growth. Effects of these factors are presented as under:

Temperature and light: The ambient temperature and available light in the plant's environment affect significantly to growth behavior of the plant. In greenhouse these effects are very strong for plant growth. Comparatively, the plants grown in warm environment (high temperature) and receive sufficient light intensity, require high rate of PGR application; and vice-versa. On this ground, it is therefore, suggested that the application rate of PGR must be adjusted as per season of the crop, i.e., the summer and winter seasons crops, carefully.

Growing media: The composition of growing media directly affects the efficacy of drench application in case of certain PGRs. It is general finding that in the growing media, as the level of organic contents becomes more the effect of PGR drench gets decrease on plant growth.

Water quality and quantity: The response of certain PGR's is governed by the quality of water used for irrigation to the plants. As per research findings, on the application of water with high pH, i.e., more than 7 and high alkalinity level (more than 100 ppm $CaCO_3$ equivalent), the effectiveness of many PGRs gets reduce in context to plant growth. Similarly, the effect of water quantity used for application of plant growth regulators is also likely to change on growth aspects of the plants.

Physical and Chemical Factors

The followings are the main factors affecting the effects of PGRs in context to plant growth:

(i) Residual chemical effects
(ii) Application rate
(iii) Application time
(iv) Dosage
(v) Chemical uptake and translocation
(vi) Coverage
(vii) Spray drop size.

These are described as under:

Residual chemical effect: It refers to the time span up to which the PGR remains active in plant, after its application. As per residual chemical effects the PGRs are further classified as under:

- ***Short duration*:** Normally, the products containing *Daminozide or Chlormequat chloride* (e.g., Citadel and Cycocel) have short duration residual effects on plant growth.
- ***Moderate duration*:** The products containing *Ancymidol* (e.g., Abide and A-Rest) or *Flurprimidol* have relatively moderate duration in respect to their residual effect.
- ***Long duration*:** Those products which contain *Paclobutrazol* (e.g., Bonzi, Paczol, and Piccolo) have long duration residual impacts.

Application rates: PGR application rate varies with the growth rate of the plant, concern. In the early of the plant growth the application rate is low. On the other hand, in the crops which are vigorously growing or have already vigorously grown, require high rate of application. In addition, PGR application rate also depends on the solar light, temperature, relative humidity, watering and fertilization practices, followed. Normally, in the situation of high temperature, high sunlight, vigorous growing varieties, moderate to high fertility (phosphorus), warmer days than the night and closely plantations or growing in small containers, a high level of PGR application is required.

Application time: Application time of PGR is very important to have a proper effect on plant growth/development or regulation, as well. It should be done just before attaining a rapid shoot growth. Normally, it is preferred to perform as per below:

- 1 to 2 week after transplanting the plug.
- After the roots are established.
- As the plant resumes active growth.
- In case of pinched plants, it is done after appearance of new shoots; and they are also started, elongating.

Application dose: The PGR dose is kept relatively lesser than the insecticides or pesticides used for crop protection. Its overdose may result negative effects on crop growth and also on other aspects, too. Overall, the plant growth regulators are applied in precise way and in low concentration. This is followed as the care about its application.

Chemical uptake: The uptake as well as translocation of chemical constituents in plant body varies among different PGRs. For example, the PGR Bonzi, Concise and Sumagic with same active ingredients, are efficiently extracted by the plant roots, and are readily transported to the shoot tips. However, there are so many other PGRs, in which it is not so.

Coverage: It refers to the amount or volume of PGR solution applied (sprayed) per unit area of the soil surface. In case of pot or container type growing media the coverage denotes the volume of solution (PGR) applied per pot.

Droplet size: In greenhouse cultivation the nutrients or PGRs are applied in precise way using sprayers, foggers, misters, etc. of suitable size. This is done to have a greater area coverage and penetration in the canopy. In spraying mode of application, the spray materials fall in the form of droplets on the crop/plant canopy. However, in case of fogging the droplet size is very small (fine) resulting into drifting effect. This leads to take greater time for deposition of droplets on the crop canopy. In addition, there is also requirement of air circulation for making a good level of penetration of PGR contents in canopy.

11.27.3 Methods of Application—PGRs

The application method to be followed plays significant role in effectiveness of PGRs application about growth control of the plants. There are so many methods for use, but to a most suitable and cost effective method must be given priority for use. The method should also ensure uniformity of application and penetration, as well. The most commonly used methods are mentioned below:

(i) Spraying method
(ii) Drenching method
(iii) Watering method
(iv) Sprenching method
(v) Plug and liner dips method
(vi) Bulb soaking method

Spraying method: This method is generally used, when a short-term response of PGR is desired. In addition, when small to moderate effect on plant height growth is required by the PGR, the spraying is also found suitable for application. In this method, it is taken care that when PGR is applied in the form of foliar spray, the sprayed materials must be properly absorbed or transported within plant canopy. Also, the active ingredients of PGR must move through cuticle layer of leaf or the stem and then in the plant tissues, is one of the very important points followed in this method. In addition, there are some more points to consider in context to effective application, given as under:

- The plants to be sprayed or treated using PGR should be healthy, turgid and unstressed (never wilted).

- The plant should have sufficient foliage or number of stems to absorb the sprayed PGR solution, properly.
- The spraying should be consistent and uniform.

Drenching: This is also a common method for application of plant growth regulators. In this method, the drenches are applied on the top of growing media with little or moderate contact to the plant foliage. The plant roots absorbed the applied materials, and translocate them to the growing parts of the plant. This results into inhibiting the elongation of growing points. In addition to above, the drenching is also applied to inhibit the extension or elongation of stem for a long period of time. This method follows following points to accomplish better application:

(i) Growing media should be properly moist. This ensures better uniformity of PGR distribution in the substrate of growing media.

(ii) Application amount should be adequate, so that the root mass may get completely wetted with the PGR solution.

Watering-in method: This method is one of the type of chemigation techniques. In this method, the PGR is applied along with irrigation water at pre-scheduled time to the crop or plant. The rate of application is kept very low. This method is easy and cost effective as compared to the drenching technique. In addition, a more consistent control on plant height can also be achieved by correctly performing the application.

Sprenching method: This is an improved method over spraying and drenching techniques. Sprenching technique is found suitable when a long-lasting response of PGR is required; and a moderate effect on plant height control is also desired. This accomplishes overhead application in the form of high volume spray and light watering-in, as per requirement, by means of hose. The foliar application results into runoff effect in growing media; and thus creating drenching effect, there.

Plug and liner dips method: This is another method used for application of plant growth regulators to control the plant height. It is also referred to as the liner dip, plug dip, or sometimes the liner soak, also. In liner dip technique the growing media tray with rooter liner is partially submerged in the PGR solution and also allowed to get absorb the chemical in the growing media. When it is required to perform for large-scale liner's treatment, then it is done, mechanically. On the other hand, in case of small number of liner's treatment the hand dipping is being more practical. After completion of dipping action, the plants are allowed to get dry for at least 12 hours' duration; thereafter, they are used for transplanting in the container placed with the growing media.

Bulb soaking method: In this method, bulbs are dipped in PGR solution to soak the chemicals. This is done before planting the bulbs in growing media. This method is advantageous over spraying and drenching techniques. In bulb soaking method, many bulbs can be easily treated with a less volume of solution. In addition, the same PGR solution can also be reused for treatment, without any adverse effect.

PRACTICE QUESTIONS

Descriptive Type Questions

1. Describe different elements required for plant growth.
2. Write significance of nutrition in crop growth.
3. Describe nutrient's deficiency and their symptoms in plant body.
4. Describe the methods used for predicting nutrient's deficiency.
5. Narrate the effect of excess application of fertilizer dose on crop growth; and its remedial measures.
6. Explain basics of plant nutrition.
7. Describe various measures followed for reducing nutrients loss.
8. Define fertigation and explain its importance/advantages.
9. Describe fertigation, chemigation and insectigation.
10. Describe venturi and its various modules used for fertigation.
11. Enlist and describe the commonly used fertilizers for fertigation.
12. Narrate the criteria used for selecting suitable fertilizer for fertigation.
13. What do you mean by plant growth regulator; writes its functions and advantages.
14. Describe fertigation of phosphoric and potassic fertilizers.
15. Explain various factors affecting the response of PGRs on plant growth.

Multiple Choice Type Questions

1. The numbers of essential elements for plant growth are
   (a) 5 (b) 18
   (c) 16 (d) 15
2. The plant uptake of Carbon (C), Hydrogen (H) and Oxygen (O) is largely met from
   (a) Air (CO_2) (b) Water
   (c) Soil (d) Both (a) and (b)
3. The plant growth gets accelerate when level of ambient CO_2 is available in the range of
   (a) 800 to 1000 ppm (b) 180 to 1000 ppm
   (c) 80 to 100 ppm (d) 8 to 10 ppm
4. Normal CO_2 level in atmosphere is about
   (a) 350 ppm (b) 180 ppm
   (c) 500 ppm (d) 8 to 10 ppm
5. Excess Nitrogen may cause
   (a) Inhibiting root activities (b) Very high evapotranspiration (ET)
   (c) Very high shoot growth (d) Very high nutrient uptake

6. In majority of the plant leaves the normal concentration of Manganese varies to the tune of
   (a) 10 to 20 ppm
   (b) 20 to 45 ppm
   (c) 150 to 180 ppm
   (d) 30 to 125 ppm
7. Which of the following is the mobile fertilizer in soil media?
   (a) Nitrogen and Potassium
   (b) Magnesium
   (c) Phosphorus and Sulphur
   (d) All above
8. Which of the following is the immobile fertilizer in soil media?
   (a) Nitrogen and Potassium
   (b) Magnesium
   (c) Phosphorus and Sulphur
   (d) Calcium and Copper
9. Calcium uptake is affected by the ions such as
   (a) NH_4
   (b) K
   (c) Mg
   (d) All above
10. Which of the following is the primary nutrient for plant uptake?
   (a) Nitrogen (N),
   (b) Potassium (K)
   (c) Phosphorus (P)
   (d) All above
11. Which of the following is the secondary nutrient for plant growth?
   (a) Calciusm (Ca)
   (b) Magnesium (Mg)
   (c) Sulphur (S)
   (d) All above
12. Which of the following is the micro-nutrient for plant growth?
   (a) Iron (Fe)
   (b) Molybdenum (Mo)
   (c) Boron (B)
   (d) All above
13. Which of the following is the trace element for plant growth?
   (a) Calcium (Ca)
   (b) Magnesium (Mg)
   (c) Boron (B)
   (d) Potassium (K)
14. In micro-irrigation system the function of venturi is
   (a) Supply filtered water
   (b) Pressure control
   (c) Fertigation
   (d) Safety guard to control unit
15. Fertilizer solubility depends on
   (a) Water pH
   (b) Water temperature
   (c) Grain size of fertilizer
   (d) Both (a) and (b)
16. Nitrogen percentage in Urea is
   (a) 50
   (b) 75
   (c) 46
   (d) 35
17. Which of the following fertilizer is not recommended for fertigation in fruit crops and strawberry?
   (a) Potassium chloride
   (b) Potash
   (c) Urea
   (d) Ammonium sulphate
18. The main objective of plant growth regulator (PGR) is to
   (a) Increase shoot growth
   (b) Retard the plant growth
   (c) Reduce nutrient uptake
   (d) Decrease irrigation level

19. Which of the following plant growth regulator (PGR) is used for increasing lateral branching?

(a) Benzyladenine (BA; Configure) (b) Methyl esters (off-Shoot-O)
(c) Ethephon (Florel) (d) All above

20. Which of the following plant growth regulator (PGR) can be used for increasing the number of flowers?

(a) Florgib 4L (b) Methyl esters (off-Shoot-O)
(c) Ethephon (Florel) (d) All above

Answers

1. c	**2.** d	**3.** b	**4.** a	**5.** a	**6.** d	**7.** d	**8.** d	**9.** d	**10.** d
11. d	**12.** d	**13.** c	**14.** c	**15.** d	**16.** c	**17.** a	**18.** b	**19.** d	**20.** a

BIBLIOGRAPHY

Anonymous (1987). Handbook for Pesticides Applicators and Disinsers. Ministry of environment, Victoria.

Anonymous (1989). Irrigation methods for feedlot effluent management noted the cross section. High plains Undergroundwater Conservation District No. 1 Lubbock, TX 79405.

Chemigation in Kansas. Certified equipment operator Examination Manual Kansas Department of Agriculture, Division of plant Health, Topeka, Kansas.

Goldammer T. (2019). Greenhouse Management: A Guide to Operations and Technology. Apex Publishers, USA.

Ogg, Dowler, Martin Lange, and Heilkes (1998). Application of Herbicides, through Irrigation systems. U.S Dept. of Agriculture, Extension serves.

Suresh R. (2010). Micro-Irrigation—Theory and Practice. Standard Publishers and Distributors, Nai Sarak, Delhi.

Ted W. Van Der Gulik, and P. Engg (1993). Chemigation Guidelines of British Columbia. Soil and Engineering Branch, B.S Ministry of Agriculture, Fisheries and Food, Abbotsford, B.C, V2S2C5.

W.L. Trimmer, T.W Ley, G. Clough, and D. Larsen (1992). Chemigation in the Pacific Northwest, PNW 360.

CHAPTER 12

Water Quality—Greenhouse Use

In greenhouse cultivation system the availability of water with better quality has prime importance in context to its use for irrigation of the crops, greenhouse environment control and other purposes, as well. Broadly, water quality signifies the presence of dissolved and suspended contents/materials in water either it is groundwater or surface water. Water quality decides its suitability for use. Suitability of water varies sector to sector. Say, for example, a given quality water may be suitable for irrigation purpose but that may not be fit for drinking purpose.

In greenhouse crop farming system the water quality is important in the aspect of its use for irrigation and maintenance of drip and environment control system, mainly. The water quality for irrigation point of view advocates the presence of foreign contents (dissolved or suspended) should be in such a range, that it would be fit for complete greenhouse farming system. Similarly, the water quality in respect to maintenance of drip system is concerned; the water should not contain any such elements which cause chocking problem in pipeline and water emitting system, as well. In this chapter the water quality is dealt in context to suitability of water for greenhouse based crop irrigation point of view and maintenance of drip system, both.

12.1 WATER QUALITY

Water quality is defined in different aspects depending on source, characteristics of the substances existing and presence of factors like bacteria, viruses and pathogenic contents in water. For greenhouse crop farming point of view, the water quality in terms of (i) Agronomical use; and (ii) Irrigation system are the main concern. In which, agronomical water quality signifies the suitability of water for better crop uptake without any harmful effect on crop growth; and irrigation system based water quality denotes to the water not creating pugging problem in pipeline and water emitting devices. In greenhouse system both the qualities of water must be satisfied any how; otherwise, the performance of greenhouse and the crop yield will get drastically affected. There are certain parameters defining the water quality, are presented below.

12.2 WATER QUALITY PARAMETERS

The water quality of a place specific is defined on the basis of following parameters called water quality parameters. Value of each parameter is different to define suitability of water for a particular use.

pH: It represents the concentration of hydrogen ion in water. Mathematically, pH is expressed as the logarithmic of H^+ ion concentration. The concentration of hydrogen ion makes the water in saline or alkaline. In this way, this parameter defines the water quality in terms of saline or alkaline in nature. In general, pH level varies from 0 to 14. In which pH 7 denotes the neutral condition of water. On the other hand, pH less than 7 defines the water quality as acidic. Similarly, the pH more than 7 classifies the water quality as alkaline. The pH value gets changed because of dissolved constituents in water, mainly. The pH of irrigation water varies from source to source of water and season-to-season, both. In drip irrigation system the pH of irrigation water is causative to affect the pipeline used for distributing the water across the crop field. Mainly, it is responsible to create chemical plugging problem in pipeline. Overall, the accepted range of pH for majority of the water cases varies from 6 to 9.

Electrical conductivity (EC): It depends on concentration of dissolved ions and their electrical charge in water specific. It is expressed in the unit of milli-siemen/cm, deci-siemen/m and milli-Mhos/cm. EC varies with the available concentration of solution in the water. This parameter also signifies salinity level of water, or total dissolved solids (TDS) in water. The TDS of water can be computed by using the following relationship:

$$\text{TDS (mg/l)}.1.56 = \text{E.C (micro-siemens/cm)} \quad \ldots(12.1)$$

Totally dissolved solids (TDS): This parameter expresses the concentration of dissolved salts in the water. It is denoted in the unit of mg/lit. It provides a general view about compatibility level between water quality and its effect on crop and soil media, as well.

Chlorides (Cl): It is also one of the parameters deciding water quality. In water its main source of availability is the dissolved cooking salts. Its concentration significantly affects the salinity level, and accordingly the suitability of water for concern use, too. In context to irrigation system (drip) an excess concentration of chloride beyond acceptable limit causes plugging problem in pipeline.

Alkalinity: It is because of presence of Calcium (Ca) and Magnesium (Mg) ions in water. Alkalinity denotes the ability of water or solution to counteract acidity and also to retain a non-variable pH level. In addition to Ca and Mg, there are several other ions/contents that affect the water alkalinity.

Hardness: Water hardness is expressed in terms of concentration of Calcium and Magnesium ions in the form of Carbonates. It is expressed in the unit of mg/lit or milli-equivalent. This parameter is considered to be very important regarding drip system. In drip pipeline the formation scale or chemical deposits is mainly because of concentration of Calcium (Ca^{++}) ions. On the other hand, the effect of Magnesium (Mg) ion is very less as compared to Ca ion.

Turbidity: It indicates the cleanliness and transparency level of water. Turbidity is predicted by measuring the refraction or absorption level of light beam passing through the water concerned; and is also by determining the amount of suspended particles present. The particles in the size (diameter) ranging from 0.1 to 10 micron are causative for development of turbidity effect in water. Mainly, turbidity level gets increase with increase in number of suspended particles. The effect of turbidity on water quality regarding drip system is not so significant. The possibility of plugging effect in sprinklers or drippers is about to negligible.

Total suspended solids (TSS): In deciding water quality, the TSS is assessed in terms of concentration of suspended solid particles in water. The suspended particles may be organic and non-organic materials, both. It is expressed in the unit of mg/lit. This parameter may cause plugging effect in drip pipeline system. The fine particles may choke the emitter's aperture; and accordingly to affect the emitter's flow rate.

TSS is determined by filtering a measured volume of water by using weighed filter paper. The filtered suspended particles are weighed after drying in oven at 105°C. The dry weight of suspended particles present in water sample represents the TSS level of water. Further, the filtered particles are sorted in respect to their types and sizes to divide into sand, clay and silt, as well. The size of different suspended particles is shown in Table 12.1 which can be used as guideline for dividing the plugging particles/materials in different classes.

Table 12.1 Size of different types of particles

S. No.	Particle	Size (micron)
1.	Sand	200 to 2,000
2.	Fine sand	50 to 200
3.	Silt	2 to 50
4.	Clay	Less than 2

Volatile suspended solids: These suspended solids are causative to develop a kind of quality in water concern. The volatile suspended solids get evaporate in the oven from left solids of previous test at 550°C temperature. Its concentration is expressed as mg/lit.

Algae and chlorophyll: The presence of algae and chlorophyll in water, and thereby formed water quality is judged by the appearance of green tinted colour along with brown and blue as additional shades in water. Level of their presence is expressed in terms of density, which is determined by using a transparent vessel and looking the water visually. Appearance of thick color shows to a high density; and vice-versa. The algal growth takes place in that water which is directly exposed to the sunlight. It is found in variety of types and density both; accordingly, the water quality also becomes different due to this reason. Their types and density affect the quality of irrigation water. Level of chlorophyll depends on the concentration of algae in the water. Chlorophyll concentration is measured in terms of amount of micrograms/liter.

Biochemical oxygen demand (BOD): It represents the presence of organic materials in the water. BOD is assessed by determining the amount of oxygen consumed under bacteriological activities for oxidizing the organic contents available in water. As for as, quality is concerned the water with its BOD equal to 5 is considered to be standard water quality.

Chemical oxygen demand (COD): It reveals the materials existing in water do chemical oxidization. COD is expressed as mg/lit. It is determined by oxidizing the materials present in water, first; and then determining the amount of oxygen consumed in the process.

Agronomical factor: This is also being an important water quality parameter, especially for irrigation point of view. However, it does not responsible to cause plugging problem in drip pipeline system. Agronomical factor mainly includes the nutrients and other solutions available in water. These factors affect the crop and soil, both.

Nutrients: The nutrients applied for plant growth also affects the water quality. In general, the phosphorus, nitrogen, potassium and quartz are essential nutrients for development of plants. These are found in soil and water both. In addition, they are also found available in the form of additives (fertilizers/and other nutrients). On application of these additives a part of that gets leach to the water table; and accordingly there is effects on water quality.

***Nitrogen*:** In water it is found in the form of compounds. Most commonly the Nitrogenous-Ammonia compounds (NH_4, NO_3, and NO_2) and organic Nitrogen are the examples of it. In water the appearance of nitrogen is in molecular form of N_2 which is in dissolved state. Nitrogen concentration is expressed as mg/lit for each individual compound.

***Phosphorus*:** It is also found in compound form, in dissolved and suspended state (organic compounds). Its presence in water signifies the availability of sewage or fertilizer. This chemical content can cause the development of silt residues, effective to plug the irrigation system.

***Potassium*:** It is an essential nutrient for plant growth/development. Also, it is a common fertilizer for agricultural crops. In water its presence is found in varying range. Concentration of Potassium is not causative to develop plugging effect in drip pipeline system.

***Sodium*:** This is the cation of cooking salt. Its availability is very common in majority of the water bodies. Presence of Sodium cation in irrigation water develops salinity effect in the soil media and also harms the crop growth. In addition, there is also very close bonding between sodium ions and clay particles. This leads to develop sealing effect in soil. In result there is retardance in water absorption. In soil media the absorption of sodium gets affected by several overriding factors such as sodium availability in water, soil types and bonding between concentrations of sodium and bivalent cations such as Calcium and Magnesium in water and soil, both. The relationship among concentration of Sodium, Calcium and Magnesium is expressed by a term called "Sodium Absorption Ratio" (SAR), is given as under:

$$SAR = \frac{Na}{\sqrt{\frac{(Ca + Mg)}{2}}} \quad \ldots(12.2)$$

In this equation the cations are expressed in the unit of meq/lit. Solved problem 12.1 Illustrates the computation of SAR of a given water quality.

PROBLEM 12.1 In course of determining the quality of a given water sample the concentrations of Na, Ca and Mg are determined to the tune of 7.5, 2.3, and 1.30 meq/lit, respectively. Compute SAR of said water.

***Solution*:**

Given that,

(i) Concentration of Na = 7.5 meq/lit

(ii) Concentration of Ca = 2.3 meq/lit

(iii) Concentration of Mg = 1.3 meq/lit

Using the following formula for determining the SAR:

$$SAR = \frac{Na}{\sqrt{\frac{(Ca + Mg)}{2}}}$$

In which, the values of Na, Ca and Mg are given as 7.5, 2.3, and 1.30 meq/lit, respectively. Substituting these values in above equation and after solving, we have

$$SAR = \frac{7.5}{\sqrt{(2.3 + 1.3)/2}} = 5.59$$

The determined SAR is 5.59. **Ans.**

***Boron*:** It develops poisonous effect in water at its higher concentration. This chemical content is found in most of the plants, but in very small range. Boron falls in the category of micro-nutrients. In soil media its concentration 0.5 mg/lit develops poisonous effect in boron sensitive plants. Similarly, its concentration more than 0.6 mg/lit in irrigation water alarms to take precaution about use of such water for irrigation purposes. Normally, such quality water is used as per suitability of the crop and soil. The sources of born may be the detergent and sewage water. In sewage water its concentration is normally found beyond acceptable range, i.e., poisonous in nature.

***Aluminum*:** It falls in the category of light metal. In water media it is found in very small quantity/concentration. Its effect on soil and crop is not so adverse like other chemicals. However, in the areas having low pH water and local rocks are rich in Aluminum content, the level of Aluminum gets increase to that extent, at which the Aluminum becomes poisonous to many of the plants.

12.3 WATER QUALITY FOR IRRIGATION

The suitability of water to be used for irrigation depends on concentration of different chemical contents available. The concentration should not be beyond tolerable limit; otherwise, there is development of harmful effect on the crop. There have been framed the limits of chemical concentration for different uses of water in terms of classes. The important amongst them are narrated below.

Water quality classes as per EC and salt concentration: On this aspect, water quality is divided in following four classes:

(i) Class–C_1,
(ii) Class–C_2,
(iii) Class–C_3, and
(iv) Class–C_4.

Class C_1: This class water involves following main properties:

(a) Low salinity level.
(b) It can be frequently used for irrigating the crops grown in majority of the soils.

(c) No risk of soil salinity development.
(d) In normal irrigation practice leaching is essential.

Class C_2: Important characteristics are as follows:

(a) Water contains medium salinity level.
(b) Water can be used for irrigation, but with moderate leaching arrangement.
(c) Salt tolerant crops can suitably be grown without salinity control measures.

Class C_3: The followings are important nutshell points:

(a) Water includes high salinity level.
(b) Not suitable for irrigation point of view.
(c) If water is used for irrigation the soil is required to follow salinity control measures on priority basis. However, highly salt tolerant crops can be cultivated.

Class C_4: It includes following features:

(a) Very high salinity level.
(b) This quality water is completely restricted for irrigation purposes under ordinary condition.
(c) Its use can be in (i) highly permeable soils; (ii) soils with adequate drainage facility and leaching; and (iii) crops are highly salt tolerant.

The limits of EC and salt concentration in afore-mentioned water quality classes are presented in Table 12.2.

Table 12.2 Water quality classification based on EC and salt concentration

Water quality	Electrical conductivity (1×10^6 mhos per cm)	Salt concentration (g/lit)
C_1	0 to 250	Less than 0.16
C_2	250 to 750	0.16 to 0.5
C_3	750 to 2250	0.5 to 1.5
C_4	2250 to 5000	1.5 to 3.0

(*Source*: http://ecoursesonline.iasri.res.in/mod/page/view.php?id=1530)

Water quality as per SAR and other parameters: Besides above water quality classes for agricultural concerns, Christiansen (1973) also proposed the ratings of irrigation water (quality) on the basis of EC and concentration of different chemical constituents, is shown in Table 12.3.

Table 12.3 Rating of irrigation water quality

Water quality rating	EC (mmhos/cm)	Sodium concentration Na^+	SAR	Na_2CO_3 (meq/lit)	Cl^-	EC(meq/lit)	Boron (ppm)
1	0.5	40.0	3.0	0.5	3.0	4.0	0.5
2	1.0	60.0	6.0	1.0	6.0	8.0	1.0
3	2.0	70.0	9.0	2.0	10.0	16.0	2.0
4	3.0	80.0	12.0	3.0	15.0	24.0	3.0
5	4.0	90.0	15.0	4.0	20.0	32.0	4.0
6			Higher than 5				

(*Source*: Christiansen, 1973)

12.4 PLUGGING FACTORS

The micro-irrigation system (drip and micro-sprinkler) is used in greenhouse for supplying irrigation to the planted crops. This irrigation system is totally pipeline based along with water emitting device called dripper/emitter. The water quality plays significant role on service life and water distribution performance of the system. In poor water quality condition, either it is chemically or physically the system gets badly affected. If water contains the chemicals beyond undesirable limit the pipeline gets affected by salt deposition or chocking of emitters to emit the water. Similarly, if water contains fine soil particles, the emitters are also likely to get block with the soil particles. This leads to deliver a poor performance of drip irrigation system.

In general, the water quality concern to micro-irrigation system refers to such water which could be regularly used for irrigating most of the crops without any harmful effect or problem on the crop and system, both. In poor water quality condition, the drip system is likely to get affected by the problem called "Plugging", which denotes the problem of system choking due to deposition of chemical residues and blocking of emitters either due to chemical contents in the form of deposits of precipitates or entry of fine soil particles in the micro-holes of emitters. On this ground, therefore, the analysis of water for its quality evaluation becomes most essential. And it is also suggested that, if water quality is not favourable or good then there should not be compulsion to use such water for irrigation.

The development of plugging effect in drip system is because of physical, chemical and biological factors. Accordingly, plugging factors are grouped as under:

(i) Chemical plugging factors,
(ii) Physical plugging factors, and
(iii) Biological plugging factors.

Micro-irrigation system gets badly affected because of these plugging factors acting over. In this condition the system may become incapable to discharge the water at rated capacity.

Chemical plugging factors: This is due to dissolved chemicals in water. This type of plugging factor becomes effective during water flow through pipeline system; and also while passing through the emitting unit. In the course of water flow, the dissolved chemicals get crystallized and settle in the pipeline. This leads into formation of plugging effect in pipeline system. Basically, the deposits of Calcium, Iron and Manganese are the main plugging agents. However, sometimes, the fertilizers and additives based deposits are also causative for chemical plugging. The dissolved chemicals (fertilizer content) and additives in water are crystalized and settled in the pipeline and create clogging problem, there. This form of clogging can be treated by modifying the water pH, oxidization process, removing chemical deposits and also by selecting suitable fertilizers for fertigation. Table 12.4 illustrates the parameters causing chemical pugging, their upper threshold value and treatments, followed.

Table 12.4 List of parameters causing chemical pugging, their upper threshold value and treatments

S. No.	Plugging parameters	Upper limit of threshold value	Treatment	Remark
1.	Calcium	300 mg/lit*	(i) Softening (ii) pH rectification	It depends on pH
2.	Iron	0.2 mg/lit	(i) Oxidization (ii) Iron removal	It depends on pH and oxidization level
3.	Manganese	0.1 mg/lit	(i) Oxidization (ii) Manganese removal	It depends on PH and oxidization level
4.	Sulphide	0.1 mg/lit	(i) Oxidization (ii) Disinfection	It depends on disinfection
5.	Dissolved Oxygen	0.5 mg/lit (Lower threshold)	Treatment at: (i) Water source (ii) Pumping point	Depends on organic materials and time span in pipe.
6.	pH	5< pH < 9** (Recommended)	(i) pH rectification	
7.	Phosphorus	10 mg/lit	Treatment at (i) Water source. (Fertilizers or sewage)	It depends on pH and concentration of Calcium

* Each water source is assessed individually owing to a strong association to pH, alkalinity and temperature factors.

** pH value less than 5 does not cause plugging, but is liable to cause corrosion problem in pipeline system.

Physical plugging factors: This is considered as the potential plugging problem in water flow pipeline system. It is because of deposition of suspended solids existing in the water flow through pipeline. The suspended solids may be in the nature of organic or non-organic depending on water source. In which the sand particles, mud, silt or clay are the non-organic solids, are very common to cause physical plugging of pipeline system. These materials are mainly found in canal water used for irrigation through drip system. Apart from above causes of physical plugging, the corroded water is also being effective for this kind of plugging. The corroded materials get deposit in pipeline and clog that. The living entities such as algae, etc. are the organic materials cause physical plugging effect. These materials are basically sucked in pipeline; and thus result into blockage effect in pipeline. Table 12.5 shows the parameters causing physical pugging, their upper threshold limits and treatments followed for removal, as well.

Table 12.5 Physical plugging factors, their threshold value and treatments, followed

S. No.	Plugging parameters	Threshold value (upper limit)	Treatment
1.	Particle diameter	150 microns	(i) Filtering
2.	Suspended solids	30 mg/lit	(i) Pumping, (ii) Sedimentation (iii) Filtering

(Contd.)

S. No.	Plugging parameters	Threshold value (upper limit)	Treatment
3.	Sand	> 2 mg/lit	(i) Pumping (ii) Sedimentation (iii) Filtering
4.	Silt	30 mg/lit	(i) Pumping (ii) Sedimentation (iii) Filtering
5.	Clay	30 mg/lit	(i) Sedimentation (ii) Filtering
6.	Algae Chlorophyll.	0.1 mg/lit	(i) pH rectification (ii) Oxidization level

Biological plugging factors: In drip system this form of plugging effect gets develop because of following reasons:

(a) Bacterial growth forming slims like coating in the pipes and accessories.
(b) Colonial protozoa, fungi, sponge, snails and shells create biological plugging effects in pipeline system.
(c) Entities adopting the irrigation system and accessories for their breeding purposes.
(d) Intrusion of roots in drippers.

The responsible biological parameters, their upper threshold values and treatment followed are narrated in Table 12.6.

Table 12.6 List of biological parameters, their upper threshold values, source and treatments followed

S. No.	Plugging parameters	Threshold value (upper limit)	Source	Treatment
1.	Heterotrophic Bacteria	♦ As little as possible. ♦ Check the possibility of development	(i) Organic material (ii) Sewage	(i) Treatment at water source level (ii) Doing purification
2.	Sulphuric Bacteria	♦ Check the possibility of development	(i) Sulphide presence	(i) By removing sulphide (ii) Doing purification
3.	Ferric & Manganese Bacteria	♦ Check the possibility of development	Presence of reduced (i) Iron and (ii) Manganese	(i) Removing Iron and Manganese (ii) Doing purification
4.	Colonial Protozoa	♦ Check the possibility of development	(i) Organic material (ii) Flow velocity	(i) Doing regular purification
5.	Snails and Shells	♦ Check the possibility of development		(i) Light filtering at water source level (ii) Extermination by copper sulphide

(Contd.)

S. No.	Plugging parameters	Threshold value (upper limit)	Source	Treatment
6.	BOD effluent	60 mg/lit	(i) Irrigation by sewage	(i) By sewage treatment (ii) By filtering (iii) By chlorination
7.	Roots in sub-surface drip irrigation	♦ Check the possibility of development	(i) By replacing suitable type of dripper. (ii) By avoiding root intrusion	(i) By routine irrigation (ii) By Treflan treatment

12.5 WATER QUALITY—SPRINKLER AND DRIP SYSTEMS

In deciding water quality suitable for drip or micro-irrigation system the plugging effect is considered as one of the main factors, because this is liable to affect the whole irrigation system regarding deliverance of water uniformly. The common plugging factors likely to be occurred in drip or micro-irrigation system have been described above. Besides plugging factors, the water quality is also assessed in terms of its suitability to the grown crop inside greenhouse. Overall, the most suitable way to decide the required quality of water for irrigation is done on the basis of plugging factors, so that the system may not get clog by any way. However, the sensitivity or resistance level of drippers to plugging effect is not being same but varies with the cross-section and length of water passage, flow rate and mode of water emission, as well. About these effects the sprinklers are being more resistant as compared to the drippers/emitters. The high discharge capacity drippers are being more resistant than the lower capacity drippers. Considering various factors, the water quality suitable to sprinkler and drip systems is divided into three classes, namely (i) Good water quality; (ii) Medium water quality; and (iii) Poor water quality, are presented as under:

12.5.1 Good Water Quality

In good water quality all the plugging parameters are found in low level. The values of different parameters defining good water quality are presented in Table 12.7.

Table 12.7 Range of different parameters defining good water quality for drip and sprinkler systems

S. No.	Parameter	Value	Treatment
1.	Suspended solids (mg/lit)	<20	♦ Pumping ♦ Sedimentation and ♦ Filtering
2.	Sand (mg/lit)	<1	♦ Pumping ♦ Sedimentation ♦ Filtering
3.	Silt and Clay (mg/lit)	<20	♦ Pumping ♦ Sedimentation ♦ Filtering

(Contd.)

S. No.	Parameter	Value	Treatment
4.	Calcium conc. (as $CaCO_3$) (mg/lit)	<50	♦ Softening ♦ pH rectification
5.	Iron (mg/lit)	<0.1	♦ Oxidization ♦ Iron removal
6.	Manganese (mg/lit)	<0.02	♦ Oxidization ♦ Manganese removal
7.	Sulphide (mg/lit)	<0.01	♦ Oxidization ♦ Purification
8.	Algae (Chlorophyll a) (mg/l)	<0.3	♦ Treatment at water source ♦ Filtering ♦ Chlorination
9.	Plankton: Caldocera Copepod Rotifer	 <2 <5 <50	♦ Treatment at water source ♦ Filtering
10.	Dissolved oxygen (mg/l) (Does not lead directly to plugging of drippers)	<0.5	♦ Treatment at water source ♦ Pumping point
11.	pH	<7.5	♦ pH rectification
12.	Phosphorus (mg/l)	<1	♦ Treatment at water source
13.	Hetrotropic bacteria (bacterial slime)	0	♦ Treatment at water source ♦ Purification
14.	Sulphuric bacteria	0	♦ Sulphide removal ♦ Purification
15.	Iron and Manganese bacteria	0	♦ Iron and manganese removal ♦ Purification
16.	Colonial Protozoa	0	♦ Regular purification
17.	Briozoa	0	♦ Purification and filtering
8.	Snails and shells	0	♦ Check development
19.	BOD sewage (mg/l)	<10	♦ Sewage treatment ♦ Filtering ♦ Chlorination

12.5.2 Medium Water Quality

In medium water quality, the values of majority of the plugging parameters are in medium range, i.e., little more than the good water quality. The range of parameters designating medium water quality is illustrated in Table 12.8.

Table 12.8 Values of parameters defining medium water quality for drip and sprinkler systems

S. No.	Parameter	Value	Treatment
1.	Suspended solids (mg/lit)	20–60	♦ Pumping ♦ Sedimentation ♦ Filtering

(*Contd.*)

S. No.	Parameter	Value	Treatment
2.	Sand (mg/lit)	1–5	♦ Pumping ♦ Sedimentation ♦ Filtering
3.	Silt & Clay (mg/lit)	20–60	♦ Pumping ♦ Sedimentation ♦ Filtering
4.	Calcium conc. (as $CaCO_3$) (mg/lit)	50–300	♦ Softening ♦ pH rectification
5.	Iron (mg/lit)	0.1–0.5	♦ Oxidization ♦ Iron removal
6.	Manganese (mg/lit)	0.02–0.3	♦ Oxidization ♦ Manganese removal
7.	Sulphide (mg/lit)	0.01–0.2	♦ Oxidization ♦ Purification
8.	Algae (Chlorophyll a) (mg/lit)	0.3–0.8	♦ Treatment at water source. ♦ Filtering ♦ Chlorination
9.	Plankton: Caldocera Copepod Rotifer	 2–20 5–50 50–200	♦ Treatment at water source ♦ Filtering
10.	Dissolved oxygen (mg/l) (Does not lead directly to plugging of drippers)	0.1–0.5	♦ Treatment at water source. ♦ Pumping point
11.	pH	7.5–8.5	♦ pH rectification
12.	Phosphorus (mg/lit)	1–10	♦ Treatment at water source.
13.	Hetrotropic bacteria (bacterial slime)	Presence	♦ Treatment at water source. ♦ Purification
14.	Sulphuric bacteria	Presence	♦ Sulphide removal ♦ Purification
15.	Iron & Manganese bacteria	Presence	♦ Iron and manganese removal ♦ Purification
16.	Colonial Protozoa	Presence	♦ Regular purification
17.	Briozoa	Presence	♦ Purification and filtering
8.	Snails and shells	Presence	♦ Check development
19.	BOD sewage (mg/lit)	10–50	♦ Sewage treatment, ♦ Filtering ♦ Chlorination

12.5.3 Poor Water Quality

In poor water quality one or more parameters are in very high range, while some are in medium range. The values of different parameters defining poor quality water is presented in Table 12.9.

Table 12.9 Values of parameters defining poor water quality for drip and sprinkler systems

S. No.	Parameter	Value	Treatment
1.	Suspended solids (mg/lit)	>60	♦ Pumping ♦ Sedimentation ♦ Filtering
2.	Sand (mg/lit)	>5	♦ Pumping ♦ Sedimentation ♦ Filtering
3.	Silt and Clay (mg/lit)	>60	♦ Pumping ♦ Sedimentation ♦ Filtering
4.	Calcium conc. ($CaCO_3$) (mg/lit)	>300	♦ Softening ♦ pH rectification
5.	Iron (mg/lit)	>0.5	♦ Oxidization ♦ Iron removal
6.	Manganese (mg/lit)	>0.3	♦ Oxidization ♦ Manganese removal
7.	Sulphide (mg/lit)	>0.2	♦ Oxidization ♦ Purification
8.	Algae (Chlorophyll a) (mg/lit)	>0.8	♦ Treatment at water source. ♦ Filtering ♦ Chlorination
9.	Plankton: Caldocera Copepod Rotifer	 >20 >50 >200	♦ Treatment at water source ♦ Filtering
10.	Dissolved oxygen (mg/lit) (Does not lead directly to plugging of drippers)	>0.5	♦ Treatment at water source ♦ Pumping point
11.	pH	>8.5	♦ pH rectification
12.	Phosphorus (mg/lit)	>10	♦ Treatment at water source
13.	Hetrotropic bacteria (bacterial slime)	Growth	♦ Treatment at water source ♦ Purification
14.	Sulphuric bacteria	Growth	♦ Sulphide removal ♦ Purification
15.	Iron and Manganese bacteria	Growth	♦ Iron & manganese removal ♦ Purification
16.	Colonial Protozoa	Growth	♦ Regular purification
17.	Briozoa	Growth	♦ Purification & filtering
18.	Snails and shells	Growth	♦ Check development
19.	BOD sewage (mg/lit)	>50	♦ Sewage treatment ♦ Filtering ♦ Chlorination

12.6 WATER QUALITY ISSUES RELATED TO DRIP SYSTEM

The drip system for irrigating greenhouse crops is very sensitive to water quality, either it is in terms of physical, chemical or biological clogging. This is because of the reason that the irrigation water passes through pipeline system and finally gets deliver through drippers in the form of drop near plant stem in root zone area. A poor water quality always keeps the pipeline and water emitting device on risk about their blockage due to deposition of soil particles, entry of soil particles in drippers' aperture and intrusion of roots in the same. Similarly, the deposition of chemical deposits or precipitates in the pipeline and drippers also make the system inefficient to deliver the water at rated capacity. In addition, the biological factors such as bacterial growth, snails, etc. are also causative to affect the performance of drip by resisting the flow through pipeline system. In nutshell, the water quality based some of the important issues are narrated as under:

- Negative effect of improper quality water on performance of drip system because of emitter's/sprinkler's plugging.
- Existing of inorganic solids such as silts and sands in irrigation water, undesirable to drip system.
- Organic solids like algae, bacteria, slime existing in irrigation water, causing system failure to deliver the water in terms of irrigation.
- Dissolved chemicals such as calcium, iron, manganese, etc. in water to be used for irrigation through drip system, create negative impact on greenhouse irrigation.
- Testing of water quality before placing for use.
- Compulsion on use of existing water of any quality. In this condition, water needs proper treatment to make it fit for use.
- Problem of root intrusion in drippers (inline). This problem needs special attention to prevent.
- Use of technology for solving water quality based problems.
- Requirement of high quality water for trouble free operation and better performance of drip system.
- Requirement of adequate filtering of surface water containing mosses, fish, snails, seeds and other organic contents to prevent plugging effect.
- Groundwater containing high level of minerals cause dripper chocking, needs care about its use through drip system.
- Groundwater extracted from the depth less than 100 feet often produce plugging effect because of bacterial growth, requires its use with great care.

A general guideline on water quality in context to plugging potential in micro-irrigation system, and crop irrigation and toxicity points of view for greenhouse use are presented in Tables 12.10 and 12.11, respectively. These can be followed for deciding suitable water for irrigating greenhouse crops.

Table 12.10 Water quality related to plugging potential in micro-irrigation system

S. No.	Water quality parameters	Concentration level		
		Low	Moderate	High
		Plugging Potential		
1.	pH	< 7.0	7–8	> 8.0
2.	Iron (mg/lit)	< 0.2	0.2–1.5	> 1.5
3.	Manganese (mg/lit)	< 0.1	0.1–1.5	> 1.5
4.	Hydrogen sulphide (mg/lit)	< 0.2	0.2–2.0	> 2.0

(Contd.)

S. No.	Water quality parameters	Concentration level		
		Low	Moderate	High
5.	Total dissolved solids (TDS) (mg/lit)	< 500	500–2000	> 2000
6.	Suspended solids (mg/lit)	< 50	50–100	> 100
7.	Bacteria Count (Numbers/ml)	< 10,000	10,000–50,000	> 50,000

Table 12.11 Water quality related to crop irrigation and toxicity context

S. No.	Water quality parameters	Concentration level		
		Low	Moderate	High
		Irrigation (crop use)		
1.	EC (mmhos/cm)	< 0.75	0.75–3.0	> 3.0
2.	Nitrate (mg/lit)	< 5	5–30	> 30
		Toxicity effect (special ions)		
2.	Boron-mg/lit	< 0.7	0.7–3.0	> 3.0
3.	Chloride-meq/lit	< 4	4–10	> 10.0
4.	Chloride-mg/lit	< 142	142–355	> 355
5.	Sodium (Adj SAR)	< 3.0	3–9	> 9

(*Source*: https://edis.ifas.ufl.edu/publication/AE032)

PRACTICE QUESTIONS

Descriptive Type Questions

1. Define water quality and write its importance in greenhouse farming system.
2. Describe different parameters deciding water quality.
3. What do you mean by plugging factor; and also write causes of plugging problems in drip system?
4. Classify plugging factors; and describe each in detail.
5. Describe chemical plugging problem in drip/sprinkler system. Also, narrate the limits of different parameters.
6. Describe physical and biological plugging problems in drip system; and also narrate the limits of associated parameters.
7. Narrate water quality suitable to drip system.
8. Write water quality issues related to drip system.
9. Write treatments/measures followed for removing plugging effects from drip system.
10. Write water quality suitable to greenhouse crops.

Multiple Choice Type Questions

1. Water with its pH less than 7 is defined as

   (a) Acidic (b) Sodic

   (c) Alkaline (d) Suitable for irrigation, only

2. Water with its pH more than 7 is defined as
   (a) Acidic (b) Sodic
   (c) Alkaline (d) Suitable for use
3. The concentration of Calcium and Magnesium ions in the form of Carbonates represents
   (a) Water hardness (b) Biological plugging
   (c) Physical plugging (d) All above
4. In drip system the chemical plugging is due to
   (a) Calcium deposits (b) Dissolved chemicals in water
   (c) Root intrusion (d) Bacterial slims
5. The upper limit of Calcium concentration in water causing chemical plugging in pipelines is
   (a) 300 mg/lit (b) 0.2 mg/lit
   (c) 150 mg/lit (d) 100 mg/lit
6. The upper limit of Iron concentration in water causing chemical plugging in pipelines is
   (a) 0.2 mg/lit (b) 2.0 mg/lit
   (c) 1.5 mg/lit (d) 15 mg/lit
7. The threshold limit of Manganese concentration in water causing chemical plugging in pipelines is
   (a) 0.10 mg/lit (b) 12 mg/lit
   (c) 2.5 mg/lit (d) 15 mg/lit
8. The threshold limit of BOD effluent in water causing biological blockage in pipelines is
   (a) 0.10 mg/lit (b) 12 mg/lit
   (c) 60 mg/lit (d) 15 mg/lit
9. The upper limit of particle size causing physical blockage in drip pipeline is
   (a) 100 micron (b) 150 micron
   (c) 250 micron (d) 200 micron
10. The upper limit of suspended solids concentration in water causing physical plugging in drip pipeline is
    (a) 100 micron (b) 150 micron
    (c) 250 micron (d) 200 micron
11. Threshold limit of size of sand particles in water causing physical plugging is
    (a) > 2 mg/l (b) > 10 mg/l
    (c) > 20 mg/l (d) > 35 mg/l
12. Threshold limit of concentration of clay particles in water causing physical plugging is
    (a) 30 mg/lit (b) 50 mg/lit
    (c) 15 mg/lit (d) 5 mg/lit

13. Threshold limit of concentration of silt particles in water causing physical plugging is

(a) 30 mg/lit (b) 50 mg/lit
(c) 15 mg/lit (d) 5 mg/lit

14. The upper limit of concentration of Algae Chlorophyll a in water causing physical plugging in drip pipeline is

(a) 0.1 mg/lit (b) 50 mg/lit
(c) 15 mg/lit (d) 5 mg/lit

15. In good quality water for drip/sprinkler system the concentration of suspended solid is about

(a) 0.1 mg/lit (b) <20 mg/lit
(c) 15 mg/lit (d) 5 mg/lit

16. In good quality water for drip/sprinkler system the concentration of silt & clay is about

(a) 0.1 mg/lit (b) <20 mg/lit
(c) >20 mg/lit (d) 5 mg/lit

17. In good quality water for drip/sprinkler system the concentration of Manganese is about

(a) <0.02 mg/lit (b) <20 mg/lit
(c) >20 mg/lit (d) 5 mg/lit

18. In medium quality water for drip/sprinkler system the concentration of suspended solid is about

(a) 20 to 60 mg/lit (b) 120 mg/lit
(c) 20 mg/lit (d) 105 mg/lit

19. In poor quality water for drip/sprinkler system the concentration of sand particle is

(a) 20 to 60 mg/lit (b) >5 mg/lit
(c) 20 mg/lit (d) 105 mg/lit

20. In poor quality water for drip/sprinkler system the concentration of silt and clay is about

(a) 20 to 60 mg/lit (b) >60 mg/lit
(c) 20 mg/lit (d) 105 mg/lit

Answers

1. a **2.** c **3.** a **4.** b **5.** a **6.** a **7.** a **8.** c **9.** b **10.** b
11. a **12.** a **13.** a **14.** a **15.** b **16.** c **17.** a **18.** a **19.** b **20.** b

BIBLIOGRAPHY

Christiansen J.E. (1973). Effect of Agricultural Use on Water Quality for Downstream Use for Irrigation. *Environmental Science.*

Fereres, Elias. (1981). Drip Irrigation Management. Leaflet 21259. Division of Agriculture, University of California.

Ford, H.W. and D.P.H. Tucker. (1975). Blockage of Drip Irrigation Filters and Emitters by Iron-Sulphur- Bacterial Products. *Hort Science* 10 (1): 62–64.

Ford, H.W. (1979b). The Use of Chlorine in Low Pressure Systems Where Bacterial Slimes are a Problem. *Fruit Crops Mimeo Report FC* 79–5. Gainesville: University of Florida Institute of Food and Agricultural Sciences.

Ford, H.W. (1977). Controlling Certain Types of Slime Clogging in Drip/Trickle Irrigation Systems. *Proceedings of the 7th International Agricultural Plastics Congress*, San Diego, California.

Goldammer T. (2019). Greenhouse Management: A Guide to Operations and Technology. Apex Publishers, USA.

Haman, D.Z., A G. Smajstrla, and F.S. Zazueta (1987c). Water Quality Problems Affecting Micro-irrigation in Florida. *Agricultural Engineering Extension Report* 87–2. Gainesville: University of Florida Institute of Food and Agricultural Sciences.

Nakayama, F.S. and D.A. Bucks (1986). Trickle Irrigation for Crop Production. Elsevier Science Publishers. Amsterdam, Netherlands.

Pitts, D.J., J.A. Ferguson, and J.T. Gilmour. (1985). Plugging Characteristics of Drip-Irrigation Emitters Using Backwash from a Water-Treatment Plant. *Bulletin* 880, Arkansas Agricultural Experiment Station, University of Arkansas, Fayetteville.

Pitts, D.J. and P.L. Tacker. (1986). Trickle Irrigation: Causes and Prevention of Emitter Plugging. MP 271, Cooperative Extension Service, University of Arkansas.

https://edis.ifas.ufl.edu/publication/AE032)

http://ecoursesonline.iasri.res.in/mod/page/view.php?id=1530

https://extension.colostate.edu/topic-areas/agriculture/irrigation-water-quality-criteria-0-506/

Greenhouse – Insect Pests and Disease Management

CHAPTER 13

Greenhouse cultivation is an advanced crop farming technique over traditional technologies. A greenhouse serves the purpose of multi-layered cropping system and off-season cropping, simultaneously providing a kind of protection to them against adverse environmental conditions, and diseases and pests, as well. The adverse environmental conditions may be because of extreme temperature, intense precipitation or disease incidence. Greenhouse comprises a fixed land area covered with protected layer of U.V. Polyethylene film. The greenhouse super structure may be erected using metal/steel or non-metallic materials. The U.V. polyethylene film is placed over the super structure and is rigidly fixed. Greenhouse also consists of inlet and exit points to facilitate requisite operations, smoothly. In nutshell, the whole structure resembles a well-defined shape of house, called polyhouse. Since, inside polyhouse there creates greenhouse effect; therefore, it is also called greenhouse. Greenhouse environment comprises a special type of climate, which is quite different over outside, called micro-climate. The temperature, humidity, solar radiation and the other parameters forming micro-climate are in controlled form (controlled greenhouse) by means of automation system. Overall, the humidity and temperature inside greenhouse is always greater than the outside because of grown crops and their watering.

In uncontrolled condition the relative humidity and temperature create a favourable situation for development of disease problem to the grown crops. As per reported data, there is great loss of the crop due incidence of insects/pests and diseases in absence of control measures against them in greenhouse cultivation system. And also there is huge expenditure of money for application of chemicals to control that. For example, in southern Spain the average cost of pesticide application in vegetable crops under greenhouse environment is reported to the tune of USS 0.14 m^2 (Cabello and Cañero, 1994).

In this chapter the details about greenhouse insects/pests, management strategies, greenhouse crop diseases, and their symptoms, commonly used insecticides/pesticides applications methods, etc. are presented in forthcoming heads.

13.1 GREENHOUSE INSECT PESTS

Greenhouse environment is quite different over outside because of variations in climatic parameters such as humidity, temperature and others. Normally, the temperature, humidity and other weather variables are in greater extent inside greenhouse because of the formation of greenhouse effect and retaining evaporated moistures within the greenhouse zone. This leads to cause growth of pest population at accelerated rate. In order to prevent or control the pest borne problems, the detection and diagnosis of insect pest presence at early stage becomes very essential to follow the control measures against them; and accordingly, to save the crop losses likely to be, there. In greenhouse the most common insect pests likely to attack the crop are shown in Table 13.1, below:

Table 13.1 List of common insect pests in greenhouse crops

S. No.	Pests	S. No.	Pest
1.	Aphids	7.	Caterpillars
2.	Fungus Gnats	8.	Leafminers
3.	Shore Flies	9.	Mites
4.	Bloodworms	10.	Slugs
5.	Thrips	11.	Snails
6.	Whiteflies		

These are described as under:

Aphids: These are small, sluggish and soft body insects. They have a pair of cornicles or tube, resembling exhaust pipe on their abdomen. They cluster in colonies on the plant leaves and also on the stems. Normally, Aphids are found on or under the youngest leaves. Growth rate of Alphid is very fast. In greenhouse environment a female aphid of 7- days age becomes fully able to give birth. An adult alphid can give the births ranging from 6 to 10 young per day over life span. The life span of Aphid varies from 20 to 30 days. In this way, within a short time period they generate a huge population.

Aphids insert their beaks into the leaf or stem and extract the sap from there. The sucked sap passes through their body, which gets drop on the leaf surface called "honeydew". The ants existing on the tree eat the honey dew. The ants are also a very dominating part in infestation due to aphid and problems borne, thereby. The honeydew also develops black sooty mold on the leaves. Apart from above problems, these are also causative to transmit a serious viral disease. The aphid-borne infestations can be checked by applying insecticides, which should be done, repeatedly 2 to 3 times at 3 to 7 days' interval. However, its application numbers and interval are decided on the basis of severity of the infestation. Sometimes, they are also appeared tan or off-colour in comparison to other aphids, called "mummies". These are basically parasitized aphids, cut a round hole in the upper portion of abdomen of dead aphid. The other features about aphids are mentioned below:

- These are found in varieties of colors may be green to brown, red, black or purple, too. Even in the same colony some species have different colors.
- More than 20 aphid's species infest the greenhouse crops.
- Most of the aphids have soft exoskeleton. However, some of the species also produce waxy cotton like strands to cover the body surface.
- They have clearcut sucking mouthparts to suck the saps.
- These involve the character of quick reproduction in warm weather.

- Their generation cycle gets completed in the period from 6 to 7 days.
- The female aphids reproduce without matting.
- The young aphid is called nymph.
- Aphids have the tendency to cover their body skin several times.

The view of Aphid is shown in Figure 13.1.

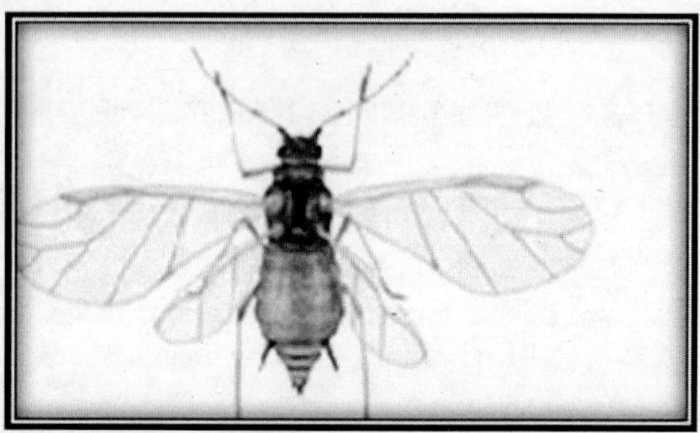

Figure 13.1 Pictorial view of Aphid

Fungus Gnats: These are small about 1/8-inch size like black flies. In appearance they have long legs and antennae, tiny heads and clear wings. Gnats' larvae are legless and have one black colored head. In greenhouse environment a Gnat completes its generation in the period ranging from 20 to 25 days.

Gnats are very much susceptible to increase their population in humid environment. The greenhouse environment contains a high level of humidity and moist growing media with organic materials provides a best place for breeding of Gnats. In addition, the outdoor places such as the accumulated water for several days, etc. is also used as breeding place by them. The larvae of Gnats are serious pests for some of the greenhouse plants. Larvae are scavengers. They feed the decayed organic matters available in the soil. In addition, the root hair is also fed by the larvae of some species. They can also enter the roots and attack the crown or stem part. Their severe attack or infestation may cause the plant wilt. In soils the larvae are found in cluster form. Few important points about Fungus Gnats are narrated as under:

- These are common greenhouse pests.
- These are dark in color and delicate.
- Appearance is just like mosquitoes.
- Wings are light grey to clear.
- These are recognized as the major insect pests in greenhouse.
- In heavy moist conditions these are very effective to cause infestation.

Pictorial view of Fungus Gnats is shown in Figure 13.2.

Shore flies: These are the insects, similar to the Fungus Gnats. Shore flies have heavy dark body with small antennae and red coloured eyes. Wings (2 numbers) have clear spots, throughput. They are easily seen inside greenhouse. In appearance, these resemble just like a winged Aphid. Life cycle is similar to the Fungus Gnats. Larva colour is yellow to brownish. Their length is up to 0.25 inch, and there is no apparent head. Shore flies rarely damage the

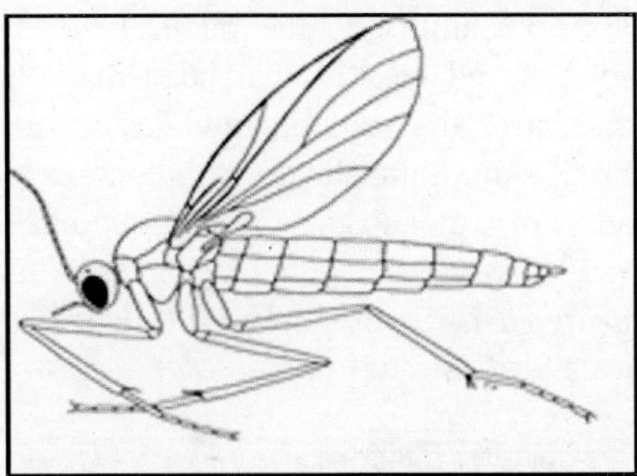

Figure 13.2 View of Fungus Gnat

plant tissues. On the other hand, an adult fly may cause pathogenic effect in greenhouse soil media. Some of the important points about shore flies are mentioned as under:

- These are the nuisance pests in greenhouse.
- These insects thrive in a moist greenhouse environment.
- The larvae are not known to feed on live plant tissues.
- Their life cycle is similar to the Fungus Gnat.
- Larva reaches to its mature length (about 2.5 cm) in 3 to 6 days.

The appearance of Shore flies is shown in Figure 13.3.

Figure 13.3 View of Shore fly

Bloodworms: These are just like striking red worms. Bloodworms are commonly found in stagnant water, watering trough or at any accumulated water place. These generally live in water. Its colour is red, which is because of hemoglobin. Hemoglobin allows them to get develop in the water at very poor oxygen level. Bloodworms are closely related to the mosquitoes. However, an adult bloodworm does not bear mouth parts to suck the blood, i.e., they are not blood feeder. On the other hand, the larvae involve chewing mouth parts to chew the materials. Normally, larvae are dependent for feeding on algae and organic contents lying in the water. They are also found in the plant roots growing through the bottom of the floating trays, but they do not cause serious injury to the plant. Resemblance of larvae includes a long and cylindrical shape, no legs and bear a clear head in brown colour. The best control measure of bloodworms is to remove the standing puddles from the area and also keep the exposure of water surface area to a minimum level. In greenhouse these pests can be checked by avoiding excessive application of water to the growing media. The soils with high level of organic contents and the potted growing media with peat are very attractive places for egg-laying. Spraying *Bacillus thuringiensis* Serotype H-14 (Gnatrol) solution the larvae can be controlled. View of Bloodworms is illustrated in Figure 13.4.

Figure 13.4 View of Bloodworm

Thrips: These are very small in length (about 1/25 inch) slender insects. Thrips are found in different colours, i.e., light brown to black. In resemblance, they have four numbers of wings, fringed with long hairs in rows and flat over the back. For feeding they rasp the plant surface and suck the exuding saps. They infest the flowers, buds and also to the young fruits of the crop/plant. For most of the greenhouse crops thrips are very infective. However, the most susceptible crops are the azalea, calla lily, croton, cyclamen, cucumber, fuchsia, ivy and rose. Some of the thrip's species also transfer or spread the plant diseases. In which, the Western Flower thrips and Onion thrips are the most dominating. In addition, these are also the vectors of tomato spotted wilt virus as well as the impatiens necrotic spot virus, attack to variety of plants. The preventive measures against infestation due to Thrips may be the use of (i) Screens on ventilators; (ii) Inspection of new materials entering the crop environment (greenhouse); and (iii) Controlling weeds. The other important features of thrips are presented below:

- In greenhouse various species of thrips are found. In which the flower thrips (*Frankliniella tritici*), western flower thrips (*Frankliniella occidentalis*), and chilli thrips (*Scirtothrips dorsalis*) are common and problematic, also.
- Color varies from white to straw yellow to brown.
- Life cycle is strongly influenced by the humidity and temperature of the place, concerned.
- In comparison to outdoor environment, they have short generation time in warm greenhouse environment.
- These pests' involve rapid developmental. In fluctuating temperature situation, the time between egg laying to become an adult varies from 7 to 15 days.

- Reproduction rate is quiet high.
- In greenhouse the development of thrips may continue throughout the year, in uninterrupted way, provided suitable crops are there.

Figure 13.5. Presents the view of Thrips.

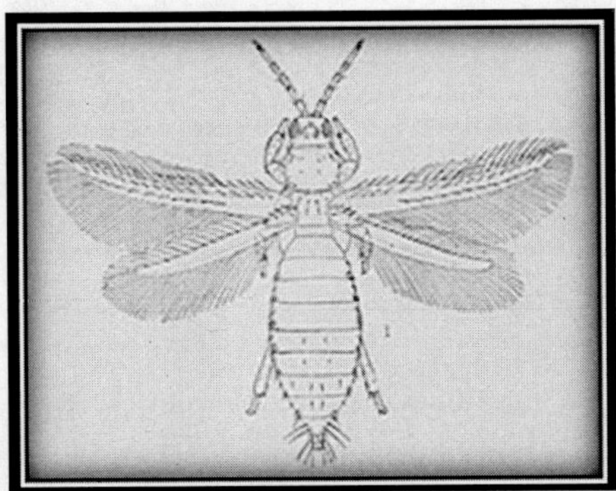

Figure 13.5 View of thrips

Whiteflies: In greenhouse these are the very serious type pests, effective to infest the crops such as fuchsias, poinsettias, cucumbers, lettuce and tomatoes, as well. These are sap sucking insects. Their life cycle is short, may be from 20 to 25 days, depending on greenhouse environment. In appearance, the greenhouse whiteflies and sweet potato whiteflies are being similar to each other, but they differ in context to their biology and control measures to be adopted. The whitefly species get develop at underside of leaves. Egg laying rate of female Whiteflies is about 25 eggs per day. A proper sanitation plays an important role in controlling the whitefly vectors. The other important features are narrated as under:

- These are the most common and difficult insect pests in greenhouses to control.
- These are tiny (smaller than 2mm) and sap-sucking insects.
- Whiteflies mostly infest the vegetables in greenhouse.
- Notable species of whiteflies are sweet potato whitefly or silver leaf whitefly (*Bemisia tabaci*), and the greenhouse whitefly (*Trialeurodes vaporarorium*); and also sometimes, the banded winged whitefly (*Trialeurodes abutilonia*).
- The life stage of whitefly comprises the (i) Adult; (ii) Egg; (iii) Three nymphal instars; and (iv) Instar or pupa stage. All these four stages get complete at underside of the leaves.
- The first nymph stage is also known as crawler stage.
- The pupa which is the final stage, develops a waxy fringe and appears in elevated form on leaf surface.

Figure 13.6. shows the view of Whiteflies.

Caterpillars: These are the immature stages of moths, are also called by different names such as loopers, cutworms, borer and armyworms, as well. The loopers are also named as the cabbage looper, horn worms, and inch worms. The cutworms are the soil pests. In immature larval stage these insects are very damaging. On the other hand, at adult stage either they do

Figure 13.6 View of whitefly

not feed or feed on nectar. They chew the leaves, stems and fruits of many kinds of plants. Infestation gets start when moths enter through ventilators or when infested plants are brought into the greenhouse environment. The adult moths are attracted to enter the greenhouse due to lighting effects; and also to lay the eggs, there. The other features are presented below:

- The cutworms can be serious pests to the younger plants.
- In daytime the cutworms get hide in the soil or below the mulch materials lying on the soil surface. In contrast, at night they feed the plant.
- The cabbage looper can be a pest especially for the lettuce grown in greenhouse.
- Infestation of caterpillars is noticed in the form of cut plants or leaves with appearance of large sections of holes.
- Generalization of caterpillar's life cycle is difficult because they have so many species.
- Some of the species of caterpillar lay the eggs on plants; some lay the eggs in soil media during daytime and come outside at night to feed, while some always stay on the plants.

Pictorial view of caterpillar is shown in Figure 13.7.

Figure 13.7 Pictorial view of caterpillar

Leafminers: These are the larvae of small flies (Figure 13.8). Leafminers are characterized by their black colour with yellow spots on the back. These are found in several species such as serpentine Leafminers in the genus Liriomyza, columbine Leafminers in the genus Phytomyza, and the relatively new daylily leafminer, *Ophiomyia kwansonis*. However, in greenhouse environment the commonly found species to infest the crops are *Liriomyza trifolii*, *American serpentine* leafminer, etc. Leafminers damage the plants by feeding the leaf from its upper and lower surface. The appearance of damaged area is generally in light colour, narrow and winding. The other salient features of Leafminers are narrated as under:

- Larval growth is symptomized by increase in its width. At full growth stage the larva may pupate in the tissues of the leaf; or sometime get emerge from the leaf and fall down over ground surface to pupate.
- Life cycle duration depends on the environmental or media temperature, plant and extent of day length.
- The female fly lays the eggs in the number of 50 to 100. After 2 to 4 days, the eggs start hatching and larvae begin feeding/mining in the tissues of the leaf.

Figure 13.8 View of leafminer insect

Mealybugs: These insects have small length (about 1/8-inch) and body is soft (sluggish) in nature. In appearance, it is just like aphids (Figure 13.9). They feed on the plant sap. Mealybugs are coated with thick layer of mealy or waxy secretions (powder) to provide protection from the contact of insecticides. Some species of Mealybugs are egg laying, while some give direct birth to the live young. These insects often produce a huge amount of honeydew like aphids, which forms a sooty mold on the leaf surface and also on the other parts of plant, too. Sometimes, the ants also use the honeydew as the food; they are closely associated to the mealybug's infestation. This type of insects is causative to infest many of the greenhouse crops. However, they are often seen on crotons, bamboo palms, etc. The significant species infesting the greenhouse crops are the citrus mealybug (*Planococcus citri*) and the long tailed mealybug (*Pseudococcus longispinus*). The other points related to the Mealybugs are presented as under:

- The cluster of mealybugs appears just like a cottony mass.
- These are the serious greenhouse pests as they spread at very fast rate.
- They exist under bud scales and within leaf axils.
- They feed on a wide range of host plants.
- The vegetables such as tomato, cucumber, and eggplant can be the main hosts for mealybugs.

Figure 13.9 Pictorial view of Mealybug

Mites: These are the pests and more closely related to the spider and ticks (Figure 13.10). An adult mite has eight legs; however the eriophyid mites have four legs. Mites do not have

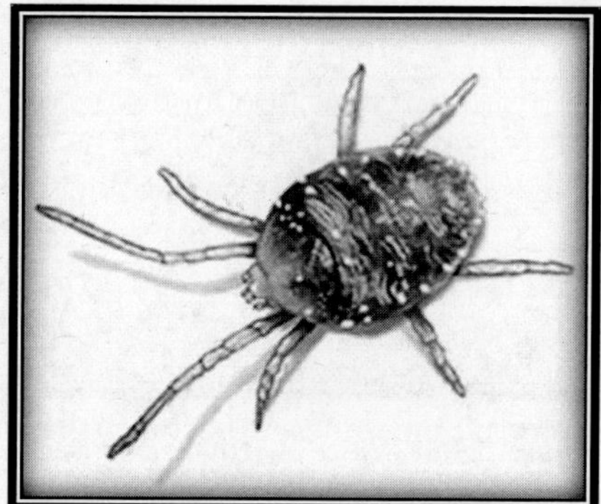

Figure 13.10 Pictorial view of mite

antenna. They suck the sap from the plants. Mites are damaging to a wide range of greenhouse plants. Mites are found in variety of species such as the Broad mite (*Polyphagotarsoeneumus latus*), Carmine spider mite (*Tetranychus cinnabarinus*), Cyclamen mite (*Phytonemus pallidus*), Lewis spider mite (*Eotetranychus lewisi*), and the Two-spotted spider mite (*Tetranychus urticae*). The Two-spotted spider mites and Cyclamen mites can cause serious problem in persistent way. Mites take their feed with mouthparts by piercing the tissues and sucking the contents of the cell. They are mostly lying undersides of the leaves and within tender buds and flowers at depth. These positions of their lying make them difficult to detect and applying measures to control in effective way. The other salient points about mites are narrated as under:

- An environment or place with the temperature ranging from 21 to 27°C along with a low humidity, is most favourable for development of broad mites.
- The female mites (broad) lay the eggs on leaf surface at 8 to 13-day period.
- The larvae hatch in 2 to 3 days; and immediately start feeding.
- Broad mites are expected to complete their life cycle (i.e., from egg to become adult) in about 7 days' period.

- The Cyclamen mites get develop fully in the environment with high relative humidity, i.e., ranging from 80 to 90% and temperature 16°C.
- In greenhouse the species namely Cyclamen and Two-spotted spider mites are typically found during fall and winter months.
- The adult female Cyclamen mites can live up to 1-month and can reproduce without mating.
- Infested plants due to mites may turn yellow and also get dry, besides losing the vigor and die, ultimately.
- The female mites can lay 200 eggs in hot and dry weather situation.
- The flowers such as Marigolds, Crotons, Chrysanthemums, Roses, Impatiens, Parlor palms, Bamboo palms and *Ivy geraniums* are highly susceptible to Two-spotted spider mites.
- The Cyclamen mites can infest the whole plant body, but sometimes they are also concentrated around the buds.
- Infested leaves get distorted; and sometimes they are also curl inward. In addition, the plant foliage also becomes dark in comparison to a healthy leaf.

Scales: These are the insects, commonly found in greenhouses. Scales have different species, but belong to two families, namely (i) Coccidae (soft scales); and (ii) Diaspididae (armored scales). They live below a waxy coating, which protect them against various agents like predators, parasitoids and pesticides, as well. The Coccidae or soft scales secrete a waxy layer on their body which is inseparable. In addition, they also excrete sugary honeydew.

The Diaspididae or armored scales also live beneath a waxy cover, but cover is not on their body. In this way, by removing waxy coating from the plant, the hidden or existing scale can be easily detected. The Armored scales do not produce honeydew. Armored scales are highly damaging pests for greenhouse crops. Sometimes, it becomes difficult to manage this pest from the infested crop, effectively. The other points related to scales are mentioned below:

- These have three-stage life cycle, i.e., egg to nymph and nymph to adult.
- Adult females lay the eggs underneath their protective cover.
- The eggs hatch over a period of 1 to 3 weeks.
- The eggs hatch into the mobile nymphs, called crawlers. The crawlers are active stage that can move between plants.

The pictorial view of scale is shown in Figure 13.11.

Figure 13.11 View of scale

Slugs/Snails: These also infest the greenhouse crops, especially, when greenhouse humidity is very high. In appearance slugs are seen fleshy and slim. They feed mainly at night time. During day hour they prefer the cool and moist places for hiding. They rasp on the leaves, stems, flowers and roots, also. They attack the leaf and make holes. However, sometimes, they also scar the leaf surface. In field, their presence is noticed by a silvery slime trails. Best control measure is to keep the place well sanitized. In addition, the greenhouse must be kept clean from the debris, leaves, bricks, stones, etc. The view of slugs/snails is shown in Figure 13.12.

Figure 13.12 View of slugs/snails

13.2 INSECT AND MITE MANAGEMENT STRATEGIES—GENERAL

The problem of insects and mites is found to be very common in greenhouse environment, which control or management is essential to realize better income from the grown crop, as well as a greater service life of the greenhouse structure (life span), itself. The management of insects and mites in greenhouse farming system is accomplished mainly based on following two main aspects:

(i) Cultural management strategies, and
(ii) Biological management strategies.

In which, the cultural management strategizes suggest to apply the practices solely based on use of non-chemical means, such as sanitation, cleaning, removing weeds from the environment, etc. On the other hand, the chemical management strategies comprise the application of chemicals, i.e., the fungicides, etc. to control the effect of disease from the crops. These are described in detail as under:

13.2.1 Cultural Management Strategies

Most commonly, the arrival or entry of pests in greenhouse environment is due to introduction of new planting materials. It is also through ventilation systems, especially, during summer season when they are kept open to reduce the inside temperature. Amongst pests many of them get survive for a short period, i.e., upto the harvest or plant removal, while some are retained to the period of next crop. In context to check the pest's impacts the cultural practices are being very effective in terms of primary control against their infestations on the plant body. The common points followed to prevent the pest's infestation are narrated as under:

- Thoroughly inspection of new planting materials to be used for plantation as greenhouse crop.
- Maintenance of doors, screens and ventilation system in proper order.
- Keeping the soil surface of greenhouse, very clean.
- Sterilization of soil to be used as growing media.
- Cleaning or sterilizing the common tools, flats and other equipment, to be used.
- Maintaining the outside area of greenhouse clean, so that the possibility of pest's invasion may be checked. The weeds lying outside provide place for their development.
- Removing the standing water located in the periphery of greenhouse, as these places provide space for algal and moss growth. This leads to develop the Fungus Gnat and shore fly based problems, etc. there.
- Disposing unwanted materials like trashes, boards, old debris, etc. from the greenhouse area.
- Allowing the greenhouse to freeze especially in winter season. This is done to destroy or eliminate the tender insects from there. However, this practice is not so easy to accomplish.
- Avoiding excess watering.
- Keeping a good level of ventilation to minimize wetness of the greenhouse area.
- Avoiding to wear the cloths of that colour which is attractive to the insects/pests. Normally, yellow colour is being more attractive for many of the insects/pests.
- Keeping the greenhouse weed free all the times.
- Removing the heavily infested plants from the greenhouse.

13.2.2 Biological Management Strategies

This is carried out by means of natural enemies of insect pests. The list of such agents is placed in Table 13.2. These agents or natural enemies require sufficient time to disperse in the infested area after their release at the site. In this measure the following points are required to follow for better result:

- After detecting the pest incidence or infestation, the natural enemies of suitable type should be released very soon without making further delay.
- In order to have proper monitoring and better effect the study of pest's biology is very important, as it provides guideline for selecting a most suitable agent for application.
- The application of unnecessary insecticides/miticide before and after release of natural enemies should be avoided. However, if it is felt essential then a light treatment may be allowed to the hot spots, only rather entire greenhouse area. However, the selective and short residual pesticides should be preferred. For example to control the caterpillars the application of *Bacillius thuringiensis* (Bt) products may be most suitable to apply, as this is not being so harmful to the natural enemies.

As demerits, few points are mentioned below:

(a) It requires more time to develop its effects on control, as compared to the chemical measures.

(b) Its rate of control is slow.

(c) In case of heavy infestation these are not found fit to eradicate.

Table 13.2 List of natural enemies for control of insect pests

S. No	Name of Pest	Beneficial organism
1.	Whiteflies	(i) Parasitic wasps (ii) *Encarsia formosa*
2.	Scale	(i) Parasitic wasps (ii) *Aphytis melinus*
3.	Serpentine Leafminers,	(i) Leafminer parasite
4.	Angus	(i) *Dacnusca sibiriica*
5.	Gnats	(i) *Diglyphus isaea*
6.	Spider mites	(i) Predatory mites (ii) *Amblyseius* (iii) *Phytoseiulus longipes* (iv) *Phytoseiulus persimilis*
7.	Thrips	(i) Predatory mites (ii) *Amblyseius cucumeris* (iii) *Amblyseius mclenziei*
8.	Soft-bodied insects and eggs	(i) Lady beetles (ii) *Hippodamia convergens* (iii) *Cryptolaemus montrouzeri* (iv) Green lacewings (v) *Chrysoperia carnea*

13.3 MONITORING OF INSECT PESTS

An early detection and diagnosis of infestation due to pests is always beneficial to apply the measures in context to their check or control the problem. Otherwise, at greater time gap the applied measures could become ineffective to eradicate the problem. In this regard, the weekly monitoring or inspection is most desirable, which should be done from all the parts of greenhouse production zone. It is also very important to collect the infected plant samples from all the species of crops grown in greenhouse. The plants located near to the ventilators, doors and fans are given priorities for collecting samples from there. From these locations of greenhouse at least 1% plants are considered for their examination in context to pest's infestation in each monitoring schedule or visit. In addition to plant sampling, the other techniques are also there for monitoring of pest infestation problem in greenhouse such as use of sticky cards of different colors, sticky tapes, etc. These are presented below:

(i) Yellow sticky cards
(ii) Blue sticky cards
(iii) White sticky cards, etc.

The yellow sticky cards attract the winged aphids, leafminer adults, whiteflies, leafhoppers, thrips, etc. besides various flies and insects. The blue cards can also be used in case of thrips. The white colour sticky cards are primarily used to detect the insect infestation. In addition, the white sticky cards can also be used to detect the Fungus Gnat adults, besides detecting the presence of pests like hot spots in greenhouse environment. These cards are suspended vertically above the top of plants in greenhouse. The insects are trapped as they come in contact to these cards. The recommended rate of use of cards varies from 1 to 3 per 1000 sq feet area of the greenhouse for a period of one week. After one week these are changed. In order to control the insect problem, these are used in large numbers to capture the insects in mass from the area. Also, to maintain a better effectiveness the cards or tapes must be in dry condition and the area should also be debris free.

13.4 PEST MANAGEMENT

Broadly, the following methods are followed to manage the pest problems in greenhouse crops:

(i) Cleanliness of production area,
(ii) Use of pest-free planting materials,
(iii) Early detection of pest's incidence,
(iv) Consideration of all management tactics.

Cleanliness of production area: In pest management this is one of the preventive measures, is carried out by maintaining a good level of cleanness in and around greenhouse area. In this context, the greenhouse is fumigated before planting a new crop. The cleanness of production area inside greenhouse is also done by pruning and removing the clippings and other debris materials from the area, in proper way. This causes elimination of places for harboring the pests. In addition, the weeds lying in and around greenhouse structure are also removed to eliminate the host plants (weeds) for pests.

Use of pest-free planting materials: It is well known, that the introduction of infested planting materials for planting, is one of the dominant sources to cause the incidence or damage of the crop due to insect pest based infestations. In the context to control the insect pest borne problems; therefore, the selection and use of pest free plants is very important. For this purpose, those plants, plugs, cuttings or transplants are selected which are completely pest free. All the plants are inspected very carefully, before placing them for plantation in greenhouse. The infested plants are also discarded or sometimes, treated with suitable chemicals. In addition, the remaining planting materials are also quarantined for a certain period.

Early detection of pests: An early detection of pests is very essential and important task in regards to application of suitable measures, either it is preventive or curative to control the pest's infestation in the crop. This job can be accomplished by following means:

(i) Using sticky cards or tapes.
(ii) Conducting regular inspection.
(iii) Using pheromones.

***Using sticky tapes or colored cards*:** These have sticky surface, because of which the pests are trapped. This leads to provide information about the source of infestation. The sticky tapes or colored cards are placed in and around the greenhouse area to detect the movement of whiteflies, thrips, adult leafminer flies, Fungus Gnats, aphids, etc. at the early of the planation. In addition, the sticky tapes and colored cards are also placed in sufficient numbers to trap more number of insect pests or to control the incidence of pest problems, effectively. This measure also provides information about source of incidence, which helps to select a suitable measure or chemical for control of incidence.

***Regular inspection*:** The regular inspection about incidence of pests or any kind of disease is also one of the most effective methods, towards prevention against occurrence of disease in the crop. A regular inspection along with paying attention on the infected leaves or parts of the plant in sincere way, is most desirable. In course of inspection, if any part of plant is found infected, then by beating that particular portion of plant, the small pests are dislodged from there and they are collected on off-white paper. This method is found suitable to detect those pests which are very hard to see, such as the spider mites and thrips. In greenhouse crop this approach is found very effective in detecting the insect pests.

***Pheromones*:** This is another method to detect the incidence of pests at the early days. The Pheromones are the natural chemicals produced by the animals. This natural chemical acts as signal to attract the insect pests. Broadly, the Pheromones are of three basic types, as mentioned below:

(i) Aggregation pheromones
(ii) Sex pheromones
(iii) Trail pheromones
(iv) Synthetic pheromones

Aggregation pheromones: These are being effective to attract many of the insect pests.

Sex pheromones: These are found effective to attract one sex of a species to another sex of species.

Trail pheromones: These Pheromones are released and deposited on the walking path, which provides the way to follow the other insects. This is very common in case of ants.

Synthetic pheromones: These mimic the natural chemicals; and are used to attract the pests to trap and also disrupt the mating.

Consideration of management tactics: Under this head of control aspect, the following considerations are taken into account:

(i) Economic,
(ii) Toxicological-towards worker safety, phytotoxic potential and pesticide residues, and
(iii) Environmental effects of all control options.

Besides above, if there is no alternative to follow except chemicals, then following points must be taken into account,

- Selection of least toxic chemicals.
- Target specific application.
- Priority to the most effective and affordable materials for use.

13.4.1 Control Methods

Broadly, the following methods are very common for controlling insect pest's problems:

(i) Cultural practices
(ii) Physical manipulation
(iii) Mechanical measures
(iv) Biological measures
(v) Chemical measures

Cultural practices: In context to pest management the cultural practices are treated as the first line of defense. In this respect, the following points are taken into consideration to achieve best effects on pest's control:

- The site selection for crop growing must be proper in all aspects.
- The planting materials to be used for planting must be healthy and pest free.
- The fertilizer to be used for application should be in slow releasing nature.
- Rate of water application should also be proper, so that there may not be high level of moisture content in greenhouse environment. A highly moist condition invites the pests for infestation to the crop.
- Control of weeds in and around greenhouse area, because weeds act as host plant for development or growth of pests.

Physical manipulation: It denotes the control of pest problem by manipulating the micro-climate of production area, with the help of light, humidity and temperature, mainly. The light is single parameter, by varying which in terms of its intensity and quantity, a significant control on pest's population along with their damage level could be achieved. The yellow "bug" light around the plant used at night, keeps away the insects such as moths, crickets and June beetles, as well. The other parameters such as temperature and humidity also play significant role in control of insect pests. These two are also manipulated to reduce the level of pest survival. Attempt is always made to maintain the level of temperature and humidity to an optimum range.

Mechanical measures: This includes so many provisions to use for controlling the insect pests' problems, such as use of:

(a) Screens
(b) High pressure water sprays
(c) Trapping of insect pests

***Screens*:** These are directly placed around the area to check the entry of insect pests, inside. Screens are available in various sizes of perforations or screen apertures. The selection of screen with proper aperture size to check the entry of insect pest, is one of the main requirements. In case of greenhouse structures, the placing of screen just in front of fan causes reduction in rate of air flow, which is not desirable. This issue should be taken care during placing of screens in greenhouse structure.

***High pressure water sprays*:** The use of high pressure water sprays is found beneficial regarding dislodging of spider mites and aphids from the host plants, which leads to check the insect pest population.

***Trapping*:** This is also one of the means to check the insect pest infestation in the crop. In this method the insect pests are trapped by using the devices such as light traps, yellow sticky traps, sticky-surfaced pheromone traps and sticky tapes, mainly. These trappers are being sticky in nature from their outer surface, and also have attracting colour to attract the insect pests. This type of measure is being best for monitoring the pest population over certain time duration, besides detecting pest infestation at early. Sometimes, this is also used for determining the impact of other management practices followed for controlling the pest problem. As per research findings, this method provides best result, especially when:

- Same brand of sticky traps are used throughout the crop and monitoring period.
- Trappers are changed at weekly interval, as the level of stickiness of trappers gets reduce due to sunlight, moisture, etc.
- Trappers are used in appropriate numbers per unit area. For example, in greenhouses the recommended rate is 1 trap per 10,000 square feet area. Their placing is done at the interval of at least 150 feet.
- Traps must be placed above the plant canopy in hanging mode.

Biological control measures: In this control measures the natural enemies are used to suppress the pests. The list of such enemies has been shown in Table 13.2. In biological measures the following points are essential to know for proper implementation of control measures.

Importation: It refers to the classical biological control, in which reuniting the pests with their natural enemies is carried out.

Conservation: It denotes the conservation of beneficial biological agents or natural enemies, such as predators, parasites; pathogens and the pests, which are used to control the insect pests. Actually, these biological agents are killed because of application of chemicals. The conservation of natural enemies to the pests can be accomplished by using non-chemical pesticides/control methods.

Augmentation: This advocates the release of natural enemies in a defined quantity at once or over time to suppress the pests in context to control their attack on the crop. However, it depends on environmental conditions and their availability. In this case, it is very important to know that a particular species of natural enemy is being effective for a specific group of pests; for others it is not so or being ineffective. In this way, the other group of pests become uncontrolled by using the natural enemy of a particular class. Accordingly, if any chemical is applied to control them, there is possibility of development of damaging effect on the natural enemy, used. The application of microorganisms in the way as the conventional pesticides, is one of the modes of augmentation. For this purpose, the used product is termed as "microbial insecticides." The product *Bacillus thuringiensis* is one of them is used to control certain caterpillars, beetles and flies. However, it does not affect to arthropods. The microbial insecticides are found most effective, especially at early stages of pest development and also their lesser availability.

Chemicals: The chemicals called pesticide are used for this purpose. As far as definition of pesticide is concerned, any chemical which kills the pests is known as pesticide. Most commonly, pesticides are the chemicals. In general, the pesticides are found in following forms:

(i) Broad spectrum based insecticides
(ii) Target-specific insecticides
(iii) Short-term insecticides vs. residual
(iv) Miticides
(v) Fungicides
    (a) Protectants
    (b) Eradicants
(vi) Nematicides
(vii) Molluscicides

***Broad spectrum insecticides*:** These are found very effective to destroy or kill the varieties of insects. Because of this reason such types of insecticides are commonly used as the killers, especially, when production area is affected by different groups of insects. The *Pyrethroids* and those which contain *Acephate, Chlorpyrifos, Diazinon and Carbaryl* fall in the category of broad spectrum insecticides.

***Target-specific insecticides*:** These are also known as narrow spectrum insecticides. These insecticides are very selective, i.e., suitable for a certain pests or group of pests. In other words, for killing a particular insect the suitable insecticide if there, should be used for application. The Chitin inhibitors and insect growth regulators can be an example for this. The Chitin refers to the primary structural chemical available in the body wall of an insect. The Chitin inhibitors play their role in interfering the plant growth and also for molting the insects (immature) as well. On the other hand, the Insect Growth Regulators (IGRs) mimic the natural juvenile hormone of an insect. The IGR works on the principle of preventing an immature insect to become adult by interfering certain processes associated to their growth. The Kinoprene-containing products fall in this category of IGR. As demerit, these have slow response about development of effect. In general, their effects are noticed in terms of:

(i) Abnormal molting,
(ii) Twisted wings,
(iii) Loss of mating behavior, and
(iv) Sometimes, the death to embryos in eggs, also.

***Short-term insecticide*:** The chemicals known as the insecticides or pesticides are being in the nature of short lasting and long-lasting, both. The short-lasting chemicals/insecticides tend to break down very quickly in the form of non-toxic contents as by-products. These chemicals are found to be the best, especially, when pests are found non-returning, and there is also the possibility of damage of non-target plants due to long-term exposure of chemicals. The active products containing insecticidal soap, pyrethrins or resmethrin fall in the category of short-term residual insecticides.

In contrast, some of the pesticides remain in active form for killing the insect pests for a long period of time called long-term residual insecticides. These are being very effective to control persistent type pest problems. However, they are causative to create environmental problem and health hazards. In long-term residual insecticide's category, the products containing pyrethroids, chlorpyrifos or imidacloprid are the main.

***Miticides*:** In greenhouse the mites which are just like tiny spider, are also found very damaging to the grown crops. These can be effectively controlled by the application of chemicals called Miticides. The Miticides and Insecticides are about to the same. The products containing Avermectins come in the category of Miticides.

***Fungicides*:** These are used to control the fungi causing molds, rots and so many diseases in the plant. More commonly, the fungicides are used as the preventive measures rather curative. Fungicides are directly sprayed on the affected object or portion to kill the Fungus. The following types of fungicides are commonly used, given as:

(i) Protectant type fungicides, and
(ii) Eradicant type fungicides.

In which, the protectant type's fungicides are used to prevent the occurrence of plant diseases, while eradicant types for curing the disease. In detail these two are described below:

Protectant type fungicides: These are used as the protectant chemicals, just like vaccinations in human body as the disease preventing agents. In other words, the protectant fungicides prevent or inhibit the fungal growth. Application of protectants is essential and beneficial, especially when a particular disease or group of disease is expected to occur, year after year. In addition, the protectants are also used as routine precautionary agents in fruits and vegetable crops, too. Depending on activeness of the Fungus, the application of fungicides needs to continue, regularly, to keep the crop in protected mode.

Eradicant type fungicides: These fungicides perform their functions just like penicillin and antibiotics used to cure the diseases in human body. Eradicant type fungicides are quite different in action over the protectant type fungicides. Often, the application of eradicant is suggested in the conditions, when:

(i) Protectants are not available.
(ii) Cost of fungicides is very high or, too expensive.
(iii) Protectant type fungicides are applied very late after occurrence of infestation.
(iv) Disease appears unexpectedly.

Nematicides: In greenhouse the nematodes are also found as one of the important crop loss making agents. In appearance, they are just tiny hair-like worms. Majority of the nematodes live in the soil media and feed on the plant roots. These can be suitably controlled by application of chemicals called Nematicides. In addition, the fumigants are also used in soil media for this purpose. Besides, the nematicides and fumigants, few contact insecticides and fungicides are also used to control such small worms existing in the soil media.

Molluscicides: These are also one of the chemicals used to control the snails and slug's problems in greenhouse crops. These chemicals come in action when they are eaten by the infesting pests. In addition to the Molluscicides, the baits are also used to attract and kill the snails or slugs in production area.

13.5 MANAGEMENT OF GREENHOUSE INSECT PESTS

In order to check or control the damaging effects of different insects/pests on greenhouse crops, their management at field level in proper way, is very essential to achieve better crop yield grown in greenhouse environment. Among various insects and mite pests most of them impose habitual problems, which are very difficult to check/control; and thus they damage the crop/ plant canopies, flowers and the fruits as well to a significant level. Comparatively, a successful management of insects and mites in greenhouse is more tedious to that of the open field. Prior to adopt the management measures regarding insects and mites control, it is very essential to know or perform following points:

(i) Identification of pest.
(ii) Understanding the biology and behavior of pests.
(iii) Knowing about feeding habit of pests.
(iv) Information about entry of pests in greenhouse environment.

(v) Information about pest's reproduces.
(vi) Information about status of crop damage including early damage in life cycle
(vii) Knowhow about clues regarding their presence.

The management strategies for each individual insect/pests is described, below,

Aphids

These damage the crop by removing the plant sap by inserting mouthparts in the phloem. It is in their common habit that they move or shift to another host plant for searching a soft and fresh tissue to get feed. The young terminals or lower surface of leaves are the most favourable parts for feeding. Because of this reason, the aphid fed leaf becomes discolored; and sometimes, there is also distortion in leaf, i.e., leaf curling facing down or upward. Presence of aphids can be detected or monitored by using yellow sticky cards, placed vertically at 4 to 6-inch height above standing crop canopy. For better result the sticky cards are also placed near the doors or other points from where there is possibility of aphid's entry in greenhouse. The sticky cards should be changed at weekly intervals; or when they have become completely covered with the aphids.

Management strategies

This includes following management strategies:

(i) Cultural management strategies
(ii) Physical management strategies
(iii) Biological management strategies
(iv) Chemical management strategies

Cultural management strategies: In this respect the following measures are adopted:

- Keeping proper sanitation in and around the production area.
- Careful inspection of entry of new planting materials for plantation regarding their infestation.
- Strictly avoidance of infested plants or cuttings for plantation.
- Removal of weeds in and around the greenhouse, because these are the host plants for them.
- Discarding old stock of planting materials.
- Removing the baskets and "pet" plants, if these are inside greenhouse.

Physical management strategies: This includes the measures to place the screens on the doors and ventilations of greenhouse, especially during fall and spring seasons. This is done to prevent the entry of aphids inside greenhouse.

Biological management strategies: In this management strategy the predators and parasites are used for controlling the pests. In general, the Aphids are highly attracting to many of the predators and parasitoids. Comparatively, parasitoids are more effective than the predators to reduce the population of aphids. However, in warm weather condition the parasitoids are found ineffective to control the aphids.

The parasites such as *Aphidius ervi*, *Aphidius colemani*, and *Aphelinus abdominalis* can be suitably used for this purpose. In which, the parasite called *Aphidius colemani* is found suitable to control Green peach aphids and Melon aphids but not to the Foxglove or Potato aphids.

In predators the *Aphidoletes aphidimyza* and *Chrysoperla rufilabris* are commercially used for controlling aphids.

***Insecticidal soaps*:** In some cases the insecticidal soaps are also being effective to control the aphid's population. Also, the refined horticultural oils are found fruitful in control of aphid. However, it is always advised to the users that they must go for testing them, before their use; otherwise, on application of the same, if there is no any effect, then there is likely of crop damage and making huge monitory loss of the growers.

***Microbial*:** These are normally found effective when level of infestation is small. In heavy infestations its effects is not so.

Chemical management strategies: More commonly, the systemic or translaminar insecticides are found most effective in control of aphid as compared to the contact insecticides. However, insecticides must be available in sufficient amount at the feeding point/place of aphids. In general, the systemic insecticides are being very effective for control of those aphids which feed on new growths. Similarly, the contact insecticides provide better effect in the condition of thorough spray coverage and their penetration in canopy to a good level.

Caterpillar

Most of the caterpillars damage the crop or plant by eating their parts such as the foliage and the flowers, as well. In worse situation, the entire leaf except mid-vein is consumed in eating. Particularly, the species such as Beet armyworm can destroy the Chrysanthemums by eating their tender buds and shoot tissues. Regular monitoring of production area and scouting of infested plants are the best preventive measures in this regard. In scouting, those plants are seriously checked which are located close to the vents, doors, louvers, and sidewalls as these are the points from where the adults enter the greenhouse.

Management strategies

The management strategies followed to control the caterpillars are described as under:

Cultural management strategies: It includes following measures to achieve the goal:

- Maintaining a good level of sanitation in and around the greenhouse.
- Cleaning the weeds and plant debris from the surroundings because these places act as the host for caterpillars.
- Placing insect proof nets at all such places from where the adults are likely to enter the greenhouse.
- Using clean and healthy planting materials.
- Keeping the greenhouse fully maintained, so that there may not be any hole or cut through which the adults could enter inside.

Biological management strategies: In this management strategy the parasitized eggs are laid in the eggs of caterpillar pests. This leads to generate new wasps (mini-wasp). Life cycle of new wasps is moving very fast ranging from 7 to 10 days' period, i.e., within this period the eggs are converted into adults. Biological strategies follow the following measures to control the caterpillars:

***Microbial*:** The control of caterpillars using microbial is one of the bio-rational management strategies. In this measure the biological control organism such as *Bacillus thuringiensis* is applied, especially, when caterpillars are at young stage. Its effectiveness depends on consumption of ingredients by the caterpillars.

Chemical management strategies: In this management strategy the chemical agents, i.e., insecticides are used to control the caterpillars. In this regard the contact type insecticides are found most effective, while systemic insecticides are not so effective. Contact type insecticides provide better result when all parts of plants are thoroughly covered with applied insecticide. Normally, application is carried out with the help of sprayers of suitable capacity.

Fungus Gnats

In case of Fungus Gnats, the adults are not so damaging. Female gnats lay the eggs, which get hatch into larvae. The larvae damage the plants significantly, by feeding the roots of the plant. In general, the larvae prefer to grow in the growing media containing high level of moisture content; and dependent on fungi as the food source for them. In greenhouse environment, the Fungus Gnat larvae also dependent on a wide range of ornamental plants, grown. The larvae affect more to the young plants or seedlings as compared to the mature plants. In context to its control or management, the monitoring plays significant role, which may be accomplished by using the yellow sticky cards. Since, Fungus Gnats are found on the soil surface; therefore, placing of sticky cards, horizontally, rather vertically, is being more effective. In greenhouse, besides the attack of Fungus Gnats there is also incidence of other pests such as shore flies, etc. which monitoring is also being most essential. On consideration of this fact, it is therefore found better to place the sticky cards not only in horizontal direction but also in combination of horizontal and vertical order, both. This exercise must be done before plantation of seedlings or plantlets.

Management strategies

In control of Fungus Gnats, the management strategy comprises same aspects as in previous case. They are presented below:

Cultural management strategies: In this head of management strategy, the followings measures are suggested to follow:

- Follow up of proper water management in greenhouse crops.
- Proper sanitation in growing media.
- Avoiding excess irrigation and fertilizer application to become as the waste from the production area.
- Making appropriate provision for efficient drainage.
- Keeping greenhouse soil dry as much as possible.

Biological Management Strategies: The parasitoids and predators are used as biological management tools for Fungus Gnats. The predators such as predacious mites (*Hypoaspis miles*), entomopathogenic nematodes (*Steinernema feltiae*), and rove beetle (*Atheta coriaria*), etc. are found most effective to control the Fungus Gnats. However, they must be used before population blast of Fungus Gnat. The details about parasitiods and predators are as follows:

***Parasitoids*:** The *Hypoaspis miles* as one of the most commercially available parasitoids, is used to manage the larval population in greenhouse crops. For better result they must be released at early before blasting of population. Its effect is stretched for the period of 6 to 8 weeks. In favourable condition of greenhouse environment, these predators get spread throughout greenhouse production area. The *H. miles* shows better performance at the temperature between 15 and 30°C.

***Predators*:** The predator named *Atheta coriaria* (rove beetle) is very popular to control the Fungus Gnats. It feeds the eggs and larvae of Fungus Gnat, Shore flies and Thrips pupae. In greenhouse they remain in flying form. The larvae and adults both are dependent on pests for their feed. The temperature ranging from 18 to 27°C and relative humidity from 50 to 85% constitute a good environment for their survival.

Bio-rational management strategies: In this head of management strategy, the microbial, which is the biological insecticide named "*Bacillus thuringiensis*" (var. *Israelensis*) is found most effective. Its application at weekly basis is desirable; and that should be continued till significant reduction in Gnats population.

Chemical management strategies: In greenhouse crops the chemicals called insecticides are commonly used for this purpose. However, in the condition of development of pesticidal resistance the control of Gnats using insecticides becomes difficult. This is because of the reason that most of the insecticides are applied to the growing media as drench, while larvae stage is most damaging to the plant.

Leafminers

Female Leafminers have the characteristics of taking feeds from soft and succulent leaves by piercing the surface. In this action there develops several wounds on leaf surface. The formed wounds are known as "stipples", are appeared as the raised small circular scars. This effect leads to decline the photosynthesis action; and accordingly retardence in plant growth. The monitoring is best option for its control, which could be done by using the yellow sticky cards (traps) for capturing the adult leafminers. The traps are placed horizontally, close to the ground surface, as greater number of leafminers are localized there. The recommended use rate of trap is to the tune of 1 trap per 10000 sq. feet area. The weekly monitoring is found better. In addition to the strip cards, a carful inspection of mined or stippled leaves and taking measures for that, is also being very effective in control of leafminers.

Management strategies

Like others, this is also carried out through adoption of cultural, biological and chemical based acivities, described as under:

Cultural management strategies: Under this management task the following measures are followed:

- Removal of infested plants and cuttings from the production area.
- Careful inspection of new planting materials regarding leaf stipples and active mines. It is also suggested to keep them away for several days for watching about development of mines from the leaf stipples.

Biological management strategies: In this management strategy the parasitic wasps (*Diglyphus isaea and Dacnusa sibirica*) are applied for control of leafminers. These parasitic wasps lay the egg over young leafminer larva and decline their effects. As per research recommendations, the use of parasitic wasp named Diglyphus is found better in summer season, because during summer there is possibility of migration of few more insects/pests in greenhouse from outside, naturally.

Chemical management strategies: The insecticides are used in the form of contact spray to control the leafminers. Spraying should be repeated at 3 to 4 days interval for destroying adult leafminers. The larvae can be effectively killed by using the systemic insecticides.

Mealybugs

Mealybugs feed the leaves and soft parts of the plant through their mouth parts by piercing and sucking actions. This leads to cause the plant stunted and leaves appear in yellow color; and sometimes distorted, also. In addition, Mealybugs also excrete honeydew like Aphids do. The honeydew develops black sooty molds that affects cosmetic properties of the plant, specific. In concern to monitoring of Leafminers, their early detection plays important role. The climbing of ants on the plant is an indication of this problem.

Cultural management strategies: The following measures are followed under this head of management:

- Discarding the heavily infested plants from production area.
- Cleaning of pots, tray's edges and other items existing in the production area.
- Careful inspection of newly introduced planting materials.

Biological management strategies: The parasitic wasps and several predatory beetles are used for this purpose. The wasp attracts the insects and kills them. The parasitic wasp named *Leptomastix dactylopii* is found most efficient to control the Mealybugs (citrus). Also, in the condition of heavy infestations, this parasitic wasp in conjunction with Mealybug destroyer, i.e, *Cryptolaemus montrouzieri* performs very well. However, for other Mealybug species it is not so effective.

Bio-rational management strategies: This is a microbial based management control measure. In this context, the *Beauveria bassiana,* which is a Fungus, is used for the purpose. This Fungus secretes an enzyme, in which the insect's cuticle gets dissolve. After dissolving, that enters the insect's body and produces a toxin there, which leads to decline the immune system of insects. In order to have better result, a thorough spray coverage is essentially done, so that the contact between fungal spores and insect may be created in proper way. Also, as per level of infestation the application should be done repeatedly, several times.

Chemical management strategies: In this management the contact insecticides are applied during crawler stage of the insect, repeatedly, for creating proper contact. Spraying interval varies from 0 to 3 days, depending on residual effectiveness of the insecticide, used. In addition, through spreader-sticker the coverage, penetration and residual activity, can be appreciably enhanced. However, there is high risk of phytotoxicity.

Mites

In greenhouse production area the mites are also found as one of the crop damaging insects. They pierce the plant tissues and remove the fluids with the help of their mouthparts. In addition, some of the Mite's species also inject a toxin element in their saliva at feeding time and develop effect, so. Their damage is more visible on the upper surface of plant's leaf in the form of mottling or speckling. The level of damage varies with the Mite's species and plant's species, both. Sometimes, in the absence of control measures, the Mite (cyclamen) infests the entire plant body and also gets concentrate around the buds. Infested plants/leaves may turn into yellow colour. At severe infestation the plant loses its vigor and also gets dry. Majority of the Mite's species have very wide range of hosts. This results into development of severe effects on many of the greenhouse crops. For example, the Two-spotted spider mites are very common pests, infest many plant species.

The monitoring to assess the presence of mites can be accomplished by conducting inspection of the greenhouse crops/plants, sincerely. In this regard, a more attention is given to the spots like pathway inside greenhouse and the area close to the greenhouse entrance. In addition, those plant species/varieties which are most susceptible to mite's infestation are also kept on attention. Besides above, the places or areas close to the greenhouse which are prone to mite's infestation are also taken at priority for their monitoring.

Management strategies

The suitable management strategies followed in line of Mite's control are narrated as under,

Cultural management measures: In this head of management, the following cultural practices are followed:

- Careful vigilance about infestation of plants, continuously.
- Not allowing to infested planting materials in greenhouse.
- Controlling to grow unwanted vegetation at greenhouse surroundings.
- Removing infested plants from the greenhouse.

In addition, in case of Two-spotted spider mite the following cultural practices are also followed to prevent the problems:

- Careful inspection on new planting materials about infestations in them.
- Removal of weeds in and around greenhouses premises.
- Disposal of old planting materials such as the pet plants, etc. lying at greenhouse. These materials provide space for harboring the insects.
- Avoid overfertigation of nitrogen-based fertilizers because these fertilizers create vigorous vegetative growth, which is highly favourable to such type of mites.

Biological management strategies: Like other insects, in this case also the predatory mites are used to control the problems. In case of controlling Two-spotted spider mites the predators such as *Phytoseiulus persimilis, Galendromus occidentalis, Neoseiulus (Amblyseius) californicus, Amblyseius andersonii, Amblyseius fallacis, and Feltiella acarisug*, etc. are used. However, amongst them the predator named *Phytoseiulus persimilis* is found most effective for two-spotted spider mite's control. These predatory mites are released, immediately at the early of getting the sign of infestation. As compared to the Miticide used for control, the predatory mites take more time to control the infestation. It is also to note that the predators get die without Spider mites. The research evidences advocate that the control of new mites borne infestation requires introduction of new predators.

In addition, the predatory mite called *Phytoseiulus persimilis* is also found effective to control Spider mites; and it can be successfully used in many greenhouse crops. This predator is found year-round active. The *P. persimilis* predatory mites consume the eggs, larvae, nymphs and adults of spider mites, too. Especially, for short-term crops or bedding plants its suitability is highly significant. In order to have better result on control, it is released in the condition of low population of Two-spotted spider mite or when it is detected, initially. In this case, it is also advised that the release of predatory mites should be preferred near to the infested places or localized hot spots. At week interval two treatments can be appropriate.

Chemical management strategies: Residual pesticidal resistance is one of the main problems with miticide application. Although, in current situation, varieties of miticide are available for use, but before using them their resistance testing is more important. For better result, the application of contact type miticide is beneficial, because infestation is at both the sides of leaves.

Scales

In greenhouse the scales also create problem in the grown crop to an appreciable level. At its greater infestation the plant's leaves turn yellow in colour and they also drop down; even they can also stunt the new growth. In line of controlling this problem, an early detection of the problem is most important. It is also advised to the growers that they must have proper training in regards to identification of these pests and their symptoms indicating crop damage, also. As thumb rule, the climbing of ants on the plant is considered as one of the indicators for development of scale's borne problems.

Management strategies

These are narrated as under:

Cultural management strategies: Under this management strategy the following activities are followed:

- Follow up of proper sanitation.
- Cleaning of the greenhouse production area.
- Inspection of plants and cuttings placed inside greenhouse about presence of scales, exoskeletons, tests or honeydew on them.

Biological management strategies: The parasitoids and predators are used as biological control measures for controlling scale borne problems. In parasitoids the *Metaphycus helvolus,* which is a parasitic wasp, is used as preventive measure. In course of action the adult wasps get caught in the honeydew, because of their tiny size. In addition, the adult wasps give one egg inside each scale, which gets converted into a larva. The larvae consume the scale from within; and in a due course of time a new parasitoid is emerged from the scale. Among predators the *Cryptolaemus montrouzieri*, which is predatory ladybird beetle is used for controlling the Scales. These predators hide under the leaves and also in the plant crevices, where the scales are feeding; and create effects.

Bio-rational management strategies: The insecticidal oils and soaps are used for the purpose. These are found more effective to kill the scales by damaging their life stages as compared to many of the contact insecticides. However, they are failing to provide residual control. In addition, there is also the problem regarding their full coverage. Apart from above, the insect growth regulators (IGR) are also used for controlling scales. In action the IGRs plays significant role in disrupting their development, i.e., preventing eggs and nymphs. In this regard the *Buprofezin* and *Pyriproxyfen* are commonly used IGRs.

Chemical management strategies: The contact insecticides are used for the purpose. Its application at crawler stage is found more effective. In addition, repeatedly application is also being essential to cover the critical or susceptible stages as and when they appeared. However, depending on residual effectiveness of already applied insecticides, the spraying of contact insecticides may be done at the interval ranging from 0 to 3 weeks. The use of spreader-sticker can further improve the coverage, penetration, and residual effectiveness, as well, but there is possibility of development of heavy phytotoxicity.

Shore Flies

The Shore flies cause *fly specks,* which might be due to excrement left on the foliage of seedlings/cuttings and the mature plants. The adult flies are implicated in spreading the Fungus spores. They can be monitored with the help of yellow sticky cards. The sticky cards should be placed in vertical position for better result. In propagation area its monitoring on weekly basis is recommended to be the best. Monitoring should be done by inspecting the plants and soil surface, regarding presence of shooflies, there.

Management strategies

The suitable management strategies for controlling shore flies-based problems in greenhouse environment, are narrated as under:

Cultural management strategies: The followings are important treatments followed for the purpose:

- ♦ Proper water management
- ♦ Proper sanitation of greenhouse
- ♦ Avoiding over fertigation
- ♦ Providing good drainage facility
- ♦ Keeping greenhouse soil media dry as much as possible.

Biological management strategies: Predatory mites are used under this management strategy. The predatory mite named "*Hypoaspis miles*" is commonly used. These mites feed the larvae of the insect; and thus decline the insect population. Predatory mites work well only on soil surface; not in standing water. Shore flies reproduce in water just as damp soil.

Bio-rational management strategies: In this management strategy the microbials are used for control of larval stage of shore flies. The microbial are applied in the form soil treatments, especially, in case of vegetable crops grown in greenhouse. The *Azadirachtin* is one of the main microbial. On its application, the larvae absorb it. This leads into interruption of molting process, significantly.

Chemical management strategies: In this chain of management, the insecticides are applied at larvae or adults stage of shore flies. However, larval is the most appropriate stage for its application. Its effects on control of shore flies remains for a long-term. Application in the form of spraying or wetting the surface of growing media is found most effective to kill the larvae. Amongst various available insecticides, some of them are not being so effective to kill the eggs or pupae. In such cases, they are applied, repeatedly, several times.

Thrips

These are very serious type insects. They feed by piercing the plant cells and suck the cellular contents. Because of this action the plant cells are damaged in Thrips incidence. This leads to develop the effect in terms of deformation in flowers, leaves and the shoot's growth of the plant. As symptom there is formation of streaking of silver colour and flecking on expanded leaves. In addition, Thrips often deposit small size greenish-black fecal specks on the leaves when they feed, is treated as the symptom of thrips borne problem.

In context to monitoring of thrips an early detection is most desirable, which may be performed by placing sticky cards above the plant or crop canopy at the rate of 1 card per 500 square feet area. In addition, the places near to the doors, vents, etc. are also being most suitable points for putting the sticky cards. There are different types of sticky cards such as blue cards and yellow sticky cards. Among these two, the blue sticky cards are more effective to trap the thrips, than the yellow sticky cards. The yellow sticky cards are found effective for flying pests (greenhouse) such as winged aphids, whiteflies, and Fungus Gnats. On weekly basis the number of thrips trapped per card is determined to see the severity of insect attack.

Management strategies

These are narrated as under:

Cultural management strategies: It includes following practices:

- Proper weed control in and around the greenhouse, especially, near vents and doors, because weeds act as refuge for thrips. This can be done by using black colour plastic film covered with coarse gravel materials. The course gravels placed on plastic film create an unfavorable location for pre-pupal and pupal stages of thrips.
- Maintenance of proper sanitation.

Biological management strategies: This is carried out by means of following biological sources:

(i) Predatory mites
(ii) Minute pirate bugs
(iii) Nematodes.

***Predatory mites*:** List of predatory mites used for thrips control is shown in Table 13.3.

Table 13.3 List of predatory mites used for thrips control (Goldammer, 2019).

S. No.	Predatory Mites	Remark
1.	*Neoseiulus cucumeris*	♦ Very effective to control immature thrips in greenhouse crops such as peppers, cucumbers and several ornamental crops as well.

(*Contd.*)

S. No.	Predatory Mites	Remark
		♦ Performs better at cool temperature. ♦ It should be released early before increase in thrips population.
2.	*Amblyseius swirskii*	♦ Very effective to control immature thrips in greenhouse crops such as peppers, cucumber and several ornamental plants. ♦ Performs better at warm temperature. ♦ It should be released early before increase in thrips population.
3.	*Amblydromalus limonicus*	♦ It should be released early before increase in thrips population.
4.	*Lphiseius degenerans*	-do-
5.	*Orius insidiosus*	-do-
6.	*Hypoaspis Gaeolaelaps or Stratiolaelaps*	-do-

***Minute pirate bug*:** This is also a predator used for thrips control. The predator named "*O. insidiosus*" (winged predator) is commonly used for the purpose. This consumes all moving thrips and also feed on pollen, spider mites, aphids, whiteflies, moth eggs, and young caterpillars.

***Nematodes*:** More commonly the nematode named "*Steinernema feltiae*" is used to control the thrips in greenhouse crops. This particular nematode attacks many of the soil-dwelling insects, i.e., pupating thrips and Fungus Gnats larvae. In addition, nematodes also enter the insect hose from the places of body openings and produce bacteria which kills the host insects. Since, nematodes are very sensitive to UV light; therefore, they are preferably applied either in evening hours or in cloudy weather condition.

Bio-rational management strategies: In this management strategy the horticultural oils and microbials are commonly used to control the thrips. In horticultural oils the neem oil, insecticidal soaps of low toxicity or pyrethrins are effectively used for temporary reduction in thrips number. Application becomes more effective when they are applied at first appearance of thrips. In microbial the "*Beauveria bassiana*" is treated as one of the pathogenic agents for insect. In order to make more effective or lethal, the fungal spores must be in direct contact to the pest.

Chemical management strategies: As per documented reports, the control of western flower thrips using chemicals is difficult, because they have potential to tolerate most of the insecticides. In addition, they also feed either from deep within flower head or on growing larvae. This feature of western flower thrips causes difficulty to denote a clear-cut target point for application of insecticides. In this condition, it is suggested to apply the insecticides for thorough coverage of infested place. It is also very essential to note that the application of insecticides must be in rotation, so that there would not be effect of residual resistance on them. In this regard, it is also advised that the use of an effective insecticide should be maintained for more than one generation of pest, prior to use other insecticide of a particular class.

Whiteflies

This insect completes its several generations, annually, in greenhouse environment. Normally, within 21 to 25 days an adult whitefly is formed, depending on the environment's temperature. The Nymphs and adults are located at the lower side of plant's leaves; and suck the plant fluids, on which they are dependent for feed. Sucking action is done by their mouthparts. In case of high population of whiteflies taking their feed from the plants, the plant's foliage becomes yellowish in colour. In addition, the Nymphs also secrete honeydew. The honeydew acts as growing media for development of black sooty mold fungi on leaves. The sooty molds on leaves declines the photosynthesis. This results into reduction in growth and yield potential of the crop, concerned. Similarly, if honeydews are deposited on fruits, the fruit quality also gets reduce, significantly. In addition to above, the whiteflies may also serve as the vectors for different viral diseases.

Monitoring of whiteflies can be easily done by using yellow sticky cards; and also by maintaining a proper inspection on existing eggs, nymphs and pupate lying on lower side of the plant's leave. The recommended rate of Yellow sticky card is to the tune of 1 card per 1,000 sq. ft production area. Cards are placed just above the crop canopy; and they are replaced on weekly basis. However, in case of susceptible crops and occurrence of greater attack, a more number of cards are required to place for proper monitoring. In addition, at the other places such as below the benches and near to the doors and vents additional sticky cards are placed. The placement of cards in vertical position above the canopy is found most effective. However, their height may also be raised because of increase in plant height; and thereby the canopy, too.

Management Strategies

This comprises following strategies regarding control of Whiteflies based problems:

Cultural management strategies: The main objective of this management strategy is to remove all possible resources or reasons responsible to cause infestation in greenhouse crops due to whiteflies. The important amongst them are narrated as under:

- Thoroughly removing all the weeds and debris materials lying inside and outside greenhouse, immediately, as these provide place for harboring immature and adult whiteflies. It is also being more effective, if the weeds and debris materials are kept in plastic bag in sealed form.
- Keeping infested plant debris in closed container, because on keeping them in open condition there is full possibility of production of adult whitefly, which may likely to return back into the greenhouse and create infestation problems, there.
- Inspecting new planting materials to be used for plantation in greenhouse regarding their infestation. This should be done before their plantation. The inspection should be in context to the presence of nymphs, pupae, eggs and the adult Whiteflies, as well. This type of inspection is essential because survival of Whiteflies is totally dependent on the plant, as adult whiteflies cannot live without feeding on host plants.

Biological management strategies: In this management strategy the following biological substances are commonly used for the purpose:

(a) Predatory wasps,
(b) Predatory mites, and
(c) Black beetle.

***Predatory wasps*:** Two predatory wasps namely *Encarsia Formosa* and *Eretmocerus eremicus* are commonly used for controlling whitefly infestation. In which, *Encarsia Formosa* predatory wasp attacks the larval stage of whitefly, is considered as the primary natural enemy of greenhouse whiteflies, and also for banded-winged whiteflies and sweet potato whiteflies. The predatory wasp *E. formosa* controls by killing the Whiteflies either in the form of laying eggs into immature stages or by directly feeding on nymph of young whiteflies.

***Predatory mites*:** The predatory mites such as *Amblyseius swirskii* and *Amblydromalus limonicus* are found very effective against the infestation caused due to all the species of whiteflies and thrips. The predatory mite named *Amblyseius swirskii* feeds on thrips, whitefly eggs and crawler, is considered as one of the effective whitefly predator mites. Because of this reason, *A. swirskii* is found highly compatible with the whitefly controlling parasitic wasps.

***Black beetle*:** This is also called *Delphastus pusillus*, is noticed to be very effective in the situation of heavy population or infestation of whiteflies. Although, at high population condition the growers apply the pesticides for immediate control of whiteflies, but the Black beetle can also be the best alternative for control of whiteflies. Black beetles are well capable to control all species of whiteflies and they can also be used with the parasitic wasp.

Bio-rational management strategies: In this management strategy the microbials and insect growth regulators (IGRs) are used for controlling whitefly based infestations in greenhouse crops. In microbials the Fungus *Beauveria bassiana* is found most effective, which kills the eggs, immature whiteflies, and adult whiteflies, too. Its application at low population of whitefly is highly beneficial. Foliar application along with good coverage is most desirable for productive result. In addition, the timely application and more in number of applications is also essential. In case of insect growth regulators (IGRs) the pesticides such as *Distance (pyriproxifen)* and *Pedistal (novaluron)* as the IGR, are commonly used.

Chemical management strategies: Insecticides are used for controlling the whitefly based infestations. The foliar application is not very effective as the nymphs and eggs are localized underside of the foliage. In result their contact with insecticide's spray is not being proper. In contrast, the adult whiteflies are effectively controlled by spraying the insecticides. In this context, the systemic insecticides are more effective, provided they are applied early during crop development stage. As per level of infestation or population of Whiteflies the application at 3 to 4 weeks' interval, repeatedly, results better effect. In addition, sometime, the whiteflies get develop resistance against a given insecticide. In this condition; it is therefore, suggested to rotate the insecticides of different chemical classes i.e., Pyrethroids, organo-phosphates, insect growth regulators, etc. for application.

13.6 GREENHOUSE CROP'S DISEASE

Greenhouse contains a special type of climate inside, called micro-climate, which is totally developed due to grown crops, soil moisture content, solar radiation, humidity and the temperature. In addition, it is also formed artificially as per requirement of the grown crop. Inside greenhouse the humidity, temperature and wetness are the major factors for inviting disease problems in grown crops. Once the crop gets infested with any kind of disease, the chance of crop to result desired yield gets badly affected, provided no control measures are adopted properly and at proper time. The presence of high humidity and moisture for a long period of time, is the most favourable situation for germination of conidia and infection due to many of the pathogens such as bacteria, fungi and viruses, as well. The fungi are causative to fungal disease, in which plant gets infected because of nutrients stealing and also by breaking down of tissues. The bacteria are the single cell organisms, without nucleus. On the other hand, the viruses are sub-microscopic and infectious type particles, which gets multiply inside living host cells. In unmanaged or neglected situation regarding application of control measures, the population of pathogens gets continue in increasing mode, till infection susceptible plant tissues are available, there. This condition leads to develop disease in the plant.

13.6.1 Common Plant Diseases and their Symptoms

There are varieties of plant diseases to infest the crops. In general, the plant diseases are grouped in two classes, namely (i) Abiotic disease; and (ii) Biotic/non-infectious disease. The non-infectious diseases are because of air pollution, nutritional deficiencies or toxicities, as well. As far as, plant symptom is concerned, it is abnormally in or on the plants, gets develop due to disease or nutrient's disorder. The abnormalities may be in visible form or in detectable range. In nutshell, the symptoms are resulted because of morphological disorder/change in plant body in the forms of alteration and damage of plant tissues or cells due to interference in metabolism action.

As per studies, about 85% plant diseases are due to fugal effect; and other diseases are due to virus and bacterial organisms. Besides, few plant diseases are also due to some specified nematodes. In viral diseases the crop growth gets badly reduced and also there is drastic change in the color may be noticed as the plant's symptom. Overall, the common symptoms appeared in viral diseases are follows,

(i) Stunning
(ii) Mottling
(iii) Mosaic pattern
(iv) Reduction in flowering
(v) Chlorosis or change in normal development of leaves and buds.

The important and common plant diseases of greenhouse crops are listed in Table 13.4.

Table 13.4 List of common greenhouse diseases

S. No.	Disease	S. No.	Disease
1.	Black Rot	8.	*Pythium* Root Rot
2	*Botrytis* Blight	9.	Rhizoctonia Root Rot
3.	Downy Mildew	10.	Rusts
4.	Fungal Leaf Spots	11.	Sclerotinia Disease
5.	*Fusarium* Root and Stem Rot	12.	Leaf Spots
6.	Phytophthora Root Rot	13.	Canker
7.	Powdery Mildew	14.	Root Rots

The above diseases are described in next page:

Leaf spots: These are the localized infected spots on leaf surface, mostly caused by fungi or bacteria. However, these are also appeared because of hail fall, insects, pesticide applications and moisture stress. In case of fungal effect, the spots are in round shape, while it is in angular shape when they are formed due to bacterial effects.

Rusts: In greenhouse this type of disease is caused by fungi. The rust can be removed by rubbing the materials with the fingers. Appearance of rust on plant body is in the color, i.e., yellow to reddish spore mass. The rust forming fungi have multiple stages of spores. The fungi may require many hosts to complete their life cycle.

Canker: These are nothing but dead areas or spots lying on the twigs, branches, stems and trunk, also. The reasons for development of canker are the hail fall, sunscald, pruning wounds, damage of plant body due to improper staking and attack of infectious agents, mainly. Sometimes, the cankers are also caused by disease organisms, appear in the form of sunken area on branches and trunk parts. On drying, the barks lying in sunken area get split or tear out.

Root rots: This disease is found difficult to diagnose clearly, as the roots are lying below the soil. In order to diagnose this disease with better conformity, it is always suggested to remove the entire root system of the plant; and carefully inspect the infested parts in that. On infestation of this disease the plant root system gets badly damage. And the plants may also like to die back or wilt the small leaves.

13.6.2 Fungal Diseases in Greenhouse Crops and their Management Strategies

Amongst various diseases infesting the greenhouse crops the fungi are one of the major, as they yield largest number of plant based pathogens. Fungi cannot make their food themselves as they do not have chlorophyll contents in them. They take their foods by living on another materials or organisms. As for as reproduction is concerned, majority of the fungi reproduce via spores. Spores are being very effective to spread the fungi to a wide scale. This is because of the reason that the spores are being weightless. Spores can be transmitted to the distance of mile or more by blowing winds. In addition, these can also be displaced by splashing water droplets during rainfall. Spores are also susceptible to enter the soil media and infect the same. In greenhouse soil or growing media, occurrence of this possibility is very common. Fungus can also enter the plant tissues; and thus affect the plant growth, severely. The important fungal diseases are described, below:

Black Rot

This disease is caused by the Fungus named "*Thielaviopsis basicola*", which seriously threats to the pansies, petunias and vinca. In addition, the same may also infect the cyclamen, calibrachoa, poinsettia, primula, impatiens, snapdragon, verbena, phlox, begonia, and nicotiana. The symptom of black rot is not very prominent. Sometimes, it creates confusion about appearance of symptoms similar to the nutrient deficiencies. Especially, in greenhouse, it is easily overlooked due to healthy-appearing of plants. On the other hand, the Fungus called *Thielaviopsis* causes serious growth reduction and crop yield in some of the highly susceptible cultivars. It damages the root system; and accordingly, there is reduction in nutrient absorption or uptake by the plant. This results into nutrient's deficiency based symptoms in the plant. The occurrence of black rot disease can be identified by the following symptoms:

- Stunting with older leaves shriveling.
- Leaves may turn into yellowish colour.
- The youngest leaves may become stunted and tinged with red.
- At mid stage the older leaves become yellow-green. However, veins are in their original green color.

Management strategy

This is divided in two categories, i.e. (i) Cultural; and (ii) Chemical management strategies. These are described as under:

Cultural management strategies: This is done as per below:

- Maintaining proper sanitation of cropped field, as spores of the pathogen (Fungus) can persist on the floor mats, benches, and pots lying inside greenhouse.
- Disallowing for reusing the plug trays for growing those crops, which are susceptible to *Thielaviopsis*. However, if it is compulsion to reuse the pots or trays, then selection should be made to those which are relatively less susceptible to *Thielaviopis*. The pots must be rinsed to a good level, so that the organic debris may be removed from there. The organic debris provides space to harbor them.
- Disinfecting and thoroughly cleaning the containers and plug trays. For this purpose, the Hydrogen Peroxide (H_2O_2) can be used. It can also be done by bleaching the containers and tray plugs, using Chlorine (10% solution).
- Thorough cleaning the greenhouse area after end of crop season.

Chemical management strategies: It is carried out with the help of fungicides (chemicals) of suitable concentration. The suitable chemicals are listed in the Table 13.5.

Table 13.5 List of fungicides used for black rot control

S. No.	Fungicide	Remark
1.	Containing active ingredient Thiophanate-methyl	♦ Best and most reliable fungicide
2.	Containing Benzimidazole ingredient	♦ Best control effect
3.	Containing action ingredient (i) Azoxystrobin, (ii) Fludioxonil, and (iii) Triflumizole.	♦ These have good efficacy but not consistent as Thiophanate-methyl.
4.	Polyoxin D.	♦ Very effective but not as the Thiophanate-methyl

***Botrytis* Blight**

This is one of the most common fungal diseases in greenhouse crops. This is caused by *Botrytis cinerea*. Sometimes, the *Botrytis* Blight disease is also referred as the Gray-mold disease. This is because of the reason that it produces gray fuzzy-appearing spores on plant surface where tissues have been infected. In greenhouse these spores get germinate on the plant surfaces in high humidity condition, and within wide range of temperature. In addition, they also get germinate in deposited water drops on plant surfaces. This disease can infect the plant at its any stage. However, the new tender growth, freshly injured tissues, and the dead tissues parts are most susceptible to this type of fungal disease. The other important points about this disease are narrated as under:

- This fungal disease also attacks the healthy, soft, nutrient-rich flower or bract tissues of many flowers such as Cyclamen, Geranium, Rose, and Poinsettia.
- In high humidity condition and to a soft plant material this disease occurs very easily.
- In the greenhouses with stagnant moist air and greater fluctuations in day/night temperatures resulting into condensation of moisture on the plant surface, the occurrence of this disease is very high.
- The container crops and dense seedling beds are also highly infected by this kind of fungal disease.

The occurrence of *Botrytis* Blight disease is mainly noticed by the symptoms of very fast development of gray "fuzzy" growth on the flowers, and also on the other infected parts of the plant. In flowers the sepals and petals often show its symptoms, first.

Management strategies

This is divided in following two main categories,

(i) Cultural management strategies, and
(ii) Chemical management strategies.

Cultural management strategies: The *Botrytis* Blight disease gets commonly occur because of improper management. In this regard the suggested management practices are narrated as under:

- Keep the plant canopy dry during dusk to dawn.
- Apply watering or irrigation by drip system; not through sprinkler system.
- Do proper sanitation before, during and after each crop cycle
- Maintain the greenhouse area (in and out) clean to a high level.
- Disinfect the path, sitting benches, recycled container and other objcets related to the greenhouse, frequently with the help of best quality approved disinfectant. It should be done when greenhouse is empty.
- Heat and ventilate the greenhouse to reduce its humidity level. Reduced humidity declines the fungal growth and sporulate, as well. As per recommendation the relative humidity must be below 85%. At night the humidity can be reduced by maintaining the greenhouse warm and proper ventilation.

Chemical management strategies: This is accomplished by using suitable fungicides. For this purpose there is variety of fungicides are available in the market. In use of fungicides it is very important to know that few fungi get develop their resistance against a given chemical or fungicide. In this condition, the application of that particular chemical or fungicide becomes ineffective to discharge the control action. Therefore, to avoid this type of situation, it is always advised to use the chemicals or fungicides in rotation. For example, the *Botrytis* populations have residual resistance against the chemicals such as Chlorothalonil, Iprodione, and Fenhexamid, as well.

Downy Mildew

This is also one of the damaging diseases to many of the greenhouse crops. Downy Mildew disease is difficult to control by using fungicides after its establishment in the crop/plant. This types of diseases are caused by a group of Fungus like organisms, similar to the species such as *Pythium* and *Phytophthora*. It is also observed that most of this disease fungi are the host specific; and accordingly they infect the plants of a specified family. The *Peronospora*, *Bremia*, Plasmopara, and *Basidiophora* are the pathogens species. In field the Powdery Mildew disease often creates confusion with the Downy Mildew, because of appearance of few similar features. The temperature and humidity of the place causes vital effect on development of pathogens and spreading of this disease, as well. The common symptoms of Downy Mildew disease are pointed below:

- At beginning they blight the foliage, but in continuation they spread very rapidly into fresh tissues of growing tips and flower buds. This leads to result stunning and distortion effect.
- Appearance of Blotchy yellow or brown lesions on leaves, i.e., yellowing in general.
- Development of leaf distortion.
- Taking place of leaf stunting.

Management strategies

It comprises following two different aspects:

Cultural management strategies: In greenhouse medium, the occurrence of this kind of disease to a significant level is because of cool temperature and high humidity of the site specific. In general, an extended period of coolness and damp weather leads to cause many of the epidemics. Spore germination takes place at fast speed in moist environment. The management strategies for control of this disease are as follows:

(i) Keep the greenhouse (in and out) dry and clean.
(ii) Maintain the humidity in optimum range.
(iii) Maintain the temperature in proper range.

Chemical management strategies: It comprises following measures:

- Follow immediately the proper control measures.
- Ensure good level of protectant fungicides.
- Apply the fungicide every 7 to 10 days' periods.

As precautionary measure, the fungicides of varying chemical classes should always be used; otherwise, there is the possibility of development of resistance against a specific fungicide of a particular chemical class.

Fungal Leaf Spots

This disease is also due to fungal effects. The prolong wetness of leaf surface invites this disease. Its symptoms are highly varying. The fungi namely *Alternaria, Ascochyta, Cercospora, Colletotrichum (anthracnose), Phyllosticta, Gloeosporium, and Septoria* are very common to cause this type of fugal disease. However, some of them are leaf spot fungi, which are seed-borne. The ornamentals plants such as bedding plants, cut flowers and cut foliage, tropical foliage plants, and woody crops are highly susceptible to fungal leaf spots. The life cycle of many leaf fungal spot diseases is about the same. Spores get spread to a wide range by blowing winds. In addition, spores are also splashed due to watering effect. The important symptoms of this disease are mentioned below:

(i) In presence of organisms, there is formation of blights or spots on leaves, stems and flowers, etc.
(ii) Its symptoms or attack on the plant root.
(iii) The blights or spots appear on lower foliage and moves up through canopy.

Management strategies

It is described under following two different aspects:

Cultural management strategies: It comprises following management strategies to check the disease:

- Regular inspection of plants in context to the disease infestation.
- Discarding symptomatic plants from greenhouse.
- Reducing greenhouse humidity.

Chemical management strategies: Although, a lot of fungicides are available to use for controlling the fungi-based diseases, but their selection amongst them as per symptoms of disease concern, is very essential and important; otherwise, their application may cause no effect on the disease and accordingly, there is damage to the crop. In order to control the Fungus leaf spot disease, few suitable fungicides have been shown in Table 13.6.

Table 13.6 List of fungicides, suitable to leaf spot disease (Goldammer, 2019).

S. No.	Fungi/disease	Fungicide	Remark
1.	*Alternaria*	(i) Chlorothalonil (ii) Mancozeb	♦ It can be controlled by many of the fungicides. ♦ The old fungicides such as chlorothalonil and mancozeb are found excellent to control. ♦ However, these two leave unacceptable residues in the media.
2.	*Colletotrichum* (Anthracnose)	(i) Copper (ii) Mancozeb (iii) Chlorothalonil (iv) Pageant Intrinsic (combination of FRAC groups 7 and 11) (v) Copper Sulphate Pentahydrate with Pageant	♦ It is due to *Colletotrichum* spp. ♦ Use of Copper Sulphate Pentahydrate with Pageant in rotation results good effect on control without excessive residues.

Fusarium Root and Stem Rot

This disease is caused by the *Fusarium* species in varieties. The *Fusarium* species are a cosmopolitan group of fungi spread the disease to a very wide range in greenhouse crops. The most common species are *F. lateritium, F. solani, and F. oxysporum.* In ornamental plants this disease causes root rot and crown rot and also stem cankers, mainly. These are being very persistent as facultative parasites. They also have the characteristics to survive in adverse conditions by entering in dormancy stage in the form of chlamydospores; and also in saprophytic state on dead root fragments. It starts with the stage of chlamydospores, which is single celled, round in shape and thick walled. Chlamydospores are produced in abundance in dead tissues or localized mass of organic substances lying in the soil media. Chlamydospores cause or allow the pathogens to lie inactive in the soil media in unfavorable situations such as drought or very low temperature. The pathogens lying on, become inactive when seedling roots grow close to the Chlamydospores. The extreme wet or dry conditions accelerate the development of *Fusarium*. The symptom of *Fusarium* is observed at rapid scale, especially, in drought stress situations. The important symptoms of *Fusarium* rot and Stem rot diseases are narrated as under:

- Rotting of taproot (usually to the lower portion) and lateral roots and turning into black or brown colour.
- Decay of outer layer of the roots.
- Indication of vascular discoloration.
- In prolong situation of this disease the oldest leaves begin to yellow and stunting of younger leaves before flaccid.

Management strategies

Like other diseases this disease also includes the cultural and chemical management strategies for its control, narrated below:

Cultural management strategies: Important strategies are pointed as under:

- Restrict the host plant stress from the other pathogens, because the plant may likely to have an increased vigor; and that can also withstand the fungi very promptly.
- Clean the greenhouse surface, thoroughly.
- Properly disinfect all bench surfaces, pots and their mixes, tools, trays, containers, and the equipments placed there for use.

Chemical management strategies: If the crop field involves the problem of *Fusarium* root rot disease from long back, then fungicide treatment becomes essential to nullify the infestation. In case of protectant fungicides which can manage the *Fusarium* root rot, the fungicides have comparatively less or little effect on *Fusarium* vascular wilts.

Phytophthora Root Rot

It is just like or closely related to the *Pythium*, also causes root rot problem. A wide range (variety) of plants are susceptible to *Phytophthora*, which have several species and host specific. The Poinsettia, Fuchsia, Vinca, Gloxinia, Lantana, African violet, Begonia, and ornamental peppers are the common hosts of this disease. It can be devastating and difficult to control the problem. In floricultural crops it is very dangerous type disease. It becomes difficult to control after its establishment on the crop. In hydroponic systems and also in greenhouse environments this disease is very much susceptible to occur. Spores are in various types which allow persisting them to a significantly changing environmental conditions. Especially, the zoospores and Chlamydospores can get easily survive on the pots, floors, media and other surfaces available in greenhouse. On the other hand, the zoospores can be in swimming mode for a small distance say few inches on water surface. The symptoms of this disease are mentioned below:

- Infected plants wilt and overall they decline with dark lesions called canker at the plant's crown. Because of cankers the flow of water and nutrients in plant body, i.e., between root and stem gets decline.
- In acute situation the plants are likely to die. In few cases the plant's crown gets infected at first and thereafter proceed to the stem and foliage close to the petiole.

Management strategies

These are grouped as under:

Cultural management strategies: The control of *Phytophthora* spp. is normally being difficult. In this situation the *Phytophthora* should be kept away from the greenhouse. In floricultural crops this is particularly found difficult to manage due to existing of prefinished plants in large amount, in the periphery. It is also very common that the plants infested by this disease do not show clear cut symptoms, but when infection becomes fully established or the plants become dominantly stressed, then its symptoms are appeared to show.

Chemical management strategies: Fungicides are used for this purpose. The commonly used fungicides in greenhouse crops are the *Adorn (fluopicolide), Micora SC (mandipropamid), Orvego SC (ametoctradin/dimethomorph),* and *Stature (dimethomorph).* These are found very effective to control various *Phytophthora* species in greenhouse crops. In addition, the Phosphorus acid products such as Alude and Vital can also be used for controlling this disease; but these involve poor consistency, causing they are not found so reliable to control the *Phytophthora* disease. Sometimes, the standard Subdue *MAXX (mefenoxam)* are also suggested to use for controlling the *Phytophthora* but they must be applied in rotation with others, suitable and effective products.

Powdery Mildew

This is also one of the most common and widely covered plant diseases in greenhouse production system. The Powdery mildew disease belongs to the group of fungi, encompassing genera *Erysiphe*, *Leveillula*, *Microsphaera*, and *Sphaerotheca*. These are characterized by producing grey or white powdery growth. This particular disease causes significant loss in many of the greenhouse crops including floricultural crops such as roses, violas, African daisy, zinnias and vegetables—tomatoes, cucumbers crops, mainly. Although, by this disease the plants do not destroy (death), but the aesthetics of crop and its value get drastically hampered. As for as, life cycle of this disease is concerned, they have very simple life cycle. The spores form a long chain on short erected fungal stalks, create "fluffiness". The relative humidity about 95% or approximately zero vapour pressure deficit (VPD) for 3 to 4 hours or more is required for the spores (Conidia) to germinate and penetrate in the leaf or stem epidermal cells of the plant. The spores or conidia are being in powder form which gets easily disseminated due to air in greenhouse environment. Important symptoms of this disease are pointed as under:

- These are detected by the symptom of white colour powdery growth of Fungus on infected patches of the host plant.
- Appearance of fungi colonies varies, i.e., fluffy or sometimes in white to sparse and gray.

- Attack on young growing shoots, foliage, stems, and also to the flowers.
- Colonizing of mature tissues in plant.

Management strategies

This is carried out in two ways, i.e., (i) cultural; and (ii) chemical strategies, are described as under:

Cultural management strategies: The followings are the important points to consider under this management strategies:

- Regular monitoring of the crops.
- Rogueing of infected plants.
- Pruning of diseased tissues, if there at any part of the plant body. Note that the rogueing of infected plants or pruning of diseased tissues should be done when plant's surface is wet. Also, the diseased parts/materials should be immediately placed in the plastic bag so that the spores may not spread outside.

Chemical management strategies: The following points are followed under this head of management strategy:

- In favorable situations the application of fungicides plays significant role in control of this disease.
- Mostly, the fungicides of eradicative (eradicant) and protective (protectant) nature are used. The protectant type fungicides are used as preventive measure to check the further development of Powdery Mildew.
- Protectants (fungicide) are applied in favourable condition to outbreak the disease. On the other hand, the eradicants are used to stop the pathogenic development from any kind of further damage because of fungal infestation.
- Eradicants are preferred to apply, especially, when there is expectance of pathogens in the crop field.

Pythium Root Rot

The *Pythium* Root Rot disease is caused due to Pathogen called "*Pythum*". This lives in water, where it produces sporangia, which is the fruiting body. The sporangia get change into zoospores, which remains around the roots of the plant and infect that and also colonize there. The zoospores significantly disseminate the pathogens of this disease. In addition, the *Pythium* also forms Chlamydospores and Oospores, which are the resting structures, allow them to survive in the pores or spaces of floating trays. In this way, in float system used for crop growing it serves the purpose of primary inoculum. This disease can infest to any greenhouse crops/plants but the geranium, poinsettia, and snapdragons are often found most affected. *Pythium* Root Rot disease is very common and persistent in greenhouse crops. In greenhouse environment the three species of root-rotting *Pythium* are most dominant, they are the (i) *Pythium irregular*; (ii) *Pythium ultimum*; and (iii) *Pythium aphanidermatum*. Important characteristics of this disease are mentioned below:

(i) Stunted plant's growth.
(ii) Most susceptible in wet or saturated soil condition.
(iii) Hibernate on dirty plant containers, benches, hoses, and greenhouse pathways, as well.

Apart from above characteristics, the salient symptoms of this disease are mentioned as under:

- In this disease the juvenile tissues such as the root tips are infested badly.
- Once, the *Pythium* enters the roots, there starts rapid black rotting of entire primary root system. And after laps of time if proper measures are not adopted, they move in stem tissues. However, as the soil gets dry the new roots start appearing and the plant recovers themselves. In wet or high moisture condition a large extent of roots are destroyed; and plants are also wilt due to this disease. Because of this reason there develops confusion about actual source causing effects on the crop.
- In this disease the bulbs of susceptible plants turn to black in color; desiccate gradually and even form a hard mummy.

Management strategies

This is divided in two parts, namely the cultural management strategies and chemical management strategies, described as under:

Cultural management strategies: The cultural based management strategies to control *Pythium* Root Rot disease includes following activities to follow:

- Scout the infested plants.
- Sanitize greenhouse crop environment.
- Clean the pathways, benches, etc. inside greenhouse and also disinfect them using suitable disinfectant.
- Control over irrigation and fertigation, both.
- Restrict the use of poorly drained growing media.
- Avoid to place the pots or trays in standing water.

Chemical management strategies: In this management the chemicals are used to control the disease, described below:

- Apply fungicides suitable to *Pythium*. However, in worse situation, i.e., when *Pythium* has significantly infested the plant leading to result badly rotting of root system, the fungicides become not so effective to control the disease. Most commonly the products, namely, *Subdue MAXX (mefenoxam), FenStop (fenamidone) and Truban* and *Terrazole (etridiazole)* are found effective in controlling *Pythium* Root Rot disease.
- Especially, in greenhouse crops, if the *Pythium* is found resistant against Subdue MAXX, then *Truban* or *Terrazole* can also be used to control the disease.

Rhizoctonia Root Rot

This disease is found very common to occur in highly changing environmental conditions. Pathogens of *Rhizoctonia* spp. are soil borne; live in the soil and also in potting medium. It can persist several years in the soil media. In many of the seed producing crops, it produces pre- and post-emergence "damping off" effects. The other features of this disease are mentioned below,

- It does not produce spores.
- It spreads due to movement of soil particles caused by water flow or blowing winds.
- Sclerotia gets germinate in the soil.

- Mycelium tends to colonize at the part of plant surfaces, where nutrients are available.
- It infested the plants at the soil line, in result there is loss of root system as well as constriction of stem and accordingly, there is girdling and death of the top, also.
- Pathogens of this disease can also attack the leaves of the plant. This effect is very severe in the crops grown at closer spacing and moist medium
- The entire stock beds are likely to lost in few days in presence of favourable condition for *Pythium*.
- In herbaceous greenhouse crops such as dianthus, impatiens, coreopsis, ageratum, chrysanthemum, and petunia the *Rhizoctonia* Root Rot disease is very common to take place.
- Dry soil is more favorable for development of this of type of disease.
- In greenhouse the *Rhizoctonia* spp. occurs in potting media and can cause effects in leaves and stem.

Besides above features of *Rhizoctonia* Root Rot disease, its important symptoms are pointed as under:

- It lesions on lower parts of stem.
- Roots are often get dry.
- Roots turns to light in color.
- Damping off of young seedlings.
- *Rhizoctonia* is very active in upper soil layer.

Management strategies

It is accomplished under cultural and chemical management treatments, described below:

Cultural management strategies: Since, pathogens are soil borne; therefore, they can escape very easily and cause serous loss of the crops, before their detection in the field. In this condition, as compared to control its prevention is more important. Normally, in cultural management strategies the following measures are followed in line of its prevention/control.

- Using healthy plants for plantation.
- Using new or sterilized pots or potting media.
- Avoiding direct transplantation of the plants. Plants must be inspected about any kind of disease infestation in them.

Chemical management strategies: The fungicides such as *Terraclor (PNCB), Terraguard (triflumizole), Cleary's 3336/OHP 6672 (t-methyl), and Medallion (fludioxonil)* are found very useful in preventing and checking *Rhizoctonia.*

Rusts

This disease is also one of the fungal infections, is more common in the ornamental crops such as aster, campanula, carnation, chrysanthemum, daylily, fuchsia, goldenrod, hollyhock, iris, marigold, penstemon, poinsettia, rose, snapdragon, switch grass, statice, veronica, violet, and zonal or bedding geranium, etc., mainly. It is treated as serious disease, affects the production, significantly. There develops reddish to orange blister-like swellings on the infected parts of the leaves or stem of host plant. This swelling is also referred to as "pustules". In this disease, the host plant is rarely killed. However, in gross the health and appearance of plant gets adversely affected. Rust is found in different species, affect majority of the greenhouse crops/plants. In general, most of the rust species affect single plant family.

As far as life cycle is concerned, they involve very complex life cycle. In case of few rusts only one host is required to begin their life cycle, while in others, two different types of hosts are required for their pathogens to complete the life cycle. The other important features of this disease are mentioned below:

- Rust fungi produce a large quantity of spores in a very short-time span. Because of this reason a small number of infected plants can create epidemic in the cropped field.
- This disease can get spread through air and water both.
- Spores are blown away by blowing winds.
- Splashing water also transmits this disease to the plants, especially in greenhouse.
- In greenhouse it is also due to introduction/plantation of infected plants.
- The cool temperature of growing zone, high relative humidity of crop canopy and dense planting are the critical conditions to invite this disease.

Important symptoms of this disease are as follows:

- Development of lesions (pustules) on lower surfaces of plant leaves. The size of lesions gets increase. And eventually rupture the epidermis and release spores.
- The pustules may also be on the upper surface of the leaves, which can coalesce to form a large necrotic area.
- Spores are typically bright in color.

Management strategies

Like other diseases, this disease also involves the cultural and chemical management strategies to control, are narrated as under:

Cultural management strategies: Few measures are as follows:

- Careful inspection of all new planting materials about disease infection in them, before their plantation.
- Maintenance of proper environmental conditions in context to the temperature, humidity, etc.
- Proper sanitation of environment. Sanitation is always found better than the treatment with fungicides.

Chemical management strategies: This includes following measures:

- Using effective fungicides. However, mostly the available fungicides are preventive type; not as the curative fungicides.
- In case of fungicide treatment, it is always suggested to follow the rotation between fungicides to be applied; otherwise, there is full possibility of development of resistant against a particular pesticide, which is not being appropriate.

Sclerotinia Disease

Sometimes, this disease is also called white mold. Although, it is very common in outdoor crops, but also observed occasionally in greenhouse environment. This disease can cause the root rot, stem rot and blighting of foliage and leaf petioles, as well in majority of the crops grown inside greenhouse. In general, the greenhouse crops namely the Alyssum, Begonia, Gazania, Geranium, Gerbera, Gloxinia, Larkspur, Lobelia, Petunia, Stocks, Vinca, and Zinnia are most susceptible to this disease. Few important points about this disease are mentioned as under:

- Its cycle is started from acrospores, which are produced from "apothecia". Feature of apothecia is brown in colour; shape-just like cup; fruiting body and diameter varies from 5 to 15 mm.
- The acrospores can move to a very long distance.
- In greenhouse they enter through vents or doors, mainly.
- High humidity condition, and/or wet surfaces are found best to thrive *Sclerotinia.*
- The temperature ranging from 15 to 21°C is found best for their development. However, they can also grow in the environment having 2 to 32°C temperature.
- Incidence of this disease can be very extensive in the situation of prolong favourable temperature and moisture.

The important symptoms of this disease are as follows:

- The *Sclerotinia* fungi can cause blighting or rotting of any parts of plant body lying above or below the ground surface.
- At beginning its appearance is patchy or spasmodic.

Management strategies

The control management strategies are divided as under:

Cultural management strategies: Under this head of management, the following measures are adopted to control the disease:

- Maintaining proper sanitation.
- Avoiding the use of unsterilized field soils in pot type growing media.
- Keeping proper weeds control.
- Maintaining plant foliage in dry condi§tion, which can be done by minimizing the overhead watering and dripping.
- Maintaining a good air circulation through crop canopy, which can be done by ensuring a proper spacing among.

Chemical management strategies: In regard to control of this disease, there are varieties of fungicides are available in the market, but majority of them are the preventative type; not the curative. The important points in their application are as follows:

- Applying fungicides in rotation to avoid the possibility of development of resistant against a particular fungicide.
- Using contact type fungicides in rotation is preferred.

13.7 PESTICIDE'S APPLICATION EQUIPMENT

In disease control the application of control measures in proper way within time frame is very important, besides selection of most suitable eradicating materials. Overall, the followings are few important points which play significant role in successful control of crop diseases using pesticides:

- Exact location of target place or area.
- Correct information on infesting pests and their threshold economic level.
- Control strategies to minimize the input level of pesticides to be used.
- Uniformity in application.
- Uniformity in application dose.
- Timely and safe application.
- Use of most suitable application equipment.

In order to achieve-above mentioned target points regarding effective application of insecticides/chemicals to eradicate the problems or diseases from the crop concerned, the use of machines for application of the same is very essential, because uniformity in application rate and to cover a large areal tracts (infested), manually not possible. The use of machines is only alternative. There are varieties of machines/devices available for application of chemicals in liquid form, can be smoothly used for application. However, the selection of most suitable equipment among them is very important. As far as, in greenhouse use is concerned, the selected machine or equipment must be simple in operation. Mostly, the backpack sprayer, air-assisted low-volume sprayer, or ultra-low volume sprayer, i.e., the foggers are found most suitable for application of pesticides and others in greenhouse crops. Some of such equipment are described as under:

Sprayer: This is the machine used for application of chemicals in liquid form to the standing crop, either it is grown inside greenhouse or in open field. The mode of application is in the form of fine water droplets mixed with chemical contents. Sprayers are found in different types and capacities. The nozzle is main component by which the application is made in the form of fine water droplets, uniformly throughout target area. The commonly used nozzles are described as under:

Nozzle: This is one of the main components of sprayer or spraying device, which emits the liquid in the form of fine droplets, dispersed over the target area. Nozzles are characterized by their flow rates, spray angle, droplet sizes and distribution pattern, as well. In general, a nozzle performs following functions:

(i) Regulation of flow rate.
(ii) Atomization of mixture (liquid) into droplets.
(iii) Dispersal of droplets in a specific pattern.
(iv) Capacity of good area coverage.
(v) Uniformity in application rate.

In context to achieve best spraying performance from the sprayer, the selection of suitable size nozzle plays an important role. It is always taken care that there must be uniformity in application, besides a good level of area coverage. Nozzles are made of brass, nylon, stainless steel, hardened-stainless steel, tungsten carbide, thermoplastic, and ceramic materials, as well. However, among all the brass made nozzles are very common. Although, the brass nozzles are expensive over others, but they have a high level of wear tolerance with abrasive materials such as liquid fertilizers, etc. In contrast, the steel made nozzles are resistant to wear, but their cost is high.

Nozzles type: There are several types of nozzles available in the market; and they all have their own characteristics. In general, the nozzles are grouped in following three groups:

(i) Hydraulic nozzles,
(ii) Air-shear nozzles, and
(iii) Rotary atomizers.

In which, the hydraulic type nozzles utilize hydraulic pressure to create water droplets. The air-shear type nozzles work on the principle of venturi effect to force the liquid into air stream and formation of droplets, thereby. The rotary atomizers utilize the centrifugal force to create water droplets. The centrifugal force is generated due to rotating cage or discs attached to the system. These three types of nozzles are described, below:

***Hydraulic nozzles*:** These nozzles work on the principle of hydraulic force concept. Liquid is directed under pressure through orifice. The diameter of orifice is very small than the supply line. This results into a very high velocity of liquid flow, which in turn to cause the stream of liquid coming out from the nozzle, instable. The instability in out coming discharge from the nozzle, causes breaking of discharged liquid into fine drops. The variation in drop size is governed by the hydraulic pressure acting on the flowing liquid. Hydraulic nozzles are also found in various types depending on flow rates, distribution patterns and spray angles. The common types are namely (i) Cone type; (ii) Flat-fan type, and (iii) Air induction type nozzles.

***Air-shear nozzles*:** These nozzles are also known as the air resisted nozzles, work on the principle of breaking the liquid into very small droplets due to very high air jet speed. The liquid is directly discharged in the air stream against air blast. This causes the formation of small droplets. In this sprayer, if liquid is discharged at 90° to the air-stream the size of droplets becomes large. At fast air blast and greater flow rate the size of droplet gets reduce; and vice-versa.

Rotary atomizer: The rotary atomizer is also a spraying device used for application of insecticides. It is a rotating disc to discharge the liquid at high-speed forming a hollow cone spray. Its rotational speed controls the drop size. The size of droplet formed by this device also depends on fluid properties such as density, viscosity and surface tension between fluids. A small-size atomizer (10 cm diameter and 30,000 rpm) can cover the area at the rate of 490,000 m/s^2.

13.7.1 Commonly Used Sprayers

In pesticide application the extent of area coverage and making a good level of contact between the insect pest and the pesticides applied, have prime importance. The extent of area coverage depends on the capacity of sprayer to be used. In greenhouse crops for application of pesticides the list of suitable sprayers is shown in Table 13.7.

Table 13.7 List of sprayers, commonly used in greenhouse crops

S. No.	Sprayer
1.	Hydraulic sprayers
	(i) Compressed air sprayer
	(ii) Backpack sprayer
	(iii) Skid-mounted sprayer
	(iv) Irrigation boom sprayer
	(v) Central pesticide application system

(Contd.)

S. No.	Sprayer
2.	Targeted low-volume sprayers (i) Backpack mist blower (ii) Air-assisted low-volume sprayers (iii) Electrostatic sprayers
3.	Fog or ultra-low volume sprayers (i) Mechanical foggers (ii) Thermal foggers

Above three types of sprayers are categorized on the basis of flow rate, operating pressure, and droplet's size, produced, are described, below:

Hydraulic sprayers: These are the high volume sprayers, are used to wet highly dense foliage. For its use, a large volume of water is required for applying the chemicals at standard rate. However, volume of water requirement depends on the type of sprayer, nozzle, spraying methodology to be followed and size of the crop foliage. It is always suggested that before using any sprayer, they must be calibrated.

Targeted low-volume sprayers: These are the low volume sprayers, mainly used to apply the insecticides, fungicides, disinfectants and fertilizers, also, to the greenhouse crops. Average size (diameter) of water droplets formed by this type of sprayer varies from 40 to 70 micron, at the pressure from 1,000 to 3,000 psi. At high pressure the size of droplets becomes very fine; and they are discharged at high velocity. As soon as the spray cloud hits the target the high velocity gets easily diffused. This phenomenon leads to develop a swirling spray cloud with high degree of turbulence within foliage. The types of targeted low volume sprayers are described below,

- ***Backpack mist blower*:** In this spraying machine a high velocity air stream is created with the help of small capacity gas engine and fan system. Spraying is done by injecting the liquid in the air stream with a special type of nozzle equipped in the spray unit. As compared to hydraulic sprayer, this sprayer involves more complicated spraying mechanism.
- ***Air-assisted low-volume sprayers*:** Application is performed by striking a high speed air current to the stream of liquid flow. This results into formation of small droplets, which get spread on the crop canopy.
- ***Electrostatic sprayers*:** These sprayers are capable to produce the water droplets of uniform in size, which are also likely to disperse, more evenly. Droplet size varies from 30 to 60 micron, are electrically charged. The area coverage is at par to the high-volume sprayers.

Fog or Ultra-low volume sprayers: These sprayers are also known as foggers. In use of this sprayer comparatively small quantity of water is required to complete the pesticide application. The size (diameter) of water droplets is smaller than 25 micron. In mass, such small size water droplets form "fog" in a closed area like greenhouse. Due to formation of fog near to the target, the application of pesticides becomes more effective because of development of proper contact between pests and the chemicals, applied. Proper circulation of air in the area is essential to achieve a good level of spraying or application of pesticides by this spraying machine. Different types of foggers are described below:

***Mechanical foggers*:** This machine performs the spraying work by developing a very high pressure. At high pressure the nozzle discharges the liquid in the form of very fine droplets, which results into formation of fog". The size of droplets is around 25-micron or less. In such application, there is good level of contact between applied insecticides and the pests, which is very effective to control the problem.

***Thermal foggers*:** These are the special type of spraying machine used for application of liquid chemicals to a very large areal coverage. Its system is just like jet engine. This device consists of a big capacity tank to contain chemical solution for spraying. The liquid pesticide is injected into a very hot and fast moving air stream. This results into vaporization of injected chemicals; and simultaneously the formation of very fine droplets, thereby. The size (diameter) of droplets is lesser than 10 to 50 microns. Such small size water droplets are able to move to a long distance from the point of emission. Because of this reason, these sprayers are found well capable to spray the chemicals to a greater distance in regards to disease control. A large capacity thermal fogger is capable to propel the fog about 100 feet in seconds from the machine's location and about 50,000 sqfeet area can be easily sprayed in less than 15 seconds time. Overall, the area coverage depends whether the chemical to be applied as wettable or liquid formulation.

PRACTICE QUESTIONS

Descriptive Type Questions

1. Enlist most common type of insect pests problems in greenhouse crops.
2. Describe management practices followed for controlling effects of insect pests in greenhouse crops.
3. Narrate management strategies for controlling Aphid infestation in greenhouse crops.
4. Describe management strategies for controlling greenhouse insect pests.
5. Describe insect and mite management practices in greenhouse farming system.
6. Describe biological management strategies for controlling Whiteflies in greenhouse crops.
7. Describe common plant diseases and their symptoms in greenhouse environment.
8. Describe pest management practices in greenhouse crops.
9. Narrate fungal diseases and their management strategies followed in greenhouse crops.
10. Describe chemical and mechanical management strategies for controlling fungal leaf spot disease in greenhouse production area.
11. Describe management strategies followed to control *Rhizoctonia* root rot disease.
12. Describe biological and mechanical control strategies for Mealybugs
13. Describe common plant diseases and their symptoms in context to greenhouse farming system.
14. Describe biological control measures followed for insect pest's management.
15. Describe various equipments used for application of insecticides/pesticides.

Multiple Choice Type Questions

1. Leafminers is the
(a) Insect (b) Pest
(c) Disease (d) Both (a) and (b)

2. Snail is the example of
(a) Pest (b) Insect
(c) Disease (d) Both (a) and (b)

3. Aphids can be controlled by application of
(a) Pesticides (b) Insecticides
(c) Herbicides (d) Ammonium phosphate

4. A favourable environment for growth of Fungus Gnats is
(a) Arid environment (b) Dry environment
(c) Humid environment (d) None of above

5. The loopers, cutworms, borer and armyworms, etc. are associated to
(a) Caterpillar (b) Whitefly
(c) Aphids (d) Fungus Gnats

6. The loopers, cutworms, borer and armyworms, etc. are associated to
(a) Predators (b) Caterpillar
(c) Snails (d) Fungus Gnats

7. Which of the following is the main host plant for Mealybugs?
(a) Tomato (b) Cucumber
(c) Eggplant (d) All above

8. Caterpillars can be controlled by using
(a) Insecticides (b) Pesticides
(c) Herbicides (d) Soil solarisation

9. The biological control measures for scale borne problems is
(a) Insecticides (b) Predators
(c) Parasitoids (d) Both (b) and (c)

10. Which of the following is the parasitoid used for controlling scale borne problems?
(a) *Metaphycus helvolus* (b) Predators
(c) Sodium sulphate (d) Both (b) and (c)

11. The infestation of plant root system is associated to
(a) Root rot disease (b) Flashy leaves
(c) Shoot system (d) Both (b) and (c)

12. The *Fusarium* root rot disease can be controlled by
(a) Fungicide treatment (b) Herbicide treatment
(c) Chemical treatment (d) Proper fertigation

13. The control of caterpillars can be done by using
(a) *Bacillius thuringiensis* (*Bt*) (b) Cleary's 3336/OHP 6672 (t-methyl)
(c) Terraclor (PNCB), (d) Medallion (fludioxonil)

14. The infestation of Whiteflies can be controlled by using parasitic wasps, namely

(a) *Bacillius thuringiensis* (*Bt*) (b) *Encarsia formosa*
(c) *Eretmocerus eremicus* (d) Both (b) and (c)

15. Which of the following are the predatory mites?

(a) *Amblyseius swirskii* (b) *Encarsia formosa*
(c) *Amblydromalus limonicus* (d) Both (a) and (c)

16. In greenhouse crops the most common symptoms of viral-based diseases are

(a) Stunning (b) Mottling
(c) Blights (d) Both (a) and (b)

17. Thrips can be controlled by

(a) Predatory mites (b) *Amblyseius cucumeris*
(c) *Amblyseius mclenziei* (d) All above

18. Whiteflies can be controlled by

(a) Parasitic wasps (b) *Amblyseius cucumeris*
(c) *Encarsia formosa* (d) Both (a) and (c)

19. Spider mites can be checked by

(a) Predatory mites (b) *Phytoseiulus persimilis*
(c) *Encarsia formosa* (d) Both (a) and (b)

20. The disease "Fungal leaf spot "is due to

(a) *Alternaria* (b) *Ascochyta*
(c) *Cercospora* (d) All above

Answers

1. b	**2.** a	**3.** b	**4.** c	**5.** a	**6.** b	**7.** d	**8.** a	**9.** d	**10.** a
11. a	**12.** a	**13.** a	**14.** d	**15.** d	**16.** d	**17.** d	**18.** d	**19.** d	**20.** d

BIBLIOGRAPHY

Aylsworth, Jean (1993). Biological controls catch on with growers. Greenhouse Grower. December. 8081.

Batavia, IL., Chase, A.R. (1998). New bactericides and fungicides for disease control on ornamentals. Greenhouse Product News. December. Casey, Christine (1997). Integrated Pest Management for Bedding Plants. IPM No. 407. Cornell University Cooperative Extension, Ithaca, NY. 109 p.

DeAngelis, J.D. (1991). Introduction to Biological Pest Control in Greenhouses. Oregon State Univ. Extension Service, Corvallis, OR.

Gindrat, D. (1979). Biological soil disinfection. p. 253287. In: D. Mulder (ed.) Soil Disinfection. Elsevier Scientific Publishing Co., New York, NY.

Gill, Stanton and John Sanderson (1998). Ball Identification Guide to Greenhouse Pests and Beneficial. Ball Publishing, Batavia, IL.

Goldammer T. (2019). Greenhouse Management: A Guide to Operations and Technology. Apex Publishers, USA.

Green, Thomas A. (ed.) (1998). IPM Almanac. Gemplers, Belleville, WI.

Gillespie, D.R. (1995). Development of integrated pest management and biological control systems for the production of greenhouse crops.

Goldammer T. (2019). Greenhouse Management: A Guide to Operations and Technology. Apex Publishers, USA.

Hussey, N.W. and N. Scopes (1985). Biological Pest Control: The Glasshouse Experience. Cornell University Press, Ithaca, NY.

Kuack, David (1995). Janet Bandy on implementing an effective IPM program. Greenhouse Management and Production. April.

Powell, Charles C. and Richard K. Lindquist (1997). Ball Pest and Disease Manual, 2nd edition, Ball Publishing,

Roberts, Dan R. (1992). Insect-, disease-suppressive mixers help growers minimize crop losses. Greenhouse Manager. September. 7071.

Steiner, Marilyn Y. and Don P. Elliot. (1987). Biological Pest Management for Interior Plantscapes, 2nd edition. Alberta Public Affairs Bureau, Edmonton, Alberta, Canada.

https://en.wikipedia.org/wiki/Aphid)

https://www.sciencedirect.com/topics/agricultural-and-biological-sciences/Fungus-gnats

https://www.britannica.com/animal/aphid

https://hort.extension.wisc.edu/articles/Fungus-gnats-and-shore-flies

https://www.britannica.com/animal/bloodworm-annelid

https://en.wikipedia.org/wiki/Frankliniella

https://hort.extension.wisc.edu/articles/whiteflies

https://en.wikipedia.org/wiki/Caterpillar

https://en.wikipedia.org/wiki/Agromyzidae

https://ipm.ucanr.edu/PMG/P/I-HO-PFIC-CO.001.html

https://www.orkincanada.ca/pests/mites

https://www.britannica.com/animal/scale-insect

https://www.agric.wa.gov.au/pest-animals/snail-and-slug-control

TERMINOLOGIES AND CONVERSION TABLES

TERMINOLOGIES

Absolute humidity: It is the ratio of mass of water vapor to the unit volume of space.

Absolute drought: A drought is said to be absolute when at least 15 consecutive days or more with as much as 0.25 mm rainfall.

Advection: It is the process in which the solutes are transported by the bulk mass of flowing fluid.

Agricultural drainage: It is the removal of excess water from agricultural fields.

Aridity index: It is defined as the ratio of annual water deficiency to the annual water required, expressed in percent.

Artificial recharge: Recharge at a rate greater than the natural, carried out artificially, is called artificial recharge.

Basic intake rate: It is the final and constant infiltration rate.

Bulk density: It is the weight of soil in a given volume. Soils with a bulk density higher than 1.6 g/cm^3 tend to restrict the root growth. Bulk density increases with compaction and tends to increase with depth. Sandy soils are more prone to high bulk density.

Capillary action: It is the movement of water in the interstices of a porous medium due to capillary forces.

Capillary conductivity: It is the property of an unsaturated porous medium to transmit liquid.

Capillary head: It is the potential expressed in terms of head of water, causing the water to flow by capillary action.

Capillary potential: It is the scalar quantity representing the work required to move a unit mass of water from the soil to a selected point and energy state.

Capillary rise: It is the height of water rise above free water surface due to capillary action.

Capillary water: The water held in the soil above the phreatic surface by capillary forces is called capillary water.

Cation exchange capacity: It is the sum total of exchangeable cations that a porous medium can absorb. It is expressed in moles of ion charge per kilogram of soil.

Coefficient of permeability: It is the property of soil, which describes how easily a liquid will move through a soil. It is also referred to as the hydraulic conductivity of a soil.

Connate water: The water entrapped in the interstices of a sedimentary or extrusive igneous rock at the time of its deposition is called connate water.

Consumptive use: It refers to total water used through ET and 1% of ET in metabolic action.

Critical flow: It is the state of flow when Froud's number is equal to 1.

Critical depth: The depth of critical flow in the channel is called critical depth.

Crop coefficient: It is ratio of evapotranspiration (ET) to pan evaporation.

Crop management practice factor: This is one of the factors of the Universal Soil Loss equation, which depends on the crop and cropping practices followed for soil erosion or soil control.

Darcy's law: The law, which states that the velocity of flow through porous medium is directly proportional to the hydraulic gradient, assuming the flow is laminar and inertia can be neglected.

Deep percolation: It is the flow of soil water downward by gravity below the maximum effective depth of root zone.

Desorption: It is the reverse process of sorption.

Diffusion: The process by virtue of the ionic or molecular constituents move under the influence of their kinetic activity in the direction of their concentration gradient is called diffusion.

Dispersivity: It is the property of porous medium which determines the dispersion characteristics of the medium by relating the components of pore velocity to the dispersion coefficient.

Distribution coefficient: It is the quantity of solute, chemical or radionuclide sorbed by the solid per unit weight of solid divided by the quantity dissolved in the water per unit volume of water.

Drought: It is an event of prolong shortage of water supply, whether atmospheric, surface water or groundwater. A drought can last for months or years, or may be declared after as few as 15 days.

Drought index: It is the accumulated average daily rainfall during the period in which no effective rainfall is there.

Drought year: A year with total rainfall less than $\bar{x} - SD$ is called drought year.

Effective rainfall: The rainfall amount effective for creating direct runoff is called effective rainfall.

Evaporation: It is the removal of water in gaseous form from the water surface.

Evapotranspiration: The combined loss of water from a given area by evaporation from the land and transpiration from plants.

Field capacity: It is the level of moisture content in the soil, which is retained after draining the excess or gravitational water from the soil.

Fluid potential: The mechanical energy per unit mass of a fluid at any given point in space and time with regard to an arbitrary state and datum is called fluid potential.

Flume: It is device used for measuring the discharge rate of canal or stream. It is constructed in the shape of channel.

Fresh water: The water which contains less than 1,000 mg/l of dissolved solids is called fresh water. Generally, the water containing more than 500 mg/l is treated as undesirable for drinking and many industrial uses.

Froud's number: The ratio of inertia forces to gravity forces is called Froud's number. It is a dimensionless parameter. It decides the characteristics and state of flow in open channels. The expression of Froud's number is given as under:

$$F = \frac{V}{\sqrt{gD}}$$

in which, V is the velocity of flow, D is hydraulic depth of flow and g is the acceleration due to gravity.

Gravitational head: It is component of total hydraulic head related to the position of a given mass of water in reference to an arbitrary datum.

Gravitational potential: It is the energy per unit volume of water required to move an infinitesimal amount of pure, free water from the reference elevation to the soil water elevation.

Gravitational water: The water moving into, through, or out of the soil or rock due to influence of gravitational force is called gravitational water.

Groundwater: The water retained in saturated zone is called groundwater. In other terms, it is the retained water in the aquifer.

Groundwater discharge: It is the flow of water from the zone of saturation.

Groundwater divide: It is the potentiometric surface from which groundwater moves away in both the directions normal to the ridge line.

Groundwater flow: The movement of water in the zone of saturation is called groundwater flow.

Groundwater recharge: The process in which the surface water is added to the water table or groundwater is called groundwater recharge.

Groundwater travel time: It is the time required to move the groundwater from one point to another.

Hail: It is solid form of precipitation consisting balls or irregular lumps of ice, each of which is called a hailstone.

Heterogeneity: It is the characteristic of a medium in which material properties do not remain same everywhere in the soil media.

Homogeneity: It is the characteristic of a medium in which material properties remain same everywhere in the soil media.

Hydraulic barrier: It refers to the barrier across groundwater flow system to restrict or impede the movement of contaminants.

Hydraulic conductivity: It is the measure of a soil's ability to transmit water.

Hydraulic gradient: The slope of water table or potentiometric surface is called hydraulic gradient.

Hydraulic head: The height above a datum such as sea level of the column of water that can be supported by the hydraulic pressure at a given point in a groundwater system, is called hydraulic head.

Hydrometrology: It is the science which deals the hydrology and metrology.

Hydrostatic pressure: The pressure exerted by the weight of water at any given point in a body of water at rest, is called hydrostatic pressure

Infiltration: The downward entry of water into the soil is called infiltration.

Infiltration capacity: The maximum rate at which a soil is capable of absorbing water is called infiltration capacity.

Infiltration gallery: It is a horizontal drain made from open jointed or perforated pipes, which is laid below the water table and collects groundwater.

Infiltration index: It is defined as the rate of rainwater loss such that the volume of rainfall excess is equal to the direct runoff.

Infiltration rate: The rate of water entry into the soil is the infiltration rate.

Injection well: It is the well, used for injecting the water into the sub-surface soil formation.

Intermittent stream: These streams carry the flow during monsoon season when rainfall takes place in frequently. Ground flow is very limited.

***In-situ*–rainwater harvesting:** It is the practice of harvesting the rainwater in the field itself.

Intrinsic permeability: Pertaining to the relative ease with which a porous medium can transmit a liquid under a hydraulic or potential gradient is called intrinsic permeability. It is a property of the porous medium and is independent of the nature of the liquid or the potential field.

Irrigation: Artificial application of water to irrigate the crop is called irrigation.

Irrigation interval: It the time difference between two successive irrigation.

Irrigation return flow: The part of artificially applied water that is not consumed by evapotranspiration and that migrates to an aquifer or surface water body.

Laminar Flow: The flow of a fluid when each particle of the fluid follows a smooth path which never interferes with one another is called laminar flow.

Leaching requirement: It is the fraction of irrigation water that must pass through the root zone in order to prevent soil salinity from reaching a level that would result in reduced growth to crops, trees, gardens or landscape plants.

Lysimeter: A device used for measuring the evapotranspiration is called Lysimeter.

Matric potential: The energy required to extract water from a porous medium to overcome the capillary and adsorptive forces is called matric potential.

Mean annual rainfall: It is the average rainfall of the year of a particular area/region.

Mean areal precipitation: It is the average precipitation of an area/region.

Mean monthly precipitation: It is average rainfall of a particular month.

Mist: It is the form of precipitation; normally thin fog is the mist.

Mixing ratio: It is the ratio of mass of water vapor to the mass of dry air, usually expressed as gram/kilogram of dry air.

Monsoon: The wind system with annual oscillations, blowing from oceans to the continents in summer and from continents to the oceans in winter is called monsoon.

Moisture content: It is percent water retained in a soil.

Moisture equivalent: The ratio of weight of water to the weight of solid particles is called moisture equivalent, expressed in percent.

Moisture tension: It is equivalent negative pressure of water in an unsaturated porous medium equal to the pressure that must be applied to the medium to bring the water to hydraulic equilibrium through a porous permeable material with a pool of water of the same composition.

Moisture volume percentage: The ratio of the volume of water in a soil to the total bulk volume of the soil, is called moisture volume percentage.

Moisture weight percentage: It is the moisture content expressed as a percentage of the oven-dry weight of a soil.

Normal rainfall: It is the long-term average rainfall based on 30-year duration.

Osmotic potential: It is the soil water potential borne by dissolved solutes in water. The dissolved salts develop osmotic pressure in the range of 0.01 to 0.2 MPa in moist soil.

Pan coefficient: It is defined as the ratio of lake evaporation to the pan evaporation.

Perched water: It is the water body located above the main water table.

Percolation: It is the downward movement of water through unsaturated zone.

Permeability: It is the property of the soil to transmit water and air.

Piezometer: A devise used to measure groundwater pressure head at a given point.

Pore space: It is the space not occupied by solid content in soil media.

Porosity: The ratio of total volume of voids to the total volume of the porous medium is called porosity.

Pressure head: It is the height of a water column that corresponds to a particular pressure exerted by the water column on the base of its container.

Pressure potential: It is the energy per unit volume of water required to transfer an infinitesimal quantity of water from a reference pool of water at the elevation of the soil to the point of interest in the soil at reference air pressure and temperature.

Rainfall: It is the liquid form of precipitation, utilizable for crop cultivation.

Rainfall frequency: The number of times during a specified period of years, that precipitation of a certain magnitude or greater occurs or will occur at a station is called rainfall frequency.

Rain gauge: A device used for measuring the rainfall is called rain gauge.

Rainfall intensity: It is the rate of fall of rainfall, expressed in mm/h or cm/h.

Relative humidity: It is defined as the ratio of amount of moisture present is a given space to the total amount which that volume contains at saturation stage.

Recharge: It is the process by which surface water is added to the groundwater.

Recharge area: The extent of area in which groundwater recharge is taking place, is called recharge area.

Recharge capacity: It is the maximum rate at which recharge is taking place in to the ground-water.

Saturated zone: It is the soil water zone in which all the pore spaces are filled with water.

Sediment yield: This the amount of eroded soil mass delivered into the flow system. It is equal to the multiplication of gross erosion and sediment delivery ratio.

Soil moisture: It is the water stored in the soil, and is affected by precipitation, temperature, soil characteristics, etc.

Sorption: It is the process of absorption and adsorption.

Sorptivity: It is defined as a measure of the capacity of the medium to absorb or desorb the liquid by capillarity. In other words, the sorptivity expresses the tendency of a material to absorb and transmit water and other liquids by capillarity. This term was introduced by John Philip in the year 1957.

Specific capacity: The rate of discharge of water from the well divided by the drawdown of the water level within the well, is called specific capacity.

Specific discharge: The rate of discharge of groundwater per unit area of a porous medium measured at right angle to the direction of flow, is called specific discharge.

Specific retention: It is the ratio of the volume of water that a given soil media will hold against the gravity force to the volume of the soil media itself. It is usually expressed as a percentage.

Specific storage: The volume of water released from or taken into storage per unit volume of the porous medium per unit change in head, is called specific storage.

Specific yield: It is the ratio of the volume of water that a saturated soil yields under gravity effect to the total volume of the soil. Specific yield is usually expressed in percentage.

Static head: It is the total vertical distance that a pump raises the water. It has two components.

Static lift: It is the elevation difference between the water source and the pump.

Static discharge: It is the elevation difference between the discharge point and the pump.

Steady flow: A flow in which the velocity of the fluid at a particular point does not change with time, is called steady flow. It is also known as stationary flow.

Surface water: The water collected on the soil surface is called surface water.

Sub-surface water: The water retained in the voids of porous media is called sub-surface water.

Sub-irrigation: It is one of the irrigation methods, in which irrigation is applied to the plant roots. Sub-irrigation is also known as seepage irrigation.

Soil moisture tension: It is the measure of amount of work done to move the water in soil media. It is generally expressed in Pascal, bar, or atmospheres.

Tensiometer: A device used to measure the soil moisture tension in the unsaturated zone is called Tensiometer.

Total dissolved solids (TDS): The total concentration of dissolved constituents in solution, usually expressed in milligrams per liter is called TDS.

Transmissivity: It is the rate of groundwater flow under a unit hydraulic gradient through a unit width of aquifer of thickness m. It is equal to the product of hydraulic conductivity (K) and thickness of aquifer (b).

Transpiration: It is the process in which water is lost through living plants during respiration process.

Underground water: The water below the soil surface, normally stored in the aquifer is called underground water.

Unsaturated flow: The movement of water in a porous medium in which the pore spaces are not completely filled with water. In other words, the movement of water in unsaturated zone is called unsaturated flow.

Unsaturated zone: The zone between land surface and the water table is called unsaturated zone.

Vadose zone: It is also termed as unsaturated zone, is the part between the land surface and the top of the phreatic zone, at which the groundwater is at atmospheric pressure. Vadose zone is extended from the top of the ground surface to the water table.

Void: In the soil mass it represents the pores between the solid particles including the volume of water and the volume of air. The volume of void basically relates with the Void ratio, Porosity and Degree of saturation.

Void ratio: The ratio of volume of void space to the volume of solid particles in a given soil mass is called void ratio.

Volumetric water content: It is the measure of soil moisture, defined as the ratio of water volume to soil volume.

Water content: The amount of water present in the soil media is called water content.

Water year: The time duration from start of rainfall to the end of rainfall during year is called water year. In India it is from 1st June to 31st May.

Wash load: It is the form of sediment load which concentration is greater than the suspended load.

Water harvesting: It is the collection of rainwater, which may be in the depressions, ponds, river, steams, reservoirs, etc.

Water intake: It is the process of entry of water into the soil depending on soil wetness, soil type, surface characteristics, etc.

Wind: Moving air is called wind. Or air in motion is called wind.

Wind break: It is the mechanical measures used for wind erosion control. Wind breaks are established by means of live or dead materials.

CONVERSION TABLES

Length			
1 millimeter	0.001 meter	1 inch	2.54×10^{-2} meters
1 centimeter	0.01 meter	1 foot	0.3048 meters
1 decimeter	0.1 meter	1 angstrom	1×10^{-10} meters
1 decameter	10 meters	1 fermi	1×10^{-15} meters
1 hectometer	100 meters	1 light year	0.946×10^{16} meters
1 kilometer	1000 meters	1 mile	1.609344 kms

Area	
1 sq. inch	6.4516×10^{-4} square meter
1 sq. foot	9.2903×10^{-2} square meter
1 acre	4.0468×10^{3} square meter
1 hectare	1×10^{4} square meter
1 sq. mile	2.5888×10^{6} square meter
1 barn	1×10^{-28} square meter

Volume	
1 milliliter	0.001 liter
1 centiliter	0.01 liter
1 deciliter	0.1 liter
1 decaliter	10 liters
1 hectoliter	100 liters
1 kiloliter	1000 liters
1 cubic inch	1.639×10^{-2} liters
1 gallon	3.785 liters
1 cubic foot	28.316 liters
1 milliliter	0.001 liter
1 centiliter	0.01 liter
1 deciliter	0.1 liter
1 decaliter	10 liters
1 hectoliter	100 liters
1 kiloliter	1000 liters
1 cubic inch	1.639×10^{-2} liters
1 gallon	3.785 liters
1 cubic foot	28.316 liters

Mass	
1 milligram	0.001 gram
1 centigram	0.01 gram
1 decigram	0.1 gram
1 decagram	10 gram
1 hectogram	100 gram
1 kilogram	1000 grams
1 stone	6350.29 grams
1 pound	453.592 grams
1 ounce	28.3495 grams

Time	
1 minute	60 seconds
1 hour	60 minutes 3600 seconds
1 day	24 hours
1 week	7 days
1 year	365 days

Energy	
1 BTU (British thermal unit)	1055 Joule
1 erg	1×10^{-7} joule
1 foot-pound	1.356 joule
1 calorie	4.186 joule
1 kilowatt-hour	3.6 × 106 joule
1 electron volt	1.602×10^{-19} joule
1 liter atmosphere	101.13 joule

Power	
1 erg/sec	1×10^{-5} watt
1 BTU/hr	0.2930 watt
1 foot-pound/sec	1.356 watt
1 horsepower	745.7 watt
1 calorie/sec	4.186 watt

Force	
1 dyne	1×10^{-5} newton
1 pound	4.448 newton

Density	
1 slug/cubic ft	515.4 kilogram/cubic meter
1 pound/cubic in	2.768×10^{4} kilogram/cubic meter

Viscosity	
1 poise	0.1 kg/m.s
1 slug/ft	4.79×10^{1} kg/m.s

Index